W9-BMK-573

IMPORTANT

HERE IS YOUR REGISTRATION CODE TO ACCESS MCGRAW-HILL PREMIUM CONTENT AND MCGRAW-HILL ONLINE RESOURCES

To obtain 30-day trial access to premium online resources for both students and instructors, you need THIS CODE. Once the code is entered, you will be able to use the web resources.

Access is provided for examination purposes only to assist faculty in making textbook adoption decisions.

If the registration code is missing from this examination copy, please contact your local McGraw-Hill representative for access information. If you have adopted this textbook for your course, contact your local representative for permanent access.

To gain access to these online resources

1. **USE** your web browser to go to: www.mhhe.com/brannan2

2. **CLICK** on "First Time User"

3. **ENTER** the Registration Code printed on the tear-off bookmark on the right

4. After you have entered your registration code, click on "Register"

5. **FOLLOW** the instructions to setup your personal UserID and Password

6. **WRITE** your UserID and Password down for future reference. Keep it in a safe place.

If your course uses WebCT or Blackboard, you'll be able to use this code to access the McGraw-Hill content within your online course. Contact your system administrator for details.

The McGraw-Hill Companies

 Higher Education

Thank you, and welcome to your McGraw-Hill Online Resources.

0-07-320468-4 T/A BRANNAN, AIE T/A A WRITER'S WORKSHOP, 2/E

KTMO-XHFO-UC3L-77AJ-06B9

REGISTRATION CODE
REGISTRATION CODE

Praise for *A Writer's Workshop*

"I must say that Brannan did a fabulous job putting together a textbook that covers every topic essential for developmental courses. CONGRATULATIONS!"

—Joanna A. Benavides, *Laredo Community College*

"Brannan's book is informative, illuminating, and the most logical resource for the new millennium. . . . I believe this book will be an unequalled resource for building writing skills."

—Marilyn Garrett, *Texas Southern University*

"The strengths of *AWW* are numerous, and the revisions in this edition target the needs of the developing writer dead center. Brannan has seemingly looked into the minds of student writers and their teachers and emerged with an engaging, fine-tuned product that will prove to be an invaluable tool in the writing classroom."

—Eric Cash, *Abraham Baldwin College*

"The writing is direct, simple, and very empathetic. It helps the reader acknowledge that while writing is tough, it's an eminently doable activity."

—Greg Underwood, *Pearl River Community College*

"The (modes) chapters are wonderfully written and seem to anticipate all the issues/questions for each organizational pattern. I especially like the introductory sections and the use of pictures for each section. The annotated student model provides students with a 'true' view of the writing process."

—Yolanda W. Page, *Dillard University*

"The revision coverage is excellent."

—Susan Brant, *College of the Canyons*

"The writing samples are really pretty wonderful and very effective. They far exceed the value of the writing samples in my own text and I would like to use them in my class next semester."

—Rebecca Busch Adams, *Naugatuck Valley Community Technical College*

"I find the use of previous paragraphs for development into essays remarkably effective. . . . The emphasis on revision that this text appears to offer is long overdue."

—Tracy Peyton, *Pensacola Junior College*

"Brannan does an outstanding job of showing how to turn the paragraph into an essay."

—Jeanette Palmer, *Motlow State Community College*

"I have not found any other text to have the same clarity and effective balance of elements. . . . It lays out basic writing skills with respect for the student. Students with a wide range of sophistication have found it clear and engaging."

—**Diane Thompson,** *Harrisburg Area Community College*

"I would encourage my department to adopt Brannan's text because he explains and models the writing process very well and offers hands-on instruction in all areas, not just the areas he thinks need the most attention."

—**Nita Wood,** *Tidewater Community College*

"Instead of beating us over the head with traditional grammatical terms, the author describes the way our language works (i.e., pausing at the end of a complete thought is signaled in writing by a period). For developmental students, I have found that this approach makes much more sense and is not as intimidating as a traditional approach."

—**Karen Roth,** *Garden City Community College*

"The author needs to be commended for the in-depth coverage of the various writing modes. The student should gain confidence by following the paragraph and essay building process presented in this book."

—**Judith G. Best,** *Garrett College*

SECOND EDITION

A Writer's Workshop

Crafting Paragraphs, Building Essays

Bob Brannan

Johnson County Community College
Overland Park, Kansas

Boston   Burr Ridge, IL   Dubuque, IA   Madison, WI   New York   San Francisco   St. Louis
Bangkok   Bogotá   Caracas   Kuala Lumpur   Lisbon   London   Madrid   Mexico City
Milan   Montreal   New Delhi   Santiago   Seoul   Singapore   Sydney   Taipei   Toronto

Higher Education

A WRITER'S WORKSHOP: CRAFTING PARAGRAPHS, BUILDING ESSAYS

Published by McGraw-Hill, an imprint of The McGraw-Hill Companies, Inc., 1221 Avenue of the Americas, New York, NY 10020. Copyright ©2006, 2003. All rights reserved. No part of this publication may be reproduced or distributed in any form or by any means, or stored in a database or retrieval system, without the prior written consent of The McGraw-Hill Companies, Inc., including, but not limited to, in any network or other electronic storage or transmission, or broadcast for distance learning.

This book is printed on acid-free paper.

1 2 3 4 5 6 7 8 9 0 WCK/WCK 0 9 8 7 6 5

ISBN   0-07-288222-0 (student edition)
ISBN   0-07-288224-7 (annotated instructor's edition)

Editor in Chief: *Emily Barrosse*
Publisher: *Lisa Moore*
Senior Sponsoring Editor: *Alexis Walker*
Director of Development: *Carla Samodulski*
Marketing Manager: *Lori DeShazo*
Senior Media Producer: *Todd Vaccaro*
Media Supplement Producer: *Marc Mattson*
Managing Editor: *Melissa Williams*
Production Editor: *Chanda Feldman*
Permissions Editor: *Marty Granahan*
Manuscript Editor: *Tom Briggs*
Art Director: *Jeanne Schreiber*
Design Manager: *Cassandra Chu*
Text Designer: *Maureen McCutcheon*
Cover Designer: *Yvo Riezebos*
Art Editor: *Katherine McNab*
Photo Research: *Brian J. Pecko*
Production Supervisor: *Tandra Jorgensen*

Composition: 10/12 Palatino by GTS-LA
Printing: PMS 307, 45# Pub Matte, Quebecor Versailles

Cover: © J.L. de Zorzi/Corbis

Credits: The credits section for this book begins on page C-1 and is considered an extension of the copyright page.

Library of Congress Cataloging-in-Publication Data

Brannan, Bob.
    A writer's workshop : crafting paragraphs, building essays / Bob Brannan.—2nd ed.
        p. cm.
    Includes index.
        ISBN 0-07-288222-0 (student ed. : alk. paper) — ISBN 0-07-288224-7 (alk. paper)
        1. English language—Paragraphs—Problems, exercises, etc. 2. English language—Rhetoric—Problems, exercises, etc. 3. English language—Grammar—Problems, exercises, etc. 4. Report writing—Problems, exercises, etc. I. Title.
    PE1439 .B69 2005
    808'.042—dc22   2005041609

The Internet addresses listed in the text were accurate at the time of publication. The inclusion of a website does not indicate an endorsement by the authors or McGraw-Hill, and McGraw-Hill does not guarantee the accuracy of the information presented at these sites.

www.mhhe.com

Bob Brannan

Bob Brannan is a professor at Johnson County Community College in Overland Park, Kansas, where he has taught composition for the past ten years. He received his M.A. in composition/rhetoric from Iowa State University and began his teaching career as a "freeway flyer," shuttling between community colleges and carrying his office in a bag. Over the years he has taught a number of writing classes—including developmental, first- and second-semester composition, business and technical writing, advanced composition, and honor's seminars—but he focuses much of his attention on the pre-college-level writer. *A Writer's Workshop* is his first composition textbook.

When not working in a writing classroom, Bob spends much of his time with his family, frequently attending his daughter's tea parties, where his voice imitations are in great demand, and climbing trees with her in his backyard.

v

PREFACE

A Writer's Workshop is a text for developing writers that is based on three assumptions:

- Students learn to write best by writing.
- They need to revise their work significantly.
- They deserve comprehensive instruction to show them how to revise effectively.

To this end, I have tried to create a text filled with opportunities for the least- to the most-skilled students to write often within a rhetorical context and to critically evaluate their work.

As you explore *A Writer's Workshop,* you will no doubt notice that it is more focused on writing assignments than other composition texts at the same level. Almost three-quarters of the book is devoted to process instruction and support for students as they develop their paragraphs and essays. While many composition texts claim to thoroughly explore an assignment with students, these texts devote only a few pages to this instruction, shifting the focus instead to grammar, spelling, and punctuation. *A Writer's Workshop* has a well-developed handbook section in Unit Five, but the focus stays on the larger concerns of producing a written text.

If students are to succeed in their writing, they need specific answers to their questions. When they ask, "What do you mean by 'dominant impression'?" "How do you build toward a climax?" or "How can I keep my examples from being underdeveloped?" their textbook ought to supply the answers. *A Writer's Workshop* does this and more. Through the chapter introductions, the skills sections, the engaging student models, the step-by-step process instruction, and the annotated student models, *A Writer's Workshop* gives students the help they need to become skillful writers.

Of course, no textbook can replace a talented and dedicated teacher. The detailed instruction that *A Writer's Workshop* provides will, however, free teachers from the need to track down models, create heuristics, prepare checklists, and concoct editing practice, so that they can spend more time with their own students' writing—the true focus of a composition course. In addition, students *can* take a book home with them, so the clearer and more detailed the instruction a book provides, the better able students are to help themselves. My goal for this second edition of *A Writer's Workshop* has been to make it even more readable and to improve the features that allow both students and teachers to do their best work.

Organization of the Book

A Writer's Workshop is divided into six units:

UNIT ONE, Getting Our Feet Wet, covers the processes of writing and reading.

- **Chapter 1** gives students many opportunities to practice essential writing strategies like prewriting and organizing and ends with several assignment options that instructors can use to assess student skill levels.

- **Chapter 2** helps students to improve their reading skills and read more effectively. A logical extension of Chapter 1, Chapter 2 makes the reading/writing connection clear by explaining the reading process as a matter of locating thesis and topic sentences and working with the writer to actively understand the main point. Activities are linked to Chapter 3 so that instructors can quickly move students into the assignment chapters of *A Writer's Workshop*.

UNIT TWO, Working with the Paragraph, introduces the paragraph.

- **Chapter 3** offers a comprehensive treatment of paragraph structure and development.
- **Chapter 4** offers detailed suggestions for revising paragraphs, from rough drafts through final drafts. As they work through their assignments in chapters 5–11, students can refer to this chapter for specific, well-illustrated suggestions for improving their work.
- **Chapters 5 to 11** cover seven patterns of development (leaving out definition and argument, which are treated in Unit Three), taking students through all phases of the writing process.

UNIT THREE, Working with the Essay, moves students from writing paragraphs into writing essays.

- **Chapter 12** focuses on essay form and development and devotes special attention to introductions and conclusions.
- **Chapter 13** offers thoroughly illustrated advice for revising rough, second, and final drafts.
- **Chapter 14** helps students either expand a paragraph written in response to an assignment in Unit Two or begin an essay focusing on one of the patterns of development. The three chapters that follow, **Chapters 15, 16,** and **17,** which cover definition, persuasion, and essay exam skills, emphasize the combination of patterns of development that students have worked with in Unit Two.

UNIT FOUR, Polishing Style, helps students with many elements of style.

- **Chapter 18,** "Creating Sentence Variety," helps students increase their syntactic fluency with extensive sentence-combining exercises that also reinforce the use of correct punctuation.
- **Chapter 19** helps students learn to control their tone, select language carefully, and eliminate clutter.

UNIT FIVE, Practicing Sentence Sense, includes chapters that cover common problems developmental writers have with grammar, spelling, and punctuation.

The operating principle in this unit is that less is more. The assumption behind these chapters is that students can learn to punctuate effectively, express themselves clearly, and achieve a degree of syntactic fluency without an overemphasis on grammar and punctuation rules. These chapters also demonstrate a number of basic stylistic options, and a substantial chapter is devoted to the special concerns of ESL students.

UNIT SIX, Additional Readings, offers fifteen professional readings.

The selections in Unit Six are appropriate to the course in length and complexity and model key principles introduced in the assignment chapters.

The **appendix** is a step-by-step guide to writing a brief research paper.

Features of the Assignment Chapters in Units Two and Three

Because the focus of *A Writer's Workshop* is on students' writing, the assignment chapters in Units Two and Three are the heart of this text. Each assignment chapter includes the following elements:

- The **Introduction** offers a vivid illustration that helps focus students' attention on the type of writing covered in the chapter.
- **Setting the Stage** summarizes the chapter's goal in a paragraph.
- **Linking to Previous Experience** shows students what they already know about the type or types of writing covered in the chapter, linking the material to their personal, work, and academic lives and to the writing they have already practiced in the text. (Informed by reading theory—the goals is to activate a student's "schema"—this approach is used throughout the text.)
- **Determining the Value** shows students the relevance of the chapter to their personal, work, and academic lives and to larger concerns of personal growth.
- **Developing Skills and Exploring Ideas** helps students with skills essential for understanding and writing the chapter assignment. The skills are thoroughly explained and reinforced with activities.
- **Analyzing Student Models** offers strong-but-attainable student sample work, accompanied by a prereading paragraph and questions to help students actively read it, and by a postreading bulleted list to help students analyze key features of good writing that they can apply to their own compositions. The Questions for Analysis that follow the student models focus on organization, development, and style, helping students see how their own writing can be improved.
- **Summarizing the Assignment** describes the requirements and goals of the paragraph or essay students are being asked to write.
- **Establishing Audience and Purpose** provides a rhetorical context for the writing assignment that follows.
- **Working through the Assignment** provides detailed guidelines for each step of the writing process. It includes the following subsections:
  - **Discovering Ideas** offers extensive **Topic Lists** that are geared to student interests.
  - **Prewriting** is modeled for each assignment.
  - **Organizing Ideas** gives specific guidance on developing and integrating essential elements like topic and thesis sentences, complete with examples.
  - **Drafting** offers several important reminders to help students prepare their first drafts.

it easier for students to understand concepts and strategies important to writing each chapter assignment.

- **Helpful hints and cautions in the margin:** These marginal "hints" and "cautions" reinforce the instruction in the text by emphasizing key points that students need to pay attention to.

- **Online support for writing and research, powered by *Catalyst:*** The Online Learning Center for *A Writer's Workshop* includes exercises and activities, along with support for online research. For this second edition of *A Writer's Workshop,* the Online Learning Center has been vastly expanded to include resources from *Catalyst,* McGraw-Hill's powerful online resource for student writers, including thousands of grammar exercises, with feedback for each response, writing tutors for the different patterns of organization, a tutorial on how to avoid plagiarism, and more. Computer icons in the margin of the text let students know when more help is available in the Online Learning Center.

- **New reading selections in Unit Six:** Four of the reading selections in Part Six are new: "The Jacket" by Gary Soto, "Friends, Good Friends, and Such Good Friends" by Judith Viorst, "The Fine Art of Complaining" by Caroline Rego, and "They Gotta Keep It: People Who Save Everything" by Lynda W. Warren and Jonnae C. Ostrom.

Supplements Package

Supplements for Instructors

- **The Annotated Instructor's Edition** (ISBN 0-07-288224-7) consists of the student text complete with answers to all activities. Marginal Teaching Ideas provide suggestions for using the text in class.

- **The Web site accompanying the text (www.mhhe.com/brannan)** offers password-protected instructional aids and resources for instructors. The Web site includes the Instructor's Manual, which provides comprehensive commentary on every chapter in the text, sample syllabi, alternative writing assignments, peer response worksheets, and more, as well as additional online resources for writing instructors.

- **PageOut!** helps instructors create graphically pleasing and professional Web pages for their courses, in addition to providing classroom management, collaborative learning, and content management tools. PageOut! is FREE to adopters of McGraw-Hill textbooks and learning materials. Learn more at http:/www.mhhe.com/pageout/.

- **Partners in Teaching: Teaching Basic Writing Listserv (www.mhhe.com/tbw).** Moderated by Laura Gray-Rosendale of Northern Arizona University and offered by McGraw-Hill as a service to the developmental composition community, this listserv brings together senior members of the college community with newer members—junior faculty, adjuncts, and teaching assistants—to address issues of pedagogy, both in theory and practice. Access to the online newsletter, instructional modules, and the accompanying discussion groups is free—and commercial-free.

Supplements for Students

- As noted previously, the *Online Learning Center* accompanying the text (www.mhhe.com/brannan), now powered by *Catalyst,* offers a wide variety of additional resources for students, including grammar exercises with feedback, writing activities for additional practice, guides to doing research on the Internet and avoiding plagiarism, useful Web links, and more.

- Available on the Web site, *Working with Your Computer* (formerly Appendix 1 in the text) is a guide to basic word processing using Windows and the common word processing software Microsoft Word. This document, which consists largely of screen images, is a simplified user's manual with some practical suggestions and warnings to help students with the many questions they ask their instructors in class: "How do I double space, insert page numbers, spell check, word count . . . ?"

Dictionary and Vocabulary Resources

The following supplements are available at a discount when packaged with *A Writer's Workshop.*

- **Random House Webster's College Dictionary** (ISBN 0-07-240011-0) This authoritative dictionary includes over 160,000 entries and 175,000 definitions. The most commonly used definitions are always listed first, so students can find what they need quickly.
- **The Merriam-Webster Dictionary** (ISBN 0-07-310057-9) Based on the best-selling *Merriam-Webster's Collegiate Dictionary,* the paperback dictionary contains over 70,000 definitions.
- **The Merriam-Webster Thesaurus** (ISBN 0-07-310067-6) This handy paperback thesaurus contains over 157,000 synonyms, antonyms, related and contrasted words, and idioms.
- **Merriam-Webster's Vocabulary Builder** (ISBN 0-07-310069-2) This handy paperback introduces 3,000 words and includes quizzes to test progress.
- **Merriam-Webster's Notebook Dictionary** (ISBN 0-07-299091-0) An extremely concise reference to the words that form the core of English vocabulary, this popular dictionary, conveniently designed for 3-ring binders, provides words and information at students' fingertips.
- **Merriam-Webster's Notebook Thesaurus** (ISBN 0-07-310068-4) Conveniently designed for 3-ring binders, this thesaurus provides concise, clear guidance for over 157,000 word choices.
- **Merriam-Webster's Collegiate Dictionary and Thesaurus, Electronic Edition** (ISBN 0-07-310070-6) Available on CD-ROM, this online dictionary contains thousands of new words and meanings from all areas of human endeavor, including electronic technology, the sciences, and popular culture.

Please consult your local McGraw-Hill representative or consult McGraw-Hill's website at **www.mhhe.com/english** for more information on the supplements that accompany the second edition of *A Writer's Workshop.*

Custom Options

A Writer's Workshop can be customized for brevity or for courses that place different amounts of emphasis on the paragraph or the essay. The text can also be expanded to include your course syllabi, semester schedule, or any other materials specific to your program. Spiral binding is also available. Please contact your McGraw-Hill representative for details, or send us an email at english@mcgraw-hill.com.

ACKNOWLEDGMENTS

This second edition of *A Writer's Workshop* has benefited from the input of many people, including the editorial team at McGraw-Hill. I thank Alexis Walker, senior sponsoring editor, who has listened to my concerns patiently and helped me make the right strategic decisions for the second edition. Carla Samodulski, senior developmental editor, has done a wonderful job of working with me to cut superfluous text and improve clarity. Carla has also helped in the reorganizing effort, making this edition even more student friendly. The daily struggle with line-by-line concerns has fallen to Randee Falk, who has helped me to simplify and clarify, often pointing out where one example, rather than three, would do the job well.

A number of reviewers and class testers from across the country have helped me tighten and polish this edition, and I would like to acknowledge my debt for their many practical revision suggestions:

Judith G. Best
Garrett College

Roy L. Bond
Richland College

Nellie Boyd
Texas Southern University

William Carroll
Abilene Christian University

Eric Cash
Abraham Baldwin College

Frank Cronin
Austin Community College

Frank J. D'Andrea
Portland Community College—Sylvania

Brenda Kay Driver
University of Memphis

David D. Glaub
University of Wisconsin-Parkside

Bonita Hilton
Broward Community College

Janet Burnett Huchingson
Tarrant County College—SE

Judith McKenzie
Lane Community College

Mary Mocsary
Southeastern Louisiana University

Safa Motallebi
Auburn University Montgomery

Yolanda W. Page
Dillard University

Sandra Provence
Arkansas State University, Newport

Brenda Rawson
College of Eastern Utah

Karen Roth
Garden City Community College

Diane Thompson
Harrisburg Area Community College

Sandra Torrez
Texas A&M University—Kingsville

Greg Underwood
Pearl River Community College

Linda VanVickle
St. Louis Community College—Meramec

I would also like to thank those reviewers who provided valuable suggestions for the first edition:

Rebecca Busch Adams
Naugatuck Valley Community Technical College

Linda Bagshaw
Briar Cliff College

Sandra Barnhill
South Plains College

Joanna A. Benavides
Laredo Community College

Karen L. Blaske
Arapahoe Community College

Susan Brant
College of the Canyons

Vicki Covington
Isothermal Community College

Crystal Edmonds
Robeson Community College

Marilyn Garrett
Texas Southern University

Eddye Gallagher
Tarrant County College

Maria A. Garcia
San Antonio College

Jeanne Gilligan
Delaware Technical and Community College

Huey Guagliardo
Louisiana State University at Eunice

Faye Jones
Northeast State Technical Community College

Laura Kasischke
Washtenaw Community College

Patsy Krech
University of Memphis

Eleanor Latham
Central Oregon Community College

Marcia B. Littenberg
SUNY, Farmingdale

Joyce L. Maher
Eastern Shore Community College

Sebastian Mahfood
St. Louis University

Randy R. Maxson
Grace College and Seminary

Aubrey Moncrieffe, Jr.
Housatonic Community College

Jeanette Palmer
Motlow State Community College

Myra Peavyhouse
Roane State Community College

Tracy Peyton
Pensacola Junior College

James Read
Allan Hancock College

Al Reeves
Montana State University College of Technology

Carole Rhodenhiser
Fort Valley State College

Lola Richardson
Paine College

Linda C. Rollins
Motlow State Community College

Harvey Rubenstein
Hudson County Community College

Patricia S. Rudden
New York City Technical College

Julia Ruengert
Ozarks Technical Community College

Karen Sidwell
St. Petersburg Junior College

Pauline Simonowich
Pitt Community College

Alvin Starr
Community College of Baltimore

Christina Vick
Louisiana State University at Eunice

Ted Wadley
Georgia Perimeter College

Beverly Walker
North Central State College

Fred Wolven
Miami–Dade Community College

Nita Wood
Tidewater Community College

William W. Ziegler
J. Sargeant Reynolds Community College

I would particularly like to thank the following colleagues at Johnson County Community College who have helped me enormously by reviewing and using the first edition, giving me much thoughtful feedback on how to improve the text:

Jay Antle

Andrea Broomfield

Mark Browning

David Davis

Kami Day

Maureen Fitzpatrick

Mary Grace Foret

Keith Geekie

Jack Halligan

Shaun Harris

Sandy Calvin Hastings

Monica Hogan

Pat Jonason

Bill Lamb

Mary Pat McQueeney

Ellen Mohr

Paul Northam

Judy Oden

Larry Rochelle

Ted Rollins

Marilyn Senter

Finally, I want to thank my friends and family members who, as I have worked on the new edition, have once more put up with my many absences from their lives. As always, I am renewed daily by my wife, Beth Johnson, and daughter, Lauren, who have both come to understand that my sense of time ("I'll be through with this chapter in five more minutes!") may be forever hopelessly skewed.

Bob Brannan

CONTENTS

UNIT THREE

Working with the Essay *273*

Chapter 12
Introducing the Essay *274*

Chapter 13
Revising Essays *312*

Chapter 14
Expanding Paragraphs into Essays *324*

Getting Our Feet Wet

Practicing the Writing Process

How Do We Begin to Write?

Teaching Idea
Developmental students generally need a great deal of encouragement to overcome their initial self-definition as incapable of success at writing. To dispel this false impression, you can discuss it in class.

The first step in beginning to write is to think of yourselves as writers—not necessarily easy to do. Depending on past experiences, you may have already labeled yourselves as OK, not so hot, or downright terrible. Many view the act of writing as mysterious and think successful writers have lucked into their talent. But most people who write are not geniuses. Just like you, accomplished writers have to work hard at their craft. They can be confused at first, uncertain and anxious about where their ideas will come from. Often they produce some genuinely bad writing in their early drafts and agonize over the final shape of their words—and what others will think of the work.

Whatever your past experiences with writing, you share in the common experience of everyone who seeks to commit words to paper. When you write, be it a brief paragraph or long essay, you *are* a writer, with all the hard work, the aggravation, and the satisfaction that comes with it.

How do writers get started? To focus your efforts before beginning to write, you should ask yourself several questions.

Questions to Ask at the Start of a Writing Project

1. What is my purpose?

People write for many reasons, often having several for the same project, although one purpose usually predominates. Primary reasons for writing are to entertain, explain ideas and information, and persuade. There are, of course, other reasons for writing, such as to express emotions or explore ideas.

2. Who is my audience?

Most student writing is done for teachers. However, in "real-world" writing, you need to be able to communicate effectively with different readers, ranging from fairly general audiences to very specific ones. Knowing who your audience is will help you decide what and how much to say.

3.   What, exactly, is the project?

If you are writing for yourself, you may know just what you want to say, but writing out your goals will still help you to focus your thoughts. In class your instructor will give you an assignment guide, or you will follow the assignment instructions in the text. In any case, from the outset you should determine what the project calls for: purpose, audience, overall organization, length, and draft due dates.

4.   How can I develop a real interest in the project?

Teaching Idea
It is important to establish from the outset that students must take responsibility for their own success in the course. Committing themselves to succeed in writing is the same as striving to do well in any other activity they prize: sports, cars, dance, music, and so on.

The worst approach to any writing assignment is to take a passive attitude, to say, "I don't care, what*ever.*" Sometimes you will have to write to specific requirements, sometimes not. When a topic is assigned, you can still find some part of it that is appealing. When you can choose a topic, take time to find an interesting one, rather than going for the first or seemingly easiest one. If you can commit to the project, you are more likely to enjoy the writing process—and you will probably end up with a better grade.

Good writing is not easily accomplished; it takes time. To achieve the best results, first gain a clear overview of the project, and then apply effective study skills.

KEY STUDY SKILLS

1. Listen carefully in class, ask questions, and take notes, especially when your instructor writes on the chalkboard, uses the overhead projector, or posts information on a class website.
2. Take handouts home to study or complete.
3. Participate fully in class activities and discussion: this approach will help you understand every writing assignment.
4. Pay attention to supplemental instructions your instructor gives you to clarify writing projects in this text.
5. Study the textbook's student models for further guidance.

After Breaking Ground—into the Writing Process

Teaching Idea
Rather than prescribing *the* writing process, talk of many writing processes and try to help students improve on the habits they bring to class.

We all have gone through steps to produce written paragraphs and essays, so we all have *a* writing process. For some of us, that process has worked well; for others . . . not so well. The rest of this chapter explains the writing approach many of us already unconsciously use. However, the writing process varies with individuals, and you should freely adapt it to what works best for you.

Steps in the Writing Process

Gathering and shaping ideas and putting words on paper are a natural sequence for most of us, but writers seldom move through this process like a train moving on a track, beginning at one point and progressing to the final destination.

In fact, you will often find yourself brainstorming for ideas in the middle of a paper, editing as you notice an error, and sometimes substantially reorganizing when the work seemed nearly complete.

> **THE WRITING PROCESS**
> 1. Discover ideas
> 2. Organize ideas
> 3. Draft
> 4. Revise
> 5. Edit
> 6. Proofread

Discovering Ideas

Teaching Idea
To help students overcome resistance to prewriting methods like freewriting, try some in class, having students share their results.

CAUTION! The danger in freewriting is mistaking what you have produced for a final draft—or even a solid first draft!

HINT: No ideas at all? Try freewriting.

How many times have you been faced with a writing project and found that you have nothing to say? It is a common, frustrating occurrence. Instead of smacking your keyboard in frustration or simply giving up, why not try one or several of the following methods for discovering ideas?

Freewriting

Freewriting is rapid, uncensored writing. You may already have used it to produce a rough draft. Fast drafting or freewriting lets you get ideas on paper— some of which may be usable. To practice this method, set aside time—say, 5 to 10 minutes—and write nonstop, without censoring ideas or worrying about grammar, spelling, and punctuation. Even if you run out of thoughts, keep writing or typing.

If you have no idea of what to write, freewriting can help you uncover ideas. Freewriting for this purpose commonly produces sentences like the following:

> Well I don't know what to say at this point and I think this freewritng stuff isnt going anywhere fast. Whose idea was it for me to try this king of writing anyway. May be Ill humor the teacher and keep it going for a few more minutes. Geez I just looked at the clock and I've got 7 motre minutes to write!

The point is to keep producing words even when you do not seem to be getting anywhere. Although no one has been able to explain why, the mere act of writing triggers more words and, often, usable ideas. Then, with a topic in hand, you can try **focused freewriting**—uncensored writing on a general topic. The following example is a brief focused freewrite:

HINT: Focused freewrites can give your writing direction.

> I get to chose from a list of places or come up with my own place. I don't k ow what the best way is. Maybe I'll try some of the outside places on the list I like the outdoors fishing, hnting, hiking in themountains. I like being aroung the trees and plants. I seem to have always liked being outside ever since I was a little kid. How about that trrehouse my brother and I built when we were how old? About 11 and 13. Eric was pretty good at figuring out how to get the main platform built and braced into the trees. He was always better at building stuff than I was but we worked preety ell on that job. Let's see I'm supposed to be comeing up with a descriptionof

something. May be the treehouse could work. I wonder if it's still there? I could drive back into the oldneighborhood and look I guess. How many trees, 3. We had to nail on to those big old catalpa trees in our backyard in South Bend. Dad would only let us put it up about ten-twelve feet from the ground. No way to get up high into those huge branches. . . .

In this freewrite, the author discovers several ideas for a descriptive paper. The backyard, the tree house, or the author's former house might make interesting subjects to explore.

ACTIVITY 1.1 Focused Freewriting

Select a topic from the list below and write nonstop on it for 5 minutes. Remember, don't worry about grammar, spelling, or punctuation or whether ideas get tangled.

airport	football field	restaurant
attic	gym	swimming pool
beach	interstate	wharf
cafeteria	kitchen	woods
car wash	library	zoo

Teaching Idea
The prewriting methods in Chapter 1 are slanted toward description, a common jumping-off place for developmental writing courses. You might want to combine some of the chapter activities with Chapter 5, Picturing a Place.

Clustering

Clustering is another good prewriting technique. With this method you write a single word in the center of a page and then jot down around it any words that the center word brings to mind. After linking several words to the original word, you connect more words to the second set. Keep extending your network of linked words until you find a grouping that seems interesting.

Consider the following cluster:

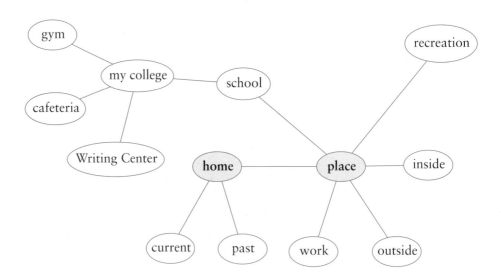

If the author wanted to select the "home" cluster to begin a more **focused cluster,** the next step might look like this:

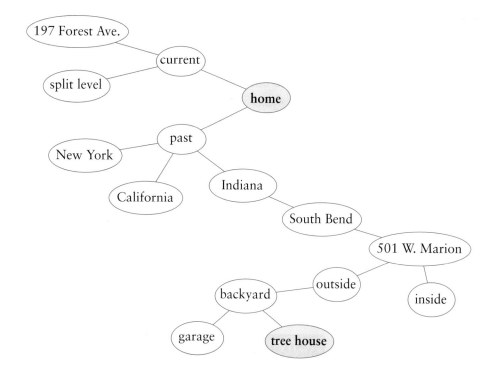

Now the author has arrived at the tree house as a possible topic for his description paragraph. He might choose to cluster again for specific details, or he might try another method for generating ideas, like brainstorming or listing.

ACTIVITY 1.2 Focused Clustering

Select a topic from the list in Activity 1.1 (or continue with the one you have already chosen), and create a focused cluster like the one preceding. Work for 5 minutes, trying to fill a page with word associations.

Brainstorming (Listing)

In **brainstorming,** either by yourself or with others, you list in a word or phrase every idea that occurs to you when you think about a general topic. If we extended the tree house topic from the clustering activity, we might end up with a list like this:

Tree House

mine and my brother's	dad got the shingles
no one else allowed	climbing the rope
sturdy	sleeping outside
good in rain	water balloon fights
our gang	creaking in the wind

If we **focus** the list, we can concentrate primarily on generating the specific words and sensory details that make up a good description. (For more on description, see p. 77.)

Teaching Idea
Students who resist formal outlines often see the value in brainstorming to create a loose list. You can help them develop outlines by condensing and arranging ideas on the board.

Revising

HINT: Revision = adding, cutting, and rearranging material.

Diagnostic Editing Test

If going easy on yourself was important during the first rough draft, now you need a different attitude. Revising requires a critical (but not negative) frame of mind and a willingness to look closely at your work, knowing that it can be improved. As you rework your draft, by yourself and with others, you will be looking to add, shift, and delete material.

Nothing about revision is easy; in fact, it may be the hardest part of the writing process. To revise effectively, you need to learn what problem areas to look for, gain insight into what you want to say, and let go of words and sentences that aren't working. Sometimes you will even need to throw out that first rough draft and start over. If you want to see your writing improve, you must join the many professional writers who may moan and groan as they revise, but who do so until they shape a product they can be proud of.

After giving the draft some time to "cool off" (try for at least a day), remind yourself again of your purpose and audience, and look closely at your topic or thesis sentence. Taken as a whole, does your paper seem to grow from your main point? Jot down any reactions you have, positive or negative, and then reread the draft, following this list of priorities:

Revision Priority List

1. **Content:** The content of your work is the most important feature.
   - Check your ideas for clarity: Can you and other readers understand your point?
   - Be sure you have enough examples and details to convey your meaning and satisfy readers' curiosity.
   - Check for unnecessary points, examples, or details—anything that is repetitive or will distract readers from the central idea.

2. **Organization:** Make sure readers can follow your ideas.
   - Check your topic or thesis sentence to see if it still clearly guides readers.
   - Review the overall organizational pattern. If you chose a spatial arrangement, for instance, make sure you have been consistent in ordering details.
   - Look closely at how your sentences and paragraphs flow together. If transitions or other connectors are needed, use them.
   - Check your ending: Does it link to the main point of your paper and leave readers with something to reflect on?

3. **Style:** Word choice and arrangement can make writing easy or difficult to follow.
   - What words are not working well?
   - Is your meaning fuzzy?
   - Do you repeat words unnecessarily?
   - Do you have enough variety in the length, type, and beginnings of your sentences?
   - Where can you tighten sentences, eliminating words that serve no purpose?

4. **Mechanics:** The last element to check in your paper is mechanics— grammar, spelling, and punctuation. When you move into more polished drafts, you will edit out mechanical errors that keep you from communicating clearly.

As you practice revising, you will get better at it. Moving slowly through your drafts and focusing on one category to revise at a time will make this process more manageable.

Group Revising

HINT: Use constructive criticism to help you revise.

HINT: You don't have to be an English whiz to help others revise.

Teaching Idea
It helps to address head-on the misconception of many students that they don't know enough to help each other in group revision.

What if you have tried to revise by yourself in the past without much luck? Fortunately, in your writing class, you will have the help of fellow students and your instructor.

To profit most from collaborative work, you should be open to constructive criticism. Although none of the students in your group is an English teacher, you don't have to be an expert to respond to each others' drafts. Simply letting a student author know that an idea is unclear or that a paragraph seems to be drifting can be invaluable.

Each assignment chapter in this book gives advice on discovering ideas, organizing, drafting, and beginning to revise. Also, the revision chapters, 4 and 13, offer step-by-step suggestions for improving your drafts. However, for some general suggestions to make group revising productive, read through the following lists:

HOW THE WRITER CAN HELP THE READER

1. In a sentence or two at the top of your draft, specify your audience and purpose.
2. Tell your reader your main point.
3. Direct the reader to any part of the paper you have specific concerns about—for example, "I'm not sure about my topic sentence. Does it tell you what I think is the main point?" or "Do you think I might have too many details about sound in the first half of the paragraph?"
4. After your paper has been read, listen carefully to the reader's responses, and then ask for clarification of any comments you didn't understand.
5. Do not let a reader overwhelm you. Be selective in the advice you follow. Have several other readers comment on suggestions for revision, especially if a suggestion feels wrong for your paper.

Teaching Idea
Some students will blindly accept any suggestion another student makes about their writing. It is important for students to learn to evaluate each other's feedback.

HOW THE READER CAN HELP THE WRITER

1. Ask about the audience, purpose, and main point.
2. Read the draft quickly and tell what you liked or thought the author did well.
3. Answer any questions the author has about the draft.
4. Reread the draft again slowly, using the revision checklists in each revision chapter. Jot notes in the margins of the paper. A helpful shorthand is to draw a straight line under words, phrases, and sentences that you particularly like and a wavy line under any part that seems questionable.
5. Share your honest reactions with the author. But remember, neither of you should expect the other to be the "teacher." Your job is simply to give the best response you can as you understand the assignment requirements.
6. Remember to role-play the designated audience as you read, and respond as you think that person or group would.

words in the title, even small ones like *is* and *do,* except articles (*a, an, the*), prepositions (*of, in, to,* etc.), and coordinating conjunctions (*and, but, so,* etc.). If articles, prepositions, or conjunctions begin or end a title or follow a colon, however, capitalize them.

3. Spell check any additional required material, such as outlines. Staple or paperclip your pages. Avoid putting the paper in a plastic sleeve, which most instructors consider a nuisance.

ACTIVITY 1.10 Proofreading

Proofread your paper and hand it in to your instructor. Be sure to read your teacher's comments and corrections carefully when he or she returns the paper, and then list all errors on your Improvement Chart.

Diagnostic Writing Assignments

Before you begin any of the assignments below, review this chapter's advice on discovering ideas, organizing, and drafting. Try at least one prewriting method, and aim to write a single paragraph of 200 to 300 words. After you have a revised draft in hand, be sure to edit and proofread it carefully. Because your instructor may ask for them, save your prewriting and organizing notes so you can turn them in along with your draft.

Option 1: Description

Describe a room that you are familiar with and comfortable in. If you can visit the room (e.g., a room in your home), you might try listing details of the surroundings and then arranging the details spatially (one side to the other, front to back, bottom to top—see p. 88). Remember to state some central point or main idea about the room in your first sentence.

Option 2: Narration

Tell a story about some event in your life that you remember well and that has affected your view of yourself, another person, or the larger world. You could use several of the discovery methods discussed in this chapter to find ideas, but you might begin with general clustering and then try a focused cluster. Arrange your details chronologically (as if you were reliving the event from beginning to end—see p. 128). State some main point or reason for telling the story in your first sentence.

Additional Links on Writing

Option 3: Exposition

Explain why you are in college and what you hope to gain from this experience. You could use several of the discovery methods discussed in this chapter to find ideas, but you might begin with general freewriting and then try a focused freewrite. Arrange your reasons, starting your paragraph with the least important one and ending with the most important (see p. 144). State some overall point or reason for being in school in your first sentence.

Chapter Summary

1. Clarify the writing project.
2. Commit yourself to the work.
3. Practice the writing process:
   A. Discover.
   B. Organize.
   C. Draft.
   D. Revise.
   E. Edit.
   F. Proofread.
4. Be flexible in approaching the writing task. Try alternatives when necessary.
5. Don't despair. Help for your writing abounds, but you must become an active learner, seeking out the help that you need to succeed.

especially when the text is crammed with information. Here are three useful approaches:

1. **Skim** all signposts: titles, chapter previews and summaries, headings and subheadings, analytical questions, text boxes, and highlighted, boldfaced, and italicized print.
2. **Skim** beginnings and endings.
3. **Link** new information to previous knowledge.

Signposts

HINT: Signposts create a chapter outline.

All textbooks use signposts (visual aids) to help readers focus on the main points in each chapter. The title itself will usually contain the main idea of the chapter. After the title you will often find chapter previews, sometimes in the form of lists or brief summaries. Within the chapter, the major headings and subheadings form a chapter outline. Brief summaries or lists of essential points often appear at the ends of main sections, and many chapters conclude with a summary of or questions on the chapter's primary ideas. Text boxes and marginal notes highlight significant points and ask questions to help readers reflect on the material. Finally, words and passages are boldfaced, italicized, or shaded to emphasize a point. Skimming through a chapter and noting these reading aids may take a few minutes, but it is time well spent.

Beginnings and Endings

Chapters in textbooks are organized in much the same way as paragraphs and essays. Each chapter has a central focus (thesis), which divides into several topics. These, in turn, are divided into subtopics, all of which are then developed through examples, details, and explanations. Before you read the body of the chapter, it helps to read the chapter introduction and concluding paragraphs or chapter summary. For more in-depth knowledge, you can then skim the body paragraphs, focusing on the first and last sentences of each. All paragraphs should contain a unifying idea, and that idea will frequently be stated as a clear topic sentence at the beginning of the paragraph and may be restated as a summary sentence at the end.

Connections: Linking New to Previous Knowledge

After you have previewed a chapter, noting the signposts and perhaps skimming the beginnings and endings of paragraphs, pause for a moment of reflection. What have you just read? What does it mean to you at this point? How do the terms and ideas fit into your previous experience? We all have a large store of experience and knowledge to draw from. When you link new information to what you already know, you remember more efficiently. For example, if you have trouble with the concept of the Internet as a means of global communication, you might think of it as a vast net or spider web of telecommunication lines connecting people's computers all over the earth. Within almost all new material, you can usually find something familiar to help fix the new information in your mind. If you have little actual experience with a topic, you will still have associations with it and can make useful comparisons that will help you understand and remember it.

ACTIVITY 2.1 Previewing a Chapter

Turn to Chapter 3, Introducing the Paragraph, and skim the signposts, the beginning, and the ending. Remember not to read the body of the text; simply sample what the chapter will present in more depth. After 5 minutes of skimming, answer the following questions. (You may need to flip to the chapter, but avoid in-depth reading.)

1. What is the chapter focus? _Learning about body paragraphs_

2. What are three essential parts of a body paragraph? _Topic sentence, body sentences, concluding sentence_

3. What are three ways of organizing ideas within a paragraph? _Spatial, chronological, importance_

4. What is a topic sentence? _Sentence containing the main idea of the paragraph_

5. What are the three ways of developing a paragraph? _Examples, details, explanations_

6. What does it mean when we say that a paragraph is coherent? _All the sentences are linked by connectors._

7. What are five ways to achieve coherence in a paragraph? _Transitions, repetition, synonyms, pronouns, reference to main idea_

8. Based on your prior knowledge, how would you describe the concept of *coherence* in a paragraph? What does the word *coherence* mean to you? What image or association comes to mind when you think of it? For example, the text uses the image of glue or tape. _Answers will vary. Possible responses: Coherence means making sense. Images include thread stitching fabric together, nails holding two-by-fours together, and rivets holding sheet metal together._

Reading: Processing Ideas

Teaching Idea
Some students mistakenly believe that effective readers can understand even difficult material quickly and retain it easily. We can help them to see that there is sometimes virtue in reading slowly.

After previewing a chapter, the next step involves active reading, in which you read the body of the text, adding to your initial understanding of the material. During active reading you may often pause to think about the author's message, sometimes backing up to reread. Complicated material requires careful reading; seldom can you sprint through a college textbook. As active readers move through a text, they interact with it, asking questions, anticipating the author's next point, agreeing or disagreeing with ideas, and linking new information to their previous knowledge.

HINT: Active reading is a deliberate, often slow process.

HINT: Active readers interact with the text.

Teaching Idea
Encouraging students to interact with an author's text is another step in moving them to interact with their own writing.

Teaching Idea
Encourage class discussion about visualizing by having students continue to add details to the park picnic scene, either orally or in writing.

Here are three useful habits to develop as you read through any text:

1. **Anticipate** and **react** to the author's points.
2. **Visualize** what the author is explaining or detailing.
3. **Link** new ideas to previous ones.

Anticipating and Reacting

When you preview a chapter, you guess at what the body of the text will assert. Then, as you read, you react to the more detailed information. For example, if an author makes an arguable statement like "The Second Amendment provides for militias, not individual gun ownership," you can tentatively agree or disagree, depending on the examples and explanations that follow. In a passage in which the author develops an extended comparison of, for example, a school to a prison, a reader might respond in several ways:

- **Uncertainty:** "What in the world does the writer mean by this comparison?"
- **Guesses:** "I wonder if he means school before college, when education is still mandatory?"
- **Disagreement/agreement:** "I don't/do see many similarities here."
- **Comprehension:** "Oh, I see. He means the teachers are like prison guards."

Experienced readers carry on a running *internal* conversation with the text, but they also sometimes express themselves *aloud*.

Remember that all writing—from the comic section of the Sunday newspaper to a calculus textbook—comes from people who are trying to communicate but not always succeeding. When writers don't communicate clearly, readers must puzzle out meaning for themselves. Interacting with a text is the most important habit you can develop to help you become a more effective reader.

Visualizing

Another active-reading technique is to visualize what the author is saying. To one degree or another, we all form images in our minds. For example, what kinds of pictures do you see in the following description of a family picnic?

The redwood table was covered with summer picnic food just right for the park: bowls of potato salad, cold pasta, baked beans, deviled eggs, sweet pickles, and potato chips. Hot dogs sizzled on the grill alongside hamburgers, soaking up flavor from smoking mesquite chips. Mom and Dad rested on the bench for a moment, sipping iced tea and gazing fondly at their three children laughing as they pushed their swings higher and higher still into the clear blue sky.

This brief paragraph includes only a few of the details we would see if we were actually there. But if we work with the writer, we can fill in others, making the scene come alive. For example, does the picnic table have a tablecloth? If so, what kind and color—possibly plastic with a red-and-white-check pattern? Maybe there are trees nearby, other families lounging on blankets in the grass, and other children climbing monkey bars and sliding down slides. Writers select details to stimulate readers' imaginations. Active readers then do most of the work themselves.

Even writers who are not purposely writing a description will include many details to illustrate their points. Active readers form pictures in their minds as key words trigger images. For example, you might read a passage like the following:

> In mid-September of 1835, the *Beagle* arrived at the Galápagos Islands, a volcanic archipelago straddling the equator 600 miles west of the coast of Ecuador.

Even though several of the words may be unfamiliar, words like *island, volcanic,* and *equator* probably create pictures in your mind. Perhaps you visualize sandy beaches and palm trees or a volcano spewing molten lava and hot gases; possibly you envision a black line circling a globe. We all form images differently, but creating vivid pictures helps us remember material—and makes reading more interesting.

Linking New to Previous Knowledge

Just as in prereading, as you read, it is crucial to connect new ideas to previous knowledge. For example, linking the *Beagle*'s arrival at the Galápagos Islands to some other event of the mid-1800s you are familiar with—say, the beginning of Queen Victoria's reign—will help you put Charles Darwin's voyage in context—an important step toward understanding. Whenever you link previous knowledge to new ideas through associations and comparisons, you help yourself understand and remember.

ACTIVITY 2.2 Developing Active-Reading Habits

This activity returns you to Chapter 3, this time to read in more depth. Turn to the pages listed for each of the three topics below. Read the material carefully, and then practice the three active-reading habits discussed previously: anticipating and reacting to the text, visualizing (creating a mental picture), and linking previous knowledge to new ideas.

EXAMPLE

Turn to page 40 and read the information on revising topic sentences.

A. Anticipate and react: *Oh, jeez, more about topic sentences. Now I'm supposed to make the topic sentence more interesting? What if I'm not even all that interested in this topic?*

B. Visualize: *When I think of a* tool, *I see hammers, saws, rakes, pliers, wrenches, drills—I just need to create a picture in my mind of my garage.*

C. Link to previous knowledge: *Specific words fall into a "more limited category" than ones like them. This makes sense to me if I think of cars in general or my own Toyota Corolla, which is more specific than hundreds of other kinds of cars.*

1. Read about examples and details versus explanations (pp. 41–42).

   A. Anticipate and react: *Possible response: This writing stuff doesn't seem so hard. Give examples and then tell about them—big deal.*

B. Visualize: _Possible response: I can picture the little girl in the bathroom, but I wouldn't have worried about her either until I heard the explanation._

C. Link to previous knowledge: _Possible response: I have had to explain myself with examples many times, like with the baseball example. I agree with the writer about boring games._

2. Read about layering examples (p. 43).

A. Anticipate and react: _Possible response: I can see how this "layering" can make my sentences grow._

B. Visualize: _Possible response: I would rather have a three-layer cake than one layer._

C. Link to previous knowledge: _Possible response: This sounds like the upside-down triangle we learned about my sophomore year in high school._

3. Read about unity (pp. 45–46).

A. Anticipate and react: _Possible response: How am I supposed to write anything that's interesting if I have to cut every little idea that isn't related to the topic sentence?_

B. Visualize: _Possible response: I can picture the woman mowing the yard, and I don't think her paragraph would be unified if she started talking about how hot and sweaty she got while mowing._

C. Link to previous knowledge: _Possible response: I've mowed my lawn enough to know what the advantages are. A disadvantage that would break the unity of the paragraph would be getting a sunburn._

Reading: Focusing and Recording Main Ideas

Knowing a few common patterns for organizing and developing ideas will make your reading easier and more efficient the first time through. Also, using a pencil and highlighter will make the material easier to review.

Here are several strategies to help focus your reading and record the information you have located:

1. **Look** for thesis, topic, and summary sentences.
2. **Focus** on primary (essential) examples.
3. **Look** for repeated material.

4. **Notice** the patterns of development.
5. **Learn** to annotate, outline, summarize, and paraphrase.

Looking for Thesis, Topic, and Summary Sentences

Thesis sentences contain the main idea of an essay; **topic sentences** contain the main idea of a paragraph. Both sentences state, "This is my topic, and this is what I'm going to say about it." Essays and textbook chapters usually have a thesis statement in the opening paragraphs. Within body paragraphs, the first or second sentence is often a topic sentence, and at the end of the paragraph, there may be a summary sentence that reiterates the main idea. Look for these sentences when you preview a text, and then concentrate on them while reading. In the following paragraph, the topic sentence is shaded. (For more on thesis, topic, and summary sentences, see pp. 294–295.)

Developing Body Paragraphs

After a writer has established a workable topic sentence, he must next move into the heart of his paragraph, the support sentences. Depending on the writer's purpose, the audience's expectations, and the topic itself, these supporting sentences might range from several to several dozen. "Twenty-four sentences!" you might think to yourself when faced with a lengthier paragraph or essay assignment. "How in the world am I ever going to fill up all that white space?" The answer is, the same way that writers have been filling up paragraphs, essays, books, and other kinds of writing since words were first pressed into wet clay. After you have declared your main point, you will illustrate it with **examples, details,** and **explanations.** These are the simple tools of the trade. And no matter how long the writing project runs, writers use the same kinds of material over and over to "fill up the space," sometimes artfully, sometimes not. In the next few pages, we will take a look at exactly what solid support is: what it consists of, how much is enough, when it is relevant, and how to be sure it is clear to your readers.

Focusing on Primary (Essential) Examples

Teaching Idea
To help students understand essential versus nonessential examples, have them read the student model "Dangers in a Deli" in Chapter 3 before and after the second-level examples were removed.

Paragraphs are built from detailed examples and explanations. However, not all of these are critical to a reader's understanding of the paragraph's main idea. Writers often use secondary examples and explanations simply to reinforce their most important points. When reading for information, you should concentrate on the primary examples and most important explanations. Don't be distracted by the less-important ones. In the paragraph above, the main points that support the topic sentence are in bold type (not unusual in a textbook). The other supporting points—the possible text length, a writer's reaction to a long project, and the reference to clay tablets—are secondary and useful primarily to develop the main idea.

Looking for Repeated Material

Textbooks in particular will repeat and elaborate important ideas, providing many examples and explanations. When you notice repeated material within a paragraph or chapter section (often highlighted in lists, charts, summaries, headings, and boxes), pay special attention; it is probably important. In the paragraph above, notice that the idea of support, in the boxed phrases, is repeated several times.

Noticing the Patterns of Development

In Chapter 1, we looked briefly at the patterns of development, which writers use to expand and clarify their ideas. While body paragraphs are usually developed with detailed examples, writers use those examples in predictable ways. For instance, in the paragraph above, we find imagined dialogue, which is a narrative element. Then the paragraph begins to tell how writers develop their ideas—the process-analysis or how-to pattern. Illustrating through examples, using vivid descriptive details, comparing things, speculating about causes and effects, defining terms—when we begin to recognize these patterns, the ideas and information contained within them become easier to understand and to recall.

Writing to Learn Exercises

Here's the main point.

No set length for a paragraph!

What does this "wet clay" reference mean?

Learning to Annotate, Outline, Summarize, and Paraphrase

Annotating and Outlining

After discovering the main points in a text, active readers often **annotate,** the process of underlining or highlighting important points and then writing marginal notes to record reactions to the material. It is common to write questions, agree/disagree with a point, express surprise, link an idea with one found elsewhere in the text, and so on. You might number examples, star passages, circle prominent facts, and connect information with arrows.

There is no one best way to annotate, but in general highlight selectively. It will not help you to focus on critical parts of the text if you highlight three-fourths of it. Less is better.

Following is an example of how our paragraph excerpt might be annotated:

Sample Annotation

After a writer has established a workable topic sentence, he must next move into the heart of his paragraph, the <u>support sentences</u>. Depending on the writer's purpose, the audience's expectations, and the topic itself, these supporting sentences <u>might range from several to several dozen</u>. "Twenty-four sentences!" you might think to yourself when faced with a lengthier paragraph or essay assignment. "How in the world am I ever going to fill up all that white space?" The answer is, the same way that writers have been filling up paragraphs, essays, books, and other kinds of writing since words were first pressed into <u>wet clay</u>. After you have declared your main point, you will illustrate it with **examples, details,** and **explanations**. These are the simple tools of the trade. And no matter how long the writing project runs, writers use the same kinds of material over and over to "fill up the space," sometimes artfully, sometimes not.

How can this be? Over and over? It's got to be more complicated than that.

Informal "scratch" outlines can also be useful for retaining information. Here is how we might outline the paragraph above:

Sample Scratch Outline

Topic sentence: After a writer has established a workable topic sentence, he must next move into the heart of his paragraph, the support sentences.

Supporting points:

1. There is no set length in paragraphs.
2. Examples, details, and explanations develop paragraphs.

Paraphrasing and Summarizing

Paraphrasing and summarizing material that you read helps you remember it because doing so requires you to put the ideas in a text into your own words. In a **paraphrase,** you retain both primary and secondary examples. Therefore, a paraphrase is longer than a **summary,** which consists only of the main idea and significant examples. Here is how the excerpted paragraph might be paraphrased or summarized:

Sample Paraphrase

The main point of this paragraph is how to develop paragraphs. The author says that paragraphs have no set length but that their size depends on what the writer wants to accomplish, what readers expect to hear, and maybe how complicated the subject is. Support sentences consist of examples, details, and explanations.

Sample Summary

This paragraph states that writers need to use examples, details, and explanations when developing paragraphs.

Teaching Idea
Paraphrasing and summarizing are critical skills, especially if you assign students a paper that requires them to use sources. Asking students to read and then summarize selected passages from the text in class will give them practice in summarizing and help them learn important concepts.

ACTIVITY 2.3 Focusing and Recording Main Ideas

Read through the paragraph excerpt below, underlining the topic sentence and any primary examples. (Remember that topic sentences are usually the first or second sentence but can be located elsewhere in a paragraph.) Next, annotate in the margins to show your reactions. Finally, write a brief scratch outline and a one-sentence summary of the paragraph.

Organizing Body Paragraphs

So far we have looked closely at the parts of a body paragraph and discussed a number of important ways to focus and develop them.

But paragraphs and essays also benefit from an overall organizational plan, and there are several methods that are useful, depending on what you want to accomplish. If your primary goal is to describe, you might choose a **spatial** method of arrangement, organizing the parts of your description from side to side, front to back, near to far, inside to out, or bottom to top. If your primary goal is to tell a story—to entertain, explain, or persuade—you would choose a **chronological** pattern, relating events as they unfold in time. If you are most interested in communicating information—telling how something works, defining an idea, giving some history—or persuading, you might select **order of importance**, that is, beginning with your least important or interesting idea and ending with the most significant. Whatever overall method you choose, keep in mind that, especially in writing longer papers, you will often combine methods. For instance, a persuasive essay with reasons primarily arranged from least to most convincing might include a story that is arranged chronologically, or the essay might need to arrange some scene spatially.

Scratch Outline

Topic sentence (main point): But paragraphs and essays also benefit from an overall organizational plan, and there are several methods that are useful, depending on what you want to accomplish.

Supporting points:
1. Spatial arrangement is good for descriptive writing.
2. Chronological order is good for narratives.
3. Order of importance is useful for informative and persuasive writing.
4. Essays often combine these methods.

Summary (one sentence): Paragraphs can be arranged by space, time, or importance.

Postreading: Retaining Ideas

Teaching Idea
You might relate postreading to the revision or editing stage of the writing process. Postreading requires patience too, but it pays off by completing the job and fixing knowledge in place.

When you finish a reading assignment, you can simply slam the book shut and move on to the next item on your to-do list, or you can take a few more minutes to review, making your future recall of the material easier. When you stop reading, keep interacting with the text by asking questions like "What do I think of the material just covered? How does it fit with my experience? Are there any special points that I agree or disagree with, any ideas or suggestions that I will use from now on or that I think are useless?" Forming opinions will help you remember important ideas.

There are many ways to review effectively, and you have probably tried some of them: silently skimming main points, stating them aloud, or organizing your thoughts on paper. Here are some specific suggestions that will help you review any reading assignment:

1. **Repeat the prereading step,** especially focusing on signposts (chapter previews and summaries, headings, and so on).

2. **Summarize or outline the main points.** This may only require pulling together the paragraph summaries you have already written or listing the main points that you underlined when you annotated.

3. **Quiz yourself** on the material as if your instructor were asking the questions. If you can't answer your own questions, you know you have to reread.

4. **Try to define any important term or idea** in a sentence of 20 words or less. Can you remember (or come up with) an example that helps to define the term or support the idea?

5. **List** what you feel are the three most important points from your reading.

Additional Links on Learning

ACTIVITY 2.4 Practicing Postreading Strategies

Using any of the five suggestions above, review Chapter 2, and then list the *essential* points about reading that you need to remember. Limit your list to 10 points.

Chapter Summary

1. There are techniques to help people read more effectively.

2. Most people can read more efficiently if they practice reading techniques.

3. Reading can be divided into three stages: prereading, reading, and postreading.

4. Interacting with the text is the most important habit a person can develop for improving comprehension and recall.

5. Three useful ways to preread are to look for signposting devices, skim beginnings and endings, and link new to previous knowledge.

6. Three habits to form while reading are to anticipate the author's points and react to them, form a mental image from points in the text, and link new to previous knowledge.

7. Four points in a text to focus on while reading are thesis, topic, and summary sentences; primary examples; repeated material; and patterns of development.

8. Four methods to help record information in a text are annotating, outlining, summarizing, and paraphrasing.

9. People who practice postreading retain more information.

10. Five ways to postread are repeating the prereading step, summarizing, self-quizzing, defining important terms, and listing important points.

Working with the Paragraph

Introducing the Paragraph

What Is a Paragraph?

Teaching Idea
You can work through parts of Chapter 3 concurrently with an assignment chapter. Also, it will be useful to return to this chapter several times as students move through Unit Two.

In the preceding photo, the three women are solving a puzzle, putting the many pieces together to make a complete picture. As a writer, you are also working on a puzzle, looking closely at the pieces that together help make your writing effective. So far we have discussed the writing and reading processes, reviewing in general how compositions grow. Now we will look more specifically at one writing unit—the paragraph—to see how it works in relation to larger units of writing.

A **paragraph** is a collection of related sentences that are clearly connected to one another and that make some point. Paragraphs come in several varieties:

- Introductory
- Body
- Concluding
- Transitional

HINT: Paragraphs usually work together.

HINT: Paragraph = focused topic, interesting development, decisive conclusion.

NOTE: To see a student model paragraph with the parts labeled, turn to pages 43–44.

Although each of these "specialty" paragraphs serves its own purpose, our focus in this chapter will be on the body paragraph. We will be developing paragraphs as a single unit of thought while remembering that paragraphs generally work together in essays. We will practice focusing a paragraph with a topic sentence; developing that main idea with specific, relevant support; and concluding the paragraph forcefully.

There is no set length for a paragraph; the kind of writing and the audience for it usually determine the number of sentences. For example, newspapers favor shorter paragraphs, whereas articles in academic journals often include paragraphs that fill a page. The paragraphs you write in Unit Two will usually run 250 to 300 words, or around fifteen sentences.

To contrast the paragraph with the essay and to get a sense of the parts of a paragraph, take a look at the following diagram:

Body Paragraph   Essay

Topic sentence = topic + statement

Body of paragraph (contains sentences to support the topic sentence):

1. Connector
2. First example, reason, or detail
3. Support for first example

1. Connector
2. Second example, reason, or detail
3. Support for second example

(Additional examples, reasons, or details as needed to develop paragraph)

Concluding sentence:
1. Connector
2. Link to topic sentence
3. Expanded thought

Introductory paragraph

Body paragraph 1

Body paragraph 2

Body paragraph 3

Concluding paragraph

The **body paragraph** has three basic parts: topic sentence, support sentences, and concluding sentence. As you can see, the essay also has an introduction and a conclusion, but they are entire paragraphs, not single sentences. Unit Two covers writing single paragraphs, but not introductory and concluding paragraphs. We will study these types of paragraphs in Unit Three.

Writing a Topic Sentence

All effective paragraphs have a **main point,** that is, some reason for their author to put that group of sentences together. In body paragraphs, writers frequently state explicitly what the paragraph will be about, and they often make this statement the first sentence. This statement is called a **topic sentence.** Topic sentences indicate the direction of the author's and the readers' mental journey. Like a compass guiding a backpacker through unfamiliar terrain, the topic sentence can help readers find their way from one end of a paragraph to the other, without taking needless detours along the way.

Consider the following sentences. Which one both limits the topic and makes a statement or expresses an opinion about it that you think the author could develop in a single paragraph?

    A. I have a brother named Jason.

    B. Many families have more than one boy.

    C. My brother Jason is a great guitarist.

Sentences A and B are simply factual observations that give the reader no sense of what else the writer might want to say about them. The reader is tempted to say, "So what?" Sentence C, on the other hand, limits the topic ("Jason") and makes a clear statement or assertion about it ("is a great guitarist") that we would expect the author to discuss further. A clearly expressed opinion or statement combined with a well-focused topic gives you and your readers the direction you need to move through the rest of the paragraph. As you begin to write topic sentences, remember the following points:

HOW TO WRITE A TOPIC SENTENCE

1. Limit the topic.

Since we are working only with paragraphs, your scope must be fairly narrow. For example, instead of trying to take on the topic of global environmental problems, you might discuss a personal commitment to recycling.

Sometimes writers list several parts of their topic in a forecasting statement like this: "If people want to begin to recycle, all they need to do is call Deffenbaugh Waste Disposal, make a bit of extra room in their garage, and be prepared to separate the 'hard' from the 'soft' trash."

2. Make a clear statement about it.

Your topic sentence should state an opinion or controlling point. For instance, don't say, "Many people recycle in the United States"—a general factual statement that could lead in many directions. Instead, express a point, like this: "I learned the hard way how important it is to recycle."

3. Use specific word choices.

Strive to make your topic sentence interesting, since it is your introduction to the rest of your paragraph. You might begin with a rough topic sentence like "My brother is a great guitarist." But by adding more specific details, you could write a far more interesting sentence, such as this one: "My brother Jason toured all last summer with Pearl Jam, playing some terrific solo riffs."

ACTIVITY 3.1 Recognizing the Parts of Topic Sentences

In the following group of topic sentences, underline the topic once and the statement being made about it twice.

Teaching Idea
If you work through Activity 3.1 in class, you might have students add an example or two to these sentences orally, warming them up for paragraph development.

EXAMPLE
My dad, Charlie Martin, had a way of making us smile in the middle of difficult situations.

1. My best friend had a horrible experience in a pawnshop last week.
2. Hot air balloon rides are fun but more dangerous than most people think.
3. "Road rage" affects people from all walks of life.
4. All day care facilities should require a state license.
5. I think cemeteries are very restful places.

Focusing Topic Sentences

Good topic sentences are broad enough to let the writer develop a subject with specific examples, explanations, and details but narrow enough to allow the subject to be covered in a paragraph. Notice how the following broad topic sentences can be narrowed:

UNFOCUSED   Most people look forward to holidays.

WORKABLE   I always look forward to spending Thanksgiving with my relatives in Dallas.

UNFOCUSED   In the fall nature slows down and prepares for winter.

WORKABLE   While much of nature slows down in the fall, squirrels seem to be in perpetual motion as they prepare for the long winter months ahead.

ACTIVITY 3.2 Focusing Topic Sentences

Revise the following topic sentences to narrow their focus. As you decide how to limit each statement, imagine that you will have to write a paragraph based on your revised topic sentence. Consider drawing on your own experiences or general knowledge to make a specific point about each topic.

Teaching Idea
In Activity 3.2 you might want to help students begin to see the distinction between paragraphs developed through personal experience versus general knowledge. Possible answers in this annotated edition for sentences 2–4 suggest development through general knowledge versus personal experience in sentences 1 and 5.

EXAMPLE
Having to stay in the hospital can be a miserable experience.

Revised and limited: _One of the most miserable experiences of my life was being hospitalized for knee surgery last June._

Answers will vary.

1. Many people enjoy rock concerts.
   Possible response: The most fun I have had at a concert was at the Rolling Stones Kansas City performance in the summer of 1973.

2. Education costs a great deal in this country.
   Possible response: Fifty dollars a credit hour is too much to charge at Johnson County Community College.

3. Computers are often used by students to word process their writing assignments.
   Possible response: Computers are especially helpful to students when they revise and edit.

4. There are many SUVs on the road today.
   Possible response: Because most SUVs are larger than passenger cars, SUVs put many drivers at risk.

5. Most people take precautions when they learn that a tornado has been sighted in their vicinity.
   Possible response: Last summer when a tornado was sighted near K-10, my wife and I began preparing the house for high winds.

Often, when you reread drafts of your paragraphs, you will see that the supporting sentences take you in a slightly different direction than what you stated in the topic sentence. Sometimes this requires deleting or modifying the supporting sentences, and sometimes it means reshaping the topic sentence.

ACTIVITY 3.3 Deducing Topic Sentences

Read each of the following groups of sentences from the body of a paragraph, state a topic that matches the given sentences, and then write a suitable topic sentence.

EXAMPLE

- Jinyi opened her first present and clapped her hands in delight.
- Her parents, brothers and sisters, and the rest of the family wished her well.
- Jinyi's mother brought the cake, with 10 candles blazing, into the room.
- Her father hugged her and whispered, "You are the best daughter a father could ever hope for."

Possible topic: _Jinyi's tenth birthday party_

Possible topic sentence: _Jinyi had a wonderful time on her tenth birthday._
Answers will vary.

1. • One major mistake new college students make is too much partying.
   - Another problem many students have is zoning out in class.
   - Whereas cramming used to cut it in high school, daily study is now required.
   - It is difficult to balance schoolwork with jobs.

Possible topic: _Problems for college students_

Possible topic sentence: _Students new to college will soon find out the pitfalls that stand in the way of their education._

2. • I never realized that marriage would have so many bumps in the road.
   - Being a good partner requires more than giving 50-50.
   - A couple must communicate daily.
   - Another important practice is regularly showing affection.

Possible topic: _Problems in marriages_

Possible topic sentence: _To help a marriage succeed, a couple must work hard at it._

3. • Dad told us to burn the leaves, and my older brother Jim thought gasoline would help.
   - After we had the leaves raked in a big pile, Jim poured on a mayonnaise jar full of gas.
   - "Go ahead and light them," he ordered me.
   - When the leaves exploded, I was knocked flat on my back.

Possible topic: <u>A story about a yard accident</u>

Possible topic sentence: <u>Following orders one day without thinking about</u>
<u>them nearly put me in the hospital.</u>

Revising Topic Sentences

A **rough topic sentence** is enough to begin a draft of your paragraph with, but why stop with "rough"? When you polish a topic sentence, you can make it more informative and interesting. One way to improve a topic sentence is to use *specific* words wherever possible. Selecting a specific word simply means choosing a word that fits into a more limited category than another, similar word.

Consider the following word lists, and decide which list includes general words and which includes words that are more specific.

A	B
tool	hammer
plant	rose bush
person	Thomas Jefferson
energy source	coal
animal	horse

You can see that the words in column B are more specific; that is, they are part of a larger group that the words in column A represent. For instance, the first word in column A, *tool*, includes the first word in column B, *hammer*, as well as such items as a screwdriver, wrench, paintbrush, shovel, and more. The more specific the word you choose, the sharper the image it creates—and the more interesting the sentence becomes.

Take a look at the following topic sentences. The first one in each pair is the rough topic sentence, and the second has been polished by adding specific words (underlined).

ROUGH TOPIC SENTENCE	My vacation didn't turn out too well.
REVISED TOPIC SENTENCE	My vacation to <u>Ft. Lauderdale</u> was a <u>disaster</u>.
ROUGH TOPIC SENTENCE	Our day care center has had a problem recently.
REVISED TOPIC SENTENCE	<u>Peppermint Patty's</u> day care has sent <u>six children</u> home this week with <u>pinkeye</u>.
ROUGH TOPIC SENTENCE	My family's table manners need some work.
REVISED TOPIC SENTENCE	<u>Elbows on the table, arms stretched across plates</u> <u>as hands reach for the salt shaker, brothers and</u> <u>sisters outshouting one another</u>—my family's table manners need some work.

(For more on specific language, see pp. 78–80, 483–484.)

Teaching Idea
Activity 3.4 introduces the concept of specific language that will be revisited in Chapter 5, Picturing a Place. You might also encourage students to add sensory details and active verbs to the topic sentences.

ACTIVITY 3.4 Polishing Topic Sentences

Rewrite the following sentences, making them more interesting by adding specific words where appropriate.

Answers will vary.

1. Rough topic sentence: I like working on my car.

   Revised topic sentence: I like working on my '66 convertible Mustang.

2. Rough topic sentence: I didn't much care for some teachers in high school.

   Revised topic sentence: The most boring teacher I had to suffer under in high school was my American history teacher, Mr. Armor.

3. Rough topic sentence: I know now why I am finally back in school.

   Revised topic sentence: After digging holes in rotten weather for too long, I'm leaving landscaping behind as soon as I finish college.

4. Rough topic sentence: My husband has to work too much.

   Revised topic sentence: Because my husband is now working 60 hours a week, our family life has suffered in many ways.

5. Rough topic sentence: Living in a new country is difficult.

   Revised topic sentence: Moving to the United States from Korea, I have faced three special challenges.

Developing Body Paragraphs

Teaching Idea
To help students understand paragraph development, ask one or two of them to say something about a vacation they have recently taken. If they reply with a laconic "awesome," you can ask what they did that was such fun, building on their responses until the vacation begins to come clear. Separating examples from supporting explanations can help students see the importance of both.

After writers establish a workable topic sentence, they must next write sentences that support it. These sentences are developed with examples, details, and explanations—the basic tools of the trade. No matter how long the writing project, we use these tools over and over to "fill up the space," sometimes artfully, sometimes not.

The next few sections explore support: what it is, how much is enough, when it is relevant, and when it is clear.

Kinds of Support

Writers support their topic sentences with specific examples, details, and explanations.

Examples

An **example** illustrates some part of a statement by showing a specific instance of it. Whenever you are asked for more information to help someone understand an idea, chances are that you will give an example. For instance, you might say to a friend, "Baseball is boring." Your friend, a baseball fanatic, immediately replies, "What do you mean by that?" When you tell her that the game lacks action, that the pitcher and the catcher have most of the fun, that half the time the infielders and outfielders are so stationary they might as well be asleep, and that you would like to see a little more body contact, like in football, you have provided a list of examples.

Personal examples are based on your own experiences. When you talk about how frustrating preschoolers can be and illustrate your point by telling about the time your 4-year-old sister locked herself in the bathroom and refused to come out for 2 hours, you are using a personal example.

Examples outside your personal experience include some of the possibilities below:

TYPES OF EXAMPLES

1. **Facts:** commonly accepted truths—for example, "Some trees lose their leaves in the fall."
2. **Statistics:** numerical facts—for example, "The earth is 93,000,000 miles from the sun."
3. **Information** gathered from print sources (books, newspapers, magazines, etc.), electronic sources (including the Internet), interviews, TV, and radio.
4. **Second-hand anecdotes:** things that happened to someone else.
5. **Comparisons,** including metaphors/similes—for example, "The flute is basically a pipe with holes drilled in it."
6. **"What-if" situations:** speculation about what could happen, such as what would happen if you decided to stop working on Fridays.
7. **Dialogue** created or reported to express a point.

Details

Just as we need examples to illustrate general statements, we need **details** to make examples more interesting. Details help sharpen an image or clarify an idea. To make the example of your little sister's locking herself in the bathroom more vivid, you could name some parts of the scene, then add **modifiers** and **sensory details:**

> My 4-year-old sister slammed the hard wooden door of the bathroom, and I heard the lock click shut. Then she shrieked at me, "I hate you!" When I tried to calm her down, she turned on both taps of the sink full blast and began flushing the toilet to drown me out.

Explanations

You can use examples to develop much of your writing, but sometimes you need more. What if the reader does not understand the example or how it relates to your point? You can offer **explanations**—reasons that justify behavior, tell how things work, anticipate possible outcomes, and more. Explanations are vital when you develop a main point because they fill in the gaps between examples and guide readers through your ideas.

Suppose a reader's reaction to the detailed example of the preschooler's behavior above is "That doesn't seem so frustrating to me. Why didn't you just walk away and forget it?" The writer would need to explain that the child was his responsibility and that it would have been too dangerous to leave her locked in a bathroom by herself, especially while she was having a tantrum.

Explanations work with details and examples to "fill up the white space." In the following paragraph, you will find three major examples to support the topic sentence, an explanation following each major example, and details throughout to make the examples and explanations more vivid for the reader.

KEY

Topic sentence

Examples

Details

Explanations

Dangers in a Deli

More frequently than people realize, there are dangers in deli work. [1.]One concern for potential deli workers is slippery floors. If the counter is packed with anxious customers, and workers are hustling about taking care of their orders, a wet floor is not going to take top priority. During the rush what's going to stop an employee from running too fast, which could result in a serious wipeout? [2.]In addition to slippery floors, working around chemicals should not be taken lightly. When cleaning the glass, you might end up with ammonia sprayed in your eyes. Both pan degreaser and sanitizer are used at dish time, and it only takes one splash in the sink to send someone on her way to the emergency room. [3.]But the part of the job that is most dangerous is using the meat and cheese slicer. Whether operating the slicer or simply cleaning it, you risk cutting yourself. With just one careless slip near the sharp blade, you could end up with one less finger. **A new person on the job might be a little nervous because of the possible injury that deli work entails, but luckily safety training is a requirement.**

Sufficient Support

Detailed examples and clear explanations are important; you must have enough of them to fully illustrate your ideas. However, all too often inexperienced writers think a topic has been fully presented when the development is thin or repetitive.

To avoid underdevelopment, fill your paragraphs with layers of specific examples: the further a reader moves into a paragraph, the more specific it should become. Each major point should be clarified with detailed examples and explanations that increasingly limit and focus the paragraph's main idea:

Relatively general → Main point (topic sentence)

First-level example + details

Second-level example + details

Relatively specific → Third-level example + details

Teaching Idea
For a closer look at this "layering" principle, refer students to the Chapter 7 prewriting suggestions. In addition to the terms *first level/second level*, you might ask students to explain a statement by answering the questions "What do you mean by that? Can you give me an example?" This technique will often open up students' ideas wonderfully.

HINT: Layer examples from general to specific.

rain and high winds. Behind me I can hear the clink of bottles and glasses from the bar, and I wonder whether I'm feeling too lazy to go get another drink. In a minute, I think. What's the rush? But maybe I ought to speed it up a bit to catch the office back home before they close. I should check the McWard portfolio this afternoon. A white seagull eyes me hopefully, standing on the sand about 10 feet away, anticipating another piece of the sandwich that I have been sharing. Other seagulls circle overhead, squabbling and attacking each other over what looks like a piece of trash. About 50 yards down the beach, I can see a young couple—newlyweds?—laughing and drawing shapes in the wet sand. Beyond them the surf is gentle, breaking softly on the flat shelf of the beach. In the distance, rocking gently in the swells, a boat heads out to sea, its red flag with white diagonal stripe flapping. I glance down at the snorkeling gear I brought and think maybe it's time for a little action, but then the bartender is standing by my chair, another glass of soda and lime in hand. "Michael," he says smiling, "how about a little refresher?" There goes my resolve. "Thanks, I think," I tell him. As I flop back onto the lounge chair, I remind myself that this is my vacation. There is a time for work and a time for rest, and a wise person knows when each is appropriate.

ACTIVITY 3.6 Determining Relevant Support

Look closely at the following paragraph and then underline any sentences that seem to stray too far from the topic sentence. In the space after the paragraph, explain why each sentence you marked does not belong.

Primary audience: American college students ages 18–22.

Teaching Idea
Activity 3.6 might generate some discussion on the relevance of the sentence about the overly competitive brother. Students can successfully argue for or against the sentence, demonstrating the need for the author to control unity by providing clear explanations.

When I was 10 years old, I used to live for baseball. Summer signaled the time school was finally over, and my friends and I could hit the park. We never wasted any time. Eight boys ranging in age from 7 to 15 met at our house for breakfast, filled up their water bottles, and headed down to the park. We almost always had it to ourselves. Of course, there was one time when the city held their Fourth of July celebration there. Down went the Frisbees to mark the bases, out came the gloves, bats, and balls, and then began the all-day games. You might think that a group of kids couldn't stay focused on anything all day, but we did. This was like our little World Series. Part of it was just love of the game; part of it was the competitive spirit. We all wanted to win. My brother was the most competitive of all of us and would fight over the strikes and the foul or fair balls. After countless innings, balls chased into the street, and blisters from swinging the bat too many times, we would call it a day. I knew that later in the evening I might sneak a quick game of basketball in with my brother in our driveway. The sun would finally set on the eight of us, sweating, dehydrated, and covered in dirt from sliding into bases and diving for grounders. Whoever had the most wins, it didn't really matter. We went home happy, knowing that the next day we could play baseball again.

1. *Of course, there was one time . . . This sentence is a clear break in the narration.*

2. *My brother was the most competitive . . . Some students will leave this in, citing the mention of competition in the previous sentence. Others will point out that the paragraph's focus is on love of the game, not winning. This discussion can help with the sometimes slippery nature of paragraph unity.*

3. *I knew that later that evening . . . This sentence, too, is a clear break in the narration.*

Clear Support

HINT: Clarity = clear explanations and precise word choices.

After revising your paragraph for sufficient, relevant, and clear support, you might think that you are home free. But there is still one more vital thing to check for—clarity. Achieving **clarity**—explaining examples, reasons, and word choices completely—is essential if readers are to fully understand your paragraph. One of the surest ways to check for clarity is to imagine a specific audience reading your work so that you can anticipate and answer their questions.

For example, in the baseball paragraph from Activity 3.6, there are several words, phrases, and ideas that might puzzle someone unfamiliar with American culture. Consider the phrase "my friends and I could hit the park." This is an idiomatic expression that native speakers understand but that could easily be misinterpreted. (Why would young people want to beat the ground at the park?) In the next sentence, even audience members who are familiar with American culture might wonder about 7-year-olds playing baseball with 15-year-olds. Are the ages accurate; is any more explanation needed here? The stated audience would not have any difficulty with words and phrases like *Fourth of July, Frisbees, World Series, foul or fair balls, strikes, sliding into bases,* and *diving for grounders,* but other readers might.

HINT: Role-playing your audience can help with clarity.

As you reread your work, checking for clarity, try to role-play your audience. And as other readers give you input, ask these questions frequently: "Do you understand all of my ideas? Are my examples and explanations clear? Do any of the words puzzle you or seem to need further explaining?"

ACTIVITY 3.7 Achieving Clarity in Word Choices

Teaching Idea
Activity 3.7 is oriented toward process instruction and is a good one to revisit if you teach the process analysis chapters. Audience is, of course, especially important in process instructions.

As you read the following paragraphs, think about the audience and what they might know; then underline any word or phrase that might need additional explanation.

EXAMPLE
Audience: 12-year-olds learning about fly-fishing

First you must select the proper fly for the weather and water conditions. I would suggest a <u>dry</u> fly number 12, perhaps a Royal Wulff. Your leader should be <u>tapered</u>, with <u>no more than a 3X tippet</u>, and you must be particularly careful using the <u>improved clinch knot</u> with which you will attach the fly to the tippet.

An Oak Deeply Rooted—or a Tumbleweed?

Many people would define the ideal life as one in which they can live where they want to, when they want to. The Midwest appeals to people from all over the country who want housing that is still affordable, a small city with lots of green spaces, and an environment that is relatively low in crime. But when summer comes, people head for the mountains in droves. In an ideal situation a couple would have a small, well-furnished cabin in a rugged mountain chain like the Rockies and spend time there from July through September. They could spend time backpacking, fishing the lakes and streams, rafting the rivers, horseback riding, and mountain biking. However, mountain winters are rugged, so there comes a time when many people feel the most desirable destination is the beach. In January, when the temperatures in the middle and northern part of the country are dipping well below zero, in a mass exodus, winter-shy crowds head for the southern rim of our country and beyond. And why not? Who wants to bundle up in four layers of clothes and a down coat just to waddle outside to check the mail? Beach residents can look forward to sailing, motorboating, jet skiing, windsurfing, fishing, snorkeling, diving, and strolling along the beach. Aside from the gentler weather and fun activities, it seems easier to find large groups of like-minded people of various ages to socialize with. _____

_____

HINT: Any of the possible concluding sentences could be inserted here.

Teaching Idea
Students often have difficulty articulating the implications of their own ideas. To prepare students for their later work with concluding paragraphs, introduce the notion of the expanded thought in a concluding sentence and help students see that there are many ways to carry their main point one step further at the end of their papers.

POSSIBLE CONCLUDING SENTENCES

A. It would be fun to have the freedom and money to live wherever a person wanted to, and it is a shame that more people in this affluent country of ours can't do it.

B. But if people want this kind of lifestyle, they need to work hard and save so they can earn it.

C. With so many places to visit and new experiences awaiting us, who wouldn't want to travel the country as the seasons turn?

D. In the long run, although it would be wonderful to have the freedom and the money to move from place to place, attitude and health probably count more than wherever people live.

E. But even with the opportunities for fun that multiple homes could bring, I think I would miss my friends and family too much to stay away from my *home* home too long.

F. So, if you like this vision of a future, be sure to take it easy while you're young, don't work too hard, don't worry about an education that will lift you upward, and by all means max out those credit cards today—you'll be living the ideal life before you know it.

HINT: Try several concluding sentences to end your draft.

Any of these possible conclusions could be the "right" way to end this paragraph. You might try several possible endings as you revise your drafts, searching for the one that seems to best fit your topic, purpose, audience, and tone (humorous, serious, sad, angry, and so on).

ACTIVITY 3.9 Selecting Concluding Sentences

In the following three sets of sentences, you will find a topic sentence and three concluding sentences. Circle the letter of the one you feel is the strongest closing sentence, and in the space provided, explain why you think it works best.

1. Topic sentence: Whenever I close my eyes trying to remember the "good old days," the first thing that comes to mind is my friends calling me scaredy-cat.

    Possible concluding sentences:

    A. I have a career goal today, which I am close to achieving, of becoming a travel agent.
    B. Several of my childhood friends are currently in jail.
    C. Although I wouldn't want to relive these childhood experiences, they have helped me become more sensitive to other people's fears and insecurities.

    Sentence C: This sentence uses a connector, links with the topic sentence, and expands the main thought.

2. Topic sentence: I was 15 years old and had never before lost a tae kwon do tournament, but this St. Louis match was a big one, and I was a little worried.

    Possible concluding sentences:

    A. With only 5 seconds left, my opponent's parents began to cheer with tears in their eyes.
    B. But losing this tournament helped me to see that there will always be someone better, so I should never stop learning and practicing what is important to me.
    C. Martial arts are a good way to stay in shape if you are willing to spend the time at them.

    Sentence B: This sentence uses a connector, links with the topic sentence, and expands the main thought.

3. Topic sentence: So, as my life in America began, I was surprised at the great difference between Korean high school and American high school.

    Possible concluding sentences:

    A. Though I miss my home and friends, I'm glad that I was able to experience the freedom I found in my American high school.
    B. In Korea, I had no choice; there was a required academic program that couldn't be disputed by the students.

the writer has written. In your own work, you should become aware of the devices listed below, which will help your writing "stick together":

METHODS FOR ACHIEVING COHERENCE
1. Transitions
2. Repetition
3. Synonyms
4. Pronouns
5. Reference to a main idea

Teaching Idea
It can be a bit misleading to refer to all the methods for linking sentences as transitions (although they certainly function this way). You may find the term *connectors* useful when referring to the five methods listed in *AWW*.

Transitions

Transitions (also called "connectors" in this text) are the most common method writers use to create coherence. Transitional words and phrases guide a reader through your writing like street signs help you to find your way in a city. Table 3.1 lists common transitions.

TABLE 3.1 Common Transitions

FOR LOCATING OR MOVING IN SPACE (PARTICULARLY USEFUL IN DESCRIPTIVE WRITING)			
above	east (west, etc.)	inside	over
against	elsewhere	in the distance	surrounded by
alongside	far off (away)	into	there
around	farther on	near	through
at the side (end)	forward	next to	to
backward	from	off	to the right (left)
behind	here (close to here)	on	under
below	in	on the other side	up
beyond	in back	onto	upstairs
by	in between	opposite	
down	in front of	out of	

FOR MOVING IN TIME (PARTICULARLY USEFUL IN NARRATIVE WRITING)			
after	first (second, etc.)	next	suddenly
afterward	immediately	now	then
at last	in the meantime	often	time passed
awhile	in the past	once	until
before	later	previously	when
earlier	long ago	recently	while
finally	meanwhile	soon	

All References to Calendar Time and Calendar Events

ago (days, weeks, months, years)

one day (days of the week, months of the year, seasons, holidays)

that morning (afternoon, evening)

today (tonight, yesterday, tomorrow)

All References to Clock Time

any clock numbers used with A.M./P.M. (12:00 A.M., 1:00 P.M., etc.)

a few minutes (seconds, hours)

All References to Regular Meals

during breakfast (brunch, lunch, dinner)

FOR ADDING MATERIAL (PARTICULARLY USEFUL IN WRITING THAT EXPLAINS HOW SOMETHING WORKS)			
again	as well as	furthermore	likewise
also	besides	in addition	moreover
and	further	last	next

FOR GIVING EXAMPLES AND EMPHASIS (PARTICULARLY USEFUL IN EXPLANATORY AND PERSUASIVE WRITING)			
above all	especially	in particular	one reason
after all	for example	in truth	specifically
another	for instance	it is true	surely
as an example	indeed	most important	that is
certainly	in fact	of course	to illustrate

FOR COMPARING (PARTICULARLY USEFUL IN WRITING THAT FOCUSES ON SIMILARITIES AND DIFFERENCES)			
alike	both	like	resembling
also	in the same way	likewise	similarly

FOR CONTRASTING (PARTICULARLY USEFUL IN WRITING THAT FOCUSES ON SIMILARITIES AND DIFFERENCES)			
after all	dissimilar	nevertheless	still
although	even though	on the contrary	though
but	however	on the other hand	unlike
differs from	in contrast	otherwise	whereas
difference	in spite of		yet

FOR SHOWING CAUSE AND EFFECT (PARTICULARLY USEFUL IN EXPLANATORY AND PERSUASIVE WRITING)			
accordingly	because	hence	then
and so	consequently	since	therefore
as a result	for this reason	so	thus

employees that <u>Bill</u>'s office project would be handled quickly and that <u>Bill</u> would be back on the front line with his co-workers before they knew it.

If version A seems difficult to understand, you might notice the overuse of *his.* Pronoun reference becomes especially tricky when a pronoun could be referring to several different nouns, as is the case with Bill and Jim. A good general rule when revising for both coherence and clarity is to check pronouns several times to be sure the noun they refer to will be clear to your readers. (For more on pronoun reference problems, see pp. 582–584.)

ACTIVITY 3.13 Achieving Coherence through Pronouns

Teaching Idea
Activity 3.13 will help students see the importance of clarity, and also tone, in pronoun reference. The reference errors (head removed, put the mother down?) seem laughable, damaging the author's serious, sad tone.

In the following paragraph excerpt, cross out unneeded or confusing pronouns, and write in the replacement words in the line above.

Smokey lived with me for $8\frac{1}{2}$ years and was my good friend. But then she contracted a feline virus comparable to AIDS in humans. During the time she was sick, she also got cancer, which caused a lump on her neck just behind her head. We had ~~it~~ *the lump* removed once in hopes that ~~it~~ *the operation* would save her life, but instead ~~it~~ *the lump* came back. When it returned, it was twice as big as ~~it had been~~ *before*, and ~~it~~ only took half the time to form. My mother and I decided that it would be best to put ~~her~~ *Smokey* down. It was the hardest decision of my life, but I loved ~~her~~ *my cat* too much to see her in such pain.

Reference to Main Ideas

You can also achieve coherence within and between paragraphs by linking main ideas or examples. For instance, notice how the following paragraph excerpt begins to develop the idea of *merciless teachers* in the topic sentence, continues with the synonym *cruel,* and reinforces the idea of cruelty with the word *punish.*

As I think back on middle school in Korea, I remember that I was afraid of the <u>merciless</u> teachers who wanted me to enjoy studying by forcing it on me. One of my teachers, for moral education, was short and fat, just like the whip he carried. "I see you haven't done your homework, Jeong," he said. With my palms up, he began to whip my hands harshly. Somehow the pain ended with me crying and begging, "I will do it next time, teacher!" Another <u>cruel</u> man, my history teacher, liked to use his green baby bamboo stick to <u>punish</u> me when I didn't score more than 80 percent on his exams.

Effective writers rely on all five methods we have discussed—transitions, repetition, synonyms, pronouns, and references to the main idea—to achieve coherence, often using several in the same sentence.

Selecting a Title

Teaching Idea
During their final revising sessions, you might have students review the pointers on writing effective titles and then compare theirs. Next, have several students read their titles aloud to get some feedback from the class and from you.

HINT: You may find a good title in a phrase or sentence in your draft.

With your paper almost finished, it is time to expend one last bit of creative energy—choosing a title. But why do you need one in the first place? Especially if your paper is short, why not let the reader just jump right in? Think for a moment about all the writing you have read over the years—books, stories, poems, newspaper and magazine articles—and the television programs and movies you have seen. How many did not have a title? If professional writers give a great deal of thought to titling their work, they must have a good reason for doing so.

A title's primary purpose is to attract readers. In "real-world" writing, authors are competing for their readers' attention, time, and money, so any device that increases the authors' chances of success is welcome. You, too, are competing for your audience's attention. Whether you are working on a personal project, a business proposal, or a paper for a professor, including a title captures your readers' interest and sets up a positive expectation.

As you draft, be alert to any image or phrase that might make a good title. If nothing seems promising, brainstorm alone or with others when the paper is complete. Whenever you create your title, remember that it should accomplish two goals: interest readers and indicate your slant on the topic.

If you had to choose one of the following papers to read on the basis of the title, which would most interest you?

1. A profile of a hard-working mother:
   A. "My Mom the Worker"
   B. "She Kept the Ship Afloat"
2. A story about a child sneaking one too many cookies:
   A. "Children Should Mind Their Parents"
   B. "Slamming the Lid on Andrew"
3. A personal narrative about a serious accident:
   A. "A Bad Wreck"
   B. "Crawling through the Wreckage"

In each case, version B is more vivid and inviting. The following suggestions will help you create titles that are more like them:

HOW TO WRITE EFFECTIVE TITLES

1. Keep titles short (roughly 1 to 8 words). People can read and process a shorter title more efficiently than a longer one. Readers confronted with a long title may think that the paper to follow will also be hard work.
2. Link the title to your main idea or dominant impression.
3. Create an image:
   A. Use a metaphor or other comparison. Notice the first title example above. What do you suppose "the ship" refers to? (For more on metaphors, see pp. 505–506.)
   B. Use specific words, sensory details, active verbs, and words with *-ing* endings. Notice that the second and third title examples use *-ing* words to convey action. (For more on action words ending in *-ing*, see p. 66.)

3. **Are you choosing "active" verbs to describe action?**

Verbs show action or states of being. Verbs that show action are usually a better choice than more "static" verbs (*be, do, have,* and *make* are common culprits). Compare the following two sentences. Which creates the sharper image in your mind?

 A. The children <u>are having</u> a good time bowling.

 B. The small children <u>are jumping, clapping, and screaming</u> as their balls <u>hit</u> the pins.

Revise your own sentences to add active verbs wherever they are needed. (For more on active verbs, see p. 516.)

4. **Are you using any *-ing* words?**

Present participles (verb forms with an *-ing* ending) can also convey action. Compare the following two sentences. Which creates the sharper image in your mind?

 A. I can hear the trees move.

 B. I can hear the leaves <u>rustling</u> and branches <u>brushing</u> against each other.

Revise your own sentences, adding *-ing* words wherever they are needed. (For more on *-ing* words, see Chapter 23.)

5. **Are the sentences in your paragraph varied in length?**

Your writing can be more interesting when you vary the length of your sentences. After polishing word choices, count the words in each sentence. If you find that more than three or four sentences in a row are roughly the same length (say, 14, 17, 12, and 15 words), either combine two of them or divide a longer one. (For more on overall sentence variety, see Chapter 18.)

6. **Are the beginnings of your sentences varied?**

If even two sentences in a row in your draft begin with the same word, such as *the,* you might need to change an opening or combine sentences to break up the pattern. Also look for too many similar openings, even if the sentences are not together. (For more on variety in sentence openers, see Chapter 18.)

7. **Have you repeated a word or phrase so often that it becomes noticeable?**

While some repetition is fine, too much becomes boring. Compare the following sentences. Which sounds repetitive?

 A. I like to spend time at the <u>pond</u> because the <u>pond</u> is a relaxing place. Of all the <u>ponds</u> I have visited in the last 20 years, this <u>pond</u> is the one that will forever live in my memory.

 B. I like to spend time outdoors in relaxing surroundings, and there is one <u>place</u> in particular that I enjoy. Of all the <u>ponds</u> I have visited in the last 20 years, this is the <u>one</u> that will forever live in my memory.

Revise your own sentences to cut or replace words that are repeated too often. (For more on unnecessary repetition, see pp. 510–511.)

8. **Have you included words that serve no purpose?**

Everyday speech is full of nonessential words, but writing should not be. Cluttered writing can bore and confuse, whereas concise writing involves readers and clarifies ideas. Compare the following two sentences. Which is concise, and which cluttered?

A. The meat hotdogs, long and thin, sizzle with a sizzling sound as they cook, roasting, and drip meaty hotdog juices off the end of the wooden stick.

B. The hotdogs sizzle as they cook and drip juices off the end of the stick.

Revise your own sentences to cut nonessential words. (For more on unneeded words, see pp. 487–495.)

Teaching Idea
Given half a chance, students will reply to revision questions with vague statements or simply fall back on revising for mechanics. Journal Entry 4.2 again asks for specifics and will be most useful if student responses are discussed in class and then collected for review.

> ## JOURNAL ENTRY 4.2 (Continues Journal Entries from Assignment Chapters 5–11)
>
> To help you focus on revision and alert your instructor to your progress, list three *specific* changes you have made or feel you ought to make to your second draft. Refer to the second-stage draft questions, answering them specifically. (Example: Question 4: "I noticed that although I am describing people in a restaurant, I hadn't used any *-ing* words, so I found a good place for these in my fourth and eighth sentences.") Next, in several sentences state what you like best about your draft so far.

Editing

Like many students you might be tempted to hurry through the editing stage. This impulse is understandable—it is often a long journey from brainstorming to final draft. Writers can stumble at the end of this journey, much like the overexcited backpacker who has survived uninjured in the mountains for a week and a half, and who, seeing the lodge just down the trail, trips and sprains her ankle.

Of course, aside from being overanxious to complete the writing excursion, you often don't know what to look for in your final draft. After all, if you don't know the rule that tells you where to put the comma, how are you supposed to recognize the spot where the comma is missing?

Well . . . it would be great if there were a quick fix for grammar, spelling, and punctuation errors, but the simple truth is that you will be grappling with them for a long time. All writers do. But it may help to remember that the mechanics of writing are truly the least important element (though still significant). And even if you are not a "comma whiz," you can quickly catch many mistakes if you are willing to read your work *slooowly* and carefully.

The following paragraphs have a number of these common mechanical errors:

Correction Symbols

COMMON ERRORS
- Misspelled words
- Sound-alike words
- Missing words
- Wrong words
- Sentence fragments
- Comma splices
- Run-on sentences
- Faulty capitalizations
- Incorrect apostrophes
- Missing commas
- Unneeded commas
- Faulty pronoun reference
- Faulty pronoun agreement
- Verb tense shifts

HINT: Editing these practice paragraphs will help you with your own revision.

HINT: To edit your work effectively, slow your reading to a crawl.

Teaching Idea
These editing review paragraphs can be especially useful if reviewed on a day when students are preparing to edit their own papers.

Test your editing skills by reading through each paragraph slowly, putting a finger on every word if necessary, to see how many mistakes you catch.

Editing Review

1. As I glance down at the windowsill I often, think, about the many dead insects, lying their one can only assume that the bugs want there last moments alive too be my porch. Its small body makes quite a feast, for the two Barn Spiders that share my porch with me. The webs' are always filled with one delicacy, or anothr, one spider, in particular has, woven quite a spectacular web, against the old, paint-chipped corner. While I am inhaling, my first cup of morning fuel. A magnificent gust of wind blows thru. The sweet smell my neighbors freshly cut grass fills the air so flagrantly, that I can barely notice the thick humidity building for the day ahead.

    (To see the corrected version of this excerpt, turn to p. 92 and look at the first half of "Waking Up the Right Way.")

2. When I went to Middle School in korea. I was afraid of sevral merciles teachers, who seemed too want me to enjoy studying forcing it on me. My Moral Education Teacher was one of these crule educators, he was short, and fat like the whip he carried to enforce there every whim. "I see you have'nt done your homework Jeong", he would say. He orders me to hold my palms up and, then he begins to whip my hands harshly.

    (To see the corrected version of this excerpt, turn to p. 150 and look at the beginning of "Teaching with Whips.")

3. Panick and fustration our a sure fire recipe, for tears but I fought them of and strugled too remain calm, for my girls. Suddenly I hear a voice, say "Listen I have a cell phone, do you want to call someone to come pick you up". As I turned toward the voice I saw an older gentleman, who looked a lot like my dad. Begining to cry I explained how helples I felt.

    (To see the corrected version of this excerpt, turn to p. 136 and look at the middle of "Do Unto Others . . .")

4. In order too help customers shop more efficiently, in Toys "R" Us, the store is divided into three overrall categories: areas for older children, toddlers, and babies. The older chidren have four major areas. Blue, Pink, R-Zone, and Silver piles of toys for everyone. Boys mostly head for the blue section, and items like the GI Joe's Hotwheel's and Lego's. In no time, at all, the boys can have Lego race tracks assembled, on he floor, and be racing miniature batmobiles after the "bad guys."

(To see the corrected version of this excerpt, turn to p. 180 and look at the beginning of "Shopping the Easy Way.")

5. Marrying, while still teenagers, can be a bad decision creating many problems for young couples. First when teens marry in or just out of high-school. They're relationships often change drasticaly instead of spending with there individual former friends newlyweds often find that that there spouse did not like some or all of the others friends' so the husband, or wife has to chose—"them or me."

    (To see the corrected version of this excerpt, turn to p. 203 and look at the beginning of "Making the Promise Last.")

6. Living in the country as a child a sling shot is what I longed for to play, and hunt with and finally decided would make one. Collecting the materials' for my treasure through did not come eazy. It recquired the most perfect forked branch form a Pine tree. A square of leather to hold the stone and a peice of rubber band. Any old rubberband will not do, though, it has too be surgical tubing light brown, and hose shaped, for the power I wanted.

    (To see the corrected version of this excerpt, turn to p. 229 and look at the beginning of "A Boy's Best Friend.")

7. Raisin hell, and living for the moment where all I use to care about but now that Im moving in my thirties life has change. When I was just entering, my twenties, I was still living at home. Although you never would have known it, by the way I come and go, telling none any thing. But, I have come along way sense then.

    (To see the corrected version of this excerpt, turn to p. 256 and look at the beginning of "Breakin' Through.")

Well, how did you do? If you caught all but two or three errors in any paragraph, congratulations; you are a careful editor! If you missed more than five or six, try to slow down even more. The following are a few reminders of errors to look for in your own draft.

Problems to Watch for When Editing

The following list will help you edit your paragraphs for problems with spelling, word choice, grammar, and punctuation.

1. **Spelling errors:** Use your computer's spell checker first, and then try to find at least one other reader who is a fairly good speller. Remember, too, to consult a good dictionary. (For help with spelling problems, see Chapter 27.)

2. **Sound-alike words:** A common example is using *there* for *their* or *they're*. Keep adding soundalike words that cause you problems to your Improvement Chart (Appendix 2), and try to memorize these repeat errors. Writers usually keep making the same handful of mistakes—unless they identify and correct them—till doomsday. (For help with sound-alike words, see Chapter 27.)

3. **Missing words:** Read slowly to detect these errors. Sometimes reading each sentence backwards—though tedious—can help, and covering the sentence ahead of the one you are editing can keep you from jumping ahead too quickly.

4. **Wrong words:** Be suspicious of words that sound too fancy. If you often thumb through a thesaurus looking for words, you might be using the words incorrectly. You probably already know words that express your meaning well, and smaller, more common words are usually the best choices. Your readers can help by alerting you to words you may be using incorrectly, and then you can use a dictionary to decide. (For more on achieving clarity by using small words, see pp. 497–499.)

5. **Sentence fragments:** Remember two common types of incomplete sentences:

PHRASE FRAGMENT	Running to the store for bread and a six-pack of Coke. (The word group lacks a subject and a verb and is not a complete thought.)
SUBORDINATE CLAUSE FRAGMENT	Because he is the kind of man we want for mayor. (The word group has a subject and verb, but the subordinating word *because* makes it an incomplete thought.)

   You can correct most fragments by joining them to another sentence or adding words to make them complete sentences. (See pp. 555–560.)

6. **Comma splices/run-ons:** These errors happen when two sentences are joined incorrectly with only a comma or with no punctuation at all:

COMMA SPLICE	The cement is freezing, it instantly numbs my feet.
RUN-ON	The cement is freezing it instantly numbs my feet.

   There are at least five easy ways to fix these errors. (See pp. 548–554.)

   > **Note:** In dialogue, be careful to avoid this kind of comma splice:
   >
   > Roxanne shouted, "Get out of here, nobody gives a damn about you anyway!"
   >
   > Instead write:
   >
   > Roxanne shouted, "Get out of here! Nobody gives a damn about you anyway!"
   >
   > People often speak in short sentences and fragments. Don't be afraid to use this kind of sentence in your dialogue.

7. **Capitalization:** Capitalize each proper noun (a specific/unique person, place, or thing; see Chapter 26). In your titles capitalize most words, even little ones like *is* and *one*. But do not capitalize articles

Teaching Idea
If you have students edit in class, it is useful to list the three major comma categories on the board along with some "cue" words: *because, who/which, and/but.* You will also find selected editing review sheets in the Instructor's Manual.

(*a, an, the*), prepositions (*to, on, of, in,* etc.), and coordinating conjunctions (*and, but, so,* etc.) unless these words begin or end a title or follow a colon.

8. **Apostrophes:** Use to show ownership or to mark the omission of a letter in a contraction: "Maria's calculator isn't working." (See Chapter 26.)

9. **The Big Three comma categories:** These categories govern perhaps half the common uses of the comma:

   A. Use commas to introduce single words, phrases, and subordinate adverb clauses before a main clause (cue words: *because, as, if, when,* etc.). (See Chapter 26.)

      EXAMPLE   If I finish my paper early, I will watch *The Matrix Reloaded.*

   B. Use commas to enclose nonessential words, phrases, or clauses within a main clause or to set them off at the end of a main clause (cue words: *who/which,* etc.). (See Chapter 26.)

      EXAMPLE   *The Matrix Reloaded,* which continues *The Matrix,* uses more computer animation and special camera effects than the first film.

   C. Use commas to divide main clauses joined by *and, but, or, so, yet, for,* or *nor.* (See Chapter 26.)

      EXAMPLE   Neo gains more powers in this sequel, and he uses them outside of the Matrix against the machines.

10. **Unnecessary commas:** As you learn the handful of rules that help with comma placement, you will move away from the old standby: "I put commas where I hear pauses." Using your ear helps with punctuation— but only about half the time. Most of us don't want a 50 percent average, so learning a few rules is the way to go. Try to avoid unneeded commas such as those in the following examples:

    INCORRECT   I went to Burger King for lunch, and then to McDonald's for dinner. (Your ear might tell you to pause, but a comma is not needed unless the two word groups you are joining with *and* are complete sentences.)

    CORRECT   I went to Burger King for lunch and then to McDonald's for dinner.

    INCORRECT   I eat three 13-ounce bags of potato chips every day, because I want to have a heart attack. (You might naturally pause before *because,* but it begins an essential clause that explains *why* this person eats so foolishly and so should not be set off with a comma.)

    CORRECT   I eat three 13-ounce bags of potato chips every day because I want to have a heart attack.

    (See Chapter 26 for more on finding, and correcting, unnecessary commas.)

11. **Faulty pronoun reference and agreement:** Pronouns must refer to a specific noun, and they must agree with that noun in number:

    REFERENCE ERROR   Florence was talking to Abby when *she* saw the accident. (Clarify *she* reference: *she* = Abby.)

    AGREEMENT ERROR   *Each* of the players want a raise. (*All . . .* want . . .)

    (For more on pronoun problems, see Chapter 26.)

Sample Paper (No Title Page)

1/2 inch

1 inch

Gwin 1

Double-space
heading and
paragraph.

Terry Gwin

Professor Brannan

Composition 100, Section 37

September 28, 2004

Title centered
No underline
No quotation marks

Death Strikes

1 inch

1 inch

  There were many people in the water waiting to put their boats on their trailers at Hillside Lake on that tragic July afternoon. I felt hot and sticky waiting on the lake, frantically maneuvering my small aluminum boat closer to the ramp, but I knew my turn was still a long way away. Slowly, ominous black clouds that had been building on the horizon rolled closer and closer. Thunder shook the huge lake as if it were a glass of water, vibrating, nearly ready to fall off some gigantic rock and shatter on the ground. Suddenly, the sky began to pour, as if someone had opened a faucet. I remember looking at the old man in the boat next to me and how his head turned so quickly. I can remember hearing a high-pitched hum, like a camera flash charging up. Quickly, instinctively, I jerked my head around to my left toward the shore and saw the massive bolt of lightning fly down from the sky into a man's chest. He arched his back and was thrown into the water. The lightning hit him as though a refrigerator had been dropped on him. He was only thirty-three years old, and he died right in front of me, a sight that will stay in my memory, like a stain, forever. Death can strike anyone at any time, and I know now that eighteen does not mean immortal.

at least 1-inch margin

JOURNAL ENTRY 4.4 (Continues Journal Entries for Assignment Chapters 5–11)

Reflecting for a moment on the work you did in and out of class to produce this paragraph, take 5 minutes to write a paragraph telling your instructor about what challenges you had to overcome, how you dealt with them, and what strategies you think might be most important to apply to your upcoming writing assignments this semester.

CHAPTER 5

Picturing a Place

What Are We Trying to Achieve and Why?

Setting the Stage

When you look closely at the picture on the opposite page, what do you notice? A family is celebrating Kwanzaa, smiling happily and applauding the young girl who has perhaps just performed for them. What feelings come to you as you observe this family? If you had to sum up this picture in a few words, what would they be? If you said "happiness" or "comfort" or "family togetherness," you have just identified a **dominant impression** and gotten to the heart of this chapter on description.

Describing is the process of relating details to help another person see what we have seen. It is the act of painting a picture with words. But good descriptions do more than just give readers a picture of a scene; they use the other senses (hearing, touch, taste, smell) to involve the audience more completely. When we provide (and listen to) descriptions that offer unique points of view on a subject—subjective descriptions—we enrich our lives, communicating personal experiences and extending the boundaries of what we can know through our senses alone.

In this chapter, we will learn about describing in general and about describing a place in particular.

Linking to Previous Experience

What describing have you done in the past—how about vacations, skiing perhaps. What did the mountains look like? How much snow fell while you were there; was there a deep base? What were the temperatures? How crowded were the lift lines? If you have not been on a vacation for a while, when was the last time you described a scene or an individual closer to home? Perhaps you have detailed another person's clothing to a friend or described your child for an acquaintance who also has a youngster in your preschool. Perhaps you have tried to create a favorable image of that "blind date" you were trying to persuade your friend to go on. We describe daily, and being able to do it well is a useful skill.

Determining the Value of Description

Besides being part of our social lives, descriptive skills make us better readers and improve our writing at work, home, and school. But even more valuable is developing the ability to observe our surroundings closely. By the time you have worked through the activities in this chapter, analyzed the model paragraphs, taken notes for your own descriptions, and workshopped drafts, you will find yourself noticing more of the world around you—and seeing it more clearly.

Teaching Idea
Journal Entry 5.1 can get students talking about description as they use it in their own lives and can be done in class on the day that you introduce this chapter.

JOURNAL ENTRY 5.1

Name three things, people, or places you have described recently (e.g., a new car, a friend, or a workplace). Briefly develop one of those descriptions for your instructor. What value do you see in being able to describe well?

Developing Skills and Exploring Ideas in Descriptive Paragraphs

Teaching Idea
This chapter introduces several concepts crucial for developing students' writing: specific and concrete words and sensory details.

To understand more fully the composition concepts from Chapters 1 and 3 and to use them in our own descriptions of places, we will practice the following:

1. Using specific, concrete language
2. Using the five senses
3. Establishing and strengthening the dominant impression
4. Organizing the description by using a spatial arrangement
5. Locating the reader in space and time

Using Specific, Concrete Language

To create effective descriptions, writers should understand the concept of **general versus specific language.** (For more on this, see p. 40.) If you make a relatively general statement (e.g., in a topic sentence), you should support it by using the most specific words you know. Specific language will help you create vivid images. The larger the group—or category—that contains a word, the more

HINT: Use specific words to build images.

general the word is. And, conversely, the smaller the group, the more specific the word is—as shown by the nested circles below:

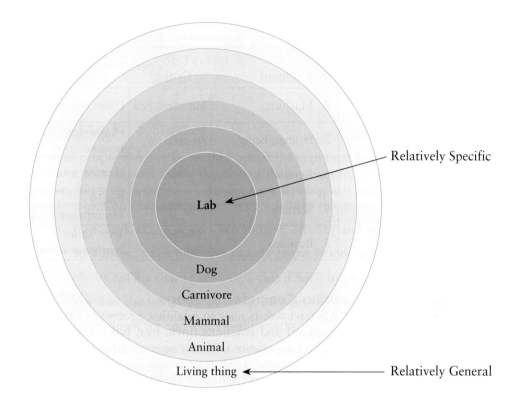

The same concept is illustrated by the Language Line below:

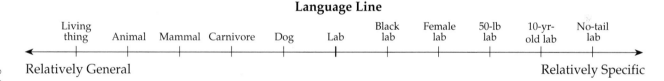

You will probably notice that as we move along the Language Line, choosing more specific nouns, the group the word belongs to shrinks, in the process creating an image. To make the image even sharper, you can add details (modifiers such as *small* and *old*). Using concrete, specific words results in a fairly clear picture of a small old black lab missing her tail. We could probably pick this dog out of a group of other dogs running in a park, and she is a far cry from the opposite end of the spectrum (a "living thing"). You can easily apply this process of narrowing the category to your own descriptions.

ACTIVITY 5.1 Narrowing the Category

For each of the five words in column I on page 80, select a more specific word for column II and an even more specific word for column III, and then add two modifiers to the words in column IV.

Teaching Idea
The Language Line works well for many words, particularly nouns. You might draw the line on the board, have the class suggest a word, and then have them help you develop the word. Try having students begin by making the word more general.

you removed all the sensory details, would this description be less interesting to you?

> Jumping feet first off the gently rolling boat, the salty taste of seawater in my mouth, I feel the warm Caribbean waters close over my head. Sinking slowly in a swirl of frothy silver bubbles, I look back up to the surface to see the dark hull of the dive boat steadily receding. Beneath me broken shafts of sunlight filter past the tips of my black fins as I kick back and forth, keeping the descent under control. At 30 feet I begin to kick harder and inflate my BC, the sudden sound of compressed air rushing past my ear. Another 10, 20, 30 feet, and there I hover, weightless, over the plateau. Spread out to 100 feet in all directions, green and purple sea fans bend gently in the mild surge as rainbow-colored parrotfish graze on the reef, the sound of their teeth grinding chunks of coral audible even under 60 feet of water.

Teaching Idea
To supplement Activity 5.3 by showing cluttered writing, have students write two or three sentences that include as many sensory details as they can cram in. Then have them trim the sentences back so they are effective.

Sensory Chart

Sight	Sound	Touch	Smell	Taste
Boat	Compressed air	Warm water	None	Salty
Silver bubbles	Teeth grinding	Sinking		
Shafts of sun		Weightless		
Black fins		Rolling		
Green and purple sea fans				
Rainbow-colored parrotfish				

CAUTION! Too many sensory details can be too much of a good thing.

Note: The point of using sensory details is not to cram as many into a paper as possible, or even to represent all five senses, but rather to use these details selectively wherever they can enhance an image.

ACTIVITY 5.4 Using the Five Senses

Brainstorm sensory details for one of the following places. Be alert to any details that might help show a central focus or dominant impression/feeling. Don't be surprised if you come up with more details under sight and sound than any other sense.

Answers will vary.

1. Cafeteria at lunch hour (dominant impression: activity/fast pace, maybe even confusion or chaos!)

2. Church wedding (dominant impression: excitement/happiness, maybe even communal spirit of love)

3. Zoo (dominant impression: *either* depression/confinement, maybe even animals in misery, *or* relaxation, maybe even contentment, animals happy to have a life so easy—try for one of these, remembering that, as always in focused description, you *choose* the details that you want your readers to see)

4. Summer camp (dominant impression: happy confusion/expectation/fun)

expanded thought
alone again till the next time they come back to their

home away from home.

ACTIVITY 5.8 Concluding Sentences

Items 1–4 contain rough topic sentences that could work to begin a paragraph that describes a place and rough concluding sentences that might work to end the paragraph well. Circle the number of any sentence that would make an acceptable *rough* conclusion.

1. My kitchen is an easy place to work in. (rough topic sentence)
With all this equipment to work with, my kitchen is efficient. (rough final sentence)

2. My house has a relaxing place to spend time in. (rough topic sentence)
If I plastered and repainted, all the rooms would look better. (rough final sentence)

3. My home office is well organized. (rough topic sentence)
I really don't use my home office very much. (rough final sentence)

4. For a memorable place to vacation, skiing is the best. (rough topic sentence)
Snow skiing in the mountains is great fun. (rough final sentence)

Now, for a more interesting ending, revise one of the rough concluding sentences you circled, remembering to include a connector, the place, and the dominant impression. The following example will help you revise:

To make a concluding sentence stronger, use an expanded thought, specific words, sensory details, or an action.

EXAMPLE

ROUGH TOPIC SENTENCE — Farm ponds are pretty busy places.

ROUGH CONCLUDING SENTENCE — With so much going on in them, farm ponds are fun to visit.

REVISED CONCLUDING SENTENCE —
connector **dominant impression** **place**
With all the frantic animal action at my uncle's pond,

some people might think no one could rest there, but
expanded thought
for me, it's one of the most relaxing places I can spend
specific words
time at on a late spring afternoon.

Your choice of rough concluding sentence from the list of four: Answers will vary: Snow skiing in the mountains is great fun.

Your revised concluding sentence: Having finally mastered the bunny hill, I now love skiing and can't wait to challenge myself on the blue slopes next year.

Organizing Descriptions by Using a Spatial Arrangement

All writing that is easy to read follows an organizational strategy. In writing description, an author will often choose a **spatial arrangement,** which simply means organizing details from one point in space to another so readers can more easily visualize the scene. In describing a person or an animal, you might progress from the head to the feet; for an object like a car, you could proceed from the outside to the inside; for a place like a room, you might begin at the ceiling and work down to the floor or perhaps begin at the entrance and then move inward.

Spatial arrangement is usually flexible, giving writers freedom to choose an approach, which they should then follow consistently.

Activity 5.9 Organizing Descriptions

The following lists of place details are jumbled. Read through them, and then number the details using the spatial arrangement given in parentheses, with 1 as the first detail in a paragraph and 6 as the last.

EXAMPLE

Topic sentence: My attic is the dirtiest place in the house. (Arrange details from bottom to top.)

___2___ The floorboards are covered with dust.

___4___ Two small windows are streaked and smeared.

___6___ The rafters have cobwebs hanging from them.

___1___ I can feel grit beneath my feet on the stairs going up.

___3___ Old furniture has the dust of ages accumulating on it.

___5___ Boxes of ancient books are piled to the ceiling.

1. Topic sentence: First Watch on a busy Sunday morning is a study in efficiency. (Arrange details from front to back.)

    ___1___ Outside the restaurant a host is taking names for seating.

    ___6___ At the far end of the line, I can see the cooks efficiently cranking out the food.

    ___2___ In the lobby, coffee and tea are set for waiting customers.

    ___3___ At the front desk a manager greets people while checks are being processed in an orderly way.

    ___4___ Bussers clear, wipe, and reset tables quickly.

    ___5___ Behind the food line I can hear the dishwashers hard at work.

2. Topic sentence: The poolroom grew quiet, and time seemed to slow as everyone around the table concentrated on the last shot of the game. (Arrange details from bottom to top.)

    ___5___ The TV sets on the walls seemed to blur out, and the sound became just so much white noise.

    ___6___ Overhead, the blades of the ceiling fans were frozen in place.

    ___1___ People stopped shuffling their feet.

_____3_____ Lucky Ed was draped over his cue—the stick, cue ball, and eight ball his whole universe.

_____4_____ As Ed's right hand drew the cue back, the crowd leaned forward in anticipation.

_____2_____ Bottles of Budweiser were dangling at their sides—no one dared to move before the shot.

3. Topic sentence: Monastery Beach on a hot July afternoon is full of activity. (Arrange details from distant to closer as you stand in the parking lot at the edge of the beach.)

_____4_____ Scuba divers are putting their fins on at the edge of the surf.

_____5_____ In the middle of the beach, a handful of giggling kids tries to get a kite up into the air.

_____1_____ In the distance a fishing boat loaded with tourists chugs along.

_____2_____ Forty yards out from shore a sea otter floats on his back in the kelp, banging away at an abalone he has wrenched from the ocean floor.

_____3_____ Waves pick up height 10 yards from the beach as they curl and break over the few brave swimmers.

_____6_____ Where the beach meets the parking lot, seagulls cluster around trash cans, squabbling among themselves for scraps.

Locating the Reader in Space and Time

Teaching Idea
Students can clearly see the value of "space" transitions in scene building, and you can use these connecting words as a semester-long reminder whenever you discuss coherence devices.

As we learned in Chapter 3, linking sentences with connectors is essential for readers to follow the flow of your ideas. Aside from repeated words, synonyms, pronouns, and references to the main idea, description especially benefits from time and space transitions like the following:

FOR LOCATING OR MOVING IN SPACE			
above	by	in between	over
against	east (west, etc.)	into	there
alongside	far off (away)	near	to the right/left
around	in	next to	under
at	in the back	on	upper

FOR MOVING IN TIME			
after	first (second, etc.)	next	suddenly
afterward	immediately	now	then
at last	in the meantime	often	time passed
awhile	in the past	once	until
All references to calendar time and calendar events: last week, a few months ago			
All references to clock time			

(For a more complete list of transitions, turn to pp. 54–55.)

ACTIVITY 5.10 Locating the Reader in Space and Time

In "Ground Zero" underline all the space connectors once and time connectors twice (there are only a few time connectors). Use the preceding lists and the complete lists on pages 54–55 to locate the transitions.

Ground Zero

My bedroom is a mess. I can't seem to hang a picture straight on the walls, and my poster of The Dave Matthews Band has come untaped at the upper right corner so that it sags a little. The queen-sized bed is a disaster; it looks more like an animal's nest than a place for humans. There are three pillows propped up against the oak headboard and two lying on the carpet. The elastic has worn out around the pale-blue bottom sheet, so it has curled up at the corners. I like to snack in bed, so I have left the remains of old meals spread on and under it: an old pizza crust with the red sauce . . . well, kind of dark red sauce now, a Big Mac box, an old French fry or two, and some kind of crumbs—no, I think it's sand. A red-and-green quilt is lying in a pile by the end chest, where it slipped off a month ago, and I'm afraid to look under the bed for what I might find there. My desk is littered with papers and old Kleenexes, and there is usually an open can of Coke on it, sticky at the bottom. The wastebasket overflows. My parents can't believe I'm comfortable living like this, and I wouldn't mind having it cleaner, but, hey, messy is so much easier.

ACTIVITY 5.11 Locating the Reader in Space

Fill in the blanks with the space transitions from page 89.
Answers will vary.

1. After walking into the movie theater, you have to go _to the right_ or _left_ to get to the film you came to see.

2. Driving _into_ the garage, I could see my work cut out for me.

3. The weight room is located _in the back_ of the club.

4. In most houses you can find a mirror _above_ the vanity.

5. The boathouse is _next to_ the dock.

Descriptive Paragraphs: Analyzing Student Models

The following models show ways to describe inside and outside locations: how to develop and arrange details, and how to polish sentences for readability. As you focus on each model, take a few minutes to read the prereading and postreading commentaries and then to carefully answer the questions for analysis. This commentary and analysis will help you better understand why the writing is successful, so you can write stronger descriptive paragraphs yourself.

➧ Prereading Exploration for "Untitled"

The following paragraph was written to describe a place. The author's purpose is to communicate a special feeling she has about the place to her classmates so that they might get to know her a bit better. Before you jump into the reading, think about the elements of effective descriptive writing that we have discussed. Next, answer these questions:

1. How should the author try to focus the paragraph? _Through a_ _dominant impression_

2. What kinds of details do you suppose the author will use to develop the paragraph? _Sensory details_

3. What is the difference between a relatively general and a relatively specific word, and which tends to create the most vivid image? _Larger vs. smaller category of words—specific_

Before continuing with the paragraph, read the first and last sentences, and then, as you read, look for descriptive details and explanations that reinforce the dominant impression.

Teaching Idea
The student model "Untitled" is a fine example of description without any interaction among people. You might want to contrast it to the other two Chapter 5 models, which use people as part of the description.

Untitled

The most peaceful place I know of on a clear, dry night is my grandparents' pond, where I can relax around an open campfire. As the brilliant yellow moon shines down, reflecting off the pond, little waves ripple across the surface. Gazing at the sky, I can see millions of sparkling stars and, from time to time, even view a falling star. The blazing embers leave a smoke trail rising upward from the fire. Through the darkness, I can see the shadows of the trees, silhouettes of the horses, and swooping bats. The sounds of the night surround me: the murmur of voices in the distance, leaves rustling, and branches brushing against each other. From the nearby pond and surrounding trees, I can hear the unique chorus of the tree frogs and bullfrogs. As the train whistles by, the cries of howling coyotes drift on the wind. From time to time, I can even hear the lonesome hooting of an owl. When the popping and crackling of the fire dies down, the embers are ready for cooking. The hotdogs sizzle as they begin to cook and drip their juices off the end of the stick. Refreshing aromas of trimmings from the apple and pear trees add sweetness to the oak branches as they burn. Nearby, the smell of the horses is carried in the breeze. While fire heats the hotdogs, I can smell the meat cooking. The hot, white melting marshmallows fresh from the fire stick to my fingers. After eating and feeling contentedly full from the hotdogs and sticky chocolate/nut smores, I have time for solitude. While the chilly breeze blows, the radiating warmth of the fire draws me in. This is my favorite

4. Name one or more action descriptions that support the dominant impression, and then explain how the action does this.

5. Name three specific words, and list a more general word for each (see pp. 78–79)

6. List sensory details, trying to find several for each sense.

7. List at least three time and three space connectors (see p. 89).

8. Name three active verbs and three -ing words that the author uses to show action. (Active verbs show specific action: the horse *gallops* versus moves; the cardinal *sings* versus makes a song.) (For more on active verbs, see p. 515.)

9. What is your favorite image in this paragraph? Why do you like it?

10. To improve the paragraph, what three sensory details or specific words could be added to support the dominant impression?

11. In the seventh sentence of "Waking Up the Right Way," the author asks a question. Is there any value in asking readers an occasional question? Why do you think Becker does it? (For more on question sentences, see pp. 463–465.)

12. What would make a good title for Andrea Turner's paragraph, and why? (For more on titles, see pp. 59–60.)

WRITING A DESCRIPTIVE PARAGRAPH
Summarizing the Assignment

Write a single paragraph of roughly 250 to 300 words that paints a verbal portrait of a place. The place can be indoors and more or less surrounded by four walls (a room in a house, a store in a shopping mall, a library), or outside (a park, a favorite fishing hole, a basketball court). Your goal is to focus on a general feeling or overall impression you want your readers to have about the place. This dominant impression will help shape and develop the paragraph.

Establishing Audience and Purpose

Teaching Idea
High on the list of conceptual problems for student writers is communicating with a specific audience. While description is not the best assignment to convincingly demonstrate the need for a target audience, it is a good place to begin.

Select any person or group you think might be interested in the location you will describe, and write your paragraph for that audience. For instance, if you chose a favorite fishing pond—say, on a friend's farm in southern Miami County, Kansas—you could write your description specifically for your friend, knowing that you would both share memories of the place. Or you could choose a larger audience—say, the readership of a conservation magazine like *Kansas Wildlife & Parks*—in which case the audience would know something about the land near the pond but would not actually have been there. (**Note:** Your composition instructor is always at least a secondary audience, so write to show him or her that you are learning descriptive strategies.)

Your overall purpose is to convey information and a feeling about a place, to help readers see it through your eyes.

Working through the Writing Assignment

Discovering Ideas

Writing Tutor: Description

HINT: Try to get involved with your project.

HINT: Choose several possible places before you fix on one.

Teaching Idea
Many students will want to settle for a descriptive topic that is familiar and seems easy, like their bedroom (see "Ground Zero" in Activity 5.6), but you might urge them to stretch themselves a bit. If students choose several topics for initial brainstorming, they are more likely to find one that they care enough about to invest some energy in.

Your instructor may assign one place for the whole class to write about. If the choice is left to you, however, there are many possible topics. The good news is that you can select a place that you know well and care about. The bad news is that too much freedom can cause a writer to feel overwhelmed. You might be tempted to put off choosing a place and fall behind on the assignment, or you might settle on a first, quick choice, whether you care about it or not. Because you will work on the paper for several weeks, why not find a topic that really interests you? (Involving yourself in a writing project is a trick of the writer's trade that will help you have more fun with writing and will usually produce better work.)

The following topics lists may help get you off to a good start.

Topics Lists

INSIDE PLACES TO DESCRIBE

- Any room in your house
- Attic
- Tool shed
- Restaurant
- Auto repair shop
- Department store
- Museum
- Gym
- Bowling alley
- Arcade
- Library
- Cafeteria
- Nature center
- Riverboat
- Dance studio

- Church/synagogue
- Pet store
- Pawn shop
- Music store
- Hospital
- Movie theater
- Art gallery
- Fishing boat
- Beauty salon
- School (any level)
- Day care center
- Bus depot
- Airport
- Subway station
- Train station
- Boxing arena

- Doctor's office
- Police station
- Grocery store
- Florist shop
- Furniture store
- Stable
- Recycling center
- Funeral home
- Hardware store
- Toy store
- Veterinary clinic
- Greenhouse
- Barn
- Trade show
- Tattoo/piercing shop

OUTSIDE PLACES TO DESCRIBE

- Your property
- Beach
- Park
- Mountains
- Pond, lake, or river
- Stadium
- Zoo
- Field
- Interstate (at rush hour)
- Parking lot
- Car wash
- Fountain

- Trailer court
- Municipal landfill
- Pig or cattle pen (corral)
- Woods
- Summer camp
- Construction site
- Wharf
- Race track (car, horse, dog)
- Tree house
- Basketball court
- Football field

- Tennis court
- Swimming pool
- Wildlife sanctuary
- Garden (any type)
- Historic site
- Cemetery
- Rodeo
- Outdoor concert
- Amusement park
- Nursery (for plants)
- Field (corn, wheat)

CAUTION! Limit how much of your location you describe.

HINT: Visit your place and take notes!

If you haven't found a possible topic from these lists, think of the places where you regularly go: home, work, and school. Also consider the places where you pursue your interests. What hobbies do you enjoy? Do you target shoot, play in a band, or prepare gourmet meals? How about sports, team and individual? We all lead varied lives that offer many possible place topics.

Whatever place you select, limit how much of it you describe. For instance, a college campus is too large a topic for this paragraph assignment, but the school cafeteria could be just right. The Lake of the Ozarks is, again, too large, so settle for a particular part of it that you know well.

After you have decided on a place, go there if you can and take a few notes. While you can draw many details from memory, you will probably miss important ones. Even professional storytellers, who are paid to create scenes from their imagination, often visit a place to record details. Here are several suggestions to help with your own note taking:

Prewriting

1. Sit quietly at your place for a few minutes. Look around, listen carefully, and open your senses—all five of them. Remember, you are looking for a dominant impression to focus on. Is the place busy and loud or slow and quiet? Is it full of angry people or pleasant people? Are you outside in the middle of one of nature's spectacles—sunset/sunrise, snowstorm, fog, or electrical storm? If you do not form a dominant impression on the first visit, you may need to visit your place again.

HINT: Listing is one of several useful prewriting methods for description.

2. Now create a list of sensory impressions: sight, sound, touch, smell, and taste. Sight and sound are often the most noticeable. Name objects as specifically as possible, and try to include colors.

3. Take notes about the people in your place and how they interact. Are they friendly, cooperative, competitive, angry, isolated, quiet, busy, rowdy, or what?

4. Record the dimensions of the area and where important objects are in relation to each other.

5. As you observe the place, try to create a comparison, perhaps as a metaphor or simile—for example, "The waiter was as busy as a squirrel burying acorns in autumn." (For more on metaphor/simile, see p. 505.)

7. Listen to people, and write down some of their dialogue.

HINT: Working with others can save you work.

If a dominant impression is not yet clear, don't despair; but don't write an unfocused description either. Look for help. Your instructor, writing group members, writing center staff, friends, and family can all give useful input.

PREWRITING—SUMMING UP

1. Decide on several places or choose several from the topics lists.
2. Limit the size of the places you intend to describe.
3. If possible, go to the places and take detailed notes of the things and people there.
4. In your list include sensory details, specific details, and actions.
5. Decide on a dominant impression.

Teaching Idea
Journal Entry 5.2 is important because it helps clarify the problematic concept of *dominant impression* for students. Incorporating their journals into the regular class curriculum is one way to track student progress on the assignment.

JOURNAL ENTRY 5.2

How can you describe the overall feeling of your place in a few words? Is there much activity? Are people in a good mood? Is the action chaotic? Is your place restful or soothing? Have you picked an outdoor area that is rugged and wild? Review your prewriting notes, and then state the dominant impression in one sentence. (Remember, a place can feel different to different people, and there are often several ways to express a dominant impression.)

HINT: Delete distracting details—keep only those details that show the dominant impression.

Organizing Ideas

After listing the sensory details, specific things, and actions that you experienced in your place, it is time to choose and arrange these details to show an overall impression. You will probably find unneeded details in your lists, and even some that contradict the dominant impression. These details should be cut. As you begin to draft, other useful details will come to mind, so be receptive to them. Good ideas come to writers *throughout* the process of drafting and revising.

Following is a prewriting list for Jo Lucas's place paragraph, "Our Family Outing" (pp. 104–105), with several details crossed out that distract from the overall impression she wanted to show of activity and family fun:

Sight	Sound	Touch	Smell	Taste
40 lanes: kids having fun, black bumper pads, computer scoring, Cosmic Bowl (dark with black lights), smoke	Noisy games		Lane oil smell	All the food
Bowling balls: blue, pink, orange, green, yellow				
Walls: red, blue, green, yellow	Laughing children	Hot cheese	Hamburgers, chili cheese fries, popcorn	
Arcade games: blue print carpet	People talking			
Main service desk	Game tokens clatter			
Snack bar	Sizzling hamburgers			
Backstop restaurant: TVs, pool tables, batting cages, birthday parties, ~~lazy food servers, husband and wife arguing, dad yelling at his son~~		~~AC too cold~~		~~Bad taste of hotdog relish~~

Teaching Idea
You might ask students why they think the author of the annotated student model chose to delete the details of "lazy food servers" and so on under the sight column.

Teaching Idea
Even if you strongly
emphasize a focusing
dominant impression, some
students will still leave it out
of their topic sentence. You
might spot-check for the
dominant impression at this
point by having students
read their topic sentences
aloud.

HINT: Move from the
topic sentence directly
into the description.

Arrange the specific words and details that you decide to keep in a roughly spatial order. Jo Lucas organized her description as she progressed into and through the family fun center. However you arrange your details—top to bottom, front to back, and so forth—be consistent in the order you use.

After organizing your details, write a topic sentence that names your place and states your dominant impression, as in the following topic sentences from the student models in this chapter. The <u>place</u> is underlined once and the <u><u>dominant impression</u></u> twice:

A. The most <u>peaceful</u> place I know of on a clear, dry night is <u>my grand-parents' pond</u>, where I can relax around an open campfire.

B. With my morning cup of coffee in hand, I head toward the most <u>tranquil</u> part of my house, <u>my front porch</u>.

Follow the topic sentence with description, and locate readers within the scene by using space and time transitions (words like *above, near, next to, first, after,* and *finally*). (For more transitions, see pp. 53–58.)

ORGANIZING—SUMMING UP

1. Write out your dominant impression in a word or two.
2. Cut any details from your prewriting list that conflict with the dominant impression.
3. Arrange your details spatially.
4. Review the list of transitions—especially space transitions—and other connectors on pp. 53–58.
5. Write a rough topic sentence that names the place and states the dominant impression.

JOURNAL ENTRY 5.3

How will you organize the details of your description—from top to bottom, outside to inside, one side to another, or far to near? Can you picture yourself in a fixed spot inside a room, or do you see yourself walking through the place? After reviewing your notes, write a brief paragraph explaining how you will organize your description and why this method makes sense to you.

Drafting

Teaching Idea
Although you may have
already covered drafting in
Chapter 1, it helps to review
this material again the day
before student drafts are due.

With the preliminary work done, you are almost ready to write the first draft. But before plunging in, review the drafting suggestions in Chapter 1 (pp. 12–13). Also, keep the following suggestions in mind:

1. Describe a place; do not tell a story. A story is a series of actions connected by time, leading to a high point and resolution of action. Your description may have action, as all the student models in this chapter do, but the actions are there only to reinforce the dominant impression.
2. Feel free to include action description along with dialogue.

3. Occasionally, tell readers what to think about your details and how you feel about them (for more on this, see the student models in this chapter).

4. Add plenty of details. Specific words and sensory details are essential. Even if you overdescribe in the first draft, you can cut unneeded material later.

JOURNAL ENTRY 5.4

After completing the first rough draft, think about your work, and then write two paragraphs of four to five sentences each. In the first paragraph, tell what you like most about your draft and why; in the second, tell what you like least and why. Be specific. This self-assessment can help you decide where to begin revising.

Revising Drafts

First-Stage Drafts

At this stage, you should focus on content (scene description: specific words, sensory details, thoughts, and feelings) and organization (arranging and connecting ideas).

1. **Are you really describing a place and not slipping into a narrative (story)?**

   While a well-told story will have lots of action leading to a high point or climax, a descriptive paragraph may have little or no action. A story follows a person through a series of actions and has an uncertain outcome, whereas a description does not try to build suspense.

2. **Is your topic sentence effective?**

   If you have included the place being described and a limiting statement about it, you have a good start. Now add a word or two of sensory detail (a detail about color, sound, or touch perhaps), and make a word more specific, particularly the name of the place. (The topic sentences in the student models show general and specific words—for example, family fun center = Incred-A-Bowl.) Also, try for a medium-length topic sentence (15–20 words) rather than a shorter one (5–10 words) or a longer one (25–40 words). (For more on topic sentences, see pp. 36–41.)

3. **Does your description have an overall point (dominant impression)?**

   Many rough drafts include random details of sight, sound, and other senses. Remember, you are not merely a camera recording any picture that comes in front of your lens. You are a person with a point to make about your place, so your details should reinforce that point. For example, if the dominant impression of your bedroom is relaxation, do not include details such as the piled-up textbooks and overdue homework assignments on your desk, both of which are making you nervous. (For more on the dominant impression, see pp. 83–84.)

4. **Are you occasionally telling your readers what to think about the details?**

   Readers often need some brief explanation within a sentence to reinforce a dominant impression. For example, in "Our Family Outing" (pp. 105–106), the author mentions the pool tables and batting cages and then notes that parents bring their children to practice there, adding to the paper's focus on family togetherness. (For more on clarifying the dominant impression, see pp. 83–85.)

5. **Are you occasionally letting your readers know how you feel about the place?**

Because this is a subjective description, you should let your reader know what you feel and think about the place—as long as the thoughts and feelings help reinforce the dominant impression. (For more on thoughts/feelings in description, see "Waking Up the Right Way," pp. 92–93.)

6. **Are you using enough specific language?**

One main goal in this assignment is to learn the difference between specific and general words and the value of each. Your second draft will be stronger when you make some of the images more specific. (For more on specific words, see pp. 78–79.)

7. **Are you using sensory details?**

Remember that we often overrely on sight and use too few of the other senses—especially sound and touch—in building images. Sometimes, too, we overdescribe, cramming too many details into a sentence. (For more on sensory detail, see pp. 81–82.)

8. **Is your concluding sentence effective?**

The final sentence should include a connector, a word that echoes the dominant impression, and a comment about your place (expanded thought). Since you are not yet writing an essay, you should avoid using three or more sentences for your conclusion. Stick with one or, at most, two sentences, and you will end your one-paragraph paper effectively. (For more on concluding sentences, see pp. 48–52.)

9. **Are all the sentences in the paragraph well connected?**

First drafts often need more time and space connectors. Reread each sentence, imagining that you are directing a photographer who is filming your place. You will tell the photographer what to shoot, using phrases like "to the left of the mirror," "in front of the picture window," and "next to the refrigerator." (For more on connectors, see pp. 53–58.)

> ## JOURNAL ENTRY 5.5
>
> To help you focus on the revision process and alert your instructor to your progress, list three *specific* changes you have made or feel you ought to make in going from your first to second draft. Refer to the first-stage draft questions, answering them specifically. (Example: Question 3: "I felt like my dominant impression was unfocused. I had to cut some details [*list* these details] because they were off the main point.") Next, in several sentences, state what you like best about your draft.

Second and Final Drafts

For advice on revising and then editing further drafts of your work, turn to Chapter 4.

ANNOTATED STUDENT MODEL: "OUR FAMILY OUTING"

Let's look closely at how another student successfully worked through the writing process: gathering ideas, drafting, revising, and editing to create a well-focused, vivid description of a family fun center. (To see the prewriting list for this paragraph, turn to pp. 86–87.)

As you read, keep in mind that revision seldom occurs in tidy stages. Sometimes, for example, you will edit early in the process of writing a draft and change content later. However, the following draft stages will help focus your revision efforts.

First-Stage Draft

As you work through your first draft, watch for these problem areas:

- Unfocused dominant impression
- Too many sentences leading into the description
- Weak concluding sentence
- Too few specific words and sensory details

It's Friday night, and the whole family is wondering what to do. We could go catch a movie or save some money and just rent a video. They just built a new Blockbuster down the street, so it's easy to pick one up. After a little debate, we finally decide on bowling. We all pile in the car and my husband drives and soon we are there—Incred-A-Bowl. And it is pretty incredible, there's so much there for a family to do. As you walk in the place you can see all kinds of activity. People are laughing and talking, employees are busy checking out bowling shoes, and you can see the balls rolling down the alleys into the pins. There is a huge arcade with brightly lit and noisy arcade games. You can also see people helping customers. Further along is the snack bar. You can smell the aroma of freshly popped popcorn and hamburgers on the grill. If you keep looking, you will see the Backstop restaurant with televisions mounted around the room, near the ceiling. Each television is on a different sports channel, so you don't miss a play of any sport. They have put the bumper pads in the gutters for the small kids so they can knock over a few pins. Tonight is the Cosmic Bowl. This means turning the regular lights off and turning the black lights on. They turn the smoke machines on and this gives the effect of outer space. The bowling balls glow as they roll down the lanes. Everyone is laughing and enjoying themselves.

Second-Stage Draft

SPECIAL POINTS TO CHECK IN REVISING FROM FIRST TO SECOND DRAFTS
1. Add sensory details.
2. Add specific words.
3. Add locator phrases.

Topic sentence revised

Sensory details added: colors, smells, sounds

Action shown through -ing endings

Specific words added

Another location added

Locator phrases added

Action shown through -ing endings

Expanded thought in conclusion

Closing sentence added

It's Friday night, and we are at the Incred-A-Bowl, it is the largest and busiest family fun center in Johnson County. As we walk through the main entrance of the fun center you can immediately detect the scent of the lane oil. The wall above the pins at the end of the forty shiny synthetic lanes is painted in florescent red, blue, yellow, and green colors. Off to the left is the huge arcade with its blue print carpet, and brightly lit and noisy arcade games. There are children everywhere laughing and screaming as they play there games and collect their tickets. You can hear the clatter of tokens, as parents get change for their bills in the token machine. To the right of the entrance, where we came in, is the control desk. Here people are talking, laughing, and helping customers. Further down the crowded concourse is the snack bar. You can smell the aroma of freshly popped popcorn, and hamburgers sizzling on the charbroil grill. To the left of the snack bar is the Backstop restaurant. It is decorated with all kinds of sports memorabilia. There are thirteen-inch televisions mounted around the room, near the white ceiling. Each television is on a different sports channel, so you don't miss a play of any sport. Upstairs in the restaurant are pool tables and batting cages. Back downstairs there are some birthday parties going on. They have put the bumper pads in the gutters for the small kids. They are now jumping, clapping, and screaming as their pink, blue, yellow, green, and orange balls hit the pins. The computerized scoring is a nice feature. Because it allows the parents to participate in the fun instead of having to keep score. Tonight Incred-A-Bowl is having a Cosmic Bowl. This means turning the regular lights off and turning the black lights on above the lanes. They also turn the smoke machines on and this gives the effect of outer space. The blue, pink, orange, green, and yellow bowling balls glow as they roll down the lanes. Everyone is laughing and enjoying themselves. This is a great place to keep family ties close.

Third-Stage Draft

Teaching Idea
To prepare students for editing, you might want to have them edit the third-stage draft in groups and then check their versions against the final edit.

Moving into a third-stage draft, Jo polished her work for word choices and sentence variety.

SPECIAL POINTS TO CHECK IN REVISING FROM SECOND TO THIRD DRAFTS

1. Add sensory details.
2. Add specific words.

Teaching Idea
Many students who write drafts at the first and second stages resist revising a strong draft to make it even better. The third-stage draft can be particularly beneficial to them.

Title added

Material added

Material added

3. [Combine sentences for variety.]
4. **Substitute synonyms for repeated words.**
5. ~~Delete unneeded words.~~

Our Family Outing

It's Friday night, and we are at the Incred-A-Bowl, it is the largest and busiest **family fun center** in Johnson County. As we walk through the main entrance ~~of the fun center~~ you can immediately detect the scent of the lane oil. The wall above the pins at the end of the forty shiny synthetic lanes is painted in florescent red, blue, yellow, and green colors. Off to the left is the huge arcade with its blue print carpet, and brightly lit, ~~and~~ noisy arcade games. There are children everywhere laughing and screaming as they play there games and collect their tickets. You can hear the clatter of tokens, as parents get change for their bills in the token machine. To the right of the entrance, where we came in, is the control desk. Here seven people are talking, laughing, and helping customers. [Further down the crowded concourse is the snack bar where you can smell the aroma of freshly popped popcorn, and hamburgers sizzling on the charbroil grill.] Someone has just purchased an order of chili cheese fries. It looks so sinful, with its homemade chili and hot nacho cheese. [To the left of the snack bar is the Backstop restaurant, which is decorated with all kinds of sports memorabilia.] There are thirteen-inch televisions mounted around the room near the white ceiling. Each **tv** is on a different ~~sports~~ channel, so you don't miss a play of any sport. Upstairs in the **restaurant** are pool tables and batting cages. This is where many parents take their **sons and daughters** to practice batting the upcoming baseball season. Back downstairs there are some birthday parties going on. [They have put the black bumper pads in the gutters for the small **kids** who are now jumping, clapping, and screaming as their pink, blue, yellow, green, and orange balls hit the pins.] The computerized scoring is a nice feature. Because it allows the parents to participate in the fun instead of having to keep score. [Tonight Incred-A-Bowl is having a Cosmic Bowl which means turning the regular lights off and turning the black lights on above the lanes.] They also turn the smoke machines on and this gives the effect of outer space. The ~~blue, pink, orange, green, and yellow~~ multicolored bowling balls glow as they roll down the lanes. [Everyone is laughing and enjoying themselves here at Incred-A-Bowl, a great place to keep family ties close.]

Final-Editing Draft

Teaching Idea
It is worth the time to take students back to Chapter 4 as they revise and edit their first several assignments. The Final-Draft Checklist is mirrored in Chapter 4, so if students need more in-depth reminders than the checklist provides, they will not have to search through the text. The information is accessible in a few consecutive pages.

Here is the last draft of "Our Family Outing," the one that Jo has carefully edited. Now is the time to slow down, focusing on each word and applying the grammar and punctuation rules you have learned so far, especially for the use of commas.

SPECIAL POINTS TO CHECK IN EDITING FINAL DRAFTS

1. Misspellings
2. Sound-alike words
3. Missing words
4. Wrong words
5. Sentence fragments
6. Comma splices/run-ons
7. Faulty capitalizations
8. Incorrect apostrophes

9. Comma(s) needed
   a. Introductory words/phrases/clauses
   b. Nonessential word groups
   c. Main clause with coordinating conjunctions
10. Unneeded commas

Our Family Outing

It's Friday night, and we are at the Incred-A-Bowl, It [6] which is the largest and busiest family fun center in Johnson County. As we walk through the main entrance,[9a] you [4] I (or we) can immediately detect the scent of the lane oil. The wall above the pins at the end of the forty shiny synthetic lanes is painted in florescent [1] fluorescent red, blue, yellow, and green colors. Off to the left is the huge arcade with its blue print carpet,[10] and brightly lit, noisy arcade games. There are children everywhere laughing and screaming as they play there [2] their games and collect their tickets. You [4] I (or we) can hear the clatter of tokens,[10] as parents get change for their bills in the token machine. To the right of the entrance, where we came in, is the control desk. Here seven people are talking, laughing, and helping customers. Further down the crowded concourse is the snack bar,[9b] where You [4] I (or we) can smell the aroma of freshly popped popcorn and hamburgers sizzling on the charbroil grill. Someone has just purchased an order of chili cheese fries. It looks so sinful,[10] with its homemade chili and hot nacho cheese. To the left of the snack bar is the Backstop restaurant, which is decorated with all kinds of sports memorabilia. There are thirteen-inch televisions mounted around the room near the white ceiling. Each it [7] TV is on a different sports channel, so you [4] customers dont [8] don't miss a play of any sport. Upstairs in the restaurant are pool tables and batting cages. This is where many parents take their sons and daughters to practice batting for [3] the upcoming baseball season. Back downstairs there are some birthday parties going on. They have put the black bumper pads in the gutters for the small kids[9b], who are now jumping, clapping, and screaming as their pink, blue, yellow, green, and orange balls hit the pins. The computerized scoring is a nice feature[5] because it allows the parents to participate in the fun instead of having to keep score. Tonight Incred-A-Bowl is having a Cosmic Bowl[9b], which means turning the regular lights off and turning the black lights on above the lanes. They also turn the smoke machines on[9c], and this gives the effect of outer space. The multicolored bowling balls glow as they roll down the lanes. ~~Everyone is~~[4] All the people are laughing and enjoying themselves here at Incred-A-Bowl, a great place to keep family ties close.

—Jo Lucas

FINAL-DRAFT CHECKLIST

Before turning in your final draft for a grade, review this checklist. You may find that, as careful as you think you have been, you still missed a point or two—or more. (For more on any of these points, see Chapter 4.)

☐ 1. Are you describing a place and not slipping into a narrative (story)?
☐ 2. Does your description have an overall point (dominant impression)?
☐ 3. Are you occasionally telling readers what to think about the details?
☐ 4. Are you letting readers know how you feel about the place?
☐ 5. Are you using enough specific language?
☐ 6. Are you using enough sensory details?
☐ 7. Is your topic sentence effective?
☐ 8. Is your concluding sentence effective?
☐ 9. Are all the sentences within the paragraph well connected?
☐ 10. Are you using active verbs and *-ing* words to describe action?
☐ 11. Have you varied the length and beginnings of your sentences?
☐ 12. Have you used synonyms for words that are repeated too often?
☐ 13. Have you cut unneeded words?
☐ 14. Have you written an interesting title? Have you checked its capitalization?
☐ 15. Have you prepared your paper according to the format expected by your instructor? (Check to see if you need to include a title page, double space, leave at least 1-inch margins, and use a 12-point font.)
☐ 16. Have you edited closely (including having at least one other person proofread)? Have you checked your Improvement Chart for pattern errors?
☐ 17. Have you looked specifically for the following errors: misspellings, soundalike words, missing words, wrong words, sentence fragments, comma splices/run-ons, faulty capitalizations, incorrect apostrophes, missing commas, and unnecessary commas?

Chapter Summary

1. Describing is the process of using details to build vivid images.
2. Descriptive writing relies on specific words and sensory details.
3. Words can be relatively general or relatively specific—the more specific a word, the clearer the image.
4. Description is often found in narrative, expository, and persuasive writing.
5. Writers often focus description with a dominant impression.
6. A topic sentence in a paragraph describing a place should name the place and state the dominant impression.
7. Descriptions are often organized spatially.
8. Time and space transitions are needed in descriptive writing.
9. Subjective descriptions are strengthened by the inclusion of thoughts and emotions.
10. Action—including people moving and speaking—is often part of description.
11. Writing is not complete until it has been revised and carefully edited.

ALTERNATE WRITING ASSIGNMENTS

While the focus of this chapter has been on illustrating a place, there are many other uses for description. For this assignment, be sure to do the following:

1. Decide on a dominant impression.
2. State the dominant impression in your topic sentence.
3. Use specific words and sensory details to develop the dominant impression.
4. Conclude with a sentence that restates the dominant impression and makes a final point.
5. Connect your sentences with time and place transitions.

ASSIGNMENT OPTIONS

1. Describe a person. Find someone you know well or someone you are around enough to observe his or her appearance (physical look and clothing) and actions (the way he or she walks, stands, and sits; his or her body language and mannerisms). Listen to the person and record some characteristic dialogue. Your goal is to create a verbal portrait so that someone who has not met this person would recognize him or her from your description. Focus your description with a dominant impression, such as sloppy, well groomed, athletic, lazy, talkative, shy, funny, or angry.

2. Describe an object. Select an object and detail its appearance. This object could range from the small and ordinary (salt shaker, toaster oven, wrench) to the large and more unusual (construction crane, new Corvette, office building). Your goal is to capture the dominant impression of the object through description. For instance, your salt shaker might be exceptionally functional. You could describe what it looks like and how well it does its job of dispensing salt. The construction crane might suggest power. You could describe the large metal parts and then show the machine in action.

3. Describe an animal. Select a household pet (dog, cat, hamster, iguana), a farm animal (cow, horse, pig, chicken), or wild animal in your neighborhood (squirrel, rabbit, bird, garter snake). Again the trick is to focus the description through a dominant impression, a defining trait of the animal. It might be easy and obvious to choose a trait like sloppiness for a pig. But it could be more challenging to show the intelligence or lovable qualities of the pig.

4. Describe a product. There are a zillion possible products you could describe. Limit the field by sticking to one you use regularly. For instance, you might describe your favorite breakfast cereal. Why do you find it appealing? You could focus your description on characteristics like taste, texture, and length of time it stays crunchy.

5. Describe an event. Rather than create a story with organized action leading to a high point, capture the feeling of the event. Perhaps, as in the accompanying photo, you have witnessed a dramatic moment at a sporting event and can communicate that feeling. This picture shows the soccer players' joy in scoring—the dominant impression. You could help readers understand the excitement at the game by describing how people reacted, what they said and did. The players are jumping in the air, clapping hands, smiling, and shouting to one another. Undoubtedly, the coaches and spectators are also showing their happiness. Think about an event that you remember well or, better yet, go to one with the purpose of capturing a dominant impression through close observation and detailed note taking.

CHAPTER 6

Telling Your Own Story

What Are We Trying to Achieve and Why?

Setting the Stage

Teaching Idea
To introduce personal narrative, you can begin asking questions about students' experiences with storytelling. Often, they don't realize that TV shows and films are largely narrative, and at least with these media they have lots of experience.

People have been in the storytelling business for a long time, perhaps for as long as humanity has existed. A universal impulse, spanning all cultures, moves people to share their experiences with one another. Just as the Native Americans shown on the preceding page are drawn closer together by the tales of the tribe's elder, so too are we drawn together by the stories of our own culture. Whenever we tell someone what we have done during the day—the bargain we got while shopping, the algebra exam we aced, the ticket we got speeding to school—we are telling a story, or **narrating.**

Narration comes naturally to us. Since we first learned to speak, we have been telling those around us about our lives, stories that have helped us release emotions, reveal some part of ourselves, influence others, and entertain. In this chapter, you will work more consciously with the elements of personal narrative, learning how to fashion them into a focused and interesting story. As you gather material, you will look for the significance of your story and test this definition of personal narrative: *Someone doing something somewhere for some reason.*

Linking to Previous Experience

What experience do you already have with narrative? Consider film and television. Movies begin as screenplays, and most TV programming is scripted. Much of what we read for entertainment is fiction, beginning with the picture books read to children and progressing into short stories and novels.

We also create our own narratives. Though few of us have the skills of an accomplished fiction writer, we all talk about ourselves, work associates, friends, and family members (perhaps too much sometimes!). Whenever you begin a conversation with a line like "You'll never guess who I saw Ted Wilson's wife with last night," you are launching into a narrative.

In addition, many of us occasionally write narratives. If you have ever kept a diary or e-mailed a friend, you were probably writing narrative. In elementary, middle, and high school, you probably were asked to write about your life. If you worked through Chapter 5 in *A Writer's Workshop,* you have written a description of a place, an assignment that contains many elements of narration: specific language, sensory details, active verbs, clearly linked sentences, and a unified dominant impression.

Determining the Value of Narration

Getting better at telling stories can help you in many ways. For example, on the job, you might have to defend yourself by narrating a conflict you had with a customer or fellow employee. In school, you might be called on to narrate events in your classes. For instance, in political science, you might be asked to tell about the 2004 presidential campaign; in sociology, you might need to illustrate with personal examples a discussion of violence in movies and its effects on teens; and in composition, you might recount an event that helped you see yourself in a different light.

Improving your narrative skills will also enrich your personal life. Knowing more about storytelling can increase your enjoyment of stories and films. Telling your stories in class will help you speak more comfortably in front of people. And as you work through the process of remembering an event, you will reflect on your behavior and the behavior of others, thinking about the meaning of your story and how the events helped make you who you are.

Teaching Idea
As with many of the journal entries, Journal Entry 6.1 can be written in class and used to stimulate whole-class or group discussion of personal narrative. Students will often want only to summarize their stories, so it is useful to stress their purpose in telling the story and to ask them about its possible significance.

JOURNAL ENTRY 6.1

Recall instances during the past week when you told someone about something that happened to you. List three of these, and summarize in a couple of sentences what happened in each. Next, list whom you told your story to and what your purpose was: to release frustration, communicate information, express your feelings, persuade, or simply make her or him laugh. How well did you succeed in each instance?

Developing Skills and Exploring Ideas in Narrative Paragraphs

To learn how to write effective personal narrative, we will practice the following:

1. Creating a narrative that has conflict, suspense, and a climax
2. Finding the significance or meaning of a story
3. Building a story that shows as well as tells
4. Using effective dialogue
5. Including metaphors and similes to add clarity and interest

Teaching Idea
To help students with the idea of suspense in narrative, you might have them discuss some especially suspenseful moments in a popular film.

Teaching Idea
Students often see narrative conflict as a confrontation between people, forgetting about internal conflict and conflict involving a person coping with his or her environment.

Creating Conflict, Suspense, and a Climax

Perhaps it is human nature to be more interested in narratives that involve conflict than those that do not. As a species surviving many centuries of struggle with other species and with natural forces, we may well have no choice in the matter. Our instincts might simply tell us, "Look out: possible negative outcome. Pay attention!" Whatever the case, you will find **conflict**—the potential for events to go wrong—critical to your story, and you should arrange the action so as to keep your reader in **suspense** (wondering) about the outcome or **climax.**

The central conflict in your story might be one of these:

- A person dealing with another person or group—for example, your boss treats you poorly.
- A person dealing with her- or himself—for example, you are learning to control your temper.
- A person coping with the environment—for example, your air conditioner is broken, and it is 100 degrees outside.

In the first example, we might have two very different stories to tell:

1. My boss is a great guy who treats me wonderfully.
   A. I am paid more than most people in my position.
   B. I get four annual merit bonuses.
   C. I have all the time off a person could want.
   D. My boss insists that I leave the office every day by 3:00 P.M.
   E. I have a beautiful office.
2. My boss is a tyrant who makes my life a living hell.
   A. I am working for next to nothing.
   B. No matter how hard I work, I have never gotten a raise.
   C. I am lucky to get part of the weekend off, much less a vacation.
   D. My boss insists that I work a minimum of 10 hours a day.
   E. I work in a cramped cubbyhole with poor lighting and ventilation.

Most of us might envy the fortunate soul in version 1, but we would probably be more interested to know how the poor stiff in version 2 is going to improve his or her life.

If we were to create a brief narrative based on version 2, we might choose a few hours in the day of our person—let's call him Oscar Jamieson—when it looked like his life was going to take a turn from bad to worse. Oscar will be arriving at 7:30 A.M. at the Sprint building where he works.

Action Outline

Conflict: Oscar has a confrontation with his boss today.

Lead-in: He is worrying about the big billing statement he completely mishandled yesterday.

Developing the conflict—actions to build suspense:

- Hearing through a co-worker on the way to his office that he is in big trouble
- Finding a brief "come-see-me" note in his in-box from his boss
- Wondering, worrying, and avoiding the confrontation all morning
- Getting a phone call from the boss, who orders him to "Get in here now!"

- Seeing the assistant look up, shake his head, and look down at his desk
- Entering the boss's office and seeing her scowl from behind her desk
- Standing helplessly while the boss rages about the billing statement mess
- Listening to the dreaded words "You're fired!"

Climax: Seeing his boss suddenly fall back in her chair, clutching her chest; calling the secretary, but, too late (darn), the boss drops dead

Resolution: Finding out that Oscar's best friend has been promoted to the boss's position and that Oscar, too, is up for a promotion

Hurray for Oscar! What looked like a horrible day for him (the good guy) turned out instead to be a terminal day for his boss (the bad guy). Although this action outline is a bit simplistic—people are seldom simply good or bad—it demonstrates several important elements of story structure:

- **Lead-in:** a brief introduction to arouse interest and set the stage
- **Conflict:** the problem a person encounters in the story
- **Suspense:** the reader's uncertainty about the outcome of the conflict
- **Climax:** the high point of the action
- **Resolution:** the result of the climax—the point of the story (significance)

Teaching Idea
You might have students compose their own "action outlines" using participial phrases to encourage action. This activity has the added benefit of illustrating parallelism in outlining.

Teaching Idea
Activity 6.1 might take 20 minutes or so and is a good way to get students thinking about specific action in their own narratives.

ACTIVITY 6.1 Creating Conflict, Suspense, and a Climax

With group members, choose a topic from one of the three categories listed below (or from the topics listed on pp. 122–123), and decide what the conflict is. If you choose an event that actually happened to a group member, ask questions about the event. Next, describe the conflict in a single sentence, and then write an action outline as illustrated above.

1. An embarrassing moment: speaking in public, asking for a date, having forgotten your wallet or purse in a restaurant when the bill is presented, being caught in a lie
2. An unpleasant moment as a consumer: returning defective merchandise, being overcharged, suspecting a mechanic of cheating
3. A public confrontation: handling a traffic accident, being pulled over by a police officer, arguing in a restaurant, dealing with a neighbor, protecting your property

Answers will vary.

Action Outline

Topic: A person eating at a restaurant has forgotten his wallet.

Conflict: Alex is on his first date with Sonya, and as the bill comes, he realizes that he has no money!

Lead-in: Alex has finally found the courage to ask Sonya, whom he is infatuated with, out on a date. They are finishing a pleasant dinner.

Actions to develop conflict and build suspense:

A. Alex telling Sonya what a good time he has had.

B. Sonya responding similarly, saying how glad she is that Alex finally asked her out.

C. Both exchanging soulful looks.

D. Waiter leaving check at the table.

E. Alex frantically searching for his wallet.

F. Alex desperately trying to think of a solution: Did I leave my wallet in the car or at home? Do I know anyone here I can borrow money from?

Climax: Alex tells Sonya about his problem.

Resolution: Sonya laughs about the affair, says no problem, and uses her own credit card to pay the bill. She shows her sympathetic nature and proves her quality of character to Alex, who likes her even more as a result.

Finding the Significance of a Story

A story should have a point. Without one, the story is likely to be confusing, boring, or both. In Oscar Jamieson's narrative, we can see that he has been freed from a tyrant who has been making his life miserable. There is a clear progression from the anxious beginning of his day to the triumphant end. But even in a story with a clearly resolved conflict, the writer can directly state the action's significance. For example, here are several points that could emerge from Oscar's story:

HINT: Writers choose the meaning of their stories.

- After people have suffered enough, if they have faith and can hang on, they may eventually be rewarded.
- There is justice after all.
- Bullies and tyrants tend to come to a bad end.
- It's pointless to feel too worried or depressed about a bad situation before you know the outcome.
- Having experienced cruelty, people often resolve to become kinder.

Any of these ideas or a combination of them could be the main point of the story. It is the author's privilege to choose. The main point, however, should come naturally from the event and not feel tacked on at the end. For example, it would seem forced to use Oscar's story as a warning to people to eat better and exercise to avoid a heart attack or to show how a friend can help you get promoted. In your own narratives, the significance will not always be clear at first, but as you tell the tale, a point should emerge.

HINT: The significance of a story won't always be clear to you at first.

ACTIVITY 6.2 Finding the Significance of a Story

Skillful writers of serious fiction often imply many shades of meaning. Less experienced writers, though, need to focus on one meaning and make it clear. The following story, "On the Brink," has several possible points, but none that are explicitly stated. If the writer were part of your group, what suggestions could you give to clarify a meaning? Read and discuss the model, and then write out three possible points the story could make.

On the Brink

As I prepared for surgery at the vet clinic where I now work, I was administering anesthesia to a miniature black poodle when respiration stopped, and the heart stopped beating. I scrambled to the side of the small poodle to start respiration, also giving epinephrine (adrenaline) and dopram, trying to get the heart beating again. Not sure what else to do, I yelled frantically for Dr. Erickson, and he came into the room saying, "What the hell is going on in here?" After assessing the situation, he began to assist me in trying to revive the limp, almost lifeless poodle lying on the surgical table. It seemed there was no hope for the small black poodle when a single breath came from its lungs, then another, and another. However, the battle had just begun, for the dog had no heartbeat, but it was breathing. The doctor and I had never seen anything like it before. Often there will be a heartbeat and no breath, but never the other way around. After a few more minutes, we got the dog's heart beating, but the big question then was whether we should go ahead with the exploratory surgery as planned or let the animal come out of anesthesia, in which case it would risk dying from the abdominal swelling. We decided to go ahead with the surgery, trying to save the poor poodle from certain death. As we cut open the body cavity to find out what was causing the swelling, the uterus expanded and swelled out of the animal's body cavity. We immediately removed the infected uterus, sutured the body cavity, and quickly brought the dog out of anesthesia to observe it for other difficulties.

List of Possible Meanings

EXAMPLE
It amazes me to see how creatures can hold on to life.

Answers will vary.

1. Teamwork can save a life.

2. Remaining calm is important in a crisis.

3. Making the right decision under pressure can be difficult.

Building a Story That Shows as Well as Tells

Creating a story requires the ability both to show and to tell. When you **show** readers something, they are able to interpret the scene or idea for themselves. When you **tell** readers about something, you interpret for them. Which of the two following passages do you think tells and which shows?

A. We were growing more frightened by the moment.

B. As late as it was, one of my cousins, my brother Tama, and I were still

up, talking over some gruesome scenes from *The Exorcist*, in our minds once again hearing Linda Blair roar out "MERRIN!" in her demon voice and seeing her head turn completely around. Suddenly, we all heard a scratching sound at the outside of the door and an awful noise that sounded like someone groaning in pain: "Ooohhh-aaaghh!"

HINT: Showing and telling work together in an effective narrative.

If you chose passage A for telling and passage B for showing, you are correct. You might notice that telling is more economical; it gets the point across fast. However, telling often involves only the mind, leaving out the heart. And while showing requires more words, if done well it can involve readers on several levels as they react to the characters' speech and actions, and experience the sensory details. Good writers interweave showing and telling as they build the scenes that make up their narratives, using one to clarify and reinforce the other, as in the following passage:

As late as it was, one of my cousins, my brother Tama, and I were still up, talking over some gruesome scenes from *The Exorcist,* in our minds once again hearing Linda Blair roar out "MERRIN!" in her demon voice and seeing her head turn completely around. <u>We were growing more frightened by the moment</u> when suddenly we all heard a scratching sound at the outside of the door and an awful noise that sounded like someone groaning in pain: "Ooohhh-aaaghh!"

Rough drafts often suffer from too much telling and too little showing. But if you realize the power of showing and are willing to work at it, you can create narratives that truly move an audience.

CAUTION! First drafts often tell too much and show too little.

Teaching Idea
Have students read aloud their "showing" answers to Activity 6.3 (or let them trade in groups) to see how many ways there are to show.

ACTIVITY 6.3 Building a Story That Shows *and* Tells

The following sentences tell a reader how to interpret a situation. Write a sentence that shows the same statement. (You can show with sensory details, a person's actions, and a person's statements.)

EXAMPLE
Telling: My brother was concerned about my grandfather lying on the floor.
Showing: My brother screamed, "Mom, help, grandpa is dying!"
Answers will vary.

1. Telling: Josh felt sick again today.

   Showing: After throwing up three times in 30 minutes, Josh crawled back to his bed.

2. Telling: The whole family felt sad as they gathered around the casket.

   Showing: Grandfather quietly cried while his three granddaughters placed roses in the casket with their father. The older man looked down at his 45-year-old son and muttered again, "The old should not have to bury the young. It just ain't right."

3. Telling: The customer service representative did not appear interested in my story.

   Showing: <u>Stifling a yawn and turning for the third time to laugh at a joke from his friend behind the counter, the customer service representative at Best Buy did not seem much interested in my story.</u>

4. Telling: ~~Now I finally understood that Adrian was a bigot.~~

   Showing: <u>"It's the Jews who own all the banks. They're the ones who control the interest rates in this country." Hearing this remark from Adrian, I finally realized that he was a bigot.</u>

5. Telling: Batur was overjoyed when his semester grades arrived.

   Showing: <u>Kissing his grade report, Batur danced a little jig and shouted to his wife, "Another 4.0—I'll get a scholarship for sure."</u>

Teaching Idea
To help students see the value of dialogue in narrative, ask them how often they get together with friends and then listen to one person talk the whole evening. If they have been stuck in this situation, how are they likely to judge the speaker—as boring or controlling or self-centered? Dialogue creates variety.

Using Effective Dialogue

Dialogue—the words people speak—is an important way to show. Whereas narratives can be written without dialogue, stories usually benefit from it. Having the characters in your story speak can reveal their qualities, add important information, and make the mood or feeling of the story stronger. When you tell the story by speaking as its **narrator,** you also add variety and reveal more of yourself. (Remember, narrators must follow the conventions of standard edited English, so their writing "voice" will differ somewhat from their speaking voice.)

There are three kinds of "speech" in narrative: direct and indirect dialogue and revealed thought. **Direct dialogue** reproduces the words spoken by a character and is the most powerful:

DIRECT DIALOGUE   I couldn't keep my mouth shut any longer: "I'm not going to sit here and listen to you bad-mouth my brother one more second!"

Notice that within the quotation marks the verb tense shifts from the narrator's past tense to the present tense.

Indirect dialogue reports what someone else said, but not in his or her exact words:

INDIRECT DIALOGUE   My brother Tama told me he didn't believe in any of this supernatural nonsense.

Compare this to "Tama said, 'I don't believe in ghosts and all that other creepy stuff.'" Notice how the words change as the brother speaks for himself.

We use indirect dialogue when what is said has less importance to the story than direct dialogue would give it. We also use it to make the story go faster, to move readers more quickly to important events.

Revealed thought is the narrator thinking aloud:

REVEALED THOUGHT   I was thinking, "Oh my God, I am not dreaming. It is real!"

NOTE: In dialogue, put periods, question marks, and exclamation points *within,* not outside, the quotation marks at the ends of sentences.

Notice that when the narrator reveals thought, instead of just telling the story, the verb tense shifts from past to present. This tense shift helps readers feel more involved with the story, as if they are really in the scene.

ACTIVITY 6.4 Using Effective Dialogue

In the following passages, note the underlined indirect dialogue, and write out direct speech that seems appropriate to the speaker and situation.

EXAMPLE

Mrs. Hill sat silently at the front of the room, grading papers. I decided I would just use my study card to get started on the exam. So I cautiously reached down to retrieve the card, which had suddenly become my cheat sheet. I slid it under my leg and began filling in my exam. Then I heard Mrs. Hill's pencil fall to the floor, and she rose from her chair. My heart stopped as she reached my desk. I was asked to rise from my chair. As I stood, I felt as though my knees would buckle beneath me. My cheat sheet fell to the floor. Mrs. Hill, my most admired teacher, now had my test in hand and began shredding it.

HINT: Note that the first comma and exclamation point are *inside* the quotation marks.

Direct dialogue: _"Anita," Mrs. Hill said sternly, "get up from your seat—now!"_

Answers will vary.

1. It's a cool spring night at Qualcomm Stadium in San Diego, and I am preparing for my most exhilarating start ever, and my last as a pitcher for the all-Marine baseball team. As my teammates and I walk down the long hallway to the field, all I can hear are the cleats clicking on the cement floor. I see the nervous tension on their faces increase as we reach the field. They look like kids at their first big league game. Their mouths fall open as they stand on the field and see thousands of cheering fans filling the stadium. My coach turns to the team and lets us know that we should be calm, that if we relax we will do a good job tonight.

   Direct dialogue: _"Boys, this is just another game. You're great players. You've already proved it. Just settle down and play ball, and we'll do fine."_

2. Running down to the bullpen, I can feel the beads of sweat dripping down my face. While I am going through my warm-up pitches, my good friend C. J. gives me a few words of encouragement. He tells me that I should think of this game as any of the past 50 we have played. He says that I should forget about the pressure and just try to have fun like we always do.

   Direct dialogue: _"Listen up, Brandin, this game's a cakewalk," my friend C. J. says, tossing me a can of Skoal. "It's no different than a dozen other games we've played this season. Loosen up. Let's have some fun, and I'll let you buy me the first beer after the game."_

Including Metaphors and Similes to Add Clarity and Interest

Metaphors and **similes** are figures of speech that compare things.

METAPHOR	The ancient, bent oak tree at the wood's edge is the old man of the forest.
SIMILE	The ancient, bent oak at the wood's edge looks like an old man.

In both cases, the comparison is between a man and a tree. Notice that the simile uses *like*. Similes also use *as*.

Figures of speech like these can add color and clarity to your writing and focus readers on important parts of your story. Compare the following sets of sentences for a literal description versus a figurative one:

LITERAL	Suddenly, it began to rain hard.
FIGURATIVE	Suddenly, the sky became an open faucet, pouring rain on all of us below.
LITERAL	I will always remember the sight of the man who died in front of me.
FIGURATIVE	The 33-year-old man died right in front of me, a sight that will stay in my memory, like a stain, forever.
LITERAL	She was the biggest woman I had ever seen.
FIGURATIVE	She was huge, like an NFL linebacker.

In the literal versions, the meaning is clear, but the figurative versions take the meaning one step further, adding emphasis, clarity, and color. In fact, metaphors and similes are common in everyday life. Try reading an article in *Sports Illustrated* or listening to a sports broadcast; expressions like "the shot came low, like a heat-seeking missile" or "her speed is her ticket back to the Olympics" are common. In your own writing, try experimenting with metaphors and similes, especially when you revise for style. (For more on metaphors and similes see p. 505.)

As you practice metaphors and similes, be wary of creating **clichés**—figures of speech grown stale from overuse. Avoid clichés like these:

Caught between a rock and a hard place	Got a handle on the situation
Seemed to last for an eternity	Began to see the light
Sent chills down my spine	Felt butterflies in my stomach
Moved like lightning	Felt his heart pounding like a drum
Re-created the wheel	Stood still as a statue

(For more on clichés, see pp. 506–507.)

ACTIVITY 6.5 Including Metaphors and Similes

To practice figurative language, for the following literal expressions, create a metaphor or simile that expresses the same thought.

Answers will vary.

EXAMPLE

Literal: The sun shone down on the wet street.

Figurative: The street had been transformed by the rain into a river of light.

1. Literal: Bill was angry as he approached the return desk.
   Figurative: Bill looked like a volcano about to erupt as he stormed up to the return desk.

2. Literal: Dilated to 9 centimeters, Alice was in terrible pain.
   Figurative: Every contraction felt like a sharp steel spring uncoiling inside Alice, stabbing her cervix and making her scream, "Someone get this baby out of me."

3. Literal: Asking Elise out on their first date, Eduardo felt awkward and embarrassed.
   Figurative: Asking Elise out on a first date, Eduardo felt like a toad before a princess.

4. Literal: All of his files were locked within a nonfunctioning computer.
   Figurative: As if possessed by some idiot demon, Lori's computer continued to flash the warning message "You have performed an illegal function."

5. Literal: Professor Davis droned on, once again boring his captive students.
   Figurative: Ben tried to stay awake in Professor Davis's class, but it was like trying to fight off sleep at 3:00 a.m. while staring at an infomercial on TV.

Narrative Paragraphs: Analyzing Student Models

Teaching Idea
The model "Sixteen and Mother of Twelve" is a good one to show that a personal narrative does not have to be about a car wreck or the death of a loved one to be interesting and well written.

The student narratives that follow should give you ideas for your own. As you read them, look for narrative strategies that you like, and use them in your own story. Also, read the prereading and postreading commentaries, which will help you understand why the stories work well.

➤ Prereading Exploration for "Sixteen and Mother of Twelve"

The author, Lani Houston, wrote this narrative for her class members to help them understand one of her important personal insights. To further define her audience, she noted that anyone with military or leadership experience might be interested in her story. Before you jump into the reading, answer these questions:
Answers will vary.

1. Think about the title. Does it make you want to read on?

hearing the sounds grow louder as we approached. I was thinking, "Oh my God, I am not dreaming. It is real!" When I finally opened the door, I was shocked to see grandfather. My so-serious, blind grandfather, who never got up at night—this was how he would pay us back for our noise. Toothless, his hair ruffled from sleep, and wearing loose white pajamas, he was standing in front of me, leaning forward to scratch on the door again and continue his joke. Only not being able to see that I had opened the door, he fell forward onto the floor, and I lost my balance as I tried to catch him, falling too. For some reason I decided that he must be having a heart attack and needed help. My brother, who obviously thought something similar, screamed, "Mom, grandpa is dead!" Suddenly, the whole house was up—my aunt and uncle, two sisters, mom and dad—everyone crowding into the hall asking, "What happened? Who's hurt? Is grandfather all right?" I lay on the floor, paralyzed, and grandfather couldn't talk, not because he was hurt, but because he was laughing so hard. The more he laughed, the more we thought he was having some kind of seizure. Dad ended up calling an ambulance before grandfather calmed down enough to say what had happened, to assure everyone that he was really all right, and to apologize for the disturbance. I still think back on this joke that backfired whenever I'm tempted to try one of my own pranks, remembering what kind of disaster can follow a little "harmless fun."

—*Anna Suarez*

POSTREADING ANALYSIS: KEY POINTS FOR BUILDING NARRATIVE

- **Topic sentence:** states the event and implies the significance.
- **Concluding sentence:** restates the event and adds a final (expanded) thought.
- **Context:** in the second sentence, gives a reason for the action.
- **Suspense:** spooky mood set with *The Exorcist* (familiar to her audience).
- **Direct dialogue:** used to increase suspense and add humor—for example, "What is it?" and "Mom, grandpa is dead!"
- **Revealed thought:** builds suspense—for example, "Oh my God, I am not dreaming. It is real!"
- **Time connectors:** *"as late as it was," "when suddenly."*
- **Specific words:** *loose white pajamas* versus nightclothes, *3:00 A.M.* versus in the morning.
- **Action words:** verbs (*roar*) and *-ing* words (*scratching* sound).

Questions for Paragraph Analysis

Note: These questions apply to both student models.

1. In the topic sentence, what words name the event, and what words make a limiting statement about it?

2. What words in the concluding sentence link to the topic sentence?

3. What is the expanded thought in the final sentence? Does it end the story smoothly, or does the point seem "tacked on"? (For more on the expanded thought, see p. 49.)

4. Create an action outline of the characters' major movements from place to place, beginning each phrase with an *-ing* word. Limit the outline to eight actions. (For action outlines, see Activity 6.1.)

5. How much time does the story cover?

6. What details about the setting has the writer provided? (For more on setting, see p. 126.)

7. List any sensory details that you can find. Does this narrative have more or fewer details than you found in the descriptive models in Chapter 5?

8. Name three specific words, and list a more general word for each (see pp. 78–79).

9. Name three active verbs and three *-ing* words the author uses to show characters in motion. (For more on active verbs, see Chapter 23.)

10. Find two instances of showing and two of telling. How does the showing make the story interesting? (For more on showing and telling, see pp. 114–116.)

11. How does the dialogue add to the story? What does it show about the narrator and the other characters? (For more on dialogue, see pp. 116–117.)

12. List at least three time and three space transitions. How do the time transitions help readers move through the story? (For more on transitions, see pp. 54–55.)

13. What is your favorite image in this story? Why do you like it?

WRITING A NARRATIVE PARAGRAPH
Summarizing the Assignment

Building on the descriptive skills you practiced in Chapter 5, create a short narrative of 250 to 300 words that tells the story of a significant event in your life. Your story should include a topic sentence that draws readers in, actions arranged chronologically (by time order) that involve you and another person(s), and a final sentence that refers to the story's point and adds a final, expanded thought. Describe the setting well enough to help your readers follow the events and learn about the characters, but concentrate on narration, or telling and showing what the people are doing, feeling, and thinking. Whereas the dominant impression helped you focus your descriptive paper, the significance will help you focus your narrative. Remember, the story must have a point. How has the event affected your view of yourself? What does the event say about the larger world or your relation to it?

HINT: Try several topics before you commit to one.

What was the result: Mrs. Swanson came to the door with a bowl of mini Hershey bars and was handing them to us when she suddenly noticed the soaped mirrors in her hallway. She confronted us—not in a mean way; she was hurt—saying she had just been out there a few minutes before we had come. We were caught but felt forced to lie. I could see that she didn't believe us. I felt guilty about it and stopped soaping windows after that. But the worst part was being forced into the pointless lying.

When using a prewriting technique like this one, you may have better luck writing a little about several topics rather than a lot about your first choice. After you have decided on one event, you can extend your prewriting by asking more specific questions. For example, what were the boys' and Mrs. Swanson's ages? Further details could help set the mood (a cold, rainy evening) and sharpen the setting (details of the hall). If one prewriting method doesn't work, switch to another.

To further focus your prewriting, think about one aspect of your story at a time, setting aside half a page for each and listing memories as they surface. Try gathering material on the following important story elements:

Teaching Idea
You might want to help students through part of their prewriting in class by having them choose an event, answer the journalist's questions, and then freewrite on one or more of the six narrative points.

- **Setting:** In narrative, the setting or scene is merely a backdrop against which characters move, so you will seldom go into great detail. However, some details are needed to show the characters in relation to one another and to help set the mood. For example, consider how the darkness and silence of the house in "What a Joke!" (pp. 121–122) add to the children's feelings of fright. Jot down details about physical objects (car, chair, tree) as you recall them, including their size and location, color, sound, and smell. You won't use them all, but it is good to have them to draw on.

- **People:** You and perhaps one other person are important enough to describe in any detail in your event paper. You need to provide only a brief sketch (approximate age, overall physical look, maybe hair or eye color, some article of clothing). Then you can focus on the action and your thoughts and feelings.

Teaching Idea
Remind students that dialogue that approximates what was said is fine.

- **Dialogue:** While not all narratives include spoken dialogue, most do. Dialogue is a powerful device for showing what people feel and think. You can use it to vary your narrator's voice and to provide information that adds to the story. Try to write down dialogue as accurately as you can.

- **Action:** Without action, narrative dies. The action does not have to be dramatic or violent (Arnold Schwarzenegger firing another Stinger missile to blow up a helicopter), though. Remember that mental and emotional action can be compelling as well. However, as you gather ideas, try to recall physical movement. How did you cross the room? Where did the other person sit? Did you lean back on one arm, slouch in your chair, or slice the air with your hand as you emphatically said, "No!"?

Teaching Idea
Because some students have difficulty discovering the point of their narrative (and, of course, sometimes there simply isn't one), you might model a Q/A exchange with one student, using the prompts under "Significance." Then students can split into groups and do the same with one another.

- **Thoughts and feelings:** As you reflect on the event, try to recall what you thought and felt immediately before, during, and after the action. Often, you will capture only a piece of the thought or feeling you had at the time and then elaborate on it based on your current thoughts and feelings.

- **Significance:** In our personal narratives, we need to discover why the memory is important enough to write about. The meaning may not be clear at first or may be limited to one point, but it is important. The following questions will help you discover your meaning:

- How did my behavior reflect on who I was at the time?
- How did my behavior affect who I am now?
- What did the other person's (people's) behavior indicate about her or him (them)?
- What were the positive or negative effects of the action?
- What could have resulted?
- Have I learned anything about myself, another person, or the world from the event?
- Has the event changed my behavior, thinking, or feeling?

(For more on significance, see p. 113.)

HINT: Get reactions from others.

Whether you have finalized your topic or not, now is a good time to hear from others. Talk to people about your event. If they think it can be shaped into an interesting final story, you may feel more confident in moving ahead.

PREWRITING—SUMMING UP

1. Decide on several events or choose several from the topics list.
2. Use a prewriting technique to get an overview of your events.
3. Choose an event and briefly summarize it.
4. Prewrite to generate ideas for the setting, people, action, and significance.
5. Summarize your story for someone else to see the person's reaction.

JOURNAL ENTRY 6.2

Review your prewriting notes, particularly the ones that cover significance. Do you feel that your story has a point yet? Does your material reveal something about you? In a brief paragraph, explain the meaning of your narrative.

Organizing Ideas

The following points will help you shape and focus your material before you start your draft. First, write out at least a rough topic sentence. The topic sentence does not have to reveal the outcome of your story, but it should hint at it and give readers a sense of your direction with a limiting statement. It may state the significance outright. (For more on topic sentences, see pp. 36–41.) In the following topic sentences, from the student models in this chapter, the topics are underlined once and the limiting statements twice.

HINT: Try hinting at the significance of your event in the topic sentence.

A. At the Civil Air Patrol Encampment of 1996, when I was only 16, I learned how satisfying it can be to lead a group successfully.

B. At 3:00 A.M. one morning my grandfather decided to play a joke on us that didn't turn out to be as funny as he thought it would be.

Teaching Idea
Insisting that they limit the lead-in to their narratives will save some students from having to do major cutting and refocusing in their first draft.

HINT: Limit the amount of time or number of scenes in your narrative.

Once you have a rough topic sentence, organize your paragraph chronologically (as the clock moves), beginning close to the high point, or climax, of the action and keeping your buildup to the climax short. For example, a one-paragraph story on the birth of a child should begin on the day of the delivery, leaving out the other 9 months.

Here are two ways to manage time problems in one-paragraph narratives:

1. Limit the time of the event. Many terrific short narratives cover only a few minutes, as do the student models in this chapter. If you try to cover more than a few minutes, be sure to summarize, using time transitions like *the next morning, when we got there,* and *by 8:00.*

2. Stick with one or two scenes in which all the action occurs. For example, in the student model "What a Joke!" the story is set entirely in Anna's room.

Remember to use strong connectors between sentences, as in this shortened list of time and space transitions. (For more on connectors, see pp. 53–58.)

Teaching Idea
If you worked through Chapter 5, you might remind students that the time and space transitions are the same ones they have already used.

FOR LOCATING OR MOVING IN SPACE			
above	east (west, etc.)	in between	over
against	elsewhere	in the distance	surrounded by
alongside	far off (away)	into	there
around	farther on	near	through

FOR MOVING IN TIME			
after	first (second, etc.)	next	suddenly
afterward	immediately	now	then
at last	in the meantime	often	time passed
awhile	in the past	once	until

All references to calendar time and events: one day, days ago, tonight, afternoon

All references to clock time: a few minutes, 12:00 A.M., three hours

All references to regular meals: during breakfast, lunch, dinner

ORGANIZING—SUMMING UP

1. Write out a rough topic sentence that hints at the outcome or significance of your event.

2. Limit the time span of the story and the number of scenes in it.

3. Cut any unneeded lead-in to the main part of your story.

4. Arrange your narrative material chronologically using an action outline (see pp. 109–110).

5. Review the list of transitions—especially time and space transitions—above and the other connectors on pages 53–58.

Teaching Idea
If students limit their "action" outlines from Journal Entry 6.3 to, say, six to eight major actions, they will be less likely to write 500-word paragraphs.

JOURNAL ENTRY 6.3

To help focus your draft, try an action outline that lists the major actions of your event as they occurred. (To see an action outline for this journal entry, see pp. 111–112.)

Drafting

Teaching Idea
Although you may have already covered drafting in Chapter 1, it helps to review this material again the day before student drafts are due.

With the preliminary work done, you are almost ready to draft. But before plunging in, review the drafting suggestions in Chapter 1 (pp. 12–13). Also keep the following suggestions in mind:

1. Visualize the setting. Close your eyes and try to envision the setting of your story. If the narrative occurs inside, what does the room look like? What kind of furniture is there? How is it arranged? Is it day or night? Warm or cold? Summer or winter? Sometimes it helps to establish a larger frame for the picture before moving in to capture the details. Imagine that you are hovering in a helicopter filming from a hundred feet above the scene. What do you see?

2. Use your "creative memory." Few people can remember everything they want to put into a story. Feel free to fill in the blank spaces of your memory with details and dialogue that could have happened.

3. Summarize action to move readers quickly through your story.

4. Describe a scene in detail when you want the reader to slow down and pay attention, especially when you are close to the climax of your story.

HINT: Summarizing speeds up the pace of a story; detailing slows it down.

Teaching Idea
To help students understand how summarizing and detailing affect narrative pace, you might have them skim the first few sentences of the annotated student model to show summarizing and then skim the detailing of the author's thoughts and emotions. They should be able to see that the detailing slows down the pace and emphasizes the material.

JOURNAL ENTRY 6.4

After you have written your first draft, reread it and note the climax. Is it near the end of your story, and do you then wrap up the paragraph within a sentence or two? Explain how the action in your story logically leads up to this climax.

Revising Drafts

First-Stage Drafts

At this stage, you should focus on content (main story elements: action, climax, resolution, setting, thoughts, and feelings) and organization (arranging and connecting ideas).

1. Has your narrative paragraph grown too long?

Once you get rolling, it is easy to include interesting side details that nonetheless distract readers and weaken your main point. So find the center of your tale—the high point of the action and its meaning—and then cut whatever doesn't get readers there quickly. Use only a sentence or two to set up a context for the action, and move immediately from the climax to the concluding sentence (or two). Also, limit the time span the narrative covers—a few minutes to a few hours works well for a paragraph.

HINT: Move straight from your topic sentence into the action.

2. Is your topic sentence effective?

Sometimes, it is effective to begin a personal narrative with an action sentence like the following: "After finishing a lunch of greasy fries and burgers, I dashed through the parking lot toward room 130." However, this sort of beginning does not give readers (or you) a clear sense of the paper's direction. To focus your brief story, it is usually best to begin with a topic sentence that hints at the climax or states the meaning of the event. (For more on topic sentences, see the models in this chapter and pp. 36–41.)

3. Does the story have conflict, suspense, climax, and resolution?

HINT: Conflict and movement are crucial to your story.

For your narrative to work, it must have conflict: person versus person, person versus the external world (forces of nature, animals, machines), or person versus him- or herself (an internal struggle). For the story to have suspense, it must keep readers wondering what will happen next. If the action is well organized, it will move chronologically to a climax, where the action stops. As you reflect on the action in the final sentence (or two), you can create a resolution for the story by highlighting a significant point or meaning. (For more on these points, see pp. 111–113.)

4. Have you sketched the setting sufficiently?

In narrative, readers need only a few well-chosen details to visualize a setting—just a sketch will usually do. Remember to use specific words (*Mustang* vs. *car*) and sensory details (sight, sound, touch, smell, taste). (For more on specific language and sensory details, see pp. 78–79.)

5. Have you described people sufficiently?

Although narrative emphasizes people's actions, thoughts, and emotions, you should provide some physical details about the main characters. Notice how the brief description of the grandfather in "What a Joke" (pp. 121–122) adds interest to the tale: "Toothless, his hair ruffled from sleep, and wearing loose white pajamas, he was standing in front of me, leaning forward to scratch on the door again and continue his joke." Also, you might show how your main characters move—what gestures they make, and how they walk, sit, or stand.

6. Have you included effective dialogue?

Because dialogue is a powerful device for showing people's thoughts and emotions, it is used frequently in stories. You may not need dialogue in your story, depending on the topic (see the student model "Death Strikes"), but your story probably will benefit from it. Check to make sure the dialogue sounds convincing. (For more on dialogue, see pp. 116–117.)

7. Have you revealed your thoughts and feelings?

Narratives become slow and boring when writers "tell" too much of the story rather than showing the action. However, when writers tell about their thoughts and feelings and then show them, stories become more interesting.

8. Is the significance of the event clear?

Your event may have several meanings to you, but you should focus on one, sharing that insight with your audience. A clear point adds substance to your story and helps readers connect with you, the author. (For more on significance, see p. 113.)

9. Is the concluding sentence effective?

Your final sentence should contain a connector (transitional word or repeated word) and clearly indicate the significance of the event. But don't conclude with a cliché or worn expression. (For more on concluding sentences, see pp. 48–52, and for more on clichés, see pp. 506–507.)

10. Are sentences within the paragraph well connected?

HINT: Summarizing actions can link scenes and speed up the pace of the story.

First drafts of narratives usually need more time and space connectors, especially time transitions. Sentences can also be more strongly linked using synonyms, repeated words, and pronouns. Also, remember that time transitions such as "in the meantime" or "a few moments later" can speed up the pace of the story. (For more on sentence connectors, see pp. 53–58.)

> **JOURNAL ENTRY 6.5**
>
> To help you focus on the revision process and alert your instructor to your progress, list three *specific* changes you have made or feel you ought to make in going from your first to second draft. Refer to the first-stage draft questions, answering specifically. (Example: Question 9: "My story was going off track, so I had to cut out the first three sentences and use the fourth one as my topic sentence.") Next, in several sentences, state what you like best about your story.

Second and Final Drafts

For advice on revising and then editing further drafts of your work, turn to Chapter 4.

ANNOTATED STUDENT MODEL: "DO UNTO OTHERS . . ."

Teaching Idea
If you assign the annotated student model in stages that parallel students' own progress through their papers, you can use the annotated drafts to ease students into their own peer revising groups.

To help with your narrative, read through the Annotated Student Model that follows. In examining Chris Potts's drafts, you can profit from her hard work and head off some of the problems that are likely to creep into your own drafts.

As you read, keep in mind that revision seldom occurs in tidy stages. Sometimes, for example, you will edit early in the process of writing a draft and change content later. However, the following draft stages will help focus your revision efforts.

First-Stage Draft

Teaching Idea
This first-stage draft clearly alerts students to the problem of having an overlong lead-in.

Total words = 538 (need to focus)

First drafts are for getting words on paper, so, naturally, there will be plenty to change. While many narratives initially leave out important parts of the story, other first drafts include too much. Notice in this first draft how much of the lead-in was not needed.

"Come on, Joelle, we need to hurry up," I said, trying to motivate my three-year-old girl toward the car. "Coming, mommy, I gotta get my babies!" Oh, no, I thought, this could take forever, and I don't have forever. I had to get to the bank to pick up some papers for the house. Jordan, her nineteen-month-old sister, looked on, playing with her "babies." She was not getting ready to move any faster than her big sister. "Listen, sweetie, we are in a hurry, like a race. Ready. Set. Go!" Neither of my girls were cooperating today, so I scooped them both up and headed for the garage. After wrestling the girls into their car seats, I slowly backed down the driveway. It was getting more difficult each day to maneuver the car with my ever-increasing midsection—the girls' little brother, 4 weeks till delivery—getting in the way. But we made it into the street and were on our way to the bank. What I hadn't counted on was taking a turn too hard. I flattened a tire. I didn't know what to do since there was no one around to help me, and I couldn't do the job anymore myself. Panic and frustration are a sure-fire recipe for tears, but I tried to stay calm and composed so my girls wouldn't catch my mood. Suddenly, I heard a voice. "Listen, I have a cell phone. Do you want to call someone to come pick you up?" As I turned toward the voice, I saw an older guy who looked a lot like my dad. I explained to him that everyone who could help was out of reach and I wasn't sure what I was going to do. As I spoke, I had no control over the tears. "Are you sure you've thought through all your options?" he asked. "How about Triple-A? Do you have any other family or friends who could help?" I just shook my head. "Well, then," he said as he rolled up his sleeves I still no how to fix a flat. If you don't mind me taking a run at it? Show me where the jack and spare are, and I'll see what I can do. "Why don't you wait inside the bank while I put the spare on?" I nodded yes, and opened the door to get the keys. Then I unbuckled the girls and ushered them out of the car. As Joelle jumped out, she called the man "Papa," thinking he might be my dad, but she wasn't sure about it. To really confuse her, the man, said, "Hi, Peanut," which is the name my dad calls her. The girls and I went into the bank, retrieved our papers, and headed to check on the man's progress. "Well, you're back in buisness," he said. "It's just a spare tire. You shouldn't go over 45 miles per hour with it." As he spoke, I offered the cash envelop to him. Then I attempted to utter a profound thank-you. Gratefulness was still caught in my throat, and I was crying again. He said that he didn't want the money in the envelop and added, "You don't have to do that, but I will ask you to do a favor for me. The next time you see who needs help, stop and help them." I said "I will" and a few "thank-yous" and we headed our seperate ways.

Second-Stage Draft

Teaching Idea
This second-stage draft illustrates the common problem in narratives of insufficient showing.

Teaching Idea
Here is another clear reminder to students to revise for suspense/tension.

First drafts of narratives often have unnecessary details, especially in the beginning, and the topic and concluding sentences often need to be revised. If your draft seems too predictable, you may not have developed much suspense yet or shown the conflict clearly. Double-check dialogue for realism and brevity. Finally, look closely at the setting and people. Are all pieces of your scene adequately described to help readers follow the action?

SPECIAL POINTS TO CHECK IN REVISING FROM FIRST TO SECOND DRAFTS
1. ~~Delete unnecessary material~~.
2. Add material to increase tension/suspense.
3. Show as well as tell.
4. Describe physical actions.
5. Check time and space connectors.
6. Tighten topic and concluding sentences.

Teaching Idea
Although the pronoun *you* is frequently overused in student writing, it can be effective when the writer actually intends to speak to her audience as Chris Potts does in her topic sentence, using a question to draw her readers in.

Topic sentence revised

Lead-in condensed from first draft

Material added to increase tension

Added: sound, action, specific details

Examples added to *show* helpless condition

Explaining added to *show* emotion

*Unneeded dialogue deleted

Specific detail added for clarity

Action added

Have you ever been stuck, needing help, with no place to turn? One day several years ago, I found myself in a rush to get to the bank. I needed to sign papers vital for the closing of our first house. We desperately needed a larger house for our growing family. With my two girls in there car seats in the back, we neared the parking lot of the bank. I thought we would make it before the bank closed but I hadn't counted on the accident. Bang! A nasty metallic sound told me what to expect. As I got out I could see it, yes, the tire was flat. The rim touched the ground. What was I going to do? I ran through my options quickly. My husbands plane wouldn't land for another hour and a half. My friend Angie had left town with her family that morning. I knew how to change flat, but, I was pregnant. And then what would I do with my daughters in the back seat? Panic and frustration are a sure-fire recipe for tears, but I tried to remain calm and composed so my girls wouldn't catch my mood. Suddenly I heard a voice say, "Listen, I have a cell phone. Do you want to call someone to come pick you up?" As I turned toward the voice. I saw an older guy, who looked a lot like my dad. I explained to him that everyone who could help was out of reach and I wasn't sure what I was going to do. As I spoke, I started crying.* "Well, then," he said as he rolled up his sleeves, "why don't you wait inside the bank while I put the spare on. You have a spare, don't you?" I had no words. Gratefulness had swallowed panic and frustration but had gotten caught in my throat as I simply nodded yes. The girls and I went into the bank, retrieved our papers, made a cash withdrawal, and headed back outside. The man had just shut the trunk, and was rolling down his sleeves. "You're back in buisness," he said with a smile." As he spoke, I offered him the cash envelop. Then I attempted to utter a profound thank-you. Gratefulness was still caught in my throat, and I was crying again. He said that he didn't want

Conclusion revised to reinforce significance

Expanded thought added.

CAUTION! Beware of clichés and tired phrases in the final sentence.

the money in the envelope and added, "You don't have to do that, but I will ask you to do a favor for me. The next time you see who needs help, stop and help them." I said, "I will" and a few "thank-yous," and we headed our seperate ways. Later, after I had returned the favor I understood why he hadn't excepted the money I had offered. *No reward could be as satisfying as the good deed itself.*

Third-Stage Draft

Teaching Idea
You might want to point out to students that they will find lots of mechanical errors in even the third-stage draft.

By this point, Chris has her draft in good shape. The content is mostly in place, and the organization is effective. Topic and concluding sentences work well, and time and space connectors firmly anchor her reader in the story. Now she will deal with sentence- and word-level problems to polish the draft.

> **SPECIAL POINTS TO CHECK IN REVISING FROM SECOND TO THIRD DRAFTS**
> 1. Add specific words.
> 2. [Combine sentences for variety.]
> 3. **Replace clutter and repeat words with synonyms and phrases.**
> 4. Delete unneeded words.
> 5. Add active verbs and *-ing* words.

Title added

Teaching Idea
In the third-stage draft, Chris uses a question to draw readers in (topic sentence) and then several sentences later effectively uses another question to help develop her narrative. You might want to link this use of questions to the section on questions in Chapter 18.

Material added to *show* difficulty

Do unto Others . . .

Have you ever been stuck, needing help, with no place to turn? [One day several years ago, I found myself in a rush to get to the bank to sign papers vital for the closing of our first house, a house we desperately needed for our growing family.] [With my two girls in there car seats in the back, nearing the parking lot of the bank, I thought we would make it before the bank closed] but I hadn't counted on the accident. Bang! I had hit a curb hard and a nasty metallic sound told me what to expect. As I got out, I could see it. [Yes, the tire was flat the rim touching the pavement.] What was I going to do? I ran through my options quickly. My husbands plane wouldn't land for another hour and a half. My friend Angie had left town with her family that morning. I knew how to change flat, but, 8 months pregnant, I was lucky still to be tying my own shoes. And then what would I do with my daughters in the back seat? Panic and frustration are a sure-fire recipe for tears, but I fought them off and struggled to remain calm and composed (so my girls wouldn't catch my mood) for my girls. Suddenly I heard a voice say, "Listen, I have a cell phone. Do you want to call someone to come pick you up?" As I turned toward the voice. I saw an older gentleman who looked a lot like my dad.

(~~I explained to him that everyone who could help was out of reach and~~ ~~I wasn't sure what I was going to do. As I spoke I started crying.~~) **Beginning to cry. I explained how helpless I felt.** "Well, then," he said as he rolled up his sleeves, "why don't you wait inside the bank while I put the spare on. You have a spare, don't you"? I had no words. Gratefulness had swallowed panic and frustration but had gotten caught in my throat as I simply nodded yes. The girls and I hustled into the bank, retrieved our papers, (~~made a cash withdrawal~~) **withdrew cash,** and headed back outside. Our good samaritan had just shut the trunk, and was rolling down his sleeves. "You're back in business," he said with a smile." ⌈As he spoke, I offered him the cash envelop, and attempted to utter a profound thank-you, but gratefulness was still caught in my throat, and the tears were in full force again.⌋ He (~~said he didn't want the money in the envelope~~) **declined** the envelope **saying** "You don't have to that, but I will ask you to do a favor for me. The next time you see who needs help, stop and help them." I squeaked out an "I will" and a few "thank-yous," and we headed our seperate ways. Later, after I had returned the favor I understood why he hadn't excepted the money I had offered. No reward could be as satisfying as the good deed itself.

Metaphor added

Final-Editing Draft

In this last draft, Chris slows her reading to a crawl, editing closely, word by word, line by line. It is a tedious process, but she knows that she still has many errors to correct.

Teaching Idea
To prepare students for editing, you might want to have them group edit the third-stage draft and then check theirs against the final draft.

SPECIAL POINTS TO CHECK IN EDITING FINAL DRAFTS

1. Misspellings
2. Sound-alike words
3. Missing words
4. Wrong words
5. Sentence fragments
6. Comma splices/run-ons
7. Faulty capitalization
8. Incorrect apostrophes
9. Comma(s) needed
   a. Introductory words/phrases/clauses
   b. Nonessential word groups
   c. Main clauses with coordinating conjunctions
10. Unneeded commas

Do unto Others . . .

Have you ever been stuck, needing help, with no place to turn? One day several years ago, I found myself in a rush to get to the bank to sign papers vital for the closing of our first house, a house we desperately

Teaching Idea
Although we teach our students to avoid fragments most of the time, they can be used to good effect, as Chris Potts does with the one word "Bang!" You might ask students to compare her intentional fragment with the two unintentional ones later in the draft to see which fragment they feel accomplishes a special purpose.

needed for our growing family. With my two girls in ~~there~~[2] their car seats in the back, nearing the parking lot of the bank, I thought we would make it before the bank closed[9c], but I hadn't counted on the accident. Bang! I had hit a curb hard[9c], and a nasty metallic sound told me what to expect. As I got out, I could see it,[6]. Yes, the tire was flat[9b], the rim touching the pavement. What was I going to do? I ran through my options quickly. My ~~husbands~~[8] husband's plane wouldn't land for another hour and a half. My friend Angie had left town with her family that morning. I knew how to change[3] a flat, but, 8 months pregnant, I was lucky still to be tying my own shoes. And then what would I do with my daughters in the back seat? Panic and frustration are a sure-fire recipe for tears, but I fought them off and struggled to remain calm for my girls. Suddenly, I heard a voice say, "Listen, I have a cell phone. Do you want to call someone to come pick you up?" As I turned toward the voice.[5], I saw an older gentleman who looked a lot like my dad. Beginning to cry.[5], I explained how helpless I felt. "Well, then," he said as he rolled up his sleeves, "why don't you wait inside the bank while I put the spare on? You have a spare, don't you?" I had no words. Gratefulness had swallowed panic and frustration but had gotten caught in my throat as I simply nodded yes. The girls and I hustled into the bank, ~~recieved~~[1] retrieved our papers, withdrew cash, and headed back outside. Our good samaritan[7] Good Samaritan had just shut the trunk,[10] and was rolling down his sleeves. "You're back in ~~buisness~~[1] business," he said with a smile. As he spoke, I offered him the cash ~~envelop~~[4] envelope,[10] and attempted to utter a profound thank-you, but gratefulness was still caught in my throat, and the tears were in full force again. He declined the envelope saying, "You don't have to do[3] that, but I will ask you to do a favor for me. The next time you see someone[3] who needs help, stop and help them." I squeaked out an "I will" and a few "thank-yous," and we headed our ~~seperate~~[1] separate ways. Later, after I had returned the favor[9b], I understood why he hadn't ~~excepted~~[2] accepted the money I had offered. No reward could be as satisfying as the good deed itself.

—Chris Potts

Teaching Idea
It is worth the time to take students back to Chapter 4 as they revise and edit their first several assignments. The Final-Draft Checklist is mirrored in Chapter 4, so if students need more in-depth reminders than this list provides, they will not have to search through the text. The information is accessible in a few consecutive pages.

FINAL-DRAFT CHECKLIST

Before you turn in your final draft for a grade, review this checklist. You may find that, as careful as you think you have been, you still missed a point or two—or more. (For more on any of these points, see Chapter 4.)

☐   1. Has your narrative paragraph grown into an essay?

☐   2. Is your topic sentence effective?

☐   3. Does the story have conflict, suspense, a climax, and a resolution?

☐   4. Have you sketched the setting fully?

☐   5. Have you described people sufficiently?

☐   6. Have you included effective dialogue?

☐   7. Have you revealed your thoughts and feelings?

☐   8. Is the significance of the event clear?

☐   9. Is your concluding sentence effective?

☐ 10. Are all the sentences within the paragraph well connected?

☐ 11. Have you used specific language?

☐ 12. Are you using active verbs and *-ing* words to describe action?

☐ 13. Would a metaphor or simile strengthen your story?

☐ 14. Are your sentences varied in length and beginnings?

☐ 15. Have you used synonyms for words that are repeated too often?

☐ 16. Have you cut unneeded words?

☐ 17. Does the paper have an interesting title? Have you checked its capitalization?

☐ 18. Have you prepared the paper according to the format expected by your instructor? (Check to see if you need to include a title page, use double spacing, leave at least a 1-inch margin, and use a 12-point font.)

☐ 19. Have you edited your work closely (including having at least one other person proofread)? Have you checked your Improvement Chart for pattern errors?

☐ 20. Have you looked for the following errors: misspellings, sound-alike words, missing words, wrong words, sentence fragments, comma splices/run-ons, faulty capitalizations, incorrect apostrophes, missing commas, and unnecessary commas?

Chapter Summary

1. A narrative tells about events and usually involves people. Narratives have many forms, but when we tell a story, we are usually talking about "someone doing something somewhere for some reason."

2. Narratives involve conflict and suspense: a chronological arranging of actions leading to a high point and having a point.

3. The setting serves as a backdrop for the action.

4. Narratives reveal characters' thoughts and feelings and usually use dialogue.

5. Well-organized narrative paragraphs require topic and concluding sentences. Time and space connectors are essential.

6. Both showing and telling are used to develop stories. Of the two, showing requires the most energy from the writer but has the most power.

7. Specific words and sensory details help build memorable scenes.

8. Figures of speech like metaphors and similes add clarity and color to narratives.

9. Like any writing, a narrative is not complete until it has been revised and carefully edited.

ALTERNATE WRITING ASSIGNMENTS

Here are a few more assignment options that may be of interest. For this assignment, be sure to do the following:

1. Create a narrative that has conflict and tension.
2. Choose a story that has clear significance or meaning.
3. Build a story that shows as well as tells.
4. Use effective dialogue.
5. Include metaphors and similes to add clarity and interest.

ASSIGNMENT OPTIONS

1. Interview your parents and ask them to relate a story or two from your early childhood that involves you. You might help them recall a moment by mentioning several possible topics:

   - How they picked your name
   - How they prepared for your arrival in the home
   - What life was like during your first 6 months
   - When you first crawled, talked, or walked
   - When you made the move from a crib to a bed
   - Any other significant developmental moment

   Retell one of their stories about you as a narrative with a beginning, middle, and end. Arrange the action chronologically, build suspense, detail a setting, and move toward a climax. The significance of your event could involve a realization you have about your parents or parenting in general. Since you will rely on your parents' memories for details, ask plenty of questions and take careful notes.

2. Role-play someone you have recently disagreed with. This person could be close to you (father, mother, child, etc.) or someone you don't know well. The point is to get inside the person's skin and then retell the argument from her or his perspective. As you narrate the event, use lots of dialogue, but don't neglect the setting and a brief lead-in to set up the disagreement. What did it stem from, and how serious is it? Remember that you are the other person, so you can only guess at your actual thoughts/feelings. The significance of the event may be how sympathetic you became to the other person's perspective.

3. Write an extended joke or retell a humorous story that has a point. For example, you might recall a time when you used poor judgment and suffered from it. Perhaps the "great deal" you got on a $500 used car turned out not to be so hot. Maybe you took 21 credit hours in one semester and learned how stressful academic life can be. Or your first experience with credit cards might have shown you how much fun 20 percent interest rates can be on a $5,000 balance.

Follow narrative conventions, organize using a topic and concluding sentences, and be sure to make the significance of the event clear.

CAUTION! This is probably the hardest of the five alternate assignments.

4. Create a fictional story starring you or another character. Your story should have conflict as well as physical, mental, and emotional movement. The story should be brief—only one or two scenes. Since it must have a point, you might avoid a purely action sequence—guns blazing and cattle stampeding—in favor of one that shows something about who people are and what they are worth.

5. Interview your grandparents to learn about some significant event in their lives. A grandparent, as in the photo above, can be a wonderful source of information. You might ask him or her to time travel, moving back 40 or 50 years to an era that probably seems like ancient history to you. Memorable events in most people's lives include births, engagements, weddings, illnesses, deaths, relocations, and career changes (see the topics list, pp. 124–125). You could write your retelling of their story in the third person (he said/thought, etc.) or assume the identity of the grandparent and write from that first-person perspective.

Illustrating through Examples

What Are We Trying to Achieve and Why?

Setting the Stage

Teaching Idea
You might begin Chapter 7 with a brief review of examples from Chapter 3 in the section "Developing Body Paragraphs."

What is it about amusement parks that appeals to people in general? What activities appeal to you specifically? Suppose a friend asks you what you like best about a local theme park—Disney World, Six Flags over Texas, Worlds of Fun, Coney Island. If you say, "The rides" or, more specifically, "Roller coasters, especially the wooden ones like the Timber Wolf!" you have given an example. Whenever people make a statement and then follow it with an example to show their meaning, they are illustrating a point. Examples are the building blocks of all writing.

In this chapter, we will build on the narrative/descriptive skills you developed in Chapters 5 and 6, using specific word choices, sensory details, comparisons, focus, and well-connected sentences. We will go one step further, however. Instead of focusing on a single place or story, we will work with *several* examples, each introduced by a **subtopic sentence.** In addition to personal examples, we will use general knowledge of the world and close observation to create a slightly more formal tone.

Teaching Idea
Some students have difficulty moving on from the single-place or single-narrative assignments in Chapters 5 and 6. It helps to stress the use of three to four examples.

Linking to Previous Experience

Teaching Idea
To help students shift from the purely personal "I" voice, you might begin by having a student describe the experiences of a friend—for example, "Give me an example to show how rotten a friend's boss is." The next step, of course, is to ask for an example from the student's general knowledge or imagination—how bad could a boss be?

If you worked through Chapters 5 and 6, you have already used examples to express a dominant impression and an event's significance. Also, our own lives are full of examples. When we attempt to clarify a statement for another person, we usually do so with an example. You might say, "I can't stand my job," and a friend responds, "Why?" If you answer by mentioning the long hours, monster of a boss, and low pay, you have given examples. If you discuss bad jobs in general, you might leave your personal experience out, instead citing examples

141

typical of bad jobs: a rotten boss, low pay, long hours, unpleasant co-workers, and poor work environment. We often give examples to explain ourselves or defend a position, based on what we have read or heard.

Determining the Value of Examples

Specific examples help us share our experiences, discuss ideas, and plan for the future. Unsupported statements like "I can't stand Shannon," "The Royals are a second-rate ball club," and "This policy will lead the country to ruin" raise questions that well-chosen examples can answer.

Examples also help us understand our own feelings and thoughts. Why do we trust one co-worker and not another? What examples can we give to explain these feelings? When we prepare for an essay exam, we gather as many examples as we can remember. Why is Martin Luther King, Jr., considered a pivotal figure in the civil rights movement in this country? Why do some people believe in the conspiracy theory behind the assassination of President John F. Kennedy? If we can offer specific examples to support our answers, we will probably do well on the exam.

As we develop examples in Chapter 7, we will learn to communicate more effectively and to clarify our own thinking.

Teaching Idea
Journal Entry 7.1 can be done in collaborative groups and is a good way to get students thinking about development through specific language, sensory details, explanations, and comparisons.

JOURNAL ENTRY 7.1

Think about several occasions in the recent past when you used examples to explain, defend a position, or entertain. List several instances, summarizing the situation in a sentence or two. Was one example in each instance sufficient to achieve your purpose, or were more needed? How much detail did you give? Did you re-create part of a scene using specific language, sensory detail, dialogue, and so on, or did you explain at length, perhaps using comparisons?

Developing Skills and Exploring Ideas in Illustration Paragraphs

To learn how to use examples effectively, we will practice the following:

1. Using subtopic sentences to introduce each major example
2. Arranging major examples by order of importance
3. Linking all sentences, especially subtopics, with connecting words
4. Developing examples with specific words, details, and explanations

Teaching Idea
Activity 7.1 introduces the subtopic sentence and relates it to the topic sentence it will become when students start writing essays. You might want to link this activity to the analysis of "Dangers in a Deli" in Chapter 3 and/or the comparison of subtopic to topic in "Teaching with Whips" in Chapter 14 under "Drafting."

Organizing Examples through Subtopic Sentences

As we have seen, most paragraphs should begin with a topic sentence that tells what the paragraph will be about. When writers develop a paragraph with several major examples, they often use subtopic or minor topic sentences, in addition to the topic sentence, to tell what each major example will be about.

Each subtopic sentence should begin with a <mark>connector word or phrase</mark> (shaded in the following examples), state the <u>example</u> (underlined once), and then make a <u>limiting statement</u> about it (underlined twice).

TOPIC SENTENCE   I will never know how I <u>survived</u> my <u>adolescent years</u>.

The topic sentence predicts a paragraph about the writer's dangerous youth.

FIRST SUBTOPIC SENTENCE   <mark>Although</mark> I was <u>never more than bruised</u> while doing it, <u>jumping onto the tops of boxcars</u> from a low bridge was one of my earliest <u>dangerous stunts</u>.

The first subtopic sentence gives the first major example of a dangerous act: jumping onto boxcars. This sentence would be followed by several more sentences giving details (sights, sounds, smells, etc.) that show what jumping onto boxcars was like.

SECOND SUBTOPIC SENTENCE   <mark>More</mark> <u>dangerous (and stupider)</u> than <u>train jumping</u> was my 16-year-old's effort at <u>flying a '69 convertible Firebird from an off-ramp</u>.

The second subtopic sentence gives the second major example: "flying" a Firebird. More details would follow to develop the scene: an explanation of how the driver lost control, sensory details, thoughts, and feelings.

THIRD SUBTOPIC SENTENCE   The <mark>closest</mark> <u>I came to death</u> was when I was just thirteen and <u>thought the ice on Granite Lake would support me</u>.

The third subtopic sentence gives the third major example: walking on weak ice. More details would follow: the action of walking onto the ice, the sound of ice cracking, and the feeling of being immersed in freezing water.

ACTIVITY 7.1 Subtopic Sentences

For the topic sentences that follow, decide on three major examples that could illustrate a paragraph about them and then complete each of the subtopic sentences with your examples.

EXAMPLE
Topic sentence: To be a <u>good parent</u>, a person must either be born with or develop <u>several essential personality traits</u>.

Subtopic sentence 1: <u>The first trait a parent should have is a love of play.</u>

Subtopic sentence 2: <u>Another important quality is a vivid imagination.</u>

Subtopic sentence 3: <u>However, the most necessary quality for a parent is patience.</u>

Answers will vary.
1. Topic sentence: When people <u>lose control of their anger</u>, there are often <u>severe consequences</u>.

   Subtopic sentence 1: One negative effect is <u>that they damage property.</u>

   Subtopic sentence 2: Angry people will also <u>hurt themselves.</u>

   Subtopic sentence 3: The worst result of losing control is <u>when we hurt other people.</u>

Teaching Idea
To practice development, you might ask students to give a few additional examples or details for any of the subtopics in the section preceding Activity 7.1.

NOTE: Many paragraphs focus on only one main example and therefore do not need subtopic sentences.

Teaching Idea
Activity 7.1 can also help students with connecting subtopic sentences and indicating order of importance.

the transitional words in the lists provided and/or any other connector that works. (For more on connectors, see pp. 53–58.) Circle all connectors.

FOR ADDING MATERIAL			
again	as well as	furthermore	likewise
also	besides	in addition	moreover
and	best	last	one
	first		worst
	further		next

FOR GIVING EXAMPLES AND EMPHASIS			
above all	especially	in particular	one reason
after all	for example	in truth	surely
another	specifically	it is true	that is
as an example	for instance	most important	to illustrate
certainly	indeed	of course	
	in fact	one example	

EXAMPLE

Topic sentence: A good coach has to know how to relate to his or her players.

Subtopic sentence 1: A coach should be patient.

Rewrite with connectors: (One important quality) in a coach is patience.

Subtopic sentence 2: A coach should be a good listener.

Rewrite with connectors: (Another ability) a coach needs is to be a good listener.

Subtopic sentence 3: A coach should be sympathetic.

Rewrite with connectors: While being a (good listener) is important in coaching, being sympathetic is the (most important trait) of all.

1. Topic sentence: James Hanson is one of the most boring people alive.

   Subtopic sentence 1: He speaks in a monotone

   Rewrite with connectors: One boring habit of his is speaking in a monotone.

   Subtopic sentence 2: All he ever talks about is football.

   Rewrite with connectors: Besides a monotonous tone, James is always stuck on one topic—football.

   Subtopic sentence 3: Once he has someone cornered, he won't let the person go.

   Rewrite with connectors: His worst habit, though, is cornering people.

2. Topic sentence: Fishing is a relaxing sport for many people.

Subtopic sentence 1: Tossing a line in the water and reeling it back in is simple.

Rewrite with connectors: For example, tossing a line in the water and reeling it back is simple.

Subtopic sentence 2: The natural surroundings are pleasant.

Rewrite with connectors: Besides the ease of fishing, the natural surroundings are pleasant.

Subtopic sentence 3: A person can get away from routine distractions.

Rewrite with connectors: But the most pleasant part of fishing is that a person can get away from routine distractions.

3. Topic sentence: Urban living has a number of disadvantages.

Subtopic sentence 1: Pollution can be a problem.

Rewrite with connectors: First, pollution can be a problem.

Subtopic sentence 2: Traffic is often frustrating.

Rewrite with connectors: Also, traffic is often frustrating.

Subtopic sentence 3: The crime rate is often high.

Rewrite with connectors: However, the biggest disadvantage is the high crime rate.

Developing Examples

As we discussed in Chapter 3, writers develop their points through detailed examples and explanations. Compare the following two excerpts from paragraphs about the problems of owning an older car. Which excerpt seems most interesting and most clearly makes its point? (The subtopic sentences are underlined.)

A. But none of these troubles is more important than unexpected breakdowns, and used cars are more likely than new ones to leave a driver stranded. When the car breaks down, the driver is left without transportation. He or she is going nowhere. This situation is frustrating and can be dangerous, depending on where the breakdown happens.

B. But none of these troubles is more important than unexpected breakdowns, and used cars are more likely than new ones to leave a driver stranded. Imagine driving alone down a deserted country road in the middle of nowhere at midnight when a loud bang from the engine compartment and a horrible grinding noise tells you to pull over fast. You are stuck, going nowhere. It's creepy and cold, and the trees and shrubs crowd up close to the nonexistent shoulder of the road. You can't pull safely off, even if the car would start. Luckily, you have a cell phone, and help will arrive—within the next hour! Being at the mercy of a used car this way is frustrating and sometimes dangerous, and drivers left stuck at a stoplight in the middle of a busy intersection or stalled out on a road trip must wonder just how good that "good" deal was when they decided to buy used instead of new.

HINT: Specific words, sensory details, and action descriptions help to develop paragraphs.

If you decided that version B is more interesting, there are several reasons you might prefer it. Version A says little after the initial subtopic sentence that introduces the main example. The second and third sentences merely repeat the idea of the first sentence, and the final sentence only makes general statements about "frustration" and "danger." In contrast, version B develops the statement about unexpected breakdowns with a "what-if" example that includes action, specific words, sensory details, and explanation. The examples and details help clarify how unpleasant being stranded could be. The final sentence reinforces the main point of the excerpt, providing several more specific examples. (For more on developing body paragraphs, see pp. 41–48.)

ACTIVITY 7.4 Developing Examples

Teaching Idea
If you have students work in groups on Activity 7.4, you might encourage them to include more examples/details than they would actually use. Each group member can write his or her own examples, and then they can compare, select, and combine into one subtopic.

The two paragraph subtopics that follow are general and repetitive. Rewrite the sentences in each of the subtopics, using more specific examples and details. As you revise them, ask yourself, "What does the writer mean by these statements?" and "What kinds of examples, details, and explanations can I add to make the statements more clear?"

EXAMPLE

Topic: What constitutes a healthy diet?

Subtopic sentence: Low-fat foods are an important part of a healthy diet.

Poorly developed subtopic:

Unlike other food, vegetables are low in fat. They will not put weight on a person because they do not contain much fat. Vegetables are low in calories and so do not cause a person to gain weight; therefore, they can keep a person healthy.

Revised subtopic with specific, detailed material:

Most vegetables, such as broccoli, asparagus, and cauliflower, have no fat but plenty of fiber and essential nutrients. In fact, snacking vegetables like carrots and celery have so few calories that a person burns most of the calories they contain just by chewing. On the other hand, dairy products like whole milk, cheese, and ice cream are loaded with fat and low-density cholesterol, which can clog arteries and cause heart attacks.

1. Topic: What makes a person interesting?

   Subtopic sentence: One way to be interesting is to be a good listener.

   Poorly developed subtopic:

   A good listener is someone who knows how to listen well. He or she pays attention and tries to hear what a person is saying. Paying close attention, a good listener follows a conversation and does not drift away from what is being said.

   Revised subtopic example with specific, detailed material:
   Good listeners do not just stay in the same room with you while you are talking. They will often sit close to you, frequently make eye contact, nod their heads, and respond in other ways. Good listeners ask questions occasionally to clarify what the speaker is saying, but they do do not try to control the conversation.

2. Topic: What fears did I have as a child?

   Subtopic sentence: The most terrifying moments for me came at night.

   Poorly developed subtopic:

   I especially hated being alone in my dark room. Because the room was so dark, I could too easily imagine things that were not there. Seeing imaginary creatures always frightened me and made me want to be anywhere but in my bedroom.

   Revised subtopic example with specific, detailed material:
   I especially hated being alone in my dark room. As soon as my mom and dad kissed me good night and closed the door, I would begin seeing monsters. A chair with my jacket on it became a bear; my model airplanes hanging from the ceiling became spiders slinking down their threads; the closet door creaked, and I knew a demon was ready to leap out on me.

Illustration Paragraphs: Analyzing Student Models

The following model paragraphs will help you write effective illustration papers. "Teaching with Whips" and "Dying to Have Fun" were developed using the "I" voice of personal experience. "Dangers in a Deli" and "Nothing Worthwhile Comes Easy" use the "they" voice, which shifts the readers' focus away from the author.

Teaching Idea
Ask students, before or after they read this paragraph, how they feel about corporal punishment in schools. Is it ever justified? Is there a better way to maintain discipline in school, and if so how? The examples students give of their own school experiences will reinforce the idea of specific development.

► Prereading Exploration for "Teaching with Whips"

Jeong Yi wanted to share some of his personal experiences with classmates so that they could compare their own education with his and learn about some of the cultural differences between them. Jeong also noted that teachers might be interested in the paper because he discusses using force to make students learn.

1. Having read the chapter introduction and worked through several activities, how many main examples might you expect this paragraph to contain?

   Three or four

2. What kind of sentence would you expect each major example to begin with?

   A subtopic sentence

Teaching with Whips

When I went to middle school in Korea, I was afraid of several merciless teachers who seemed to want me to enjoy studying by forcing it on me. My moral education teacher was one of these cruel educators. He was short and fat like the whip he carried to enforce his every whim. "I see you haven't done your homework, Jeong," he would say. He ordered me to hold my palms up, and then he began to whip my hands harshly. Somehow the pain ended with me crying and begging, "I will do it next time, teacher. I promise!" Another spiteful man was my history teacher, who liked to use his green baby bamboo stick to punish me when I didn't score more than 80 percent on the exams. When I would see him headed my way with that certain glint in his eye, slapping the stick into his own hand, I knew what was about to happen. "Why," I wanted to shout at him, "why don't you let us feel some interest in history. Maybe then we would be more responsible!" But these words never left my lips, although his did. "If you don't study, you won't succeed," he barked as he dealt quick whips. I muttered curses with his final blow. The most memorable of all these tyrants was the despised art teacher nicknamed Poisonous Snake. None of the students got along well with him. He seemed to dislike all of us equally. The black tape wrapped around the long, powerful stick that he used so frequently increased all our fear. I could only anticipate the pain I would feel the day I scored poorly on an exam I'd just taken. Burning with anxiety, I thought the only way to prevent these pains would be to study more diligently. If the goal of

Poisonous Snake and the rest of my teachers was just to make me study harder, they succeeded. But if they were concerned at all whether or not I learned to like education, then they all failed miserably.

—Jeong Yi

POSTREADING ANALYSIS: KEY POINTS FOR BUILDING ILLUSTRATION

- **Topic sentence:** names the topic and makes a limiting statement.
- **Concluding sentence:** restates the topic and adds a final (expanded) thought.
- **Subtopic sentences:** name each main example and make a limiting statement—for example, "My moral education teacher was one of these cruel educators."
- **Sentence connectors:** transitions (*when, then, around*), repeat words (*teacher*), synonyms (*educators, tyrants*), pronouns (*another, most, my*), and reference to main idea of merciless teachers (*pain, forcing, harshly, punish*).
- **Development:** action, dialogue, scene and character details, sensory details, active verbs (*barked*), -*ing* words (*crying*), specific words (*Korea*), and telling thoughts and emotions; also, explanations of the examples ("When I would see him headed my way with that certain glint in his eye . . .").

➡ Prereading Exploration for "Dying to Have Fun"

Teaching Idea
To reinforce the importance of using specific details, you might ask students why Jeong Yi described the teachers' sticks.

Teaching Idea
You might take a few minutes of class time to discuss the questions in the prereading exploration of "Dying to Have Fun" to see if ideas for student topics emerge.

Tom Kellogg wrote this paper for himself to think through a tragedy and for people who like the outdoors and can identify with the float trip examples. Answers will vary.

1. Are there any pastimes you enjoy that others consider dangerous, exhausting, uncomfortable, or just plain tedious? _____

   _____

2. List one activity that you like, make a limiting statement about it (is it fun or dangerous or exhausting or challenging?), and then write three or four examples to illustrate your statement.

   _____

   _____

   _____

   _____

Dying to Have Fun

Paddling down Kansas and Missouri rivers is one of my favorite pastimes, but I have had some awful experiences on them. One aggravation I have learned to deal with is bad weather. Our first night on the river, everybody is excited and raising hell—till the rain comes. For some reason

of the possible injury that deli work entails, but luckily safety training is a requirement.

—Catherine Denning

POSTREADING ANALYSIS: KEY POINTS FOR BUILDING ILLUSTRATION

- **Topic sentence:** names the topic and makes a limiting statement.
- **Concluding sentence:** restates the topic and adds a final (expanded) thought.
- **Subtopic sentences:** name each <u>main example</u> and make a <u>limiting</u> statement—for example, "One <u>concern</u> for potential deli workers is <u>slippery floors</u>."
- **Sentence connectors:** transitions (*during, in addition to, but*), repeat words (*deli*), synonyms (*workers, employees*), pronouns (*which, you*), and reference to main idea (dangers: *wipeout, emergency room, risk*).
- **Development:** action, scene details, active verbs (*packed*), *-ing* words (*operating*), and specific words (*ammonia*); also, explanations of the examples ("If the counter is packed with anxious customers . . . ").
- **Audience:** potential deli employees (so Catherine uses "you").

Questions for Paragraph Analysis

Note: These questions apply to all three student models.

1. In the topic sentence, what words name the topic, and what words make a limiting statement about it?

2. What words in the concluding sentence link to the topic sentence?

3. What is the expanded thought in the final sentence? (For more on the expanded thought, see pp. 49–51.)

4. Copy each of the subtopic sentences, and underline the <u>main example</u> once and the <u>statement</u> about it twice. Circle connectors: transitions, repeat words, <u>synonyms</u>, and pronouns. (For more on connectors, see pp. 53–58.)

5. What words show that the main examples are arranged by order of importance? (See Activity 7.3.)

6. Choose an example and tell how the author's explaining (as opposed to detailing or action description) helps you better understand the author's point. (For more on detailing and explaining examples, see pp. 42–43.)

7. Choose an example and tell how the action description and detailing help you to better understand the author's point (see pp. 150–154).

8. Name three specific words, and list a more general word for each (see pp. 78–79).

9. Name three ways to further develop any example in this paragraph. Consider action, active verbs, dialogue, specific words, sensory details, description of person or setting, revealing thoughts or emotions, and further explanation.

WRITING AN ILLUSTRATION PARAGRAPH
Summarizing the Assignment

Write a single paragraph of 250 to 300 words that illustrates a point with several examples. Whereas in Chapters 5 and 6 you focused on a single place or story unified in time, now you will use *several* examples (three or four) to illustrate your point, and you will introduce each of these examples with a subtopic sentence.

You may rely on personal examples and the "I" voice to develop your topic, or you may distance yourself from the material by using the "they" voice of more general knowledge and observation.

Establishing Audience and Purpose

Teaching Idea
You might add to your discussion of audience that a writer's job is not always to talk only about what he or she wants to say any more than a speaker should always control a conversation. It is common courtesy to anticipate what the people around us might be interested in hearing and then to talk about it.

After choosing a topic, decide whom you want to write for (realizing that your composition instructor is always a member of your audience). If, for instance, you choose a topic like great spring break vacations and want to write for friends, you should use examples that will interest them. If many of them are party hounds, then you might show and tell about young people at parties on the beach, in the mountains, or in some other desirable place. But if your readers might be more interested in art galleries, museums, and historical sites, then you could develop examples of these. Writing for a specific audience will help focus your work. (For more on audience profiling, see pp. 9–10.)

You may have several purposes in mind—to entertain, persuade, or inform—but communicating ideas clearly should take top priority.

Working through the Writing Assignment

Discovering Ideas

Writing Tutor: Illustration

Before brainstorming for topics, consider two approaches to the assignment: illustrating with personal experience or with more general knowledge.

- **Personal experience:** This method lets you draw on your own experiences and use the "I" voice, illustrating your examples with brief narrative/descriptive examples, as in the student models "Teaching with Whips" and "Dying to Have Fun."

- **General knowledge:** This approach is a bit more formal, avoiding "I" and favoring the third-person "they" (see "Dangers in a Deli" and the annotated student model). You might write in this voice if you are dealing with a topic from personal experience but one that you would like to distance yourself from (divorce, addiction, death of a loved one). Or you might want to discuss a subject that you have no personal experience with but have knowledge of through talking to people, reading, watching TV, and observing. For example, you may never have played football but still have opinions on what makes a great football game or football player. Your insights can make interesting examples.

The following lists are divided to suggest topics that may be more given to an "I" or "they" approach. Many of the topics, however, can be written about using either voice.

Teaching Idea
When you assign the topics lists, you might also include the alternate writing assignments.

Teaching Idea
Students sometimes submit imperfectly written process analysis paragraphs unless they are steered away from how-to topics.

Teaching Idea
After students have listed examples, you might write several of their lists on the board and ask the class to help arrange the items from least to most important. This stimulates discussion about relative importance and the writer's responsibility to choose.

Topics List

TOPICS TO DEVELOP THROUGH PERSONAL INVOLVEMENT/EXPERIENCE
(Will use "I" and personal anecdotes to create a relatively informal tone.)

- Positive (or negative) experiences with teachers or with any office or support service on campus (counseling, admissions, writing or math centers, financial aid, etc.)
- Things your high school did well (or poorly) to prepare you for college
- Possible benefits of composition or math skills (or any other school subject) in helping you achieve career goals
- Rules at home, work, or school that you hate (or hated) to obey
- Competition with a brother or sister
- A hobby, sport, talent, game, or activity that you enjoy
- Instances when you were independent or courageous or industrious or useful; instances of being dependent or fearful or lazy or useless; or instances that illustrate any other personality trait
- A time when you did things just right (or all wrong)
- A memorable trip or trips you have taken with family or peers
- A musical or sporting event that was particularly memorable
- Childhood or adult fears or delights or fantasies
- Embarrassing moments while growing up

TOPICS TO DEVELOP THROUGH OBSERVATION AND ACCUMULATED KNOWLEDGE
(Will usually call for the use of "they," generalized examples, and a more formal tone.)

- Problems community college students have balancing school and other demands
- Qualities or practices of a good (or bad) teacher or student
- Kinds of problems for parents caused by babies (or toddlers, elementary school children, preteens, or teens)
- Qualities of a good (or bad) parent
- Good (or bad) TV programs or movies for children
- Characteristics of a good role model for children (a parent, teacher, athlete, musical artist, or cartoon or story character)
- Benefits or ill effects of any sport or form of exercise (baseball, basketball, football, soccer, rugby, jogging, swimming, walking, rock climbing, skiing, surfing, etc.)
- Characteristics of a great football player or game (or baseball, basketball, soccer, etc)
- Foods found in a healthy (or an unhealthy) diet
- Signs of alcohol or other drug abuse
- Advertising on TV (could be: creative or funny or boring or frightening or . . .)
- TV programming (too much sex or violence or profanity or stereotyping or . . .)
- Ways the Internet can affect a person's life (positively or negatively)

Teaching Idea
It is a good idea to remind students occasionally that paragraphs and essays have no preordained length.

After choosing several possible topics, prewrite (clustering, freewriting, and listing are good choices) to find five or six examples to illustrate each one. Having more examples than you will use lets you choose the strongest when you cut back to three or four. The following topic—problems of community college students—demonstrates how to list and develop examples for an illustration paragraph. (By the way, there is no "right" number of examples in a paragraph or essay. The writer uses as many as she or he feels is necessary to fully illustrate the point.)

Prewriting

Teaching Idea
Students can review "Sufficient Support" in Chapter 3 for more information on layering examples.

The first step is to come up with **first-level examples** or main examples—kinds of general or typical problems. You should develop six but keep only three or four.

PROBLEMS COMMON TO COMMUNITY COLLEGE STUDENTS

1. Money
2. Work
3. Family   } **First-level examples**
4. Study time
5. Commuting
6. Social life

Teaching Idea
If students seem troubled by the terminology of first- and second-level examples, try using "examples with detailed support." The point of the "layering" discussion is to help students see that they can achieve a more fully developed explanation if they don't give up on an idea or example too quickly.

This list of six main or first-level examples includes some important problems of community college students, only three or four of which will be used in the paper. The next step is to develop each main example by answering the question "What exactly do I mean by that?" For the first problem from the list above, you might use **second-level examples** like the following:

MONEY PROBLEMS COMMON TO COMMUNITY COLLEGE STUDENTS

1. Transportation to and from college
2. Tuition and books
3. Rent, utilities, food, and clothing   } **Second-level examples**
4. Insurance
5. Medical
6. Recreation

In this second-level list, you answer the question "What do I mean by money problems of community college students?" But can we be even more specific? What if someone wants to know more about transportation expenses? You could create a list of **third-level examples** like the following:

TRANSPORTATION MONEY PROBLEMS COMMON TO COMMUNITY COLLEGE STUDENTS

1. Gasoline
2. General car maintenance   } **Third-level examples**
3. Auto insurance

Teaching Idea
Having students review the Language Line from Chapter 5 can help clarify the need for increasing specificity in developing examples.

With each level you clarify and so develop your examples by *limiting* them. This is the same principle we used in the first assignment in Chapter 5, Picturing a Place, when we practiced specific language on the Language Line, moving from relatively general to relatively specific words (see pp. 78–79).

You can also see this concept using the graphic introduced in Chapter 3:

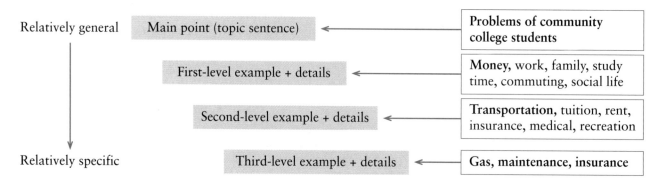

Relatively general — Main point (topic sentence) ← Problems of community college students

First-level example + details ← Money, work, family, study time, commuting, social life

Second-level example + details ← Transportation, tuition, rent, insurance, medical, recreation

Relatively specific — Third-level example + details ← Gas, maintenance, insurance

To build one subtopic in an illustration paragraph, we could use the examples developed in our prewriting lists like this:

KEY

Topic sentence

First-level example

Second-level example

Third-level example

> **Community college students have many problems standing in the way of their education.** Money always seems to be a concern. Of course, we all have to worry about *paying the rent and utilities, keeping clothes on our bodies and food in them as well.* And many of us are also footing our own *medical and health insurance bills.* But as students we also have to deal with the *cost of tuition and books,* not to mention *getting to and from the college.* Most of us can't just walk to campus, so we have the *additional expenses* of gas, general car maintenance, and car insurance.

HINT: It's best to create material and then prune.

Now readers have a fairly good idea of what we meant when we said that community college students have money problems.

PREWRITING—SUMMING UP

1. Choose several topics from the topics list, or create several of your own.
2. Make a limiting statement about each topic.
3. Prewrite to generate at least six main examples for each topic.
4. Prewrite to generate second-level examples for each main example.
5. List any third-level examples or details that come to mind.
6. Select the topic that most interests you.

Teaching Idea
Journal Entry 7.2 is a good
checkpoint to see if students
understand the principle of
developing examples.

JOURNAL ENTRY 7.2

Select a topic for your paragraph, and follow the prewriting model on page 158, which develops problems common to community college students. Write out six examples that illustrate your topic, and then develop them with second- and third-level examples.

Organizing Ideas

Teaching Idea
You might want to remind
students of the benefit of
subtopic sentences.

A topic sentence will guide you as you write the rest of the paper. If you have not yet decided on the "I" (more informal) or "they" (more formal) approach, now is a good time to do so. Here are two pairs of examples of topic sentences, one sentence in each pair using the "I" voice and the other using the "they" voice. Topics are underlined once; statements are underlined twice.

A. Topic = laziness: Although I have become more industrious as an adult, when I was a child I specialized in doing nothing.

B. Topic = laziness: In a busy country like ours, full of people working overtime, there are still plenty of people doing nothing.

A. Topic = smoking: The day I climbed a short flight of stairs to my apartment and stood there leaning on the door so winded that I almost passed out, I knew smoking was hurting me.

B. Topic = smoking: The ill effects of smoking have been well documented.

Remember that you will keep only three or four examples, arranged from least to most important and linked by connectors, including transitional words like those below. (For more on connectors, see pp. 53–58.)

FOR ADDING MATERIAL			
again	as well as	furthermore	likewise
also	besides	in addition	moreover
and	further	last	next

FOR GIVING EXAMPLES AND EMPHASIS			
above all	especially	in particular	one reason
after all	for example	in truth	specifically
another	for instance	it is true	surely
as an example	indeed	most important	that is
certainly	in fact	of course	to illustrate

ORGANIZING IDEAS—SUMMING UP

1. Write out a rough topic sentence to focus your material.
2. Decide on a formal ("they") or informal ("I") approach.
3. Choose three or four examples to illustrate your topic.
4. Arrange your examples from least to most important.
5. Review the list of transitions and other connectors (see pp. 54–55).

HINT: Ideas for expanded thoughts in the conclusion will often occur to you while you are drafting.

thought in the conclusion. For example, it might have been distracting to talk about "good times" in the body of the deli paragraph, but "good times" might work well as a final comment. (For more on concluding sentences, see pp. 48–52.)

JOURNAL ENTRY 7.5

To help you focus on revision and alert your instructor to your progress, list three specific changes you have made or feel you ought to make in going from your first to second draft. Refer to the first-stage draft questions, answering specifically. (Example: Question 2: "I realized I was only developing one example, so I added two more.") Next, in several sentences, say what you like best about your draft.

Second and Final Drafts

For advice on revising and then editing further drafts of your work, turn to Chapter 4, pages 65–72.

ANNOTATED STUDENT MODEL: "NOTHING WORTHWHILE COMES EASY"

Teaching Idea
To prevent students from writing an underdeveloped essay with weak introductory and concluding paragraphs, point out that the divisions in the annotated student model are there to demonstrate the different parts of the paragraph.

HINT: First drafts often give a new direction to your ideas.

Carefully reading the annotated student model will help clarify questions you have about your own draft.

First-Stage Draft

Bill Ross decided to explain how difficult college can be to those who have never been and those who have attended but forgotten the challenges they faced. He used listing to discover eight major examples, which he then trimmed to four. As you will see, he was not sure what tone to adopt initially, so the first draft skips back and forth between the "I" approach and the more formal "they" approach.

Note: This rough draft of a paragraph is separated into topic and concluding sentences and four subtopics to illustrate the connections among its parts. Because it is a rough draft, it includes errors in grammar, spelling, and punctuation.

Topic sentence

Refocus of paper will create *material cuts and additions*.

First subtopic

Second subtopic

Some college students have a difficult time with school and the rest of there lives.

We all want to relax sometimes, but it's hard to have a social life and still get the studying done. And if you are a partier, look out! Its hard to make grades and have fun.

Bills are another problem. Some students have it easy, scholarships or a free ride from there parents, but most community college students, anyway, are working their way through. If you have children, it's even worse. Just think of all bills having a house and family can rack up like mortgage payments, utilities, food, clothing, doctor bills, etc. Stressing out over money makes studying difficult.

Third subtopic

Need overall developing of main examples with specific support, details, and explanations

Fourth subtopic

Avoid tone shift from "they" to "I."

Teaching Idea
The first-stage draft shows a clear example of pronoun shifting from "I" to "you."

Concluding sentence

Having to work to pay the bills is another problem. Of course, almost all adults have to support themselves but most people aren't running in three different directions at once. With college students trying to study, have some kind of social life and then work forty hours a week, it can be to much.

And then there's the family hassle that students like me have to worry about. I'm a returning student who hasn't been in college for 15 years. Along the way I accummulated a wife and three children, so its especially hard for me. But I am not alone. Just look around in your classes and you will see lots of older students struggling to make it all work out. As much as I love my family, they take the biggest chunk of my time, after work. And you probably know how much a family can just wear you out. By the time my wife and I get the kids to bed, it's hard to hit the books.

College is not easy for most people, but I think it has to be harder for the older returning student with a family.

After completing the first draft, Bill made two important decisions. First, he thought that the "I" voice made him sound like he was merely complaining, so he decided to try for a more objective reporter's voice. Second, he discovered that he wanted to shift the focus of his topic from the experience of college students in general to that of nontraditional students like himself who attend community colleges.

Second-Stage Draft

Teaching Idea
This model clearly illustrates subtopic sentences along with connecting words. Here, again, students can see layered development.

First-stage drafts of illustration papers often have difficulties with focus and development. Note how much explanation and how many more examples were added to the following draft to help clarify meaning. As you work on your own draft, keep asking, "What do I mean by that last statement, example, or idea?" Also use topic, subtopic, and concluding sentences. Help your readers find their way through your paper with the least effort. They will appreciate your efforts.

SPECIAL POINTS TO CHECK IN REVISING FROM FIRST TO SECOND DRAFTS
1. Check the topic sentence: topic + statement.
2. Check subtopic sentences (first-level examples): connector + main example topic + statement.
3. Delete unnecessary material.
4. Add *second-level examples* for clarity, completeness, and emphasis.
5. *Add explanations.
6. Check connectors: transitions, repeat words, synonyms, pronouns, and references to main idea.
7. Check the concluding sentence: connector + link to topic sentence + expanded thought.

Topic sentence revised

Adult students with spouses and children have a difficult time balancing school with the rest of there lives.

Subtopic sentence revised

Second-level examples added

*Explanation added

They don't have much time for a social life, but everyone needs some relaxation. Even struggling with classes, *most students want to see an occasional movie with a friend, catch a ball game, or have diner out.* *When students take time for rest & relaxation, they are looking over their shoulder at the clock.

Subtopic sentence revised

Second-level examples added

*Explanation added

But socializing is often the least of the distractions for returning students. They constantly face the money battle. With families to care for the students have to worry about *rent and mortgage payments, utilities, car payments, car repair bills, general property maintenance, food, clothing, medical, insurance of various kinds, school (their own included), and even squeezing in a few presents* for their loved ones occasionally. *The stress of dealing with the money drain sometimes makes focusing on textbooks difficult.

Subtopic sentence revised

Second-level examples added

*Explanation added

In order to meet the financial demands, of course, most nontraditional students are full-time workers as well. Often both husbands and wives financially support the family. Though sometimes only one brings in a paycheck while the other works at home. *Spending 40 hours a week, and more outside the home selling insurance, repairing cars, waiting tables; or spending the same amount of time inside the home cleaning house, fixing meals, and chasing children around—*nontraditional students often have a kind of frazzled look around the edges.

Subtopic sentence revised—to show *most important* problem

*Explanation added

But the other stresses and distractions aside, for nontraditional students coming back to school, the family might be the biggest obstacle. Most mothers and fathers love there children and each other. But *the daily drag of diapering, feeding, carting to school, and soothing fears and hurt feelings* can drag a person down and wear him or her out. *Even the most dedicated student has a hard time studying after a full day. And those who do jam the late-night studying in are often beat in class the next day.

Concluding sentence revised

Note the expanded thought.

While other students also have difficulties, dealing with their education, and Community College students in particular, the returning adult student with family responsibilities might just have the toughest job of all.

Third-Stage Draft

Teaching Idea
The third-stage draft shows sentence combining for variety and elimination of unneeded repetition.

You might think the paper is complete by the time you have written a thorough second draft. After all, you have reorganized, deleted material, and added new examples, details, and explanations—shouldn't the paper be done? However, if you want your work to move beyond good to excellent, you usually need to write a third draft. With most of the major concerns taken care of, you can now improve your word choices and sentence variety and get rid of the clutter words that so often slip into rough drafts.

> **SPECIAL POINTS TO CHECK IN REVISING FROM SECOND TO THIRD DRAFTS**
> 1. Add specific words.
> 2. Substitute more precise or audience-appropriate words.
> 3. Combine or restructure sentences for variety.
> 4. **Replace clutter and repeat words with synonyms and phrases.**
> 5. Delete unneeded words.

Nothing Worthwhile Comes Easy

Nontraditional students with spouses and children have a difficult time balancing school with the rest of there lives.

More accurate words substituted

[Although many of them don't have much time for a social life everyone needs some relaxation.] Even struggling with a 12-hour course load, most students want to see an occasional movie with a friend, catch a ball game, or have diner out. Most of the time when they take time for rest & relaxation, ~~students~~ **they** are looking over their shoulder at the clock—classes start at 8:00 A.M.!

Sentences combined, specific words added, repetition reduced through pronoun

[But socializing is often the least of the distractions for returning students, as they constantly face the money battle.] ~~Students~~ **Their** families add to the financial worries with **parents** footing the bills for rent or mortgage, utilities, insurance, general property maintenance, food, clothing, medical, car, school (their own included), and even the occasional present for a loved one. The stress of dealing with the money drain sometimes makes focusing on textbooks difficult.

Sentences combined, repetition reduced through synonym and pronoun

In order to meet the financial demands, of course, most nontraditional students are full-time workers as well. Often both ~~husbands and wives~~ **spouses** financially support the family. Though sometimes only one brings in a paycheck while the other works at home. Spending 40 hours a week, and more outside the home selling insurance, repairing cars, waiting tables; or spending the same amount of time inside the home cleaning

Synonym replaces phrase

house, fixing meals, and chasing children around—nontraditional students often have a ~~kind of~~ frazzled look around the edges.

Clutter phrase deleted

But the other stresses and distractions aside, for ~~non-traditional students~~ **mom's and dad's** coming back to school, the family might be the biggest obstacle. [As much as most mothers and fathers love there children and each other, the daily routine of diapering, feeding, clothing, carting to school, soothing fears and hurt feelings, explaining, teaching, and just generally loving family members can ~~drag a person down and~~ wear a person ~~him or her~~ out.] Even the most dedicated student has a hard time studying at 2:00 A.M. after a full work and family day. And those who do jam the late-night studying in are easy to spot as they work to keep their heads propped up in class the next day.

More appropriate word substituted

Sentences combined, specific words added, redundant expression added

While other college students also have difficulties, dealing with their education, and Community College students in particular, the returning adult student with family responsibilities might just have the toughest job of all.

More accurate word added

Final-Editing Draft

In this last draft, Bill slows his reading to a crawl, editing closely, word by word, line by line, looking especially for the pattern errors he listed on his Improvement Chart. It is a tedious process, but he knows that he still has many errors to correct.

Teaching Idea
It is worth the time to take students back to Chapter 4 as they revise and edit their first several assignments. Chapter 4 includes more detail about the points included in the Final-Draft Checklist, so if students need more in-depth reminders than the list provides, they will not have to search through the text.

SPECIAL POINTS TO CHECK IN EDITING FINAL DRAFTS

1. Misspellings
2. Sound-alike words
3. Missing words
4. Wrong words
5. Sentence fragments
6. Comma splices/run-ons
7. Faulty capitalization
8. Incorrect apostrophes
9. Comma(s) needed
   a. Introductory words/phrases/clauses
   b. Nonessential word groups
   c. Main clauses with coordinating conjunction
10. Unneeded commas

Topic, subtopic, and concluding sentences merged to show a single, complete paragraph

Teaching Idea
You might want to focus on a single error in the final draft, such as the unneeded comma, to help students review.

Nothing Worthwhile Comes Easy

Nontraditional students with spouses and children have a difficult time balancing school with the rest of ~~there~~[2] their lives. Although many of them don't have much time for a social life,[9a] everyone needs some relaxation. Even struggling with a 12-hour course load, most students want to see an occasional movie with a friend, catch a ball game, or have ~~diner~~[1]

dinner out. Most of the time when they take time for rest & relaxation, they are looking over their shoulder at the clock—classes start at 8:00 A.M.! But socializing is often the least of the distractions for returning students,[10] as they constantly face the money battle. Their families add to the financial worries,[9b] with parents footing the bills for rent or mortgage, utilities, insurance, general property maintenance, food, clothing, medical, car, school (their own included), and even the occasional present for a loved one. The stress of dealing with the money drain sometimes makes focusing on textbooks difficult. In order to meet the financial demands, of course, most nontraditional students are full-time workers as well. Often both spouses financially support the family.[5], though sometimes only one brings in a paycheck while the other works at home. Spending 40 hours a week,[10] and more outside the home selling insurance, repairing cars, waiting tables; or spending the same amount of time inside the home cleaning house, fixing meals, and chasing children around—nontraditional students often have a kind of frazzled look around the edges. But the other stresses and distractions aside, for ~~mom's and dad's~~[8] moms and dads coming back to school, the family might be the biggest obstacle. As much as most mothers and fathers love ~~there~~[2] their children and each other, the daily routine of diapering, feeding, clothing, carting to school, soothing fears and hurt feelings, explaining, teaching, and just generally loving family members can wear a person out. Even the most dedicated student has a hard time studying at 2:00 A.M. after a full work and family day. And those who do jam the late-night studying in are easy to spot as they work to keep their heads propped up in class the next day. While other college students also have difficulties,[10] dealing with their education, and ~~c~~[7] community ~~c~~[7] college students in particular, the returning adult student with family responsibilities might just have the toughest job of all.

—*William Ross*

FINAL-DRAFT CHECKLIST

Before you turn in your final draft for a grade, review this checklist. You may find that, as careful as you think you have been, you still missed a point or two—or more. (For more on any of these points, see Chapter 4.)

☐ 1. Is your topic sentence effective?

☐ 2. Have you used three or four examples, or have you used only one?

☐ 3. Have you clearly arranged your main examples—either by time or by importance?

☐ 4. Does a subtopic sentence introduce each main example?

☐ 5. Are your main examples well developed and thoroughly explained?

☐ 6. Are all sentences well connected?

☐ 7. Is your concluding sentence effective?

☐ 8. Have you used specific language?

☐ 9. Have you chosen active verbs and -ing words to describe action?

☐ 10. Have you used a metaphor or simile (see Chapter 6)?

☐ 11. Are your sentences varied in length and beginnings?

☐ 12. Have you used words so often that they are noticeable?

☐ 13. Have you included unneeded words?

☐ 14. Have you written an interesting title? Have you checked its capitalization?

☐ 15. Have you prepared your paper using the format expected by your instructor? (Check to see if you need a title page, use double spacing, leave at least a 1-inch margin, and use a 12-point font.)

☐ 16. Have you edited your work as closely as you know how to (including having at least one other person proofread)? Have you checked your Improvement Chart for pattern errors?

☐ 17. Have you looked for these errors: misspellings, soundalike words, missing words, wrong words, sentence fragments, comma splices/run-ons, faulty capitalizations, incorrect apostrophes, missing commas, and unnecessary commas?

Chapter Summary

1. Writers use expository writing to communicate ideas, information, and opinions. After making a relatively general statement (topic sentence), they use examples, explanations, and details to develop and clarify that statement.

2. Examples may be based on personal experience or developed through close observation, accumulated knowledge, "what-if" situations, generalized or typical instances, and research.

3. Examples often include narrative/descriptive details, especially examples based on personal experience.

4. Tone is the attitude or feeling authors have toward their subjects and the relationship they want to establish with their audience. Writers vary their tone based on their material and audience.

5. Writers who adopt a more formal tone seldom use *I* and rely heavily for development on close observation, accumulated knowledge, "what-if" situations, generalized or typical instances, logical reasoning, and research.

6. Each major example in an illustration paragraph should be introduced with a subtopic sentence.

7. In expository and persuasive writing, writers often organize examples from least to most important or dramatic.

8. Transitional words and other connectors are needed to link subtopic and concluding sentences to the rest of the paragraph. The transitional phrases *for example* and *for instance* are important in illustration paragraphs.

9. To explain examples, writers limit the category to which the example belongs; they answer the question "What do I mean by that?"

10. Writing is never complete until it has been carefully revised and edited.

ALTERNATE WRITING ASSIGNMENTS

Here are a few more assignment options that may be of interest. For this assignment, be sure to do the following:

1. Use subtopic sentences to introduce each major example.

2. Arrange major examples by order of importance.

3. Link all sentences, especially subtopics, with transitional words and other connectors.

4. Develop examples with specific words, details, and explanations.

ASSIGNMENT OPTIONS

1. Although the chapter assignment asks for several examples, you will often write paragraphs within essays that rely on only one major example. Rethink any one of the major examples you chose for the chapter assignment, and then develop it further. Be sure to use plenty of second- and third-level examples. If you are drawing on personal experience, you might review Chapters 5 and 6 for reminders on the dominant impression and significance of the event. Remember to rework your topic sentence to reflect your narrowing of scope.

2. After writing the Chapter 7 assignment, rewrite it, shifting the tone. If you were especially warm and chatty, in the new version use a more distant reporter's voice. If you chose an objective tone, become more personable. Because your audience influences the tone, you may need to redefine your target reader. If, for instance, you wrote to young adults about great vacations and emphasized the partying potential, you may have used personal examples and informal diction. Changing the audience to parents who are interested in their teens' vacation plans would affect the tone and the content of the main examples.

3. Write a biographical sketch of a person, focusing on a single personality trait and using three to four anecdotes (brief stories) as examples. For instance, you might characterize your brother as selfish. What three to four instances of selfish behavior can you remember that would show this trait to a reader?

4. Select a work-related project that you will use on the job. If you work in retail sales, for example, you could characterize three or four types of customers that a new employee should be able to identify. Maybe you work at a business like Kinko's and can identify several potential problems for a person new to the job. Perhaps you are writing a job evaluation for yourself or another employee and need to supply several examples to justify a statement such as "Jasmine has great communication skills." Give your supervisor or prospective employer several specific examples demonstrating these skills.

5. Choose a topic that relates to your cultural heritage or to any group with which you closely identify. Perhaps you are of Irish descent and are interested in the mythology or music of Ireland. Coming from a western European background, you might like Renaissance festivals. Perhaps you love music and go to concerts every chance you get. What might attract you to a particular concert? Perhaps, like the woman in the accompanying photo, you like to crowd surf. What are three more reasons that you go to concerts?

CHAPTER 8

Creating and Explaining Groups

What Are We Trying to Achieve and Why?

Setting the Stage

Teaching Idea
You might ask students to give details about another supermarket aisle, breaking the aisle further down into subsections and the specific items found in them.

Imagine a store that did not divide its merchandise in some orderly way. As a shopper new to a supermarket, if you were looking for, say, strawberries, you would head to the fruit section and expect to find them there. If instead the fresh strawberries were shelved with the strawberry jelly, you would have a hard time finding them. Similarly, you would look for baked goods together: bread, English muffins, and hamburger buns. In a store that had no merchandise signs or that lumped items together randomly there would be chaos, and few people would shop there.

Teaching Idea
Having a student read one or two of these introductory paragraphs aloud is one way to focus the class's attention on the new material.

But in reality all major stores organize their merchandise systematically, using a method called **classification.** As we work through this chapter, we will practice classifying, learning to select a logical **single organizing principle (SOP)** to divide topics into groups, which we will then develop through examples, explanations, and details.

Linking to Previous Experience

What experience do you already have with classification? Well, as a shopper, you have a sense of how store managers classify. For example, in grocery stores you will often find items grouped by how they are used (such as cleaning products) or what they are most similar to (such as fruits grouped with vegetables). Similarly, at your hardware store, an aisle or part of an aisle may be devoted to, say, locks—padlocks, chain locks, bolts, hooks, and eyes. At home, most of us sort laundry from time to time—socks, underwear, pants, shirts, blouses; we classify and group these items by their use (the SOP). If you have ever moved your own belongings or an entire household, you confronted a major classification project.

173

Unless you grouped and labeled items by room, the logical SOP here, you probably had a mess on the other end.

In college, too, classifying with an SOP is common. Most teachers are grouped by discipline (the SOP): history, math, English, and so on. Textbooks are full-length examples of classification, with material divided by topic (the SOP) into units, chapters, and sections.

Determining the Value of Classification

Schoolwork also requires classifying. For example, in a history class, you might be asked to group the causes of the Civil War by the aspect of American life they related to (the SOP)—that is, to group them into economic, social, political, and other causes. In a biology class, you might be asked to classify a plant by how it reproduces (the SOP).

At home, on the job, and in school, classifying is valuable, helping us to simplify and make sense of the world. We depend on this ability and often use it unknowingly. For this reason, as valuable as the ability is, we also need to be wary of it. When we categorize things and people in haste, without much thought, we sometimes **stereotype.** Stereotyping oversimplifies complex issues and people, often creating rather than solving problems for us.

Teaching Idea
Because the chapter stresses grouping similar things—in effect, minimizing differences—it is worth spending a few minutes discussing what makes things and people unique, and sometimes impossible to classify. Your conversation can easily lead to the danger of unwarranted classification—stereotyping.

CAUTION! Misusing classification can create stereotypes.

> **JOURNAL ENTRY 8.1**
>
> List several examples of classifying you have done or seen. Indicate the SOP for each one. For example, perhaps you reorganized a clothes closet. Was use the basis for the reorganization (the SOP), so that you grouped shirts with shirts, pants with pants, and so on? Or was it frequency of use (the SOP), so that you put the clothes you use most often at the front of the closet?

Developing Skills and Exploring Ideas in Classification Paragraphs

To learn to write a successful classification paragraph, you need to practice the following:

Teaching Idea
The activities lead students through the prewriting they need to produce their first draft. You might remind the class to be alert to possible topics as they do this work.

1. Using a single organizing principle (SOP)
2. Avoiding overlapping categories
3. Including all of the important members of the group
4. Having a reason for the classification

Using a Single Organizing Principle

To group items logically, we need a standard for grouping them, or single organizing principle. For example, a restaurant menu groups items by courses—

appetizers, entrées, side dishes, and desserts—listed in the order in which they are usually served. Every item fits into one group or another, and within each group, we find only items that are similar to each other—desserts, for example, feature ice cream and pie but not pork chops.

After choosing a topic for this assignment, you will also need to think about a single organizing principle, one that will give you groups that are appropriate for your topic.

ACTIVITY 8.1 Using a Single Organizing Principle

The following topics are divided into categories, or groups, based on a single organizing principle. Put an "X" next to the category that doesn't belong, and then state the SOP.

EXAMPLE
Topic: holidays

Categories: ___ Spring ___ Summer ___ Fall ___ Winter _X_ Christmas
Organizing principle: _seasons of the year_

1. Topic: parties

    Categories: __ Home __ Friend's house __ Park _X_ Boring __ Hotel
    Organizing principle: _place where parties are held_

2. Topic: first dates

    Categories: __ Relaxed _X_ Cheap __ Tense __ Exciting __ Funny
    Organizing principle: _emotional responses to_

3. Topic: love

    Categories: __ Spouse __ Child __ Friend _X_ Erotic __ Parent
    Organizing principle: _kinds of people to love_

4. Topic: cooking

    Categories: __ French __ Greek _X_ Spicy __ Mexican __Vietnamese
    Organizing principle: _cooking of different countries_

5. Topic: movie scenes

    Categories: __ Explosions __ Gunfire __ Punching _X_ Humor __ Falls
    Organizing principle: _kind of violence_

Selecting an Organizing Principle

With many topics, the SOPs we use to classify items are obvious and predictable. For instance, in buying a car, most of us use price to group cars in terms of those we seriously look at and those we only dream about. Asked to classify insurance, most of us would list groups like life, medical, auto, and homeowners.

However, some topics are less predictably grouped. We often have the freedom to choose an SOP based on what interests us and might interest

3. Common gems: rubies, sapphires, emeralds, <u>diamonds</u>

4. Food groups: meat, fish, poultry; fruits, vegetables; grains; <u>dairy</u>

5. Continents: Africa, Asia, North America, South America, Europe, Australia, <u>Antarctica</u>

Classification Paragraphs: Analyzing Student Models

Teaching Idea
This paragraph is a good model for showing students how to take an interesting slant on a topic. Ask students to classify shoppers using another SOP, such as level of enthusiasm or efficiency, and see what groups they come up with.

The student models that follow will help you write effective classification paragraphs. Both "Mall Crashers" and "Shopping the Easy Way" are developed through generalized experience, whereas "I Do" includes several personal examples. Either method can work well.

➤ Prereading Exploration for "Mall Crashers"

During a class discussion about types of shoppers, Chanthan Srouch decided to write this paper on nonshoppers. He thought that the members of his writing group and others who frequent malls would enjoy it.

Before reading the paragraph, think about the kinds of people you have seen in a mall who are not shopping but are there for some other reason. List three categories of nonshoppers below. After reading, compare your list with the author's categories. What kind of paragraph might you have written on this same topic?

Answers will vary: window shoppers, parents bringing children for rides,

diners, people walking for exercise

Mall Crashers

Malls across America attract thousands of people every day who are not there to buy anything, but all of them have their own special reasons for being there. The first, and maybe most satisfied, of these nonshoppers is the classic window shopper. These people are the ones who only browse, looking at and trying out merchandise, but seldom buying anything. They may try on four pairs of shoes or half a dozen sweaters, but they mostly just leave the salesclerks with no money and plenty of mess. The next nonshoppers, generally teens and young adults, are the ones looking to meet a member of the opposite sex. They can be found cruising the aisles of stores, sometimes pretending to be interested in merchandise; but usually when they are spritzing cologne around or feeling fabric, their eyes are on the attractive man or woman who is really shopping. Standing in a store, sitting on a bench, or sipping a soda in a food court, they are the ones who are not much interested in picking up merchandise, but who would love picking up a date. The remaining nonshoppers, the least happy, are those who accompany the serious shoppers. This group might include friends who are dragged along for company, children who have no choice, or the reluctant spouse of a shopaholic wife or husband. These nonshoppers are easy to spot because they are often the package carriers and protectors. While their determined partners are attacking the sale racks, the poor tagalongs can be seen draped with shirts, pants, and blouses as they obediently follow the leader; or they spend their time pacing back and forth on mall sidewalks, muttering to themselves as they glance back and forth from their watch to the store. As closing time for the mall stores nears, the nonshoppers will be among the last ones to leave, many having achieved their ends, but few carrying any purchases of their own.

—*Chanthan Srouch*

POSTREADING ANALYSIS: KEY POINTS FOR BUILDING CLASSIFICATION

- **Topic sentence:** names the topic and SOP.
- **Concluding sentence:** restates the topic and adds a final (expanded) thought.
- **Subtopic sentences:** name each group and make a limiting statement— for example, "The first, and maybe most satisfied, of these nonshoppers is the classic window shopper."
- **Sentence connectors:** transitions (*first, next, when*), repeat words (*shopper*), synonyms (*people, teens*), pronouns (*they, who, these*), and reference to main idea (shopping: *browse, looking at, trying out*).
- **Development:** action, scene and character details, sensory details, active verbs (*spritzing*), -*ing* words (*standing, sitting, sipping*), and specific words (*shoes, sweaters, cologne*); also, explanations of the examples ("they are the ones who are not much interested in picking up merchandise, but who would love picking up a date").
- **Humor:** wordplay (*shopaholic*; "picking up *merchandise*" versus "picking up a *date*").

Teaching Idea
"Mall Crashers" gives the class an example of wordplay and shows how it can affect tone in writing. You might use this model as an opportunity to begin a discussion on wordplay and humor in their work.

➡ Prereading Exploration for "Shopping the Easy Way"

Teaching Idea
For students who have difficulty writing outside the first-person perspective, "Shopping the Easy Way" is a good model.

Ann Nall works in a local Toys "R" Us and chose it as her topic. She thought that her information would be especially interesting to new parents and to parents in general.

Skim the paragraph. Notice that Ann does not use any personal experiences in the paper. Would they help or seem out of place?

Answers will vary. Personal experiences are not necessary, although Ann

could easily have included some.

priced, and inexpensive. The information you give would have real meaning for your readers.

You may have several purposes in mind—to entertain, persuade, or inform—but communicating ideas clearly should be your top priority.

Working through the Writing Assignment

Discovering Ideas

**Writing Tutor:
Classification**

HINT: Having a point to make about your topic will focus your groups and guide the examples.

HINT: There are many ways to divide and classify topics from the list.

Teaching Idea
Try to head off the meaningless classification paper by asking students about their topics and why they have chosen them. For students who do not yet have a point, ask the rest of the class to suggest points that could be made.

Teaching Idea
Have the class pick a subject or two from the topics list, decide on an SOP, and give you three or four groups to list on the board.

Writing that groups things, information, and ideas can be dull. Classifying certainly helps a customer in a hardware store to locate a number-2-size Phillips head screw; however, nuts, nails, and screws may not make for a fascinating paper. As you explore topics, consider several SOPs, and think about whether they will lead to groups that you can develop with detailed examples and lively explanations. Think about whether you will be able to make a point with the resulting classification. If you don't make a point, you are likely to bore your readers and yourself. For example, merely talking about a pet parakeet, gerbil, iguana, and guinea pig because they all live in cages (the SOP) might well make the reader respond, "So what?"

The items in the following topics list all can be divided in different ways, depending on the SOP you use. For example, you might classify students (a topic in the first item, "People") according to their study habits: studies night and day, prepares most of the time, occasionally cracks a book, and never bothers to buy a book.

Topics List

- **People:** family, relatives, neighbors, students, drivers, shoppers, dates, white-collar professionals, blue-collar workers, criminals, friends, enemies, sleepers, men, women, musicians, losers, winners, leaders, followers
- **Places:** zoos, parks, sports arenas, rivers, lakes, beaches, swimming pools, cemeteries, amusement parks, national parks, websites, hotels, vacation spots, radio stations, retail stores, restaurants, libraries, schools
- **Events:** embarrassing moments, funerals, weddings, holidays, accidents, practical jokes, painful moments, stages in your life, sales calls, parties
- **Services:** dating, moving, pest control, hair styling, equipment rental, bail bonds, landscaping, employment, travel, phone, heating and air conditioning, adoption, counseling, auto repair, body shops, insurance
- **Emotional states:** happiness, sadness, love, hate, contentment, discontent, enthusiasm, boredom, desire, revulsion, depression, fear, anger
- **Behavior:** kind, cruel, responsible, irresponsible, truthful, deceptive, generous, selfish
- **Personal adornment:** jewelry, makeup, tattoos, piercing, hair coloring, hair styling, fingernail polishing
- **Clothing:** shirts, pants, shorts, dresses, blouses, jackets, coats, socks, shoes
- **Expenses:** home, work, school, recreational
- **Academic subjects:** history, math, English, science, art, music, business, accounting, computer science, foreign language, journalism

- **Career programs:** nursing, welding, paralegal, emergency medical technician, dental hygiene, fashion merchandising, hospitality management
- **Art:** drawing, painting, sculpture, pottery, metal work, photography
- **Musical instruments:** strings, wind, percussion
- **Energy sources:** renewable, nonrenewable
- **Sports:** team sports, individual sports, spectator sports

After choosing several possible topics, prewrite to explore SOPs for these topics. For each SOP you explore, you need to determine what groups will result and how you can develop these groups.

Prewriting

One way you can explore SOPs is with focused clusters, such as the following for the topic of weddings:

Expense, religion, ethnicity—any of these could be used to classify weddings, so the writer must decide which. Using clustering or another prewriting method, we could develop categories for several of the boxed terms. For example, you could choose "seasons" and list spring, summer, fall, and winter. But then you might ask, "What do I want to say about these kinds of weddings?" If you want to write for, say, a trade magazine that specializes in weddings, you could use "seasons" as the SOP and present information in a businesslike tone. But if your purpose is to entertain and reveal something about your experiences, you might use an SOP like the "prevailing emotional state of the bride and groom."

Here is how Richard Bailey, the author of the student model "I Do," grouped weddings based on the feelings of the bride and groom.

1. Blinded by love
2. Joyful
3. Happy
4. Content
5. Uncertain and anxious
6. Panicky
7. Horrified

Brainstorming list of possible categories for grouping weddings by emotional states

Brainstorming can also help you decide which groups to use. After brainstorming examples for each group in his list, Richard chose three groups: joyful, content, and uncertain/anxious weddings. To see how he developed these groups, turn to the model "I Do," on pp. 189–190.

Teaching Idea
To give students practice in discovering an SOP, have them create grocery lists of 20 items and then group the items in any way that seems logical to them. Next, have them compare lists and explain why they grouped the items the way they did.

HINT: You must decide on one organizing principle among many.

Teaching Idea
Encourage students to list as many groups as they can think of in their prewriting (the annotated student model began with seven) and then trim them to the three or four that they have the most to say about.

PREWRITING—SUMMING UP

1. Choose several topics from the topics list, or create several of your own.
2. Prewrite to generate several organizing principles.
3. Prewrite to generate categories and examples for each principle.
4. Reflect on your purpose, interests, and audience to choose a topic and an SOP.

Teaching Idea
Journal Entry 8.2 is a good checkpoint to see if students are on track. You might have them share their work in groups or in general class discussion.

JOURNAL ENTRY 8.2

List several SOPs for your topic, and then choose one that most interests you. Explain in a few sentences why this SOP interests you more than the others, is appropriate to your topic, and might interest an audience.

Organizing Ideas

To help focus and arrange categories, write a topic sentence, one that states the SOP, with or without using words like *categories, groups, kinds, types, sorts, varieties, classes,* and *divisions.* Some writers also forecast their groupings. The following topic sentences illustrate these points:

GROUPING WORD MENTIONED	The weddings I have attended over the years fall into several distinct <u>categories</u> based on the emotional state of the bride and groom.
NO GROUPING WORD MENTIONED	The weddings I have attended over the years often reflect the emotional state of the bride and groom.
GROUPINGS FORECASTED	Weddings can be divided into the four following types based on the emotional state of the bride and groom: <u>joyful, content, uncertain, and panicky.</u>

Think about your groupings and how you will organize them. In thinking about the groupings, make sure that they do not overlap—that is, that none of the examples could fit into more than one of the groups. If, for instance, you are categorizing movies, you might include action/adventures, romantic comedies, westerns, and musicals, but not films by Arnold Schwarzenegger, most of which would fall into the action/adventure category. Also make sure that you don't have more groups than you can effectively develop; three or four are usually appropriate. For overall organization, you might choose space, time, or importance:

HINT: Follow the same order in the paragraph as in the forecasting statement.

- **Space:** for a topic requiring physical grouping of objects (books in a library)
- **Time:** for a topic using brief stories to group (stages of your life)
- **Importance:** for a topic using groups that are clearly less and more dramatic (dangerous weather: thunderstorm, blizzard, tornado)

HINT: Try a scratch outline before you draft.

When you have an organization, try writing a scratch outline. At this point, you might look ahead to the drafting. Think about subtopic sentences with which to introduce each group, and think about linking groups with connectors like the transitions below. (For more on connectors and a complete list of transitions, see pp. 53–58.)

FOR ADDING MATERIAL			
again	as well as	furthermore	likewise
also	besides	in addition	moreover
and	further	last	next

FOR GIVING EXAMPLES AND EMPHASIS			
above all	especially	in particular	one reason
after all	for example	in truth	specifically
another	for instance	it is true	surely

FOR COMPARING			
alike	both	like	resembling
also	in the same way	likewise	similarly

FOR CONTRASTING			
after all	dissimilar	nevertheless	though
although	even though	on the contrary	unlike
but	however	on the other hand	whereas

ORGANIZING—SUMMING UP

1. Create a rough topic sentence to focus your material.
2. Eliminate excess categories and any that overlap. Keep three or four.
3. Arrange the categories by space, time, or importance.
4. Try a scratch outline.
5. Review the list of transitions and other connectors.

JOURNAL ENTRY 8.3

Jot down your rough topic sentence. Does it contain an SOP? Next list your categories in whichever order you have chosen. In a few sentences, explain why you think this arrangement will work well.

Drafting

With the preliminary work done, you are almost ready to write your first draft. But before plunging in, review the drafting suggestions in Chapter 1 (pp. 12–13). Also, recheck the SOP and groups you have chosen for the following:

- An SOP that effectively classifies your topic
- A clear reason for the classification, one that makes a point about your topic
- An SOP that avoids overlapping categories and makes it possible for you to include all important group members without creating an endless list

Teaching Idea
If you don't have time to pick up the students' first rough drafts, consider collecting Journal Entry 8.4 to give you a quick glimpse into their progress.

JOURNAL ENTRY 8.4

Soon after writing your first draft, reread the assignment on page 181, and then skim the draft. Does it fit the assignment? Are there three or four categories in place that are arranged effectively? What part of your draft do you like best? What part do you dislike most? Answer in a paragraph.

Revising Drafts

For help with revising first, second, and final drafts, turn to Chapter 4.

ANNOTATED STUDENT MODEL: "I DO"

Carefully reading the annotated student model will help clarify questions you have about your own draft.

First-Stage Draft

Teaching Idea
You may find the annotated student model most useful in showing the many changes often needed in going from a first to a second draft.

The groups are in place but need to be developed with detailed examples and further explanation.

Unneeded sentence between topic and first subtopic sentence

The second and third subtopic sentences need further focus.

Richard Bailey, who had been to several weddings, picked weddings as his topic and young adults thinking of getting married soon as his audience. After limiting his groups to three—joyous, content, and unhappy weddings—he wrote a fast draft to get some ideas down on paper.

Weddings come in all shapes and sizes but not all of them are happy. I have been to half a dozen over the last 10 years, and I can tell you that some were great, some were so-so, and others were disasters. One of the happiest weddings I have ever been to was my older brother's best friend. He married a terrific woman of about the same age (they were in their forties), and the church was full of teary eyes as they walked down the aisle with some old fifties tune in the back ground. Not all people getting married can be ecstatic. Some fall into another group. These kinds of weddings are with people who have grown up as childhood sweethearts and then they become friends and then they get married. Weddings like these are full of people who already know each other because of the couple's history together the conversation in the church is among people saying the wedding is long overdue. Another bad wedding to be in is the confused and panicky kind. Weddings like this are often between two people who don't belong together in the first place. Sometimes accidents force the issue, sometimes familys pressure people, and sometimes two people just chose the wrong partners. My younger brother's first marriage was this sort, and the problems were obvious even to the wedding guests. His bride's people took one-half of the church and Marks took the other half of the church. The ceremony was over fast. No one seemed sure what was happening and Mark ended up dropping his wife on the floor! As awful as Mark's wedding was and despite high divorce statistics in this country, I will probably get married someday.

Second-Stage Draft

Teaching Idea
You might want to skim the first and second drafts of the annotated model in class before students begin working on their first drafts to help them head off several potential problems.

Rough first drafts of classification papers often have difficulties with overall focus, development, and relevant material. Note the explanations and examples added to the following draft to help clarify meaning.

SPECIAL POINTS TO CHECK IN REVISING FROM FIRST TO SECOND DRAFTS
1. Check the topic sentence: topic + statement of SOP.
2. Check subtopic sentences: connector + group + statement.
3. Check the concluding sentence: connector + link to topic sentence + expanded thought.
4. Delete unnecessary material.
5. Add material for clarity, completeness, and emphasis.
6. Check connectors: transitions, repeat words, synonyms, pronouns, and references to main idea.

Topic sentence revised

Subtopic sentences revised (and shaded to help you identify them)

Supporting details and examples added throughout

The weddings I have been to over the years can be grouped into several categories based on how the bride and groom feel. When many people think of weddings, they think of deliriously happy young couples. These are the people who can't wait to get the wedding over, and the honeymoon started. I have been to several like this. However, the happiest couple I have ever seen were not young, but in their early forties. Neither Jack nor Fran had any doubt. As they stood at the altar reciting their vows to the sound of some old fiftys tune and the church was full of teary eyes as they completed their vows with a kiss. If not all marrying couple are lucky enough to be overjoyed, there are still many who are happy and content. Often these weddings are between people like my older brother and his wife. Bruce and Julie grew up together, became friends, and then fell in love. Weddings like these are often full of people who already know each other, because of the couple's history together. The conversation in the church is full of people saying stuff like "Well . . . it's about time" and "at last."

Transitional word *worst* added to show order of importance

The worst kind of state for a couple to be in is in confusion and panic. Weddings like this are often between two people who don't belong together in the first place, shouldn't be together, and who will never last. Sometimes accidents force the issue, sometimes familys pressure people, and sometimes two people just chose the wrong partners. My younger brother's first

Explanation added

marriage was this sort, and the problems were obvious even to the wedding guests. <u>Evelyns</u> people took one-half of the room and <u>Marks</u> took the other half of the room. <u>No mixing it up between the families.</u> The ceremony was quick and the reception was short. No one seemed sure what was happening, and Mark, <u>who had been drinking too much made matters worse when he dropped Evelyn as he tried to carry her across the threshold.</u> As awful as the panicky marriage can be and despite all the divorces in this country, I expect to get married one day, and I hope that mine lasts.

Explanation added

Concluding sentence revised

Third-Stage Draft

Many of us would call the paper complete by the time we have done a thorough second draft. But if you want your work to move beyond good to excellent, this third draft gives you that opportunity. With all of the major material and organizational concerns taken care of, you can now improve word choices and sentence variety and delete the clutter phrases that so often slip into rough drafts.

Teaching Idea
Whereas some students may not see the value in the sentence combining of the third-stage draft, most will recognize that the specific words and synonyms that have been added and the words that have been cut have improved the draft.

Teaching Idea
To reinforce revision for style, you might want to assign selected pages from Unit Four on the days the class is discussing the third-stage draft and working on their own developing drafts.

SPECIAL POINTS TO CHECK IN REVISING FROM SECOND TO THIRD DRAFTS
1. Add specific words.
2. Substitute more precise or audience-appropriate words.
3. Combine sentences for variety.
4. **Replace clutter and repeat words with synonyms and phrases.**
5. <u>Delete unneeded words.</u>

Title added

I Do

The weddings I have been to over the years can be grouped into several categories based on how the bride and groom feel. When many of people think of weddings they think of young couples', deliriously happy, who can't wait ~~to get the wedding over~~ **to get the rings** and the honeymoon started. I have been to several like this, however, the happiest ~~couple~~ **people** I have ever seen were not young, but in their early forties. Neither Jack nor Fran had any doubt as they stood at the altar reciting "till death do us part" to the strains of "When I Fall In Love," and the church was full of teary eyes. As they completed their vows with a kiss. If not all marrying couple are lucky enough to be overjoyed, there are still many who are happy and content. Often these weddings are between ~~couples~~ **people** like my older brother and his wife who grew up together, became friends, and then fell in love. Weddings like these are often large and full of people who already know each other, because of the couples history together. Conversation in the pews is filled with ~~stuff like~~ **phrases** like

"Well . . . it's about time" and "at last." The ~~worst kind of~~ least desirable emotional state for the ~~a couple~~ **bride and groom** is confusion ~~and~~/panic. Weddings like these are often between two people who don't belong together in the first place and who probably won't last. Sometimes accidental pregnancies force the issue, sometimes family pressure is responsible, sometimes two people just chose the wrong partner. My younger brother's first marriage was like this, and the division was obvious even in the wedding guests. Evelyns people took one-half of the church ; Marks took the other half ~~of the room.~~ The ceremony was quiet and quick, vows were mumbled, and the reception was short. No one seemed quiet sure what was happening, and even Mark's ~~who had been drinking too much~~ big attempt to lighten the mood by carrying Evelyn across a threshold at the reception hall fell flat when he stepped on her dress and dropped her. As awful as the panicky marriage can be and despite all the divorces in this country, I expect to get married one day, but I hope that mine lasts!

Final-Editing Draft

In this last draft, Richard slows his reading to a crawl, editing closely, word by word, line by line, looking especially for the pattern errors he has listed on his Improvement Chart. It is a tedious process, but he knows that he still has many errors to correct.

SPECIAL POINTS TO CHECK IN EDITING FINAL DRAFTS

1. Misspellings
2. Sound-alike words
3. Missing words
4. Wrong words
5. Sentence fragments
6. Comma splices/run-ons
7. Faulty capitalization
8. Incorrect apostrophes
9. Commas(s) needed
   a. Introductory words/phrases/clauses
   b. Nonessential word groups
   c. Main clauses with coordinating conjunction
10. Unneeded commas

I Do

The weddings I have been to over the years can be grouped into several categories based on how the bride and groom feel. When many people think of weddings,[9a] they think of young ~~couple's~~[8] couples, deliriously happy, who can't wait to get the rings on[3] and the honeymoon started. I have been to several like this,[6] ; however, the happiest people I have ever seen were not young,[10] but in their early forties. Neither Jack nor Fran had any doubt as they stood at the altar reciting "till death do us part" to the strains of "When I Fall in[7] Love," and the church was full of teary eyes as they completed their vows with a kiss.[5] If not all marrying couples are lucky enough to be overjoyed, there are still many who are happy and content. Often these weddings are between people like my older brother and his wife,[9b] who grew up together, became friends, and then fell in love. Weddings like these are often large and full of people who already know each other,[10] because of the couple's history together. Conversation in the pews is filled with phrases like "Well . . . it's about time" and "at last." The least desirable emotional state for the bride and groom is confusion/panic. Weddings like these are often between two people who don't belong together in the first place and who probably won't last. Sometimes accidental pregnancies force the issue, sometimes family pressure is responsible, and sometimes two people just ~~chose~~[4] choose the wrong partner. My younger brother's first marriage was like this, and the division was obvious even in the wedding guests. ~~Evelyns~~[8] Evelyn's people took one-half of the church,[6]; ~~Marks~~[8] Mark's took the other. The ceremony was quiet and quick, vows were mumbled, and the reception was short. No one seemed ~~quiet~~[2] quite sure what was happening, and even Mark's big attempt to lighten the mood by carrying Evelyn across a threshold at the reception hall fell flat when he stepped on her dress and dropped her. As awful as the panicky marriage can be and despite all the divorces in this country, I expect to get married one day, but I hope that mine lasts!

—*Richard Bailey*

FINAL-DRAFT CHECKLIST

Before you turn in your final draft, review this checklist. You may find that, as careful as you think you have been, you still missed a point or two—or more. (For more on any of these points, see Chapter 4.)

- ☐ 1. Have you used a single organizing principle?
- ☐ 2. Have you included all important groups?
- ☐ 3. Do you have a clear reason for your classification?
- ☐ 4. Does your topic sentence name your topic and state the SOP?
- ☐ 5. Have you arranged your groups—usually by time or importance?
- ☐ 6. Does a subtopic sentence introduce each group?
- ☐ 7. Are your main examples relevant, developed, and thoroughly explained?
- ☐ 8. Are all sentences well connected?
- ☐ 9. Does the concluding sentence have an expanded thought?
- ☐ 10. Have you used specific language?

☐ 11. Have you used a metaphor or simile?

☐ 12. Are your sentences varied in length and beginnings?

☐ 13. Have you used synonyms for words that are repeated too often?

☐ 14. Have you cut unneeded words?

☐ 15. Have you written an interesting title? Have you checked its capitalization?

☐ 16. Have you prepared your paper using the format expected by your instructor? (Check to see if you need a title page, use double spacing, leave at least a 1-inch margin, and use a 12-point font.)

☐ 17. Have you edited your work as closely as you know how to (including having at least one other person proofread)? Have you checked your Improvement Chart for pattern errors?

☐ 18. Have you looked for these errors: misspellings, soundalike words, missing words, wrong words, sentence fragments, comma splices/run-ons, faulty capitalizations, incorrect apostrophes, missing commas, and unnecessary commas?

Chapter Summary

1. Classification groups things by a single organizing principle (SOP).

2. We classify information, people, places, events, and objects to simplify our lives, making ideas more comprehensible and accessible.

3. Writers choose an SOP based on the topic and on their own and their audience's interest in the topic.

4. Classification should include all obvious groups without creating an endless list.

5. Writers should always have a reason for classifying.

6. Writing that classifies may use any of the three basic organizing strategies but frequently uses order of importance.

7. Each category should be introduced with a subtopic sentence.

8. Each category should be developed with detailed examples and explanations.

9. Writing is never complete until it has been carefully revised and edited.

ALTERNATE WRITING ASSIGNMENTS

Teaching Idea
Classifying things, as in Alternate Writing Assignment 1, initially can be less demanding than some of the other topics. However, students then have the challenge of making the classification interesting.

Here are a few more assignment options that may be of interest. For this assignment, be sure to do the following:

1. Establish a single organizing principle that includes all logical groupings.

2. Announce this principle in your topic sentence.

3. Introduce each main grouping with a subtopic sentence.

4. End with a concluding sentence that restates and expands the main idea.

ASSIGNMENT OPTIONS

1. Describe or upgrade a classifying system at your job. Secretaries and other office personnel file information according to an SOP (often

alphabetically); restaurant personnel group food, beverages, and menu items; people in retail sales arrange counters, aisles, and departments. Look closely at what you or someone else does at your job, and then either simply describe the classification system or suggest a more efficient method. Consider this a business document and adjust your tone accordingly.

2. Write a classification paragraph with a humorous intent. You might focus on events of a certain type—say, family gatherings—and classify them ranging from warm and wonderful encounters to pitched battles. You might choose behaviors of some type—say, those that children use to try to manipulate their parents—and classify them ranging from screaming tantrums to kisses and avowals of love. Or you might choose some type

of restrictions that you find annoying—say, questionable rules—and classify them according to how seriously they need to be taken.

3. Write a classification paragraph involving the field you plan to have a career in. For example, engineering could divide into mechanical, electrical, civil; teaching could split into preschool, elementary, middle school, high school, and college. If you are headed for certification in a field like HVAC or fire science, you could categorize the job elements or opportunities within it. Your goal in this assignment is to increase your knowledge of the field.

4. Write a classification paragraph in which you divide your life to date into stages, to gain insights into who you are. You might use as an organizing principle one of the following: productivity, freedom, responsibility, risk taking, or socializing. For example, a person could choose degree of freedom as an SOP and group life stages into nearly absolute freedom, much freedom, not much freedom, and almost no freedom.

5. Write a classification paragraph based on the three accompanying photos. You can see the three families enjoying themselves through different activities (the SOP): roasting marshmallows around a campfire, sledding with inner tubes, and strolling on the beach. Comment on these activities as ways to bring a family closer, and include some personal examples.

CHAPTER 9

Recognizing Causes,
Explaining Effects

What Are We Trying to Achieve and Why?

Setting the Stage

Teaching Idea
When you introduce causal analysis, it helps to use synonymous terms like *reasons* for causes and *results* for effects. (For more synonyms, see "Organizing Ideas.")

What caused the accident shown in the preceding photo? Was the driver in the overturned truck simply careless? Was there a mechanical failure? Was there a weather-related problem like ice on the road? Did the driver swerve to avoid a potential accident, thus causing his own? We ask these questions as we try to understand or assign responsibility for an action—that is, as we try to determine its **causes.** When we speculate about the outcome of an event, we are concerned with its **effects.** What will happen to the driver at fault—a ticket, a fine, jail time? How will this accident affect his career? If he has had problems in the past, will his insurance rates go up? Will he be fired? Will any other company hire him after this accident?

When we apply this question-and-answer process to the events in our lives, we are dealing with cause-and-effect thinking, the focus of Chapter 9.

Linking to Previous Experience

Teaching Idea
Students more readily understand cause/effect when you explain this pattern in terms of understanding problems and figuring out solutions, and in terms of anticipating and avoiding problems. You might want to point out how cause/effect *thinking* complements process-analysis *doing.*

People constantly face problems that need solutions. For instance, you are stuck in your driveway because the car won't start. Or in your house, you suddenly heard a splashing sound from the bathroom—it was the toilet. Now your car won't start, and the toilet won't stop. What's causing the problems? How will you fix them? What results (effects) can you expect if you tear into them with a hammer and a wrench? Maybe you should call Dad, Uncle Henry, your older sister, a plumber, or a mechanic? Solving problems and anticipating outcomes are basic survival skills that we all have practiced from the earliest age.

Within this text, we have already worked with cause and effect. In Chapter 5, when you established a dominant impression (effect), you needed to show what elements brought about (caused) the feeling. The Chapter 6 personal narrative was full of cause-and-effect relationships as your story unfolded, event A adding to event B. The significance of the event (effect) was created (caused) by the people and their actions. In Chapter 7, you made a statement (often the effect) and then used examples (causes) to illustrate it. And the categories of Chapter 8 were often developed with cause-and-effect examples.

As we move ahead in this text, we will continue to see cause and effect operating, one of many strategies for developing ideas.

Determining the Value of Causal Thinking

We also see cause and effect at work in school. In a nursing class, students must understand the possible causes of a patient's wheezing and the effects of different ways of treating this symptom. In an interior design class, students must solve the problem of making a tiny room appear larger, determining what will have the effect of creating a spacious impression. In an economics class, the professor asks students to predict the effect on mortgage loans of raising the prime interest rate.

Learning causal thinking will help you in college classes, but aside from earning good grades, you will develop a more critical frame of mind. The world is complex, and its people multifaceted. As you practice clear causal thought, you will see the world more clearly and make more reasoned judgments.

Teaching Idea
If you teach the persuasion chapter, you might want to link clear cause/effect thinking to avoiding the post hoc fallacy.

Teaching Idea
Journal Entry 9.1 is a good in-class discussion tool to help students understand how much a part of our lives cause-and-effect thinking is.

JOURNAL ENTRY 9.1

When have you recently used cause/effect thinking to understand a situation, solve a problem, or predict an outcome? Perhaps your in-laws came for the weekend. What effects did they have on your household? Maybe you just received a brand new MasterCard with a $3,000 limit. If you don't cut it in two, what effects might you predict? Summarize two situations, and tell the causes and/or effects for each.

Developing Skills and Exploring Ideas in Cause or Effect Paragraphs

Teaching Idea
You might point out to students that Activities 9.1 and 9.2 can be used as prewriting for their own topics.

To learn to write effective cause/effect paragraphs, you need to practice the following:

1. Exploring all the likely causes and effects
2. Developing causes or effects thoroughly
3. Choosing only the real causes and effects
4. Thinking critically to avoid oversimplifying

Teaching Idea
Instead of focusing on the terminology of *primary, secondary,* and so on in working through Activity 9.1, you might emphasize the various causes and effects these terms can reveal.

Discovering Causes and Effects

Most events have more than one cause and more than one effect, even when these added causes and effects are not obvious to us. For example, we might think that a student did poorly on an algebra exam because he didn't study enough. This is likely a primary, or main, cause, but perhaps there are other significant reasons, which we could explore with a list like the following:

QUESTIONS FOR EXPLORING CAUSES

- **Primary:** What causes would certainly bring about the event?
- **Secondary:** What causes might reasonably bring about the event?
- **Contributing:** What causes might play a role by creating or adding to another cause?
- **Immediate:** What is the cause closest in time that produced the event?
- **Distant:** What causes might be separated from the event by time or space?
- **Hidden:** What causes might not be readily apparent?
- **Minor:** What causes might be involved in a lesser way (and in some cases be mistaken for significant ones)?

HINT: You could use a similar series of questions to explore effects ("What effects would this event have?" and so on).

Applying these questions to the failed algebra exam, we might come up with this list:

- **Primary:** insufficient studying
- **Secondary:** argument with parents the night prior to the test
- **Contributing:** work demands cutting into study time
- **Immediate:** answering only half the problems
- **Distant:** not grasping arithmetic concepts from earlier grade levels
- **Hidden:** undiagnosed attention deficit disorder
- **Minor:** student nearby whistling throughout the exam

CAUTION! There are often several primary causes and effects.

Now we can see that there are many reasons for poor grades, and we would pick the ones best suited to our purpose, interest, and audience. Notice that what might be only a secondary reason for one person might be a primary reason for another. For example, the argument might have upset the student so much that he could not think clearly during the exam. Also, a distant or hidden cause might be crucial to the effect, so you must decide which causes or effects are most significant.

HINT: Whether a cause is primary or secondary is often the writer's judgment.

ACTIVITY 9.1 Discovering Causes and Effects

Teaching Idea
Activity 9.1 is more challenging to students if they list *possible* rather than far-fetched causes and effects.

Working in a group, discuss one of the following topics, brainstorming for causes or effects. The "Questions for Exploring Causes" may help you discover ideas. Next, list six possible causes or effects. Then decide which three are most likely, and tell why you eliminated the others.

EXAMPLE
Topic: being elected valedictorian of your graduating class

Possible causes:

1. Having overall highest GPA	2. Making A's on all final exams
3. ~~Having a parent as the principal~~	4. ~~Getting early computer training~~
5. Having good study habits	6. ~~Being rewarded by parents for A's~~

Reasons for cutting causes: Number 3 is not likely because GPA, not the principal, determines the valedictorian. Causes 4 and 6 could contribute to student success but are not as significant as causes 1, 2, and 5.

Answers will vary.

1. Topic: requiring all high school students to take a course that educates about addictive substances

Possible causes:

1. Governmental mandate	2. A few students getting caught with marijuana	
3. A trend in drug overdoses at a school	4. Several students talking about smoking pot	
5. The well-publicized death of a student	6. Mayor's campaign promise from last year.	

Reasons for cutting causes: Causes 2 and 4 are insufficient and 6 is unlikely, given how often politicians follow through on campaign promises.

2. Topic: switching careers in midlife

Possible causes:

1. Being discredited in one job and losing it	2. Secret childhood fantasy	
3. Being caught stealing (other major infraction?)	4. Friends from high school doing better	
5. Realizing that a job is being phased out	6. Being tired of a job and wanting a change	

Reasons for cutting causes: Number 2 seems least likely, though still possible, because most middle-aged people do not make major life changes based on adolescent fantasies. Number 4 does not seem sufficient, though it could contribute. Because most people cannot justify the time, money, and energy a career switch takes based on boredom, number 6 is out.

3. Topic: marrying while still teenagers

Possible effects:

1. Starting a family early	2. Seeing the world	
3. Beginning to lose touch with unmarried friends	4. Maintaining a burning infatuation	
5. Divorcing early in life	6. Graduating from college with honors	

Reasons for cutting effects: <u>Most teen marriages are caused by</u>
<u>pregnancy, and young people (or those of any age) struggling with</u>
<u>children have a difficult time achieving number 2, 4, or 6.</u>

4. Topic: watching too much television

Possible effects:

1. Studying less	2. ~~Being driven into depression~~
3. Missing out on social activities	4. ~~Learning the secret to instant success~~
5. Reading less	6. ~~Committing a "copycat" crime~~

Reasons for cutting effects: <u>TV is unlikely to account for either cause 2</u>
<u>or cause 6 without some significant contributing causes. And despite</u>
<u>late-night television real estate schemes and "psychics," cause 4 is</u>
<u>also unlikely.</u>

Developing Causes and Effects

After choosing likely causes or effects for your topic, you will develop them with detailed examples and clear explanations. You may use the "I" voice of personal experience or the more formal "they" approach. Examples can be developed through specific words, sensory details, active verbs, -*ing* words, and dialogue. You will need a subtopic sentence to introduce each cause or effect.

ACTIVITY 9.2 Developing Causes and Effects

Choose a topic from Activity 9.1 and develop one of its causes or effects with examples, details, and explanations. You can use personal experience, as in the following example, or general knowledge. After deciding how you will develop this cause or effect, write a subtopic sentence that includes the cause or effect and makes a statement about it. Then develop it in several sentences.

EXAMPLE

Topic: watching too much television

Possible effect: <u>Too little time for studying causes poor grades.</u>

Subtopic sentence: <u>When I was a sophomore in high school, my grades</u>
<u>took a nosedive when my parents gave me a TV for my room.</u>

Subtopic developed: It was great to have some privacy to watch TV and not have to fight with my older brother over who got to see what program. But I started watching the tube nonstop from the time I got home from school till bedtime. After failing three out of five classes, even I saw a problem, and my parents took the set till my grades improved.

Answers will vary.

Topic from Activity 9.1: _____

Possible cause or effect: _____

_____

Subtopic sentence: _____

_____

Subtopic developed: _____

_____

_____

_____

_____

_____

Choosing Real Causes and Effects

People are often wrong about causes and effects because they judge too quickly, assuming that, just because two actions are closely related in time, one necessarily causes or is an effect of the other. For example, children who hear thunder and see rain follow might conclude that thunder causes rain. Or a motorist caught in slow highway traffic might conclude that the driver in front of him is the problem when, in fact, the slowdown is caused by the gawkers ahead of both drivers who are staring at a stalled car on the roadside. When we slow down and think more critically, we are more likely to find the real causes and effects of an event.

ACTIVITY 9.3 Choosing Real Causes and Effects

Teaching Idea
Some students will think that all of the items on one cause or effect list are likely—for instance, that "liking the taste of beer" might cause alcoholism. This reaction can lead to some lively discussion, especially when students explain their reasoning. (You might refer students back to Activity 9.1 and the "minor" cause.)

For each topic, put an X in front of the cause and the effect that seem *least* reasonable. Next, explain why you think the cause or effect is unlikely.

1. Topic: becoming addicted to alcohol

Causes	**Effects**
_____ Having parents who are heavy drinkers	_____ Losing a job
_____ Having friends who are heavy drinkers	_____ Losing friends
_____ Suffering from overstress	__X__ Leading a happier life

___X___ Liking the taste of beer   _____ Becoming malnourished

_____ Being genetically predisposed   _____ Developing cirrhosis of
                                                 the liver

Unlikely cause: Liking the taste of beer may be a contributing cause,
but it is not a significant reason.

Unlikely effect: Few alcoholics lead happy lives, at least until they give
up drinking.

2. Topic: overusing pesticides and herbicides on a lawn

Causes	**Effects**
_____ Being ignorant of the problem	_____ Killing some plants and animals that aren't pests
_____ Being indifferent to the problem	_____ Polluting water
_____ Having no laws restricting use	___X___ Eradicating insect pests and weeds
_____ Wanting a beautiful lawn	_____ Polluting soil
___X___ Reacting to environmentalists	_____ Making animals and people sick

Unlikely cause: Few people would protest against environmentalists by
poisoning their own yard.

Unlikely effect: Lawn battles are constantly fought and never won.

3. Topic: attending the funeral of someone you never liked

Causes	**Effects**
_____ Fulfilling a family obligation	_____ Feeling good about the decision
___X___ Trying to meet new people	_____ Feeling horribly bored
_____ Acting kindly toward the family	_____ Making family members happy
_____ Fulfilling a moral obligation	_____ Reassessing feelings toward the deceased
_____ Fulfilling a work obligation	___X___ Realizing deceased was a saint

Unlikely cause: Not many people go to funerals to fill their social
calendar.

Unlikely effect: A person might view the deceased more favorably but be
unlikely to canonize him or her.

Thinking Critically

Teaching Idea
If you teach the persuasion chapter, you might want to link Activity 9.4 to the fallacy of oversimplifying.

Teaching Idea
Letting students compare their responses to Activity 9.4 in class will reinforce the message that causes and effects can be complex.

When people look for a quick explanation or solution to a problem, they often oversimplify. For instance, when you see a young person driving a $50,000 car, you might conclude that she has lots of money. But there are several other likely explanations: She is leasing the vehicle, or she is driving her parents' car, or she has a 5-year loan and barely makes the payments. To write and think critically, we often need to slow down, asking the question "Is this the only or best explanation possible?"

ACTIVITY 9.4 Thinking Critically

Read the following oversimplified statements, and list five other likely causes or effects.
Answers will vary.

1. Television is the reason so many college students do not perform better in school.

   Other causes of poor academic performance:

   A. Dealing with family problems

   B. Working too much

   C. Missing classes

   D. Avoiding homework

   E. Partying

2. If the driving age were raised to 18, there would be fewer accidents.

   Other causes of accidents:

   A. Anyone driving drunk

   B. Driving when a person is too old

   C. Careless driving by middle-aged adults

   D. Anyone driving in bad weather

   E. Anyone coping with difficult road hazards

3. If a person switches careers in midlife, he is probably failing at his job.

   Other causes for a career change:

   A. Moving

   B. Wanting more money

   C. Failing business

   D. Wanting more opportunity for advancement

   E. Having achieved financial security and looking for creative fulfillment

4. People exercise mainly to feel good about themselves.

   Other effects of exercise:

   A. Improving health

   B. Increasing longevity

C. Improving quality of life

D. Contributing to a person's social life

E. Helping an athlete perform better in an organized sport

5. Rap music makes people behave violently.

Other effects of rap music:

A. Helping people feel happy

B. Creating a good beat to dance to

C. Bringing a group of people closer together

D. Introducing people to aspects of a different culture

E. Allowing people to vent frustration without hurting anyone

Cause or Effect Paragraphs: Analyzing Student Models

The following models will help you write cause or effect paragraphs. "Making the Promise Last" is developed through generalized experience, whereas "The Thousand-Dollar Lesson" and "Building Memories" focus on personal examples. As with any writing models, do not simply reproduce the authors' work; instead, apply the principles you discover to your own writing.

➡ Prereading Exploration for "Making the Promise Last"

Teaching Idea
To promote causal thinking and to stimulate an interesting discussion, have students talk over the *positive* effects of early marriage before they read "Making the Promise Last."

In discussions with group members, Gebdao Kaiwalweroj found that they agreed with her that early marriage can lead to problems. They shared stories from which she drew some specific examples for her paper. For a target audience, Gebdao chose young people considering early marriage.

Though this paper is not a formal argument, part of the author's purpose is persuasion. Before reading further, for perspective on the issue, list four possible *positive* effects on young adults of marrying right out of high school.

Answers will vary. Possible positive effects: Two people support and nurture one another; two lives are enriched by joining; two people become even more responsible as they chart out a life together; no longer needing to play the dating game, the couple can move ahead with life goals, such as building a business or continuing their education.

Making the Promise Last

Marrying while still teenagers can be a bad decision, creating many problems for young couples. First, when teens marry in or just out of high school, their relationships with other people often change drastically. Instead of spending time with their individual former friends, newlyweds often find that their spouse does not like some or all of their friends, so the husband or wife has to choose—"them or me." Even when the old friends are accepted, many times friendships die out because a married couple's interests can be so different from a single person's. While some young couples continue to go to the same parties, concerts, and vacation spots, many more find themselves having to try to have fun with each other's in-laws instead. As the years pass, another problem begins as young couples often find themselves becoming increasingly cut off from the rest of life and dependent on one another. They have already been seeing less of old friends, many of whom are off at college or trade school or simply doing other things, but after that first baby arrives, the young couple's life becomes really isolated. A new baby also has the effect of making their life hard. If they had been thinking about more school, with the new load of bills, forget it. The newest priority becomes baby food and diapers. When the normal stress of raising a baby is added to life goals put aside and relaxation time vanishing, many young marriages begin to crumble. Now the couple experiences one of the worst effects of hasty marriage—divorce. Even without the added tension of a baby, many young adults, who are still finding out who they themselves are, soon learn in their time living together that they are not right for each other. If a child is involved, then the baby's life and the parents' lives are inevitably changed for the worse. The childless couple may split, finding a better life for themselves one day, but divorce with a baby heaps extra bills for separate maintenance and guilt on the parents. While some early marriages work out well, so many end poorly that maybe teens should wait until they know and can take care of themselves better before they stand at an altar and promise to take care of someone else.

—*Gebdao Kaiwalweroj*

POSTREADING ANALYSIS: KEY POINTS FOR BUILDING CAUSE/EFFECT

- **Topic sentence:** names and focuses the topic and predicts effects.
- **Concluding sentence:** restates the topic and adds a final (expanded) thought.
- **Subtopic sentences:** name each effect and make a limiting statement— for example, "First, when teens marry in or just out of high school, their relationships often change drastically."
- **Sentence connectors:** transitions (*first, when, now*), repeat words (*couple*), synonyms (*teenagers, newlyweds*), pronouns (*many, themselves, who*), and reference to main idea (marriage problems: *die out, cut off, stress*).

- **Development:** action, scene and character details, sensory details, active verbs (*die out, heaps*), *-ing* words (*creating, spending, vanishing*), and specific words (*high school, teenagers, newlyweds*); also, explanations of the examples ("many times friendships die out because a married couple's interests can be so different from a single person's").
- **Qualifying:** words used to soften a statement (*often, can, maybe, some, may*). (For more on qualifying, see pp. 397, 491.)

CAUTION! Qualifying cause/effect relationships is important.

➡ Prereading Exploration for "The Thousand-Dollar Lesson"

Teaching Idea
Because "The Thousand-Dollar Lesson" focuses on effects, you might also want to discuss possible causes, encouraging students to see that their own topics might be better handled as either causes or effects.

In this essay, Lucas Eimers writes for an audience of young adults who have gotten a speeding ticket or two and who have had trouble with their car insurance.

Before reading the paragraph, think about this question: If you were to write about speeding, would you focus on causes or effects? Which do you think would make a more interesting paper? Why? Since Lucas tells about the effects of speeding, focus on causes, listing four of them below:

Answers will vary. Possible causes for speeding: (1) enjoyment,

(2) emergency, (3) driving while drunk, (4) test driving a new car

_____

_____

_____

The Thousand-Dollar Lesson

While traveling last spring, I learned about the miserable consequences of speeding. My first unpleasant experience was actually getting the ticket. I knew I was in trouble from the moment I saw the red flashing lights in my rearview mirror and looked down at the speedometer to see the needle on 85. I thought I might be able to talk my way out of it until I saw the Clint Eastwood look-alike Texas highway patrol officer step up to my window. "All right, boy, let me see your license and proof of insurance," he drawled, cutting off my "Gee-I-didn't-realize-I-was-going-that-fast" line. The officer seemed to enjoy every second it took him to write that ticket out, and with an evil smirk he handed it to me, saying, "Have a nice day." I'm pretty sure he was the only one having fun. The next problem was paying the ticket. I didn't want it on my record because it would crank up my insurance rates, so I knew it would cost plenty, and it did. The ticket was only 75 dollars, but it cost 300 to have it "disappear" from my record. Yet as bad as that expense was, the next effect was worse. My parents had been paying my insurance because I was still living at home and going to college. However, after they learned of my ticket, they decided to stop helping me with the coverage. They reasoned that if I had enough money to speed, then I had enough money to pay for my own insurance. I never quite figured out their logic, but I got their point. A thousand dollars for a year's premiums is an expensive lesson. Having to cover the insurance on top of the ticket led to the worst consequence of all—work, work, work! I picked up additional hours at the golf course where I work, but that was not enough. So I turned to my parents, who were willing to help, they said, with smiles that reminded me of the Texas highway patrol officer. There were plenty of odd jobs for me to do on the weekends around the house: painting the shed, staining the deck, washing the windows, cleaning out the garage. . . . My folks were very creative and have given me lots of this kind of "help." Before this last year I thought I knew what kind of trouble speeding could cause me, but I know now, and I am more inclined to think about the consequences of everything I do now before I act.

—Lucas Eimers

POSTREADING ANALYSIS: KEY POINTS FOR BUILDING CAUSE/EFFECT

- **Topic sentence:** names and focuses the topic and predicts effects.
- **Concluding sentence:** restates the topic and adds a final (expanded) thought.
- **Subtopic sentences:** name each effect and make a limiting statement—for example, "My first unpleasant experience was actually getting the ticket."
- **Sentence connectors:** transitions (*first, next, however*), repeat words (*speeding*), synonyms (*cost, expense*), pronouns (*it, my, who*), and reference to main idea (speeding problems: *miserable, unpleasant, work*).
- **Development:** action, scene and character details, sensory details, active verbs (*drawled, handed*), -*ing* words (*cutting, painting, staining*), comparisons (*Clint Eastwood look-alike*), and specific words (*Texas highway patrol officer, rearview mirror, 85*); also, explanations of the examples ("My parents had been paying my insurance because I was still living at home and going to college").

HINT: Comparisons can help your reader better see what you mean.

Questions for Paragraph Analysis

Note: These questions apply to both student models.

1. Which words in the topic sentence name the topic, limit it, and predict cause or effect?
2. What words in the concluding sentence link to the topic sentence?
3. What is the expanded thought in the final sentence? (For more on the expanded thought, see pp. 49–51.)
4. Copy each of the subtopic sentences, and underline the cause or effect once and the statement made about it twice. Circle connectors:

transitions, repeat words, synonyms, and pronouns. (For more on connectors, see pp. 53–58.)

5. What words show that the main causes or effects are arranged by order of importance (see Activity 7.3) or in another way?

6. Choose a cause or effect and tell how the author's explaining (as opposed to detailing or action description) helps you better understand the author's point. (For more on detailing and explaining examples, see pp. 41–42.)

7. Choose a cause or effect and tell how the action description and detailing help you to better understand the author's point (see pp. 203–206).

8. Name three specific words and list a more general word for each (see pp. 203–206).

9. Name three ways to further develop any cause or effect in this paragraph. Consider action, active verbs, dialogue, specific words, sensory details, description of person or setting, revealing thoughts or emotions, and further explanation.

WRITING A CAUSE OR EFFECT PARAGRAPH
Summarizing the Assignment

Teaching Idea
AWW recommends writing about either causes *or* effects, to help students with focus and substantive development, but, of course, a student might deal with both causes *and* effects in a paragraph or essay.

Write a single paragraph of 250 to 300 words that explains the reasons (causes) something happens or the results (effects) that follow from it. While writers often develop their work with both causes and effects, to keep your paragraph focused, choose either causes *or* effects. Include a focused topic sentence that predicts causes or effects, use three or four well-developed major examples (causes or effects), and end with a sentence that links to the topic sentence and adds a final (expanded) thought about it.

Establishing Audience and Purpose

HINT: Targeting an audience will help focus your material.

One of the best ways to focus this paper is through audience and purpose. Aside from your instructor, consider who else might be interested in your topic—for example, your parents, a good friend, or a group to which you belong. (For more on audience profiling, see pp. 9–11.) If you chose as your topic the causes of poor grades in college, you could write for students who are not doing well in school. They might be interested in your insights, and you would then have a purpose: to inform these students and perhaps help them improve their academic performance. At a more general level, a cause or effect paper has one or more of the following purposes:

- To understand a situation
- To solve a problem
- To predict an outcome
- To entertain
- To persuade

EFFECTS FORECASTED   Our trip to the zoo last Sunday taught my daughter a lot about exotic creatures, helped her to overcome her fears of large animals, and helped us grow closer together.

NO EFFECTS WORD OR FORECASTING   Before our trip to the zoo last Sunday, I would not have believed so many positive experiences could come from one place.

After writing a topic sentence, look again at your list of causes or effects and make decisions, limiting your list to three or four points. Think about how these points might best be organized, and write a working outline. Brian crossed out several effects and then combined 2 with 3 and 4 with 5 to arrive at a manageable working outline with three points:

Teaching Idea
Have several students write their lists on the board while the class discusses ways to combine and arrange the causes or effects.

Effects

1. Learn about exotic animals
2. Overcome her fears
3. Encourage kind treatment of animals
4. Have fun together—bond
5. Reduce boredom
6. ~~Teach her about larger world~~
7. ~~Increase environmental awareness~~

Working Outline for "Building Memories"

A. Learning about exotic animals
B. Overcoming fear of large animals
C. Bonding with a parent

You will introduce each cause or effect with a subtopic sentence linked to the paragraph by connectors like the transitions listed below. (For more on connectors, see pp. 53–58.) Before drafting, review this list.

FOR ADDING MATERIAL			
again	as well as	furthermore	likewise
also	besides	in addition	moreover
and	further	last	next

FOR GIVING EXAMPLES AND EMPHASIS			
above all	especially	in particular	one reason
after all	for example	in truth	specifically
another	for instance	it is true	surely
as an example	indeed	most important	that is
certainly	in fact	of course	to illustrate

FOR SHOWING CAUSE AND EFFECT			
accordingly	because	hence	then
and so	consequently	since	therefore
as a result	for this reason	so	thus

FOR SUMMARIZING AND CONCLUDING			
finally	in conclusion	in short	that is
in brief	in other words	largely	to summarize

ORGANIZING—SUMMING UP

1. Create a rough topic sentence to help focus your material.
2. Decide on the main causes or effects (only three or four). To do this, combine closely related causes/effects, delete unneeded ones, and add any that are needed.
3. Arrange the main causes/effects either by importance or chronologically.
4. Create a working outline.
5. Review the list of transitions (and remember the other connectors).

JOURNAL ENTRY 9.3

Write out your working topic sentence. Does it mention causes or effects? Now list your main causes or effects. Does chronological order or order of importance seem the best arrangement for the material? Why?

Drafting

HINT: You can avoid oversimplifying your topic by using qualifying words.

With the preliminary work done, you are almost ready to write your first draft. But before plunging in, review the drafting suggestions in Chapter 1 (pp. 12–13). As you write, be sure to do the following:

1. Qualify where needed, using terms like *often, many, sometimes, usually, frequently, seldom, might, could,* and *possibly.* (For more on qualifying, see pp. 397, 491.)
2. Include important causes or effects.
3. Remember that the fact that one event occurs before another does not mean one event causes the other.

HINT: Complete all points or thoughts.

4. Complete all thoughts so readers can see the cause/effect relation. If, for instance, you said that because your parents were on vacation you almost lost your job, a reader might be confused. However, if you completed the thought by explaining that your folks usually wake you in the morning so you won't be late for work, you clarify the causal connection.

JOURNAL ENTRY 9.4

Teaching Idea
Use Journal Entry 9.4 to help focus group revision, as each student directs readers to parts of the draft that she or he is concerned about.

Soon after writing your first draft, reread the assignment on page 207, and then skim the draft. Does it fit the assignment? Are there three or four causes or effects, and are they arranged effectively? What part of your draft do you like best? What part least? Answer in a paragraph.

Revising Drafts

For help with revising first, second, and final drafts, turn to Chapter 4.

ANNOTATED STUDENT MODEL: "BUILDING MEMORIES"

Teaching Idea
You may find it helpful to assign the annotated student model in stages paralleling the students' own drafting and revision.

Carefully reading the annotated student model will help clarify questions you have about your own draft.

First-Stage Draft

Brian Peraud chose parents with school-age children as an audience. He wrote a fast draft based on his working outline.

Topic sentence needs focus.

Second sentence is unneeded.

Need further focus.

Main effects are in place but need to be developed with detailed examples and further explanations.

    I had a great time with my daughter the other day. The drive over to the zoo took longer than it should have, but that didn't keep us from having a good time. First, we both learned more about foreign animals like lions and elephants. Katy learned that they live in families called prides and the females do almost all the hunting. Then the female lions bring home the food to the head of the pride and the other lions. Another good thing about our trip together was that it helped my daughter overcome fear of big animals. When she was 3, she was knocked down by a dog, and she has been nervous around dogs since. Being close to calm animals like the elephants, made her feel more relaxed. She enjoyed seeing the mother caring for her new baby. After we had been at the zoo for awhile, Katy was relaxed enough to help me feed a giraffe. It was fun watching my little girl feed the animal. The giraffe was so tall and she was so small. She held the grass out to it standing so high above the ground. As the tongue curled around the grass, Katy squealed, yet she fed the giraffe even more. Another good thing about our trip was spending playtime together. It was fun to run around, laughing at the prairie dogs and creeping up on the peacocks shimmering in the sunlight. We both had our hands slimmed by the baby goats, and Katy got a big kick out of seeing me butted from behind. We had to keep up our strength by eating. This gave us an excuse to eat all the junky zoo food we could get our hands on: hotdogs, cheese nachos, and rainbow bomb pops. This trip to the zoo helped me realize how important it is to keep building happy memories.

Teaching Idea
In the second-stage draft, have students evaluate the revised subtopic sentences and the added detailed examples. Ask what these revisions contribute to the draft.

Second-Stage Draft

Rough first drafts of cause or effect papers often have difficulties with overall focus, development, and relevant material. Note the explanations and examples added to this draft to help clarify meaning.

SPECIAL POINTS TO CHECK IN REVISING FROM FIRST TO SECOND DRAFTS

1. Check the topic sentence: topic + statement of cause or effect.
2. Check subtopic sentences: connector + cause or effect word + statement.
3. Check the concluding sentence: connector + link to topic sentence + expanded thought.
4. ~~Delete unnecessary material.~~
5. Add material for clarity, completeness, and emphasis.
6. Check connectors : transitions, repeat words, synonyms, pronouns, and references to main idea.

Topic sentence revised to clarify effects and add specific words

Unneeded second sentence deleted.

*Explanation added

Supporting examples and details added throughout

Subtopic sentences revised (and shaded to help you identify them)

*Explanation added

Dialogue added

Transitional word *most* added to show order of importance

Taking my daughter to the zoo last Sunday had three main consequences. ~~The drive over to the zoo took longer than it should have, but that didn't keep us from having a good time.~~ One important effect was that we both learned more about foreign animals. * Both Katy and I have been around dogs and cats. But neither of us has spent much time near wild animals. Going to the zoo gave us a chance to be close to and read about the big cats, elephants, rhinos, hippos, zebras, seals, and others. Katy learned that lions , for instance , live in families and that the females do almost all the hunting. They bring home the food to the dominant male and the cubs. Another benefit to our trip together was helping my daughter overcome her fear and anxiety of large animals. When she was a little girl of 3, Katy was knocked down by a dog, and she has been nervous around even small dogs since. Being close to large, calm animals like the elephants, *peacefully flapping their ears and grazing, made her feel more relaxed. She especially enjoyed seeing the mother caring for her new baby. After we had been at the zoo for awhile, Katy was relaxed enough to help me feed a giraffe. It was fun watching my little girl—all 41 inches of her—holding grass out to the giraffe. This is an animal standing 16 feet above the ground! As the tongue curled around the tuft of grass, Katy squealed, "Ooh, its slimy!", yet she was willing to feed the giraffe even more. But for me the most important result of our trip was just that we got to spend some playtime together. It was fun to run all over the zoo, laughing at the prairie dogs in their burrows and creeping close to the male peacocks shimmering in the sunlight. We both had our hands slimmed by the baby goats as we fed them those smelly little green pellets, and Katy got a big kick out of seeing me butted from behind. We knew we had to keep up our strength by eating. This gave us an excuse to eat all the junky zoo food we could get our hands on: hotdogs, cheese nachos, rainbow bomb pops, and a wad of cotton candy that would have choked a hippo. Besides being great fun, our trip helped me again to realize how important it is in any relationship—but especially for a parent and child—to keep building happy memories.

Concluding sentence revised to connect with audience

Third-Stage Draft

This draft gave Brian the opportunity to polish his work at the word and sentence level, and to move his draft beyond good to excellent. Notice in particular how he has added more specific words to clarify images.

Teaching Idea
Many students never move their work beyond a second draft, in part, of course, because they can't see how to. This third-stage draft is uncluttered enough to allow students to focus on one or two points to try for in their own revision.

SPECIAL POINTS TO CHECK IN REVISING FROM SECOND TO THIRD DRAFTS
1. Add specific words.
2. Substitute more precise or audience-appropriate words.
3. Combine sentences for variety.
4. **Replace clutter and repeat words with synonyms and phrases.**
5. Delete unneeded words.

Title added

Building Memories

Taking my daughter to the zoo last Sunday, had three main consequences. One important effect was that we both learned more about ~~foreign~~ exotic animals. While Katy and I have been around dogs and cats neither of us has spent much time near ~~foreign~~ wild animals. Going to the zoo, gave us a chance to be close to and read about the big cats, elephants, rhinos, hippos, zebras, seals, and others. Katy learned that lions, for instance live in families called prides, and that the females— "the girls," as she said—do almost all the hunting, bringing home the ~~food~~ kill to the dominant male, and the cub. Another benefit to our trip together was helping my daughter overcome her fear ~~and anxiety~~ of large animals. When she was ~~a little girl of~~ 3 Katy was knocked down in the park by a Chow and she has been nervous around even small dogs since. Being close to large, calm animals like the elephants, peacefully flapping their ears and grazing, made her feel more ~~relaxed~~ at ease. She especially enjoyed seeing the mother caring for her new calf. After we had been at the zoo for ~~awhile~~ an hour. Katy was relaxed enough to help me feed some grass to a giraffe. It was fun watching my little girl—all 41 inches of her—holding grass out to an animal standing 16 feet above the ground!] As the dark-purple tongue curled around the tuft of grass in her hand, Katy squealed, "Ooh, its slimy!" yet she was willing to feed the giraffe even more. For me the most important result of our trip was just that we got to spend some playtime together. It was fun to run over the zoo, laughing at the little prairie dogs in there burrows and creeping close to the male peacocks shimmering blue-green in the sunlight. We both had our hands slimmed by the baby pygmy goats, as we fed them those smelly little green pellets, and Katy got a big kick out of seeing me butted from behind. [To keep up our strength, we just had to eat all the junky zoo food we could get our hands on: hotdogs, cheese nachos, rainbow bomb pops, and a wad of cotton candy that could have choked a hippo.] Besides being great fun, our trip to the zoo helped me again to realize how important it is in any relationship—but especially for a parent and child—to keep building happy memories.

Final-Editing Draft

By this point, Brian's draft is in great shape, and he can shift into low gear, moving slowly, line by line, looking for each error in grammar, spelling, and punctuation, and using his Improvement Chart to help find pattern errors.

SPECIAL POINTS TO CHECK IN EDITING FINAL DRAFTS

1. Misspellings
2. Soundalike words
3. Missing words
4. Wrong words
5. Sentence fragments
6. Comma splices/run-ons
7. Faulty capitalization
8. Incorrect apostrophes
9. Comma(s) needed
   a. Introductory words/phrases/clauses
   b. Nonessential word groups
   c. Main clauses with coordinating conjunction
10. Unneeded commas

Teaching Idea
You might focus students on the unneeded comma errors that Brian corrected in his final draft. If the class has been practicing participial phrase sentence openers, some students may be trying to set off gerund phrases used as subjects, as the first few number 10 errors illustrate.

Building Memories

Taking my daughter to the zoo last Sunday,[10] had three main consequences. One important effect was that we both learned more about exotic animals. While Katy and I have been around dogs and cats,[9a] neither of us has spent much time near wild animals. Going to the zoo,[10] gave us a chance to be close to and read about the big cats, elephants, rhinos, hippos, zebras, seals, and others. Katy learned that lions, for

ALTERNATE WRITING ASSIGNMENTS

These assignments show some of the ways we use cause-and-effect analysis and may help you find a topic. For this assignment, be sure to do the following:

1. Choose either causes or effects, and mention your focus in the topic sentence.

2. Beware of oversimplifying and underexplaining.

3. Introduce each main cause or effect with a subtopic sentence.

4. End with a concluding sentence that expands the main idea of the paper.

Teaching Idea
Ask students to carefully consider their purpose if they choose Alternate Writing Assignment 1. An author whose purpose is essentially to vent frustration will be handling a paragraph differently than an author with a persuasive intent.

ASSIGNMENT OPTIONS

1. Write a letter of complaint dealing with a situation, service, or product. For example, think of a time when you were dissatisfied with some service (lawn care, car repair, haircut) or product and discuss the outcome (effects). You might focus your effects merely on reporting, say, the stalling of your car after a tune-up or mention in detail what you will do about the poor service if it is not remedied (call the Better Business Bureau, sue, go to small claims court).

2. Write about the causes or effects of a trend in society. For example, you might have noticed an increase in young women smoking and speculate on why (advertising targeting young women, schools cutting back on health education, role models who smoke). Or you might have noticed a decrease in attendance at concerts or sporting events. What is causing it? What might be the results? Consider trends affecting entertainment, sporting events, employment, education, interpersonal relationships, consumer products, child care, health care, and other areas.

3. Write about the long-term effects someone has had on you. Think about a person who has been important in your life—a teacher, coach, boss, parent, or child—and tell about the effects he or she has had on you. For instance, you might discuss how your child helped you learn patience, humility, and appreciation for the little things in life. Or you may remember a coach who was a tyrant—overly demanding, belittling, verbally abusive—and who caused you to consciously avoid such behavior.

4. Choose a problem and find solutions to it. Think about a problem that has troubled you recently. For example, tuition costs might be hard for you to meet. How did you or will you handle this difficulty? You might continue to work part- or full-time, pick up more hours, ask for a loan from a parent or friend, apply for a bank loan, apply for a Pell grant, or buy 10 more lottery tickets and hope. The solutions will be the effects generated by the problem.

5. Select what might seem to be a small cause and look for dramatic effects. When you build your chain of effects, think about how each action affects the one that follows it. For instance, many imported species of plants and animals have ravaged their new environment. In the late 1800s, rabbits were introduced into Australia but rapidly decimated the local animal population by eating so much of the vegetation. Common dandelions have caused many lawn lovers to pour herbicides onto their grass, and when the chemicals run off or seep into the water table, another chain of destruction begins.

You might want to use the two accompanying photos to write a paragraph on effects that begin with people overusing pesticides and herbicides. Toxic runoff pours from a drainage pipe in the first illustration; fish have been killed by it in the second. What other effects might come about from this pollution? Think of other animals—large and small—that live in the river and the animals that depend on them as a food source. Also consider how the poisoned water might affect people who use the river for drinking water and recreation.

Explaining Activities: Doing Them, Understanding Them

What Are We Trying to Achieve and Why?

Setting the Stage

Teaching Idea
Many students are drawn toward how-to-do topics, perhaps because they seem simpler, but how-to-understand topics are often more challenging and interesting. You might encourage students to try both approaches before settling on one.

In the photos on the preceding page, a boy is preparing to focus his telescope on a full moon. But before he can focus the image, he will have to follow a few simple steps: loosening lock knobs, using the viewfinder to target the moon, tightening the lock knobs, and then adjusting the focus knob. If you have never handled a telescope, do you think you could follow instructions telling how to focus one? When we try to explain or understand an activity—how something is done or happens—we are involved in **process analysis,** the assignment for Chapter 10.

Process analysis can help us do something or help us understand something. An explanation of how to focus a telescope—how to physically turn knobs, point the lens, and make fine adjustments—is an example of process analysis that enables *doing*. An explanation of how the telescope works—how the lenses and mirrors reflect and refract light, for instance—is an example of process analysis that furthers *understanding*.

Linking to Previous Experience

We live in a world filled with processes to do and understand. In nature alone, we can see thousands of processes operating daily, from the cycle of rainfall and evaporation that transfers water back and forth between the atmosphere and the earth to the transformation of caterpillars into butterflies. We busily pursue our own daily routines, seldom thinking about the steps needed to complete them—until something makes them difficult (say, having an arm in a sling) or until we need to learn a new routine or explain one of our routines to someone.

School, too, has given you experience with process analysis as you have learned both to do and to understand. When you solved problems in algebra class, listing the steps, or learned about photosynthesis in biology, you used and honed your process-analysis skills.

Determining the Value of Process Analysis

Teaching Idea
Linking new knowledge to old throughout the text is a good teaching strategy, and the chapter introductions can help you achieve this. If you have worked with Chapter 9, you might, in particular, want to connect cause and effect with process analysis.

Process description is useful in many ways. For example, while you rely on cause-and-effect analysis to decide that the car won't start because the battery is dead, you need process skills to charge or replace the battery. On the job, you may regularly learn new procedures and explain procedures to fellow workers. In school, also, you often explain processes in detail; for example, students training to be dental assistants must detail every step of the preparation for a root canal.

Process skills also help us satisfy our curiosity. We wonder about the vast reaches of space and the beginning of existence; we are also curious about the smallest processes, down to the subatomic level. Learning to examine, understand, and do is an essential survival skill, and it is one of the traits that makes us human.

Teaching Idea
Journal Entry 10.1 can be handled in whole-class discussion or in groups. It will help introduce students to several key elements of process narration, including steps and definitions.

JOURNAL ENTRY 10.1

List two activities that you are familiar with, and write out six steps a friend could follow to complete or understand each one. Were six steps enough? Too many? What words in your steps might need to be explained further?

Developing Skills and Exploring Ideas in Process-Analysis Paragraphs

To learn to write effective process papers, you need to practice the following:

1. Listing all the necessary steps
2. Explaining the steps thoroughly, giving reasons and warnings
3. Defining all the terms
4. Avoiding monotonous sentence patterns

Listing All Necessary Steps

When we try to understand or perform an activity, we need to know all the important steps. If any are missing, we won't be able to understand or perform the activity. Consider, for example, this list of steps for changing a flat tire:

1. Jack up the car.
2. Take the tire off.
3. Put the spare on.
4. Jack the car down.
5. Put away the jack.

Is this enough information for someone who has never changed a tire to get the job done? Or might we need a few more steps, like these:

1. Make sure you are on a level surface.

2. Locate the jack, lug wrench, and spare tire.

3. Check to see if the spare is sufficiently inflated.

4. Locate the correct jacking point.

5. Block the wheel across from the flat tire.

6. Set the parking brake.

7. Break the lug nuts free.

8. Position the spare tire within arm's reach.

9. Raise the car slowly several inches higher than needed to remove the flat.

10. Check to make sure the car is stable.

11. Remove the lug nuts, leaving the top nut for last.

12. Remove the wheel.

13. Put on the spare.

14. Finger tighten the lug nuts in a crosswise fashion.

15. Lower the car till the tire touches the ground.

16. Fully tighten the lug nuts.

17. Fully lower the jack and pull it away.

18. Unblock the opposite wheel.

19. Put the tire, jack, and lug wrench away.

Just as we often need complete steps to understand or perform an activity, so do those we write for. When you are not sure how much your readers know about an activity, include *more* information.

Teaching Idea
After students create their lists in Activity 10.1, have them look for steps that seem to belong together and any steps that seem repeated. If they cross out the repetitious material and group some of the steps, they will be on their way to organizing a process paper.

ACTIVITY 10.1 Listing All Necessary Steps

Pick one of the following processes and list all the steps the stated audience would need to complete it.
Answers will vary.

1. Process (to perform): how to build a campfire

   Audience: 18-year-old who has never built a campfire

Gather dry wood, dry tinder, and newspaper	Check to make sure there is not a high wind
Stack close at hand	Have water close by in case fire gets out of hand
Clear a circle 18 to 24 inches in diameter	Light fire at the base
Ring the space with rocks or medium-size logs	Be ready to add more newspaper and dry tinder
Place tinder and newspaper in center of fire ring	When fire begins to catch, blow gently to help it
Stack wood on tinder in layers, smaller to bigger	As fire catches, keep adding wood as needed
While stacking, leave air spaces	

2. Process (to perform): how to housebreak a puppy

   Audience: 10-year-old who has never had a pet

Decide if you will paper train or train for outside	Take puppy on 20-minute walk each night
If training for outside, be ready to walk dog a lot	If puppy messes in house, only scold him if you catch him in act or immediately thereafter
Provide food and water at times you can watch dog	If he messes, scold, and then take outside
Right after puppy eats or drinks, take him outside	Be alert to signs that puppy wants to go outside
Wait outside for dog to pee or poop or both	Take puppy outside for brief outing many times a day
Praise puppy and give him a treat	
Never feed close to bedtime	

3. Process (to perform): how to buy a used car

Audience: 16-year-old who has just gotten her driver's license

Decide whether to consider a dealership	Size up the owner—responsible/credible?
Call in response to ads in newspaper	Check car carefully, inside and outside
Ask all necessary information about vehicle	Ask owner questions about maintenance and accidents
Determine how much you can afford	Test drive
Have money in your checking account	Have inspected
If not paying by check, bring cash	Negotiate price
Visit owner	Have cash but be ready to walk

4. Process (to understand): childbirth

Audience: First-time expecting parents

Uterine contractions begin and cervix begins to dilate	Child emerges from mother's vagina
Contractions progress, becoming more regular	Physician cuts umbilical cord
Cervix continues to dilate, averaging 13 to 14 hours for first pregnancies	Baby takes first breath
When dilation reaches 9 to 10 centimeters, baby begins to move out of the uterus	Within a few minutes, placenta is expelled
Placenta breaks and amniotic fluid escapes	
Baby slowly moves through cervix with each contraction and "push" of the mother	
Pain increases with infant's passage	

Explaining Steps Thoroughly

Teaching Idea
If students are still uncertain about warnings and explanations, you can ask them about several steps/suggestions in buying a used car, from Activity 10.1. For example, ask why a person should try to avoid a dealership or why it might be important to have the used car inspected before negotiating a price.

Beyond listing the steps necessary to complete a process, we must explain the steps fully. It does little good to give an instruction such as "locate the correct jacking point" if readers don't know what "correct jacking point" means. If you clarify the meaning by stating that it is one of four spots on the vehicle reinforced to bear the car's weight and either list the spots or include a picture, then they might be able to accomplish the step.

Aside from clarifying the meaning of a step, we must often explain the "why" behind it for curious readers. For instance, why would a person changing a tire want to remove the top lug nut last? If you explain that it is to keep the wheel centered so that it won't slip off from a side, you satisfy readers' curiosity, making them more likely to follow your suggestions.

Also, we should include warnings whenever not following a step could cause problems. For example, you might warn readers not to fully tighten the lug nuts on a tire while the vehicle is suspended because they risk knocking the car off the jack.

ACTIVITY 10.2 Explaining Steps Thoroughly—Giving Reasons and Warnings

Look at the steps you wrote for a process in Activity 10.1, and decide which need to be clarified for the stated audience. For each step needing clarification, in the relevant space, write the step number and rewrite the step so that it includes an explanation, reason, or warning. (Keep in mind that one clarification may make another one necessary.)

Answers will vary.

Process: _buying a used car_

Audience: _16-year-old_

Explanation(s)/reason(s):

Why bring cash (check), negotiate, and be ready to walk away?

People selling used cars often don't want to spend any more time on the process than they have to. If you are ready with the money, it can help the owner to decide in your favor. Always negotiate because this is part of the buying/selling game. Most people ask for more than they think they can get and expect to take somewhat less. Being prepared not to buy strengthens your position in the negotiation game. Also, you may need some time to cool down if you are overly excited by the deal.

Warning(s):

Why avoid dealerships, have an inspection, and size up the owner?

Dealerships have a lot more experience selling cars than you have buying them. They are selling for a profit and often simply lie, so you get stuck with the bad deal.

Even if the vehicle looks and sounds good, it might have many problems. An expert inspection increases your chances of buying smart. Some people are more inclined to lie than others, and many people will simply withhold information—caveat emptor.

Defining All Terms

Process analysis calls for clearly defining all terms. Just because a word is familiar to you or others does not mean that everyone knows it. For example, would you expect someone who has never changed a tire to be able to identify a lug wrench, lug nuts, or wheel block? Further, could you expect the person to know how to use the lug wrench or set the wheel block? Because you cannot know whether readers understand all your terms, you must define any that you think might be a problem for them. (For more on defining terms, see pp. 358–365.)

ACTIVITY 10.3 Defining All Terms

Again using the process from Activity 10.1, list which terms *probably* and which terms *possibly* need to be defined for the stated audience. Next, explain why you separated the "possibles" from the "probables." Remember, there is no sure way to predict readers' knowledge, so you must use your best judgment on when to define terms.

Teaching Idea
The example in Activity 10.3
will give students another
idea for writing about a
process to understand.
Students might also choose
one of their own topics here.

EXAMPLE

Process: earthquake

Audience: seventh-grade earth science class

Probable terms to define: plate tectonics, seismic activity, crust, magma, faults, Richter scale, seismograph, epicenter

Possible terms to define: shock, aftershock, earth's core

Why I separated the terms: The probable terms to define are common in the scientific community, and many adults would know them, but most 12- and 13-year-olds would not. The possible terms to define are more familiar and likely to be understood through the context of the discussion.

Answers will vary.

Process: buying a used car

Audience: 16-year-old

Probable terms to define: Blue Book value, caveat emptor, title transfer, potential mechanical defects: "valve job," "frame realignment," "losing compression," "worn timing chain"

Possible terms to define: notary public, cash, credible owner

Why I separated the terms: Probable terms to define: Many 16-year-olds have heard these terms, but most have not had to learn yet what they mean.

Possible terms to define: Notary: The reader has probably heard the term and knows that notaries certify legal documents, but the reader may not know where to find a notary or why one might be important.

Cash: Some readers will not realize that "cash" does not necessarily mean dollar bills and might have a problem carrying, say, $5,000 in hundred-dollar bills around.

Credible owner: Some young people will need more than a word or two to warn them away from a seller who is likely to lie to them—for example, a professional small-time dealer working out of his or her home.

Avoiding Monotonous Sentence Patterns

Have you ever found yourself reading through a process explanation—say, instructions for assembling a bookcase or learning to factor in algebra—and exclaiming, "Hey, this is exciting! I can't wait to read more"? If not, it is in part because most process instructions try to be as businesslike as possible; their purpose is to get a job done, not entertain. However, even the driest subject can be made more (or less) readable through the sentence structures used. Consider the following paragraph excerpt on putting up a wall shelf:

> First, I gather all my supplies. Second, I set them within reach. Third, I begin to attach the shelf brackets to the wall. Fourth, I pencil in each hole in the mounting brackets against the wall. I do this so I can drill in the correct spots. Fifth, I choose a bit one size smaller than the bracket screws. Sixth, I drill holes about half the length of the screws. I do this to help the screws grip more firmly. Seventh, I screw the brackets into the wall. Eighth, I begin the steps for attaching the shelf.

If your response is "Fairly clear writing but boring," then how can we make the information more readable? Why not combine sentences to vary their length and beginnings, and delete the monotonous string of *first, second, third,* and so forth?

> Once I have gathered all of my supplies, I set them within reach and begin the process of attaching the shelf brackets to the wall. First, I place the mounting brackets on the marks that I previously measured for the height of the shelf, and then I pencil in each bracket hole so I can drill in the correct spots. With a bit the next size smaller in diameter than the bracket screws, I drill holes about one-half the length of the screws (the smaller holes help the screws grip the wall more firmly and eliminate the problem of making holes too big for the screws). Now I line up the brackets with the holes and screw the brackets into the wall, being careful not to overtighten the screws so I don't pull them out of the soft drywall. With the brackets secure on the wall, it's time to attach the shelf.

The revised paragraph is more readable and therefore more interesting. Notice that this rewriting made it possible to include more explanations, so the paragraph is also more informative. Chapter 18 focuses on sentence variety, but you already know many ways to achieve variety and improve writing.

ACTIVITY 10.4 Avoiding Monotonous Sentence Patterns

Teaching Idea
Process-analysis instructions can quickly deteriorate into virtual outlines, but sentence variety can help prevent this problem. Whether or not you are working through Chapter 18 with your students, you might want to remind them of sentence variety (and punctuation) with Activity 10.4.

Teaching Idea
If you want students to begin focusing on grouping steps, you might ask them to separate the steps in Activity 10.4 into three groups, each introduced with a subtopic sentence, as the suggested answer in this instructor's edition demonstrates.

Read the following paragraph of 10 short sentences. Then rewrite it in the space provided, combining some sentences to vary sentence beginnings and length. Begin with a topic sentence. Feel free to add information or explanations that would strengthen the paragraph. Consult Chapter 18 for help with sentence variety, or simply try to combine sentences by using some of the following words:

because, although, as, if, since, when, where, while
and, but, so, or, for, nor, yet
who, which, that
first, second, third, last, next, then, now, after, as a result, later, soon, before, especially
Answers will vary.

Process: how to guarantee that you will get a ticket after being pulled over for speeding

Audience: a younger brother or sister

Monotonous version:

> First, act like you are trying to hide something. Second, avoid eye contact with the officer. Third, loudly protest that you weren't speeding. Fourth, refuse to show your driver's license. Fifth, throw your license at the officer. Sixth, accuse the officer of harassing you. Seventh, accuse the officer of just trying to fill a ticket quota. Eighth, try to bribe the officer. Ninth, swear at the officer. Tenth, act like you want to punch the officer.

Rewritten version with greater sentence variety:

If you want to be sure to get a ticket after you have been pulled over for speeding, just follow these easy steps. You can begin by mildly annoying the officer. Act like you are trying to hide something under the seat as he or she approaches the car. If the officer fails to ask about the suspicious behavior, still be sure to avoid eye contact and loudly protest that you weren't speeding (you might want to begin swearing). Now that you have the officer annoyed, guarantee the ticket with these pointers. First, refuse to show your driver's license; then change your mind and throw the license out the window. Next, tell the officer that he is harassing you, that you were only keeping up with the traffic and that you think he is just trying to fill his monthly quota. Now, of course, the ticket is assured, but if you want to push for more, like jail time, try these pointers. First, try to bribe the officer, and when that doesn't work, begin calling him or her names. Finally, get out of your car and try to hit the officer. Congratulations, you have just earned not only a ticket but also a ride to jail.

Process-Analysis Paragraphs: Analyzing Student Models

The following model paragraphs will help you write process papers. "A Boy's Best Friend" and "Recipe for a Red-Hot Sunday" are how-to-do paragraphs; "Staying Alive," the annotated model, is a paragraph about a process to be understood.

Process papers that tell how to do something often use the word *you*, referring to the reader. In addition to being directly stated, *you* is implied in commands ("Keep the heat at 350 degrees"—meaning *you*, the reader, must keep the heat at 350). Another approach is to use *I* throughout. "A Boy's Best Friend" uses *I*, and "Recipe for a Red-Hot Sunday" uses *you*. "Staying Alive" largely avoids both *I* and *you*, an approach that is common in writing about processes to be understood.

➡ Prereading Exploration for "A Boy's Best Friend"

Teaching Idea
To help students generate ideas, you can remind them of the many things that children build, such as "forts" made of cardboard boxes or pillows, bird feeders/houses, tree houses, dollhouses, and animal cages.

Steve Oh chose a topic from his childhood in rural Korea. He knew the topic would be manageable and thought his paragraph might appeal most to young men in any culture who had similar childhood experiences of making "weapons" for fun and as a way to gain some control over their environment.

Do you remember as a child making anything that was particularly special to you? List one thing that you made along with six steps or more that went into it. Answers will vary.

_____

_____

A Boy's Best Friend

Living in the country as a child, I longed for a slingshot to play and hunt with, and finally decided I would make one. Collecting the materials for my treasure, though, did not come easy. It required the most perfectly forked branch from an oak tree, a square of leather to hold the stone, and a piece of rubber band. Any old rubber band would not do, though; it had to be surgical tubing, light brown and hose shaped, for the power I wanted. To obtain this rarity, I biked half an hour into town to the drugstore, after begging the money from my older brothers. My brothers also helped me find the best-shaped and healthiest-looking branch from a nearby forest. Because the only leather I could find was my dad's belt, I secretly cut off a two-inch length from the end of it, praying that he would not notice. Finally, I was ready to construct my prize. With instructions from my brothers, I sawed the three ends of the oak branch to form a capital Y, each section approximately 6 inches long. Next, I peeled away the rough brown bark and sanded it with a medium grade of sandpaper until it was smooth as silk. Using the Korean equivalent to a pocketknife, on the side of the Y facing away from me, I carved notches roughly 1/8 inch deep and 1/4 inch wide about 1/2 inch from the tips. Then I wrapped the ends of the rubber band around the notches, being extra careful to tie the bands securely. (I didn't want to lose an eye if the tubing slipped from the branch when I had the slingshot fully drawn back!) With my knife I drilled a small hole in the ends of the leather patch, slipped one inch of the tubing through each hole, folded it over, and tied it together with a square knot so it, too, would not slip. My slingshot was complete. I pulled back the band to test it, let it go, and heard the best "Snap!" I could have hoped for. My childhood dream was realized, and I was ready to chase after those terrible little sparrows that had been ruining our rice crop.

—Steve Oh

POSTREADING ANALYSIS: KEY POINTS FOR BUILDING PROCESS ANALYSIS

- **Topic sentence:** names the topic and predicts how-to-do process.
- **Concluding sentence:** restates the topic and adds a final (expanded) thought.
- **Subtopic sentences:** name each <u>major step</u> and may make a <u>limiting statement</u>—for example, "<u>Collecting the materials</u> for my treasure, though, <u>did not come easy</u>."
- **Sentence connectors:** transitions (*though, also, finally*), repeat words (*slingshot*), synonyms (*treasure, prize*), pronouns (*it, he*), and reference to main idea (make one: *collecting, to obtain, to construct*).

Teaching Idea
You might stress that process instructions do not have to be dry, although there are many circumstances in which outline instructions are preferable to livelier writing.

- **Development:** action, scene and character details, sensory details, active verbs (*longed*), *-ing* words (*living, collecting*), and specific words (*oak, square, surgical tubing, 1/8 inch*); also, explanations of the examples ("it had to be surgical tubing, light brown and hose shaped, for the power I wanted").
- **Warnings:** "I didn't want to lose an eye . . . ."

➡ Prereading Exploration for "Recipe for a Red-Hot Sunday"

Teaching Idea
It can clarify the "you"/"I" issue to contrast the "you" in "Recipe for a Red-Hot Sunday" with the "I" in "A Boy's Best Friend."

Jeff Coburn decided to write about the only dish he knows how to make. He doesn't much enjoy cooking and thought he would write to readers who feel the same way but might appreciate a quick dish for a party setting. As you read, decide if the ingredients are clear and the explanations complete.

Recipe for a Red-Hot Sunday

If you are looking to spice up those cold November football Sundays, try my easy recipe for nuclear hot chili. The first step is to gather the ingredients. With the friends who are going to be watching the game with you in mind, you will need at least 2 pounds of ground beef (90 percent lean lets you avoid draining the grease after browning). Next, pick up two 14-ounce cans of kidney beans, one of chili-hot beans, one of whole stewed tomatoes, and two 6-ounce cans of tomato paste (these items are generally located in the same aisle). Your trip through the vegetable section should produce two green peppers, two habaneros (the rocket fuel!), two garlic cloves, celery, and one white onion. For spices, try a package of McCormick's Ground Beef Chili Seasoning; the salt and pepper are probably already on your shelves. With the ingredients assembled, you are ready to prepare the kitchen and veggies for cooking. Locate a sharp serrated knife and cutting board, a 1-quart bowl for holding the chopped veggies, and a large pot like a Dutch oven (12 inches across and 6 to 8 inches deep). Now slice the green peppers, celery, and onion into bite-sized chunks. Mince the garlic and slice the habaneros into slivers, being careful not to touch your eyes, especially, until after washing your hands, unless you enjoy feeling like you are being scalded! Open the canned ingredients, and you are ready to cook. First, brown the meat (draining it if you want to), and then add the chili seasoning along with salt and pepper to your taste. Next, add the garlic, peppers, tomatoes, and paste, and stir them all thoroughly. Let this mixture simmer for about 30 minutes, and then add the three cans of beans (they are precooked, so you don't want to overcook them to mush). That's it. You're done. Now just let the pot simmer till you hear the doorbell ring, and get set for a good, hot game.

—Jeff Coburn

POSTREADING ANALYSIS: KEY POINTS FOR BUILDING PROCESS ANALYSIS

- **Topic sentence:** names the topic and predicts how-to-do process.
- **Concluding sentence:** restates the topic and adds a final (expanded) thought.
- **Subtopic sentences:** name each <u>major step</u>—for example, "The first step is to <u>gather the ingredients.</u>"
- **Sentence connectors:** transitions (*first, next, now*), repeat words (*chili*), synonyms (*mixture, recipe, pot*), pronouns (*you, who, all*), and reference to main idea (making chili: *gather ingredients, prepare the kitchen*).
- **Development:** action, scene and character details, sensory details, active verbs (*mince, slice*), *-ing* words (*being, washing*), and specific words (*November, ground beef, 6-ounce cans of tomato paste*); also, explanations of the examples ("90 percent lean lets you avoid draining the grease after browning").
- **Warnings:** "being careful not to touch your eyes . . ."
- **"You":** how-to-do instructions commonly use "you" to address the reader.

Questions for Paragraph Analysis

Note: These questions apply to both student models.

1. Which words in the topic sentence name the topic and predict a how-to-do process?

2. What words in the concluding sentence link to the topic sentence?

3. What is the expanded thought in the final sentence? (For more on the expanded thought, see pp. 49–51.)

4. Copy each subtopic sentence, and underline the <u>major step</u>. Circle connectors: transitions, repeat words, synonyms, and pronouns. (For more on connectors, see pp. 53–58.)

5. What transitional words show that the steps are arranged chronologically (see pp. 229–230)?

6. Choose part of a major step in the process and tell how the author's explaining (as opposed to detailing or action description) helps you better understand one of the author's reasons or warnings. (For more on detailing and explaining examples, see pp. 41–42.)

7. Choose part of a major step and tell how the action description and detailing help you to better understand the author's point (see pp. 229–230).

8. What warning(s) does the author include?

9. Name three specific words and list a more general word for each (see p. 229–230).

10. Name three ways to further develop any step in this paragraph. (Consider action, active verbs, dialogue, specific words, sensory details, description of person or setting, revealing thoughts or emotions, and further explanation.)

Teaching Idea
You might point out that in process instructions, a major group of steps often involves gathering supplies, an organizing device used in both these student models.

WRITING A PROCESS-ANALYSIS PARAGRAPH
Summarizing the Assignment

Write a paragraph of 250 to 300 words that explains a process or activity. Rather than give three or four examples to illustrate a point, as in Chapter 7, now your paragraph should enable your readers to do or understand something. So, instead of saying "Home-cooked meals are far superior to restaurant food," and then explaining why, you might say, "Anyone can make a great home-cooked meal if he can read a cookbook and has an hour for preparation time."

Because you want an audience to be able to follow your instructions, specific examples, clear explanations, and well-defined terms are especially important. Paragraphs will be arranged chronologically (as the clock moves), with information grouped into several major steps introduced with subtopic sentences.

Establishing Audience and Purpose

Teaching Idea
To reinforce the importance of audience awareness and defining of terms, you can remind students of Activity 10.3 as they read through these two process explanations. Also, you might ask students if the comparisons in the second version help with clarity.

Which of the following two process explanations is easier for you to understand?

A. Most pelecypods move by extending the slender, muscular foot between the valves. Blood swells the end of the foot to anchor it in the mud or sand, and then longitudinal muscles contract to shorten the foot and pull the animal forward. In most bivalves, the foot is used for burrowing, but a few creep. Some pelecypods are sessile.

B. Most creatures like clams and oysters move by extending a slender, muscular part of their bodies called a foot. The foot is often smaller than a person's little finger and works a bit like a rubber band. As the animal stretches the foot from between its two shells, it digs into the sand with one end, and then moves its body forward as the "rubber band" contracts. Most of these creatures use their foot for burrowing, but a few can move across the ground. Some are permanently fixed in one spot.

If version B is easier for you to follow, it is probably because specialized terms from version a (*pelecypods, valves, bivalves, sessile*) have been simplified. Whenever you write process explanations, you should know your audience so that you can define words that might be unfamiliar to them or use simpler terms and fully explain concepts that might be difficult.

You may have several purposes—to entertain, persuade, or inform—but explaining the process in a clear way should take top priority.

Working through the Writing Assignment

Writing Tutor: Process Analysis

Discovering Ideas

Look for something that you know well or a topic you want to know more about. Hobbies and sports offer many possibilities. We work, go to school, have families, and belong to organizations—all of which involve processes. Keeping the need for manageability in mind may also help you choose a topic. For instance,

CAUTION! Limit your topic.

explaining how a space shuttle is built would be far too broad, but discussing the installation of heat-shielding tiles on the nose might work well.

The following topics list may help you find a topic. Remember, you want to write a paper to enable readers to do or understand something.

Teaching Idea
Have students skim these lists and write down six topics that they know well enough already to write about. Often, students are surprised by how much they know.

Topics List

HOW TO:

- Decide on the right pet or housebreak it
- Break a bad habit (smoking, drinking, unhealthy eating)
- Ski moguls, pitch a tent, or get up on a surfboard
- Get along with a neighbor you don't like
- Handle an embarrassing moment in public
- Organize a garage sale
- Do something with a musical instrument (hold it, clean it, tune it), or explain how a musical instrument works
- Lose (or gain) weight, or explain how the body loses or gains weight
- Build a birdfeeder
- Plan a great vacation
- Find a deer in the woods
- Get along with backpacking/hiking partners
- Condition yourself for a demanding sport
- Deal with losing (or winning)
- Catch a trout (bass, bluegill, crappie, catfish)
- Detail a car (remove a dent, tune an engine, adjust the headlights)
- Fix a broken vacuum (or any other appliance/machine), or explain how an appliance/machine works
- Avoid a speeding ticket after being pulled over
- Ask for a raise
- Deal with angry customer or handle a "rush"
- Dress appropriately for work
- Reduce boredom on the job
- Increase your gratuity as a restaurant server, or explain how gratuities are handled/divided
- Prepare for an exam, participate in class, or take notes
- Select a major or certificate program
- Create a good excuse for tardiness or absence
- Balance your schedule as an athlete and student

In thinking about how you will approach potential topics, keep in mind these two important points:

Teaching Idea
Students often try to describe too much when initially choosing a topic; they then become frustrated and are tempted to abandon a promising topic. You might head off this reaction by showing them how to narrow their topic.

1. **Limit your topic.** Choose a small part of a larger process, or select only major points in a larger process. For example, don't try to instruct someone on how to play guitar; help her learn a scale, a chord, or a strumming method.

2. **Remember that you are writing a process paper, not an illustration.** For example, if your topic is housebreaking a pet, your topic sentence might be something like "Housebreaking a puppy requires patience, planning, and time," *not* "Several funny things happened to our household while we were housebreaking Fluffy."

HINT: Decide on an approach—to do or to understand.

Once you have tentatively decided on a topic, you need to decide whether you will be writing about a process for readers to do or to understand.

Prewriting

Teaching Idea
As you begin working with the aquarium example, ask how many students have aquariums at home. Do they think that this hobby could possibly be turned into a readable process paper?

Listing can work well at various points in the process of discovering ideas. Suppose that you choose to write about aquariums and decide to take a to-do approach. You might use listing to generate more specific ideas for possible paragraph topics:

HOW TO:

- Clean salt water/freshwater
- Set up
- Choose fish for freshwater
- Create one without a pump
- Choose all invertebrates
- Keep children safe around it

Because processes involve steps, listing is especially useful in developing ideas for a process-analysis paragraph. Suppose you choose a to-understand approach and plan to explain how an aquarium functions. You might create a list of steps like the following:

HINT: List steps in the process.

1. Aquariums run on air pumps.
2. Aquariums sometimes use external filters.
3. Aquariums often use lights (sometimes lights simulating sunlight to help plants grow).
4. Aquariums need the correct chemical balance to keep fish alive.
5. Air runs to a gang valve.
6. Air pushes water up the tubes.
7. Air runs down tubes to an undergravel filter.
8. Air bubbles breaking at the surface of the aquarium help mix oxygen with the water.
9. Water carries waste from the fish, trapping it at the bottom.
10. Water moving up the tubes draws water down through the filter.

With a list of steps in hand, you can now delete, add, and arrange material.

PREWRITING—SUMMING UP

1. Decide on several possible topics, of your own or from the topics list.
2. Think about how to write about your topic in terms of a real process—one involving steps—not general explanation.
3. Limit the process enough for a one-paragraph paper.
4. Decide on a to-do or to-understand approach to the assignment.
5. Pick an audience.
6. Prewrite for a list of steps needed to explain your process.

JOURNAL ENTRY 10.2

Teaching Idea
Journal Entry 10.2 is an important process checkpoint and can be handled well in group discussion.

List your topic, approach (to do or to understand), audience, and steps. Is the topic limited enough? Based on your target audience, what steps may not be needed? What steps might you need to add? Explain in a paragraph.

Organizing Ideas

As always, a topic sentence is vital to focus your work. Here are several that could introduce a paragraph that explains how an aquarium functions:

A. An aquarium is a simple closed environment carefully designed to keep fish alive.

B. Have you ever wondered how it is possible for fish to survive in such a small space as an aquarium?

C. The watery world that captive fish survive in depends on two primary elements in a working system: an air pump and an undergravel filter.

Notice that all three topic sentences mention the topic (aquariums) and predict a process and that sentence c also forecasts two important points.

The next step in organizing is to make sure steps are arranged chronologically, delete any unnecessary steps, and add steps where needed. Guided by sentence C, you might modify your list in this way:

1. Aquariums run on air pumps.

2. ~~Aquariums sometimes use external filters.~~

3. ~~Aquariums often use lights (sometimes lights simulating sunlight to stimulate plant growth).~~

4. ~~Aquariums need the correct chemical balance to keep fish alive.~~

5. Air runs to a gang valve.

6. Air runs down tubes to an undergravel filter.

7. Air pushes water up the tubes.

8. Water moving up the tubes draws water down through the filter.

9. Water carries waste from the fish, trapping it at the bottom.

10. Air bubbles breaking at the surface of the aquarium help mix oxygen with the water.

Steps 2–4 are deleted because they are not essential to the discussion of the undergravel filter and air pump. Steps 8 and 10 are switched for a more logical order.

Now you must decide whether to group the steps. Many simple process explanations are clear enough without grouping, but complex explanations need the clarity that grouping steps under subtopic sentences provides. The mention in the aquarium topic sentence of the air pump and undergravel filter suggests the need to organize the steps into two groups.

One common grouping in process analysis is the **preliminary step,** or the gathering of supplies. This grouping is important in writing about processes like tearing apart a carburetor, hanging a picture, or preparing a dish. Notice how it is handled in "Recipe for a Red-Hot Sunday."

Before you draft, review the following lists of transitions and those on pages 53–55, and think about other connectors—repeat words, synonyms, and so on—you might use.

Teaching Idea
If students have listed steps in minute detail, they may have lengthy lists by now. It's helpful to organize several of their topics on the board.

HINT: Arrange material by time (or by order of importance).

HINT: Subtopic sentences may be useful for ordering and clarifying your steps.

HINT: A preliminary-steps grouping is often needed in process instructions.

FOR MOVING IN TIME			
after	first (second, etc.)	next	suddenly
afterward	immediately	now	then
at last	in the meantime	often	time passed
awhile	in the past	once	until

FOR ADDING MATERIAL			
again	as well as	furthermore	likewise
also	besides	in addition	moreover
and	further	last	next

FOR GIVING EXAMPLES AND EMPHASIS			
above all	especially	in particular	one reason
after all	for example	in truth	specifically
another	for instance	it is true	surely

FOR SHOWING CAUSE AND EFFECT			
accordingly	because	hence	then
and so	consequently	since	therefore
as a result	for this reason	so	thus

ORGANIZING—SUMMING UP

1. Create a rough topic sentence to help focus your material.
2. Eliminate steps not essential to the process.
3. Add needed steps.
4. Arrange the steps chronologically.
5. Use subtopic sentences as needed to group and clarify the steps.
6. Review the list of transitions and other connectors.

JOURNAL ENTRY 10.3

Write out your working topic sentence. Does it clearly indicate that your paragraph is about a process? List your steps in chronological order. Should you group steps? If so, write subtopic sentences, naming the major groupings.

Drafting

Teaching Idea
Before students begin drafting, you might reiterate that explanations and warnings are crucial to well-written process instructions.

Teaching Idea
This is a good place to remind students to avoid omitting the article *the,* as in: "When [the] butter, sugar, and cocoa are combined . . ."

CAUTION! Be consistent with pronoun use.

With the preliminary work done, you are almost ready to draft. But before moving ahead, review the drafting suggestions on pages 12–13. As you write, be sure to do the following:

1. Explain how some activity occurs or is performed.
2. Include needed steps so as not to lose your readers.
3. Explain the why behind steps, and give warnings of what to avoid.
4. Define any word that you think might puzzle your readers. You can often place the definition within parentheses following the term in question.
5. Decide whether you will use *you* or *I* in giving instructions or if you will largely avoid both. Be careful not to switch back and forth between the two.

> **JOURNAL ENTRY 10.4**
>
> Soon after writing your first draft, reread the assignment on page 232, and then skim the draft. Does it fit the assignment? Have you written a series of steps, probably grouped under subtopic sentences? What part of your draft do you like best? What part least? Answer in a paragraph.

Teaching Idea
Journal Entry 10.4 can give you some insight into students' progress and is also useful to help focus group revision.

Revising Drafts

For help with revising first, second, and final drafts, turn to Chapter 4.

ANNOTATED STUDENT MODEL: "STAYING ALIVE"

Carefully reading the annotated student model will help clarify questions you have about your own draft.

Teaching Idea
You might point out that Schumann defines her audience as having little knowledge of aquariums and have students assess the clarity of her explanations based on this definition.

Teaching Idea
The day before or on the day first drafts are due, try having one student read the first-stage draft aloud and then have another student read the final draft. Ask the class to characterize the two versions. What do they like about each?

Need more specific words

Avoid shift to *you* in process to be understood.

Need to define and explain more thoroughly

Missing a step

First-Stage Draft

Carla Schumann wrote about one of her hobbies, keeping freshwater fish. To help focus the paragraph, she picked as her audience people who do not know much about keeping fish as pets but who might like to.

> If you have ever wondered how fish can stay alive in an aquarium, the answer is, "Easily." Almost all aquariums use a pump to push air that it sucks in from around it into the water. This pumping action helps mix the air with the water and gets rid of fish waste. You can see how the air travels first thru one or two small tubes that are attached to the pump and end up in the water. The tubes can run directly into the water but are usually connected to a valve that splits the air into separate channels. Then the plastic tubing runs down to the undergravel filter. After the air is pushed down through the risers to the bottom of the aquarium, it immediately moves upward, making it rise up the tube. As the water rises, the water nearest the undergravel filter is drawn through the gravel and filter on the bottom of the tank. This pulls all the junk out of the water and traps it within the gravel and under the filter, so the water stays clear and the bacteria down enough for the fish to live. As the water comes from the risers, it splashes around on the surface of the water in the aquarium, which in turn speeds up the mixing of oxygen into the water. This process of air mixing with water keeps the tank clean and the fish lively.

Second-Stage Draft

When drafting process explanations, we often leave out steps or include unneeded ones, as is the case with Carla's first draft. Other common difficulties are underexplaining steps and not defining important terms. Role-playing your audience and/or having another person read the draft will help you with these problems.

SPECIAL POINTS TO CHECK IN REVISING FROM FIRST TO SECOND DRAFTS
1. Check the topic sentence: topic + indication of process.
2. Check subtopic sentences (if applicable): connector + major step grouping.
3. Check the concluding sentence: connector + link to topic sentence + expanded thought.
4. ~~Delete unnecessary material.~~
5. Add material for clarity, completeness, and emphasis (remember definitions).
6. Check connectors : transitions, repeat words, synonyms, pronouns, and references to main idea.

Topic sentence revised

*Explanation added

Subtopic sentence clarified

Step in the process added and explained

Subtopic sentence added

*"Filter" defined

*Explanation added

If you have ever wondered how fish can stay alive in a small glass case the answer is, "Easily." The process begins with a pump to push *ordinary room air that it sucks in from around it into the water. This pumping action helps mix the air with the water and gets rid of fish waste. You can see how the air travels first thru one or two small tubes that are attached to the pump and end up in the water. The tubes can run directly into the water but are usually connected to a valve that splits the air into separate channels. These channels have a short length of plastic tubing connected to them. The tubing is in turn connected to thin, plastic rods that descend through larger plastic tubes that attach to the filter on the floor of the aquarium. The undergravel filter is the second most important piece of equipment in the process of keeping the water livable for the fish and clear enough for pleasant viewing. *(This simple piece of plastic covers the bottom of the aquarium, resting against the glass and is covered with a layer of gravel.) After the air is pushed down through the risers to the bottom of the aquarium, it immediately moves upward. *This creates a slight pull on the surrounding water, which causes it to rise upward through the tube. As the water rises, the water nearest the undergravel filter is drawn through the gravel and filter on the bottom of the tank. This pulls all the junk out of the water and traps it within the gravel and the filter, so the water stays clear and the bacteria down enough for the fish to live. As the water comes from the top of the risers, it splashes around on the surface of the water in the aquarium, which in turn speeds up the mixing of oxygen into the water. This simple cycling of air down to the bottom and up to the top does not account for all aquarium maintenance, but it is the most essential process in keeping captive fish alive and healthy.

Concluding sentence revised

Note the expanded thought.

Third-Stage Draft

If you want your work to move beyond good to excellent, this third draft gives you that opportunity. With most of the major concerns taken care of, you can now improve your word choices and sentence variety, and get rid of the clutter phrases that so often slip into rough drafts.

Teaching Idea
This third-stage draft clearly illustrates how many specific words might still be needed in a developing draft to improve clarity and readability.

SPECIAL POINTS TO CHECK IN REVISING FROM SECOND TO THIRD DRAFTS
1. Add specific words.
2. Substitute more precise or audience-appropriate words.
3. Combine sentences for variety.
4. **Replace clutter and repeat words with synonyms and phrases.**
5. Delete unneeded words.

Staying Alive

If you have ever wondered how fish can stay alive in a small glass case, for years, the answer is—easily. The process begins with a pump to push ordinary room air into the water of an aquarium. This air travels first thru one or two narrow clear plastic tubes that are attached to the pump, and end up in the water. The tubes can run directly into the ~~water~~ **aquarium,** but are usually connected to what is called a "gang valve" that splits the air into several outlets. These outlets have a short length of plastic tubing connected to them and the tubing in turn is connected to thin hollow plastic rods that descend through larger plastic tubes called risers ~~connected~~ **attached** to the undergravel filter on the floor of the aquarium. The undergravel filter is the second most important piece of equipment in the process of keeping the water livable for the fish and clear enough for pleasant viewing. (This simple piece of slotted plastic covers the bottom of the ~~aquarium~~ **tank** from side to side, resting against the glass, and is covered with a one- to two-inch layer of gravel.) After the air is pushed down thru the risers to the bottom of the aquarium, it immediately ~~rises~~ **bubbles** upward, causing the surrounding water to rise ~~upward~~ through the tube. As some water moves toward the surface that water

Title added

You used to connect with reader in topic sentence.

You removed to cut pronoun shift in body

Sentences combined for variety and flow

Parantheses used to add definition

More accurate words substituted

☐ 12. Have you used synonyms for words that are repeated too often?

☐ 13. Have you cut unneeded words?

☐ 14. Have you written an interesting title? Have you checked its capitalization?

☐ 15. Have you prepared your paper using the format expected by your instructor? (Check to see if you need a title page, use double space, leave at least a 1-inch margin, and use a 12-point font.)

☐ 16. Have you edited your work closely (including having at least one other person proofread)? Have you checked your Improvement Chart for pattern errors?

☐ 17. Have you looked for errors involving the following: misspellings, soundalike words, missing words, wrong words, sentence fragments, comma splices/run-ons, faulty capitalization, incorrect apostrophes, missing commas, and unnecessary commas?

Chapter Summary

1. Writers use process analysis to examine an activity so that others might understand or perform it.

2. Knowing how to understand, explain, and do is a basic survival skill.

3. Writing for a specific audience is critical in process analysis.

4. Process instructions require a complete list of steps.

5. Each step or suggestion must be explained clearly and thoroughly.

6. Wherever needed, warnings must be provided.

7. Clarifying terms is essential. When readers might not understand a term, a definition should be given.

8. Sentences should be varied to avoid monotonous sentence patterns.

9. Most process instructions are organized chronologically.

10. Grouping steps using subtopic sentences is often necessary.

11. The topic sentence should state the topic and predict a process explanation.

12. Writing is never complete until it has been carefully revised and edited.

ALTERNATE WRITING ASSIGNMENTS

Here are some additional process topics that may be of interest. For this assignment, be sure to do the following:

1. Write practical instructions for doing a task, or simply explain how something is done or functions.

2. List and explain steps, and, where appropriate, give warnings.

3. Define any terms that might be unfamiliar to your audience.

4. Use a topic sentence, link sentences, and conclude with an expanded thought.

What Are We Trying to Achieve and Why?

Setting the Stage

Teaching Idea
Having students brainstorm for similarities and differences between the two photos can help them begin thinking about comparison and contrast.

What similarities and differences do you see between the two photos here? There are obvious similarities: Both show a medical examination underway; a doctor is using a stethoscope to check a patient's heart. In addition, both doctors are African American, both patients appear relaxed, and both pairs are alone. There are also some obvious differences: adults versus children and therefore a real doctor versus a child who is role-playing, females versus males, and a patient who is African American versus one who is not. Whenever we notice similarities and differences between two people, places, events, objects, or ideas, we are making a comparison and contrast—the assignment for Chapter 11. With **comparison,** the focus is on similarities; with **contrast,** it is on differences.

Linking to Previous Experience

We all have a wealth of experience with comparing and contrasting. From the 3-year-old child comparing two video covers and picking the one that most resembles her much-loved *Aladdin* film, to the young couple comparing and contrasting houses as they search for a first home, people compare and contrast daily. On the job, we discover important similarities and differences as quickly as possible. If the new boss begins to seem like the tyrant from a former job, you might soon be looking for other work. In school, you are asked to compare and contrast historical figures like George Washington and Thomas Jefferson, Ulysses S. Grant and Robert E. Lee, and Elizabeth I and Mary Queen of Scots. And in this text, you have practiced comparison/contrast in several ways, including by using metaphors and similes.

Determining the Value of Comparison and Contrast

Comparison/contrast skills help us every day to avoid making poor choices, like buying overripe bananas or avocados at the supermarket. In larger, more important ways, too, we need to compare and contrast critically to live a happier life. If we judge correctly from the start, we are more likely to avoid that unsuitable college, dead-end job, or unhappy marriage.

Developing the habit of comparing also improves our thinking and makes us more open to new experiences. Seeing similarities between an unfamiliar activity and an activity we already practice—say, between ice-skating and roller-skating—we might be more likely to try the new activity. As we move into the wider world of human experience, we can see how similar people are across ethnicities in our own country and across nationalities around the world. Learning to compare, to see ourselves in other people, can help us become more tolerant human beings.

Teaching Idea
You might use Journal Entry 11.1 as the basis for a class discussion on how common comparison/contrast is and to reinforce the value of having a point to make.

JOURNAL ENTRY 11.1

Summarize several recent instances in which comparison/contrast was used, either by you or by someone else (friend, teacher, radio announcer). What was being compared/contrasted: two people, places, or events? What was the reason: to inform, entertain, or persuade? Did the comparison/contrast achieve its purpose?

Developing Skills and Exploring Ideas in Comparison/Contrast Paragraphs

To learn to write effective comparison or contrast papers, you need to practice the following:

1. Making a meaningful comparison or contrast
2. Making an interesting comparison or contrast
3. Developing each topic thoroughly
4. Using transitions and other connectors

Making a Meaningful Comparison or Contrast

In all of your writing projects, you need to establish a purpose and point. Lacking either, you are likely to wander all over the landscape, getting nowhere fast. Can you determine the writer's point from the following outline?

Topic sentence: Ford and Chevy pickup trucks have a lot in common.

- Fords have engines, and so do Chevies.
- Fords have four wheels, and so do Chevies.
- Fords have beds in the back, and so do Chevies.
- Fords have cabs in the front, and so do Chevies.

- Fords have windshield wipers, and so do Chevies.
- Fords come in many colors, and so do Chevies.

Concluding sentence: I think you can see that Ford and Chevy pickups are similar.

If you said, "Yes, I see what the writer is trying to say—many times over—but so what?" your reaction is understandable. Merely listing similarities is not enough. You must have a point if you want to interest readers. The Ford–Chevy comparison could be focused in ways like the following:

- Ford and Chevy trucks are so similar that price should decide which you buy.
- Although Ford and Chevy trucks are similar in many ways, Ford has a better warranty.
- Although Ford and Chevy trucks are similar in many ways, Chevies have a better maintenance record.

Teaching Idea
Activity 11.1 includes several topics with a persuasive intent, but you might remind students that their purpose may also be to inform or entertain.

ACTIVITY 11.1 Making a Meaningful Comparison or Contrast

For each topic, brainstorm to uncover several similarities and differences. Next, write three statements that give the topic a point. Then compose a topic sentence based on one of the statements. Be sure to indicate in the topic sentence that you intend to compare/contrast. (For more on topic sentences, see pp. 36–41.)

EXAMPLE
Topic: jogging versus bicycling

Pointless topic sentence: Both jogging and bicycling are forms of aerobic exercise.

Points that could be made about this topic:

A. _Jogging is worse for a person's body than bicycling._

B. _Bicycling is more dangerous than jogging._

C. _Bicycling requires more dedication than jogging._

Possible topic sentence: _Although jogging is a convenient and inexpensive_ _form of exercise, it is far harder on a person's body than bicycling._

_____ (paragraph of _contrast_)

Answers will vary.

1. Topic: men versus women

   Pointless topic sentence: Men are a lot different from women.

   Points that could be made about this topic:

   A. _As a rule, men assert themselves more in conversation than women._

   B. _Overall, women have better manual dexterity than men._

   C. _Most men have a different management style than women._

   Possible topic sentence: _Whereas many men have a confrontational,_ _authoritarian management style, women tend to manage their_ _subordinates through dialogue and consensus._

   _____ (paragraph of _contrast_)

2. Topic: college classes versus high school classes

   Pointless topic sentence: Both college classes and high school classes require homework.

   Points that could be made about this topic:

   A. <u>Colleges offer a dangerous freedom seldom found in high schools.</u>

   B. <u>College professors are less concerned about student success than are high school teachers.</u>

   C. <u>A good student in high school is likely to be a good student in college.</u>

   Possible topic sentence: <u>The freedom in college classrooms as opposed to high school classrooms makes a college education much more difficult.</u>

   _____ (paragraph of <u>contrast</u>)

3. Topic: infatuation versus love

   Pointless topic sentence: Infatuation is different from real love.

   Points that could be made about this topic:

   A. <u>Infatuation requires a blindness not found in real love.</u>

   B. <u>Infatuation creates a fantasy about the opposite sex that love does not need.</u>

   C. <u>Infatuated people cling to one another whereas people in love can be apart.</u>

   Possible topic sentence: <u>While infatuation sometimes leads to love, the former thrives on self-deception while the latter grows through honesty.</u>

   _____ (paragraph of <u>contrast</u>)

Making an Interesting Comparison or Contrast

Teaching Idea
You might point out to students that choosing a less obvious comparison may make the paragraph more interesting not only to read but also to write.

It is easy to settle for a topic's obvious similarities or differences. For instance, in comparing a rowboat to a canoe, you might easily list similarities, such as that both carry people on water, require muscle power to move, can be used for fishing, are easy to transport, and are found on lakes and rivers. However, as in Activity 11.1, choosing an obvious comparison often leads to boring reading.

To minimize a dull approach to a topic, try this: If two topics seem alike, contrast them. If they seem different, compare them. Making a point about the rowboat–canoe comparison—say, that rowboats are superior to canoes for fishing—we could then list interesting differences to support that claim: Rowboats are more stable, provide more room for casting, will support more powerful motors, hold more gear, and are easier to anchor in moving water.

CAUTION! Avoid obvious comparisons.

ACTIVITY 11.2 Making an Interesting Comparison or Contrast

For each of the following paired topics, create a list of similarities and differences, decide which list would make the more interesting paragraph, and then write a topic sentence that has a point.

EXAMPLE
Topic: winter versus summer

| Differences | | Similarities |
Winter	Summer	Winter and Summer
Cold	Hot	Extreme temperatures
Snow	Rain	People need shelter
Plants sleep	Plants awake	Some pleasant days
Short days	Long days	School break
Animals scarce	Animals plentiful	Drought

More interesting list: similarities

Topic sentence: Although there are some obvious differences between winter and summer, the weather extremes affect people in much the same way.

Answers will vary.

1. Topic: high school versus college

| Differences | | Similarities |
High School	College	High School and College
Few electives	Many electives	Both 4 years
Long class days	Short class days	Both have teachers
Parental supervision	Self-supervision	Both have core curriculum
Less expensive	More expensive	Both award valuable credentials
Less freedom	More freedom	Both receive governmental financial support

More interesting list: differences

Topic sentence: Although both high schools and colleges deal in paper, pencils, and textbooks, the degree of freedom in each makes them different in some fundamental ways.

2. Topic: beach vacation versus mountain vacation

| Differences | | Similarities |
Beach	Mountain	Beach and Mountain
Warm	Cold	Night life
Lazy	Active	Dangers-sunburn
Sea level	Altitude	Beautiful scenery
Swimming	Skiing	Distant locations
Wildlife	Wildlife	Expensive

More interesting list: similarities

Topic sentence: Although some might think that a beach and a mountain vacation have little in common, the exotic locations, beautiful scenery, and night life make them seem similar in significant ways.

Teaching Idea
You might want to point out the difference in tone in using transitions like *nevertheless, on the contrary,* and *however* versus *but, yet,* and *though.*

FOR COMPARING			
alike	both	like	resembling
also	in the same way	likewise	similarly

FOR CONTRASTING			
after all	dissimilar	nevertheless	though
although	even though	on the contrary	unlike
but	however	on the other hand	whereas
difference	in contrast	otherwise	yet
differs from	in spite of	still	

ACTIVITY 11.4 Using Transitions and Other Connectors

Complete each sentence with a suitable transitional word.
Answers will vary.

1. I liked going to camp when I was young, _____even though_____ I missed my family a lot.

2. _____Although_____ living on my own has its advantages, it _____also_____ has its downside.

3. _____Nevertheless_____, living with a roommate can be a problem.

4. _____Still_____, many people prefer to live on the Plaza.

5. _____In spite of_____ all the preelection promises, I still don't expect much government reform.

6. The helicopter, _____however_____, is superior to the plane in at least two respects.

7. Most of my friends don't like museums, _____yet_____ I do.

8. _____Unlike_____ Carlo, Tony is energetic and enjoys being around people.

9. Bruce thinks I prefer electric guitar. _____However_____, I would rather hear acoustic.

10. Eleanor is going to medical school _____in the same way_____ her mother did.

Comparison/Contrast Paragraphs: Analyzing Student Models

The following model paragraphs will help you write comparison or contrast papers. "Two Different Worlds" shows **block organizing,** in which the writer first gives all of the examples, or points of comparison or contrast, for one of the two things being compared/contrasted and then all of those for the other thing. "Breakin' Through" and "The Joy of Simple Living," the annotated paragraph, illustrate **point-by-point organizing,** in which the writer discusses the two things being compared/contrasted together, point by point. (For more on these, see "Organizing Ideas," pp. 261–263.)

➡ Prereading Exploration for "Two Different Worlds"

Teaching Idea
The prereading questions for "Two Different Worlds" can stimulate some interesting class discussion and help students with topic ideas.

Dave Harrison decided to contrast the work demands in high school and those in college for an audience of college-bound high school seniors.

To find a topic for your paper, think about your own expectations of what college would be like versus what it is like.

Answers will vary.

1. What surprises have you had so far? _____

_____

_____

2. Have you changed your views about education, other people, or yourself since you started? If so, list your views before and after, and consider exploring the differences in a paragraph of contrast. _____

_____

_____

Two Different Worlds

I never realized how easy high school was until my first semester in college—that's when I hit the wall. High school, for the most part, was a breeze. I had no worries about homework, papers, or tests. When I knew a test was coming, I would read my notes and then ace the exam. At that time I thought I had it rough, although I probably only spent 30 total hours on homework my whole senior year. The only paper that was semidifficult was my government research essay my junior year. I was allowed to write this paper on any topic, the only requirements being to make it five to seven pages long and cite my sources. I chose to write about the extinction of the dinosaurs. This was an acceptable topic for my government research paper. I had an entire semester to finish the paper, and it still about killed me. Looking back now, I see just how easy high school was. When I started college, however, the level of work increased. I had fewer classes but ten times the homework of high school. I now know what work is. Every week I have completed lab reports for Intro to Electronics, done Internet research projects, or turned out papers for my writing class. On top of doing my lab reports, I spend from 6 to 8 hours a week doing the labs. Late nights are not uncommon anymore. Some nights I have been known to stay up till two in the morning, and sometimes I never sleep, period. Adjusting to the workload from high school to college has been a shock, and I have learned that if a student wants to learn and do well in school, he or she has to be committed.

—*David Harrison*

Teaching Idea
Throughout the discussion of comparison/contrast as a controlling pattern for a paragraph or essay, it is worth reiterating that writers often briefly compare or contrast as well as use the other patterns of development to clarify ideas.

POSTREADING ANALYSIS: KEY POINTS FOR BUILDING COMPARISON/CONTRAST

- **Topic sentence:** names and limits the topic, and predicts a comparison or contrast.
- **Concluding sentence:** restates the topic and adds a final (expanded) thought.
- **Subtopic sentences:** name each thing being compared and make a limiting statement—for example, "High school, for the most part, was a breeze."
- **Sentence connectors:** transitions (*at that time, however, now*), repeat words (*work*), synonyms (*homework, papers, tests*), pronouns (*that, this, it*), and reference to main idea (work: *easy, a breeze, no worries, semidifficult*).
- **Development:** action, scene details, active verbs (*hit*), *-ing* words (*looking*), and specific words (*government, junior*); also, explanations of the examples ("When I knew a test was coming, I would read my notes and then ace the exam").
- **Organization:** block (see "Organizing Ideas," pp. 261–263).

➡ Prereading Exploration for "Breakin' Through"

Teaching Idea
You might want to use "Breakin' Through" as a model for students who want to use their paragraphs as a means of introspection.

Comparison and contrast papers are a great opportunity to reflect on a person's life, as Gina Rizzo did in this paragraph, in which she contrasted her "roaring twenties" and late twenties. She wrote for members of her writing group, whom she felt would be interested since they were entering their twenties.

To generate possible topics, think back on your own life.
Answers will vary.

1. List one or two things you have done that surprised you, times when you behaved in a way that was indifferent, lazy, selfish, or cruel—or perhaps involved, active, generous, or kind. _____

   _____

   _____

2. If you have ever felt like a different person than you are now, write a short description of that person, and consider pursuing the topic in a paragraph of contrast. _____

   _____

   _____

Breakin' Through

Raising hell and living for the moment were all I used to care about, but now that I am moving into my thirties, life has changed. When I was just entering my twenties, I was still living at home, although nobody would have known it by the way I came and went, telling no one anything.

But I have come a long way since then. Even though I am 29 now, my mom knows where I am most of the time, not because she checks up on me but because I want her to know what I am doing. Being in touch with the family has become important to me. As a younger woman, I was always invited to the biggest and craziest parties. There is an old saying, "If you can't run with the big dogs . . ." Well, I was one of the big dogs. No one could outparty me. I don't recall when it happened, but I have lost the taste for drinking altogether. Somewhere down the road my body started rejecting the soothing liquid that I had begun to rely on too much. I don't go to the big or crazy parties anymore. My friends have quit inviting me, which is just as well. I don't much feel like partying that way now. I would rather remember my life instead of just hearing about it. Maybe the most important difference between my younger self and the woman of today is how I think about time. I used to live only in the present, never planning ahead, never saving money. I bartended for a living, so my money was spent just like I made it, one day at a time. I didn't plan vacations; I would decide the day before, and off I'd go, hopping another red-eye to Las Vegas. I would go anywhere I could afford with the money I had in my pocket. However, times have changed. I actually have a savings account now, and I just bought a plane ticket for my coming vacation two months in advance! Being more responsible with money ought to help me get a few more wants out of life, not just my needs. As I look back over my roaring twenties, I see a lot that makes me shake my head at myself, but I have realized that nobody comes into the world fully grown. We just have to inch forward, a bit at a time, hoping for the best.

—*Gina Rizzo*

POSTREADING ANALYSIS: KEY POINTS FOR BUILDING COMPARISON/CONTRAST

- **Topic sentence**: names and limits the topic and predicts a comparison or contrast.
- **Concluding sentence**: restates the topic and adds a final (expanded) thought.
- **Subtopic sentences**: name each point of contrast and make a limiting statement—for example, "When I was just entering my twenties, I was still living at home, although nobody would have known it . . ."
- **Sentence connectors**: transitions (*despite, however, although*), repeat words (*I*), synonyms (*self, woman, big dogs*), pronouns (*myself, nobody, anything*), and reference to main idea (contrast: *changed, come a long way, difference*).
- **Development**: action, scene details, active verbs (*outparty*), -*ing* words (*raising, telling*), and specific words (*twenty-nine, red-eye, Las Vegas*), also,

explanations of the examples ("my mom knows . . . not because she checks up on me but because I want her to know what I am doing").

- **Organization:** point-by-point (see "Organizing Ideas," pp. 261–263).

Questions for Paragraph Analysis

Note: These questions apply to both student models.

1. Which words in the topic sentence name the topic and predict a comparison or contrast?

2. What words in the concluding sentence link to the topic sentence?

3. What is the expanded thought in the final sentence? (For more on the expanded thought, see pp. 261–263.)

4. Copy each subtopic sentence. Underline the thing being compared or point of comparison or contrast once and the statement about it twice. Circle connectors: transitions, repeat words, synonyms, and pronouns. (For more on connectors, see pp. 53–58.)

5. List three transitional words that show comparison or contrast (see pp. 255–257).

6. Choose an example and tell how the author's explaining (as opposed to detailing or action description) helps you better understand the author's point. (For more on detailing and explaining examples, see pp. 41–42.)

7. Choose an example, and tell how the action description and detailing help you to better understand the author's point (see pp. 255–257).

8. Name three specific words and list a more general word for each (see pp. 255–257).

9. Name three ways to further develop any example in this paragraph. Consider action, active verbs, dialogue, specific words, sensory details, description of person or setting, revealing thoughts or emotions, and further explanation.

WRITING A COMPARISON OR CONTRAST PARAGRAPH
Summarizing the Assignment

Teaching Idea
You might want to assign the material in this section on the same day that you begin Chapter 11.

Write a paragraph of 250 to 300 words that compares or contrasts two people, places, events, objects, or ideas. While writers often develop their work with both comparison and contrast, to stay focused, pick either comparison or contrast. Also, choose a block or point-by-point method of arrangement; then develop the topic with detailed examples and clear explanations.

Begin the paragraph with a sentence that names the two things being compared or contrasted, indicates a comparison or contrast, and makes a limiting statement about the topic. Each major example should begin with a subtopic sentence, and the final sentence should make a clear point.

Establishing Audience and Purpose

What point do you want to make about your topic, and for whom? As we saw in Activity 11.1, it is all too easy to write a meaningless comparison or contrast. If, however, you choose a topic that you care about and present it to others whom you want to know about it, you will probably find a point. Consider how the authors in this chapter chose examples with their audience in mind. Most college-bound high school seniors would be interested in Dave Harrison's discovery about the college workload, and many young adults would be interested in Gina Rizzo's life changes. Finding a point and an audience to tell it to will make your work easier and more enjoyable.

You may write with several purposes—to entertain, persuade, or inform—but explaining the similarities or differences should be your top priority.

Working through the Writing Assignment

Discovering Ideas

Writing Tutor: Comparison/ Contrast

HINT: Search for an interesting topic, and try for a surprising slant on it.

CAUTION! Choose topics that can reasonably be compared.

Teaching Idea
Some students will enjoy the creative challenge in trying to make unlikely comparisons seem likely. It is worth a few minutes of class time to model how an "unlikely" comparison can be developed.

You can write about many topics, including two people, places, or events. Or you might pick two objects—say, an oak tree and a rose—and think about their relationship to one another. Perhaps, as in "Breakin' Through," you will compare one period of your life with another. The topic choices are limited only by your imagination and what you can develop in a single paragraph.

However, resist the impulse to choose a topic too quickly. Look for one that you care about, and think of how to develop it in a way that will interest readers. If you really want to discuss two similar family pets—say, a German shepherd and a Labrador retriever—surprise your readers by contrasting the animals. Because a dog and a cat seem so different, try comparing them.

But, while an "apples-and-oranges" comparison can make a creative paper, be careful in choosing your subjects. For example, a TV and a blender have little in common except that they both need electricity to run. A paper comparing them would be a stretch.

The following list may help you find a topic.

Topics List

- **Pets:** dog/cat, fish/turtle, parakeet/boa constrictor
- **Cars:** Camry/Taurus, SUV/van, Miata/MG
- **Consumer services:** MCI/Sprint, two cable providers, Yahoo/Web Crawler
- **Cultural traditions:** wedding: Italian/Jewish; funeral: Irish/Japanese
- **Family members:** brother/sister, mother/father, aunt/uncle
- **Food:** Korean/Thai, Creole/Italian, German/French, ballpark/movie theater
- **Homes:** childhood/current, house/apartment, mobile home/fixed home
- **Locations:** town/city, United States/other country, East Coast/Midwest
- **Stages of education:** kindergarten/high school, elementary school/college, high school/college
- **Groups:** football team/soccer team, marching band/choir, athletes/debate team
- **Colleges:** your college/any other, community college/university
- **High schools:** your high school/any other, U.S./other country
- **Teachers:** senior English/college English, geometry/algebra, history/speech
- **Courses:** welding/HVAC, nursing/nutrition, algebra/geometry
- **Jobs:** mowing lawns/waiting tables, military/civilian, clerical/manual labor, part-time/full-time

- **Employers:** hard-driving/easy-going, friendly/distant, generous/stingy
- **Potential careers:** electrical engineering/computer science, nursing/respiratory therapy, elementary education/secondary education
- **Working conditions:** current/past, indoors/outdoors, stress level for job A/for job B
- **Losing a job:** easy way/hard way, justly/unjustly

CAUTION! A pointless comparison is painful to write and read.

Prewriting

After picking a topic, you need to decide on a point for your paper. A general cluster can help with this. For example, if you chose a topic like town versus city living, you could begin with the question "What comes to mind when I think about both towns and cities?" and then write a cluster like the following:

Teaching Idea
After students have selected several topics, you might put one or two on the board and have the class develop a list of similarities and differences for them.

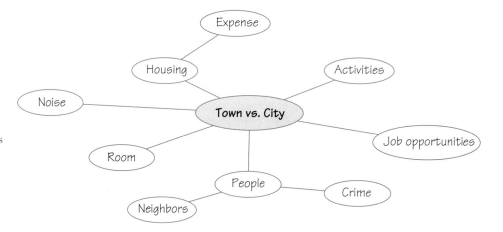

Now you can list both differences and similarities:

Differences		Similarities
Town	**City**	**Town and City**
Quieter/peaceful	Noisier	Both can be noisy
Fewer people	More crowded	People can be a problem in both
Friendlier people	Less friendly	People can be helpful in both
More living space	Less living space	Can be room enough in both
Less crime	More crime	Some crime in both
Lower cost of living	Higher cost of living	People cope with expenses in both
Lower salaries	Higher salaries	People earn an income in both
Fewer activities	More activities	Many similar activities

Listing both differences and similarities will help you see which are more interesting to you. The author of the annotated model, "The Joy of Simple Living," chose differences for her paragraph, focusing on three main examples to contrast her experiences with towns and cities.

PREWRITING—SUMMING UP

1. Pick several topics, of your own or from the topics list, and decide on one that will interest you and an audience.

2. Prewrite, including by listing, to find both similarities and differences.

3. Check your lists for focus and a point.

4. Choose either to compare or to contrast.

Teaching Idea
Journal Entry 11.2 works well in groups and can especially help those students who are having trouble deciding on a topic and focus.

JOURNAL ENTRY 11.2

List differences and similarities for the two things you will discuss. Which list will lead to the more interesting paper? Who besides your instructor might like to read about your topic? Why would the audience be interested? How will you limit the subject so it can be developed in a single paragraph?

Organizing Ideas

Write a topic sentence that includes the topic, your point, and an indication of contrast or comparison. To show how two things are alike, you can use words like *same, similar, alike, resembling, both,* and *also.* To show how two things are different, you can use words like *different, unlike, dissimilar, opposite, although,* and *whereas.*

If your rough topic sentence reads something like "Towns are different from cities," you probably have not yet decided on a point for the comparison/contrast. Go back to your prewriting lists, and see if the examples suggest a point.

From the town–city list, you might come up with a topic sentence like one of the following:

A. City living offers cultural advantages that cannot be found in small towns.

B. Although cities have many cultural advantages, small towns offer a sense of community that a city cannot easily duplicate.

C. Although small towns often have a strong sense of community, cities offer more economic opportunities.

D. For raising a family, a small town is better than a city in several ways: more room, more peace and quiet, and friendlier people.

Notice that each topic sentence indicates the topic (the two subjects—towns and cities) and the focus of the topic (the underlined words) and also tells the reader to expect a paragraph of contrast. Sentence D includes a forecasting statement (the shaded words) as well.

To organize a comparison/contrast paper, you need to pick either block or point-by-point arrangement:

- **Block method:** First state all points of comparison or contrast for one of the two subjects and then, midway through the paragraph, state all the points for the second subject, in the same order.

- **Point-by-point method:** State the first point for one subject and then the other, then the next point for one subject and then the other, and so on until you have stated all the points.

Although both methods are effective for paragraphs, longer essays are more likely to use the point-by-point method so readers don't have to try to keep in mind points from one part as they read the points in a later part.

Teaching Idea
To help students understand block versus point-by-point comparison, put one or two of their topics on the board, and have the class organize them using both methods.

Here are examples of the two methods:

Small Town versus City

Block	Point by Point
Topic sentence:_____	Topic sentence:_____

I. Small town
  1. Space for the children to play
  2. Peaceful for the whole family
  3. Relationships with the neighbors
	I. Space for the children to play
	  A. Small town
	  B. City

II. City
  1. Space for the children to play
  2. Peaceful for the whole family
  3. Relationships with the neighbors
	II. Peaceful for the whole family
	  A. Small town
	  B. City

	III. Relationships with the neighbors
	  A. Small town
	  B. City

Concluding sentence: _____	Concluding sentence: _____

In the block organization, the first half of the paragraph discusses three points about small town living, and the second half discusses the same three points about city living. In the point-by-point organization, the three points are discussed one at a time in relation to both town and city.

To show how these methods actually work, we can use material from "The Joy of Simple Living," the annotated model. (The author herself used the point-by-point method; that example has been excerpted, and the block example adapted.) Notice that the two paragraphs have the same topic sentences and the same concluding sentences.

Teaching Idea
Remind students that the paragraph models illustrating organization on pages 261–263 are shortened versions of the final draft.

Block Arrangement

Having had the opportunity to live in both cities and small towns, I find that I prefer town living for raising a family.

First, my children need space to run and play. In the town of Acton, Massachusetts, I found a spacious home on three-fourths of an acre with additional surrounding land. Also, life in Acton was peaceful and quiet. With fewer cars, we rarely heard "city" noises. Instead, the nights seemed filled with soft breezes. But what the whole family liked most about Acton were the friendly people. The children found playmates lined up on our front sidewalk, and my husband and I mixed easily with the townspeople. They were good people who would go out of their way to help.

On the other hand, when I found my home in Geneva, Switzerland, it was small with a tiny backyard. The children had to play in a parking lot, frightening me as I thought of the accidents that could happen. Also, Geneva was filled with the sounds of people coming and going in the streets, talking loudly, and sometimes shouting. Finally, I found that people in the city were less helpful.

Of course I have had many good experiences in cities as well as these bad ones, but for anyone raising a family, I recommend the slower pace and neighborliness of a town over a city anytime.

Point-by-Point Arrangement

Having had the opportunity to live in both cities and small towns, I find that I prefer town living for raising a family.

First, my children need space to run and play. In the town of Acton, Massachusetts, I found a spacious home on three-fourths of an acre with additional surrounding land. On the other hand, when I found my home in Geneva, Switzerland, it was small with a tiny backyard. The children had to play in a parking lot, frightening me as I thought of the accidents that could happen.

Also, life in Acton was more peaceful and far quieter. With fewer cars, we rarely heard "city" noises. Instead, the nights seemed filled with soft breezes. In contrast, Geneva was filled with the sounds of people coming and going in the streets, talking loudly, and sometimes shouting.

What the whole family missed most, however, were the friendly people of Acton. The children found playmates lined up on our front sidewalk, and my husband and I mixed easily with the townspeople. They were good people who would go out of their way to help. In contrast, I found that city residents were less helpful.

Of course I have had many good experiences in cities as well as these bad ones, but for anyone raising a family, I recommend the slower pace and neighborliness of a town over a city anytime.

HINT: Usually arrange points by order of importance.

With either method, use subtopic sentences to name the things being compared or contrasted. And whichever organizing method you choose, you need to decide how to order your points. These are usually ordered by importance, but occasionally spatially or chronologically.

When switching from one subject to the other or moving from one point to the next, remember to use transitions like those on pages 53–58.

ORGANIZING—SUMMING UP

1. Create a topic sentence to focus your material.
2. Limit points of comparison or contrast to three or four.
3. Arrange the points by importance (occasionally by space or time).
4. Pick either block or point-by-point organization.
5. Use a subtopic sentence to introduce each subject or point.
6. Review the lists of transitions and other connectors.

JOURNAL ENTRY 11.3

Write out your topic sentence. Does it mention two subjects, tell whether you will compare or contrast, and express an opinion/reason for making the comparison or contrast? Now list three or four points of comparison or contrast by order of importance, following either a block or point-by-point format.

Drafting

Before you begin drafting, review the drafting suggestions in Chapter 1, pages 12–13. In writing, be sure to do the following:

1. Choose either comparison or contrast.
2. Include all the points, or main examples, for one subject that you have for the other, and develop each point with at least one detailed example.

Teaching Idea
This is a good time in the writing process to reiterate that all points of comparison should be included for both topics.

Teaching Idea
Encourage students to
include an occasional
metaphor or simile (see
Chapter 19).

3. Be sure your paper makes a point. The topic and concluding sentences
   can help clarify why the subject has meaning for you.

4. Include transitions to help your readers keep track of your comparisons
   or contrasts.

Teaching Idea
Journal Entry 11.4
encourages students to
interact with their writing
and can be useful in focusing
peer revision sessions.

JOURNAL ENTRY 11.4

Soon after writing your first draft, reread the assignment on page 258, and
then skim the draft. Does it fit the assignment? Have you compared or contrasted? Have you introduced each subject or point with a subtopic sentence? What part of your draft do you like best? What part least? Answer
in a paragraph.

Revising Drafts

For help with revising first, second, and final drafts, turn to Chapter 4.

ANNOTATED STUDENT MODEL: "THE JOY OF SIMPLE LIVING"

Carefully reading the annotated student model will help clarify questions you
have about your own draft.

Teaching Idea
To stress that a point is
needed for focus, you might
refer students back to Ana's
prewriting lists (p. 260) to
show what else she could
have written about.

First-Stage Draft

Ana Maria Sauer had moved with her family many times and decided that small
towns were better places for raising children than cities. So she chose a paragraph of contrast for an audience of parents who might be considering a move.

Teaching Idea
Refer students to Chapter 24
for help with pronoun shift
errors.

Avoid *you*

Need to develop examples with more
specific supporting examples and
details

Need more connecting words to move
between town and city points

Some people go for small towns and some for cities but I would
rather live in a small town. Some people just need more space around
them than others, especially if you have kids. When we lived in Acton, we
had plenty of land and a large house. There was a ton of room for the
kids to play, and I loved watching them playing games in the neighborhood. In Geneva we were cramped. There wasn't much room in our house
and the children ended up playing in the streets, with all the problems
that meant. Life in Acton was quieter than in Switzerland. We weren't
bothered by car noises. Instead, we heard the sounds of the wind moving through the treetops. But, in Geneva we heard way too much racket.
People shouted and cars raced their engines on a regular basis which disturbed all our sleeping. I think that I most missed the good friends and
even acquaintances I made in Acton. Maybe we were just lucky to find

such a good group, but the townsfolk were almost always friendly and willing to help. In Geneva people seemed to want to ignore you. They were standoffish, and none of us really made any lasting relationships. Cities are depressing places and I'm glad we will be moving once again; you guessed it, back to Acton.

Second-Stage Draft

First drafts are often underdeveloped and unfocused. Notice how Ana Maria strengthened her paragraph by working on the following points:

SPECIAL POINTS TO CHECK IN REVISING FROM FIRST TO SECOND DRAFTS

1. Check the topic sentence: topic + point + indication of comparison or contrast.
2. Check subtopic sentences: connector + subtopic + point.
3. Check the concluding sentence: connector + link to topic sentence + expanded thought.
4. Delete unnecessary material.
5. Add material for clarity, completeness, and emphasis
6. Check connectors: transitions, repeat words, synonyms, pronouns, and references to main idea.

Topic sentence revised—contrast is implied, not mentioned directly

Supporting examples and details added throughout

Dialogue added

Subtopic sentences revised (and shaded to help you identify them)

Transitional words in contrast and others added

Having had the opportunity to live in both cities and small towns I find that I prefer town living to city living for raising a family. In the town of Acton I found a spacious home with additional surrounding land. During my walks through the neighborhood, I would smell the fragrance of the blossoming trees. I would also enjoy watching the kids playing ball. They looked happy and glad to be with each other, shouting to each other, "Throw me the ball, here, here!" On the other hand, when I found my home in Geneva, it was small with a very tiny backyard. The children had to play in a parking lot. This frightened me as I thought of the accidents that could happen. Sure enough, one day my daughter Anina came weeping and crying to me. Making me long for are safe home in Acton. Also, life in Acton was more peaceful and far quieter, with so few cars, we rarely heard "city" noises. Instead, the nights seemed filled with soft breezes the wind whispering through the treetops. In contrast, Geneva was filled with the noises of people killing time in the streets, talking loudly and sometimes shouting. Sirens, backfiring, and racing engines disturbed all our sleep, especially my daughter Sandra's. What the whole family missed most, however, were the friendly people of Acton. The kids easily found playmates and my husband and I also found friends. They were good people who would go out of their way to help. Once when I locked my keys in car, one of the people I barely knew took me home, waited for me to locate my spare key, and then drove me back to my car. In contrast, I found that people in the city were less helpful. Once when my battery died, none of the people I asked for help would bother. I ended by calling a tow service and I lost a day waiting for them to come get my car. Of course I have had many good experiences in cities as well as these bad ones, but for anyone raising a family I recommend the slower pace and neighborliness of a town over a city anytime.

Note the expanded thought

Concluding sentence revised

Third-Stage Draft

Teaching Idea
Try selecting only one point at a time for students to focus on in the third-stage draft, such as specific words.

Rather than call a second draft complete, we can focus on word choices, sentence variety, and concision—polishing a good draft to make it a great one.

SPECIAL POINTS TO CHECK IN REVISING FROM SECOND TO THIRD DRAFTS
1. Add specific words.
2. Substitute more precise or audience-appropriate words.
3. Combine sentences for variety.
4. **Replace clutter and repeat words with synonyms and phrases.**
5. Delete unneeded words.

Title added

The Joy of Simple Living

Having had the opportunity to live in both cities and small towns I find that I prefer town living to the city living for raising a family.

Clutter phrase deleted

First, my children need space to run and play. In the town of Acton, Massachusetts I found a spacious home on three-fourths of an acer with additional surrounding land. During my leisurely walks through the neigh-

More specific words added

borhood in spring, I would smell the fragrance of the blossoming apple trees, and enjoy watching the children playing ball. They looked happy

Sentences combined and specific words added

and glad to be with each other with their flushed faces', shouting to each other, "Throw me the ball, here, here!" On the other hand when I found my home in Geneva, Switzerland, the house it was small with a very tiny

Clutter phrase deleted

backyard. The children had to play in a parking lot frightening me as I thought of the accidents that could happen. Sure enough, one day my daughter Anina came weeping and crying to me with her knee bleeding. Making me long for are safe home in Acton. Also, life in Acton was more peaceful and far quieter, with so few cars, we rarely heard "city" noises.

More appropriate words substituted

Instead, the nights seemed filled with soft breezes the wind whispering lullabies through the treetops. In contrast, Geneva was filled with the ~~noises~~ **sounds** of people coming, and going in the streets, talking loudly and sometimes shouting. Sirens from police cars and ambulances, back-firing from cars and motorcycles, and racing engines disturbed all our sleep, especially my daughter Sandra's. What the whole family missed most, however, were the friendly people of Acton. The children found playmates lined up on our front sidewalk and my husband and I mixed easily with the townspeople. They were good people who would go out of their way to help.

Sentences combined and specific words added

Synonm replaces phrase

of their way to help. Once when I locked my keys the car in the grocery store parking lot, ~~one of the people~~ a **neighbor** I barely knew took me home, waited for me while I rummaged around to locate my spare key, and then drove me back to my car. In contrast, I found that people in the city were more detached, less helpful. Once when my battery died while I was parked downtown, none of the people I asked for help would bother. I ended by calling a tow service and I lost a day waiting for them to come get my car. Of course I have had many good experiences in cities as well as these bad ones, but for anyone raising a family I recommend the slower pace and neighborliness of a town over a city anytime.

Final-Editing Draft

At this point, Ana shifted into low gear, moving slowly line by line, to find errors in grammar, spelling, and punctuation that she knew were still there. She used her Improvement Chart (from Appendix 2) to locate pattern errors.

Teaching Idea
To help students edit their own papers, ask them to explain the difference between the 9c and 10 errors in the final draft.

SPECIAL POINTS TO CHECK IN EDITING FINAL DRAFTS

1. Misspellings
2. Soundalike words
3. Missing words
4. Wrong words
5. Sentence fragments
6. Comma splices/run-ons
7. Faulty capitalization
8. Incorrect apostrophes
9. Comma(s) needed
   a. Introductory words/ phrases/clauses
   b. Nonessential word groups
   c. Main clauses with coordinating conjunction
10. Unneeded commas

The Joy of Simple Living

Having had the opportunity to live in both cities and small towns,[9a] I find that I prefer town living for raising a family. First, my children need space to run and play. In the town of Acton, Massachusetts,[9b] I found a

spacious home on three-fourths of an ~~acer~~[1] acre with additional surrounding land. During my leisurely walks through the neighborhood in
spring, I would smell the fragrance of the blossoming apple trees,[10] and
enjoy watching the children playing ball. They looked happy with their
flushed ~~faces'~~[8] faces, shouting to each other, "Throw me the ball, here,
here!" On the other hand,[9a] when I found my home in Geneva, Switzerland,
it was small with a tiny backyard. The children had to play in a parking lot,[9b] frightening me as I thought of the accidents that could happen. Sure enough, one day my daughter Anina came crying to me with
her knee bleeding,[5] making me long for ~~are~~[2] our safe home in Acton.
Also, life in Acton was more peaceful and far quieter.[6] With so few cars,
we rarely heard "city" noises. Instead, the nights seemed filled with soft
breezes,[9b] the wind whispering lullabies through the treetops. In contrast,
Geneva was filled with the sounds of people coming,[10] and going in the
streets, talking loudly and sometimes shouting. Sirens from police cars
and ambulances, backfiring from cars and motorcycles, and racing
engines disturbed all our sleep, especially my daughter Sandra's. What
the whole family missed most, however, were the friendly people of Acton.
The children found playmates lined up on our front sidewalk,[9c] and my
husband and I mixed easily with the townspeople. They were good people who would go out of their way to help. Once when I locked my keys
in[3] the car in the grocery store parking lot, a neighbor I barely knew took
me home, waited for me while I rummaged around to locate my spare
key, and then drove me back to my car. In contrast, I found that people
in the city were more detached, less helpful. Once when my battery died
while I was parked downtown, none of the people I asked for help would
bother. I ended by calling a tow service,[9c] and I lost a day waiting for
them to come get my car. Of course I have had many good experiences
in cities as well as these bad ones, but for anyone raising a family I
recommend the slower pace and neighborliness of a town over a city
any time[4] anytime.

—*Ana Maria Sauer*

FINAL-DRAFT CHECKLIST
Before turning in your final draft, review this checklist. You may find
that, as careful as you think you have been, you still missed a point or
two—or more. (For more on any of these points, see Chapter 4.)

☐ 1. Have you chosen to write either a comparison or a contrast?

☐ 2. Does your topic sentence name and limit the topic, and predict a comparison or contrast?

☐ 3. Have you chosen a block or point-by-point method of arrangement?

☐ 4. Have you arranged your main points of comparison or contrast effectively?

☐ 5. Have you written a subtopic sentence to introduce each subject (block arrangement) or point (point-by-point arrangement)?

☐ 6. Have you detailed and explained three to four examples?

☐ 7. Are points of comparison or contrast and examples linked with transitions and other connectors?

☐ 8. Does the concluding sentence have an expanded thought?

☐ 9. Have you used specific language?

☐ 10. Have you used a metaphor or simile?

☐ 11. Are your sentences varied in length and beginnings?

☐ 12. Have you used synonyms for words that are repeated too often?

☐ 13. Have you cut unneeded words?

☐ 14. Have you written an interesting title? Have you checked its capitalization?

☐ 15. Have you prepared your paper using the format expected by your instructor? (Check to see if you need a title page, use double space, leave at least a 1-inch margin, and use a 12-point font.)

☐ 16. Have you edited your work closely (including having at least one other person proofread)? Have you checked your Improvement Chart for pattern errors?

☐ 17. Have you looked for errors involving the following: misspellings, soundalike words, missing words, wrong words, sentence fragments, comma splices/run-ons, faulty capitalization, incorrect apostrophes, missing commas, and unnecessary commas?

Chapter Summary

1. Comparison and contrast are the discovering of similarities and differences between two people, places, events, objects, or ideas.

2. Through comparison and contrast, we explore and evaluate unfamiliar things in the light of those we already know. Analogy, metaphor, and simile are forms of comparison.

3. Comparisons should be meaningful and interesting and made between two topics that are similar enough to be compared.

4. Two ways to organize comparison/contrast are block and point by point.

5. Transitional words and other connectors are needed to introduce new points of comparison/contrast and shifts from one subject to the other.

6. Points are frequently arranged by order of importance but can be ordered spatially or chronologically.

7. Subtopic sentences are useful for introducing new points of comparison/contrast.

8. The topic sentence should name the topic, make a statement about it, and predict a comparison or contrast.

9. The concluding sentence should begin with a connector, link to the topic sentence, and expand the main point of the paper.

10. Writing is never complete until it has been carefully revised and edited.

ALTERNATE WRITING ASSIGNMENTS

Here are some additional comparison/contrast topics that may be of interest. For this assignment, be sure to do the following:

1. First consider both similarities and differences.

2. Have a reason for your comparison or contrast.

3. Either compare or contrast.

4. Develop each of your subjects equally.

5. Use transitions and other connectors.

ASSIGNMENT OPTIONS

1. Compare or contrast a period in your life, such as early childhood, with same period in the life of someone you know well. To prepare, you could talk to an older family member (a parent or grandparent, an aunt or uncle) about his or her life growing up. Here are some points to compare or contrast:

   - Location: town/city, state
   - Home
   - School
   - Work
   - Friends
   - Recreation
   - Hopes/aspirations
   - Worries/fears

Encourage the person to tell stories related to any of these points or other points. You may decide to focus on just one of the suggested points.

2. Compare or contrast yourself with someone from another country or culture. To prepare, interview a student you know from writing class or elsewhere, asking about his or her home and culture and how they compare to yours. Points you might ask about include the following:

- Country/area in the country
- School
- Recreational activities
- Music
- Hopes/fears
- Clothing
- Dating
- Friends
- Sports

3. Write a paper that contrasts a stereotype with your own view. You might briefly describe the stereotype and then develop three or four specific points on which the stereotype differs from your own experience or general knowledge. Here are some stereotypes:

- Teenagers are bad automobile insurance risks.
- Men want sex while women want love.
- Heavy metal music is just loud noise.
- Anyone with a high GPA must be a nerd.
- High school and college athletes don't care much about academics.

4. For a comparison paper, create a profile of yourself that matches a job you would like. Lay out the necessary skills for the job, and then show how you are well suited for it. You might locate an actual job description—from your current employer, for instance, or from your school career center. Or you can make up your own description, including for a fantasy job. Perhaps you have always wanted to be a special assistant to Steven Spielberg, or a philosopher king—a ruler of your own country or maybe even of the universe. Match your imagined qualifications with those needed for the job.

5. Examine the accompanying photos and write either a comparison or contrast paragraph on them. Before you choose an approach, list similarities and differences to help find the most interesting slant on your subjects. Next, decide on a point for your paper. For example, you might want to comment on the love most parents have for their children and how they show it.

Introducing the Essay

What Is an Essay?

Teaching Idea

Although students have written essays in high school, they are often initially intimidated by moving from the paragraph to the essay. It can help reduce their anxiety to discuss their essay-writing experiences, including the essays many of them will write in other classes this semester.

Teaching Idea

If you are having students expand a paragraph they wrote for a previous assignment, you might work through Chapters 12 and 14 with them concurrently, using examples from their old assignments to help illustrate essay form and development.

Although we worked through many challenging single-paragraph assignments in Unit Two, the essay may still seem a bit intimidating. Like experienced hikers who have climbed foothills but are finally confronted with a mountain, we might think, "Too steep, too rugged, the air's too thin—I'm not goin' *there*!" In truth, though, the essay is not overwhelming; it doesn't even have to be all that big. In fact, an essay is largely an expanded paragraph, written for the same reasons (to entertain, inform, or persuade) and complete with parts you already know: an introduction, body, and conclusion.

While essays may have dozens of body paragraphs—and others to introduce and conclude them—many are relatively brief, as are the ones in this unit. While we write short essays of five to six paragraphs, we will practice all the strategies for discovering, organizing, and developing ideas we learned earlier in the term, and we will learn about an important focusing statement—the **thesis.**

Essay Form

In Chapter 3, we saw that a body paragraph and an essay have many similarities. Both should begin with a controlling point, support that point with detailed examples and explanations, and end decisively. The following illustration shows how body paragraphs and essays are related:

Body Paragraph   Essay

| Topic **sentence**: topic + statement |

Body sentences
- Subtopic sentence one: connector, subtopic, statement
- Development: examples, details, explanations

- Subtopic sentence two: connector, subtopic, statement
- Development: examples, details, explanations

- Subtopic sentence three: connector, subtopic, statement
- Development: examples, details, explanations

Concluding **sentence**
- Connector
- Link to topic sentence
- Summary
- Expanded thought

Introductory **paragraph**
- Hook
- Development
- Thesis: topic + statement

Body paragraph 1
- Topic sentence: connector, subtopic, statement
- Development: examples, details, explanations
- Summary sentence (optional)

Body paragraph 2
- Topic sentence: connector, subtopic, statement
- Development: examples, details, explanations
- Summary sentence (optional)

Body paragraph 3
- Topic sentence: connector, subtopic, statement
- Development: examples, details, explanations
- Summary sentence (optional)

Concluding **paragraph**
- Connector
- Link to thesis
- Summary
- Development (expanded thought)

The body paragraph often begins with a **topic sentence** (main point) while the essay begins with a **paragraph** that usually contains a thesis sentence (main point), often positioned as the *last* sentence in the paragraph. Notice in the illustration above how the first arrow shows this relationship. Topic and thesis sentences are comparable, except that because essays are more fully developed, the thesis may need to allow for the fuller treatment of a subject.

As we saw in Chapter 7, body paragraphs that develop several primary examples begin each example with a **subtopic sentence** to introduce the main point. Similarly, body paragraphs in essays usually begin with a **topic sentence** to predict the main point (see the second, third, and fourth arrows in the preceding illustration). Both subtopic and topic sentences are then developed with detailed examples and explanations.

Body paragraphs end with one or two sentences while brief essays end with one paragraph, as the fifth arrow indicates. In both cases, a writer finishes by referring back to the paper's main point—found in the topic or thesis sentence. Body paragraphs sometimes summarize with a few words while essays often use a sentence or more.

Teaching Idea
You might remind students that the topic and concluding sentences of the deli paragraph model are separated here for instructional purposes only.

Student Models: Paragraph and Essay

To see how a paragraph might grow into an essay, let's compare paragraph and essay student models, both of them versions of "Dangers in a Deli," especially noting the beginnings, endings, and development.

Paragraph Model

Length: 200 words

Topic sentence

Subtopic sentence 1

Sentences for development

Subtopic sentence 2

Sentences for development

Subtopic sentence 3

Sentences for development

Concluding sentence

Dangers in a Deli

More frequently than people realize, there are dangers in deli work.

One concern for potential deli workers is slippery floors. If the counter is packed with anxious customers, and workers are hustling about taking care of their orders, a wet floor is not going to take top priority. During the rush what's going to stop an employee from running too fast, which could result in a serious wipeout? In addition to slippery floors, working around chemicals should not be taken lightly. When cleaning the glass, you might end up with ammonia sprayed in your eyes. Both pan degreaser and sanitizer are used at dish time, and it only takes one splash in the sink to send a worker to the emergency room. But the part of the job that is most dangerous is using the meat and cheese slicer. Whether operating the slicer or simply cleaning it, you risk a nasty cut. With just one careless slip near the sharp blade, you could end up with one less finger.

A new person on the job might be a little nervous because of the possible injury that deli work entails, but luckily safety training is a requirement.

—*Catherine Denning*

Essay Model

Length: 575 words

Essays require an introductory paragraph.

Hook: First sentence arouses curiosity.

Sentences for development

Thesis sentence

Topic sentence 1

Dangers in a Deli

Would you like to keep all of your body parts intact today? How about your eyesight, how much do you value it, or that brain that keeps your body functioning? With all of the activity in a deli, employees rushing about, impatient customers pressuring you to hurry, and management barking orders, accidents can happen when you least expect them. Smashing your head on a slippery tile floor, splashing caustic chemicals into your eyes, and slicing off fingers are just a few of the dangers you can encounter. If you don't want to end up in the emergency room on your first day here, you need to be aware of the potential dangers in working at a deli.

One common hazard for deli workers is slippery floors. Often, especially during the lunch rush, the place gets jammed. Anxious customers crowd into one another and lean over the stainless steel counter in your face to call out three more changes to their already late

Sentences for development

orders. Trying to manage the rush, employees hustle about, carrying checks, prepping sandwiches, carting plates back and forth. When scurrying from the salad case to the register, you might not notice that freshly mopped floor, and before you know it, you are crashing into a wall and banging your head on the slick, hard tile. And if you don't trip yourself up, there are always other employees to run into you, which can also cause a serious wipeout.

Topic sentence 2

Besides the slippery floors, workers also need to be cautious around chemicals. Even when business is slow, it is easy enough to be careless: for example, when cleaning the grease and handprints off all the glass, you might suddenly spray yourself in the face with ammonia. But it gets

Sentences for development

worse when the rush begins, and the owner goes into his panic mode: "Get these dishes done! Now, now—we're filling up!" You might think you have a good grip on that slippery platter, until it slips out of your hands and splashes into a sink full of pan degreaser and sanitizer. It only takes one faceful of that hot, soapy water to send a worker to the emergency room.

Topic sentence 3

But the part of the job that is most dangerous is using the meat and cheese slicer. Whether operating the slicer or simply cleaning it, you risk a nasty cut. The shiny circular blade on the machine is as sharp as a surgeon's scalpel, and you will be using it all the time, your hand just inches away from the cutting edge. Everyone knows the kind of damage that can

Sentences for development

happen; everyone is extra careful, but then business picks up or someone is just too tired to pay attention. The blade doesn't know the difference between a piece of ham and four fingertips. Just one careless slip and you could end up with one less finger.

Essays require a concluding paragraph with a connector, link to thesis, summary, and development.

Cuts, chemicals, concussions, and other dangers—with all these ways to be injured, a new person on the job might feel a little nervous. But deli work doesn't always make you feel anxious and frazzled; in fact, it can be enjoyable. Whether you are talking to interesting customers or spending time with friends, the deli is usually a fun place to work. It can even be a great place for keeping your mind off problems at home or that algebra exam on Friday. Although accidents can happen, you are a lot less likely to have one if you keep the worst of the hazards in mind.

—Catherine Denning

As you compare the paragraph and essay models, you might notice the chief differences between them: **length, introduction,** and **conclusion.**

- **Length:** You can increase length in two ways: by adding examples and by developing them. The deli paragraph of **200** words grew into an essay of **575** words not by using more main examples but by developing those already there.

- **Introduction:** Whereas the deli paragraph is introduced by a sentence, which serves to focus what follows, the deli essay is introduced by a paragraph, which does that and much more. Specifically, the essay's thesis (main point) is similar to the paragraph's topic sentence, *and* the author has added a **lead-in sentence** to "hook" readers (like baiting a hook for a fish) along with several more sentences to maintain the readers' interest and lead into the thesis.

- **Conclusion:** Rather than ending with a single sentence, the deli essay uses a concluding paragraph. The lead sentence includes a connector, a brief summary of the essay's main points, and a link to the thesis (workers need to be aware of dangers in a deli). Instead of merely trailing off, the author adds an expanded thought to finish decisively. Note that—as may occur when you write—the expanded thought has changed in the essay, from safety training to good times.

HINT: In developing a paragraph into an essay, you might change the expanded thought.

As we move ahead in Chapter 12, you will learn how to transform simple paragraphs into more complex essays.

Introductory Paragraphs

Introductions

If you began some of your one-paragraph papers with two or three sentences you then trimmed back, you have already written partial introductory paragraphs. Often, the sentences were on their way to becoming a full-fledged introductory paragraph but, in the context of these shorter papers, would have been distracting to readers. Now, however, you can develop these sentences and arrange them for greater interest and force.

Introductory paragraphs serve an important function: engaging readers' interest. If a reader is disappointed by or disinterested in the first few sentences of an essay, why should he or she continue? Because a poor introduction often indicates that further reading will be a waste of time, the essay goes unread. To avoid this pitfall, make your introductions interesting and well focused by including the following parts:

- **Hook:** one sentence (first sentence in the introductory paragraph)

- **Development:** three to four sentences (middle sentences)

- **Thesis:** one sentence (often the last sentence in the introductory paragraph)

Thesis Sentences

Thesis

The **thesis sentence** is the most important part of your introduction. By naming the topic and making a statement about it, the thesis sentence guides readers through the essay, just as a topic sentence guides them through a paragraph. If you are expanding a paragraph from Unit Two, your topic sentence, essentially unchanged, may serve as your thesis sentence. However, if in expanding the paragraph you are adding points or changing a main example, you may need to rewrite your topic sentence so that it further focuses your essay. Even if you are not making such changes, you might still want to polish the wording. Compare the topic and thesis sentences from the paragraph and essay versions of "Dangers in a Deli":

TOPIC SENTENCE   More frequently than people realize, there are dangers in deli work.

THESIS SENTENCE   If you don't want to end up in the emergency room on your first day here, you need to be aware of the potential dangers in working at a deli.

Teaching Idea
It is worth reiterating the various positions in which thesis sentences can be placed and showing examples of this (several of the essays in Unit Six will help here).

Clearly, both sentences express the same point; however, the thesis targets an audience more precisely (potential deli employees) and uses a more specific phrase ("emergency room") for emphasis.

Writers may use several sentences to express their thesis, locate it outside the introduction, or, occasionally, only imply rather than state it. For example, when arguing to a potentially resistant audience, a writer might delay the thesis. However, to keep both yourself and your readers oriented in your essay, it helps to make the thesis the last sentence in the first paragraph—as all the student model essays in this text have done.

HINT: Position the thesis as the last sentence in your first paragraph to keep yourself and your readers oriented.

When you write a thesis sentence, as when you write a topic sentence, you should do the following:

1. Limit the topic.
2. Make a clear statement about the topic.
3. Refine the statement by explaining it clearly and using specific words, action words, and sensory details.

Limiting the Thesis Sentence

Teaching Idea
If you used the Language Line in Chapter 5, you might want to turn back to it to refresh students' memories and link the concept of general versus specific to the thesis sentence.

A thesis sentence should be midway between general and specific—general enough to need focused examples to illustrate it, and specific enough to need only as many of those examples as the writer intends to give. The Language Line from Chapter 5 can help us see the general-specific range and locate the thesis:

Relatively General		Thesis ⟶	Relatively Specific
"Deli—lots of things go on"	"A deli job—hard and dangerous"	"A deli job—lots of time spent, hard and dangerous"	"My deli job—involves long hours, hard work, and serious danger"

Often, the writer begins with a fairly general thesis and, in part through trial and error, discovers the focus needed to sufficiently limit it. Notice how the following thesis sentence becomes increasingly focused until it could guide the drafting of "Dangers in a Deli":

1. There are lots of things that go on in a deli.
2. A deli job takes plenty of time and can be hard, dangerous work, but there are good times too.
3. Working in a deli can be hard and dangerous.
4. Working in a deli involves some serious dangers.

The author has moved from the relatively general "deli" and "lots of things" to the appropriately specific "deli job" and "serious dangers," winding up with a useful rough thesis sentence.

Like a topic sentence, a thesis sentence can include a **forecasting statement.** Thus, the example could be expanded as follows:

> Working in a deli involves several serious dangers: the slippery floors, some harsh chemicals, and the meat and cheese slicer.

Making a Clear Statement about the Topic

Sometimes, the thesis sentence might be limited enough, but the statement it makes about the topic isn't clear. The problem may be in the wording of the sentence or the thinking behind it. Consider the following thesis:

> Television is full of violence that affects children in ways that no one will ever be able to understand fully.

The writer evidently wants to discuss some aspect of how TV violence affects children—a reasonably limited topic for an essay. However, as this thesis sentence is phrased, it's not clear where the essay is going. There are two possible directions, and the writer needs to revise the thesis to indicate one or the other:

A. Violence in children's programming can cause children to behave violently.

B. Though psychologists and psychiatrists think they understand the impact of TV violence on children, they have only learned part of the picture.

Aside from the thesis that goes astray through faulty wording or thinking, there is the thesis that meanders, like an old lazy river, winding around in great looping oxbows until it finally arrives at the end—sort of. Consider the following example:

> The medical profession offers many exciting career possibilities for young people who want to fully explore their potential and work within an industry that helps other people in the same selfless way that a member of the clergy might, especially if a person decides to go into an area that some would avoid because of unpleasant working conditions or patients who suffer too much, areas like respiratory therapy or geriatric care.

Besides being too long for a thesis (or most any other) sentence, this example includes too many ideas—though most are worthwhile and could be useful elsewhere in the essay.

How long is too long, or too short, for a thesis sentence? While there is no set rule, a medium-length sentence, of, say, 15 to 30 words, generally works well. Some thesis sentences can be quite short for dramatic impact; others can run to 40 words or more. As long as your thesis is clear, the word count should not be much of a problem.

Note that a thesis sentence that is well crafted can *imply* its focus; what is important is that it not *hide* it. For example, an essay dealing with effects might use either of these thesis sentences:

A. Joining the navy right out of high school had four positive effects on my life.

B. I have come to appreciate the unconscious wisdom of my decision to join the navy right after my high school graduation.

HINT: Forecasting an essay's main points can be an effective addition to a thesis sentence.

Teaching Idea
You might point out that forecasting statements, especially lengthy ones, can make brief essays sound a bit repetitive.

CAUTION! Watch out for the meandering thesis sentence.

Teaching Idea
Remind students to save their brainstorming and drafting material because, as with the meandering thesis sentence, good ideas can often be salvaged.

HINT: Thesis sentences are often between 15 and 30 words long.

HINT: Thesis sentences may artfully *imply* the focus of an essay.

Teaching Idea
Ask the class to compare the thesis sentences that forecast, imply, and waffle. Have students explain in their own words why the waffling sentence is ineffective.

Version A clearly states the topic and even uses the word "effects." But version B also clearly states the topic while implying that the essay will develop effects. Contrast these two thesis sentences to the following one:

> I had to decide what to do with my life after high school, and I thought about joining the military because so many young people go that route.

Undecided, or "waffling," thesis sentences like this make it difficult for readers to know where the essay is headed.

Polishing the Thesis Sentence

HINT: Polish thesis sentences through **specific words, action words,** and **sensory details.**

Few of us will immediately hit upon the perfect thesis sentence and then go tearing into an essay. Instead, we will most likely need to work on the thesis, revising it for clarity and style, and using **specific words, action words,** and **sensory details** to make it more interesting.

With the deli essay, we can see one example of a writer upgrading her thesis:

A. More frequently than people realize there are dangers in deli work.

B. If you don't want to end up in the emergency room on your first day here, you need to be aware of the potential dangers in working at a deli.

Version B, aside from more directly addressing readers, includes the **specific words** "emergency room" to show where they might be headed if they do not pay attention to the information in the essay.

Could we add an **action word** to this thesis? How about "bleeding"?

> If you don't want to end up your first day here bleeding all over yourself on the way to the emergency room, you should be aware of the potential dangers in deli work.

Could we also add a **sensory detail** (sight, sound, touch, smell, or taste)?

> If you don't want to see bright red arterial blood spurting from a severed index finger, you should be aware of the potential dangers in deli work.

Teaching Idea
If students wince a bit at this last thesis sentence, point out that specific language and action words evoke strong responses in readers and so are valuable rhetorical strategies.

This thesis sentence adds a visual detail, "bright red"; two action words, "spurting" and "severed"; and two specific words, "arterial" and "index." However, the point in refining your thesis is not to cram as many action words or sensory details into it as possible. In fact, sensory details may not even be right for your topic. Note that in this particular case the writer polished her thesis sentence without including these action words and sensory details. The point is to look critically at your work with an eye to making a passable thesis sentence a powerful one.

ACTIVITY 12.1 Polishing Thesis Sentences

Teaching Idea
In Activity 12.1, you might invite students to mention several examples they would use to develop their revised thesis sentences into essays. Number 2 can generate some interesting responses.

Revise the following rough thesis sentences, underlining any specific words, action words, or sensory details that you add. Use your imagination, have some fun, and remember that even small additions can be real improvements.

EXAMPLE

Rough thesis: A sense of humor has been useful to me.

Revised thesis: Being able to laugh at myself in embarrassing situations has saved me from some depressing moments.

Answers will vary.

1. Rough thesis: Winter is hard on the world.

   Revised thesis: With its Arctic wind and subzero temperatures, winter drives plants, animals, and people into hiding.

2. Rough thesis: I know how to make my wife (husband, girl/boyfriend) happy.

   Revised thesis: While my wife enjoys receiving presents on established occasions like birthdays, if I want to make her truly happy, I bring her small, unexpected presents throughout the year.

3. Rough thesis: There is one kind of party that is sure to attract the police.

   Revised thesis: Whenever I have Eric's band over to play at a keg party in my backyard, the police show up before midnight.

4. Rough thesis: Buying gifts that will be well received is not easy as you need to pick the right gift.

   Revised thesis: To buy a special gift for someone, you have to know the person well and buy her what she, not you, would value.

5. Rough thesis: Extreme sports fall into several different categories.

   Revised thesis: Leaping from a bridge with a piece of rope attached to my ankle, clinging to a sheer rock face 2,000 feet above the ground, or jumping out of a plane at 15,000 feet—my favorite extreme sports can be classified by the element of risk in each.

Developing Introductions

Teaching Idea
Let students know that there are other ways to develop introductions besides these, but if they learn several reliable methods, they will seldom be stuck for an introduction.

HINT: Some writers prefer to begin an essay draft with only a thesis, composing the introduction later.

HINT: These methods are often combined.

With a clear thesis sentence to end the introductory paragraph, you have a strong start to your essay. To lead readers to that thesis, you can use any of the following methods:

STRATEGIES FOR INTRODUCTIONS

1. Description
2. Narration
3. Comparison/contrast
4. Cause and effect
5. Definition
6. Persuasion
7. Question(s)
8. Background information/history (including why the topic is important to you)
9. Startling information
10. Reversal
11. Combination of several methods

To see these methods in action, read through the following introductions for "Dangers in a Deli." Notice that these different introductions can each lead to the same thesis sentence. The thesis sentence is shaded, and the "hook," or lead-in sentence, discussed in the next section, is underlined.

Note: In these introductions, you will see the word *you.* It is appropriate there because the author is directly addressing readers. However, *you* is frequently overused in student writing; use it only in contexts in which you are sure it is appropriate. (For more on *you* and pronoun shift problems, see Chapter 24.)

Methods for Developing Introductory Paragraphs

There are at least 10 basic methods for developing introductory paragraphs:

1. **Description:** Create a series of vivid images—perhaps three or four. Consider these images as quick snapshots rather than a continuous story. Use one sentence for each image, and develop each with actions, specific words, and sensory details (sight, sound, and touch, especially).

Irritated customers shouting orders, pans clanging together, shirts soaked through with sweat—another shift at the deli is well under way. Employees are racing to keep up with the orders. Ben is slicing bread too fast for safety, the bread knife barely missing his palm as he opens one loaf after another. Ellen slips on a wet spot on the tile floor and jams her wrist against a wall. Ramon mutters, "Damn it!" as he scalds himself in the sink. A delicatessen in a lunch rush can be a hectic, nerve-wracking place. If you don't want to end up in the emergency room on your first day here, you need to be aware of the potential dangers in working at a deli.

2. **Narration:** Tell a brief story.

Shawn came into the restaurant cracking jokes, kidding customers and fellow employees alike, and generally having a good time. Everyone liked him right away and could see that he would be fun to have around. But in the middle of his third day on the job, during the lunch rush, we lost him for good. I was taking an order at table seven, when all the loud talking, jostling, and eating stopped abruptly. Everyone in the restaurant heard Shawn scream as he lost the first joint of his little finger to the meat slicer. He learned the hard way how dangerous this job can be. If you too don't want to end up in the emergency room on your first day here, you need to be aware of the potential dangers in working at a deli.

3. **Comparison/contrast:** Compare or contrast your topic with something your readers would be familiar with. You might also compare through a metaphor or simile.

Although I have never been on a cattle ranch, I think I know what it feels like to be caught in the middle of a stampede. I don't usually think of my customers as cows (though some do eat like animals), but in the middle of a lunch rush in our deli, with the restaurant packed from the front door to the counter and frustrated people calling out orders, you too might feel like you are about to be trampled. The pressure during a rush from customers and management alike can cause employees to move faster than what is safe. If you don't want to end up in the emergency room on your first day here, you need to be aware of the potential dangers in working at a deli.

4. **Cause and effect:** Explain causes leading to or effects leading from the topic. Or create a fictional scenario—what might happen relating to your topic.

   Let's talk about Allen, a fictitious new employee at the deli, who is not paying much attention to his trainer as she talks about procedures and hazards on the job. He halfway listens as she tells him about how fast he will be expected to move in about an hour, when the lunch rush hits. "Right, yeah, OK," he says, paying more attention to Will Smith's rap in his headphones. An hour passes, people begin flooding in, and Allen begins to panic. Trying to carry a tray full of salads too quickly, he slips on the tile floor and lands flat on his back, knocking himself unconscious. Unless you are careful, you could be Allen. If you too don't want to end up in the emergency room on your first day here, you need to be aware of the potential dangers in working at a deli.

5. **Definition:** Briefly define some concept important to your topic.

   Self-preservation is an instinct that tries to keep animals out of harm's way, and it works pretty well for most of them, except for some humans. These are the people—maybe you know some like this—who refuse to listen to good advice or even to warnings that might save them from much misery. On the other hand, when a reasonable person has the opportunity to learn about job hazards that might endanger her, she listens, that good old self-preservation instinct kicking in. In this restaurant a new employee has to be careful. If you don't want to end up in the emergency room on your first day here, you need to be aware of the potential dangers in working at a deli.

6. **Persuasion:** Appeal to your readers' self-interest by showing them what they have to gain by reading your essay.

   There is no reason that you have to be hurt today. No sane person enjoys pain, and few people can afford the recovery time that serious injury on the job requires. All new employees at this restaurant get a careful orientation that includes warnings on how to avoid accidents. Intelligent people pay attention. If you don't want to end up in the emergency room on your first day here, you need to be aware of the potential dangers in working at a deli.

7. **Question(s):** Ask your readers several questions that relate to your thesis.

Would you like to keep all of your body parts intact today? How about your eyesight, how much do you value it, or that brain that keeps your body functioning? With all of the activity in a deli, employees rushing about, impatient customers pressuring you to hurry, and management barking orders, accidents can happen when you least expect them. Smashing your head on a slippery tile floor, splashing caustic chemicals into your eyes, and slicing off fingers are just a few of the dangers you can encounter. If you don't want to end up in the emergency room on your first day here, you need to be aware of the potential dangers in working at a deli.

8. **Background information:** Give information or history about your topic that would help orient your readers or show them why the topic is important to you.

As a deli manager I like to keep my fellow employees healthy, and as a reasonably good-hearted human being, I don't like to see people suffer. During our peak hours we only run five employees in the front and back of the house, even though we usually need more. In order for the operation to work, everyone has to do his or her job efficiently and with some enthusiasm. If even one person just gets the slows or, worse, is injured, the rest of the crew suffers. To help the restaurant, your fellow workers, and yourself, listen closely to this orientation. You can keep yourself out of the emergency room on your first day here, if you are aware of the potential dangers in working at this deli.

9. **Startling information:** Give facts or statistics that might seem unusual or dramatic to your reader. Or create graphic examples that would cause an emotional response in your reader.

A day rarely passes without some kind of accident in our deli. Most of the time the problem is small and the hurt to a person slight. But who wants even a little pain? It is bad enough to deal with small glass cuts and scalds from hot coffee, but when business picks up, the big accidents follow. New employees especially run the risk of breaking a wrist or slicing off a body part. If you don't want to end up in the emergency room on your first day here, you need to be aware of the potential dangers in working at a deli.

10. **Reversal:** Begin your introduction moving in one direction, but switch direction as you approach your thesis sentence.

> <u>Working in a deli can be great fun.</u> Employees dress casually, no suits and ties here. Most of us are young adults with plenty happening in our lives. I enjoy listening to Felipe brag about his date last night (knowing that at least half of what he says is a lie) and watching Gabrielle and Nathan pester each other over nothing, like sister and brother. Also, when business picks up, it is a good feeling to work closely as an efficient team, depending on one another as we get the job done. But the work is not all play. There are real, serious hazards in this business. If you don't want to end up in the emergency room on your first day here, you need to be aware of the potential dangers in working at a deli.

11. **Combination:** Focus on any one introductory paragraph method to get started, but then include other methods, as many of the paragraphs above do. For example, number 10 uses description within the reversal strategy. Number 9 includes a question, description, and cause/effect. Number 8 explains in part through cause and effect. Almost all paragraphs, including introductions, are developed through examples.

As you can see, there are many interesting ways to write introductory paragraphs. The one you choose depends on your topic, purpose, and audience. If you are writing, for example, how-to instructions for assembling a swing set, you might avoid the more colorful narrative/descriptive methods, favoring instead a simple listing and defining of parts. If, on the other hand, you are persuading someone—say, a group of teens not to smoke—you might begin with a story to capture their attention. Your tone (formal/informal), word choices, and explanations in the essay body depend on the context in which you are writing, and these choices begin in your introduction.

Remember too that lively, interesting introductions rarely just fall from the sky, a gift from the gods. You must bring beginnings to life. So apply the same prewriting methods to this paragraph that you do to the body of the essay: Plan on clustering, listing, freewriting, and so forth to discover ideas.

Teaching Idea
While some students agonize over introductions, others settle for the first one that occurs to them, whether or not it is engaging or even effective. Spend some class time having students create at least two different introductions for the same essay and then choose the one they like best.

ACTIVITY 12.2 Creating Interesting Introductions

Pick one of the thesis sentences you created for Activity 12.1. For three different introductory paragraphs, write five to seven sentences leading to this thesis. Review the 10 methods listed above, and remember that you can combine several.

Answers will vary.

1. List the method number(s): _____

Begin the introductory paragraph: _____

_____

_____

_____

_____

_____

_____

_____

_____

Thesis sentence: _____

_____

2. List the method number(s): _____

Begin the introductory paragraph: _____

_____

_____

_____

_____

_____

_____

_____

_____

Thesis sentence: _____

_____

3. List the method number(s): _____

Begin the introductory paragraph: _____

_____

_____

_____

_____

_____

_____

_____

_____

Thesis sentence: _____

_____

Hooks

Let's focus now on the **hook,** the lead sentence of the introductory paragraph. If the introduction as a whole is important to draw readers in, then its lead sentence is especially so. The first sentence should "hook" the fish, your readers, arousing their interest and encouraging them to forge ahead. In creating hooks, keep these points in mind:

1. Do not state the obvious.
2. Do say something that will interest readers.

Teaching Idea
See Chapter 12 in the Instructor's Manual for the hook method used in each essay in *AWW*.

Looking back at "Dangers in a Deli," we can see how the author, Catherine Denning, managed her hook:

> Would you like to keep all of your body parts intact today? How about your eyesight, how much do you value it, or that brain that keeps your body functioning?

Catherine wrote this essay with an audience of newly hired deli employees in mind. While most people are presumably interested in keeping all their "body parts intact," the new employee who will soon be operating the slicer might feel like paying special attention. Notice that the hook is phrased as a question and that it begins to answer a question most readers ask: "What's in it for me? Why should I read this essay?" Also note that the hook extends into the next sentence, though it does not need to. For our purposes, we will talk about the hook as the first sentence, realizing that it can be more than one sentence and that it should blend easily into the rest of the introduction.

Here are several ways to create hooks:

METHODS FOR CREATING HOOKS

1. Ask a question.
2. Begin with a line of dialogue.
3. Begin with a quotation.
4. Make a startling statement.
5. Present an unusual fact.
6. Use a vivid image.
7. Create a comparison (possibly a metaphor or simile).
8. Combination of methods.

HINT: A hook can be created by combining several methods.

Hooks, like the rest of the introduction up to the thesis sentence, are largely interchangeable, often overlapping pieces that can vary as much as a writer's imagination allows. For example, Catherine could have begun her essay with any of the following sentences:

Teaching Idea
You may need to head off the misimpression that hooks must be highly dramatic to be effective. It is useful to contrast hooks like "Want to make a million dollars?" or "The accident left Jim paralyzed from the waist down" to quieter ones like "It annoys my wife intensely when I sing in the shower, and I have tried to stop."

DIALOGUE	"Aaggh! Help, I just splashed sanitizer in my eyes!"
VIVID IMAGE	Irritated customers shouting orders, pans clanging together, shirts soaked through with sweat—another shift at the deli is well under way.
COMPARISON	Although I have never been on a cattle ranch, I think I know what it feels like to be caught in the middle of a stampede.

In contrast, here are three sentences that would make poor hooks:

A. Everybody has to have some kind of job or another.

B. I have a job in a deli.

C. Accidents can happen to people when they are at work.

HINT: Obvious statements make poor hooks.

As you can see, these obvious statements arouse no curiosity; in fact, they are just dead space, discouraging readers from enjoying what might be an interesting essay.

ACTIVITY 12.3 Polishing Hooks

Choose one of the introductory paragraphs that you wrote in Activity 12.2, and revise the first sentence to create a more interesting hook.
Answers will vary.

First sentence of one paragraph from Activity 12.2: _____

Your revision of the hook: _____

_____

_____

ACTIVITY 12.4 Creating Interesting Hooks

Revise the following boring hooks, using three of the methods suggested above or some of your own.
Answers will vary.

1. Topic of essay: The day I won the lottery

   Boring hook: *Sometimes good things happen to people.*

   Interesting hooks:

   Version 1: *Have you ever met someone who has won a state lottery?*

   Version 2: *"I won, I won!" I shouted as I danced around the 7-Eleven.*

   Version 3: *Fifty thousand dollars could be waiting for me as I scratch my lottery ticket.*

2. Topic of essay: Causes of a divorce

   Boring hook: *Sometimes marriages don't work out.*

   Interesting hooks:

   Version 1: *The neighbors could not believe it when they saw Jennifer in her driveway pouring gasoline on her wedding dress and then setting it on fire.*

   Version 2: *Two out of three marriages today end in divorce.*

   Version 3: *The party was over, but the music, the dancing, and the laughter had been fun.*

3. Topic of essay: How difficult returning to college can be for

nontraditional students

Boring hook: *A college education can be very valuable.*

Interesting hooks:

Version 1: *People who earn a college diploma are likely to earn twice as much over their working lifetime as those who have only a high school degree.*

Version 2: *As John tries to quiet his screaming baby and keep the pasta from boiling over, he notices his four-year-old daughter coloring in his algebra textbook.*

Version 3: *Once upon a time a strong back and a grade school education were all a person needed to succeed in life.*

Avoiding Weak Introductions

Introductions can go wrong in various ways—sometimes several at the same time. Try to avoid the following problems:

1. **Beginning with obvious statements**

   Consider this opener: "It was a day like any other day, with weather, people moving about, and cars going from one place to another." You might expect a boring sentence like that to breed another like this: "The weather was not particularly hot or cold, the people were not extraordinary, and the cars were not really moving all that fast either." From here, the introduction and the rest of the essay will probably go downhill.

2. **Stating that you are getting ready to write an essay about something**

   Here are two examples: "In this essay I will tell you about . . ." and "The first part of my essay will discuss . . . and the next paragraph will say . . ."

3. **Apologizing for what you may not know**

   Look at these examples: "Although I do not know much about this topic . . ." and "There are experts who know a lot more about this subject than I do . . ." and "I managed to find out a little bit about this subject, and so I can say something about it." Writers are asking readers for their time. If you begin by telling readers that you don't have much worth saying, why should they waste time reading your work?

4. **Needlessly repeating information**

   Consider this opening: "Some students have problems with their schoolwork. When they do their work, it is often difficult for them. The homework and in-class work is hard to complete, and so many students—as hard as they work—find that they have a lot of trouble getting the work done." By now, readers have gotten the point—and are probably sleeping on it. (For effective repetition, see Chapter 19.)

5. **Using clichés and worn expressions**

   Think about these tired phrases: "Caught between a rock and a hard place," "after a wait that seemed like an eternity," and "with butterflies in my stomach."

Teaching Idea
To help students understand weak introductions, have them role-play the audience for the weak introductory paragraphs. For example, how likely would they be to let a mechanic work on their car who used the apology approach: "I really don't know that much about car repair, but . . ."

If a fresh figure of speech doesn't occur to you, use a literal phrase. Say, for example, "caught in a difficult situation" in place of the first cliché. (For more on clichés and worn phrases, see Chapter 19.)

Teaching Idea
Of course, there are legitimate reasons for brief introductions—for example, in essay exams.

6. Writing overly long or overly short introductions

Introductions should be in proportion to the rest of the work. A book, for instance, might use a whole chapter, while an essay of fifteen pages might need only a paragraph or two. Our brief essay introductions will be well developed in five to seven sentences—about a hundred words.

ACTIVITY 12.5 Recognizing and Revising Weak Introductions

Decide which five of the following six introductory paragraphs are ineffective. Explain why each is ineffective. Then rewrite one of them, using a method listed or one of your own.

1. Credit cards can be a real problem for anyone, especially college students. In this essay I will first discuss how much of a problem they can be, and then I will provide some solutions to this situation. Before I am through, I will show—in paragraph four to be exact—how irresponsible it is of the credit card companies to scatter their cards around so that anyone can get one. In my conclusion I will tell readers where to go to get more information on the problem.

2. Some people argue that e-mail contributes to bad writing. After all, they say, look at how people dash off those notes, and look at all the obvious errors in them. However, e-mail can actually make people better writers.

3. Many Americans insist on driving new vehicles, even if they do cost an arm and a leg. These people seem to think that new is automatically better, but I think half the time the supposed new technology is just re-creating the wheel. Who needs electric windows when a crank will do the same job? Who needs a $500 antenna that pops up and down like a jack in the box? My old '86 Toyota pickup truck with its 115,000 miles is still as good as gold and better than most of the new products on the market. I prefer driving an older vehicle for several good reasons.

4. I don't know a lot about professional sports, but it seems to me that the players make an awful lot of money. Take for instance professional baseball players. They make a ton of money. Why I think I remember reading about a month ago how some pitcher signed a $5,000,000 contract! This seems like too much money for someone who just throws a baseball. And, even though I am no authority, I'll bet it's even worse for football and basketball. I think these guys make even more! All these high salaries are bound to have negative effects on professional sports.

5. Most people want to be happy. They want to feel good about themselves and the world around them. They like to wake up in the morning feeling good, go through the day without many problems, and then come home at night to a relaxing sleep. People don't want a lot of anxiety in their lives; they prefer to be stress free. But not everyone is lucky enough to have a good life. And if a person is not lucky, he needs to take responsibility on his own shoulders, to carry

Teaching Idea
If you review Activity 12.5 with students, ask them what they like about introduction 6 and how it differs from the others.

the weight of his own life. The fact is that happiness is not something that just happens for most people; they have to work for it.

6. "Dammit, Jack," the shift manager yelled at me, "that's the third time you burned those fries tonight! Get your head together or get a new job!" I stood there looking at my feet on the greasy tile floor, hating to take it, but apologizing anyway to keep my job. Around me rang out all the noise of a McDonald's Friday night: ovens beeping, warmers buzzing, pans clanging, deep fat fryer popping, Vera calling back for more Big Macs, kids crying up front from waiting too long in this so-called fast-food restaurant. That's when I finally decided I had had enough. I had to get a new life. Although coming back to college has been difficult, it is helping me leave the McDonald's days behind forever.

Ineffective paragraphs: _1–5 are ineffective; 6 is effective_____

Reasons that each introduction is weak: _1 talks about what the writer will____
_discuss instead of discussing it, 2 is too brief, 3 is full of clichés, 4 is___
_an apology, 5 is repetitive_____

_____
_____
_____
_____

One weak introduction rewritten: _Answers will vary._____
_____
_____
_____
_____
_____
_____
_____
_____

CREATING INTRODUCTORY PARAGRAPHS—SUMMING UP

1. Write out a working thesis sentence.
2. Skim the introductory paragraph methods, the methods for writing a hook, and the tips for avoiding weak introductions.
3. Prewrite using one or more of the introductory paragraph methods.
4. Draft your introduction.

Note: Some writers prefer to draft using only a thesis for focus and then create an introduction after the body is complete.

Body Paragraphs

Paragraph Patterns

Introductory paragraphs take the first step of attracting and then focusing a reader, but then the writer must follow through, keeping the essay interesting. We do this in the **body paragraphs,** where we present most of our information.

Essay body paragraphs begin with a topic sentence, as did the Unit Two assignments, and sometimes end with a summarizing sentence, similar to our Unit Two concluding sentence. Also, you will sometimes find a subtopic sentence useful, depending on how many points you want to develop in the paragraph. Whereas our former body paragraphs were around 300 words, now we will reduce the length to 100–200 words, around five to eight sentences.

Here are the three main parts of body paragraphs:

- **Topic sentence:** connector + topic + statement (first sentence)
- **Development:** four to six sentences (middle sentences)
- **Summary sentence** (optional): restatement of paragraph's main idea (last sentence)

Topic and Summary Sentences in Body Paragraphs

Topic sentences develop the thesis, offering the *more specific* points or examples from which the essay will grow. Within each topic sentence, it is important to name and focus the point or example and to include a link to the preceding paragraph—a transition or other connector. (To review methods for coherence, see pp. 53–58.)

Notice how the topic sentence in the following paragraph uses several connectors (boxed) to link to the previous paragraph and to link this main example (slicer) to the thesis, on the dangers of deli work.

But the part of the job that is most dangerous is using the meat and cheese slicer. Whether operating the slicer or cleaning it, you risk a nasty cut. The shiny circular blade on the machine is as sharp as a surgeon's scalpel, and you will use it all the time, your hand just inches away from the cutting edge. Everyone knows the kind of damage that can happen; everyone is extra careful, but then business picks up or someone is just too tired to pay attention. The blade doesn't know the difference, a piece of ham or four fingertips. Just one careless slip and you could end up with one less finger.

To conclude longer body paragraphs, writers sometimes create a **summary sentence** like the one underlined in the preceding paragraph. These sentences can be useful because they reinforce and clarify an author's message. However, in short paragraphs, they can become repetitive, boring readers. You must judge for yourself when summary sentences will be effective in your essays.

Developing Body Paragraphs

Whether expanding a single-paragraph assignment or beginning an essay from scratch, you need to develop your main points, which you can do by using detailed examples and explanations (see pp. 41–48), and asking yourself, "How can I more clearly show my readers what I am saying?"

By comparing a major example (subtopic) from the paragraph version of "Dangers in a Deli" with the corresponding body paragraph in the essay version, we can see how one writer used details and explanations to make her paragraph grow:

Single-Paragraph Subtopic	Essay Body Paragraph
One concern for potential deli workers is slippery floors. If the counter is packed with anxious customers, and workers are hustling about taking care of their orders, a wet floor is not going to take top priority. During the rush what's going to stop an employee from running too fast, which could result in a serious wipeout.	One common hazard for deli workers is slippery floors. Often, especially during the lunch rush, the place gets jammed. Anxious customers crowd into one another and lean over the stainless steel counter in your face to call out three more changes to their already late orders. Trying to manage the rush, employees hustle about, carrying checks, prepping sandwiches, carting plates back and forth. When scurrying from the salad case to the register, you might not notice that freshly mopped floor, and before you know it, you are crashing into a wall and banging your head on the slick, hard tile. And if you don't trip yourself up, there are always other employees to run into you, which can also cause a serious wipeout.

Subtopic sentence

Author explains what she means by "slippery floors" by naming things and giving details.

Author also uses action words to support the main idea of danger.

Topic sentence Author uses **process analysis** to show how workers manage the rush.

Author uses **cause and effect** to show what happens when workers rush.

HINT: To generate more ideas for your body paragraphs, use your favorite prewriting methods.

Notice how the single-paragraph subtopic of **57** words grew to an essay body paragraph of **121** words. The author held in mind her main idea of danger—specifically, slippery floors—and, through prewriting, found more detailed examples and explanations, which she developed using the patterns of process analysis and cause and effect.

In Unit Two, where we focused on individual patterns of development, we saw that patterns could be combined. In Unit Three, we will see even more clearly that substantial, artful development comes through combining many of these patterns:

Teaching Idea
AWW stresses development through detailed examples and explanation throughout, but this is a good place to reiterate that the patterns of development are most useful when they are used together, not in isolation.

- **Description:** using vivid details to show something about a subject
- **Narration:** telling a brief story to make a point about a subject
- **Illustration:** giving examples to illustrate some point
- **Classification/division:** grouping a subject or breaking it into parts

- **Cause/effect:** telling what actions affect a subject or what effects flow from it
- **Process analysis:** telling how a subject works
- **Comparison/contrast:** showing how a subject is like and unlike similar subjects
- **Definition:** telling the essential characteristics of a subject
- **Persuasion:** trying to move someone to agreement or action

HINT: Essays grow through many patterns of development.

ACTIVITY 12.6 Developing Body Paragraphs

Teaching Idea
To reinforce the concept of coherence, ask students to locate the connecting words in the topic sentences in Activity 12.6.

Revise the following underdeveloped body paragraphs, using several **patterns of development, detailed examples,** and **explanations.** Topic sentences are shaded. Remember that you can use description and narration to create images and show people acting in a setting. Try for paragraphs of six to eight sentences. Answers will vary.

1. Another problem with people who drink and drive is that they often can't be trusted. Sometimes they say they haven't been drinking at all. Other times they say they have had only one drink when it's clear they have had more. Frequently, they go to a party saying that they will not drink at all. Right.

Revision: _____

_____

_____

_____

_____

_____

_____

_____

_____

_____

2. However, the most annoying habit my younger brother has is fooling with the TV while we are all trying to watch it. Channel surfing is his specialty. He has many ways of sneaking the constant channel changing in. If there is a commercial, watch out. If you leave the room for a snack, it's all over.

Revision: _____

_____

_____

_____

_____

_____

_____

_____

_____

_____

_____

3. In addition to the other signs of wealth in this country, when I first
entered a supermarket, I found the abundance almost dazzling.
Americans have more of everything than we have in Russia. The aisles
seemed endlessly stocked with anything a person might need.

Revision: _____

_____

_____

_____

_____

_____

_____

_____

_____

_____

Arranging Body Paragraphs within Essays

To organize body paragraphs within essays, we use much the same logic
that we used to organize subtopics within single-paragraph papers. A writer
might choose any of these organizational patterns (for more on these patterns,
see pp. 52–53):

- **Spatial:** describing a place or other subject from front to back, side to
  side, top to bottom, and so on. You might write part of an essay, or
  even a whole essay, describing, say, a lakefront home as seen from a
  boat in the water. You could focus the first body paragraph on the dock
  and boathouse, the next on the yard, and the third on the house itself.

- **Chronological:** relating a series of actions in their order of occurrence.
  In writing personal narrative, fiction, or process analysis, you order
  your paragraphs chronologically—for example, Little Red Riding Hood
  first packed her basket of goodies, then walked into the woods, then
  met the wolf, then walked to her grandmother's house, and so on.

- **Order of importance:** arranging from least to most dramatic (or most to
  least). Much expository and persuasive writing uses this method. For
  example, in "Dangers in a Deli," the three body paragraphs go from
  least to most dangerous—from falls to chemical hazards to losing a
  finger.

Remember, also, that you may follow one of these patterns within a body
paragraph, as we did in Unit Two. Although "Dangers in a Deli" uses least to

most for overall arranging, within the body paragraphs the author relies more on time order, moving from slow to fast business while the clock ticks and customers arrive, as in this body paragraph:

Topic sentence

> Besides the slippery floors, workers also need to be cautious around chemicals. Even when business is slow, it is easy enough to be careless: for example, when cleaning the grease and handprints off all the glass, you might suddenly spray yourself in the face with ammonia. But it gets worse when the rush begins, and the owner goes into his panic mode: "Get these dishes done! Now, now—we're filling up!" You might think you have a good grip on that slippery platter, until it slips out of your hands and splashes into a sink full of pan degreaser and sanitizer. It only takes one faceful of that hot, soapy water to send a worker to the emergency room.

Using Outlines

Outlines

Another aid in organizing essays is the **outline.** Our paragraph assignments from Unit Two often required short lists, but because essays are more complex, more detailed outlines can help you keep them on track. A formal sentence outline is probably not needed for short essays, but outlining primary examples and several supporting points is useful.

Notice how we might create a working outline for "Dangers in a Deli":

Teaching Idea
Some students resist any kind of outlining, no matter how informal. You can reinforce the usefulness of outlines by periodically asking students to mention the main points or examples they will include in their essays and then saying, "Good outline."

Informal Working Outline	
Thesis	If you don't want to end up in the emergency room on your first day here, you need to be aware of the potential dangers in working at a deli.
Topic sentence	I. One common hazard for deli workers is slippery floors.
Supporting examples	A. Lunch rush B. Hurrying employees C. Fall on tile floor
Topic sentence	II. Besides the slippery floors, workers also need to be cautious around chemicals.
Supporting examples	A. Slow business still dangerous—ammonia B. Owner panicking C. Platter splashing into sink—degreaser and sanitizer
Topic sentence	III. But the part of the job that is most dangerous is using the meat and cheese slicer.
Supporting examples	A. Operating or cleaning—dangerous B. Sharp blade C. People too tired—accident

However you outline, write your thesis where you can refer to it often, and list at least the main examples with supporting examples and details.

Concluding Paragraphs

Conclusions

HINT: The conclusion should fulfill the promise made in the thesis sentence.

HINT: Introductions and conclusions should be tightly linked.

Teaching Idea
Student essays so often fizzle out in their conclusions that it is worth discussing why this happens. You might ask students to speculate on why they have difficulties at the end: deadlines, lack of inspiration, exhaustion, or something else.

Teaching Idea
Your discussion of causes of weak conclusions might lead naturally into a discussion of methods for overcoming the problems: organizing and developing.

Statement about topic is shaded .
Connector is boxed .
Summary is underlined.

Even more than introductions, conclusions can pose problems for essay writers. How do you leave readers feeling that the promise made in the thesis sentence has been met and that the essay is decisively completed?

One way to provide a satisfying ending is to *plan* a concluding paragraph. Though many longer works use several paragraphs or even a chapter to conclude, you need only five to seven sentences (a hundred words or so) for your short essays. You can make these sentences interesting by using the familiar strategy of the expanded thought.

As you draft the concluding paragraph, be sure to create strong links to the introductory paragraph, and include the following elements:

- **Lead sentence:** one sentence (connector + link to thesis)
- **Summary:** one sentence or less
- **Development:** three to four sentences (often contains expanded thought)

Writing Lead Sentences and Summaries

Just as introductory and body paragraphs have a lead sentence (the hook and the topic sentence, respectively), so do concluding paragraphs. This first sentence of the conclusion includes a connector and often touches on the thesis. It may also give a brief summary of the essay's main points. Alternatively, the summary might be in the second sentence. Notice that in "Dangers in a Deli" the lead sentence includes the summary:

Cuts, chemicals, concussions, and other dangers—with all these ways to be injured, a new person on the job might feel a little nervous.

The author could have saved the summary for a second sentence:

No employee wants to get hurt while working at the deli. So we all do our best to avoid hazards like falls, chemical burns, and cuts, and most of the time we succeed.

HINT: Effective writing leads readers carefully into the final thoughts.

The beginning of a concluding paragraph eases readers out of the main stream of the writer's ideas and into his or her final comments, which wrap up the essay.

Developing Conclusions

Teaching Idea
It is useful to reiterate at this point that conclusions and introductions are "specialty" paragraphs with their own purposes; they work differently than body paragraphs.

After leading readers into the concluding paragraph, rather than meander for half a dozen empty, repetitive sentences, you need to end your essay decisively. You can do this with the following strategies, most of which are already familiar:

STRATEGIES FOR CONCLUSIONS

1. **Frame:** return to the image, comparison, story, and so on from the introductory paragraph.
2. **Expanded thought:**
   A. Express an emotion.
   B. Give a judgment, opinion, or evaluation.

C. Show how something has affected your behavior or outlook on life.

D. Ask a related question.

E. Make a reflective statement.

F. Suggest a course of action.

3. **Combination of methods**

When you "frame" an essay, you return to the introduction and the method you used there (description, narration, comparison/contrast, and so on), extending that content. For example, here is an introduction for "Dangers in a Deli" that uses a **narrative** approach:

Introduction with a Narrative Approach

Shawn came into the restaurant cracking jokes, kidding customers and fellow employees alike, and generally having a good time. Everyone liked him right away and could see that he would be fun to have around. But in the middle of his third day on the job, during the lunch rush, we lost him for good. I was taking an order at table seven, when all the loud talking, jostling, and eating stopped abruptly. Everyone in the restaurant heard Shawn scream as he lost the first joint of his little finger to the meat slicer. He learned the hard way how dangerous this job can be. If you too don't want also to end up in the emergency room on your first day here, you need to be aware of the potential dangers in working at a deli.

We can frame the essay by writing a conclusion that extends the narrative like this:

Conclusion with a Narrative Frame

Cuts, chemicals, concussions, and other dangers—there are plenty of ways a person on a job like this can be injured. When Shawn came to us on that first day, I hoped that he would be careful enough to keep working here for awhile. We need fun people like him to make the job more interesting. But Shawn let himself have too much fun. He stopped by the day after his accident to show us his hand and say goodbye. He didn't blame anything on us, and he said he was sorry to go. His last words as he walked out the door were "Hey, the next time I'll know to listen up." So have fun while you are here, but don't become another Shawn.

Another effective way to capture readers' attention one last time is to offer an **expanded thought**. With this strategy, you take your audience one closely related step beyond the ideas in your body paragraphs, broadening your topic. You may have used this strategy in the final sentence of a one-paragraph paper, but now you can develop it. The following conclusions for the deli essay show different ways to use an expanded thought. Lead and summary sentences are shaded.

Concluding Paragraphs with Expanded Thoughts

Teaching Idea
As with introductions, it is worth taking some class time to have students write at least two different conclusions for one of their own essays to show them that there are many strong ways to conclude.

Lead and summary sentences combined

1. **Personal emotion:** Let your reader know how you feel about your topic. What emotional response has it created in you?

    Cuts, chemicals, concussions, and other dangers—there are plenty of ways for a person to get hurt on this job. I worried about it for the first month I was here, especially after I saw several other workers get hurt. But I learned that I could work safely if, when the restaurant began to speed up and people started moving fast, I kept myself at about 75 percent of my maximum speed. I can still get out the orders and keep everyone satisfied without pushing myself into an accident. Nowadays I don't need to worry much about getting hurt. I just pace myself, watch what I'm doing, and have a good time.

2. **Judgment:** Evaluate your topic or express an opinion.

    Cuts, chemicals, concussions, and other dangers—with all these ways to get injured, a new person on the job might feel a little nervous. But deli work doesn't always make you feel anxious and frazzled; in fact, it can be enjoyable. Whether you are talking to interesting customers or spending time with friends, the deli is usually a fun place to work. It can even be a great place for keeping your mind off problems at home or that algebra exam on Friday. Although accidents can happen, you are a lot less likely to have one if you keep the worst of the hazards in mind.

3. **Outlook or behavior change:** Show how your outlook on life or behavior has changed as a result of your experience with the topic.

    Cuts, chemicals, concussions, and other dangers—there are plenty of ways for a person to get hurt on this job. Before I came to work here, I used to jump right into an activity without much thought of the consequences. Frying up a skilletful of bacon, chasing a soccer ball downfield, mowing the lawn—I used to rush through them all. But now I think twice. I don't want to burn myself with hot grease, sprain an ankle, or lose part of my foot under the mower. And I have found that being more cautious hasn't taken anything from me; instead, it lets me participate more fully in everything. Fingers crossed, from now on I won't be standing around on crutches on the sidelines of anything I want to do in life.

4. **Question(s):** Ask one or more questions that might grow from your topic.

    With all these ways to be injured on the job, a person might wonder about working at a deli at all. Why should people put themselves in such a risky situation? The truth is that few jobs are altogether safe. A librarian can fall off a ladder and break a leg as easily as a waiter can slip and fall on a wet tile floor. The only sure way to reduce the chance of injury on the job is to follow the advice lots of parents give their children when they approach streets: stop, look, and listen. Slow down to live longer.

5. **Reflective statement:** Tell your readers something that your topic suggests to you beyond the points made in the body paragraphs. Think of some larger or more general application to the world around you.

    With all these ways to be injured on the job, a person might wonder about working at a deli at all. After all, no one wants to be cut, burned by chemicals, or knocked unconscious. But the truth is that no matter how careful a person might be, accidents cannot always be avoided. The world is an uncertain place, full of dangers. We like to think we can control our lives and protect ourselves absolutely. However, because this is not possible, perhaps it's best always to hope for, plan for, and work toward the best while preparing for the worst.

6. **Call to action:** Suggest that your readers or someone else act on the information you have presented.

    New employees and old hands alike can have an accident when they get too tired. Falls, scalds, and cuts are not uncommon in the deli as a result. Your best option to protect yourself is to listen to your trainer on your first few days at the job. Sure, some of the advice will sound obvious—"Don't put sharp knives into a sinkful of soapy water"—but the time you stop paying attention is the time you will start hurting. So during your training period listen carefully, watch closely, and read thoroughly all the instructions for operating equipment safely. We want to keep you on the job, not put you in the hospital.

Lead and summary sentences separated

Lead and summary sentences separated

ACTIVITY 12.7 Determining an Expanded Thought

For each of the following essays, write the thesis sentence and then, in your own words, the final expanded thought.

EXAMPLE

"Dangers in a Deli" (pp. 277–278)

Thesis sentence: "If you don't want to end up in the emergency room on your first day here, you need to be aware of the potential dangers in working at a deli."

Expanded thought: Working in a deli is not all danger and unpleasantness. The job can be fun.

Answers will vary.

1. "The Jobs from Hell" (pp. 327–328)

   Thesis sentence: "Finally I tore myself out of the nightmare and sat up in bed, remembering all too well these images from the rotten jobs I have worked in my life."

   Expanded thought: His current college education is difficult, but it will pay off in the end.

2. "A Skill beyond Price" (pp. 332–333)

   Thesis sentence: "Reading is a skill beyond price, and I see people profiting from it daily as they move through various types of reading based on the person's purpose."

   Expanded thought: Reading is the source of all external knowledge, and so people do read including, today, material on the Internet.

3. "I'll Park. You Get the Tickets—Hurry!" (pp. 347–349)

   Thesis sentence: "Some people love to watch films in a theater, but I find that watching them at home is a much more relaxing experience."

   Expanded thought: There are some good reasons for seeing films at a theater.

ACTIVITY 12.8 Creating Interesting Conclusions

Choose an introductory paragraph from Activity 12.2, and brainstorm to uncover several main examples for an essay that could grow from it. Next, write two concluding paragraphs for the essay. In one, use a frame; in the other, use one or more of the methods for writing an expanded thought.

Answers will vary.

1. Concluding paragraph using frame

   Lead sentence: _____

   _____

HINT: You might combine the lead and summary sentences.

Summary sentence: _____

_____

Development: _____

_____

_____

_____

_____

_____

_____

_____

_____

_____

2. Concluding paragraph using expanded thought (method number(s):
   _____)

   Lead sentence: _____

   _____

   Summary sentence: _____

   _____

   Development: _____

   _____

   _____

   _____

   _____

   _____

   _____

   _____

   _____

Avoiding Weak Conclusions

Even knowing how to write strong final paragraphs, we sometimes stumble. Here are some common problems to avoid:

1. Under- or oversummarizing (and repeating)

Some form of summary is used in almost all conclusions: the longer and more complex the essay, the longer and more detailed the summary might be.

However, in brief essays, readers do not need much repetition of main points. A sentence or less is enough. Here is how the author of the deli essay might have oversummarized for a weak conclusion:

> As you can see, there are plenty of dangers around a deli. It is all too easy for a person to slip and get hurt on a wet floor. And there are chemical hazards as well. Also, even experienced employees might have a serious problem with the meat and cheese slicer, so everyone needs to be extra careful around it. Because people can be seriously and permanently injured by falls, chemicals, and cuts, they should be alert on the job at all times.

CAUTION! Avoid oversummarizing in conclusions.

2. Telling readers that you are getting ready to end your essay

While you should connect your conclusion to the rest of your essay, avoid doing it with statements like these: "Well, as you can see, my essay is just about wrapped up," "In conclusion, my thesis sentence has already told you . . . ," and "In the essay you have just read, I have tried to show . . ."

3. Moving into an unrelated or too loosely related topic

Remember that an expanded thought should grow naturally from the body of the essay, an extension of the thesis. It should not move into a different topic. The following concluding paragraph for our deli essay shows this problem:

> Cuts, chemicals, concussions, and other dangers—with all these ways to be injured, a new person on the job might feel a little overwhelmed. But, you know, life is full of danger. People get hurt all the time. Why once when I was mowing a lawn, I wasn't paying attention and sliced off the front of my right tennis shoe. I learned a lesson from that scare—watch what you're doing when operating dangerous equipment, especially lawn mowers!

Clearly, the emphasis has shifted from the deli to lawn mowing.

4. Overgeneralizing

Teaching Idea
If you teach the chapter on persuasive writing, you might remind students of the problem of overgeneralizing in conclusions.

Expressing opinions and evaluating can be effective concluding strategies. However, it is important to qualify statements, so you don't claim more than you can prove. Avoid assertions like these: "And so you can see no one has a good reason for watching too much television," "Any student who tries hard can make good grades," and "Everybody loves football." (For more on qualifying, see pp. 397, 491.)

5. Apologizing

Apologizing is an ineffective concluding strategy, as is illustrated by these examples: "Although I do not know much about this topic, I have tried to show you . . . ," "Even though there are experts who know a lot more about this subject than I do . . . ," and "Although I am still kind of fuzzy about this topic, I hope you have learned something from my essay . . ." You should appear confident in the conclusion. If you have serious doubts about the essay, why not revise it?

6. Using clichés and worn expressions

Beware of clichés like these: "There were butterflies in my stomach," "All I had left was the shirt on my back," and "No one could ever fill her shoes." If a fresh figure of speech does not come to mind, use a literal phrase—for example,

"I was nervous" in place of the butterfly cliché. (For more on clichés and worn phrases, see Chapter 19.)

Teaching Idea
Of course, there are legitimate reasons for brief conclusions—for example, in essay exams.

7. Making your conclusion too long or too short

Conclusions should be written in proportion to the rest of the work. Our brief essays can support a final paragraph of five to seven sentences—about a hundred words or so.

ACTIVITY 12.9 Recognizing and Revising Weak Conclusions

Decide which five of the following six conclusions are ineffective. In each case, explain why it is ineffective. Next, rewrite any *one* of them, using a frame, one of the six methods for creating an expanded thought, or a method of your own. In each paragraph, lead and summary sentences are shaded.

1. Thesis: Rebuilding a carburetor is difficult, but with the right instructions most people can do it.

   With all of the complicated steps in rebuilding a carburetor, from initially removing it to reinstallation, you might have trouble with it like I did. I got lost in the process myself several times, and I'm not sure that I included all the steps you will need to get the job done right. But I hope that I explained clearly enough and remembered the really important warnings that you ought to follow if you don't want a big mess on your hands. If you think you can rebuild that carburetor now, then all I can say is "Good luck!"

2. Thesis: My two older brothers are as different as two people can be.

   With two brothers whose personalities are this different—one a whirlwind, the other a couch potato—a person might think that I would have a favorite. But that is not the case. I love both of my brothers equally, and I find many activities that we can share—though usually two's company, three's a crowd.

3. Thesis: One way to group friends is by how long you have known them.

   Friends are important in every person's life. There are potential friends, recent friends, and long-time friends, all of whom have their places in the overall category of friends. Potential friends might become friends someday if circumstances are right. Recent friends might be good friends, but they don't have a real track record yet. They might not hold up as good friends over the long haul. But long-time friends have proven themselves time and time again. A person knows that he can depend on long-time friends because they have been around for quite awhile and have shown their loyalty, support, and friendship many times over. For my money, the best and most valuable friends are long-time friends.

4. Thesis: A mother is much more than just the woman who carries a baby to term.

   All of these qualities are necessary for a woman to be a truly great mother. Mothers must be able to maintain their children on a daily basis, care for them when they are sick, teach and model behavior, and, most important, love them even when they are being unlovable. A friend of mine gave her baby up for adoption and was worried that when the child grew older, he might think his birth mother had abandoned him. I reassured my friend that adoptive mothers can do a terrific job of raising children and that she had made the right decision. At seventeen my friend is too young to take on the responsibility of raising a child. Giving the baby to a responsible, more mature, and financially stable parent was a wise choice.

5. Thesis: Lying to loved ones is a bad idea because it is ultimately self-destructive.

Telling even small "white" lies is dangerous in a relationship, much less the big lies that are the instant death of friendship. The guilt and worry over being caught often lead to a slow but undeniable distancing from our spouse, significant other, child, or friend. And this is, perhaps, the greatest damage done. Once the lies begin, they become easier to tell, but not easier to deal with. Instead of creating new, fun memories, we spend too much energy trying to make the stories we have told mesh. Lies take us away from the ones we love a little bit at a time. Instead of many shared memories in the house of our relationships, we have few . . . and then fewer. Even if the ones we love never catch us in the Big Lie, we can still trap ourselves, finally, in an empty room of our own making.

6. Thesis: While driving in their cars, people should use cell phones only for urgent business or emergencies.

Accidents like the ones just mentioned are the most important reason not to overuse cell phones, but wasting money, missing out on the world, and being inconsiderate to passengers are also important reasons. Cell phones are a nuisance. They don't really have any place in cars and ought to be outlawed. How in the world did people survive, after all, ten years ago (and five thousand years before that) without these obnoxious little time eaters? There is no good reason to yak away on a cell phone when people are never any farther away from a stationary phone than a 5-minute drive.

Ineffective paragraphs: _1–4 and 6 are ineffective; 5 is effective._

Reasons the conclusions are weak: _1 apologizes, 2 is too brief,_
3 oversummarizes and is repetitive, 4 drifts into a loosely related
topic, 6 overgeneralizes.

One weak conclusion rewritten: _Answers will vary._

Teaching Idea
If you review Activity 12.9 with students, ask them what they like about conclusion 5 and how it differs from the weak examples.

Teaching Idea
Remind students that other people can often see an expanded thought growing from the body of an essay even when the author cannot. Peer revision groups can help in this respect.

HINT: Review examples or ideas you cut from body paragraphs to see if one might work as an expanded thought.

CREATING CONCLUDING PARAGRAPHS—SUMMING UP

1. Look over your thesis sentence and the main points in your body paragraphs.
2. Review the discussion of writing a lead sentence and summary.
3. Draft a lead sentence and summary that link to your thesis sentence and main points.
4. Review the methods for expanding a thought and the ways of avoiding weak conclusions.
5. Decide on a frame and/or an expanded thought.
6. Prewrite, focusing on a frame or method for expanding a thought.
7. Draft the rest of your conclusion.

Creating Coherence

Coherence

HINT: Pay special attention to linking paragraphs.

In Unit Two, we learned how critical it is to create coherence by linking words within and between sentences, especially between subtopics. Essays also require strong connectors, especially *between* paragraphs. Here is a brief reminder of the five ways to create coherence:

FIVE WAYS TO CREATE COHERENCE

1. **Transitions:** using linking words in various categories, including:
   - Locating or moving in space: *above, against, around, behind, below, on, in*
   - Moving in time: *after, at last, awhile, first, next, now, often, then*
   - Adding material: *again, also, and, in addition, furthermore, as well as*
   - Giving examples: *for example, for instance, another, one reason, in fact*
   - Comparing: *alike, also, both, in the same way, similarly*
   - Contrasting: *in contrast, although, but, differs from, even though, however*
   - Cause/effect: *and so, as a result, because, consequently, since, so, then*
   - Summarizing/concluding: *finally, in brief, in other words, in short*
2. **Repetition:** repeating a significant word from a preceding sentence
3. **Synonyms:** using a word equivalent to one in a preceding sentence
4. **Pronouns:** using words like *he, she, they, that, this*
5. **Reference to a main idea:** reminding readers of some important point in a preceding sentence

(For more on coherence methods, turn to pp. 53–58.)

Teaching Idea
You might mention that writers usually link sentences unconsciously, so that coherence within a paragraph is generally less of a problem than between paragraphs.

The following concluding paragraph illustrates these coherence methods.

KEY

Transitions

Repetition

Synonyms

Pronouns

Reference to main idea

In a **relationship,** it is not advisable to tell even small "white" **lies,** much less the **big lies** that are the instant death of friendship. The guilt and worry over being caught often lead to a slow *but* undeniable distancing from our **spouse, significant other, child,** *or* **friend.** *And* this is, perhaps, the greatest damage done. *Instead of* creating new, fun **memories,** we spend our energy trying to make the **stories** we have told mesh. *Eventually, instead of* many shared **memories** in the house of our **relationships,** we have very few. *In this way, even if* the **ones we love** never catch us in the **Big Lie,** we can still trap ourselves, *finally,* in an empty room of our own making.

Selecting a Title

Teaching Idea
Chapter 3 treats titles more extensively, so it is a good idea to refer students back to this material when they need to create titles for their essays.

The title is your first opportunity to impress readers, and most of us would like to have them think, "Hmm . . . interesting, I wonder what this is about?" Creating an engaging title represents a last bit of attention to an essay, and this effort inclines readers to think that the rest of the work is developed with equal care.

The following list of reminders will help you create an interesting title when you are putting the finishing touches on your essay.

> **STRATEGIES FOR CREATING A GOOD TITLE**
> 1. Keep the title relatively short—around one to eight words.
> 2. Link the title to your main idea, central point, or dominant impression.
> 3. Create an image: Use a metaphor/simile, specific words, action words, and/or sensory details.
> 4. Ask a question.
> 5. Make a play on words.
> 6. Refer to something that your readers might know about and find interesting.
>
> (For more on titles, see pp. 59–60.)

Chapter Summary

1. An essay is a group of related paragraphs that develop an overall point.
2. Like a single body paragraph, an essay requires an introduction, development, and a conclusion.
3. The most obvious differences between a single-paragraph paper and an essay are that the essay is longer and has full paragraphs to introduce and conclude it.
4. Introductory paragraphs usually consist of a hook, development, and thesis.

5. Thesis sentences are like topic sentences except that they may be slightly more general because the essay that follows a thesis will include more complex examples, details, and explanations than found in a paragraph.

6. There are many methods for developing interesting introductions, including using one of the patterns of development, such as narration, comparison/contrast, questions, or background information.

7. Body paragraphs often begin with topic sentences and sometimes end with summary sentences.

8. Concluding paragraphs consist of a lead sentence, summary, and development.

9. Concluding paragraphs may be developed in several ways, including using a frame and/or an expanded thought.

10. Essays should be both unified (all material is relevant) and coherent (all sentences are clearly linked).

11. A title is an important finishing touch, and there are strategies for creating interesting titles.

Common First-Stage Draft Issues

1. Do you use several major examples to illustrate your thesis?

You should use enough examples to develop your main point. Resist settling for one or two major examples when three or four would better illustrate your thesis.

Longer essays may have dozens of body paragraphs, but our essays of 500 to 600 words should have two to four body paragraphs. If you have written, say, five to eight body paragraphs, you probably have not developed each one fully, or you are moving into a lengthier essay. (Check with your instructor on the length range of your assignment.)

2. Is your thesis sentence effective?

Teaching Idea
If you review these revision lists with students, you might mention again that thesis sentences can be located other than at the end of the first paragraph and point out several of the essays in Unit Six as examples.

Your thesis sentence should name the topic and make a clear statement about it. The sentence may also include a forecasting statement. If your working thesis sentence is unclear or too general, the essay may be headed for disaster. Be sure that both you and at least one other reader can easily predict where the essay is going based on the thesis sentence.

Unless you have some good reason to locate it elsewhere, make the thesis sentence the last one in your introduction.

When you begin to revise a focused thesis sentence, you can make it more effective through **specific words, action words,** and **sensory details.** (For more on thesis sentences, see pp. 279–283.)

3. Is the hook of your introductory paragraph effective?

The first sentence should arouse readers' interest; it should connect with your target audience.

Check also to see that you did not begin with an obvious statement or worn expression. (For more on hooks, see pp. 288–291.)

4. Is your introductory paragraph well developed?

Introductions in short essays should be around five to seven sentences. Be sure that you develop your paragraph using one or several of the methods listed in Chapter 12 or one of your own. (For more on methods of developing introductions, see pp. 283–288.)

Make sure, too, that you avoid problems leading to weak introductions (see pp. 291–293). There are so many effective ways to begin an essay that settling for something so-so is a shame.

5. Are your body paragraphs logically arranged by space, time, or importance?

In expository and persuasive writing, you will probably organize your body paragraphs by order of importance or, less often, chronologically. Whichever method you pick, be consistent and begin body paragraphs with transitions signaling that order. (Your material sometimes will be arranged by both time and importance, which is fine.) (For more on methods of arrangement, see pp. 297–298.)

6. Do you introduce each body paragraph with a topic sentence? If relevant, do you include a summary sentence?

Teaching Idea
You might also remind students that summary sentences can make short body paragraphs sound a bit repetitive.

While not all essay body paragraphs begin with topic sentences, many do. In your essays, for clarity and focus, each body paragraph should contain a topic sentence related to the thesis. Usually, it is the first sentence in the paragraph. Remember: Topic sentence = transition or other connector + topic + statement.

You may sometimes find a **summary sentence** useful for wrapping up a body paragraph, particularly if the paragraph is fairly long. (For more on topic and summary sentences in essays, see p. 294.)

7. **Are your body paragraphs well developed?**

All paragraphs in an essay should be necessary, appropriate to a specific audience, and well developed. Also, each body paragraph should illustrate one main idea, using detailed examples and explanations. Remember to be specific, layering examples and explanations so that one sentence adds to the next. For each example, ask yourself, "What do I mean by that statement? How can I make it more clear?"

Develop your work where appropriate through sensory details, active verbs, *-ing* words, dialogue, revealed thoughts and emotions, and descriptions of settings and people. (For more on developing body paragraphs, see pp. 294–297; for more on narrative and descriptive elements, see pp. 78–81, 110–119.)

8. **Are sentences within and between paragraphs well connected?**

All sentences in your essay should be smoothly linked, and strong connections are especially important between paragraphs. Remember to use **transitional words** (words like *first, next, for example,* and *another*) and other connectors: **repeat words, synonyms, pronouns,** and **reference to main ideas.** (For more on sentence connectors see pp. 53–58.)

9. **Is your concluding paragraph effective?**

Check your concluding paragraph for these three parts:

- **Lead sentence:** one sentence (connector + link to thesis)
- **Summary:** one sentence or less
- **Development:** three to four sentences (frame and/or expanded thought)

The first sentence of your conclusion should connect with the last body paragraph and the essay's thesis, and your main points or examples should be summarized in that sentence or a separate sentence. Make sure that you don't oversummarize and that you make the rest of your conclusion interesting by using the methods for developing conclusions in Chapter 12 or one of your own. Check for problems that result in weak conclusions. (For more on developing conclusions and avoiding weak conclusions, see pp. 304–308.)

JOURNAL ENTRY 13.1

List three changes you have made or feel you ought to make from your first to second draft. Refer to the first-stage draft questions, answering them specifically—for example, "Question 4: I decided that my introduction was weak, so I rewrote it, using method 9, startling information, which we practiced in Chapter 12." Next, in several sentences, state what you like best about the revised draft.

Revising Second-Stage Drafts

If your draft is fairly complete at this stage—with most of your concerns about content and organization under control—you can focus on revising words and sentences.

Common Second-Stage Draft Issues

1. Do you use specific language?

Your essay will include both general and specific language, but specific words create the sharpest images. You can write about someone wearing "old clothes" (a relatively general expression), but if it is important to the scene, be more specific—for example, "old blue jeans and a sweatshirt" or perhaps even "faded Levi's ripped out at the knees and a baggy KU Jayhawks sweatshirt." (For more on specific language, see pp. 78–81.)

2. Do you include sensory details?

Sensory details can be useful in expository and persuasive essays, and are often linked to specific words. For instance, in "Sixteen and Mother of Twelve" (p. 120), the author writes about "camouflage uniform pants," "black marching boots," and "brown T-shirts," placing the color detail in front of the specific article of clothing. Later, the author mentions "sweaty faces," adding a touch sensation. Of course, all spoken dialogue creates a sound impression, but linked to active verbs, the sound can become more dramatic, as in "What a Joke!" (p. 121), "when Linda Blair roars out, 'MERRIN!'" (For more on sensory details, see pp. 81–82, 98.)

3. Do you choose the most "active" verbs to describe action?

Verbs are important in conveying action, but some verbs do not convey action well (*be, do, have,* and *make* are common culprits). Consider these pairs of sentences:

A. Thunder could be heard on the lake.

B. Thunder shook the lake.

C. I moved my head around to my left toward the shore.

D. I jerked my head around to my left toward the shore.

If you think that sentences B and D create more vivid images, review the verbs in your own draft to see if any can be replaced with more active, interesting ones. (For more on active verbs, see pp. 483–484, 515; for more on passive voice, a problem in sentence A, see pp. 573–574.)

4. Do you use any *-ing* words?

Participles (one kind of word with an *-ing* ending) can also show action while helping you to vary your sentences. Consider these pairs of sentences:

A. My girls made it through all the obstacles.

B. Running, climbing wooden walls, crossing rope bridges, and playing Tarzan on a rope swing, my girls tore through that course.

C. In loose white pajamas, grandfather was in front of me to scratch on the door.

D. Wearing loose white pajamas, grandfather was standing in front of me, leaning forward to scratch on the door again.

If you think sentences B and D create more vivid images, revise your own sentences, adding *-ing* words wherever needed. (For more on *-ing* words, see pp. 66, 524–525.)

5. **Do you experiment with comparisons like metaphors or similes?**

Metaphors and similes can create fresh, sometimes startling images by comparing two seemingly dissimilar things that have something in common. Consider these two descriptions:

   A. Thunder shook the huge lake, and I could see the water move.

   B. Thunder shook the huge lake <u>as if it were a glass of water</u>, vibrating, nearly ready to fall off of some gigantic rock and <u>shatter on the ground</u>.

Comparing the lake to a glass of water is a fresh image (versus a cliché), and the fragile nature of a glass that can be smashed helps set the mood for the tragedy later in the story. If you think that sentence B has more power, then review the sentences in your own draft to see if any literal description might benefit from a metaphor or simile. (For more on metaphors and similes, see p. 505.)

6. **Are the sentences in your essay varied in length?**

Writing can be more or less interesting based on the structure of sentences alone. After polishing word choices, check the length of sentences (counting the words can help). If you find more than four sentences in a row of roughly the same length (say, 14, 17, 12, and 15 words), either combine two or divide a long one. (For more on sentence variety, see Chapter 18.)

7. **Are the beginnings of your sentences varied?**

If even two sentences in a row begin with the same word, such as *the*, change an opening or combine sentences to break up the pattern. Also, look for too many similar openings even if the sentences are far apart. For example, you might notice that you started eight out of twenty sentences with the word *As*. It is easy to change a word or combine sentences to increase the readability of the essay. (For more on variety in sentence openers, see pp. 465–478.)

8. **Do you avoid repeating a word so often that it becomes noticeable?**

While some repetition is useful, too much becomes boring. Consider the following two sets of sentences:

   A. There were many people on the <u>lake</u> waiting to put their boats in the <u>water</u> there at Hillside <u>Lake</u> on that tragic July afternoon. In my boat on the <u>lake</u>, I felt hot and sticky from waiting on the humid <u>lake water</u> as I frantically maneuvered my small aluminum boat closer to the ramp by the <u>lakeshore</u>.

   B. There were many people in the <u>water</u> waiting to put their boats on their trailers at Hillside <u>Lake</u> on that tragic July afternoon. I felt hot and sticky waiting on the <u>lake</u>, frantically maneuvering my small aluminum boat closer to the ramp.

If you think that version B is more readable, revise your own sentences, cutting nonessential words. (For more on unnecessary repetition, see pp. 510–511.)

Teaching Idea
For simplicity's sake, it is sometimes useful to discuss sentence variety in terms of length alone, because combining sentences for length often also creates variety in openers.

Teaching Idea
You might point out that cluttered writing may help students reach word count requirements but that, by the time you are through crossing out the fluff, their essays will be considerably shorter.

9. Do you avoid words that serve no purpose?

Everyday speech is full of unneeded words, but writing should not be. Cluttered writing can bore and confuse; concise writing, in contrast, involves readers and clarifies ideas. Compare the following two sentences. Which is concise and which is cluttered?

A. The meat hotdogs, long and thin, sizzle with a sizzling sound as they cook, roasting, and drip their meaty juices off the end of the wooden stick.

B. The hotdogs sizzle as they cook and drip their juices off the end of the stick.

If you think that sentence B is more readable, revise your own sentences, cutting unneeded words. (For more on unneeded words, see pp. 487–496.)

Teaching Idea
Given half a chance, students will reply to revision questions with vague statements or simply fall back on revising for mechanics. Journal Entry 13.2 again asks for specifics and will be most useful if student responses are discussed in class and then collected for review.

JOURNAL ENTRY 13.2

Skim the questions on revising second-stage drafts, looking for three ways to improve your paper (or three points you think might be a problem). After you have revised your paper, list three changes you made. Be specific in your response and refer to the questions—for instance, "Question 8: I noticed that I had used the word *car* fifteen times, so I substituted *vehicle*, *hot machine*, and *it* to eliminate five of the car references."

Editing

Teaching Idea
Try focusing students on one or two errors at a time as they edit these practice paragraphs.

HINT: Editing these practice paragraphs will help you with your own revision.

Teaching Idea
Four practice paragraphs are presented here to help on days when the class edits essays (or for students to do out of class). If you need more, you will find seven shorter practices in Chapter 4.

With your essay almost complete, now is the time to edit it closely, by yourself and with others. For practice, choose one of the following editing review paragraphs and read it slowly, trying to catch the common mechanical errors listed below.

- Misspelled words
- Sound-alike words
- Missing words
- Wrong words
- Sentence fragments
- Comma splices/run-ons
- Faulty capitalization
- Incorrect apostrophes
- Missing comma(s)
  - A. Introductory words/phrases/clauses
  - B. Nonessential word groups
  - C. Main clauses with coordinating conjunction
- Unneeded commas
- Verb tense shifts
- Faulty pronoun agreement
- Faulty pronoun reference

Editing Review 13-1

Panick and fustration our a sure fire recipe, for tears but I fought them of and strugled too remain calm, for my girls. Suddenly I hear a voice, say "Listen I have a cell phone, do you want to call someone to come pick you up". As I turned toward the voice I saw an older gentleman, who looked a lot like my dad. Begining to cry I explained how helples I felt.

(The corrected version of this excerpt is on p. 136 in "Do Unto Others . . .")

Editing Review 13-2

Another important part of true Home is that people can relax their. When we feel safe we can begin to feel at ease in are surroundings. If family members our considerat of one another they will give each other the space each need they will give each other the time, and opportunity to unwind in, whatever, way works best for each. Some listens to music some watches TV and, some just appreciates laying down on a couch. A true Home encourages relaxation. At the end of a busy stressful day out "there" we all needed to escape the pressure's of being productive.

(The corrected version of this excerpt is on p. 366 in "Finding Home.")

Editing Review 13-3

"Your'e a dummy and so's your Old Lady and Old Man!" These were fighting words for me as a child and I ended up rolling around in the dirt more than once with the kids from school who said them. Growing up with hearing impaired parents in sixties if I was not fighting some kid in an alley it seems like I was trying to explain to some other child that my family was normal, we just didnt talk much which words. Back then most people didnt no much about the deaf comunity and even, today I, often see people turn, and gawk at the hearing impaired when they are signing each other. Maybe knowing more about the deaf will make them seem less strange to the hearing world.

(The corrected version of this excerpt is on pp. 367–368 in "Deaf, Not Dumb.")

Editing Review 13-4

Being in the ocean in scuba gear, is a lot like being in outer space when a diver is floating, in silence above a deep-water coral plateau with a half mile drop into darkness a few yards away. He is in another world. Depending on the compressed air, in his cylinders, and his regulator to deliver it smoothly. The diver glides weightlessly, almost effortlessly, through "inner space." Similarly an Astronaut floats in darkness. With the deepest drop imaginble all around him. He also depend on his gear to deliver air protect him from the cold and other extremes tells him how much air he has and Orient him toward his "boat." Most of us will never have the oportunity too voyage into Outer Space but, we can learn a little about the next-best option for inner planetary travel, scuba diving.

(The corrected version of this excerpt is on p. 380 in "Get Wet.")

Well, how did you do? If you caught all but two or three errors, congratulations—you are a careful editor! If you missed more than five or six, you should simply slow down even more and apply the editing skills you are learning. The following are a few reminders about the errors listed on p. 318 and tips for looking for and fixing them:

Common Editing Problems

Teaching Idea
If you have students edit in class, it is useful to list the three "missing comma" categories on the board along with some "cue" words: *because, who/which, and/but.* You will also find selected editing review sheets in the Instructor's Manual.

1. **Misspelled words:** Use your spell checker first, and then try to find at least one other reader who is a fairly good speller. Remember, too, that the dictionary can help. (For help with spelling problems, see Chapter 27.)

2. **Sound-alike words** (*there/their/they're, to/too, then/than, your/you're,* and so forth): Keep adding these word mistakes to your Improvement Chart, and review them regularly. You probably have only a few soundalike word problems, but unless you memorize the words, you will repeat the mistakes endlessly. (For help with soundalike words, see Chapter 27.)

3. **Missing words:** Read slowly. Sometimes, reading a sentence backwards can help, and covering the sentence that follows the one you are editing can keep you from jumping ahead too quickly.

4. **Wrong words:** Be suspicious of words that sound too "writerly." If you often refer to a thesaurus to find words, you might be using them incorrectly. You probably already have enough vocabulary to express yourself well, and smaller, more common words are frequently the best choices. Your readers can alert you to *possible* poor selections; then you can work with a dictionary and someone else to make the final decisions. (For more on achieving clarity through small words, see pp. 497–498.)

5. **Sentence fragments:** Remember two common types of fragments:

PHRASE	**Running to the store for bread and a six-pack of Coke.** (The word group lacks a subject and a verb and is not a complete thought. See pp. 555–557.)
SUBORDINATE CLAUSE	**Because he is the kind of man we want for mayor.** (The word group has a subject and verb, but the subordinating word *because* makes it an incomplete thought. See pp. 558–559.)

   You can correct most fragments by joining them to another sentence or adding words to make them complete sentences. (See pp. 555–560.)

6. **Comma splices/run-ons:** These errors happen when two sentences are joined incorrectly with only a comma or with no punctuation at all:

COMMA SPLICE   The cement is freezing, it instantly numbs my feet.

RUN-ON   The cement is freezing it instantly numbs my feet.

Remember, there are at least five ways to fix these. (See pp. 551–558.)

Note: In dialogue, be careful to avoid this kind of comma splice: "Roxanne shouted, 'Get out of here, nobody cares about you anyway!'" Instead write: "Roxanne shouted, 'Get out of here! Nobody cares about you anyway!'" People frequently speak in short sentences and in fragments. Don't be afraid to show this in your dialogue.

7. **Faulty capitalization:** As a rule of thumb, capitalize proper nouns—the names of specific, unique people, places, and things. (See pp. 609–610.) In your titles, capitalize most words, even little ones like *is* and *one*. But do not capitalize articles (*a, an, the*), prepositions (*to, on, of, in,* etc.), and coordinating conjunctions (*and, but,* etc.) unless these words begin or end a title or follow a colon.

8. **Incorrect apostrophes:** Remember, use apostrophes to show ownership or mark the omission of a letter in a contraction: "Maria's calculator isn't working." (See p. 609.)

9. **Missing commas:** These three categories govern perhaps half of our common comma mistakes:

   A. Use a comma to mark where a word group at the front of a sentence ends and a main clause begins (cue words: *because, as, if, when,* etc.). (See pp. 595–597.)

   EXAMPLE   If I finish my paper early, I will watch *The Matrix Reloaded.*

   B. Use commas to enclose a nonessential word group within a main clause or to set it off after a main clause (cue words: *who/which,* etc.). (See pp. 598–600.)

   EXAMPLE   *The Matrix Reloaded,* which continues *The Matrix,* uses more computer animation and special camera effects than the first film.

   C. Use commas between main clauses joined by a coordinating conjunction (*and, but, or, so, yet, for, nor*). (See pp. 601–602.)

   EXAMPLE   Neo gains more powers in this sequel, and he uses them outside of the Matrix against the machines.

10. **Unnecessary commas:** As you learn the handful of rules that help with comma placement, you will move away from the old standby "I put commas where I hear pauses." Using your ear helps with punctuation—but only about half the time. Most of us don't want a 50 percent average, so learning a few rules is the way to go. Try to avoid unneeded commas such as those in the following examples:

   INCORRECT   I went to Burger King for lunch, and then to McDonald's for dinner. (Your ear might tell you to pause, but a comma is not needed unless the two word groups you are joining with *and* are complete sentences.)

   CORRECT   I went to Burger King for lunch and then to McDonald's for dinner.

Teaching Idea
If you write an example sentence on the board to illustrate a comma dividing compound sentences, you can use the same sentence to show an unnecessary comma by crossing out the subject in the second main clause.

INCORRECT   I eat three 13-ounce bags of potato chips every day, because I want to have a heart attack. (You might naturally pause before *because*, but it begins an essential clause that explains *why* the subject eats so foolishly and should not be set off with a comma.)

CORRECT   I eat three 13-ounce bags of potato chips every day because I want to have a heart attack.

(See pp. 604–606 for more on finding, and correcting, unnecessary commas.)

11. **Faulty pronoun reference and agreement:** Pronouns must refer to a specific noun, and they must agree with that noun in number:

REFERENCE ERROR   Florence was talking to Abby when *she* saw the accident. (Clarify *she* reference: *she* = Abby.)

AGREEMENT ERROR   *Each* of the players want a raise. (*All . . .* want . . .)

(For more on pronoun problems, see Chapter 24.)

After editing on your own, don't be reluctant to seek help. Every writer benefits from critical input. You will undoubtedly spend class time editing collaboratively, but don't stop there. Look for help from your family, friends, instructor, and writing center—all valuable resources to help you improve your work.

JOURNAL ENTRY 13.3

By now, your draft should have all the important details in place, words carefully chosen, and sentences flowing smoothly. Review your Improvement Chart to focus on pattern errors, and then *slooowly* edit your paper, word by word, line by line. List at least three errors from the editing review list that you found in your draft, and then write out the corrections.

Proofreading

Teaching Idea
Proofreading is just another name for final editing, and it is amazing how many students skip this important step. In particular, you might stress number 3: spell checking additional required material and title pages.

Proofreading is the last polishing step in preparing your paper. After you have closely edited your draft, catching mechanical errors, you will print out what could be your final copy. But before turning it in for a grade, you need to make a few last checks.

HOW TO PROOFREAD AND PREPARE YOUR FINAL MANUSCRIPT

1. Check for typographical errors such as misspelled, run-together, and omitted words. Often, when fixing errors in the editing stage, we slip up in small ways on the keyboard. **Be sure to spell check once again.**

2. If necessary, prepare a title page. (For formatting a title page or the first page of an essay that has no title page, see pp. 73–74.)

3. Check the following carefully: font size (12 point), line spacing (double space), margins (1 inch), and capitalization of title (see "Common Editing Problems," number 6).

4. Spell check any additional required material, such as outlines and audience profiles.
5. Staple or paper clip your pages. Avoid putting the paper in a plastic sleeve, which most instructors consider a nuisance.

JOURNAL ENTRY 13.4

Reflect for a moment on your work in producing this essay. Now write a page telling your instructor what challenges you faced. What are the strategies that you have learned and will apply to your next writing assignment?

FINAL-DRAFT CHECKLIST

☐ 1. Have you used several major examples to illustrate your thesis?
☐ 2. Is your thesis effective?
☐ 3. Is the hook of your introductory paragraph effective?
☐ 4. Is your introductory paragraph well developed?
☐ 5. Are your body paragraphs arranged by space, time, or importance?
☐ 6. Have you introduced each body paragraph with a topic sentence?
☐ 7. Are your body paragraphs well developed?
☐ 8. Are sentences well linked within and across paragraphs?
☐ 9. Is your concluding paragraph effective?
☐ 10. Have you used specific words, sensory details, active verbs, and *-ing* words?
☐ 11. Have you tried a comparison like a metaphor or simile?
☐ 12. Are your sentences varied in length and beginnings?
☐ 13. Have you avoided repeating words too often and including unneeded words?
☐ 14. Have you written an interesting title? Have you checked its capitalization?
☐ 15. Have you edited your work closely (including having at least one other person edit)? Have you checked your Improvement Chart for pattern errors?
☐ 16. Have you looked for errors involving the following: misspellings, soundalike words, missing words, wrong words, sentence fragments, comma splices/run-ons, faulty capitalization, incorrect apostrophes, missing commas, unnecessary commas, and faulty pronoun reference and agreement?
☐ 17. Have you prepared your paper according to the format expected by your instructor? (Check to see if you need a title page. Be sure you have double spaced, left at least a 1-inch margin, and used a 12-point font.)

CHAPTER 14

Expanding Paragraphs into Essays

What Are We Trying to Achieve and Why?

Teaching Idea
As you assign any of these patterns, you will want to use some of the material from the corresponding assignment chapter in Unit Two. It is best to remind students on *several* occasions that they are now writing essays, not paragraphs.

Teaching Idea
The expanded paragraph model for each of the patterns can help students with the specific development questions that most will have as they expand their own paragraphs.

In the accompanying photograph, we can see a family busily changing the look of home. Perhaps they have gained a new member, or just feel pressed for space as the children have grown. Rather than abandoning their home, they decided to improve it by adding to it. In this chapter, you will follow their example, developing a paragraph assignment from Unit Two into an essay. Like the home-owners with their house, you may be happy with your paragraph as a small unit, but now you can increase its size, developing the ideas and adding details to make it more interesting. Some of you may also be using this chapter to build your essay from scratch.

Having worked through part or all of Chapter 12, Introducing the Essay, you probably now have a clear sense of essay form and have reminded yourself of the primary ways of developing ideas: detailed examples and thorough expla-nations. In this chapter, you will see models for essays that follow patterns of development introduced in Unit Two—illustration, classification, cause/effect, process analysis, and comparison/contrast. For each pattern, there are two mod-els, one of which has been expanded from a paragraph model in Unit Two. These models will give you ideas for your own essay. By analyzing them carefully and by comparing essays with the corresponding paragraphs in Unit Two, you will gain a better sense of how to create effective essays, from paragraph papers or from scratch.

Whether or not you are coming to this chapter with a paragraph to expand, you should review the chapter from Unit Two on the specific pattern of development (process analysis, classification, etc.) that your essay will be following.

Illustrating through Examples (Illustration)

Writing Tutor: Exemplification

Teaching Idea
Many students will more readily understand issues of pronoun case and other elements of tone if you discuss them in terms of *I* and *they*. Chapter 19 gives students more specific guidance on tone, and Chapter 24 discusses pronoun choice.

Using examples to illustrate a point or clarify an idea is the heart of all writing, so, of course, you will find examples used in all of the patterns of development. Here, however, we focus specifically on **illustration** as the main pattern of development.

As you learned in Chapter 3, examples come in two basic varieties: those drawn from our own lives—**personal examples**—and those drawn from outside our personal experience, including facts, statistics, and information from print sources. If you made a statement about your own family—say, that they are very involved in sports—you would probably choose personal examples to show that involvement. But if you wanted to speak in general terms about American families' enjoyment of sports, you would rely not on your personal experience but on your observations and general knowledge.

Developing an essay through examples is much like developing a paragraph through examples. You make a statement or give an example and then ask yourself, "What exactly do I mean by that?" and "How can I make myself more clear?"

Note: For a more complete discussion of illustrating with examples, turn back to Chapter 7.

Illustration Essays: Analyzing Student Models

The following two models, "The Jobs from Hell" and "Teaching with Whips," will help you write illustration essays. Both authors rely on personal experience to develop their examples, and so they frequently use the pronoun "I." (To see models using the more formal "they" approach, turn back to "Dangers in a Deli" and "Nothing Worthwhile Comes Easy" in Chapter 7.)

Look closely at the introductory and concluding paragraphs; introductions and conclusions are major parts of essays, and we all need more experience with them. Also, to see how a paragraph might grow into an essay, compare the essay version of "Teaching with Whips" with the paragraph version in Chapter 7 (pp. 150–151).

Teaching Idea
Try using this prereading material to stimulate class discussion of miserable jobs *before* you discuss the essay. Draw students out, having them supply specific examples and details, and then ask them to compare their responses with Latham's essay.

➤ Prereading Exploration for "The Jobs from Hell"

Eric Latham decided on an audience of young adults between the ages of 16 and 25, thinking they might be especially interested in his examples and main point. Answers will vary.

1. Before reading the essay, look at the thesis and title. Do they give a clear idea of what to expect in the body of the paper? Why or why not?

   _____

   _____

2. Think about any unpleasant jobs you have had (or have). What makes them so miserable?

   _____

   _____

3. If you have been as unlucky as Eric and can remember three, four, or more bad jobs, list them, and then give several examples of what you most disliked about them. If you have had only one marginal job, give examples from it. If you are lucky and have had only good work experiences, list those. These ideas may help you find a topic for your essay.

The Jobs from Hell

I was trapped in a nightmare; this had to be a nightmare. Somehow I had gotten stuck back on a Payless Cashways loading dock with three managers screaming at me to get three different jobs done at the same time. As I ran inside to get a forklift, the machine turned into a commercial walk-behind lawn mower, and I was suddenly frying under a Sahara Desert sun, with no grass to cut, just endless waves of dry, stinging sand. Then I was inside a dark slaughterhouse that reeked from rotting meat and was filled with the screams of dying animals. Finally I tore myself out of the nightmare and sat up in bed, realizing with a start that all these images came from the rotten jobs I have worked in my life.   1

My first miserable work experience was at Payless Cashways when I was fifteen. I remember walking through the automatic doors on day one, excited, confident, and ready to learn. Soon I *did* learn—all about angry customers who expected me to know everything about every item in the store and how to fix every broken door hinge, light, window, and toilet they were having problems with. Then the manager began overloading me with work. Twenty hours a week was too much for a freshman in high school, so that was the first "good" job to go by the wayside.   2

When I was a senior, I found another job that, at first, looked promising. Dr. Lawn paid well, but I had to mow lawns for six to eight hours a day in the July heat, with temperatures running into the nineties. One day on the job I grew sick to my stomach and feverish and literally collapsed in back of a walk-behind mower. My manager would not let me go home because we had come in a car pool, and if I had left, it would have affected the other five people working. When I finally made it home, my dad found that I had a 105-degree fever, and we both decided that no job was worth my health.   3

4   These other bad experiences aside, the worst job I have ever had was in my sophomore year when I applied for work at Fritz's Meat House. At the time twelve dollars an hour sounded like great money, so I was as anxious to begin as I had been at Payless. However, I soon found out how disgusting the work was. The store was absolutely gross, filled with rotting meat from days ago, hanging pig carcasses waiting to be chopped, and an overflowing grease bin. The bin was located on the bottom floor of the two-story building, and all the animals parts ended up in it—chicken heads, legs, and feathers; pig feet; cow ribs; and gray intestines slippery from blood and yellow fatty tissue. Well, the bin didn't empty itself. It was my treat to empty that lovely stinking mess with a huge ladle, which I did for one week, averaging twelve-hour days. Needless to say, I soon found that the money wasn't worth it.

5   I am happy no longer to be stuck in the nightmare of these bad jobs. I am working myself away from them. After sitting out from school for a year and realizing that life was not going to shower me with opportunities unless I got an education, I decided to go back. As hard as this first year back at JCCC has been, I know that graduation is not that far away. With my AA in computer science, I'll head for KU and a four-year degree. Fingers crossed, I'm saying goodbye forever to the jobs from hell.

—*Eric Latham*

POSTREADING ANALYSIS: KEY POINTS FOR BUILDING ILLUSTRATION ESSAYS

- **Title:** arouses readers' curiosity and links to the essay's main point.
- **Introductory paragraph:** begins with a hook and ends with a thesis sentence.
- **Body paragraphs:** begin with a topic sentence, which names the subtopic and makes a limiting statement about it—for example, "My first miserable work experience was at Payless Cashways when I was fifteen"—and may end with a summary sentence—for example, "Needless to say, I soon found that the money wasn't worth it."
- **Development:** uses specific examples, action, scene and character details, sensory details, active verbs (*trapped*), *-ing* words (*stinging, rotting*), and specific words (*Payless Cashways*); tells thoughts and emotions; explains the examples ("Twenty hours a week was too much for a freshman in high school . . ."). (For more on layering examples, see pp. 43–44.)
- **Concluding paragraph:** restates the thesis, briefly summarizes, and adds a final (expanded) thought.
- **Sentence connectors:** guide readers: transitions, repeat words, synonyms, pronouns, and reference to main idea.
- **Style points:** increase readability. Italicizing words (paragraph 2: *did*) and using dashes (paragraph 2) can create emphasis. Contractions can add an informal note and prevent stilted writing (paragraphs 4, 5).

HINT: Summary sentences can be useful to end body paragraphs.

Teaching Idea
In the latter part of the semester, in particular, many students will profit from some discussion of style. Seeing elements like italics and contractions in student models can generate a useful discussion. For more on elements of style, see Unit Four.

➡ Prereading Exploration for "Teaching with Whips"

Teaching Idea
Student discussion of corporal punishment in schools is usually lively, and students will often offer well-detailed examples to illustrate their points, a good way to reinforce the point of the illustration section.

Jeong Yi wanted to share some personal experiences with classmates so that they could compare their own education with his and learn something of the cultural differences between them. Jeong also thought that teachers might be interested in the essay because of his comments on the use of force to motivate students.

Before reading the essay, think about the issue of corporal punishment in school. Some people say schools in the United States would maintain better discipline and turn out more academically prepared students if physical punishment were used. How do you feel about this issue?

Answers will vary.

_____

_____

_____

(To see this essay as a paragraph, turn back to Chapter 7, pp. 150–151.)

Teaching with Whips

When I went to middle school in Korea, I feared a beating almost every day of my life. I was not worried about fellow students or even outside gang members hurting me, the way many young people in America are. And I did not cause trouble in school, so misbehavior was not the reason for my punishment. Instead, I often did not perform academically up to many of my teachers' high expectations. My low grades meant whippings. There were several merciless teachers in particular who seemed to want me to "enjoy" studying by forcing it on me.   1

As a new middle school student, I was surprised by my first painful encounter with my moral education teacher, a short fat man who carried a short fat whip to enforce his every whim. His manner of speaking somehow did not make it seem urgent for me to thoroughly complete all the homework. Then one day he noticed that I was not prepared and made an example of me to show the class how harsh he could be to defiant students. "I see you haven't done your homework, Jeong," he said, his angry red face shaking. Straining with fear, the class was dead quiet, wondering what was going to happen at that frightful moment. "Jeong, stand up!" he ordered. His chalk-dusty hands held my two shaky little hands palms up and aimed at them as if they were targets. The punishment ended with me crying and begging, "I will do it next time, teacher. I promise!"   2

Another spiteful man was my history teacher, who liked to use his green baby bamboo stick to punish students who didn't score more than 80 percent on the exams. Many of us had felt our skin rip from that skinny bamboo rod. And when I would see him headed my way with that   3 certain glint in his eye, slapping the stick into his own hand, I knew what was about to happen. "Why," I wanted to shout at him, "why don't you let us feel some interest in history? Maybe then we would be more responsible!" But these words never left my lips, although plenty of words left his. "If you don't study, you won't succeed," he barked as he dealt quick whips. I muttered curses with his final blow.

4   None of the teachers seemed to understand that my test scores did not necessarily reflect how much I studied, and this was especially true of my art teacher. Nicknamed "Poisonous Snake," he was hated by all the students. His face was always red, like a drunken man's, and he seemed unable to smile. I never received a kind word or look from him. Instead, he gave me intimidating glares with his narrow, slanted eyes. He carried a black-taped wooden stick, which was bigger and more frightening than any of the other teachers' weapons, and it never left his hand. As he used the stick in other classes, the whacking sound echoed through the silent and empty halls. I could only anticipate the pain I would feel the day I scored poorly on an exam. Burning with anxiety, I knew the only way to prevent these pains would be to study more diligently.

5   Having had to endure the anxiety, pain, and humiliation of corporal punishment from my teachers, I was finally convinced to study. Yet early on I realized that even when I studied hard I could not satisfy the teachers in some of my classes. All the focus was on test grades—performance—and my efforts put into studying never were acknowledged. Teachers should realize that forcing students is not the only or the best way to persuade them to study and that some students are not going to do well in some subjects. What is the value of a few "A's" on a report card when the knowledge can be forgotten so quickly? Why not help students to really enjoy learning so that they can motivate themselves for a lifetime of education?

—*Jeong Yi*

Teaching Idea
To reinforce the value of narrative/descriptive elements, even in expository writing, you can focus on them in Jeong Yi's essay, asking students what images they think are most compelling and why.

KEY ELEMENTS OF ILLUSTRATION ESSAYS

Here are several important points—illustrated by the preceding student models—to keep in mind for your own illustration essay:

1. Organize by beginning each body paragraph with a topic sentence (see pp. 36–41).
2. Arrange your examples by order of importance (or time) (see pp. 144–145).
3. Use clear connectors between sentences and paragraphs (see pp. 53–58).
4. Develop your examples through details and explanations (see pp. 41–43).

Creating and Explaining Groups (Classification)

Writing Tutor: Classification

Teaching Idea
You might discuss classification more in terms of organizing than generating material.

Teaching Idea
Because the SOP can be confusing to students, it is especially useful to work through several of the activities in Chapter 8 that focus on it.

As you learned in Chapter 8, you often need to classify or divide ideas or objects into groups, and to do so in a way that makes sense. That is, you use a **single organizing principle (SOP),** a standard for grouping items. For example, people group their belongings in preparing for a move. They do not group them according to, say, color and shape—the blue living room couch together with blue jeans, and the plates together with CDs—but logically, according to what room things are going to be in, so they can unpack as efficiently as possible.

On the job, at home, and at school, **classifying** is a way of dealing with and making sense out of large amounts of information. Many essay topics, too, are usefully developed through classification. With an essay-length paper, the rules for classifying that you saw in Chapter 8—using only one principle for classifying, avoiding overlapping groups, and including all important groups—become even more essential.

Note: For a more complete discussion of classifying, turn back to Chapter 8.

Classification Essays: Analyzing Student Models

The following two models will help you write classification essays. Notice that both essays make the SOP clear in the thesis sentence, so that the readers know the basis for dividing and classifying the topic. "A Skill beyond Price" discusses groups that the author created himself, while "Shopping the Easy Way" uses a preestablished system for categorizing. Either approach can work well.

Look closely at the introductory and concluding paragraphs; introductions and conclusions are major parts of essays, and we all need more experience with them. Also, to see how a paragraph might grow into an essay, compare the essay version of "Shopping the Easy Way" with the paragraph version in Chapter 8 (p. 180).

➡ Prereading Exploration for "A Skill beyond Price"

Teaching Idea
To help students avoid the pointless classification, after they have read "A Skill beyond Price," ask them to discuss the author's purpose and point.

Ho-Chul chose reading as a topic because he strongly believes that it is a key to a successful, happy life. The people he most wants to address are those who do not read much or see any special value in it—some of his fellow students, in particular.

Answers will vary.

1. How important do you feel reading is? _____

   _____

   _____

2. Do you read often or only occasionally? _____

3. Do you think that college students today value reading more or less

   than their parents' generation? Why? _____

   _____

   _____

   _____

A Skill beyond Price

1   Frequently it is said, "No one reads anymore." I have read this observation in newspapers and magazines and heard it on television commentaries. And I have heard teachers at my college complain that their students do not even read the work assigned in their textbooks, much less read for pleasure. But I wonder if this is true. The students I spend most of my time around seem to be reading constantly, and not always just their homework. Reading is a skill beyond price, and I see people profiting from it daily as they move through various types of reading based on the person's purpose.

2   The first category can be called required reading. Most people have some kind of regular required reading. At home we sort through mail to find which pieces may be valuable and which are a waste. At work many people have to read office communications, and even service and manual labor jobs post memos and warning notices that employees should read if they want to profit or keep themselves from harm. Of course, students are surrounded by books that they are expected to read and prove that they know on exams. Sometimes we resent the have-to part of this kind of reading, and sometimes just the word "required" makes us want to put it aside. However, there is much to be gained from required reading, and I have often seen that the book that one person drags himself through is happily embraced by another person.

3   More pleasant for most people is the reading that they choose for leisure and entertainment. Some people enjoy short stories and novels—literature, westerns, romances, mysteries and detective stories, and/or science fiction. Huge bookstores like Borders and Barnes & Noble are filled with people relaxing with their favorite new story. Others prefer magazines that keep them informed about the world, such as *Newsweek* and *National Geographic,* about their profession, or about some special interest or hobby. People read daily newspapers, comic books, and letters from friends. Many people find inspiration in the Bible and other religious publications. The World Wide Web offers chat rooms, listservs, and e-mail, all of which allow people to read and write for fun and knowledge. The greatest difference between reading in this category and that which is required seems to be freedom, the choice to read or not.

4   The category of reading that is the most helpful for many people and the most enjoyable for me is the practical information found in how-to

books and magazines. After reading this kind of material, people can immediately apply the knowledge to their everyday lives. For instance, they can learn how to cook delicious food, how to make a beautiful garden, how to take photographs well, and how to decorate a house attractively. Because people have a personal interest, a clear goal, in practical reading, they can concentrate on it more than with much required reading. And I have noticed that, as with some required reading, how-to books can be interesting and fun for many people, moving these books into the more-preferred leisure/entertainment category.

People read for many reasons, and if they achieve their goal in any category of reading, then it can be said that they have profited. Even the least-preferred type of reading, that which is required, can be beneficial in many ways. It seems to me that people are still much involved with words and pages in books, magazines, and electronic sources, and how could this be otherwise since reading is the foundation of civilization? We may not like to do some kinds of reading, but all the knowledge that exists outside of one person and the people he or she can immediately speak to is contained within books. The Internet, which my generation is growing up with, is a vast library that offers a wealth of words to any who will pause to view them. I think truly that we are still in a reading world.

—Ho-Chul Sung

POSTREADING ANALYSIS: KEY POINTS FOR BUILDING CLASSIFICATION ESSAYS

- **Title:** arouses readers' curiosity and links to the essay's main point.
- **Introductory paragraph:** begins with a hook and ends with a thesis sentence that specifies the SOP.
- **Body paragraphs:** begin with a topic sentence, which names the subtopic and makes a limiting statement about it—for example, "The category of reading that is the most helpful for many people and the most enjoyable for me is the practical information found in how-to books and magazines."
- **Development:** uses specific examples, details, active verbs (*sort*), *-ing* words (*warning*), and specific words (*Borders*); tells thoughts and emotions; explains the examples ("However, there is much to be gained from required reading . . ."). (For more on layering examples, see pp. 43–44.)
- **Concluding paragraph:** restates the thesis, briefly summarizes, and adds a final (expanded) thought.
- **Sentence connectors:** guide readers: transitions, repeat words, synonyms, pronouns, and reference to main idea.
- **Style points:** increase readability. Rhetorical questions can involve the reader (paragraph 5). A short sentence after several longer ones can create emphasis (paragraph 5: "I think that truly we are still in a reading world").

HINT: Effective classification requires a single organizing principle.

HINT: Develop a paragraph by adding specific names and explanation.

Teaching Idea
These concluding paragraph sentences help reiterate Ho-Chul's point about reading and attitude.

→ Prereading Exploration for "Shopping the Easy Way"

Teaching Idea
Have students who are stumped by the toy store classification choose their own workplace as a topic or choose some other business with which they are familiar.

Ann Nall works in a local Toys "R" Us and decided that it would make a good topic for her classification paper. She thought that new parents might appreciate the information she offers, especially on items in the baby section.
Answers will vary.

1. If you have ever been in a Toys "R" Us or another toy store, how did you find your way around?

   _____

   _____

2. What single organizing principle seems logical to apply to a toy store? Present one or more methods for dividing and grouping merchandise in a toy store.

   _____

   _____

   _____

(To see this essay as a paragraph, turn back to Chapter 8, p. 180.)

Shopping the Easy Way

1   Have you ever entered a toy store and been confused by the masses of toys and cluttered aisles of seemingly endless options? Sometimes you may know exactly what you are looking for but spend half an hour just trying to find the right area to start the real search. Other times you may have only a general idea of what you want, but you still hope to see everything the store has to offer so that special gift does not pass you by. When people are overwhelmed by shelves crammed so full of toys that they cannot tell one from the other and put their lives in danger as they stumble over merchandise lying haphazardly on the floor, they are not having a pleasant shopping experience. However, Toys "R" Us is nothing like this. To help customers shop more efficiently, Toys "R" Us is neatly divided into three overall categories: areas for older children, toddlers, and babies.

2   The older children have four major areas—Blue, Pink, R-Zone, and Silver—with piles of toys for everyone. Boys mostly head for the Blue section and items like the GI Joes, superheroes, Hotwheels, and Legos. In no time at all, the boys can have Lego racetracks assembled on the floor and be racing miniature Batmobiles after the "bad guys." Girls, on the other hand, usually go for the Pink section, where there are dozens of different Barbies, complete with friends—Ken, Skipper, Stacie, Kelly, Teresa, Kira— Cabbage Patch Kids, and tea sets that help the girls build fantasies as they pretend they are older. Both sexes enjoy the video games and bicycles in

the R-Zone and Silver. Although it may seem like gender stereotyping to some, the Blue and Pink sections, especially, do help both children and parents get to the merchandise they are most interested in.

The next group of children, the toddlers, has the Red and Green areas. 3
Toys in these sections are larger than those in the older children's area and do not have as many small pieces, so the toddlers are less likely to choke. Customers shop in Red to find smaller toys such as Play Dough and building blocks to help their children develop fine motor skills. Also Red offers a variety of musical instruments, from simple shakers like maracas and tambourines to the more complicated guitars and electronic keyboards. Large outdoor play sets, made primarily of plastic, and traditional metal swing sets complete with slides and gliders are located in the Green section.

For the smallest children, moms and dads shop in Purple, and it sur- 4
prises many parents that Toys "R" Us offers so much for infants. This part of the store contains most of what parents need to get children through their first year. Each aisle is clearly marked, guiding shoppers to shelves of diapers, wipes, bottles, formula, clothes, rattles, teething toys, eating utensils (mostly spoons), and . . . well, you name it. After the baby's immediate needs have been met, the store can still help with important items like baby carriers, car seats, and strollers.

Shoppers are often confused by disorganized toy stores, but orga- 5
nizing merchandise the way Toys "R" Us does helps people readily find what they need for children of different ages. There are other places to shop for your children—Kmart, Wal-Mart, Target, K B Toys—but finding what you want in these stores can be an ordeal. As frustrating as shopping of any kind can be, with the general confusion, noise, poor service, tight schedules, and money concerns, why not try to make the venture as painless as possible? Good organization is the key to a pleasant and productive shopping experience.

—Ann Nall

Teaching Idea
Some of your students might be having difficulty choosing appropriate pronoun case. Contrast the use of *you* in Ann Nall's introduction—where she intends to speak directly to her audience—to the pronoun shift examples in Chapter 24.

KEY ELEMENTS OF CLASSIFICATION ESSAYS

Here are several important points—illustrated by the preceding student models—to keep in mind for your own classification essay:

1. Use a single organizing principle (see pp. 173–176).
2. Avoid overlapping categories (see pp. 176–177).
3. Include all important members of the group (see pp. 177–178).
4. Have a reason for the classification (see p. 175).

Recognizing Causes, Explaining Effects (Cause/Effect)

As you learned in Chapter 9, when we speculate about the reasons for and outcomes of an event, we are dealing with the concept of **cause and effect.** For example, suppose a tree falls on a house. What might have caused it? High winds are a likely immediate cause, but perhaps there are other reasons, too. Insects, disease, or drought may have weakened the tree, contributing to the fall. Beyond learning why the tree fell, the homeowner will want to know about the consequences. What will this event mean in terms of the costs of the cleanup, the inconvenience, and the ultimate appearance of the house?

In your essay, you want to focus on the causes or effects that are likely and significant and to exclude those that are not. For example, in an effects essay on the tree's falling, you would include discussion of an increase in homeowners' insurance, a likely and significant consequence. In a causes essay on that topic, you would *not* include the use of excessive fertilizer on the lawn the previous week, as this is too unlikely a "cause." In that same essay, you might also choose not to include the insect damage if you decide that, although a likely cause, it is probably not a significant one. Finally, you want to avoid oversimplifying. It would be oversimplifying to write that a call to Allstate is the primary effect of the damage; your essay would probably also need to mention the inconvenience to the homeowner, the extensive lawn damage from heavy repair equipment, and other effects.

Note: For a more complete discussion of cause and effect, turn back to Chapter 9.

Cause/Effect Essays: Analyzing Student Models

The first student model, "My Friend Who Gave Up on Life," discusses likely causes of a tragic event, while the second, "The Thousand-Dollar Lesson," deals with the effects of a questionable pastime. Essays are often developed with both causes and effects, but to help focus your brief essay, you should probably choose either causes *or* effects.

Look closely at the introductory and concluding paragraphs, because these are major parts of essays, and we all need more experience with them. Also, to see how a paragraph might grow into an essay, compare the essay version of "The Thousand-Dollar Lesson" with the paragraph version in Chapter 9 (pp. 205–206).

➡ Prereading Exploration for "My Friend Who Gave Up on Life"

While we often write for a larger audience, sometimes we do write primarily for ourselves. That is the case for Julie Hammond's introspective essay, which she wrote to reflect on a friend's death and in a small way come to terms with her grief.

If you have lost a loved one or had some other tragedy enter your life, undoubtedly you have been concerned with the "why" behind the event. Take a moment to write down an unpleasant or painful event in your life and speculate about its causes. Try to list four or more probable causes.

Answers will vary.

_____

_____

_____

My Friend Who Gave Up on Life

On July 14, 1996, at midnight, I was sound asleep when suddenly the 1
phone rang. It was my friend Austin. His voice was soft and shaky as he
told me that our friend had committed suicide. The shock of the information was hard for me to take, especially at such a late hour, and I
didn't want to grasp what I had heard. "OH NO!" rang through my mind
over and over; I didn't know what to do or think. I sat alone in the darkness of my room with tears streaming down my cheeks. The thought of
Sam following through with his drunken promises made me sick, and still
to this day I wonder what could have caused my friend to decide his life
was not worth living.

Nobody can really know what causes a suicide, but one of Sam's 2
problems was depression. His life seemed always to be falling apart.
When he was younger, it wasn't so bad, but as he moved into his teens,
he began having problems with his family, friends, and school. He couldn't
even get his car to run right. School officials started calling home about
his absences, and he began acting up in classes, one time getting suspended. Most of his friends didn't know how to handle the "new" Sam,
and a lot of them just stopped seeing him. His family wasn't much help
either, always nagging at him to straighten up. In his parent's eyes he was
just another teenager going through a stage. And after the drinking
began, his folks grew even harder on him.

By sixteen Sam was definitely an alcoholic, which must have pushed 3
him closer to the end. Alcohol was a way for him to escape a world
going wrong. School, friends, family—everyone seemed to be deserting
him. His family could see that he had a drinking problem. Their solution was to stick him in rehab and figure that should take care of it.
When he returned, he would be OK for awhile. But it didn't take long
for him to start drinking and acting up. This set his family off, and they
began yelling at him that he better shape up or else. He never did, so
they just sent him away again. Those of us who were left of Sam's
friends should have been listening more carefully. When he was drunk,
Sam began saying that he was going to kill himself. I guess deep down
inside I thought he might do it someday, but I didn't know what to do
about it.

The drinking was bad enough, but it led to another serious problem 4
for Sam, probation. In the last year he was drunk all the time; he never

seemed to take a night off. And for some reason he always seemed to get caught. Finally, he was stuck with three years of probation. We used to talk about it, and he told me how trapped he felt. The school didn't want him, his family thought he was hopeless, he couldn't keep a job, and now the probation people were hounding him, making him take drug tests that he couldn't pass and watching his every move. Those three years looked like a prison sentence to Sam, and he said he figured that it would just get worse. If it wasn't his mom and dad, it was the law; someone was just waiting to lock him up for good.

5   I'm not sure if it was the probation that pushed him over, any one reason, all of them combined, or some others that I will never know. When a friend dies this way, people want to know why. Everyone talks about it, trying to figure it out. What caused the suicide; what could we have done to stop it? All of the friends Sam had left heard him talk about killing himself, and no one said they believed him. But I wonder how many of my friends are like me, inside still thinking that they really did believe he might just do it. When a friend dies, don't we all share the blame?

—*Julie Hammond*

POSTREADING ANALYSIS: KEY POINTS FOR BUILDING CAUSE/EFFECT ESSAYS

- **Title:** arouses the readers' curiosity and links to the essay's main point.
- **Introductory paragraph:** begins with a hook and ends with a thesis sentence that predicts a cause or an effect essay.
- **Body paragraphs:** begin with a topic sentence, which names the subtopic and makes a limiting statement about it—for example, "The drinking was bad enough, but it led to another serious problem for Sam, probation."
- **Development:** uses specific examples, details, active verbs (*rang*), -*ing* words (*streaming*), and specific words (*alcoholic*); tells thoughts and emotions; and explains the examples ("Those three years looked like a prison sentence to Sam . . ."). (For more on layering examples, see pp. 43–44.)
- **Concluding paragraph:** restates the thesis, briefly summarizes, and adds a final (expanded) thought.
- **Sentence connectors:** guide readers: transitions, repeat words, synonyms, pronouns, and reference to main idea.
- **Style points:** increase readability. Capitalizing letters (paragraph 1) and using a dash (paragraph 3) can create emphasis. A semicolon can create sentence variety and emphasis (paragraph 4: "drunk all the time; he never seemed to take a night off"). A metaphor or simile can add interest and clarity (paragraph 4: "like a prison sentence").

Teaching Idea
The essay communicates quite well without dialogue, but hearing Sam's voice in the last body paragraph might add to the emotional impact of the essay.

HINT: The subtopics should be likely, real, and significant causes or effects.

HINT: Details, action verbs, specific words, and comparison can add interest to your essay.

➡ Prereading Exploration for "The Thousand-Dollar Lesson"

Teaching Idea
The intent of this prewriting question is to help students focus their topics. Clearly, some topics are more interesting treated as either causes or effects.

Luke Eimers chose an audience of young adults, particularly ones who have received speeding tickets and as a result have had trouble with their auto insurance. Before reading ahead, consider the topic of speeding tickets.
Answers will vary.

1. If you wrote an essay on this subject, would you prefer to write about causes or effects?

   _____

2. What topics do you think might be better handled as causes, on the basis of the topic itself and readers' likely interest?

   _____

   _____

3. What topics might be better handled as effects?

   _____

   _____

4. List below four possible reasons a person might speed.

   _____

   _____

   _____

(To see this essay as a paragraph, turn back to Chapter 9, pp. 205–206.)

The Thousand-Dollar Lesson

1   Sometimes you just have to drive fast, even when you know you are breaking—maybe even shattering!—the speed limit. It feels great to be on an eight-lane interstate, the traffic sparse, the day clear and dry, and the pedal to the metal. My '85 Camaro can handle the speed. I push her up to ninety (well, a hundred) all the time, and she floats over the pavement like she's riding on some kind of sci-fi antigrav. Other drivers just seem to drift past my windows as I change a lane here and there, leaving even the long-haul truckers in the dust. I wish we had an autobahn like Germany so I could drive as I want to, but we don't, and I guess I have finally found that out. While traveling last spring, I learned about the miserable consequences of my favorite pastime.

2   My first unpleasant experience was actually getting the ticket. I knew I was in trouble from the moment I saw the red flashing lights in my rearview mirror and looked down at the speedometer to see the needle on eighty-five. I knew that I had been driving that slow for at least five minutes, so even though the posted limit was seventy, I thought I might

be able to talk my way out of it. But then I saw the Clint Eastwood look-alike Texas highway patrol officer step up to my window. "All right, boy, let me see your license and proof of insurance," he drawled, cutting off my "Gee-I-didn't-realize-I-was-going-that-fast" line. The officer seemed to enjoy every second it took him to write that ticket out, and with an evil smirk he handed it to me, saying, "Have a nice day." I'm pretty sure he was the only one having fun.

3   The next problem was paying the ticket. I didn't want it on my record because it would crank up my insurance rates, and I knew taking care of the ticket would cost plenty. It did. First I had to call all my friends to dig up a lawyer who could make the ticket "disappear" without making what was left of my bank account disappear too. The ticket turned out to be only seventy-five dollars, but the lawyer cost three hundred. Everyone said I got off cheap, and I believe them, but ouch!

4   As bad as that expense was, the next effect was worse. My parents had been paying my insurance because at the time I was still living at home and going to college. However, after they learned of my ticket, they decided to stop helping me with the coverage. They reasoned that if I had enough money to speed, then I had enough money to pay for my own insurance. I never quite figured out their logic, but I got their point. A thousand dollars for a year's premiums is an expensive lesson.

5   Having to cover the insurance on top of the ticket led to the worst consequence of all—work, work, work! I picked up extra hours at my job on the golf course, but that was not enough. So I turned to my parents, who were willing to help, they said, with smiles that reminded me of the Texas highway patrol officer. There were plenty of odd jobs for me to do on the weekends around the house: painting the shed, staining the deck, washing the windows, cleaning out the garage. . . . When I got tired of manual labor, they would let me cart my younger sister around town, baby sit, and help her with her homework. My folks were very creative and have given me lots of this kind of "help."

6   The expense and extra work aside, I know that a high-speed accident is the most serious possible consequence of my fast driving. And I don't want to end up with pieces of my car and me (or others) scattered along a highway somewhere, looking like a broken up 737. I think I've learned my lesson. I can't always follow my impulses, even when everything says, "Go, go, go!" As I consider career choices now that I am in college, I have

more decisions to make, and I know they should be practical ones. I have always wanted to be a pro golfer, but my parents have questioned the wisdom of this goal. Well, I still have my Camaro; maybe it's not too late to drive a NASCAR (just joking).

—Lucas Eimers

Teaching Idea
To begin a discussion of voice and tone, ask students how the elements of humor, irony, dialogue, and comparison affect the overall "feel" of "The Thousand-Dollar Lesson." Does the essay feel relaxed and casual? How about the writer? How would students characterize him—as someone they might know or want to know?

KEY ELEMENTS OF CAUSE/EFFECT ESSAYS

Here are several important points—illustrated by the preceding student models—to keep in mind for your own cause/effect essay:

1. Explore all the likely causes and effects (see pp. 196–199).
2. Develop causes or effects thoroughly (see pp. 199–200).
3. Choose only the real causes and effects (see pp. 200–201).
4. Avoid oversimplifying by thinking critically (see pp. 202–203).

Explaining Activities, Doing Them, Understanding Them (Process Analysis)

Writing Tutor: Process Analysis

HINT: Process analysis includes steps, reasons, and warnings.

Teaching Idea
It is important to help students see the difference between a process to perform and one to understand. You might mention that while it may be more challenging to write about processes to understand, they can also be more interesting to write about and read.

As we discussed in Chapter 10, when we explain an activity so that someone can perform or understand it, we are doing **process analysis.** For example, in building a house there are many steps: clearing the ground, pouring the foundation, framing the walls, putting on the roof, and much more. An experienced builder would be able to tell us about each step in the process. The explanation would probably include definitions of new words, warnings about dangers, and reasons, for example, that one step comes before another or why one material is used and not another.

The builder could give us a detailed explanation so that we might understand the process, or he could give specific instructions so we could perform some part of it. You may take either of these approaches in your essay, writing about a **process to perform** or a **process to understand.** In either approach, you will find that breaking down an activity into steps and explaining each one clearly is a powerful tool for learning about what you thought you already knew.

Note: For a more complete discussion of process analysis, see Chapter 10.

Process-Analysis Essays: Analyzing Student Models

The following two models will help you write process-analysis essays. The first, "Jokers Wild," promotes playing practical jokes as an amusing and worthwhile pastime. The author uses humor in writing about a process to understand. The second, "A Boy's Best Friend," in which we see the author as a boy, explains a process to perform.

Look closely at the introductory and concluding paragraphs; introductions and conclusions are major parts of essays, and we all need more experience with them. Also, to see how a paragraph might grow into an essay, compare the essay version of "A Boy's Best Friend" to the paragraph version in Chapter 10 (p. 229).

→ Prereading Exploration for "Jokers Wild"

As a practical joker, Michael Feldman decided to explain the process of playing a practical joke. And as a nontraditional student returning to college after years on the job, he decided to simultaneously comment on how hard so many people work in our society. For this **process-to-understand** essay, he chose to describe the general process, rather than any one particular joke. His target audience is young, hard-working adults who might themselves be inclined to play a prank on friends.

If you have ever played a joke on or deliberately surprised someone—anything from making a crank phone call to setting up a surprise party—how did you go about it? In the space below, list six steps that you followed to surprise the person.

Answers will vary.

_____

_____

_____

_____

_____

_____

Jokers Wild

1   The world needs an antidote to seriousness. Too many people are bogged down in the day-to-day grind of making a living and taking care of all their RESPONSIBILITIES. Childhood seems to end about the time we get our driver's licenses and can haul ourselves to work. It's either school or work or, for many of us, both. We can't always take the vacations we want—sometimes it's even hard to get a weekend—and between studying, working, and taking care of the people in our lives, we get kind of dried out and wrinkly, like grapes turned into raisins. But there is one partial remedy for this condition, playing pranks. If you have a general understanding of the ground rules for playing pranks on friends, everyone can survive, and most will even have a good time.

2   The first step is to know yourself. If you are shy or introverted, practical jokes may not work for you because you may suddenly, sometimes unpleasantly, find yourself in the spotlight when/if you are discovered. If you are reasonably outgoing and think you can stand the attention, you may still have problems if the prank backfires. For example, when your friend breaks her favorite desk lamp trying to escape from the gerbil you put in her desk drawer, you may find yourself buying a new lamp and apologizing profusely, on both knees if necessary.

3   If you are the right sort for pranking, the next important point is to know your victim. While casual friends make fairly good targets, good friends are often a better choice. First, you know where they work and

play, so you can pick a good spot to lay the trap for that singing telegram or surprise birthday party. Second, and more important, if the joke really blows up in your face, a good friend is less likely to hit or sue you. A casual friend, for instance, might not be as tolerant if he discovers the identity of the person who anonymously had a truckload of gravel dumped on his driveway.

With a target and suitable prank picked out, you can begin to think about execution—of the plan, not the person. The first rule here is no dangerous jokes. If, for example, you want to drop water on someone, don't put it in a metal bucket over someone's door. Physical pain is not funny, at least to the sufferer. Next, remember that timing is critical. The singing stripper that you have visit a friend at a party might go over well with everyone there, but send her to the church picnic, and you have problems. In general, if you remember that you still have to live around your victim after the joke has passed, your sense of self-preservation should tell you when to quit.

No advice on playing pranks would be complete without a few words on the aftermath, or dealing with the fallout. Your primary concern is how well it went over. If all went well, everyone chuckled, and there were no hard feelings, terrific. Then you can accept the credit for the general good times. However, if the response was mixed or poor, and you want to escape, you have several options, depending on how many people are in on the joke (you can't really rely on anyone not to blab over time). First, admire the idea behind the prank but wish that whoever did it had used a little better judgment. Second, inconspicuously offer an airtight alibi. Third, shift the blame to another friend who is also known to play pranks. Maybe he or she will appreciate your attempt to save yourself, knowing that he or she would do the same thing in your place.

Playing practical jokes can be fun for everyone—well, almost everyone— if the joker is temperamentally suited, knows his or her victim well, chooses a suitable prank, and can deal with the aftermath. As busy as we grown-ups have become, we still need to take a break sometimes and lift our faces up from the grindstone. Whether we are planning a surprise birthday party or having someone call a friend who has just "won" the lottery, well-played jokes can help relieve the stress of too-serious lives. And as long as we have a good friend who can stand us (and another friend or two to take the blame), we will have all the opportunities we need. Happy pranking!

—*Michael Feldman*

of hateful sparrows with my slingshot, as seldom as I actually hit one, is a boyhood experience I would never erase. Thinking back to my simpler life, I sometimes feel confused today. Surrounding me are my computer, fax machine, cordless phone, television, and stereo—products of technology and my new city life. At one time I was content with almost nothing, just a few toys I had made with my own hands. But now I am hardly content with an apartment full of adult toys, needing more and more to be satisfied. I have gained many things in growing up, but I fear that I have lost the boy who knew how to be happy with nothing more than a slingshot.

—Steve Oh

KEY ELEMENTS IN PROCESS-ANALYSIS ESSAYS

Here are several important points—illustrated by the preceding student models—to keep in mind for your own process-analysis essay:

1. List all the necessary steps (see pp. 222–224).
2. Explain the steps thoroughly, giving reasons and warnings (see pp. 224–225).
3. Define all the terms (see pp. 225–226).
4. Avoid monotonous sentence patterns (see pp. 226–227).

Explaining Similarities and Differences (Comparison and Contrast)

**Writing Tutor:
Comparison
and Contrast**

Teaching Idea
Comparing and contrasting are such fundamental methods of development that it is worth reminding students that they will often use brief comparisons and contrasts within other overall organizational patterns. Chapter 15 discusses such combinations at more length.

As we saw in Chapter 11, **comparing and contrasting** ideas, people, and things is the process of discovering similarities and differences among them. Topics often lend themselves to both. For example, we could *contrast* the players at a football game to the cheerleaders. The football team is entirely male while the cheerleading squad is mostly female. One group wears pads, helmets, and spiked shoes while the other wears light clothing and tennis shoes. Those in one group have serious, almost grim, expressions while those in the other are smiling and enthusiastic. One group is riveted on the action on the playing field while the other is turned outward and upward toward the crowd.

We could also *compare* the two groups. Both are the focus of the spectators' attention, both consist of athletes, both work as teams whose members depend on one another for success, both have leaders, both have organized plays or routines, and both are working toward the goal of winning the game. Thinking about it for a moment, we can uncover many differences and similarities between the groups.

Longer essays often explore both comparisons and contrasts. However, to keep your brief essay focused, you would do better to choose either comparison or contrast, as in the student model essays here.

Note: For a more on comparison and contrast, see Chapter 11.

Comparison/Contrast Essays: Analyzing Student Models

The first model, "I'll Park. You Get the Tickets—Hurry!" focuses on differences between watching movies at home and in a theater. The second, "Break on Through to the Other Side," also focuses on differences, this time between two stages of the author's life. The first model uses **block organization;** the second uses **point-by-point organization.**

Look closely at the introductory and concluding paragraphs; introductions and conclusions are major parts of essays, ones with which we can all use more experience. Also, to see how a paragraph might grow into an essay, compare the essay version of "Break on Through to the Other Side" with the paragraph version in Chapter 11 (p. 256).

➡ Prereading Exploration for "I'll Park. You Get the Tickets—Hurry!"

Hugh Edwards picked a topic he thought most people could identify with—watching movies at home versus going to a movie theater. Of the many ways to compare and contrast movies at home and movies out, Hugh chose to contrast the *experience,* focusing on the extent to which he finds it relaxing in each case.

Think about your own movie-going experiences, and then list ways in which watching a movie at home is preferable to going to the movies. How many of your examples matched the author's?

Answers will vary.

_____

_____

_____

Teaching Idea
Having students list the points the prereading activity asks for will help focus them when they read Hugh Edwards's essay.

Teaching Idea
This introduction illustrates another example of the intentional use of *you* to connect with the audience. You can contrast this use to accidental pronoun shift.

"I'll Park. You Get the Tickets—Hurry!"

The room is warm and inviting, the lighting low, your recliner soft. With a cool drink in hand, you push play, and a great movie appears on the big-screen TV in front of you. Cut to next scene: This room is cold, almost black, your chair sticky with spilled something. Clutching a softening waxed cup of watered-down soft drink, you pull your feet back as someone steps on them again and spills part of a drink on your legs. It is crowded, noisy, and uncomfortable. You can't see well (maybe the film is out of focus), and it is a hundred yards to the nearest restroom. Welcome to Saturday night at the movies, at home or out. Some people love to watch films in a theater, but I find that watching them at home is a much more relaxing experience. 1

There are many good reasons to stay home for movies. One is snacking. When I am home, I have the run of the kitchen, and I am likely to end up with a light meal of cold chicken, green salad, side dishes of black 2 and jalapeno-stuffed olives, whole wheat rolls, and several beverages of my choice. Since my 27-inch TV is only 10 feet from the kitchen, I can easily watch a film while I nibble on my snack. And if I choose to get even more comfortable, I can move to the best seat in the house, my La-Z-Boy recliner, putting my feet up with a TV tray in my lap. With an extra pillow from the bedroom behind my neck, I am in heaven. But even more important than snacking and seating for my movie-watching pleasure is the freedom I have at home. When I have set myself up for the evening, I can choose any time to start, pause, or stop the movie. If I don't like my first choice, "Eject." Then I pop in the next. If it gets too late to finish one, I just save it for the next night. And I never have to miss a minute if another cold beverage or the bathroom calls. The most relaxing part of my home-viewing evening, though, is no people problems. My roommate is almost never around, so I have the apartment to myself. The only noises I don't want to hear come from the neighbor down below, and I just crank the volume up a notch to take care of him.

3   In contrast, too often when I see a movie out, I run into problems that kill my fun. First, half the time I spend ten minutes waiting in line to get junky movie-house food: popcorn with something that resembles butter, stale nachos with melted Cheese Whiz, and Jujubes that want to yank out my fillings. With this "feast" in hand, spilling popcorn as I go, I have to search for a seat in the dark and usually find one too close to the screen, too far away from it, or at a bad angle. Then comes the balancing act where I usually manage to dump at least a handful of popcorn in my lap to sit on for the next two hours, mystery butter and all. And once I am in my seat, if the theater is crowded and the movie is exciting, I am trapped. In the first place I don't want to walk over people to get to the aisle; it's embarrassing. In the second place there is no pausing the film. Who wants to miss the best scene when that half gallon of Coke finally cycles through, and it's bathroom or bust? Even though I don't like to pop back and forth from my seat to the lobby, it seems like everyone else in my row does. It always caps off my night out at the movies to have people yakking in my ear, blocking my view of the screen, and stepping on my toes on their way out. "Sorry, pal, this is the last time."

4   Watching a movie at a theater can be downright unpleasant. Because we have less control over our surroundings, we have to put up with more annoyances than we would ever stand for in the security of

our own homes. But despite the potential aggravations, there are some good reasons for abandoning the La-Z-Boy. First, if you want to see the newest releases, you have to go out. Second, some films, like those with great special effects, are made to be viewed on a huge screen. And finally, seeing movies out can be a good social experience—and a safe first date.

—Hugh Edwards

POSTREADING ANALYSIS: KEY POINTS FOR BUILDING COMPARISON/ CONTRAST ESSAYS

- **Title:** arouses readers' curiosity and links to the essay's main point.
- **Introductory paragraph:** begins with a hook and ends with a thesis sentence that predicts a comparison or contrast essay.
- **Body paragraphs:** begin with a topic sentence, which <u>names</u> the subtopic and makes a <u>limiting statement</u> about it—for example, "There are many <u>good reasons</u> to <u>stay home for movies</u>."
- **Development:** uses specific examples, details, active verbs (*steps*), *-ing* words (*clutching*), and specific words (*27-inch TV*); tells thoughts and emotions; and explains the examples ("I can choose any time to start, pause, or stop the movie"). (For more on layering examples, see pp. 43–44.)
- **Concluding paragraph:** restates the thesis, briefly summarizes, and adds a final (expanded) thought.
- **Organization:** uses block for overall arrangement and order of importance and chronological order within body paragraphs.
- **Sentence connectors:** guide readers: transitions, repeat words, synonyms, pronouns, and reference to main idea.
- **Style points:** increase readability. Using a series, rather than separate sentences, makes writing more concise (paragraph 2: "cold chicken, green salad, side dishes of . . ."). Short sentences create emphasis (paragraph 2: "One is snacking"). A colon can create emphasis (paragraph 1).

Teaching Idea
This is a good place to remind students of the value of their narrative/descriptive skills.

HINT: Body paragraphs often benefit from order of importance organizing.

➤ Prereading Exploration for "Break on Through to the Other Side"

Teaching Idea
Nontraditional students respond particularly well to this essay. But even the youngest students should be able to identify several stages or "phases" of their lives.

Comparison and contrast papers can help us reflect on our lives, perhaps to gain some perspective on them. Gina Rizzo chose to divide her twenties into her "roaring twenties" and late twenties and to contrast the two for her writing group, students just entering their twenties. Gina felt that young adults moving into the years she had just lived through might be interested in her experiences and how they had shaped her recent decisions.

Answers will vary.

1. Think back on your own life. Have you ever done anything that

   surprised yourself? Were you unexpectedly indifferent, lazy, selfish,

   or cruel (or involved, active, generous, or kind)? _____

   _____

2. If you have ever felt like a different person than you are now, even briefly, describe that person, and consider pursuing the topic in an essay of contrast.

_____

_____

_____

(To see this essay as a paragraph, turn back to Chapter 11, p. 256.)

"Break on Through to the Other Side"

1   Raising hell and living for the moment were all I used to care about. I could see through glassy eyes, somewhat clearly, all the way from one day till the next morning. Then, when I would roll out of bed hungover and crawl toward the bathroom, I would remind myself how much fun I was having. These were the good old days, the days of my roaring twenties. I had some fun, learned a little, and came through, surprisingly, with few visible battle scars. But now that I am moving into my thirties, life has changed.

2   When I was just entering my twenties, I was still living at home, although nobody would have known it by the way I came and went, telling no one anything. But I have come a long way since then. Despite my being twenty-nine now, my mom knows where I am most of the time, not because she checks up on me but because I want her to know what I am doing. Being in touch with the family has become important to me.

3   As a younger woman, I was always invited to the biggest and craziest parties. There is an old saying, "If you can't run with the big dogs . . ." Well, I was one of the big dogs. No one could outparty me. I don't recall when it happened, but I have lost the taste for drinking altogether. Somewhere down the road my body started rejecting the soothing liquid that I had begun to rely on too much. I don't go to the big or crazy parties anymore. My friends have quit inviting me, which is just as well. I don't much feel like partying that way now. I would rather remember my life instead of just hearing about it.

4   Another important difference between my younger self and the woman of today is how I think about time. I used to live only in the present, never planning ahead, never saving money. I bartended for a living, so my money was spent just like I made it, one day at a time. I didn't plan vacations; I would decide the day before, and off I'd go, hopping another red-eye to Las Vegas. I would go anywhere I could afford with

the money I had in my pocket. However, times have changed. I actually have a savings account now, and I just bought a plane ticket for my coming vacation two months in advance! Being more responsible with money ought to help me get a few more wants out of life, not just my needs.

As I began to think more about a future, maybe the most dramatic change came over me when I finally decided to stop playing follow the leader. Like lots of young people I wanted to be in there doing what everyone else was doing. For me that included becoming a Deadhead after my first Grateful Dead concert. The other Deadheads became my family, and we followed our leaders around the country, living the Dead life, pushing ourselves to the limit, right up to the end on that warm night in August when Jerry Garcia died. His death stopped me short. "Is this what I want?" I asked myself. "Do I also want to 'break on through to the other side'?" I decided no. It was time to make another kind of break, this time with the pack. I was ready to become an individual, to take some responsibility as I'd need to do if I expected to survive as an adult. Among other changes I made, the Deadhead has become a college student.

As I look back over my roaring twenties, I see a lot that makes me shake my head at myself: the hiding from my family, the hard partying, the child's sense that there is no tomorrow. But I realize, too, that nobody comes into the world fully grown. Infant, child, teen, adult—we move through stages, learning a little or a lot as we go. I am satisfied with what I have learned so far, and the wild-child-who-was helped to get me here. I hope now that I am on the right path, the one that leads to a long, peaceful, and happy life. But no one can know. We can only think and plan and work for the best. Probably the only thing I can be sure of is that the woman of thirty-nine will be as different from me today as I am from the nineteen-year-old—and as much the same.

—*Gina Rizzo*

Teaching Idea
Gina Rizzo's final comment can provoke an interesting class discussion on the ease or difficulty of accomplishing fundamental changes in behavior and personality. This discussion may encourage some students to choose life changes as topics.

KEY ELEMENTS IN COMPARISON/CONTRAST ESSAYS

Here are several important points—illustrated by the preceding student models—to keep in mind for your own comparison/contrast essay:

1. Make a meaningful comparison or contrast (see pp. 248–250).
2. Make an interesting comparison or contrast (see pp. 250–252).
3. Develop each point of comparison or contrast thoroughly (see pp. 252–254).
4. Use transitions and other connectors (see p. 254).

Teaching Idea
The questions for analyzing essays are fairly generic because they cover the five patterns of development in the chapter. You will find points more specific to each essay in the postreading analyses.

Teaching Idea
Chapter 12 of the Instructor's Manual includes lists that identify methods used in *AWW* essays for introductions, conclusions, hooks, and summary sentences.

Questions for Essay Analysis

Note: These questions apply to all ten model essays in this chapter—not just "Break on Through to the Other Side."

1. Where is the thesis located? What is the topic, and what statement limits it?

2. Why is the hook effective? Which of the hooks discussed in Chapter 12 has the author used? (For more on hooks, see pp. 288–291.)

3. What method(s) from Chapter 12 has the author used to develop the introductory paragraph? (For developing introductions, see pp. 291–293.) Why might the introduction interest the audience stated in the prereading exploration?

4. Why might the lead sentence in the concluding paragraph be effective? (For lead and summary sentences, see p. 294.)

5. What method(s) from Chapter 12 has the author used to develop the concluding paragraph? What is the expanded thought? (For developing conclusions, see pp. 299–308.) Why might the conclusion interest the target audience? (Think of how the conclusion links with the introduction.)

6. For each topic sentence, what are the topic, the limiting statement, and the connecting words? (For more on connecting sentences, see pp. 308–309.)

7. How are the body paragraphs arranged: chronologically or by order of importance? What connector words reveal this?

8. For a paragraph in which the author explains an example clearly, how does the explanation help you to understand the paragraph's main point?

9. For a given paragraph, why do you think it is well written? Consider topic sentences, connecting words, sensory details, specific words, action description, dialogue, metaphors/comparisons, sentence variety, and clear explanations.

10. What are five instances of specific language?

WRITING AN ESSAY
Summarizing the Assignment

Teaching Idea
You can work through the next few pages concurrently with Chapter 12 to move students more quickly into their first essay assignment.

Whether you are expanding a paragraph already written or starting with a new topic, the goal is the same: to write a clear, well-organized, and well-developed essay of approximately 500 to 600 words. To do this, you should focus your topic with a thesis sentence, which you will then expand with two to four body paragraphs, each beginning with a focused topic sentence. Because introductory and concluding paragraphs are such crucial parts of essays, you should pay close attention to them. (For more on introductions and conclusions, see Chapter 12.)

Establishing Audience and Purpose

We all are experienced in speaking to different audiences—don't we, for example, speak differently to a close friend than to someone we have just met at work? When it comes to writing, though, we sometimes forget about shaping what we say for our audience; we feel almost as if we are writing for ourselves. However, precisely because we are removed from our audience, and don't have their reactions as immediate feedback, it is especially important that we keep them in mind. Do they understand? Are they interested? Are we offending someone? Choose an audience who might care about your message, and visualize them as you write. By keeping a specific audience in mind, you will often be better able to select ideas, explanations, and even individual words. The result will be a more focused, and thus more interesting, essay.

> **HINT:** Writing to a specific audience helps focus material.

You may have several purposes—to entertain, inform, or persuade—but clearly communicating ideas should take priority.

Working through the Writing Assignment

Discovering Ideas

Any of the prewriting methods we have worked with this semester (clustering, listing, freewriting, etc.) can be useful for uncovering a topic for your essay or for expanding examples from a former paragraph. To review prewriting techniques, turn back to pages 5–9 in Chapter 1. For topics lists appropriate to specific patterns of development, see the following pages:

1. Illustration: p. 156
2. Classification: pp. 182–183
3. Cause and effect: p. 208
4. Process analysis: p. 233
5. Comparison and contrast: pp. 259–260

> **Teaching Idea**
> Some students will want to abandon a topic used for a paragraph assignment and begin with a new topic for their essay. However, there is value in developing the former paragraph, not the least of which is that students will have to make substantial additions to the paragraph—in other words, engage in real revision.

You may find that the examples you used in your paragraph assignment are right for your essay and simply need to be developed, or you may want to change or add an example, group, cause, or step. However, check with your instructor before making major changes in content. He or she may want you to work with the content of your paragraph as much as possible.

Organizing Ideas

> **HINT:** Thesis and topic sentences are the keys to solid organization.

A thesis sentence is essential to keep an essay on track, so you should write one at the top of your paper before beginning to draft. The topic sentence from a paragraph assignment may work as your thesis, but, again, you may need to revise it, particularly if you have added or dropped major examples. Remember, too, that topic sentences are just as important in your essay body paragraphs as they were in your one-paragraph papers.

> **HINT:** Use connecting words between sentences and paragraphs.

To arrange your body paragraphs overall, use either time or order of importance. Whichever method seems most appropriate for your topic, include transitions and other connectors throughout the essay—but especially between paragraphs. (For connecting sentences and paragraphs, see pp. 53–58.)

Drafting

As you develop examples, remember the principle of **layering,** first discussed in Chapter 3, by which you add sufficient examples, details, and explanations to

Teaching Idea
You might refer students
back to pages 327–328 in this
chapter to see the remainder
of "The Jobs from Hell," a
well-developed illustration
essay.

help readers see exactly what you mean. In this excerpt from the illustration essay "The Jobs from Hell," we can see how the author layered meaning:

> When I was a senior, I found another job that, at first, looked promising. Dr. Lawn paid well, but I had to mow lawns for six to eight hours a day in the July heat, with temperatures running into the nineties. One day on the job I grew sick to my stomach and feverish and literally collapsed in back of a walk-behind mower. My manager would not let me go home because we had come in a car pool, and if I had left, it would have affected the other five people working. When I finally made it home, my dad found that I had a 105-degree fever, and we both decided that no job was worth my health.

HINT: Asking questions
about your statements
will help you develop
them.

What does Eric mean by "sick"? His stomach ached, he had a 105-degree fever, and he collapsed on the job. Why did he become ill? He had to mow lawns for six to eight hours a day in ninety-degree heat. Why was his illness a special problem? His boss wouldn't let him go home. As you ask and answer questions about your own examples, more material will come to you, and your paragraphs will grow.

To see how you might develop a former paragraph assignment, notice how Jeong Yi made a subtopic in his illustration paragraph, "Teaching with Whips," into a body paragraph in the essay he later wrote. The added material has been shaded:

Single-Paragraph Excerpt: 71 Words (complete paragraph on p. 329)

> My moral education teacher was one of these cruel educators. He was short and fat like the whip he carried to enforce his every whim. "I see you haven't done your homework, Jeong," he would say. He ordered me to hold my palms up, and then he began to whip my hands harshly. Somehow the pain ended with me crying and begging, "I will do it next time, teacher. I promise!"

Teaching Idea
Comparing these two
excerpts graphically
illustrates how to expand
a former subtopic. During
group work with essay drafts,
have peer reviewers compare
the subtopics in an author's
paragraph with the body
paragraphs in his or her
essay to see if there has been
substantial revision.

Essay Body Paragraph: 157 Words (complete essay on pp. 329–330)

> As a new middle school student, I was surprised by my first painful encounter with my moral education teacher, a short fat man who carried a short fat whip to enforce his every whim. His manner of speaking somehow did not make it seem urgent for me to thoroughly complete all the homework. Then one day he noticed that I was not prepared and made an example of me to show the class how harsh he could be to defiant students. "I see you haven't done your homework, Jeong," he said, his angry red face shaking. Straining with fear, the class was dead quiet, wondering what was going to happen at that frightful moment. "Jeong, stand up!" he ordered. His chalk-dusty hands held my two shaky little hands

palms up and aimed at them as if they were targets. The punishment ended with me crying and begging, "I will do it next time, teacher. I promise!"

Jeong developed this paragraph through further explanation, examples, and details. You can do the same if you ask the critical question "What do I mean by what I just said?" and answer it with a specific audience in mind.

Revising Drafts

In Unit Two, we revised body paragraphs for content and organization. In addition to revising body paragraphs, we now need to pay attention to introductory and concluding paragraphs:

- Does your introductory paragraph have a strong hook? Have you developed the paragraph with three to five sentences to interest readers? Is there a thesis sentence stating the main point of the essay?
- Does your concluding paragraph have a lead sentence with a connector and link to your thesis? Have you summarized main examples? Does the paragraph frame the essay and/or expand the thesis?

If you take time to revise your essay in several stages, dealing first with larger issues of content and organization and then working toward style and editing concerns, you will produce a superior final draft.

For step-by-step suggestions on revising, editing, and proofreading your drafts, refer to Chapter 13.

ALTERNATE WRITING ASSIGNMENTS

For additional writing assignments, turn back to the chapter in Unit Two featuring the specific pattern of development.

CHAPTER 15

Defining Terms, Clarifying Ideas

What Are We Trying to Achieve and Why?

Setting the Stage

Teaching Idea
This chapter—even more than Chapter 14—stresses using many of the patterns of development to explore ideas. Students can find guidance on any patterns that have not yet been covered in Chapter 1, the Unit Two chapter introductions, and Activity 15.5.

Teaching Idea
You might want to begin this chapter by reiterating that the patterns of development are natural ways in which people think and express themselves, as well as writing strategies. Rather than seeing patterns like comparison/contrast in isolation, you can encourage students to recognize many of the patterns in their own writing and use them as methods for generating ideas.

Most of us will immediately recognize the object in the accompanying photo: a box. We probably view the word *box* as uncomplicated, its meaning clear. But how simple is it?

In a dictionary, we find a number of definitions. Do we mean "a container typically constructed with four sides perpendicular to the base and often having a lid or cover"? How about "a square or rectangle" or "a compartment . . . in a theater"? If we were British, we might mean "a gift or gratuity." *Box* is also a verb, so we might mean "to slap or hit," as in "box his ears." If we were collecting sap for making maple syrup, we might mean "to cut a hole (in a tree)," or if we were painting, we might mean "to blend (paint) by pouring alternately between two containers." Or maybe we just want to put a few old clothes in storage—"to box them up."

Does *box* still seem simple? Whenever we try to limit the meaning of a word, to clarify it and separate it from other meanings, we are **defining.** This is the essence of Chapter 15. As we move through the chapter, you will see how you can use brief definitions together with expanded definitions based on the patterns of development from Unit Two to develop definition essays. (For more on the patterns of development, see pp. 8–9, 363–365, 372–374.)

Linking to Previous Experience

In our own lives, we define daily. At home, your six-year-old son wants to know what you mean by *responsibility*, so you tell him about the jobs people have, providing several examples to illustrate. At work, the waiter you are training knows nothing about wine, so you find yourself defining terms like *cabernet* and *chardonnay*. In school, you might have to define terms like *democracy*, *republican*, and *free enterprise*. Whenever we explain a word with another word, a phrase, a comparison, or an example, we are defining.

In this text, we have defined in every chapter. Consider these examples: In Chapter 6, Lani Houston uses narration to reveal what *leadership* means to her; in Chapter 8, Chanthan Srouch defines *mall crashers* by classifying three groups; in Chapter 11, Dave Harrison uses contrast to help define the meaning of *hard work* in college. All the patterns of development that we have worked with in this course are forms of definition.

Also, each pattern of development depends on examples, and as we work our way through examples, we answer the question "What exactly do I mean by that word or statement?" This, too, is definition.

Finally, definition ties to the essential concept of the Language Line, introduced in Chapter 5. When we define, we *limit* the meaning of a term, making it more specific.

Teaching Idea
To overcome the impression students frequently have that definition consists of brief phrases in a dictionary, you can emphasize the broader sense of extended definitions, pointing out the defining students have done all semester in their assignments.

Determining the Value of Definition

Teaching Idea
You can link defining of terms to the process-analysis assignment.

Words that are clear to us because we have been familiar with them for years are not always clear to others. If you talk about rebuilding an engine, using terms like *overhead cam, stroke, compression,* and *valve clearance,* mechanics understand without a second thought, but the uninitiated soon become lost. You need to define your terms.

Also, murky meanings can create serious problems. For example, think of the trouble that vague language like "employer will contribute to moving costs" might cause in an employment contract. Clear definition can help satisfy all parties.

Finally, writing out definitions helps us understand our own ideas. We may not feel as strongly as the novelist E. M. Forster, who said, "How can I know what I think until I see what I say?" but defining allows us to examine significant words carefully so we can be sure we know our own mind.

Teaching Idea
Journal Entry 15.1 can help students see the need to have a reason for their definitions.

JOURNAL ENTRY 15.1

Have you recently defined something or heard someone else doing so (a friend, radio announcer, teacher, etc.)? What was being defined—a technical term like *website*, a personal term like *loved one*, a job like *veterinary technician*, or an abstraction like *beauty*? Was the definition intended to entertain, inform, or persuade? Did the definition accomplish its purpose? In a paragraph, summarize the definition and tell what its purpose was and whether that purpose was accomplished.

Developing Skills and Exploring Ideas in Definition Essays

The methods for developing brief and extended definitions, covered in this section and summarized in the following points, will help you to thoroughly define terms and to write definition essays.

Teaching Idea
If you are pressed for class time, have students do the activities out of class and then discuss the work in class.

1. Brief definitions:
   - Synonyms (similar words)
   - Negation ("not that but this")
   - Comparisons (metaphors and similes)
   - Formal (grouping and detailing)
2. Extended definitions: the various patterns of development (description, narration, illustration, etc.)

Defining with Synonyms

One method for developing a definition is to use a **synonym**—a word that is roughly equivalent in meaning to the one being defined. For example, if you say, "Granddad is feeling cantankerous today," you could substitute *grouchy* or *disagreeable*. However, if you used *angry*, you would be saying something different—intensifying his irritable mood. Words often have subtle shades of meaning, so writers must take care when choosing substitutes. Keep in mind also that, to be useful, the synonym should be more familiar to readers than the word being defined.

HINT: Choose a synonym that is more familiar than the word being defined.

ACTIVITY 15.1 Defining with Synonyms

Using a dictionary, find two synonyms (one can be a phrase) for each underlined word in the following sentences. Next, with group members and a dictionary, come up with an inaccurate synonym—a word whose meaning is near that of the original but in some way alters it. Then explain why this word is different from the original.

EXAMPLE
Because Jason won't listen to others, I would call him a maverick.

Synonyms: dissenter, independent in thought and action

Inaccurate synonym: radical   Reason: Radical suggests "extreme" behavior, and Jason can be independent without being extreme (although he might be extreme too).

Answers will vary.

1. Nobody trusts Mark anymore; he's a weasel.

   Synonyms: sneak, person who is sneaky or treacherous

   Inaccurate synonym: cruel   Reason: Mark can be sneaky without also being cruel.

2. Sonya spends too much time making decisions, vacillating continually.

   Synonyms: wavering, indecisive

   Inaccurate synonym: fearful   Reason: A person may vacillate for other reasons than fear.

3. Angelina's accident ruined her Subaru.

Synonyms: <u>wrecked, destroyed</u>

Inaccurate synonym: <u>damaged</u>   Reason: <u>Damage is only partial; to</u>
<u>ruin is to damage beyond repair.</u>

4. Isabella's premonition about her uncle's death was correct.

Synonyms: <u>foreboding, feeling</u>

Inaccurate synonym: <u>guess</u>   Reason: <u>A guess implies volition,</u>
<u>whereas a premonition is involuntary.</u>

5. The virus mutated in less than a year.

Synonyms: <u>changed, altered</u>

Inaccurate synonym: <u>grew</u>   Reason: <u>Mutations do not</u>
<u>necessarily involve growth.</u>

Defining by Negation

Another way to narrow a word's meaning is through **negation.** When you negate, you say what the word is not and then what it is or, in some cases, what you will argue it is in your essay. For example, you might say, "*Marriage* is not just a legally binding contract between two people in love; it is a deeply felt personal lifelong commitment." Or you might say, "Being *loyal* is not just supporting a person when everyone else does; it is sticking by the person when almost no one else will."

Defining by negation is especially useful when an audience might disagree with your definition (persuasive writing, for instance, often uses negation).

Even when a reader doesn't view your definition differently, the word may simply have close shades of meaning that you wish to clarify. For instance, you might say, "Emily is assertive, not aggressive" or "Jack is a person with opinions but not an opinionated person."

ACTIVITY 15.2 Defining by Negation

Using either a dictionary or your own knowledge, work with group members to write a one- or two-sentence definition by negation for the following terms. Remember to include both what the term is not and what it is.

EXAMPLE
Landscaping: <u>Landscaping is not just the activity of planting shrubs,</u>
<u>trees, and so on around a property; it is a skilled profession that requires</u>
<u>a great deal of horticultural knowledge and an art that demands a sense</u>
<u>of esthetics.</u>

Answers will vary.
1. Rap music: <u>Rap music is not, as some may think, just music that</u>
<u>celebrates violence and female degradation; it is a legitimate art</u>
<u>form with many themes appealing to a large subculture in the United</u>
<u>States and elsewhere.</u>

2. Work: Work should not just be about collecting a paycheck; it should be about feeling productive and creative each day and contributing something to the world.

3. Environmentalism: Environmentalism is not just Greenpeace and other activists protesting dolphin kills and other specific issues; it is an ongoing commitment to the health of the planet.

4. Teenager: Teenagers are not just accidents waiting to happen; they are young adults busily testing boundaries and making the many mistakes that must be made before people can mature.

5. Vacation: A vacation is not just hopping a plane to an island; it is finding someplace to recharge—the backyard, the living room couch, or the end of a bungee cord.

Defining with Comparisons

Brief definitions can be given using **metaphors** and **similes,** figures of speech that compare things. A metaphor makes the comparison indirectly by simply substituting one thing for another; a simile makes it directly by including the word *like* or *as.* For example, in explaining how water moves up through a tree, we could use:

METAPHOR Phloem and xylem are pathways for carrying nutrients—river channels in the main trunk, becoming streams in the branches and trickles in the leaf stems.

SIMILE Phloem and xylem are like pathways for carrying nutrients . . .

Here are two tips for using metaphors and similes: First, compare the term being defined to something readers would know and accept as an accurate comparison. Second, avoid clichés, such as "Websites are sprouting like weeds." (For more on figures of speech and clichés, see pp. 505–512.)

ACTIVITY 15.3 Defining with Comparisons

In a sentence, create a brief metaphor or simile for the following terms.

EXAMPLE
A prison is like a moon, spinning in space, a separate world for the unwilling colonists, cut off from the mother planet a short space flight away.

Dating is a minefield from which few leave without wounds.

Answers will vary.
1. Depression is like being in solitary confinement, alone in the darkness with no way out.

2. Freedom is finishing the last final and seeing school in the rearview mirror.

3. Alzheimer's is _looking into a mirror and seeing a stranger staring_ _back._

4. A rain forest is _like a time machine carrying us back to a world that_ _used to be in balance._

5. Skiing is _controlled flight._

_____

Defining Formally

Teaching Idea
If you used the Language Line in Chapter 5, you might turn back for a brief review of it to link prior knowledge with the new concept of formal definitions.

HINT: Examples and details separate a term from other members of its group.

Another way to define is with a **formal definition,** such as those found in dictionaries. Formal definitions are often a good jumping-off point for developing definition essays.

To create a formal definition, put your term in a group or category and then add examples, details, and explanations that separate it from other members of the group. A formal definition therefore has three parts:

TERM	GROUP OR CATEGORY	EXAMPLES, DETAILS, EXPLANATIONS
Beagle	Breed of hound	Short legs; drooping ears; white, black, and tan markings
Aerobics	System of physical conditioning	Designed to enhance circulatory and respiratory efficiency; involves vigorous sustained exercise—jogging, swimming, cycling, and so on
Culture shock	Mental and emotional condition	Characterized by the confusion and anxiety that occur when a person is suddenly exposed to an alien culture or milieu

If this method looks familiar, it may be because we have used it throughout this book, beginning with the Language Line in Chapter 5 and the discussion in Chapter 7 of developing paragraphs by becoming increasingly specific with examples, details, and explanations.

In writing out a formal definition, use a verb like *is* or *means* to link a term with its group and identifying features—for example, "A beagle is a breed of hound with short legs, drooping ears, and white, black, and tan markings."

Here are three common problems in writing formal definitions:

1. **Vague, general groups and details**
   - If you indicated the group as "kind of animal" instead of "breed of hound," readers would miss an essential defining element—a beagle is a dog.
   - If you omitted the details "short legs" and "white, black, and tan markings," a bloodhound might also fit the description.

2. **Circular defining** (using a term to define itself)
   - You tell readers little if you say, "Aerobics is a form of aerobic exercise."

3. *Where* **and** *when* **replacing categories**
   - Readers lose information if you say, "Culture shock is *when* a person is confused and anxious after coming in abrupt contact with a culture different from her own." Instead of *when,* give the category: "mental and emotional condition."

ACTIVITY 15.4 Defining Formally

Teaching Idea
As you call on students to answer Activity 15.4, you might listen for the *where/when* words that are often used in place of a limiting group and then point out the usage to students.

Using a dictionary, write out a one-sentence formal definition of each of the following terms. You may quote directly or put the definition in your own words. Underline the group or category each term falls into, and include specific examples, details, and explanations.

EXAMPLE

Aerobics is <u>a system of physical conditioning designed to enhance</u> circulatory and respiratory efficiency and involving vigorous sustained exercise, such as jogging, swimming, or cycling.

Answers will vary.

1. Affirmative action is <u>a policy or program that seeks to redress past</u> discrimination by increasing opportunities for underrepresented groups, such as African Americans and Hispanics, in areas like employment and education.

2. A bar mitzvah is <u>a ceremony that initiates a thirteen-year-old Jewish</u> boy into adulthood and his moral and religious responsibilities.

3. A piñata is <u>a decorated container filled with candy and toys and</u> suspended from a height, intended to be broken by blindfolded players with sticks in a game of Latin American origin.

4. Kwanzaa is <u>an African-American cultural festival, celebrated from</u> December 26 to January 1.

Teaching Idea
Remind students that these topics, too, could work as extended definition essays.

5. Ursa Major is <u>a constellation in the region of the north celestial</u> pole near Draco and Leo, containing the seven stars that form the Big Dipper.

Creating Extended Definitions

Sometimes, particularly when dealing with complex terms, you need to extend a definition to essay length. For definition essays, you will use not only brief definitions but also several of the patterns of development from Unit Two: description, narration, illustration, comparison/contrast, classification, cause/effect, and process analysis. That is, you create extended definitions by mixing several patterns. Notice how such mixing, which characterizes well-developed professional writing, is used to help define the term *scuba* in the following paragraph from "Get Wet," the chapter's annotated student model:

In addition to knowing about the gear, people interested in scuba should know about the certification process. Just as a person has to learn the rules of the road and pass a driving exam before she gets her driver's license, so too must divers learn the rules of the ocean and how to

Process analysis comparison

operate the equipment safely. Without basic certification, diving is dangerous, and few reputable dive shops will rent equipment to uncertified divers or take them out on their boats. There are many professional dive groups (PADI, SSI, NASDS), the course fees are nominal, and a person can become certified in a matter of weeks; so there is little reason not to get the training. If a person is in good health, can swim, and is not inclined to panic in the water, the process is easy. After classroom instruction and study in a text, people move to a pool and practice with the equipment until they are ready for a lake or ocean journey. Then the real fun begins.

Cause and effect process analysis

ACTIVITY 15.5 Creating Extended Definitions

Teaching Idea
Encourage students to use a term they might want to focus their essay on so that they can use this material as prewriting.

With group members, choose one of the terms from the list below, brainstorm, and then define the term in four different ways, using each of these patterns of development:

1. **Comparison/contrast:** showing how the term is like/unlike similar terms
2. **Classification/division:** putting the term into a group or separating it from others like it
3. **Cause/effect:** telling what actions can affect the term and what effects can flow from it
4. **Process analysis:** telling how some part of the term works

Include specific examples and details. Don't be surprised if a pattern incorporates several others—for instance, if description and narration occur within a comparison.

Teaching Idea
Activity 15.5 can help students see how they might begin to work several developmental patterns into their essays. Also, to reiterate the need for a reason behind their definitions, ask them if they can see some point beginning to emerge from the prewriting example on pregnancy.

Terms to choose from (or choose from the Topics List, pp. 371–372):

dating   teenager   vegetarianism   ideal vacation   greed

cheap   workaholic   hero   water skiing   sexual harassment

EXAMPLE

Term to define: pregnancy

1. Comparison and/or contrast: In my first trimester I felt like I was terminally seasick and permanently at sea. I threw up constantly, was dizzy and bumping into walls, and was confined to my "cabin" so much I longed to be anywhere else.

2. Classification/division: Pregnancy can be divided into three stages: the first, second, and third trimesters.

3. Cause/effect: Not only was I sick for the first six months of my pregnancy, but I watched in horror as my weight climbed through the ceiling. By my eighth month I weighed fifty-five pounds more than I had before and looked like a walrus.

4. Process analysis: I knew my baby needed the food I was shoveling in. I had seen the pictures of gestation and watched as the embryo grew,

beginning as a few cells; developing a head, arms, and legs; and finally transforming into a beautiful child. Protected in other ways by the placental wall, he would still starve to death without the nutrients flowing through the umbilical cord. I had a duty to feed my baby, and oh brother, did I ever!

Definition Essays: Analyzing Student Models

Teaching Idea
To stimulate a more productive discussion, try giving the class one or two minutes to skim an essay before you begin to analyze it. This gives even the students who have not read it as homework a chance to reconnect with the class.

As you read through the following essays—"Finding Home," "Deaf, Not Dumb," and "Get Wet"—look for the ways of defining we have discussed: synonyms, negation, metaphors/similes, formal definitions, and the patterns of development. Also note that none of the essays examines its topic exhaustively. When you write your essay, you will need to decide how to focus it.

➤ Prereading Exploration for "Finding Home"

Teaching Idea
Discussing several other points that could be made about a home will help students see the possibilities for development of a concept.

April Griffin defines the concept of *home*. Because home is a universal concept, her potential audience is huge, but she narrowed it by specifying families that do not support one another as much as they should.

1. Reflect for a moment on the meaning of home. How do you define this concept? Answers will vary.

2. List three things you see as an important part of an ideal home. Answers will vary. Possibilities: safety, family, neighborhood, esthetics, utility, comfort

Teaching Idea
Paragraph 2 uses cause/effect and comparison/contrast (negation is also implied in the "house/home" contrast). Paragraph 3 uses cause/effect and process analysis. Paragraph 4 uses cause/effect, comparison/contrast, process analysis, and negation.

Finding Home

"Welcome to Our Happy Home." Perhaps you have read this phrase in an entryway or hanging over a doorway. I know that I have seen the welcome many times when entering my friends' and family members' homes. What makes the home happy? Is it the house, decorated in warm, inviting colors, furnished with all the modern conveniences, or is it the people who live inside? I believe a home is not defined by the physical structure but by the people who live in it. Home is a place where a person feels safe, relaxed, and loved.

The most basic requirement of a home is that a person can feel safe there. Of course physical safety is essential—protection from the weather, animals, and people—but there are also emotional and mental securities. It is hard to feel comfortable in a home surrounded by people who attack each other in small ways. "What do you have to be so down about?"

"You'll never make the team." "He's too good for you." These kinds of comments make a person feel small and uncertain. And it can be just as bad when a person's ideas are belittled. "You don't know what you're talking about." "That's a stupid thing to say." Buildings with families that behave this way are more houses than homes, places where people stay out of habit and need but not because they feel secure.

3   Another important part of a true home is that people can relax there. When we feel safe, we can begin to feel at ease in our surroundings. If family members are considerate of one another, they will give each other the space each needs; they will give each other the time and opportunity to unwind in whatever way works best for each. Some listen to music, some watch TV, and some just appreciate lying down on a couch. A true home encourages relaxation. At the end of a busy, stressful day out "there," we all need to escape the pressures of being productive. If we can find this room in our homes, we can recover our perspective and gather energy again to face a new day. A home in which a person can relax is a home in which she can stay sane.

4   But to me what most defines a home is love. In a loving home people do not just avoid hurting one another and then leave each other alone. They try to involve themselves in each other's lives. If someone has had a hard day at work or school, and she looks depressed or frustrated, people in a caring family talk to her, share their thoughts and feelings, and try to help her out of her bad mood. In a loving home people know what matters to each of the others and what activities each is involved in. In contrast is the house or apartment empty except for one person who wants no one else in his life, or the house shared with another person, not with love but for convenience.

5   A real home is not just a place where a person can safely hang her hat and be left alone. A real home consists of people—no matter what structure they live in—who try to create a loving environment. A house, apartment, cabin, wigwam, or grass hut—all can be true homes. A church group, sports team, or group of friends—all can be families, and where they gather can be a home. As long as a person is loved, he can feel at home in any place or with any group. One part of a definition from *The American Heritage College Dictionary* calls a home "the center or heart of something." What better thing comes from the heart than love?

—April Griffin

POSTREADING ANALYSIS: KEY POINTS FOR BUILDING DEFINITION ESSAYS

- **Title:** arouses readers' curiosity and links to the essay's main point.
- **Introductory paragraph:** begins with a hook and ends with a thesis sentence.
- **Body paragraphs:** begin with a topic sentence that <u>names</u> each main example and makes a <u>limiting statement</u> about it—for example, "The most basic <u>requirement of a home</u> is that a person <u>can feel safe</u> there"— and may end with a summary sentence—for example, "Buildings with families that behave this way are more houses than homes . . ."
- **Development:** uses specific examples, action, dialogue, active verbs (*attack*), *-ing* words (*loving*), and specific words (*American Heritage*); tells thoughts and emotions; and explains the examples ("And it can be just as bad when a person's ideas are belittled"). Uses brief definitions: synonyms (*house = home*), negation (paragraph 1), and patterns of development (cause/effect and comparison/contrast, paragraph 2). (For more on layering examples, see pp. 43–44.)
- **Concluding paragraph:** restates the thesis, briefly summarizes, and adds a final (expanded) thought.
- **Sentence connectors:** guide readers: transitions, repeat words, synonyms, pronouns, and reference to main idea.
- **Style points:** increase readability. Using questions and the pronouns *you* and *we* to *intentionally* speak to the audience can involve your readers (paragraphs 1 and 3). Dashes can set off lists in sentences (paragraph 2) and provide emphasis (paragraph 5). Imagined dialogue can create variety (paragraph 2).

Teaching Idea
The dialogue personalizes the essay, helping readers to identify with the point the author is making.

➤ Prereading Exploration for "Deaf, Not Dumb"

Teaching Idea
These prereading prompts can help students choose topics that they have a real interest in.

Bruce Hayworth has a clear purpose in this essay about the hearing impaired. He thought that people who have little experience with the deaf could use the information he provides, but he particularly wanted to speak to fellow college students.

1. Name a group you are part of that is little understood and possibly misrepresented. _Answers will vary._

2. Consider racial or ethnic minorities, groups drawn together by a common interest (heavy metal, knitting, books), or cliques in high school. List one group and three inaccurate statements you have heard made about it. _Answers will vary. Possibilities: knitting group: inaccurate statements: only old women knit, not many people knit, people who knit just need patience and not creativity_

Deaf, Not Dumb

Teaching Idea
Paragraph 2 uses cause/effect and comparison/contrast. Paragraph 3 uses process analysis and comparison/contrast. Paragraph 4 uses cause/effect.

"You're a dummy, and so's your old lady and old man!" These were fighting words for me as a child, and I ended up rolling around in the dirt more than once with the kids from school who said them. Growing up with hearing-impaired parents in the sixties, if I was not fighting some

1

kid in an alley, it seemed like I was trying to explain to some other child that my family was normal. We just didn't talk much with words. Back then most people didn't know much about the deaf community, and even today I often see people turn and gawk at the hearing impaired when they are signing to each other. Maybe knowing more about the deaf will make those in the hearing world see them as less strange.

2   Everyone knows that *deaf* means the inability to hear, but not everyone knows what causes it or to what degree it can affect people. First, not all hearing-impaired people have profound or complete hearing loss. There are many degrees of partial hearing loss, with some occurring progressively as people get older. Those who have been able to hear somewhat from birth are more likely to articulate well, while those completely deaf from birth have problems speaking clearly. Hearing loss might be caused by congenital nerve damage or by diseases like meningitis, rubella, and chickenpox, especially in early childhood. Worldwide there are 300 million people with some form of hearing impairment.

3   Many, though not all, of these people communicate through some form of sign language. In the United States most of the deaf learn American Sign Language (ASL), which differs from sign used in other countries like England or Japan. ASL communicates primarily through gestures and signs made with the hands and arms but also frequently adds the fingerspelling of words, using letters from the English alphabet. Signing is visual, often theatrical, and can be beautiful, depending on how skilled the signer is. People express their personalities in how they sign. Some are reserved, their signing and body language economical. Others are expansive, exaggerating their gestures and body language to make the "listener" laugh. Some signers can be as entertaining as professional mimes, and even nonsigners can follow and enjoy the story.

Teaching Idea
To help students see the writer–reader connection, ask them how the main example in paragraph 4 relates to Hayworth's stated audience.

4   ASL serves the deaf community well, but their most serious communication problems are in the hearing world. Few hearing people sign, so most of the hearing impaired have learned to read lips, but this has its limitations. Often only part of the message gets across because the speaker says the words too quickly or turns away, requiring the deaf person to frequently ask for clarification or miss the point. When, for instance, this noncommunication happens often enough in a classroom, the hearing students sometimes think the deaf student is unintelligent,

rather than merely missing the words spoken so clearly to those who can hear. If hearing-impaired students have enough difficulties in a classroom that cannot or will not understand them, their education suffers, which affects their future employment prospects and so the rest of their lives.

The deaf have many difficulties to overcome to compete in the larger world of those who hear. Maybe knowing something about the causes of hearing impairment, how widespread it is, how the deaf "speak," and how they can be helped or hurt by the hearing, will make the general public more sensitive to this minority. In the same way that we might go out of our way to be courteous to a nonnative speaker, say, a visitor from Russia or Thailand, we should do so for the hearing-impaired. Sometimes we do need to slow our lips down or at least allow them to be seen. Being willing to write and read notes can also help, and learning a little basic ASL is a way to welcome the non-native "speaker" into our hearing world. In a society as privileged as ours, is a moment's worth of consideration for those who have so much to offer too much to ask?

—Bruce Hayworth

POSTREADING ANALYSIS: KEY POINTS FOR BUILDING DEFINITION ESSAYS

- **Title:** arouses readers' curiosity and links to the essay's main point.
- **Introductory paragraph:** begins with a hook and ends with a thesis sentence.
- **Body paragraphs:** begin with a topic sentence that names each main example and makes a limiting statement about it—for example, "Many, though not all, of these people communicate through some form of sign language."
- **Development:** uses specific examples, action, dialogue, active verbs (*gawk*), -*ing* words (*hearing*), and specific words (*Japan*); tells thoughts and emotions; explains the examples ("There are many degrees of partial hearing loss . . ."). Creates brief definitions, including through synonyms (*hearing impaired = deaf*) and negation (the title), and extended definitions through patterns of development (process analysis and comparison/contrast, paragraph 3). (For more on layering examples, see pp. 43–44.)
- **Concluding paragraph:** restates the thesis, briefly summarizes, and adds a final (expanded) thought.
- **Sentence connectors:** guide readers: transitions, repeat words, synonyms, pronouns, and reference to main idea.
- **Style points:** increase readability. Using exclamations can arouse interest (paragraph 1). Proper nouns can be represented by initials after the first mention, for economy (*ASL*, paragraph 3). Similes can be implied (ASL signers compared to mimes, paragraph 3). Rhetorical questions (statements disguised as questions that produce a predictable response from readers) can engage readers (paragraph 5).

Teaching Idea
See Chapter 12 of the Instructor's Manual for lists that identify methods used in *AWW* essays for introductions, conclusions, hooks, and summary sentences.

Questions for Essay Analysis

Note: These questions apply to both "Finding Home" and "Deaf, Not Dumb."

1. Where is the thesis located? What is the topic, and what statement limits it?

2. Why is the hook effective? Which of the Chapter 12 hooks has the author used? (For more on hooks, see pp. 288–291.)

3. What method(s) from Chapter 12 has the author used to develop the introductory paragraph? (For developing introductions, see pp. 291–293.) Why might the introduction interest the audience stated in the prereading exploration?

4. Why might the lead sentence in the concluding paragraph be effective? (For lead and summary sentences, see p. 299.)

5. What method(s) from Chapter 12 has the author used to develop the concluding paragraph? What is the expanded thought? (For developing conclusions, see pp. 299–308.) Why might the conclusion interest the target audience? (Think of how the conclusion links with the introduction.)

6. What patterns of development or brief definition strategies has the author used? How did any three of these help you further understand the term being defined?

7. For each topic sentence, what are the topic, the limiting statement, and the connecting words? (For more on connecting sentences, see pp. 53–58.)

8. How are the body paragraphs arranged: chronologically or by order of importance? What connector words reveal this?

9. For a paragraph in which the author has explained an example clearly, how does the explanation help you to understand the paragraph's main point?

10. For a given paragraph, why do you think it is well written? (Consider topic sentences, connecting words, sensory details, specific words, action description, dialogue, metaphors/comparisons, sentence variety, and clear explanations.)

11. What are five instances of specific language?

WRITING A DEFINITION ESSAY
Summarizing the Assignment

Teaching Idea
Stress here that students are still developing their essays through detailed examples and explanation. The developmental patterns simply help generate ideas.

This assignment asks you to define a word as completely as possible within a 500- to 600-word essay. The word may name a physical object, place, activity, group, or person. Or it may name a **concept**—an abstraction not knowable through the senses. Concepts include ideas, emotions, and qualities; words like *freedom*, *love*, and *goodness* name concepts. A major goal for this assignment is for you to *consciously* work with patterns of development from Unit Two (description, narration, comparison, etc.). This work will help your writing become more diverse and interesting.

Your paper will consist of about five to six paragraphs, three to four of which will be in the body. Because introductory and concluding paragraphs are such crucial elements in essays, you should work hard on them. You should also, of course, begin each body paragraph with a strong topic sentence.

Establishing Audience and Purpose

Teaching Idea
You might reiterate that people often write for several audiences—a more general one (students' favorite) and a smaller group within that general audience. Thinking about the more specific audience can help students focus their material.

Writing effective definitions depends on understanding your readers and what they need or want to know about your term. For example, a writer might *over*explain *aerobic exercise* if he forgot that his target reader commonly jogs twenty miles and rides her bicycle one hundred miles each week. Or a writer could easily *under*explain a complicated term and quickly confuse readers. For example, if a biology major wrote the formula

$$6CO_2 + 12H_2O \xrightarrow{\text{light}} C_6H_{12}O_6 + 6O_2 + 6H_2O$$

and began talking about light and chemical energy, carbon dioxide, and chlorophyll without first explaining that he was defining *photosynthesis* and giving a general description of photosynthesis, most readers would rapidly be lost.

Furthermore, if a writer has no sense of readers' understanding of the term, how can she know when negation might be useful, what synonyms might work best, or what metaphor or simile readers might respond to? Having a clear sense of audience will help you choose material your readers will be interested in and understand.

As usual, you may have several purposes—to entertain, persuade, or inform—but defining clearly should be the top priority.

Working through the Writing Assignment

Discovering Ideas

Writing Tutor: Definition

Teaching Idea
Concepts often make for more interesting writing and reading than do object definitions, and students will choose them more readily if you show them how to develop the concepts through examples.

HINT: Choose only one meaning of your term.

As you search for topics, remember the distinction between abstract and concrete terms: **Abstract terms** cannot be known through the senses, whereas **concrete terms** have weight, texture, color, and so forth. A rose is concrete; grab one quickly and you may feel the prick of its thorns. You might define *rose* as a concrete term and develop an extended definition around it, but you could also treat it as a specific example illustrating a more abstract term, say, *beauty* or *symmetry*. The topics list gives suggestions for both concrete and abstract terms, with most of the abstractions in the concepts group.

Whether you choose a term from the list or one of your own, a good way to begin prewriting is to look the term up in a dictionary. However, if your term has multiple meanings, to focus your essay, select one meaning. To further focus the essay, you should, in addition, ask yourself the following question: "What part of this subject am *I* most interested in; what part is an *essential*, defining element; what part would my *audience* care about?"

> **Topics List**
>
> - **Family:** mother, father, brother, sister, uncle, aunt, grandmother, grandfather, husband, wife, son, daughter, baby, toddler, child, teenager
> - **Occupations:** nurse, lawyer, architect, engineer, accountant, minister, salesperson, coach, counselor, teacher, musician, carpenter, brick mason, welder, machinist, mechanic, firefighter, mail carrier, paramedic
> - **Fields:** welding, paralegal work, nursing, dental hygiene, fashion merchandising, hospitality management, travel, veterinary science, fire science, cosmetology, electronics technology
> - **Groups:** sports teams, choir, debate team, Girl Scouts, Shriners, clubs (gun club, book club, Trekkies, Dead Heads, sewing circle), PTA, African Americans (Irish, Asian, Hispanic, Native), Democrats, gang, minority

- **Places:** zoos, parks, sports arenas, lakes, beaches, swimming pools, cemeteries, amusement parks, websites, vacation spots, radio stations, retail stores, restaurants, libraries, schools (any kind), arcades, automobile dealerships, hospitals
- **Activities:** dating, shopping, driving, moving, playing sports (baseball, football, climbing, hiking, diving), traveling, landscaping, dancing, doing aerobics, vacationing
- **Behavior:** kind, cruel, responsible, irresponsible, truthful, deceptive, generous, selfish, charitable, courageous, cowardly, loyal, honorable, disciplined, sexist
- **Personal adornment:** jewelry, makeup, tattoos, piercing, hair coloring, hair styling, fingernail polishing
- **Illnesses/dysfunctions:** AIDS, smallpox, diphtheria, malaria, measles, mumps, chickenpox, cancer, meningitis, alcoholism, cirrhosis, herpes, common cold, headache, migraine, arthritis, ulcers, angina, stroke, heart attack, osteoporosis, cataracts, diabetes
- **Concepts:** credit, health, confinement, freedom, culture, subculture, pop culture, marriage, divorce, family, environmentalism, ecology, organic food, vegetarianism, capital punishment, emotional states (love, hate, envy, joy, depression), beauty, good, evil, God, devil, hero, villain, con artist, fun, work, charity, discipline, home, addiction, music, old age, middle age, childhood, employer, employee, co-worker, perfectionist, neighbor, winner, loser, bore, leader, follower, man, woman, art, education, charity, health, interior design, color, pet, assisted living, maturity, work, play, body language, slang, intelligence, sex appeal, fashion, peer pressure, self-esteem, discrimination

Prewriting

Teaching Idea
You can link these prewriting suggestions with Activity 15.5 to generate material for students' topics.

After you have chosen several terms, explore them by using any of the prewriting methods from Chapter 1 together with the methods for developing brief and extended definitions:

METHODS FOR DEVELOPING DEFINITION ESSAYS

1. **Brief definitions**
   - Synonyms (similar words)
   - Negation (not that, but this)
   - Comparisons (metaphor/simile)
   - Formal (grouping and detailing)

2. **Extended definitions:** patterns of development
   - Narration: telling a brief story to make a point about the term
   - Description: using vivid details to show something about the term
   - Illustration: giving examples to make a point about the term
   - Comparison/contrast: showing how the term is like and unlike other, similar terms
   - Classification: putting the term into a group or separating it from others like it
   - Cause/effect: telling what actions can affect the term and what consequences can flow from the term
   - Process analysis: telling how some part of the term works

Teaching Idea
It helps students understand the patterns as prewriting strategies if you work through a topic or two in class.

Teaching Idea
After students review the prewriting cluster, have them skim part of the final draft of "Get Wet" to show how the prewriting might translate into an essay.

For example, using the questioning prewriting method, you can ask questions that apply the brief definition methods to your term. For the term *scuba*, you could ask questions like these:

1. What is a synonym for *scuba*? Answer: diving.
2. What is *scuba* not like? Answer: swimming in a pool.
3. What metaphor or simile could describe *scuba*? Answer: space flight.
4. What is the formal definition of *scuba*? Answer: "A portable apparatus that contains compressed air and is used for breathing under water."

Or you can combine clustering with the patterns of development for extended definitions:

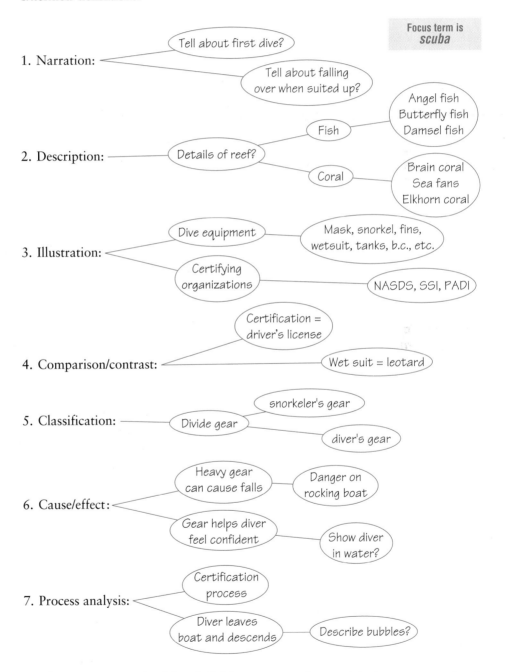

Because one goal of the definition essay assignment is to use several patterns, thinking about all of them during your initial brainstorming, as illustrated above, can move you quickly into a substantial first rough draft.

To see how the author of "Get Wet" used the material gathered from questioning and clustering in his essay, turn to pages 380–381.

PREWRITING—SUMMING UP

1. Choose several topics from the list, or choose several of your own.
2. Consider defining a concept rather than a concrete term.
3. Try both questioning and clustering, using the methods discussed previously.
4. Decide on a purpose and point for your definition essay.

JOURNAL ENTRY 15.2

Teaching Idea
Journal Entry 15.2 is a good checkpoint to see if students have come up with a reason for their definition.

Write a paragraph telling why you have chosen your term. What about it makes you want to explore it further? Who do you think will be interested in reading your essay, and what do you want to tell them about the term? What words in your definition will you need to explain?

Organizing Ideas

To stay focused as you proceed, write out a **thesis sentence.** Remember to name the term and make a statement about it that lets readers know a definition is forthcoming. You might use the word *define* or *definition* (as in "one way to define XYZ is . . .") or follow your term with the verb *is* or *means* (see sentence C below). You might also include a forecasting statement (see sentence C). Here are sample thesis sentences from the chapter models:

CAUTION! Resist the temptation to include a formal definition in your thesis in this overworked way: "As stated in *Webster's New World Dictionary,* home is . . ."

A. Maybe knowing more about the deaf will make those in the hearing world see them as less strange.

B. Most of us will never have the opportunity to voyage into outer space, but we can learn a little about the next best option for inner planetary travel, scuba diving.

C. Home is a place where a person feels safe, relaxed, and loved.

Because an essay is complex, you should create a rough outline that lists your major points and give several supporting examples for each. (To review outlines, see pp. 11–12.)

You will probably arrange your body paragraphs by time or, more often, order of importance. However, a single body paragraph might differ from the overall pattern. For example, the essay could be arranged from least to most important, but one process-analysis or narrative paragraph might be ordered chronologically.

Remember to begin each body paragraph with a topic sentence linked by connectors like the ones below. (For more on connectors, see pp. 53–55.)

- **Locating or moving in space:** *above, against, around, behind, below, on, in*
- **Moving in time:** *after, at last, awhile, first, immediately, next, now, often, then*

- **Adding material:** *again, also, and, in addition, furthermore, as well as*
- **Giving examples:** *for example, for instance, another, one reason, in fact*
- **Comparing:** *alike, also, both, in the same way, similarly*
- **Contrasting:** *in contrast, although, but, differs from, even though, however*
- **Showing cause/effect:** *and so, as a result, because, consequently, since, so, then*
- **Summarizing/concluding:** *finally, in brief, in other words, in short, to summarize*

ORGANIZING—SUMMING UP

1. Create a rough thesis sentence to focus your material.
2. Limit body paragraphs to three or four.
3. Create a rough outline.
4. Arrange body paragraphs by time or order of importance.
5. Plan on using a topic sentence to introduce each body paragraph.
6. Review the list of transitions.

JOURNAL ENTRY 15.3

Write out your thesis sentence. Does it state the term and indicate that a definition will follow? Create a rough outline, and list each developmental pattern you will use. Do you have enough material to thoroughly define your term?

Teaching Idea
After students have done the prewriting cluster with the patterns, you might have them write Journal Entry 15.3 in class and then discuss it in groups.

Drafting

With the preliminary work finished, you are almost ready to write a first draft. But before moving ahead, take a moment to review the drafting suggestions in Chapter 1 (pp. 12–13), and then do the following:

1. Remember that negation may be useful in your introductory paragraph (see "Finding Home," pp. 365–366).
2. Insert synonyms and phrase definitions in sentences, set off with commas, parentheses, or dashes (see "Get Wet," pp. 380–382).
3. With body paragraphs, use a single pattern of development or, as the model essays in this chapter do, mix several. But be sure to rely on specific, detailed examples.
4. Be sure to include information that is essential to defining your term, and tell your readers that the information is essential.
5. Be sure to give your first draft a clear point, so that your writing will have energy and interest. The essays in this chapter can hold an audience's attention partly because each writer is interested and has a point to make. One writer has an opinion on what a good home is, another encourages people to be more sensitive to the needs of the hearing impaired, and the third is excited about scuba diving.

SPECIAL POINTS TO CHECK IN REVISING FROM FIRST TO SECOND DRAFTS
1. **Introduction:** hook, engaging support sentences, thesis
2. **Body paragraphs:** topic sentence with connector
3. **Overall development:** examples, details, explanations; brief definitions and extended definitions using patterns of development
4. **Conclusion:** connector, summary, expanded thought

A Definition of Diving

Introduction reworked, adding descriptive details to strengthen comparison

1   Being in the ocean in scuba gear is a lot like being in outer space. When a diver is floating in deep water, he is in another world. He depends on the compressed air in his cylinders and his regulator to deliver it smoothly. The diver swims weightlessly through "inner space." Similarly an astronaut floats in darkness with the deepest drop imaginable all around him. He also depends on his gear to deliver air, protect him from the cold and other extremes, tell him how much air he has, and orient him toward his "boat." Most of us will never have the opportunity to go into outer space, but we can learn a little about the next best option for inner planetary travel, scuba diving.

Thesis revised

Topic sentence added

2   To understand something about scuba as a sport, we can take a look at some of the gear. Basic diving equipment can be divided into two categories. The first is gear for a snorkeler, and the second is gear for a diver. A snorkeler or breath-hold diver needs a face mask, swimming fins, a snorkel, and sometimes a wet suit, depending on the temperature of the water. The wet suit is a skin tight coverall of rubber used to keep warmth in. Putting one on is a pain. It is much like squeezing into a really tight leotard that stretches from the neck to the ankles. A scuba diver most often wears a wet suit of varying degrees of thickness (there is a dry suit for really cold water), and in addition to the snorkelers' gear wears a heavy cylinder (or tank) of air with an attached regulator for delivering the air, weight belt, diving vest, gauges for monitoring amount of air and time underwater, and a compass. If this seems like a lot of equipment, it is. And until a diver gets into the water, the diver is overloaded, uncomfortable, and prone to falling down. A complete set of scuba equipment is expensive (more than a thousand dollars), but many certified divers own only snorkeling gear and rent the rest.

Classification added

Comparison added

Examples of equipment added with explanations

Cause and effect added

Transition added to topic sentence

3   In addition to knowing about the gear, people interested in scuba diving should know about the certification process. Just as a person has

Comparison added

Examples added

Explanation added

Topic sentence added

You pronoun replaced

Gender pronoun *he* shifted to *she*

Examples, details, action words added

Brief summary added

Conclusion rewritten to focus the point—sharing

to learn the rules of the road and pass a driving exam before she gets her driver's license, so too must divers learn the rules of the ocean and how to operate the equipment safely. Without basic certification diving is dangerous. Few reputable dive shops will rent equipment to uncertified divers or take them out on their boats. There are many professional dive groups (PADI, SSI, NASDS), and the course fees are nominal. Also a person can become certified in a matter of weeks; so there is little reason not to get the training. If a person is in good health, can swim, and is not inclined to panic in the water, the process is easy. After classroom instruction and study in a text, divers move to a pool and practice with the equipment until they are ready for a lake or ocean journey. Then the real fun begins.

The most exciting part of scuba diving, naturally, is being in the water. The pool may have seemed fascinating at first, but it pales by comparison to open water, especially the waters of a reef. Teetering on the dive boat, all gear in order, the diver "strides" out and splashes into the ocean, and the diver feels in her element. The equipment she is wearing makes her part of the environment, like she belongs, something of a fish. Down the diver sinks, clearing the pressure in her ears, trailing bubbles, equalizing buoyancy till she is floating, weightless, above the reef. Stretching in every direction are forests of tall, jagged corals. Light-brown brain coral ranging in size from basketballs to boulders dot the pale sandy bottom with purple sea fans rocking at their feet. Scattered throughout the coral are the cousins of all those captive saltwater aquarium fish: brown and white damsels; orange- and white-striped clowns; yellow butterfly fish; lime-green and blue angels. The new diver hovers, amazed by the beauty of inner space, eager to see more.

Scuba is a wonderful sport that only requires the right equipment and proper training to open a new world to the diver. It is a safe sport for all ages, and one that brings people together. Because a number one rule in diving is to pair up before going under, people meet quickly. They help each other with their gear. Then they dive together and share their experiences back on board. "Did you see the size of that lobster?" "How about those amber jacks?" "The mantas looked like flying saucers!" This is the essence of scuba diving: people cooperating and sharing their excitement as they explore the new world of inner space.

4

5

ages and one that brings people together. Because a number one rule in diving is to pair up before going under, people meet quickly. [They help each other with their gear, dive together, and share their experiences back on board.] "Did you see the size of that lobster?" "How about those amber jacks?" "The mantas looked like flying saucers!" This is the essence of scuba diving: people cooperating and sharing their excitement as they explore the new world of inner space.

—*Kyle Jennings*

Chapter Summary

1. Definition is the act of limiting and clarifying the meaning of a word, of separating it from other, similar terms.
2. We define daily at home, school, and work.
3. Brief definitions—synonyms, negation, comparisons, and formal definitions—are often part of a paragraph or essay being developed with a single pattern.
4. Brief definitions may be a single word or a short phrase, often enclosed by commas, parentheses, or dashes.
5. Definition essays often use brief definitions and extended definitions based on several patterns of development.
6. Definition depends on thoroughly explained and detailed examples.
7. Transitional words and other connectors are especially important in bridging the gap between paragraphs.
8. Definition essays can be organized chronologically but are frequently arranged by order of importance.
9. A thesis sentence is the first step in focusing an extended definition essay.
10. Outlining is a valuable organizing technique.
11. Topic sentences are an essential part of a coherent body paragraph.
12. Writing is never complete until it has gone through several revisions and careful editing.

ALTERNATE WRITING ASSIGNMENTS

The following assignment options may help you focus your definition essay. For this assignment, be sure to do the following:

Teaching Idea
When introducing students to the chapter topics list, you might also point out these alternate assignments.

1. Review brief definitions and the patterns of development, and use several methods to develop your essay.
2. Have a point for your definition, and make the point clear to your reader.
3. Write to a specific audience.
4. Review methods, in Chapter 12, for creating introductions and conclusions.
5. Create a controlling topic sentence for each body paragraph.

ASSIGNMENT OPTIONS

1. Write an essay defining the term *home* in a way that either adds to or differs from the definition in "Finding Home" (pp. 365–366). Perhaps, for example, you don't agree with April Griffin's feeling that a home requires more than one person. Brainstorm for ideas based on your personal experience, and if you plan to disagree with points from "Finding Home," consider using negation in your introduction to show how your definition will differ from the author's.

2. Write a definition essay that treats a term—for example, a person, place, or activity—as the best or worst of its kind. For instance, you might discuss a person and tell what makes for a terrific or terrible boss, leader, co-worker, parent, child, grandparent, athlete, or neighbor. Or you could choose a place like an amusement park, stadium, or beach or an activity like a vacation, sporting event, or date. You may include personal experiences, perhaps using narration as one method of development.

3. Write an essay defining a term important in a career you are interested in or defining the career itself. For example, if you are thinking about computer science as a career, you might want to know more about terms like *RAM, ROM, mother board,* or *modem.* Or you might want to learn about the education required, employment prospects, or potential salary. If you research the career, remember to limit your findings to three or four significant points.

4. Write a definition essay on one word that best describes you. You might know immediately what that word is—*hard working, athletic, lazy, funny,* or *loyal*—or you might struggle with two or three before you pin it down. If you are not sure yourself, try asking a good friend or family member. One of them may surprise you with the defining word. Another approach is to imagine a setting and audience. If you were in a job interview and asked to define yourself in a word, what would you say? How would you support your definition? Presuming you want the job, you would, of course, select your word with care.

5. Write an extended definition that reacts to some term regularly applied to you individually or as a representative of a group. For example, perhaps your friends have often called you "out of control" just because you love high-risk activities like free climbing, hang gliding, skydiving, and bungee jumping, like the young man in the accompanying photo. If you agree with them, write an essay that clarifies what "out of control" means in your life. If you disagree, either define "out of control" at length or offer another term to describe your lifestyle, and then develop it through definition.

Another approach to this assignment is to agree or disagree with a term someone applies to you as a member of a group. For example, you may be tired of hearing generation Xers referred to as "politically apathetic," the Irish as "alcoholics," or feminists as "radical." As in the preceding option, define the term at length as you see it, or define an alternative term that better describes your group.

CHAPTER 16

Writing Persuasively

What Are We Trying to Achieve and Why?

Teaching Idea
Many teachers of developmental writing believe that argument is better left for Comp 1. However, brief arguments based primarily on students' own resources can be managed by developmental writers and will help better prepare them for Comp 1.

Setting the Stage

What do you think the four photos have in common? In the picture at the top left on page 386, a lawyer questions a witness while a judge weighs the evidence. Next, two politicians present their positions, each challenging the other's statements and defending his own. The third picture is filled with advertising. And the last shows a family eating dinner, enjoying one another's company and at some point perhaps talking over the day's events. If it's a typical conversation, the parents want the kids to do more around the house, the kids want to do more almost anywhere but in the house, and the dog just wants a few more table scraps.

Each of the pictures involves **persuasion**—the attempt to convince someone to accept an idea or policy (as with the politicians) or to take some action, such as find a defendant innocent or guilty, buy a product, clean a room, or feed a dog. This is the focus of Chapter 16.

Teaching Idea
It is a good idea to reiterate from the beginning of this chapter the importance of audience considerations in persuasive writing.

The chapter will focus especially on a form of persuasion known as **argument.** By *argument*, we don't mean raised voices and fists pounding on the table, but rather a reasoned exchange of ideas between people with different opinions on an issue. Our goal is to learn to come up with an issue (an arguable topic), frame a position on the issue, explore it through **reasons** backed by **evidence,** expand the argument with several patterns of development, and, finally, influence an **audience** to accept or at least respect our position on the issue.

Linking to Previous Experience

Teaching Idea
Activity 16.3 deals with the Communication Triangle, but you might want to frame this abstract concept in terms of "mind, heart, and self."

Trying to get what we want from others is basic to humans. As babies, as soon as we learn that food will come if we cry loudly enough, persuasion begins. During childhood, we quickly learn what strategies we can use on our parents to get the things we want. We appeal to them unconsciously on all three levels that

387

operate in more formal argumentation: mind, heart, and self. "If we're going to get the bike, now's the time because it's on sale for 50 percent off" (appeal to the parents' minds with a bargain); "I need a new bicycle because the brakes on my old one are shot, and I might get hurt" (appeal to the parents' hearts); and "You promised that if I did well this term in school you would buy the bike" (appeal to the parents' sense of you as hardworking and of themselves as fair).

Of course, our parents are not the only targets of our persuasive attempts. We work on (and are worked on by) other family members, friends, significant others, fellow employees, employers, teachers, and even the police officer about to write us a speeding ticket. Sometimes we succeed, sometimes not.

Also, many of you have already written papers that are at least partly persuasive. When you created a dominant impression in describing a place, for example, you chose details that would encourage readers to feel what you wanted them to. When you narrated a story, you manipulated plot, dialogue, and description to interest the audience. In establishing causes and effects, you may have influenced your readers to change a behavior to avoid negative consequences. In short, much of what you have written has had a persuasive component, but now persuasion becomes your main goal.

Determining the Value

Clearly, people influence one another, and those who are good at it profit. Persuasive skills help us negotiate purchases, land jobs, and meet significant others. But knowing persuasive strategies can also help us resist the professional persuaders—politicians, salespeople, advertisers, and others—and make reasoned rather than manipulated decisions. The process of examining and building arguments can help us think more clearly.

Further, as people living in a society, we need to think carefully about the many issues that unite and divide us. Should abortion remain legal? Do we support capital punishment? Do we need stricter gun control laws? Should sex education be taught in schools? Through argument, we can arrive at reasoned positions on these issues, in the process helping to shape the society in which we want to live.

Teaching Idea
Use Journal Entry 16.1 to begin a discussion of persuasion as it affects our everyday lives. As you have students speculate on why the persuasive attempts succeeded or failed, you can begin introducing basic elements of argument: reasons, counterreasons, evidence, appeals, qualifications, and so forth.

JOURNAL ENTRY 16.1

What persuading have you tried recently or seen others try? Maybe you wanted to see one film and a friend another. Perhaps you tried to talk your boss into giving you a raise, time off, or a shift change. Maybe you watched a teacher try to persuade her class to find value in some subject. Summarize an instance of persuasion. Did the persuader accomplish his or her purpose, and if so, how?

Developing Skills and Exploring Ideas in Persuasive Essays

The activities in this section will show you what you need to do to write an effective persuasive essay, as summarized in the following points. Remember that you are trying to persuade not only those who are neutral on your issue but also those who disagree with you; dealing with that "opposition" is a large part of effective persuasion.

Teaching Idea
To help students understand a split audience, you might draw stick figures on the board, showing them at podiums with an audience off to one side. If you are a rotten artist like me, your illustration will get a few laughs, but it will also enable you to show with arrows the interaction between the two debaters and the audience. This is a good device for clarifying possible audience objections versus an opponent's counterreasons.

Teaching Idea
If students have written a process analysis, they should define terms as carefully in their arguments as they did in their process explanations.

Teaching Idea
Ask students which terms need to be clarified in Activity 16.1 to focus the arguments.

1. Define the issue and clarify terms.
2. Present reasons and support.
3. Connect with the audience.
4. Avoid errors in logic.
5. Qualify assertions.
6. Counter opposing reasons and audience objections.

Defining the Issue

Many arguments fail because the writer has not defined the issue clearly for readers. Consider the following thesis sentence: "Minors who break the law should get the same treatment that adults do." Does "minors" mean anyone from age three to seventeen? And what exactly does "get the same treatment that adults do" mean? Should minors be prosecuted the same way adults are? Someone reading this thesis sentence might imagine the writer arguing that, say, a five-year-old caught stealing a candy from a store should have to appear in court on a misdemeanor charge or that a thirteen-year-old caught joyriding in a stolen car should be prosecuted as an adult and locked up with adult criminals. Presumably, the writer would not take these positions, but her unfocused thesis sentence implies that she would.

Because arguments can easily be misinterpreted, writers must carefully define—limit and clarify—their issue and all terms. Limiting is also important for another reason: Issues that are too broad cannot be supported, especially within the confines of a brief essay.

ACTIVITY 16.1 Defining the Issue

The following thesis sentences are unfocused and might be misinterpreted by readers. Rewrite each of them to limit and clarify the issue, as well as any unclear terms. Write out a thesis that you think you could support in your own argument.

EXAMPLE
Unfocused issue: Children should be able to leave school whenever they want to.

Focused issue (thesis): Students who have parental consent should be allowed to quit school by the age of sixteen.

Answers will vary.

1. Unfocused issue: Birth control should be available to anyone who wants it.

   Focused issue (thesis): Birth control should be available in high school to students with parental consent.

2. Unfocused issue: Schools should have fewer rules.

   Focused issue (thesis): High schools should not require school uniforms.

3. Unfocused issue: Playing sports is bad for young people.

   Focused issue (thesis): Playing contact sports like football is bad for children under twelve.

4. Unfocused issue: People should be protected from television violence.

Focused issue (thesis): <u>Parents should protect their children from</u> <u>television violence.</u>

5. Unfocused issue: Everyone should value the environment more.

Focused issue (thesis): <u>If people want to preserve air quality, they</u> <u>should buy fuel-efficient cars.</u>

Teaching Idea
The term *evidence* can be problematic for some students, so you might refer to it as *support*, a term that is accurate and one they should be familiar with.

Presenting Reasons and Providing Support

After focusing an issue, writers must present reasons and evidence to support their position. **Reasons** are the main points made about the issue; **evidence** supports those points. For example, to argue that fireworks should be outlawed, you could list reasons like the following:

1. Fireworks hurt people.
2. Fireworks cause property damage.
3. Fireworks annoy many people.

Note that, unsupported, these reasons are not very convincing. If, however, you add specific evidence, an argument begins to take shape. For instance, to support reason 1, you could begin by stating the statistic that last year 17,000 people were injured by fireworks. Next, you could add an example, noting that the red-hot wires from sparklers burn people. And you might continue with an anecdote (a brief story, first- or secondhand) about the time a younger brother shot someone in the face with a Roman candle.

Here are several forms of evidence, most of which we have already worked with, that are useful for developing arguments:

1. **Facts/statistics:** commonly accepted truths in words and numbers
2. **Authorities:** information from people who are generally recognized as experts in their field
3. **Examples:** specific illustrations
4. **Anecdotes:** brief stories
5. **Scenarios:** "what-if" situations, speculating about causes and effects
6. **Logical interpretations:** explanations of how the reasons and evidence support the thesis

Teaching Idea
If students choose an issue like removing handguns from homes with young children, the primary reason—safety of the children—may be the only reason they need to support. (Of course, they will also need to refute the main counterreason—protecting the home.)

As you explore your argument, you will probably find several sound reasons to support your position and will develop a body paragraph around each. However, occasionally, one reason is so strong that a whole argument may rest on it. In this case, the rest of the essay will be evidence to support the reason and/or refutation of the opposition's reasons.

ACTIVITY 16.2 Presenting Reasons and Providing Support

Discuss with group members each of the following topics, looking closely at the thesis and reason given to support the thesis. Now try to support each reason with *three* pieces of acceptable evidence.

Teaching Idea
Tell students that they may manufacture facts and authoritative statements to fit the topic they choose in Activity 16.2.

EXAMPLE

Topic: Outlawing fireworks

Thesis: Fireworks should be prohibited in this country.

Reason: Many children are injured by them each year.

Evidence:

- Fact: Last year there were 17,000 injuries nationally on July 4th.

- Authority: Dr. Horace Caruthers, director of the Johns Hopkins Trauma Center, has stated that bottle rockets alone are responsible for hundreds of eye injuries on July 4th.

- Example: Even relatively harmless fireworks like sparklers can cause severe burns when children grab the glowing wires in their hands or step on them with bare feet.

- Anecdote: When my younger brother was nine years old, he shot me in the face with a Roman candle.

- Scenario: Imagine your eleven-year-old son teased into holding and throwing lit cherry bombs or M-80s. Now imagine how you would feel if his hearing were damaged or his fingers were blown off, or if he were blinded.

- Logical interpretation: Because children get caught up in the moment and so often don't think of consequences, they will continue to be injured by fireworks.

Answers will vary.

1. Topic: Freedom of choice in high school curriculum

   Thesis: High school students should be allowed to choose more of their own curriculum.

   Reason: If students are more interested in their studies, they will perform better.

   Evidence:

   - I chose a senior English class that emphasized poetry and have carried this interest into college.

   - During our senior year, my best friend chose a real estate course and was so excited about it that he did better in all his courses, knowing that his improved grades might help him get a job with a realtor.

   - The Tech Prep courses at my high school have saved half the people I know from dropping out.

2. Topic: Teachers accepting late homework

   Thesis: Teachers should accept late homework from students with legitimate excuses.

Reason: Students who have worked hard on homework assignments are demoralized and angered when they cannot turn them in for credit.

Evidence:

- I have seen more than one confrontation at the beginning of a class session between a teacher and a student who had been absent.

- Teachers are always telling students that half the educational battle is won through attitude, but then teachers undercut a student's positive attitude by homework policies that seem unfair.
- My friends tell me that many of their other teachers accept late work with legitimate excuses, so they feel it's unfair that some teachers won't accept late work.

3. Topic: Changing sports teams' names

Thesis: Professional sports teams that feature names related to Native Americans should change them.

Reason: Many Native Americans understandably feel demeaned by such team names.

Evidence:

- The Washington Redskins, Kansas City Chiefs, Atlanta Braves, and Cleveland Indians are all related to Native Americans—no professional teams use teams related to other ethnic groups.
- When teams have these names, their mascots, accessories, and fan behavior (the "tomahawk chop," "Chief Wahoo," etc.) often reflect stereotypes about Native Americans.
- Some Native American groups have spoken against the use of Indian names.

4. Topic: Privacy of HIV victims versus need to know by parents

Thesis: Parents should be informed of any child carrying HIV in their children's school.

Reason: Parents should know of any potential danger to their children.

Evidence:

- In many cities parents can learn when convicted child molesters move into the neighborhood.

- Children get cuts while playing, and blood can pass the HIV virus.

- HIV is so deadly that parents have the right to know even if the chance of infection is minute.

_____

Teaching Idea
Students usually have the most difficulty with ethos and pathos in argument, but this simplified graphic, along with the two following examples, will help them see the impact of persona and the need to consider readers' emotional responses.

Teaching Idea
For more help with the concept of persona, create some scenarios for students in which they would consciously try to manipulate their image. For example, how might they dress for an important job interview with a corporation like Sprint? Why wouldn't they wear faded blue jeans, an old sweatshirt, and unlaced tennis shoes?

Teaching Idea
It is helpful to emphasize the *overlapping* nature of the three appeals.

Connecting with the Audience

How can you connect with your audience in order to persuade them? We have already discussed one way: through a careful presentation of ideas, with a well-defined issue and clear reasons effectively supported by evidence. However, there are two other major ways to consider: **presenting yourself well** and **influencing readers' emotions.** As the figure below shows, in persuasive writing, you need to think about each of the three interrelated parts of communication—the text, the writer (you), and the reader.

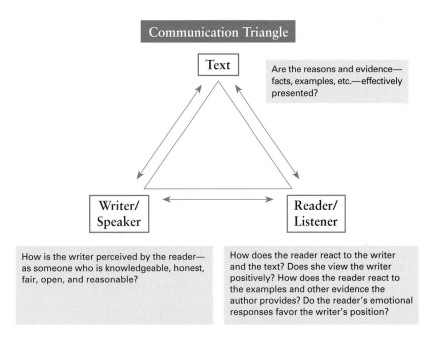

Most of us respond positively to those whom we see as reasonable, fair, and honest. In writing, we create this impression of ourselves—our **persona**—by what we say and how we say it. If our persona is a good one, it advances our argument; if not, it hinders it. For example, if you were to argue that drivers over age seventy should take an annual physical and driving exam, which of the following statements would create a more positive persona?

A. Old farts shouldn't be on the road any longer if they can't handle a grown-up's responsibility. They don't deserve to drive, and I hate it whenever I'm stuck near one in traffic.

B. Though many of our senior citizens have driven responsibly for years, when through no fault of their own the aging process diminishes their capacity to drive safely, in order to protect them and others, we ought to ask them to take an annual physical and driving exam.

HINT: It is always a mistake to antagonize the reader you are trying to persuade.

Clearly, version A creates an unsympathetic persona, and readers might suspect the writer's motives for proposing a driving exam. In contrast, version B shows a writer who seems to respect the older driver and proposes an annual exam only because it would serve the greater good.

Along with considering persona, a writer should consider the potential emotional responses of readers and choose examples that cause them to respond favorably. Which of the following two paragraphs promoting a driving exam for the elderly would be more likely to influence an audience including people with seniors in their family?

A. Like I said, these old fogies have got to go. They aren't capable anymore, they get in the way, and they cause accidents. Blue hairs and other semigeriatric cases belong more in wheelchairs than automobiles. If they have a hard time getting out to buy their Geritol without driving, let the city foot the bill for taxis or let their families do the driving. However we get them off the road, the sooner the better.

B. Neither of my grandfathers wants to endanger anyone, and they both have to get from place to place just like everyone else. But their failing physical and mental health made them unsafe drivers, so they finally stopped driving, luckily before anyone was seriously injured. As a result, my folks and I and the rest of our family are pitching in to shuttle our grandparents around. It is inconvenient. And family members are annoyed by the chore on occasion. But this "chore" has the benefit of bringing us more often in contact with each other. I see all of my grandparents more frequently now than before they stopped driving. The family profits because we are sharing a task that is right. Our older generation took care of their children and their children's children in their time. Now it is our time to take care of them.

Most of us would probably choose paragraph B because it evokes a more sympathetic emotional response. Effective argumentation requires a clear sense of your audience so that you can shape your persona and choose effective emotional appeals.

ACTIVITY 16.3 Connecting with the Audience

Discuss with group members the Communication Triangle and the appeals of persona and emotion. Next, rewrite *one* of the following paragraphs on a separate sheet of paper, making the persona more positive and trying for emotional appeals that might influence the stated audience. Consider including yourself in the audience, as in the paragraph on elderly drivers, and using pronouns like *we, us,* and *our.* Answers will vary.

1. Issue and position: Schools should enforce dress codes.

Audience: Public high school students

It should be obvious to anyone that these high school students ought to be wearing uniforms. Just look at what they are doing to one another in their own schools! They beat each other up for a pair of tennis shoes and form packs like animals to hunt each other down. And teachers have to suffer from it too. If they are not risking their

Teaching Idea

Paragraph B is the conclusion of the chapter's annotated student model. You might remind students of Activity 16.3 if you go through the model with them, pointing out the revisions the author made to create a more persuasive persona.

Teaching Idea

Tell students that they can add or delete material to improve the persona in Activity 16.3.

lives breaking up knife fights in the halls, they are having to beg the students to stop admiring each other's new sunglasses and pay attention to the lesson. I know that some students are going to whine about personal identity and freedom, but who ever said school was supposed to be a democracy after all?

2. Issue and position: People should only use cell phones for urgent business while driving.

Audience: Owners and frequent users of cell phones

Telephones have no business in cars. Aside from the rare emergency call, people just yak away while they buzz down the highway, paying little attention to the traffic and other drivers around them. And what are these pressing conversations that can't wait five minutes till the driver gets to his or her destination? "Hi, Judy, remember to bring the potato salad to Jan's on Friday." "Hello, dear, would you be sure to defrost the hamburger for dinner?" "Bill, it's killin' me. I gotta know the name of the lead in *Braveheart.*" Cell phone addicts are a menace on the road as they weave in and out of traffic, speed up, slow down, and cut off other drivers as the phone freaks swerve to make almost-missed exits. My request to cell phone owners is this: "Shut up. Even your friends don't want to hear from you that much."

3. Issue and position: Andrea Hoffman wants a raise from eight to nine dollars an hour at Family Tree Nursery.

Audience: Andrea's immediate supervisor

Dear Mr. T. Ightwad:

I have been working at this dive for a year now, and I've made it to work most of the time. When I'm here you can ask anyone—well, you better ask Glen or Annette—and they will tell you I work hard. Whenever you need someone to come through for you with overtime or weekend work, I am right there sometimes, and I stayed late twice last year. Besides, I need the money. I took two classes at the community college last year, and my books were almost a hundred dollars (what a rip-off!). I really do like working at the nursery all right, and I'll probably stick around for awhile, so I hope you will consider giving me the raise that I really do deserve.

P.S. No hard feelings if you don't give me what you owe me. Besides I know where you park your Lexus. Ha, ha, just kidding.

Avoiding Errors in Logic

Logical reasoning—the way you connect your reasons to your evidence—is another important part of persuasive writing. If readers don't think what you are stating makes sense, even if you have plenty of good evidence, they are not likely to believe you. Below are some common **logical fallacies,** or errors in logic.

Teaching Idea
Once you introduce logical fallacies, have students try to locate suspect thinking in one another's arguments during group work. Even when they can't name a fallacy, they often sense when a statement is not logical. It helps to stress *oversimplifying* and *underqualifying* as major culprits.

LOGICAL FALLACIES

1. **Oversimplifying complex issues:** As discussed in Chapter 9, events rarely have only one cause or effect. When you reduce a complex issue in this way, ignoring other significant causes and effects, you have oversimplified.

Example: "Sexual harassment in the workplace is just a case of too many sexually frustrated men acting like schoolboys." *Is* sexual frustration a cause or the only cause of sexual harassment at work? Beware of words and phrases like *simply, just a case of, always, never,* and *every.*

2. **Reducing a complex situation to two sides or solutions,** only one of which is acceptable: More oversimplifying, this either/or thinking clouds issues and lessens options for compromise.

   Example: "If we outlaw guns, only outlaws will have guns." Gun control legislation wouldn't prohibit police officers, gun collectors, or hunters from having guns.

3. **Overgeneralizing** from limited evidence: This fallacy involves drawing a conclusion too broad to be supported by the evidence.

   Example: "Because eight fans were trampled to death at the Pearl Jam concert in Denmark a few years ago, people who don't want to die should stop going to Pearl Jam concerts." This event was a tragedy, but 49,992 fans made it out alive, and subsequent concerts have gone off without a hitch.

4. **Drawing an unwarranted conclusion:** Whereas overgeneralizing involves drawing a conclusion too broad for the evidence, this fallacy involves drawing an incorrect conclusion.

   Example: "That little boy's face is dirty, and his clothes are old; his parents must not care much about him." This conclusion is incorrect if, for example, the boy was outside playing, and his parents dressed him in old clothes for that purpose.

5. **Confusing time order with cause:** As we discussed in Chapter 9, just because a possible cause precedes an event does not mean it is a real cause.

   Example: "Emily always chats with her math instructor before exams, and she always makes A's on them, so her schmoozing is paying off." Perhaps Emily studies diligently.

6. **Using a faulty analogy:** As we have discussed in several chapters, comparisons through metaphor, simile, and analogy are useful support, but they can be carried only so far as evidence in an argument. Analogies relied on too heavily as proof often break down.

   Example: "Of course we should execute people convicted of murder. We shoot mad dogs to protect people from them, don't we?" Dogs are not people, and the punishment of one is not valid support for the punishment to the other. Think of carefully selected analogies as useful support, but as only one piece of evidence among many.

7. **Attacking a person,** not an argument: Sometimes when people cannot present their own reasons and evidence persuasively or refute those of the opposition, they resort to name-calling and trying to defame the opponent. This tactic, frequently used in political campaigns, is known as "mudslinging."

   Example: "How can anyone want to reelect a governor like Jackson, who has been divorced three times and still sees a therapist twice a month?"

8. **Running with the crowd:** This fallacy relies on a common human trait, the herd impulse. People often feel more comfortable doing what others have done or are doing. The logic goes, "If so-and-so is doing it, then it must be right."

   Example: "I guess I shouldn't use the TV as a baby-sitter so much, but all the people I know do, and their kids don't seem ruined." Even though many people may be doing something, it still may not be a good idea.

Writers often succumb to fallacies like these when they allow their emotions to replace more critical judgment. Also, we hear fallacies so regularly from other people and from advertisements that faulty logic can become second nature.

One way to avoid fallacies is to **qualify** statements where needed:

TOO BROAD   Sexual harassment in the workplace is just a case of too many sexually frustrated men acting like schoolboys.

QUALIFIED   One reason behind sexual harassment in the workplace is that some men let their sexual frustration rule their behavior around their female co-workers.

HINT: Qualifying can reduce logical fallacies.

HINT: Qualify where needed but not unnecessarily.

Writers qualify statements based on how much evidence they have. In general, the less qualified an assertion, the more evidence is needed to support it.

Here are some qualifying words: *seems, appears, apparently, could be, can, may, maybe, perhaps, likely, often, sometimes, seldom, usually, frequently, most, many, few.* (For more on qualifying, see pp. 491–492.)

ACTIVITY 16.4 Avoiding Errors in Logic

Teaching Idea
To avoid overstating their case, some students begin overqualifying, which also damages their argument. You might stress the "still makes a point" part of the instructions for Activity 16.4.

With group members, identify the logical fallacy or fallacies in each of the following sentences. Next, rewrite the sentence so that it still makes a point but does not have errors in logic. Where relevant, include evidence as defined on page 390, and qualify statements.

EXAMPLE
Vegetarian diets must be bad for people because one of my friends got sick when she tried to go vegan.

Fallacy: _Overgeneralizing_

Revised sentence: _If vegetarians don't handle their diets carefully, especially taking into account the body's need for protein, they are likely to make themselves sick._

EXAMPLE
Because the state of Kansas has decided to let individual school districts decide whether or not to teach the theory of evolution, Charles Darwin's theory is dead in Kansas.

Fallacy: _Unwarranted conclusion_

Revised sentence: _Because the state of Kansas has decided to let individual school districts decide whether or not to teach the theory of evolution, some school districts will no longer teach evolution._

Answers will vary.

1. Because in football people learn to get back up after they've been knocked down, and this is an important lesson in life, children should play football.

   Fallacy: _Using a faulty analogy_

   Revised sentence: _Football may be one way for some children to learn the life lesson of getting back up when you have been knocked down._

2. Requiring automobile manufacturers to produce either hybrid gas/electric or totally electric cars is the only way to save this country's air quality.

   Fallacy: _Reducing a complex situation_

   Revised sentence: _Requiring automobile manufacturers to produce either hybrid gas/electric or totally electric cars may be the best current solution to a large part of the country's air pollution problem._

3. If we do not pass a law making English the national language, soon our country will be divided into a dozen "minicountries," each speaking its own language.

   Fallacy: _Drawing an unwarranted conclusion, reducing a complex situation_

   Revised sentence: _Passing a law making English the national language will facilitate communication among nonnative speakers from many different places and between nonnative and native speakers of English._

4. That self-confidence tape I bought paid off; I played it every night last week, and, when I talked to my boss, I got the raise!

   Fallacy: _Confusing time order with cause, drawing an unwarranted conclusion_

   Revised sentence: _The self-confidence tape I played last week was a major reason why, when I talked to my boss, I got my raise._

5. We could win the war on drugs if the United States would wipe out all the coca leaf production in South America.

   Fallacy: _Oversimplifying_

   Revised sentence: _Controlling coca leaf production in South America would make a sizeable dent in the cocaine problem in the United States._

6. Now that I'm in college, most of my friends drive after drinking a few beers, and none of them has ever had a problem, so I've decided it's all right to drink and drive.

   Fallacy: _Running with the crowd, overgeneralizing_

   Revised sentence: _Although heavy drinking seriously impairs the ability to drive, I feel confident that I can drink a beer or two and drive with no problem._

Countering Opposition

Because issues have at least two sides, there is more to argument than presenting reasons. You must deal with the opposition's major reasons and also with objections that readers might have to your own reasons. When you show that you know the other side of the issue and can answer the reader's question "Yes, but did you think of this?" you increase your credibility and strengthen your position.

Writers handle opposing reasons and objections to their reasons by first acknowledging them, in some cases **conceding** points that are true, and then **refuting** them, showing how they are wrong. Refutation often involves giving more evidence (such as facts and examples), further clarifying your reasons, and showing how opposing reasons or objections are poorly defined, incomplete, or illogical (knowing logical fallacies can help here).

What you should not do is attack the character of the opposition—for example, "Pro-choice advocates have no feeling for murdered babies"—or insult your readers. Refutation should be tactful, aimed at persuading, not forcing agreement from, the audience.

ACTIVITY 16.5 Countering Opposition

As a group, choose one of the following thesis statements, and assume you are going to argue for it based on the reasons favoring it. Discuss reasons for opposing the thesis, and then list three of those reasons. Next, brainstorm for ways to refute the reasons you listed. You might need to concede a point, offer evidence as defined on page 390, explain your reasoning, and show how an opposing reason is poorly defined, incomplete, or illogical.

EXAMPLE

Thesis: Doctors should be allowed to assist patients who are terminally ill and in great pain to commit suicide.

Reasons Favoring Assertion	Reasons Opposing Assertion
1. Patient's free will	1. Sanctity of life
2. Compassion for patient	2. Possibility of cure
3. Compassion for family	3. Depressed patients making bad decisions

Refuting Opposing Reasons

1. Sanctity of life

While it is true that many people think of human life as sacred, as a society we allow the taking of life in several ways: executions, warfare, and abortion. Perhaps there are justifiable reasons for taking human life.

2. Possibility of cure

There are some cases that might warrant this wait-and-see attitude, but shouldn't that be the doctor's area of expertise? For the rest of the suffering patients, holding out futile hope is cruel. If a terminally ill patient is riddled with cancer and is gasping out her last few months, it is pretty obvious there's not going to be a miracle cure for her.

Teaching Idea
As an alternate approach to this activity (or in addition to it), have the whole class choose sides on an issue, create a pro/con list, and then argue their positions in a mediated point–counterpoint exchange.

Teaching Idea
Activity 16.5 can help students develop their own arguments—especially if they work on one of their own issues instead of those listed. Encourage students to begin any argument by choosing an audience and creating a pro/con list of reasons.

3. Depressed patients making bad decisions

   There is truth here, but the doctor should decide. If a patient is clinically depressed, he should be protected from himself. But some bleak outlooks on life are justified. If the patient is judged competent by a psychiatrist and still wants to die because he is in great physical pain, he should be allowed to.

Answers will vary.

1. Thesis: Elderly family members who are having difficulty maintaining their homes should be encouraged to sell them and move to assisted-living quarters.

Reasons Favoring Assertion	Reasons Opposing Assertion
A. Homes can be dangerous.	A. Familiar surroundings can extend a life.
B. Homes can be too demanding.	B. Assisted living is depersonalizing.
C. Homes can be isolating.	C. Assisted living reduces family contact.

Refuting opposing reasons: *A: concede, but how about when the elderly person can no longer climb stairs or falls down them? B: it can be, but assisted living can also give isolated elderly people a chance to make new friends. C: it can, but assisted living does not have to reduce family contact and may encourage it as the elderly person becomes even more social.*

2. Thesis: For most busy people, jogging is an excellent choice of aerobic exercise.

Reasons Favoring Assertion	Reasons Opposing Assertion
A. Jogging is convenient.	A. Jogging is too harmful.
B. Jogging is inexpensive.	B. Jogging is too solitary.
C. Weather seldom interferes.	C. Outdoor weather extremes are a problem.

Refuting opposing reasons: *A: concede to some harm, but jogging can be done in moderation and on low-impact surfaces. B: concede, but often solitary is good, and jogging can be social because people often run together. C: concede, but during extreme weather people can jog on a treadmill, in a gym, or in an enclosed mall.*

3. Thesis: The benefits of eating only organically grown food outweigh the drawbacks.

Reasons Favoring Assertion	Reasons Opposing Assertion
A. Organic food has fewer health hazards.	A. People cannot afford it.
B. Organic food is more nutritious.	B. Eating organic is not needed for good health.
C. Organic food often tastes better.	C. Buying organic is inconvenient—scarcity.

Refuting opposing reasons: A: concede that some cannot, but many can, especially if they curb some other excessive spending habits, like eating junk food out. B: perhaps, but cite evidence that shows that many toxic chemicals, hormones, and additives can be avoided by eating organic. C: concede, but argue that large organic grocery stores like Wild Oats are making organic food more available.

Persuasive Essays: Analyzing Student Models

As you read the following student essays, look for the argument strategies we practiced in the skills section: defining the issue and clarifying terms, presenting reasons and support, connecting with the audience, avoiding logical fallacies including through qualifying, and countering opposing reasons and objections. Also, try to role-play the stated audience, and see if you are persuaded by the authors. If you are not, ask yourself why the argument failed, and use the answer to improve your own essay.

➡ Prereading Exploration for "Just Say No"

Teaching Idea
Before students read this essay, you might have them answer the prereading questions on the topic of television. TV use/abuse is an issue they are all familiar with, and the class discussion will help them see how to develop an argument.

Marisa Youmbi wrote about children's TV viewing habits because she has to deal with the issue regularly in her household. She thought that her essay would interest parents of school-aged children, especially single parents and dual-earner parents, since many of them are also wrestling with the issue.

How do you feel about TV? Is it a blessing in your life? Do you watch much yourself? Do you watch more than you think you should? List three reasons that TV might be a blessing and three that it might be a curse.

Answers will vary.

TV a Blessing	TV a Curse
A. Informative	A. Wastes time
B. Entertaining	B. Interferes with other activities
C. Social experience	C. Presents a distorted view of the world

Just Say No

Laura is a single mother who is sitting on her bed reading her ten-year-old son's report card and shaking her head. For almost ten years she has sacrificed, worked hard to raise her son the right way. She has spent as much time as possible with Jason, helping him with his homework, but she can't do everything, and she has often turned to the TV to baby-sit when she has had work to do. Now she reads the teachers' comments again: "Jason does not do his homework." "Jason needs to pay more attention in class." She knows that TV is not solely responsible for the D's and F's, but she also knows that four hours a night of TV is too much. Like many parents Laura has a hard decision to make: Should she fight the battle with the idiot box again or just give up?

1

2   One of many good reasons for a parent to limit a child's TV intake is to keep the child physically healthy. Most kids are by nature active; they want to be up and doing things. Whether they are out on a soccer field or just tearing around in the house, they want to *Go*. But TV reaches out for them (all of us really). It casts a spell like one of the fantasy witches from one of their cartoons. I can almost see the green smoke bubbling out of the set and curling around my son's head as he sprawls out on the couch, mesmerized by the flashing lights, music, and action in front of him. "Peter?" I call his name. "Peter, are you in there?" He might as well be drugged for all the response I sometimes get. When children spend hours each day in a trance, they are not exercising. They are learning couch potato habits that will affect what they can and want to do for the rest of their lives.

3   Besides the health issue, children suffer from too much exposure to the wrong messages on TV. There has been much debate about whether violence on television influences children to behave in aggressive or violent ways. Some say that TV violence allows kids to release frustration and anger in the fantasy acts of cartoon characters, instead of punching their brothers and sisters, so at least some TV violence is good for children. Perhaps. But when I watch my own children, nieces, and nephews practice karate kicks on one another and slash away with stick swords after seeing the same behavior on TV, it makes me suspicious. Aside from the violent behavior that kids at least model after their cartoon heroes, there are all kinds of sexual, racial, and ethnic stereotypes shaping kids' views of themselves and others. My daughter does not now look like Barbie and never will. Why should she feel this is an image to live up to?

4   What most disturbs me about excessive television for children is the negative effect it has on their learning. Of course there is a lot of good programming—on the Discovery Channel, Animal Planet, Nickelodeon, Travel, and so on—that exposes children to new ideas. But the truth is that most kids are more attracted to the action/role-playing programs than to a History Channel documentary on the life of Lincoln. When children are unsupervised, they can easily spend four to six hours a day—the national average—watching junk, which leaves little time for homework or other learning activities. Schools practically beg parents to spend time with their children reading and helping with math and other course work. How can this happen when TV has captured the audience?

And schoolwork is not all that suffers. Don't we as parents want to involve our children in other learning activities like music, dance, and sports?

Television is a mixed blessing. In small doses it does not have to have the negative effects on our children's health, behavior, and learning that it often has in large amounts. In fact most of us enjoy watching TV ourselves and with our family; and, let's face it, we often need the break from the kids that the box can provide. But, as tiring as it can be, we need to keep fighting the TV battle with our kids. We need to monitor what they watch and how much. Children cannot see very far down the road. They want what they want when they want it, regardless of the consequences. It is part of our job as parents to protect them from themselves.

—Marisa Youmbi

POSTREADING ANALYSIS: KEY POINTS FOR BUILDING ARGUMENT ESSAYS
- **Title:** arouses readers' curiosity and links to the essay's main point
- **Introductory paragraph:** begins with a hook and ends with a thesis sentence.
- **Body paragraphs:** begin with a topic sentence that often contains a reason supporting the position taken, naming the reason and making a limiting statement about it—for example, "Besides the health issue, children suffer from too much exposure to the wrong messages on TV"—and may end with a summary sentence—for example, "They are learning couch potato habits . . .'"
- **Development:** uses specific examples, action, dialogue, active verbs (*sacrificed*), -*ing* words (*bubbling*), specific words (*Discovery Channel*), and qualifiers (*many, often, some*); tells thoughts and emotions; explains the examples ("When children spend hours each day in a trance, they are not exercising"); anticipates opposing reasons and objections (paragraph 4); and uses patterns of development (narrative and cause/effect, paragraphs 1 and 2). (For more on layering examples, see pp. 43–44.)
- **Concluding paragraph:** restates the thesis, briefly summarizes, and adds a final (expanded) thought.
- **Sentence connectors:** guide readers: transitions, repeat words, synonyms, pronouns, and reference to main idea.
- **Style points:** increase readability. Using rhetorical questions (disguised statements) and the pronouns *we, us,* and *our* to *intentionally* speak to the audience can involve your readers (paragraphs 4 and 5). Dashes can be used for emphasis (paragraph 4). Imagined dialogue can create variety (paragraphs 1 and 2). Short sentences can be emphatic ("Television is a mixed blessing").

Teaching Idea
"Just Say No" is a strong example of shaping an argument for a target audience. Ask students to evaluate the appeals directed to the parent audience. Are the appeals effective, and if so why?

➡ **Prereading Exploration for "Something for Nothing?"**

Matt Smith discusses another family issue: allowances. Drawing on personal experience, Matt directs his argument toward middle- and lower-income parents who want to give their children allowances but are debating whether to have

Teaching Idea
You might want to mention assumptions in arguments at this point and link the discussion with Matt Smith's assumption that his audience already favors allowances. You can frame the discussion as another method for focusing an argument.

them earn the money. Because he defines his audience as already favoring allowances, Matt can avoid complicating his argument and make it more focused.

Authors of arguments make various assumptions, with which readers—depending on their values, knowledge, and experiences—might agree or disagree. As readers' responses to your assumptions can help or hurt your arguments, you should assume with care. How do you feel about the author's assumption that money can be a strong motivator for young people from "six to sixteen," perhaps more powerful than pleasing a parent or helping the family, and more effective than being deprived of something they value?

Answers will vary.

_____

_____

_____

Something for Nothing?

1   "Josh, congratulations, you don't have to work anymore if you don't want to. You just come in whenever you please, and I'll keep writing you a paycheck every month for at least the next ten years. What do you say?" I don't know about you, but if I were Josh, I'd be thanking the Lord and not planning on many more visits to the job site. Paying a child an allowance is not quite the same as an employer paying an employee wages; but there are some similarities, and a child is likely to react like most adults would on hearing he is about to get something for nothing—take the money and run. Parents who believe in allowances for their children should consider making their children work for the money.

2   One good reason for expecting children to work for extra spending money is that most families need the help. While there are plenty of wealthy folk in this country, most of us are not, and households run on people power. Both of my parents worked when I was growing up, so neither had a lot of extra time to keep the house running smoothly. They still carried a lot of the load, but my brothers and sister and I were expected to wash dishes, vacuum, do laundry, carry out the trash, rake leaves, and mow the lawn—all the routine chores—especially if we wanted an allowance. I remember my youngest brother at six helping us rake leaves. He was proud to be a "big kid," and we all got along pretty well together.

3   Another point in favor of children's working in return for their allowance is the motivation factor. Most parents expect their children to help out around the house, whether they give the children an allowance or not. A lot of the minimal jobs are supposed to be "understood"—putting toys away, keeping clothes on hangers, putting books back on

shelves, making up a bed, and so on. But by the time children are six or so, many parents begin leaning pretty hard on them to do the daily chores. I have seen adults shout at their kids, call them names, and spank the youngest ones for not doing their jobs. I say, rather than making kids mind by punishing them, why not reward them for doing what they should? Earned allowances can be a positive motivator for young people from six to at least sixteen, especially when they can buy whatever they want with the money.

The most important reason for tying allowances to performance is that it gives children an early clear view of the real world. People have to work and produce for a living, almost everyone. Whatever we want to call it—a paycheck, grades on a report card, praise from someone we respect, or an allowance—the world turns on people's putting out effort and being rewarded, sometimes, for it. Why shouldn't children learn this lesson early in life? If they learn it well, maybe they will carry it through to other areas as they grow older, areas like good performance at work and school. I know that some might think a ten-year-old shouldn't have to think of the pressures of the "real world," that kids should be allowed just to be kids. But I am not talking about slave labor here, just a regular routine of chores that kids can reasonably be expected to handle in any day, without taking too much time from their schoolwork or probably even from their TV watching.

Expecting children to do some work for what they are given just makes sense to me. Aside from the reasons of helping the family, positive motivation, and teaching a realistic view of the world, I think that helping children learn to work and see the benefit in it instills values in children. Too many kids are going bad today, trying to take the easy way out—cheating in school, scraping by at low-status jobs they hate, drifting off into a cloud of drugs. Maybe as simple a decision by a parent early in a child's life as teaching the youngster to earn what he gets, that the world owes him nothing, maybe this lesson will help send a son or daughter off onto the road to success.

—*Matt Smith*

POSTREADING ANALYSIS: KEY POINTS FOR BUILDING ARGUMENT ESSAYS
- **Title:** arouses readers' curiosity and links to the essay's main point
- **Introductory paragraph:** begins with a hook and ends with a thesis sentence.

- **Body paragraphs:** begin with a topic sentence that often contains a reason supporting the position taken, naming the reason and making a limiting statement about it—for example, "One good reason for expecting children to work for extra spending money is that most families need the help"—and may end with a summary sentence—for example, "Earned allowances can be a positive motivator for young people from six to at least sixteen . . . ."

- **Development:** uses specific examples, action, dialogue, active verbs (*shout*), *-ing* words (*helping*), specific words (*six to sixteen*), and qualifiers (*most, some*); tells thoughts and emotions; explains the examples ("households run on people power"); anticipates opposing reasons and objections (paragraph 4); and uses synonyms (*allowance = money*), negation (paragraph 4), and patterns of development (narrative, paragraph 1; cause/effect, paragraphs 1–5). (For more on layering examples, see pp. 43–44.)

- **Concluding paragraph:** restates the thesis, briefly summarizes, and adds a final (expanded) thought

- **Sentence connectors:** guide readers: transitions, repeat words, synonyms, pronouns, and reference to main idea.

- **Style points:** increase readability. Using rhetorical questions (disguised statements) and the pronouns *we* and *us* to *intentionally* speak to the audience can involve your readers (paragraphs 2 and 4). Dashes can be used to separate a list (paragraph 4). Imagined dialogue can create variety (paragraph 1). Short sentences can be emphatic ("'What do you say?'").

Teaching Idea

If you discuss rhetorical questions in arguments, you might link Matt Smith's use of them in body paragraph 3 with Marisa Youmbi's use of them in body paragraphs 2 and 3.

Teaching Idea

After students have analyzed a model essay, ask who was or wasn't persuaded by the author and why. Then remind students that even well-written arguments don't always succeed.

Questions for Essay Analysis

Note: These questions apply to both "Just Say No" and "Something for Nothing?"

1. Where is the thesis located? What is the issue, and what statement limits it? Does the thesis sufficiently clarify the author's issue and position? In which other paragraphs does the author reiterate his or her thesis?

2. Why is the hook effective? Which of the Chapter 12 hooks has the author used (see pp. 288–291)?

3. What method(s) from Chapter 12 has the author used to develop the introductory paragraph (see pp. 283–288)? Why might the introduction interest the audience stated in the prereading exploration?

4. Why might the lead sentence in the concluding paragraph be effective? (For lead and summary sentences, see p. 294.)

5. What method(s) from Chapter 12 has the author used to develop the concluding paragraph? What is the expanded thought? (For developing conclusions, see pp. 299–308.) Why might the conclusion interest the target audience? (Think of how the conclusion links with the introduction.)

6. For each topic sentence, what are the reason, the limiting statement, and the connector words? (For more on connecting sentences, see pp. 53–58.)

7. How are the body paragraphs arranged: chronologically or by order of importance? What connector words reveal this organization?

8. Where has the author acknowledged an opposing reason or objection to his or her reasons? Has the author refuted or weakened the opposing reason or objection? How? (For more on refutation, see pp. 399–401.)

9. What are three instances of qualifying (*most, sometimes, often*) (see pp. 401, 404)?

10. What are three places in the essay where the author tries to connect with his or her audience? Consider use of the pronouns *we, us,* and *our;* mentions of shared experiences or values; and emotional appeals (see pp. 393–394).

11. Why do you think any one paragraph in the essay is well written? Consider elements like patterns of development, appeals, topic sentences, connecting words, sensory details, specific words, action description, dialogue, metaphors and other comparisons, sentence variety, and clear explanations.

WRITING A PERSUASIVE ESSAY
Summarizing the Assignment

Teaching Idea
You may find that students write stronger arguments at this level if they choose topics that they can develop from their own experience, avoiding the need for research.

In this assignment, you will tackle an **issue** (a debatable topic), taking a clear position and defending it in an essay of 500 to 600 words. There are many potential issues to write on. You might choose one that requires some research, such as drug testing in the workplace or selective admission policies in universities, or stick with one that you know about from personal experience or general knowledge, as the students who wrote the model essays did. (If you need to do research, see Appendix 1.)

Plan on a paper of five to six paragraphs, three to four of which will be in the body. Because introductory and concluding paragraphs are such crucial elements in essays, you should pay special attention to them. You should also, of course, introduce each body paragraph with a strong topic sentence, which in most cases will give a reason for your position.

Establishing Audience and Purpose

Teaching Idea
You might mention that arguments asking for a small—but real—concession or change of behavior/attitude are often more effective than those that try for sweeping changes.

Argument is, arguably, the writing that requires the most sensitivity to **audience.** Because you are asking something from your readers besides understanding—to think or act differently—you can expect your job as writer to be tougher. After all, how do you react when people call to ask you for your time or money? How anxious are you to pull out your wallet or prolong a conversation with telemarketers?

When considering an audience in persuasive writing, you need to ask questions like "How resistant are they to my position? What can I expect to accomplish in my argument? How far can I move them to action or agreement?" Maybe you will decide that the best you can do is talk them out of throwing a rock at you. In short, within your general persuasive purpose, you need to decide more specifically how far you will try to move your audience. Because of the importance of audience, successful argument depends on giving and supporting reasons readers will find convincing, countering opposing reasons and objections to your reasons, and generally showing that you are a credible writer.

Working through the Writing Assignment

Discovering Ideas

Writing Tutor: Arguments

In exploring issues for this assignment, look to your own life for inspiration. We all lead lives full of potential topics for argument, particularly when we react to situations we are unhappy with. At home, perhaps you would like more help with the housework. Who can you persuade to help? At school, you may need an extension on a class project. How do you move your instructor to grant it? At work, you know that you deserve a raise. How will you talk your boss into it?

You may also choose a topic because you want to learn more about it, perhaps something about which you have strong feelings but not clearly thought out reasons. For example, perhaps you oppose disciplining children by spanking but are not sure what ways might be better. This essay will give you a chance to find out those better ways.

As you brainstorm, remember that a topic is not necessarily an issue but that, with a little thought, most topics can become issues. Consider this example:

TOPIC   **When husbands and wives divide chores in a marriage, men often do the yard work.**

This statement is merely a topic because it is not arguable. It is a truth with which no reasonable person can disagree. However, we can frame it as an issue like this:

ISSUE   **Men ought to do most or all of the yard work in a marriage.**

Now we have a potential argument, because some people will disagree with the statement, offering reasons to prove their point. The following issues lists may help you choose an issue. Although the issues are framed as assertions, many will need to be further focused with your interests and audience in mind.

Teaching Idea
Beginning a discussion of issues by first treating them as topics will help clarify for students what is arguable and what is not.

Teaching Idea
These issues are written as assertions to help students move more quickly into an argument, and most of them can be developed through a student's personal experience.

Issues List

ISSUES FROM FAMILY LIFE

- Parents ought to control their children's access to television.
- Parents should use methods other than spanking to discipline their children.
- Parents who can afford to give their children allowances should do so without requiring the child to earn the money.
- High-schoolers should be allowed to set their own curfews.
- Teens should be allowed to choose the family functions they attend.
- Dividing household chores along gender lines is a bad idea.
- Parents should remove handguns from their house.
- People should limit their families to three children at most.
- Parents should have more than one child.
- Families should make frequent visits to older members who are in assisted-living situations or who can no longer drive themselves.

ISSUES FROM PERSONAL LIFE

- Your parents should pay for any one of the following for you: your college tuition, a car, auto insurance, a vacation.
- Your parents should rethink a negative opinion of one of your friends.

- One of your friends should rethink a negative attitude toward another friend.
- One of your friends should change a behavior toward you or others—for example, his or her anger, caustic humor, selfishness, or indifference.
- A friend should see a movie you like.
- A friend should stop or reduce some self-destructive behavior—for example, drinking, smoking, overeating, binging and purging, gambling, or couch potatoitis.
- A police officer pulling you over for speeding should not give you a ticket.
- A salesperson should reduce the price of an item you want—for example, a stereo, a computer, sports equipment, or a house.
- Your best friend (wife, husband, boy- or girlfriend, son, daughter) and you should communicate more openly about issues that annoy you both.
- Parents should not allow grandparents to "spoil" grandchildren.

ISSUES FROM SCHOOL

- Students who are not interested in high school should be allowed to drop out, rather than be required by law to stay in until they are sixteen.
- High school students, like college students, should be allowed to choose more of their own curriculum.
- College students should be able to base their GPA on the last 50 percent of their education.
- Teachers should be more lenient on any of the following: tardiness, absences, or late homework (persuade one of your teachers).
- Teachers should always drop at least one of their students' lowest grades (persuade one of your teachers to do this).
- Colleges should provide more support services for nonnative speakers.
- Campus security should be required to issue one-dollar fines to any smoker who throws a cigarette on the ground.
- Your college needs to provide more parking.
- Colleges should allow students to fulfill their language requirement with a course in American Sign Language.
- Your college ought to provide free day care to students with young children.

ISSUES FROM THE WORKPLACE

- Your company should change any form of discrimination in hiring, such as according to age, gender, or race.
- Women should react more strongly to sexual harassment on the job.
- Your boss should give you more time off.
- Your company should allow job sharing.
- Your company should change some existing policy (offer an alternative).
- Your boss should give you a raise.
- Employee X should be fired (or promoted).
- Your company should provide on-site day care.
- Your company should provide health insurance.
- Your company should allow four-day workweeks.

ISSUES FROM THE COMMUNITY

- By age seventy, people should be required by law to pass an annual physical and driving exam to prove that they can competently handle their vehicles.
- People who do not want to serve on juries should not have to.
- People should become involved with their community by volunteering.
- Sports teams that use ethnic names should change them.
- Parental consent should be required for minors to obtain birth control.
- Parents should be told of any child carrying HIV in their children's school.
- People with cell phones in their cars should use them only for emergencies.
- Halloween is too dangerous and should be dropped as a holiday.
- Your swimming pool should stay open past Labor Day for parents with preschoolers.
- Penalties in your state should be more severe for fathers delinquent on child support payments.

Prewriting

First, check to be sure you have an issue, and not merely a topic. The test is whether you have a statement with which people might reasonably disagree. For instance, if your topic is only children, and you say, "Only children have a different experience growing up than children with brothers and sisters," you have just a topic—a factual statement. But if you say, "Only children are less prepared for life than children who have brothers and sisters," you have an issue—more specifically, an assertion that takes a position on the issue.

Next, make lists of reasons favoring and opposing your position on the issue. For instance, if on the topic of elderly drivers you assert, "Drivers over seventy should be required to pass an annual physical exam and driving test to keep their driver's license," you can then brainstorm lists of reasons favoring and opposing the assertion:

HINT: Creating a for/against list of reasons is an essential prewriting strategy.

Reasons Favoring Assertion	Reasons Opposing Assertion
1. Injury to older drivers	1. Discrimination against elderly
2. Injury to other people	2. Unfair treatment of elderly
3. Inconvenience to other motorists	3. Unnecessary law
4. Failing mental abilities	4. Transportation problems the elderly face
5. Failing physical abilities	5. Infringement on civil liberty

If you are going to argue for the position, the reasons favoring it can become points you will make, and the reasons opposing it points you will argue against. How do you choose which points to use; that is, how do you focus your lists?

You can focus your lists in two ways: by defining an audience and by finding supporting evidence. Erica Hood, who wrote the annotated student model, chose as her audience mostly urban drivers with older family members who could be at risk behind the wheel. With these readers in mind, Erica decided to include the opposing reasons "discrimination" and "transportation problems." She found evidence to support her refutation of these opposing reasons: The increased risk because of failing physical and mental health would enable her to refute the point about discrimination, and the existence of alternative means of

HINT: Knowing your audience will help you to choose reasons to support and refute your argument.

transportation for seniors would help her refute the point about transportation problems.

As you gather ideas for your argument, select the reasons to support and refute that are most appropriate in light of your audience and evidence.

PREWRITING—SUMMING UP

1. Choose several topics from the lists, or choose several of your own.
2. Focus the topic as an issue.
3. Create lists of favoring and opposing reasons.
4. Select favoring and opposing reasons based on your evidence and audience.
5. Develop several reasons with evidence.

JOURNAL ENTRY 16.2

Who would oppose your position on this issue, and what is one reason they would give? How will you refute it—with one of your reasons or by showing how the reason is faulty? Perhaps the logic is flawed (see fallacies, pp. 395–397) or poorly supported by evidence (see p. 390).

Organizing Ideas

Before moving ahead, write out your thesis, stating your issue and position. When you draft your essay, you may simply imply the thesis or frame it as a question (see "Just Say No," pp. 401–403), but for now, state it directly. Most of you will put the thesis in the last sentence of the first paragraph. Remember to **qualify** and focus the thesis, and consider including a word like *should, ought to,* or *must* to clarify your position. Here are two thesis sentences from the chapter models:

A. Parents who believe in allowances for their children should consider making their children work for the money.

B. Not testing the competency of older drivers annually could be a dangerous oversight.

There are two related mistakes to avoid in the introduction in general and the thesis in particular: inappropriate use of *you* and alienating the audience. Because you are asking an audience to change an attitude or behavior, you can easily sound critical of them. To avoid communicating this impression (even if, in fact, it is true), do not use *you* and do include yourself in the audience if possible. Contrast thesis sentence A above with this alternative:

Unless *you* want to keep raising lazy kids who don't much care about *you* or their family, *you* ought to wise up and make the kids do their fair share around the house to earn their allowance, rather than continuing to spoil them.

As you can see, the original version of this thesis is far more likely to draw the audience of parents into the essay.

Teaching Idea After students have chosen topics, have them at least start a pro/con list in class, and then work with group members, playing devil's advocate to see which main reasons/counterreasons are still missing.

Teaching Idea Journal Entry 16.2 is the first checkpoint to see if students have a real sense of their audience. You might want to collect and check the entry.

HINT: Qualify and clarify thesis sentences.

Teaching Idea Remind students of the other methods for creating coherence (repeat words, synonyms, etc.).

HINT: Avoid alienating your audience at the outset.

An Argument against Older Drivers

First draft contains reasons but lacks
several counters and specific
examples as evidence.

1   Older drivers can have a hard time of it on the road. Their reflexes slow down, their eyesight deteriorates, and their hearing goes. Although some can handle their cars competently, many are accidents waiting to happen. For everyone's safety, including their own, older drivers should be willing to take a test each year to see if they are still able to drive safely.

Working thesis

Topic sentence unfocused

2   My first point is that elderly drivers are often in poor health. They have trouble moving, their joints ache, getting in and out of a car is a problem, and they neither see nor hear well. Getting behind the wheel is dangerous if these senses are impaired. When traffic is heavy, people need to see the cars all around them and hear if someone leans on the horn. Even drivers in good health with all their senses intact can drift out of their lane and only be brought back to reality by a loud horn honk.

3   Reflex time also slows down as people get older. This creates other difficulties and problem for drivers. There are many situations where people have to react quickly while driving like when an ambulance wants by or when a car slows down drastically in front of a person. In order to help out their slow reaction time, many old folks slow down, but slower driving can be as dangerous as fast driving. During rush hour when cars are racing past, you can see the older driver, poking along at forty miles an hour. This can cause accidents.

Needs further qualifiers throughout

4   As people age, many catch illnesses that lead to dangerous driving. My older grandfather on my mother's side has Alzheimer's, and the disease began lowering his competency long before he stopped driving. No one in our family knew that he had Alzheimer's, and he was driving on the very day that he was diagnosed. I am not trying to discriminate against the elderly. However, when a driver frequently endangers himself, putting himself at risk and others, steps must be taken to ensure everyone's safety.

Disclaimer

5   We all want to protect our grandparents and ourselves from harm. To do this we need to support an annual driving exam and physical checkup for older drivers. Some might oppose such a law on the grounds that once an older driver loses their license, they become housebound. But in the city there are busses and taxis. In rural areas, people can carpool, and family members can take care of their grandparents by driving them. If people want to protect and care for their grandparents' needs, they can insist on more and better public transportation. Our lawmakers can accomplish this.

Begins to refute counterreason

Conclusion needs work to improve persona.

Elderly drivers are creating problems for everyone in society because they have such a hard time driving. Their failing health puts them in danger too. Although seniors will certainly be inconvenienced and so will their family members who have to cart them around, there really is no alternative. When a person is a proven menace, through no fault of his or her own, that person must give up certain privileges for the greater good.

Second-Stage Draft

Teaching Idea
Student arguments so often suffer from underqualifying that it is worth stressing the additional qualifiers that Erica added to her second draft.

First drafts of arguments are often underdeveloped, lacking enough reasons, opposing reasons, evidence, details, and explanations. There may also be difficulties with **emotional appeals** and the writer's **persona**. Erica knew that her first draft was solid but needed more material, a stronger connection with her audience, and a more effective introduction and conclusion. This second draft addresses these concerns.

> **SPECIAL POINTS TO CHECK IN REVISING FROM FIRST TO SECOND DRAFTS**
> 1. **Introduction:** hook, engaging support sentences, thesis (clear issue and position)
> 2. **Body paragraphs:** topic sentence with connector
> 3. **Overall development:** reasons: evidence (detailed examples, clear explanations, facts/statistics, anecdotes, scenarios, authorities)
> 4. **Appeals of persona and emotion:** including connecting with audience through *we*, *us*, and *our*
> 5. **Counterreasons and objections:** pointing out logical fallacies
> 6. **Qualifiers**
> 7. **Conclusion:** connector, summary, expanded thought

An Argument against Older Drivers

Introduction revised with personal anecdote to connect with audience

Qualifiers added throughout

Thesis revised

Clarifies age group of drivers

Topic sentence revised

Further explaining

Last year my grandfather drove through the back of the garage and into the garden behind it. Of course, this can happen to anyone, but since his reflexes are so slow, half his car went through the garage wall before he was able to stop. Maybe my grandfather should no longer be driving, but once people in America take a driving test, they are usually turned loose until the day they die. Not testing the competency of older drivers annually—especially by age seventy—could be a dangerous oversight.

We all know that eyesight and hearing almost always worsen as people age. For various reasons some older people don't like to admit it. Driving is dangerous if these senses are impaired. When a solid wall of cars stops during rush hour, a driver better be able to see it, and when a semi blows its horn announcing that it is changing lanes, a driver better be able to hear it. Sometimes eye wear or even surgery cannot correct

Personal example added as specific
evidence and link to reader

Reiterates thesis

Examples added as evidence

Specific details added to example

Reveals personal response to
shape persona

More explaining as evidence

Evidence added—persona

Pronouns added to identify with
audience: *we, us, our*

Added facts as evidence

vision enough for the elderly to drive safely. And sometimes hearing aids are turned off or their batteries are low. These are just two reasons why people over seventy should take driving tests every year.

3   Reflex time also slows as people get older. This creates other difficulties and problems for drivers. My grandfather might not have caused as much damage to his car or garage if he had reacted faster. There are many situations where people have to react quickly while driving. Sometimes an emergency vehicle needs by. And then there are times when a car abruptly slows in front of another. Also, a hazard like a piece of lumber or truck tread might appear on the highway, or a child might run out into the road. In order to compensate for their slow reaction time, many elderly reduce their overall speed, but slower driving can be as dangerous as fast driving. During rush hour when cars are racing past, that old car with someone's grandmother in it who is barely able to see over the steering wheel, poking along in the high-speed lane, can cause accidents.

4   As people age, many contract debilitating illnesses that can lead to dangerous driving. My older grandfather on my mother's side has Alzheimer's, and the disease began lowering his competency long before he stopped driving. No one in our family knew that he had Alzheimer's, and he was driving on the very day that he was diagnosed. It frightens me to think that he might not have been able to find his way back home while driving or, worse, become disoriented and had a high-speed accident. I am not trying to discriminate against older drivers. My own young adult age group is often, and sometimes justifiably, bashed for reckless driving. However, when a driver frequently endangers himself, putting himself at risk and others, even though it is not through his own fault, steps must be taken to ensure everyone's safety.

5   We all want to protect our grandparents and ourselves from harm. To do this we need to support an annual driving exam and physical checkup for older drivers. Some might oppose such a law on the grounds that once an older driver loses his license, he becomes housebound, unable to take care of his needs. But in the city there are busses and taxis and in some cities the subway. In rural areas, people can carpool, and family members can take care of their elderly by driving them. If we as citizens and children of our grandparents seriously want to protect our grandparents and care for their needs, we can insist on more and better public transportation. Our lawmakers can accomplish this.

6

Neither of my grandfathers wants to endanger anyone, and they both have to get from place to place just like everyone else. But their failing health made them unsafe drivers, so they finally stopped driving, luckily before anyone was seriously injured. As a result, my folks and I and the rest of our family are pitching in to shuttle our grandparents around. It is inconvenient. And family members are annoyed by the chore on occasion. But this "chore" has the benefit of bringing us more often in contact with each other. I see all of my grandparents more frequently now than before they stopped driving. The family profits because we are sharing a task that is right. Our older generation took care of their children and their children's children in their time. Now it is our time to take care of them.

Conclusion revised to increase persona and appeals to readers' emotions

Teaching Idea
This second-draft conclusion is such an improvement on the first attempt that it is worth noting to students, especially those who regularly seem to lose inspiration at the end.

Third-Stage Draft

With most of the organizational and material concerns out of the way, Erica could focus more on style. In this draft, notice how she improved her word choices and sentence patterns.

Teaching Idea
If you are assigning this chapter at the end of the semester, you may be focusing a bit more on matters of style. This third draft can help students with common style problems that are within the ability of many developmental writers to improve.

> **SPECIAL POINTS TO CHECK IN REVISING FROM SECOND TO THIRD DRAFTS**
> 1. Add specific words.
> 2. Substitute more precise or audience-appropriate words.
> 3. Combine sentences for variety.
> 4. **Replace clutter and repeat words with synonyms and phrases.**
> 5. Delete unneeded words.

Title revised to correct negative tone—*our* added

More specific words added

More precise words substituted

Should Our Grandparents Be Driving?

1

Last year my seventy-five-year-old grandfather drove through the back of the garage and into the garden behind it. Of course, an accident like this can happen to anyone, but since his reflexes are so slow, half his car went through the garage wall before he was able to stop. Maybe my grandfather should no longer be driving, but once people in America take a driving test at sixteen, they are usually turned loose until the day they die. Not testing the competency of older drivers annually could be a dangerous oversight.

Sentences combined for variety

2

We all know that eyesight and hearing almost always worsen as people age, even though some older people don't like to admit it. ~~Driving~~ **Getting behind the wheel** is dangerous if these senses are impaired. When a solid wall of cars stops on I-435 during the 5:30 rush hour, a

Phrase replaces overused word.

Sentence divided for emphasis

driver better be able to see it. When a semi blows its air horn announcing that it is changing lanes, a driver better be able to hear it. Sometimes eye wear or even surgery cannot correct vision enough for the elderly to drive safely. And sometimes hearing aids are turned off or their

More precise words substituted

batteries are low. ~~These~~ Poor eyesight and hearing are just two reasons why people over seventy should take driving tests every year.

Sentences combined for variety   3
Redundant phrase removed

Reflex time also slows as people get older, creating ~~other difficulties and~~ another problem for drivers. My grandfather might not have caused as much damage to his car or garage if he had reacted faster.

Sentences combined for variety using colon with list

More specific words added

There are many situations where people have to react quickly while driving: when an emergency vehicle needs by, when a car abruptly slows in front of another, when a hazard like a piece of lumber or large chunk of truck tread appears on the highway, or when a child runs out into the road chasing a ball. In order to compensate for their slow reaction time, many elderly reduce their overall speed, but slower driving can be as dangerous as fast driving. During rush hour when cars are racing past at seventy-five miles per hour, that old Chrysler with someone's grandmother in it who is barely able to see over the steering wheel, poking along at forty in the high-speed lane, can cause accidents.

4

As people age, many contract debilitating illnesses that can lead to dangerous driving. My grandfather on my mother's side has Alzheimer's, and the disease began lowering his competency long before he stopped driving. No one in our family knew that Grandpa Miller had Alzheimer's, and he was driving on the very day that he was diagnosed. It frightens me to think that he might not have been able to find his way back home

Unneeded phrases removed

~~while driving~~ or, worse, become disoriented and had a high-speed accident. I am not trying to discriminate against ~~older drivers~~ **the elderly.** My

Synonym replaces overused word

own young adult age group is often, and sometimes justifiably, bashed for reckless driving. However, when a driver frequently endangers himself ~~putting himself at risk~~ and others, even though it is not through his own fault, steps must be taken to ensure everyone's safety.

Sentences combined for variety   5

If we want to protect our grandparents and ourselves ~~from harm~~, we need to support an annual driving exam and physical checkup for ~~older drivers~~ the **elderly.** Some might oppose such a law on the grounds

Gender pronoun alternated

that once an older driver loses her license, she becomes housebound, unable to take care of her needs. But in the city there are busses and

Synonym replaces overused word.

taxis and in some cities the subway. In rural areas, people can carpool, and family members can take care of their elderly by driving them. If we as citizens and children of our ~~grandparents~~ **older generation** seriously want to protect our grandparents and care for their needs, we can insist on more and better public transportation. Our lawmakers can accomplish this.

More specific words added

Italicizing *is* for emphasis

Neither of my grandfathers wants to endanger anyone, and they both have to get from place to place just like everyone else. But their failing physical and mental health made them unsafe drivers, so they finally stopped driving, luckily before anyone was seriously injured. As a result, my folks and I and the rest of our family are pitching in to shuttle our grandparents around. It *is* inconvenient. And family members are annoyed by the chore on occasion. But this "chore" has the benefit of bringing us more often in contact with each other. I see all of my grandparents more frequently now than before they stopped driving. The family profits because we are sharing a task that is right. Our older generation took care of their children and their children's children in their time. Now it is our time to take care of them.

—Erica Hood

Chapter Summary

1. Persuasion means moving someone to accept an idea or perform an action.
2. Argument is formal persuasion that tries to move a target audience, using reasons supported by evidence and refuting opposing reasons.
3. Persuasive speaking and writing are a regular part of our daily lives.
4. Argumentation requires a clearly defined issue and position.
5. An argument benefits from the writer's developing not only appeals to the mind in the form of clearly presented evidence but also emotional appeals and a positive persona.
6. Arguments should avoid errors in logic, including oversimplifying and underqualifying.
7. Writers can connect with an audience by showing that they are part of it, understand what readers need to know, and share in their beliefs and concerns.
8. Insulting or trying to intimidate an audience is a poor persuasive strategy.
9. Argument essays are frequently arranged by order of importance.
10. Writing is never complete until it has been revised and edited.

Taking Essay Exams

What Are We Trying to Achieve and Why?

Setting the Stage

The preceding photo shows a scene with which you are undoubtedly familiar—a class of students taking an exam, the clock ticking, sweat dripping. We have all lived through this situation, sometimes with only mild anxiety, other times in a state of panic. Perhaps the most dreaded exam is the in-class essay, a task that requires analysis, synthesis, and evaluation—all under the pressure of the ticking clock. Helping you with this common academic chore is the purpose of Chapter 17.

Two important aspects of essay examinations distinguish them from our other assignments this semester:

- **Process limitations:** To be successful on in-class essays, you must be particularly well prepared because you have to write quickly, with little time for revision. Although most instructors consider time constraints when they evaluate responses, they still expect a well-written essay.

- **Audience:** For perhaps the first time this term, you will be consciously writing to your teacher. Knowing the material and knowing what your instructor expects will help you succeed.

Linking to Previous Experience

We have all taken multiple-choice, matching, and fill-in-the-blank tests. Essay exams require much the same preparation and come in several familiar forms, of which short-answer (a paragraph), long-answer (an essay), and take-home exams are perhaps the most common. To develop a paragraph- or essay-length response, you can use the composition skills you have practiced all semester: unearthing ideas, organizing, drafting, and revising/editing, as time permits. Sometimes a single pattern is called for, such as comparison/contrast. Often, however, you will use several patterns together, as you have throughout *A Writer's Workshop,* particularly in Unit Three.

As in most writing, you will be dealing with a target audience you want something from—in this case, a superior grade. So keep your instructor in mind as you explain, illustrate, and define.

Determining the Value

Being able to perform well on essay exams will obviously benefit you in school. In the workplace, too, there are many writing situations that require people to quickly organize and draft a response. Examples of such responses include lawyers' reports to their clients, nurses' ward reports, police officers' accident reports, and businesspeople's interoffice memos. Being able to produce readable writing quickly is a real-world asset.

The process of preparing for an essay exam is also valuable. How often have you thought that you understood a concept until you had to explain it to an audience? Preparing for an essay exam—memorizing material, questioning ideas, making connections, and drawing conclusions—is one good way to explore a topic to ensure that you truly understand it.

Finally, learning to remain calm under stress, or to calm yourself, will give you an ability you can use repeatedly, in school and out.

Teaching Idea
Few people like to write under time constraints, and students may question the value or fairness of in-class essay exams. You might emphasize the preparation process as one of learning and the testing process as one of efficiency.

Teaching Idea
Journal Entry 17.1 helps students see that doing well on essay exams requires a strategy.

JOURNAL ENTRY 17.1

Think for a moment about your essay-exam experiences. How well, in general, have you done on essay exams? Do you have strategies for preparing? Which of the following (if any) do you usually do to prepare?

- Carefully study the material on a weekly basis.
- Ask questions in class.
- Annotate your text.
- Link related ideas.
- Take thorough notes.
- Participate in class discussions.
- Memorize key terms.
- Create practice questions.

What is one change you could make in your preparation habits?

Developing Skills and Exploring Ideas in Writing for Essay Exams

Although we all are experienced in answering test questions, we can always improve. In addition to developing strategies for preparing in advance, such as those listed in Journal Entry 17.1, you can practice the following strategies to use when actually taking the exam:

1. Analyzing the exam question
2. Writing relevant, specific responses
3. Writing brief but effective introductions
4. Writing brief but effective conclusions

Analyzing the Question

To succeed on essay exams, you must first understand the questions being asked. This seems easy enough—until a vaguely written or complicated question comes along. Consider this question from an American history exam:

> In brief, relate the economic conditions of the South in the years immediately preceding the Civil War.

What exactly does "relate" mean, and what is the professor's purpose in asking the question? Most likely, you are expected simply to summarize the economic conditions in the South at that time. However, you might also be expected to show a causal link between these conditions and the outbreak of the war.

Sometimes verbs of command like *relate, discuss, examine,* and *explore* are open to interpretation. When in doubt, ask your instructor for clarification.

The following essay question is more precise but requires analysis—that is, it gives directions that are specific if you know how to interpret them:

> The [causes] that led to the War between the States are complicated. While many have been taught that the main issue was slavery, we have learned otherwise in this class. [List] the [three] most important [factors] leading to the Civil War, but [focus on the one] that seems to be [the most significant] (as we have discussed it in class). [Include the names] of people prominent in [each] of the [causes] and [tell] something about their contribution toward the ultimate declaration of war.

The key phrase "list the three," combined with "factors" or "causes," indicates that causes are important and that you will structure the response in three body paragraphs. "Focus on the one . . ." suggests least-to-most organization, with the most attention given to the last, most significant, reason (which the question tells us is *not* slavery). Within each paragraph, you would not only *explain* the cause, giving at least one specific example, but also *identify* at least one important person and *summarize* ("tell") what the person did to help bring about war.

When analyzing an essay question, circle key words and phrases that tell you what to write about, how to write about it, and how many parts should be included. The following lists common phrases used in essay questions along with the general category of question—that is, the pattern of development—they signal.

PHRASES USED IN ESSAY QUESTIONS

General Category	Phrases to Look for in Essay Questions
1. Description	Create a verbal picture of XYZ.
	Describe XYZ.
2. Narration	Trace the beginning of XYZ.
	Tell how XYZ happened.
3. Illustration	Give several examples of XYZ.
	Discuss/explore/explain XYZ.
4. Division/classification	Divide XYZ.
	Group or categorize XYZ.
5. Cause/effect	What caused/were some reasons for/were some factors in XYZ?
	What were the results/consequences/effects of XYZ?

6. Process analysis	Explain (list the steps in) how XYZ works.
7. Comparison/contrast	Explain the similarities and differences between XY and YZ.
8. Definition	Explain the meaning of XYZ. Identify XYZ.
9. Persuasion	Argue in favor of XYZ. Take a stand on XYZ. Show how XY is better than YZ. Defend the position of XYZ.
10. Summary	In brief, tell how XYZ works. Sketch out (the beginning of) XYZ. Give the main points of XYZ, and briefly discuss them.

ACTIVITY 17.1 Analyzing the Question

Analyze the following essay questions: Circle the key words, indicate the general category of question, and then explain how students are expected to respond. Include how many parts the answer should have and how to organize it—if the question gives you these hints.

EXAMPLE

History: ⟨Compare and contrast⟩ the major ⟨advantages⟩ and the major ⟨disadvantages⟩ of the North and the South as they began the Civil War. Consider such factors as ⟨population size, economy, geography, political structure, and the military⟩.

General category: *comparison/contrast*

To complete the essay response: *Students are expected to explain similarities and differences between the North and the South as they began the Civil War that might have helped them win or made it harder for them to win. Students should focus on the five points listed. The essay might be structured by either the block or the point-by-point method.*

Answers will vary.

1. History: Explain who Pocahontas was and what she contributed to the history of the United States. Be sure to mention all figures prominent in the Pocahontas myth and to explain how this romantic myth evolved from the reality.

   General category: *illustration*

   To complete the essay response: *Students are to explain and give specific examples to show that they understand who Pocahontas was, how she is important in U.S. history, and how the myth developed. The essay might have three body paragraphs,* the first dealing with Pocahontas and several key figures, the second discussing her

contribution, and the third explaining the transformation of reality into myth.

2. Business: Explain the process of balancing a ledger.

General category: _process analysis_

To complete the essay response: _Students should list the steps_ necessary to balance a ledger. If they can divide the steps into several body paragraphs, they should do so and then arrange them chronologically.

3. Biology: Explain the principal components of the eukaryotic cell and how they function. Consider dividing your explanation into these three parts: the outer membrane, the components in the cytoplasm, and the nucleus.

General category: _process analysis_

To complete the essay response: _Students should define the cell_ parts and then explain how they work. There might be three body paragraphs, on the outer membrane, the cytoplasm, and the nucleus. The body paragraphs might explain function chronologically.

4. Computer science: Discuss similarities and differences among the human brain, a library, and a computer in terms of how they store information, retrieve it, and present it so people might work with it.

General category: _comparison/contrast_

To complete the essay response: _Students should show that they understand_ how a computer is like and unlike the brain and a library—specifically, in how it stores, retrieves, and presents information. Students might organize by the block or point-by-point method. In point-by-point, there would be three body paragraphs, on storing, retrieving, and presenting information.

Teaching Idea
Activity 17.2 is a good review of topic sentences, unity, and specific supporting examples. While some students do consciously pad essay responses, hoping that length will substitute for substance, others have not yet learned to use what they do know to answer a question. You might stress using a forecasting statement to help students stay on track.

Writing Relevant, Specific Responses

When writing an exam response, you are not likely to fool your instructor into thinking that you know the material if you don't. So answer the question as directly and specifically as possible. Stay within any length requirements, and avoid responses that meander or are "padded."

You can make sure your response is relevant and specific by including a topic (or, in a longer essay, thesis) sentence that rephrases the exam question and forecasts an answer to it.

injuries at some later point in time. Hospitals back then weren't as good as they are today, and many soldiers died from infections and just plain bleeding to death. Even though lots of good doctors (good for what they knew back then, I mean) tried hard on both sides to save the soldiers, because of poor facilities, infection, and lack of medical supplies, the doctors often failed, and so the soldiers died. Another result of the Civil War, also called the War between the States, the War of Secession, and the War of the Rebellion, depending on what part of the country you are from, was that the African Americans who were living in this country against their will as slaves were freed by a proclamation from Abraham Lincoln, who was president then.

Writing Essay-Exam Introductory Paragraphs

The introductory paragraph for an essay-length response should be brief—usually three to five sentences, or less than 100 words. Its purpose is to involve your professor in the response and to show that you know the material. When you write your introduction, be sure to do the following:

1. As with any introductory paragraph, begin with a hook, continue with material to interest your audience, and then state your thesis.
2. Remember to use the exam question in your thesis and to use a forecasting statement for clarity.

Here is one possible introductory paragraph for an essay response to the exam question from Activity 17.2:

> The dead could have been bulldozed into mountains. Six hundred and twenty thousand lives were lost during the Civil War. This fact alone would make this war, next to the Revolutionary War, the most significant in our nation's history, but there are other reasons as well: the effect it had on the nation's economy, the ratification of the Thirteenth Amendment, and the reunification of the United States.

ACTIVITY 17.3 Writing Essay-Exam Introductions

Review introductions from Chapter 12 and then return to your paragraph response from Activity 17.2. Assuming that you were going to develop that paragraph into a full-length essay, write an introductory paragraph for it of three to five sentences that would interest a history professor. Be sure to forecast the focus of the essay.

Writing Essay-Exam Concluding Paragraphs

Like introductions, conclusions for essay-exam responses should be kept to three to five sentences, or less than 100 words. You can use them to show that you understand the significance of your answer. Teachers hope to see evidence of students' ability to make connections, and conclusions are a good place to link your response to other important concepts covered in the text and/or by your instructor. When you write your conclusion, do the following:

1. Begin with a connector and brief summary, and then move into an expanded thought that reacts to the information you have presented.
2. Include a point your instructor has stressed, perhaps a relevant fact or quotation that shows you know more than what you have discussed in the body.

Here is one way to conclude an essay response to the exam question from Activity 17.2:

HINT: Limit conclusions to three to five sentences.

Transition and summary

Despite the tremendous loss of human life and the devastation of the South's economy, the Civil War brought the country back together again and began the long road to equality for African Americans. Although the war was not fought only to abolish slavery, it was an important reason and a good one. As we have discussed in class, slavery and democracy are incompatible. To deny "life, liberty, and the pursuit of happiness" to any group is to endanger it for all.

Expanded thought, stressed by instructor

ACTIVITY 17.4 Writing Essay-Exam Conclusions

Teaching Idea
Reiterate the importance of knowing the audience in creating an effective conclusion. You might help students choose a point for their conclusions that their hypothetical professor has made several times.

Review conclusions in Chapter 12, and then write a three-to-five-sentence paragraph to conclude your response in Activity 17.2. Include a connector, link to thesis, summary, and expanded thought—some reflective comment that connects the essay question to something else in the history class or in the larger world. You might include a fact or quotation.

Writing a Complete Essay-Exam Response

A good way to study for and practice writing essay exams is to create and then try to respond to your own questions based on main points in your textbook. Your response can take the form of an outline with supporting examples and then perhaps a rough essay draft to see if you know enough to answer in depth.

In the following activity, the exam question is based on material from *A Writer's Workshop*.

ACTIVITY 17.5 Writing a Complete Essay-Exam Response

Teaching Idea
You can help students with Activity 17.5 by reviewing the narrative elements in Chapter 6 and stressing an important point or two, which students might include in their introductions and conclusions. They might also divide the writing into paragraphs, with each student working on one.

Turn back to Chapter 6, Telling Your Own Story, and review the information on narrative elements in the "Prewriting" section. Then, with group members, analyze the following question, circling key words and deciding how to organize a response.

After this discussion, write an outline and then an essay response. One person might draft while the rest add wording, or you might write separate drafts.

Your essay should be concise, use only relevant examples, and be written within 45 minutes. Include a brief introduction that would appeal to your audience (your composition instructor), body paragraphs focused around each narrative element, and a conclusion with an expanded thought. Ask your

5   The last large group of early English settlers, the Massachusetts Bay Company, also got off to a shaky start. A group of 400 Puritans who founded Salem, Massachusetts, arrived in America in 1628. Their first winter was not much better than that of the Plymouth colony. Half the Puritans died. However, they were met in 1630 by a fleet of eleven ships and 700 new settlers who were far better supplied and prepared for their new life than any previous colonists had been. Even so, 200 of the new arrivers starved to death during the first winter. In 1631, with more supply ships landing, the Massachusetts Bay Colony received the reinforcements and materials it needed to prosper.

6   Colonizing the New World was no easy task. In the nearly fifty years that it took for the settlements to finally gain a secure foothold, thousands of English men, women, and children died in a world that must have seemed to many of them a nightmare. Some were motivated by greed, some by religion, others by a sense of adventure, but, incredibly, they kept coming, as new immigrants still do today.

—*Adam Fletcher*

POSTREADING ANALYSIS: KEY POINTS FOR BUILDING ESSAY-EXAM RESPONSES

- **Title:** arouses readers' curiosity and links to the essay's main point.
- **Introductory paragraph:** begins with a hook and ends with a thesis sentence that rewords the exam question and forecasts what the essay will cover.
- **Body paragraphs:** begin with a topic sentence that names the main example and makes a limiting statement about it—for example, "Sir Humphrey Gilbert and his half-brother, Sir Walter Raleigh, were the first adventurers to try colonizing America."
- **Development:** uses specific examples, including facts, statistics, dates, names, and quotations; uses active verbs (*struggled*), -*ing* words (*dying*), and specific words (*swampy*); explains the examples ("George Popham . . . was bad tempered, alienated the Native Americans, and could not hold his group together"). Uses **brief definitions** and synonyms (*settlers = colonists*), and **patterns of development** (illustration and cause/effect, paragraph 3). (For more on layering examples, see pp. 156–157.)
- **Concluding paragraph:** restates the thesis, briefly summarizes, and adds a final (expanded) thought.
- **Sentence connectors:** guide readers: transitions, repeat words, synonyms, pronouns, and reference to main idea.
- **Style points:** Dashes can create emphasis (paragraph 3). A series saves space and can increase clarity ("starvation, illness, injury . . . ," paragraph 1). An appositive phrase saves space when defining and adds clarity ("George Popham, the president . . . ," paragraph 4).

Teaching Idea
"Clinging by Their Fingers" is a good example of how students will sometimes need to interpret an essay-exam question.

➡ Prereading Exploration for "Natural Selection"

Teaching Idea
Before students read this essay, ask them to explain what they currently know about natural selection, have them read the essay, and then ask them to evaluate Perez's explanation. Does her response thoroughly answer the essay question?

Emma Perez wrote this essay to practice for a final exam in principles of biology. Even though it was written for her professor, a biologist, to explain concepts Emma mainly relied on ordinary, nontechnical language and examples. As you read, see how well you can follow her explanations. Important concepts do not necessarily require obscure or "big" words.

Question: Explain Charles Darwin's theory of natural selection, and discuss two weaknesses in it that science has since resolved.

Natural Selection

"Charles Darwin effected the greatest of all revolutions in human thought," wrote Sir Julian Huxley, "greater than Einstein's or Freud's or even Newton's. . . ." This praise refers to Darwin's theory of evolution, which is a cornerstone for the biological sciences. At the heart of this theory is the concept of natural selection, which, with the exception of two points, convincingly explains organic evolution. 1

First, Darwin said, all organisms show variation, meaning that no two creatures are identical. No mouse is exactly like another even from the same litter; no person is an exact replica of another. Organisms differ in height, weight, color, intelligence, behavior, personality, and in many other ways. He cited the breeding of domesticated animals and cultivated plants as instances of human beings taking advantage of inherited variations to shape a species. If people can engineer the selection of desirable traits, then so can nature, and so the term "natural selection." 2

Next, Darwin discussed the struggle within a species that favors creatures with beneficial variations. He noted that all living things reproduce more of themselves than the original parents. Even a slowly reproducing species like the elephant can produce millions of descendants from a single pair given enough time, and a plant species like an elm tree produces tens of thousands of seeds each season. If all offspring survived, the species would crowd itself into extinction. However, it is clear that not all or even most offspring survive, especially when resources become scarce. Members of a species must compete for limited resources, as when two elm seedlings compete for the same nutrients in the soil or two lions struggle for the same gazelle. Because *variation* exists, the creature with the most favorable variation will ultimately win this contest for limited resources and pass its characteristics down to succeeding generations, and so the term "survival of the fittest." 3

Teaching Idea
You might treat this assignment as an in-class final essay, giving students a real test environment to prepare for.

the material. If you don't have an exam coming up, you might ask an instructor from another class to create a question for you to use as a study guide or to answer for extra credit.

Plan on studying information from a text, making a detailed outline, and then writing your essay *in class* within one period, just as you would for an actual timed essay exam. You will include a brief introduction and conclusion and several body paragraphs. Because this is an in-class project, preparation is critical to your success.

Establishing Audience and Purpose

Your instructor is, of course, the audience for an essay-exam response, and your purpose is to show him or her what you know. Here are several points to keep in mind as you brainstorm for material:

Teaching Idea
This is a good point at which to review tone in writing and ways to avoid common lapses from an academic voice, such as the inappropriate use of *you*, slang, and inappropriate contractions.

1. Remember that your instructor's goal in giving the exam is to see what you have learned and how you can apply it. Not everything you have studied will be on the exam, so part of your preparation ought to involve finding out what the exam will focus on.

2. Recognize that your writing does not have to be eloquent, but it does have to be clear and specific. Make sure you will be able to show how your examples fit together and how they help answer the question.

3. Keep tone in mind. Most instructors—even if their classrooms are usually informal and relaxed—expect a fairly formal, academic voice on an essay exam.

Working through the Writing Assignment

Discovering Ideas

Almost all of your material for this essay will come from one of your textbooks and your class notes. Therefore, you should plan on studying outside of class, even if the essay exam is open book. Trying to piece together a strong answer from several chapters you are not familiar with while the minutes tick away is a discouraging experience.

The following topics list may help you create your own exam question, or you may simply want to choose and answer one. Most of the questions contain cues to help you develop and organize the answers.

Topics List
• Biology: Describe the seven major categories in the taxonomic classification system of Carolus Linnaeus.
• Computer science: Discuss the similarities and differences among the human brain, a library, and a computer in terms of how they store information, recover and process it, and present it so people can work with it.
• Environmental science: Define the term *ecosystem*, and develop several examples with specific details.
• HVAC: Name and explain the five factors that must be controlled in providing heating, ventilation, and air conditioning for human beings.

- Sociology: Define the term *social stratification,* and explain the systems it is based on, giving a specific example for each.
- Music: Define the term *harmony,* and explain how it relates to chord progressions.
- Nursing: Explain how the AIDS virus suppresses a human being's immune system, and discuss several common effects of the virus.
- Accounting: Explain the four basic steps in the process of balancing the general ledger of a small company that uses a cash-based accounting system.
- Chemistry: List and explain the three physical states of matter, and then classify the three forms that matter is found in.
- Art history: Describe what is meant by *impressionism,* name three significant artists representative of the movement, list one important work from each, and explain why the work falls into the category of impressionism.
- Zoology: Compare and contrast mitosis and meiosis. Next, describe each of the four major phases of mitosis.
- Photography: Explain the relationship between aperture diameter and shutter speed in controlling the amount of light entering a lens. Next, describe three photo shoots where the light varies significantly, and explain what settings to use for f-stop and shutter speed to achieve the effect you hope for.
- Botany: Describe the water cycle. Include specific examples that illustrate the terms *precipitation, transpiration, percolation, runoff,* and *evaporation.*
- Hospitality management: Explain the differences and similarities among the red wines of France, Italy, and the United States.
- Forestry: Define *timber management,* and explain the process. Be sure to include the three factors a forest manager must take into account when he or she first analyzes a new forest, and include the major problems the manager is likely to encounter.
- Fire science: Explain what is meant by class "A," "B," and "C" fires. Then describe what kind of fire extinguishers are effective on them, and explain the rating system used to determine how large a fire each extinguisher can control.

Preparing for an Exam out of Class

No matter how hard you study each week, reviewing for an exam may seem an overwhelming task. Here are some points to keep in mind:

Teaching Idea
You might want to review the part of Chapter 2 on active reading at this point and remind students that the need for focus in preparing for an essay exam is another way of saying "I need a thesis that I can support."

1. Recognize that you don't have to know every fact and detail. Your instructor will usually help focus your studying by indicating key pages in the text, handing out study sheets, and offering practice (or actual) essay questions.

2. If you feel uncertain about some aspect of the exam, ask questions in class or talk to your instructor. She may be able to clarify any conceptual problems and give you some further direction for studying.

3. If you don't have a study guide with trial questions, create your own questions. To figure out what text material to write questions on, look at chapter headings, subheadings, introductions, conclusions, and summary boxes, and words in **boldface** and *italics.*

you see cues like "compare and contrast" or "describe the process of," your knowledge of the patterns of development will help you organize the essay.

If you are not allowed to bring a prewritten outline to class, write a **scratch outline** (see the annotated student model). Include the main point of each body paragraph and one or two supporting examples. If there are several questions to answer, you might start by skimming the exam and jotting down a scratch outline for each item.

Remember to begin each body paragraph with a topic sentence linked to the preceding paragraph by connectors like the transitions listed on pages 54–55.

HINT: Prepare a scratch outline.

ORGANIZING—SUMMING UP

1. Analyze the essay question, and use parts of it in your thesis.
2. Be alert to the possible need to interpret the question.
3. Look to the question to help organize your response.
4. Write a scratch outline.
5. Plan on using a topic sentence to introduce each body paragraph.
6. Review the list of transitions on pages 54–55.

Teaching Idea
When reviewing Journal Entry 17.3, you might mention that teachers often begin to evaluate content in an essay-exam response by circling facts, statistics, dates, names, and so on that they expect to see.

JOURNAL ENTRY 17.3

Write your thesis sentence. Does it use key terms from the essay question? Make a rough outline that includes your major points and supporting examples. Be specific with names, dates, facts, and statistics. (For more on outlining, see p. 298.)

Drafting

Teaching Idea
Remind students that misspelling key terms gives the impression—often a wrong one—that the student does not know the material well.

With an outline in hand, you are ready to draft. Leave wide margins ($1\frac{1}{2}$ inches), and skip lines so you can revise as time permits. Don't be too concerned with style, but do try to write clear sentences that connect to one another. Also try to develop your ideas fully—using specific names, dates, facts, statistics, and quotations as relevant—and to connect them to your thesis. Consider using numbered lists; they can save you time.

HINT: Clear explanations and specific examples are crucial.

While drafting, keep the audience in mind. What points has your instructor stressed? Where would she want you to clarify an idea or define a term, and where wouldn't she? Are you using the language of the discipline and an academic tone?

HINT: Try to reserve time for brief revision and editing.

To improve your essay score, consider also these two time-related strategies:

1. Reserve a few minutes to revise and edit. You may not be able to revise much, but sometimes even clarifying one main example can help a lot. (See the annotated student model for an example of this and for the mechanics of adding material.) Try to correct errors in spelling, especially of key terms, and major grammar and punctuation problems.

CAUTION! Do not plan on recopying.

2. Be aware that you might still get partial credit for writing an outline of any points you did not cover because time ran out.

HINT: Out of time? Outline.

Here are some tips for dealing with several other concerns you may have during essay exams:

- **Having an anxiety attack, feeling like you know nothing on the exam:** If you attended class regularly and reviewed even a little, you undoubtedly know *something* on the exam. Take a few deep breaths and refocus. If necessary, leave the class for a moment, with your instructor's permission, to clear your head. Come back to the exam, skim the questions again, find one that you can say something about, and begin an answer.

- **Worrying about other students completing their essay first:** Often finishing early means that the student did *not* do well. Use every available minute to write and revise your responses.
- **Worrying about time running out:** Remind yourself that you have skimmed the exam, planned time for each question, and tracked your progress. You can outline any uncompleted part.
- **Wondering whether to use information you're uncertain about:** If you are not reasonably sure of facts, statistics, quotations, and so on, leave them out.
- **Wondering what to do about a question when no ideas are coming:** Sometimes you simply cannot remember the information needed to answer a question. When this happens, it's best to move forward, returning if time allows.

JOURNAL ENTRY 17.4

Does your draft answer all parts of the exam question? Is each paragraph centered around a topic sentence? Have you used detailed examples with names, dates, facts, statistics, and quotations as needed? Have you avoided "padding"? Are your introduction and conclusion brief but interesting and clear? What part of the draft do you like best, and which least? Why?

Revising Drafts

To review the detailed lists for revising drafts, turn to Chapter 13.

ANNOTATED STUDENT MODEL: EXAM RESPONSE

Teaching Idea
Encourage students to write simple, clear topic sentences. Remind them that transitional words like *first, second,* and *next* are easy for them to write and for instructors to follow.

The two drafts that follow will help you with drafting and the minimal revising essay exams allow.

First Draft

Doug Cunningham wrote this response to a question from his photography instructor. Doug knew that he would not need to explain basic concepts or terms in photography, as his instructor is an expert in the field. But Doug did need to explain concepts and terms that related to his understanding of the course material. He brought a brief outline with his thesis sentence and knew what he wanted to say in the introduction and conclusion.

Photography Essay Question

Circling key terms

Define the three essential elements of photography, and explain how they combine to create an aesthetically pleasing photograph.

Author never added title. Would it help to have one? What might you suggest?

[1]Note added

Unneeded defining eliminated

Explaining added to show full knowledge of silhouettes

While much about photography is subjective, both in the eye of the composer and the viewer, there are some features that can be found in all photographs. These features combine to create other artistic elements, in the process adding depth and complexity to the field of photography. When skillfully combined, the three essential elements—shape, tone, and color—can produce aesthetically pleasing pictures.

Shape is the outline or contour of a subject. It is the most important element in a photograph, particularly black and white.[1] On a dark, overcast night we still can find our way through a landscape because we can see the shape of the tree trunk, bush, or car in front of us. In photography the size and placement of shapes within a frame help create balance and draw a viewer's eye to one point or another. Striking images can be formed using silhouettes (a darkened shape with few, if any, features recognizable) with varying degrees of backlighting to create full or semisilhouettes. One reason shapes handled in this way are so compelling is because they simplify what the viewer sees. Without additional visual cues, the eye focuses on the central shape.

The second essential element in a photograph is tone, the contrast between light and dark portions of a picture. Tone gives definition to shape. Without the contrast between light and dark, shapes appear flat; in fact, they are silhouettes. The photographer who chooses black and white film specializes in shape and tone, in the absence of color. Black and white pictures may contain very little tonal difference or may run the full range of the light/dark spectrum. Photographs that use tone effectively can create depth and mood, in some instances more effectively than in color. In general, darker images tend to create darker moods, giving a picture a sense of "mystery or menace." On the other hand, lighter tones can give a feeling of "freedom, space, and softness." Experienced photographers work with tonal qualities of film to cause emotional responses, and they are careful not to clash meaning with tone, for example, shooting a joyous wedding in dark, somber shades.

Color is the last essential element in photography and is linked to tone. Together they give depth and substance, or form, to shapes in a picture. Color, like tone, affects a viewer's emotional response to an image. Bright, warm colors—reds, oranges, yellows—can convey a sense of liveliness and fun; cooler colors—blues, purples, greens—can create a more quiet, reflective tone. Handling color in photography is another matter of selection rather than just pointing the lens at any jumble of

[2]Note added

colored objects and clicking the shutter. The most aesthetically pleasing color images try for a single dominant color with other colors harmonizing. To achieve harmony in a photograph, the photographer composes a picture using colors closely related on the color wheel,[2] for instance, shades of blue and green as they merge with the bordering yellow and purple. When too many muted or too many bold colors are combined within the same frame, the image can become confusing, with shapes "flattening," which damages the illusion of depth.

These three essential elements—shape, tone, and color—come together to produce form, texture, and pattern, all of which together can produce beautiful pictures. However, as we have discussed in class, there are few unbreakable rules for combining these basic features of photography. Sometimes, for instance, a photographer wants to use many primary colors to create a feeling of confusion. Some of the strongest images ever recorded on film break many of the "rules," and, after considering their artistic options, people should learn to trust their own subjective response to an image.

—Doug Cunningham

NOTES

1. The reason is that shape occupies the most space within a frame and draws a person's attention immediately, even in the absence of tone and color.
2. Note on the color wheel: Photographers should be aware of the primary and secondary colors, of how they mix with, complement, and contrast with one another to create pleasing images (and other effects).

Chapter Summary

1. Successfully taking an essay exam requires out-of-class preparation: an active review of textbooks and class notes that includes annotating, summarizing, outlining, anticipating questions, and, often, writing practice responses.
2. Responses can be improved by in-class preparation: skimming the exam for an overview, figuring out how much time to allow for each question, analyzing the questions, outlining, and tracking time while drafting.
3. In-class essay exams differ from our out-of-class writing assignments in several ways, including the expert audience (your instructor), limited revision time, and shorter introductions and conclusions.
4. Like other major writing projects, essay-exam responses call for the use of the writing process: prewriting, organizing, drafting, and whatever revising and editing time allows.

Polishing Style

CHAPTER 18

Creating Sentence Variety

What Are We Trying to Achieve and Why?

Teaching Idea
This chapter may be best used after students have been introduced to basic sentence grammar in Chapter 20. However, both chapters can help students understand and overcome punctuation problems, and you might find it helpful to assign this chapter in small segments over a 5- to 6-week period.

In the right-hand photo on the preceding page, we see lines of soldiers dressed alike, all with similar serious expressions on their faces, standing in a similar posture, unmoving, at attention. There is little to distinguish one soldier from the other. Uniformity is the goal; individual expression is not. However, most of us will find that our eyes are automatically drawn to the left-hand photo of fans at a football stadium, dressed (or undressed) as they are in a variety of clothes, smiling, cheering, gesturing—in short, behaving differently. One of the reasons we are more interested in the photo of the football fans is contrast. Because there are clear differences among the fans, our eyes fix on one person and then another, seeing something new each time. In general, people want contrast and difference in their lives, at least in small doses.

The same principle holds true in our writing. Sentence after sentence constructed the same way, stretching through a paragraph and then into an essay, will, like the company of soldiers above, tend to lose readers' interest, no matter how exciting the ideas might be. The point of Chapter 18, then, is to give some suggestions for involving readers in your ideas as you structure sentences in a variety of ways.

In this chapter, we will work on the following strategies that will help you with sentence variety: varying length, type, openers, and word order.

Varying the Length of Sentences

Sometimes when we write, our sentences are too similar in length. They may form a paragraph of 10 short sentences or maybe 6 or 7 longer ones. Whether they are short, medium, or long, too many sentences of the same length strung together can become monotonous.

What is your reaction to the following paragraph?

> Music brings simple enjoyment. It also affects our lives in many ways. One song can bring out specific memories. It can change a person's mood from happy to sad. Music is so much more than just a rhythmic combination of sounds. It is a marvelously powerful experience. It is universal in cultures. Music bridges the cultural gap. It brings people closer together. Can you think of a society where music was or is not a part of people's lives?

If you think the paragraph feels "choppy," you are right. The 10 sentences are too similar in length, creating a start-stop feeling, not unlike being in a car with someone learning how to use a clutch, lurching down the street. We could revise the paragraph this way, combining sentences to vary their length and make them flow smoothly:

> Besides the simple enjoyment that music brings, it also affects our lives in many ways. It is amazing how hearing one song can bring out specific memories and how it can change a person's mood from happy to sad or vice versa. Music is so much more than just any rhythmic succession or combination of sounds. It is a marvelously powerful experience that is universal in cultures, bridging the cultural gap, bringing people closer together. Can you think of a society where music was or is not a part of people's lives?

Teaching Idea
Stress the point that sentence variety does not require some arcane patterning of sentences.

The revised version has only five sentences, but notice the variety in length: 15, 27, 14, 19, and 17 words, respectively. The object in varying sentence length is not to jump from long to short to medium in some preset pattern. It is simply to interrupt a string of sentences that are similar in length with a longer or shorter sentence. A good rule of thumb is to alter the length of the third or fourth sentence in a series of sentence that have roughly the same word count.

ACTIVITY 18.1 Combining Sentences for Variety in Length

Teaching Idea
Some students misinterpret sentence variety to mean no short sentences, so you might anticipate and correct this misimpression.

To reveal what you already know about sentence variety, revise the following paragraph to increase its readability by combining sentences. (For more on sentence parts, you may read ahead in this chapter.) Aim for a mix of sentence lengths, but don't eliminate all the shorter ones. A short sentence, especially following several longer ones, can draw readers' attention. You may need to drop or add words as you combine.

> "If you use a little imagination, Aaron," his mother said, "this bathtub can be an ocean full of adventure." This sounded like a good idea to Aaron. He climbed into the tub. Then he pretended to head out across the vast ocean in search of pirates. He also looked for valuable sunken treasure. Mother began washing him and lathering his hair. Soapsuds fell into the water. They became islands to sail his ship around. Mother washed his hair. Then she said, "OK, time for a rinse." Aaron didn't mind this time. He pretended to swim under his ship. There he would look at all the ocean creatures. He saw a school of huge blue whales. He saw a giant octopus squirting a cloud of black ink. He saw hundreds of pink jellyfish trailing long, stinging tentacles.

Answers will vary.

Revised paragraph:

"If you use a little imagination, Aaron," his mother said, "this bathtub

can be an ocean full of adventure." This sounded like a good idea to

Aaron, so after he climbed into the tub, he pretended to head out

Teaching Idea
Have several students read their revised paragraphs aloud in Activity 18.1. You can quickly list on the board common sentence structures they are using (e.g., participial phrases, adverb clauses, and relative clauses) and tally them to show similar sentence variety strategies. Alternately, you might have students in pairs or groups exchange and discuss revised paragraphs.

across the vast ocean in search of pirates and valuable sunken treasure. Mother began washing him and lathering his hair. When the soapsuds fell into the water, they became islands to sail his ship around. After his hair was washed, mom said, "OK, time for a rinse." Aaron didn't mind this time. He pretended to swim under his ship to look at all the ocean creatures. He saw a school of huge blue whales, a giant octopus squirting a cloud of black ink, and hundreds of pink jellyfish trailing long, stinging tentacles.

Varying the Types of Sentences

Another way to create sentence variety is by using different types of sentences. Here are four kinds of sentences:

SIMPLE	Aaron likes ice cream.
COMPOUND	Aaron likes ice cream, so he eats a lot of it. (two independent clauses joined by a coordinating conjunction)
COMPLEX	Aaron likes ice cream because it tastes sweet. (at least one subordinate clause joined to an independent clause)
COMPOUND–COMPLEX	Aaron likes ice cream because it tastes sweet, so he eats a lot of it. (two independent clauses and a subordinate clause)

Teaching Idea
This is a good point at which to mention the unnecessary comma students often use with compound verbs.

You can use two strategies to vary the types of sentences you create: **coordination** and **subordination.** When you create a compound sentence, you join relatively equal, or **coordinate,** sentence parts with one of seven words called **coordinating conjunctions** (*and, but, or, so, yet, for, nor*), as in the compound sentence above. When you **subordinate** sentence parts, you tell readers that one part of the sentence is less important than another, as in the complex sentence above. Both coordination and subordination help you create sentence variety and express your thoughts in sophisticated ways. (For more on coordination and subordination, see Chapters 20 and 21.)

Coordinating Words in Sentences

Coordination and Subordination

As you can see in the example above, a compound sentence has at least two equal parts, each a separate simple sentence joined by a coordinating conjunction (*and, but,* etc.). You can use compound sentences to reduce the number of simple sentences (as in Activity 18.1). However, you do not always need to create a *complete* compound sentence. In fact, often you can use two-part subjects, verbs, and other words to add variety to your sentence structures and eliminate unneeded words. For example, you might combine two simple sentences into a complete compound sentence *or* create a compound subject:

SIMPLE SENTENCES	My grandmother lived into her nineties.
	My grandfather also lived into his nineties.

COMPOUND SENTENCE	My grandmother lived into her nineties, and my grandfather also lived into his nineties. (Compound sentences have a comma before the coordinating conjunction.)
COMPOUND SUBJECT	My grandmother and grandfather lived into their nineties. (Compound subjects do *not* have a comma before the coordinating conjunction.)

Or you might combine sentences with a two-part verb as in the following:

SIMPLE SENTENCES	Jody smashed the ball over the left field fence. She triumphantly rounded the bases to home.
COMPOUND SENTENCE	Jody smashed the ball over the left field fence, and she triumphantly rounded the bases to home.
COMPOUND VERB	Jody smashed the ball over the left field fence and triumphantly rounded the bases to home. (Compound verbs do *not* have a comma before the coordinating conjunction.)

When revising for sentence variety, you will sometimes write complete compound sentences and sometimes only compound subjects, verbs, and other words. Remember to use a comma before the coordinating conjunction in a compound sentence but *not* with a compound subject or verb. (For more on coordination, see Chapter 21.)

ACTIVITY 18.2 Combining Sentences Using Coordination

Teaching Idea
Activity 18.2 will help students having problems with commas and compound verbs.

Combine the following sets of sentences first as compound sentences separated by a comma and *and* or *but*. Next, reduce the compound sentence by using either a two-part subject or a two-part verb, cutting any unneeded words, making necessary changes in words, and removing the comma.

EXAMPLE

Simple sentence: Muhammad Ali was a great fighter in his day.

Simple sentence: Sugar Ray Leonard was also a great fighter in his day.

Compound sentence: Muhammad Ali was a great fighter in his day, and Sugar Ray Leonard was also a great fighter in his day.

Compound subject: Muhammad Ali and Sugar Ray Leonard were great fighters in their day.

1. Simple sentence: My best friend won a lot of money in Las Vegas.

   Simple sentence: I also won a lot of money in Las Vegas.

   Compound sentence: My best friend won a lot of money in Las Vegas, and I also won a lot of money in Las Vegas.

   Compound subject: My best friend and I won a lot of money in Las Vegas.

2. Simple sentence: Beth approached the counter at Best Buy.

   Simple sentence: She asked for a refund on her DVD player.

   Compound sentence: Beth approached the counter at Best Buy, and she asked for a refund on her DVD player.

Compound verb: Beth approached the counter at Best Buy and asked for a refund on her DVD player.

3. Simple sentence: Jack learned a lot from his DWI conviction.

Simple sentence: He has given up drinking altogether.

Compound sentence: Jack learned a lot from his DWI conviction, and he has given up drinking altogether.

Compound verb: Jack learned a lot from his DWI conviction and has given up drinking altogether.

4. Simple sentence: The wedding plans had seemed headed for disaster.

Simple sentence: They finally came together.

Compound sentence: The wedding plans had seemed headed for disaster, but they finally came together.

Compound verb: The wedding plans had seemed headed for disaster but finally came together.

5. Simple sentence: This century people will explore our solar system.

Simple sentence: After that they will colonize the planets.

Compound sentence: This century people will explore our solar system, and after that they will colonize the planets.

Compound verb: This century people will explore our solar system and after that will colonize the planets.

Teaching Idea
Students often want to skip writing sentences of their own, but you might remind them that this is the most important part of the exercise.

6. Write three sentences of your own that are either compound or that contain a two-part subject or verb (use commas correctly).

Answers will vary.

A. _____

_____

B. _____

_____

C. _____

_____

Subordinating Words in Sentences

Coordination and Subordination

Aside from coordination, you can also achieve sentence variety through **subordination**—that is, making one part of a sentence less important than another. Subordination helps writers deal with shades of meaning and complex ideas, often by setting information off with commas, parentheses, and dashes.

We will focus here on the complex sentence (a simple sentence plus one or more subordinate clauses) and adjective (or relative) and adverb clauses.

Teaching Idea
For simplicity's sake, it helps to focus students on these most common relative pronouns: *who, which,* and *that.*

Adjective Clauses—Nonessential

Adjective clauses, also called **relative clauses,** are usually easy to spot, because most begin with one of these relative pronouns: *who, which,* and *that.* An adjective clause tells something about the noun or pronoun it follows. Notice the underlined clauses in the following two sentences:

A. Jason, *who* is really a very bright guy, is flunking out of college.

B. Jason has a drug problem, *which* keeps him from focusing on his studies.

HINT: The three common relative pronouns are *who, which,* and *that.*

The "who" clause in sentence A adds information about the noun "Jason": that he is "a very bright guy." The "which" clause in sentence B explains one effect of the noun "problem": that it is hurting Jason's school work.

When adjective clauses are used in this way, they are said to be **nonessential** because the meaning of the main part of each sentence would be the same without the clauses. In both examples, if we remove the relative clauses, the main clauses would still communicate the central idea. Note that *commas* are used to set off these subordinate clauses. (For more on nonessential clauses, see pp. 530, 543.)

Teaching Idea
In fact, many writers use *which* to modify a clearly stated idea in a preceding clause rather than a specific noun or pronoun, but students often create confusing pronoun reference with the misuse of *which.*

Note: It is usually best to position "which" clauses next to a single noun or pronoun rather than expecting them to describe several words or ideas. Look at this example:

AMBIGUOUS   Jason has a drug problem and is also dyslexic, which keeps him from focusing on his studies. (Is it the drug problem, the dyslexia, or both that are affecting the studies?)

ACTIVITY 18.3 Combining Sentences with Nonessential Adjective Clauses

Teaching Idea
If students seem uncomfortable with the term *modify,* you can instead use *describe* or *tell about.*

Combine the following sets of sentences by crossing out the unneeded noun or pronoun in the second sentence and replacing it with either *who* or *which.* Use *who* to refer to people and *which* to refer to animals or things. Use a comma to set off these subordinate clauses.

EXAMPLE
Eric refused to talk with anyone at the party except Simone.

~~He~~ had been treated for clinical depression last year.

Combined: Eric, who had been treated for clinical depression last year, refused to talk with anyone at the party except Simone.

1. AIDS is still spreading worldwide.

   It is a debilitating and usually fatal disease.

   Combined: AIDS, which is a debilitating and usually fatal disease, is still spreading worldwide.

2. Lucille Ball appeared on a stamp in 2001.

   She has been called "America's favorite redhead."

   Combined: Lucille Ball, who has been called "America's favorite redhead," appeared on a stamp in 2001.

3. Brown recluse spiders have a dangerous and painful bite.

   They have a violin shape on their heads and backs.

Combined: _Brown recluse spiders, which have a violin shape on their heads and backs, have a dangerous and painful bite._

4. Tiger Woods makes a fortune through endorsements.

   He is one of the finest golfers in the world.

   Combined: _Tiger Woods, who is one of the finest golfers in the world, makes a fortune through endorsements._

5. A classical guitar uses nylon strings.

   It has a wider neck than other acoustic guitars.

   The nylon strings give the instrument a more mellow tone.

   Combined: _A classical guitar, which has a wider neck than other acoustic guitars, uses nylon strings, which give the instrument a more mellow tone._

6. Write three sentences of your own. Each sentence should contain a nonessential adjective clause. Remember to use commas, and be sure that the "which" clause refers to only one noun.

   Answers will vary.

   A. _____

   _____

   B. _____

   _____

   C. _____

   _____

Adjective Clauses—Essential

As we have seen, when adjective clauses are not essential to the meaning of the main part of a sentence, we use commas to set them off. However, they can also be **essential;** that is, if we left the clause out, the meaning in the main part of the sentence would be unclear or distorted. (For more on essential clauses, see pp. 528–529, 543.)

Compare the following two sentences:

A. Senator Smithers, *who* has the backing of several major campaign donors, will challenge the incumbent governor.

B. A politician *who* has the backing of several major campaign donors will challenge the incumbent governor.

Because Senator Smithers is named in sentence A, there can be no doubt about who will challenge the governor; therefore, the relative clause "who has the backing . . ." becomes nonessential and is set off with commas. However, in sentence B, we do not know who will have the opportunity to run for governor until we read the relative clause. We ask the question "Who gets to run for the office?" and we answer it with the essential clause—the politician "who has the backing of several major campaign donors."

Teaching Idea
To further clarify the essential/nonessential distinction, try using family members—for example, "My mother, who loves to windsurf, . . ." or "My brother who works at the hospital . . ."

Teaching Idea
It is helpful to use examples from your students' writing to clarify restrictive versus nonrestrictive elements.

Distinguishing between nonessential and essential clauses can be difficult and often depends on the author's intent. In general, the pronoun *that* (not *which*) is used in essential clauses (though you will see *which* used in an essential clause). We will continue to use *who* to refer to people.

ACTIVITY 18.4 Combining Sentences with Essential Adjective Clauses

Combine the following sets of sentences by crossing out the unneeded noun or pronoun in the second sentence and replacing it with either *who* or *that*. Use *who* to refer to people and *that* to refer to animals or things. Remember that the adjective clause should follow the noun or pronoun in the first sentence that it identifies or limits. Also, do *not* use a comma to set off these subordinate clauses because they are essential to the meaning of the sentence.

Teaching Idea
You might point out to students that if they position the *who* clauses in sentences 2 and 4 immediately after the subjects, they will have created *non*essential clauses, which *do* require commas.

EXAMPLE

AIDS is a debilitating and usually fatal disease.

I̶t̶ is still spreading worldwide.

Combined: AIDS is a debilitating and usually fatal disease that is still spreading worldwide.

1. A grant allowed Wales to build a national botanical garden.

   The grant was given by the Millennium Commission.

   Combined: A grant that was given by the Millennium Commission allowed Wales to build a national botanical garden.

2. J. K. Rowling is an author of children's books.

   She has become phenomenally popular in the past few years with her Harry Potter series.

   Combined: J. K. Rowling is an author of children's books who has become phenomenally popular in the past few years with her Harry Potter series.

3. The arctic tern is a wide-ranging bird.

   It can fly as many as 22,000 miles during the round-trip of its annual migration.

   Combined: The arctic tern is a wide-ranging bird that can fly as many as 22,000 miles during the round-trip of its annual migration.

4. Martin Luther King, Jr., was a highly influential civil rights leader.

   He won the Nobel Peace Prize in 1964.

   Combined: Martin Luther King, Jr., was a highly influential civil rights leader who won the Nobel Peace Prize in 1964.

5. The tickling sensation turned out to be a cockroach.

   I felt it on the back of my neck.

   Combined: The tickling sensation that I felt on the back of my neck turned out to be a cockroach.

HINT: To avoid confusion, review the *nonessential* clauses from Activity 18.3.

6. Write three of your own sentences that contain an essential adjective clause (remember that essential clauses do *not* need to be set off with commas):

Answers will vary.

A. _____

_____

B. _____

_____

C. _____

_____

Adverb Clauses

Teaching Idea
Having students memorize a single subordinating conjunction like *because* can help them remember the larger category of subordinators.

Another form of complex sentence you can use for sentence variety combines an **adverb clause** with a main clause. Adverb clauses, like single adverbs, answer the questions *when, where, why, how,* and *to what extent* something was done. Here is a brief list of **subordinating conjunctions,** which begin adverb clauses:

SUBORDINATING CONJUNCTIONS

after	because	since	when
although	before	though	where
as	if	until	while

(For a more complete list, see pp. 518–519.)

Consider these two examples:

COMMA NEEDED — Because Jeremy stayed out too late last night, he slept through his 8:00 class.

NO COMMA — Jeremy slept through his 8:00 class because he stayed out too late last night.

Teaching Idea
You might want to remind students that adverb clauses often turn up as fragments in student papers. Remind them as well that commas are usually not needed when the adverb clause comes at the end of the sentence.

We ask the question "*Why* did Jeremy miss his 8:00 class?" and answer it with the adverb clause "because he stayed out too late last night." Like adjective clauses, adverb clauses are subordinate to or dependent on a main clause to complete their meaning. Standing alone, they are fragments, but combined with main clauses, they add variety to your sentences. (For more on fragments, see pp. 555–560.)

HINT: Adverb clauses are easy to move around.

Notice that adverb clauses, like single adverbs and adverb phrases, can be easily repositioned in a sentence to suit the writer's meaning and word flow. You should use a comma to set off adverb clauses that begin a sentence, but you do *not* usually need to use a comma to set them off when they come after the main clause. (For more on adverb clauses, see pp. 530–531.)

ACTIVITY 18.5 Combining Sentences with Adverb Clauses

Choosing from the list of subordinating conjunctions, combine the following sets of sentences by adding a subordinating conjunction to the *second* sentence in each pair. Write two versions, the first with the adverb clause beginning the sentence and the second with the clause ending the sentence. Be careful with the comma.

EXAMPLE

I had never seen such a huge alpine lake.

I visited Lake Tahoe.

Adverb clause beginning sentence: _Before I visited Lake Tahoe, I had_ _never seen such a huge alpine lake._ (comma needed)

Adverb clause ending sentence: _I had never seen such a huge alpine lake_ _before I visited Lake Tahoe._ (comma not needed)

Answers will vary.

1. I can now get to work on time.

   The city has finally synchronized its stoplights along major thoroughfares.

   Adverb clause beginning sentence: _Because the city has finally_ _synchronized its stoplights along major thoroughfares, I can now get_ _to work on time._

   Adverb clause ending sentence: _I can now get to work on time_ _because the city has finally synchronized its stoplights along major_ _thoroughfares._

2. The mudslides will soon begin.

   It does not stop raining in northern California.

   Adverb clause beginning sentence: _If it does not stop raining in_ _northern California, the mudslides will soon begin._

   Adverb clause ending sentence: _The mudslides will soon begin if it_ _does not stop raining in northern California._

3. Beijing prepares to receive the crowds.

   The world heads toward the 2008 Olympics.

   Adverb clause beginning sentence: _As the world heads toward the_ _2008 Olympics, Beijing prepares to receive the crowds._

   Adverb clause ending sentence: _Beijing prepares to receive the_ _crowds as the world heads toward the 2008 Olympics._

4. Air pollution will become manageable.

   Automobile manufacturers finally eliminate gasoline-powered engines.

   Adverb clause beginning sentence: _When automobile manufacturers_ _finally eliminate gasoline-powered engines, air pollution will become_ _manageable._

   Adverb clause ending sentence: _Air pollution will become manageable_ _when automobile manufacturers finally eliminate gasoline-powered_ _engines._

5. We came across a website dedicated to Puff the Magic Dragon.

   We were surfing the Net.

Adverb clause beginning sentence: <u>While we were surfing the Net, we</u>
<u>came across a website dedicated to Puff the Magic Dragon.</u>

Adverb clause ending sentence: <u>We came across a website dedicated</u>
<u>to Puff the Magic Dragon while we were surfing the Net.</u>

6. Write three sentences of your own that contain an adverb clause.
(Remember to use a comma only with adverb clauses that begin a
sentence.)

Answers will vary.

A. _____

_____

B. _____

_____

C. _____

_____

Varying Sentences with Questions, Commands, and Exclamations

We can also create sentence variety by occasionally using the following types of
sentences: **interrogative** (asks a question), **imperative** (makes a command), and
exclamatory (expresses strong emotion). We use **declarative** sentences, or statements, most often in writing, but occasionally mixing one or more of the other
three types can make our work more interesting.

Teaching Idea
Remind students that
questions can be quickly
*over*used.

Questions

You will usually use two kinds of questions: the **rhetorical question,** which is a
disguised statement, and the question that you ask and then answer.

A rhetorical question looks like this: "Do we really want our 10-year-olds
addicted to crack?" No sane person would respond with a yes. The question is
actually a statement: "We do not want our 10-year-olds addicted to crack."
Rhetorical questions, often used in persuasive writing, encourage readers to
agree with the writer's view. Here is an excerpt from the Chapter 16 argument
essay "Just Say No":

> Schools practically beg parents to spend time with their children reading, learning
> math, and helping with other course work. <u>How can this happen when TV has
> captured the audience?</u> And schoolwork is not all that suffers. <u>Don't we as parents
> want to involve our children in other learning activities like music, dance, and
> sports?</u>

Both rhetorical questions evoke a predictable response in the reader. The question that a writer asks and then answers, on the other hand, does not call for
agreement from the reader but promises further information. Here is an example
from the Chapter 15 definition essay "Finding Home":

> <u>What makes the home happy? Is it the house decorated in warm, inviting colors,
> furnished with all the modern conveniences, or is it the people who live inside?</u> I

islands to sail his ship around. After his hair was washed, mother said,

"OK, time for a rinse."

As a general rule, it is best to interrupt the subject-first pattern after three or four sentences. You can vary sentence beginnings by using adverbs, phrases, and clauses.

Varying Sentence Beginnings with Adverbs

Adverbs give more information about verbs, adjectives, and other adverbs by answering the questions *when, where, why, how,* and *to what extent.* Most adverbs end in *-ly,* so they are easy to spot: *noisily, swiftly, sadly.* Single adverbs can be positioned in several places in a sentence, including at the start. Notice the following sentences:

A. Florence <u>swiftly</u> climbed the rope to the top of the tent.

B. Florence climbed the rope <u>swiftly</u> to the top of the tent.

C. Florence climbed the rope to the top of the tent <u>swiftly</u>.

D. <u>Swiftly</u>, Florence climbed the rope to the top of the tent.

When you make a style choice such as shifting an adverb, you should do so because the positioning best suits the meaning and rhythm of the sentence. If, for instance, you wanted to emphasize "swiftly," you would place it at the beginning or end of the sentence.

You might also use two adverbs to open a sentence:

<u>Swiftly and gracefully</u>, Florence climbed the rope to the top of the tent.

While some writers omit the comma after single adverbs beginning sentences, most often the comma is used, and paired adverbs always take a comma.

ACTIVITY 18.7 Creating Variety in Sentence Beginnings with Adverbs

Rewrite the following sentences with the adverb or adverb pair at the beginning. Remember to use a comma following the adverb or adverb pair.

EXAMPLE
Sonya dragged herself slowly out of bed.
Slowly, Sonya dragged herself out of bed.

1. The wrecking ball effortlessly leveled the building.
    Effortlessly, the wrecking ball leveled the building.

2. The Border collie instantly leaped into the air and snared the Frisbee.
    Instantly, the Border collie leaped into the air and snared the Frisbee.

3. Juan's best friend shouted at him and angrily left the party.
    Angrily, Juan's best friend shouted at him and left the party.

4. Aunt Diana slowly and patiently explained to her five-year-old niece why the frog could not sleep under the pillow.

Slowly and patiently, Aunt Diana explained to her five-year-old niece

why the frog could not sleep under the pillow.

5. The winds from the storm blew violently and continuously until 4:00 A.M.

Violently and continuously, the winds from the storm blew until

4:00 A.M.

6. Write three sentences of your own that begin with one or more adverbs.
Answers will vary.

A. _____

_____

B. _____

_____

C. _____

_____

Varying Sentence Beginnings with Phrases

Teaching Idea
Gerund phrases are not included here because, used as subjects, they are less helpful in breaking up subject/verb beginnings than the other kinds of phrases.

Most often, the sentence parts that can help you to vary your sentence beginnings are phrases. A **phrase** is a group of related words lacking a subject or a verb. Phrases can be placed in various positions within a sentence, including the beginning. We will work with five phrase types: prepositional, participial (present/past), absolute (present/past), infinitive, and appositive.

Prepositional Phrases

Prepositional phrases are the workhorses of your paragraphs—you can scarcely write a sentence without one—and they are easy to spot once you know a few cue words. Every prepositional phrase begins with a preposition (often a word that tells location) and ends with a noun or pronoun (*in* the ocean, *after* you). These phrases can function as either adjectives or adverbs to describe other words in a sentence, and a phrase functioning as an adverb can be moved from one location to another. Here is a brief list of common prepositions (for more, see p. 518):

Teaching Idea
It helps students to remember prepositions if you define them as short words that often tell location and then ask students to memorize one or two (*on, in*). In discussions of prepositional phrases, try mentioning several prepositions and having students attach any words to them that come to mind (however, be alert to infinitive phrases).

COMMON PREPOSITIONS

above	behind	in	over
across	below	of	to
at	by	on	with

Single prepositional phrases often begin sentences:

Above the door you will find the house key.

Together, the three words "above the door" tell *where* the key is located, so the phrase functions as an adverb. Notice that we could shift the phrase to the end of the sentence: "You will find the house key *above* the door."

When using two or more prepositional phrases to begin a sentence, set them off with a comma:

Above the door on the north side of the house, you will find the house key.

ACTIVITY 18.8 Combining Sentences with Prepositional Phrases

Combine the following sentences by cutting the unneeded words at the beginning of the *second and third* sentences. Reposition the remaining prepositional phrases at the beginning of the first sentence. Remember to use a comma.

EXAMPLE

You will find the reference section.

~~It is~~ on the first floor.

~~The floor is~~ of the library.

On the first floor of the library, you will find the reference section.

1. I witnessed a terrible four-car pileup.

   ~~The accident was~~ at the intersection.

   ~~The intersection was~~ of 85th and Metcalf.

   At the intersection of 85th and Metcalf, I witnessed a terrible four-car pileup.

2. I watched the hotel under construction rise to completion seemingly overnight.

   I watched through a hole.

   The hole was in a wooden fence.

   Through a hole in a wooden fence, I watched the hotel under construction rise to completion seemingly overnight.

3. Jake set off to seek his fortune in the land of his dreams—California!

   He set off with only 25 dollars.

   The money was in his pocket.

   With only 25 dollars in his pocket, Jake set off to seek his fortune in the land of his dreams—California!

4. John Wayne holds a special place.

   That place is in the hearts of fans.

   They are fans of the mythic West.

   In the hearts of fans of the mythic West, John Wayne holds a special place.

5. A single determined cricket kept Bruce awake far into the night.

   The cricket was outside a bedroom window.

   The window was on the north side of the house.

Outside a bedroom window on the north side of the house, a single

determined cricket kept Bruce awake far into the night.

6. Write three sentences of your own that begin with at least two prepositional phrases. Be sure to use a comma.

Answers will vary.

A. _____

_____

B. _____

_____

C. _____

_____

Participial Phrases—Present Tense

Participial phrases consist of a participle—a verb form with an *-ing* ending in the present tense or an *-ed, -en,* or *-n* ending in the past tense—and words that describe a noun or a pronoun. As single-word openers, present participles can be effective:

Singing, Andrew enjoyed the sound of his voice echoing in the shower.

Who is singing? Andrew. The participle tells readers about a noun. We might want to add an adverb to create a brief phrase:

Singing happily, Andrew enjoyed the sound of his voice echoing in the

shower.

To give even more information, we could include a prepositional phrase:

Singing happily and with great volume, Andrew enjoyed the sound of

his voice echoing in the shower.

Participial phrases can be used at the beginning, in the middle, or at the end of a sentence and usually come directly before or after the noun or pronoun they are describing. A participial phrase placed next to a word that it does not describe is called a **misplaced** or **dangling modifier.** Confusing and sometimes amusing sentences can result, as in the following:

CONFUSING   Singing happily, the shower echoed with the sound of Andrew's voice.

While it is true that pipes can sometimes make a ringing sound, it is not likely that Andrew's voice would be coming from them.

Teaching Idea
Students are sometimes more comfortable saying "*-ing* words" rather than "participles." As long as students don't confuse gerunds and the present progressive tense with participles, this *-ing* reference can be useful.

Teaching Idea
For more on misplaced modifiers, see Chapter 25.

CAUTION! Beware of misplaced and dangling modifiers (see p. 597).

ACTIVITY 18.9 Combining Sentences with Participial Phrases (Present Tense)

Combine the following sets of sentences by changing the first part of the *second* sentence into a participial phrase. Locate the verb in the *second* sentence, and then convert it into a present participle by adding *-ing.* Next, cross out any unneeded noun or pronoun, and attach the resulting participial phrase to the front of the first sentence. Use a comma.

EXAMPLE

Lori daydreamed of the warm sands and tropical weather of Fort Lauderdale.

~~She~~ smiled at the thought of Spring Break.

Smiling at the thought of Spring Break, Lori daydreamed of the warm sands and tropical weather of Fort Lauderdale.

1. Angelina asked herself again if Katy was really right for her younger brother.

   Angelina worried about the upcoming wedding.

   Worrying about the upcoming wedding, Angelina asked herself again if Katy was really right for her younger brother.

2. Richard screamed "Aaggh!" when he grasped what felt like a handful of wriggling snakes.

   He reached blindfolded into the box.

   Reaching blindfolded into the box, Richard screamed "Aaggh!" when he grasped what felt like a handful of wriggling snakes.

3. Crosby, Stills, Nash, and Young surprised many people by not just being alive but still being fine musicians.

   They jammed hard for three straight hours.

   Jamming hard for three straight hours, Crosby, Stills, Nash, and Young surprised many people by not just being alive but still being fine musicians.

4. The boys threw down their icy snowballs and tore down the alley.

   They tried to escape from an angry driver with a dented door.

   Trying to escape from an angry driver with a dented door, the boys threw down their icy snowballs and tore down the alley.

5. Isabella ignored the speed limit in several places.

   She hoped to catch the 8:00 ferry to Victoria.

   Hoping to catch the 8:00 ferry to Victoria, Isabella ignored the speed limit in several places.

6. Write three of your own sentences that begin with a present participial phrase. Remember to use a comma.

   Answers will vary.

   A. _____

   _____

   B. _____

   _____

   C. _____

   _____

Participial Phrases—Past Tense

Just as with the present participle, the **past participle** can help you vary sentence beginnings. Past participles of regular verbs are formed by adding an *-ed* or a *-d* to the end of the verb (play = play*ed*, frighten = frighten*ed*, excite = excit*ed*). The past participles of irregular verbs are not formed in a consistent way; see Chapter 23 for a list.

Single-word participles can be effective sentence openers:

Overjoyed, Samantha made a beeline for the bank with her 3000-dollar tax refund.

Who is overjoyed? Samantha. The participle tells us about a noun. Or we might give even more information by adding two prepositional phrases:

Overjoyed by the size of her check, Samantha made a beeline for the bank with her 3000-dollar tax refund.

As with the present participle or present participial phrase, be sure to set off the past participle or past participial phrase with a comma, and avoid creating dangling or misplaced modifiers by keeping the participle next to the noun or pronoun that it modifies.

ACTIVITY 18.10 Combining Sentences with Participial Phrases (Past Tense)

Combine the following sets of sentences by changing the *second* sentence into a past participial phrase. Cross out the subject (noun or pronoun) and helping verb (*am, was, were*), and attach the resulting participial phrase to the front of the first sentence. Be sure to use a comma.

EXAMPLE
I basked like a walrus on the cement at the pool's edge.

~~I was~~ chilled after a dip in the cool water.

Chilled after a dip in the cool water, I basked like a walrus on the cement at the pool's edge.

1. We went to bed without unpacking.

   We were exhausted after the long drive home.

   Exhausted after the long drive home, we went to bed without unpacking.

2. Mitch promised himself that he would actually buy textbooks next term.

   He was disappointed by his semester grades.

   Disappointed by his semester grades, Mitch promised himself that he would actually buy textbooks next term.

3. Mark could barely sleep for a week.

   Mark was excited by the opportunity to intern at Channel 9 News.

   Excited by the opportunity to intern at Channel 9 News, Mark could barely sleep for a week.

4. One of the bank tellers actually tried to eat some paper money.

The teller was locked in the vault for 48 hours.

Locked in the vault for 48 hours, one of the bank tellers actually tried to eat some paper money.

5. Tens of thousands of people have donated money to help preserve their environment.

The people are impressed by the Nature Conservancy's plan to protect wilderness and wildlife by owning and leasing the land.

Impressed by the Nature Conservancy's plan to protect wilderness and wildlife by owning and leasing the land, tens of thousands of people have donated money to help preserve their environment.

6. Write three sentences of your own that begin with a past participial phrase. Remember to use a comma.

Answers will vary.

A. _____

_____

B. _____

_____

C. _____

_____

Absolute Phrases

The **absolute phrase** is closely related to the participial phrase and consists of a noun or pronoun placed in front of a participle. In the following examples, the nouns are boxed and the endings of the participles are shaded:

ABSOLUTE PHRASES WITH PRESENT PARTICIPLES

A. The 737 encountering severe turbulence, passengers without seat belts fastened were tossed about like loose bales of hay.

B. Its brown moss–covered fur blending with the surrounding foliage, a three-toed sloth is difficult to spot.

ABSOLUTE PHRASES WITH PAST PARTICIPLES

A. Our expectations shattered, we left New York and headed back to Philadelphia.

B. The tips of his skis pointed straight downhill, Eric started his run for the bottom of the mountain.

HINT: If a phrase can be turned into stand-alone sentences by adding a helping verb, it is an absolute phrase.

Absolute phrases modify the main clause they are attached to and are always set off with commas, whether at the beginning, middle, or end of a sentence.

Note that you could turn any of the absolute phrases above into stand-alone sentences by adding a helping verb like *is, are, was,* or *were*—for example, "The

Teaching Idea
Students often have difficulty devising their own absolute phrases. You might want to show them on the board how to create a simple sentence with a helping verb and then delete the helping verb to form the absolute phrase.

737 *was* encountering severe turbulence" or "The tips of his skis *are* pointed straight downhill." When creating absolute phrases, writers deliberately leave the helping verb out to create variety in sentence structure, rather than stringing a series of simple sentences together.

ACTIVITY 18.11 Combining Sentences with Absolute Phrases (Past and Present Tense)

Combine the following sets of sentences by changing the *second* sentence into an absolute phrase. Cross out any unneeded helping verb (*am, are, was, were*), and attach the resulting absolute phrase to the front of the first sentence. Be sure to use a comma.

EXAMPLE

The singer croaked out a few measures before she gave up.

Her throat ~~was~~ aching from laryngitis.

Her throat aching from laryngitis, the singer croaked out a few measures before she gave up.

1. Enrique decided it was time to take it to the shop.

   The car was stalling at every other intersection.

   The car stalling at every other intersection, Enrique decided it was time to take it to the shop.

2. Ellen greeted her friends at Union Station.

   Her hand was waving frantically.

   Her hand waving frantically, Ellen greeted her friends at Union Station.

3. Frank let himself dream for a moment about world unity.

   The flags from dozens of countries were rippling together in front of the UN building.

   The flags from dozens of countries rippling together in front of the UN building, Frank let himself dream for a moment about world unity.

4. Skyscrapers collapsed weeks after the earthquake.

   Their internal support was weakened.

   Their internal support weakened, skyscrapers collapsed weeks after the earthquake.

5. Florence wondered, "Since when does being nine months pregnant make me communal property?"

   Her stomach was constantly patted by people she hardly knew.

   Her stomach constantly patted by people she hardly knew, Florence wondered, "Since when does being nine months pregnant make me communal property?"

6. Write three sentences of your own that begin with an absolute phrase. Remember to use a comma.

Answers will vary.

A. _____

_____

B. _____

_____

C. _____

_____

Infinitive Phrases

Teaching Idea
You might reiterate how maneuverable adverbs can be.

Infinitive phrases, which can appear in various positions within a sentence, are another way to vary sentence beginnings. Infinitives are easy to spot because they always consist of the word *to* and the present tense form of a verb (*to love, to laugh, to run*). Infinitives can function as nouns, adjectives, and adverbs, but we will concentrate on their use as adverbs, telling *why, where, when, how,* and *to what degree or extent.*

Here is a two-word infinitive opener:

To think, Rachel needed quiet.

Why did Rachel need quiet? To think. The infinitive works as an adverb. Notice that we could also position the infinitive at the end of the sentence: "Rachel needed quiet to think." We can also add another adverb:

To think deeply, Rachel needed quiet.

To give even more information, we could include a prepositional phrase:

To think deeply about her future, Rachel needed quiet.

Infinitive phrases used at the beginning of sentences, like participial phrases, sometimes are not clearly attached to the word they modify. Be careful not to construct sentences like the following:

CAUTION! Beware of misplaced and dangling modifiers.

To think deeply about her future, the radio must be turned off, or Rachel will be distracted.

While the radio can be entertaining, it does not generally have much on its mind.

ACTIVITY 18.12 Introducing Sentences with Infinitive Phrases

Complete each of the following infinitive phrases by attaching a main clause of your choosing. Be careful not to follow the infinitive immediately with a verb like *is* or *was*, which would turn the infinitive into a subject rather than a phrase that describes another word in the sentence. Be sure to use a comma.

EXAMPLE

To approach the president in public,

Not this: To approach the president in public is a dream of mine.

But this: To approach the president in public, people must first be cleared by the Secret Service.

Answers will vary.

1. To scale the last 2000 feet of the mountain,

   the climbers needed oxygen.

2. To make it to the store before it closed,

   Harry ran two red lights.

3. To enjoy the concert,

   I always arrive an hour early.

4. To beat the heat on a scorching summer day,

   people flock to the pool.

5. To adjust to a new culture,

   many people begin reading about it before they visit the country.

6. Write three sentences of your own that begin with infinitive phrases. Be careful to create infinitives that describe rather than infinitives that act as subjects, and be sure to use a comma.

   Answers will vary.

   A. _____

   _____

   B. _____

   _____

   C. _____

   _____

Appositive Phrases

Teaching Idea
Students sometimes confuse appositive phrases with participial phrases. Point out that participles have *-ing/-ed* endings and that appositives are synonyms for the nouns they precede or follow.

The **appositive phrase,** a word group (like this one) that renames a noun or pronoun, also helps with sentence variety. *Nonessential* appositives are set off by a comma wherever they occur in a sentence: beginning, middle, or end.

Here is a brief opening appositive:

A bodybuilder, Arnold Schwarzenegger had greater ambitions.

What was Schwarzenegger? A bodybuilder. The appositive phrase tells about a noun. Notice that the phrase could follow the subject: "Arnold Schwarzenegger, a bodybuilder, had greater ambitions." We could also add several other descriptive words:

A former award-winning bodybuilder, Arnold Schwarzenegger had

greater ambitions.

For even more information, we could add a prepositional phrase:

A former award-winning bodybuilder of international fame, Arnold

Schwarzenegger had greater ambitions.

To stuff in about as much information as the opening of a sentence will bear, we could include an essential relative clause as well:

A former award-winning bodybuilder of international fame who won

the Mr. Olympia title seven times, Arnold Schwarzenegger had greater

ambitions.

3. A fisherman nodded underneath a willow tree on the riverbank.

   Underneath a willow tree on the riverbank nodded a fisherman.

4. A baby stroller rolled down Johnson Drive and through a busy intersection.

   Down Johnson Drive and through a busy intersection rolled a baby stroller.

5. Great white sharks often lurk in the deep, cold water of Monterey Bay.

   In the deep, cold water of Monterey Bay often lurk great white sharks.

6. Write three inverted sentences of your own. Follow the pattern of the previous six sentences, and begin with at least one prepositional phrase.

   Answers will vary.

   A. _____

   _____

   B. _____

   _____

   C. _____

   _____

Chapter Summary

1. Writers create sentence variety by varying the length, types, and beginnings of sentences.

2. Sentences in a paragraph should be a mix of lengths: short, medium, and long. Three or four sentences in a row may be roughly the same length, but the next one should be shorter or longer.

3. Sentences can be compound, with a subject and verb on both sides of a coordinating conjunction (*and, but, so, or, for, nor, yet*): "I like 7-Up, and I drink a quart a day." A comma comes before the conjunction.

4. Sentences may contain several parts connected by *and*, such as a compound subject: "Jim and I both like 7-Up." Or they can contain a compound verb: "I like 7-Up and drink a quart a day." Compound subjects and verbs are *not* separated by a comma.

5. You can subordinate ideas in a sentence in many ways, including with adjective clauses, which are often introduced by *who, which,* or *that.*

ESSENTIAL (THAT AND WHO)	The baseball game that we saw tonight was boring.
NONESSENTIAL (WHICH AND WHO)	My mother, who calls me every evening, says she wants me to become more independent.

6. You can also subordinate information in a sentence with an adverb clause: "Because I was late, I missed the last ferry." When the clause begins the

sentence, it is set off with a comma. When it ends the sentence, it is not usually set off with a comma.

7. Sentences may begin with adverbs (-*ly* words: happi*ly*).

8. Using occasional questions, commands, and exclamations is another way to create sentence variety.

9. Phrases create sentence variety and can be especially useful in varying sentence beginnings. Phrases should be set off with a comma.

   A. Prepositional phrase: "In the drawer next to the file cabinet, you will find the hammer."

   B. Participial phrase (present): "Slipping on the wet tile, Maria wrenched her back."

   C. Participial phrase (past): "Thrilled by his good fortune, Dale carried the trophy home."

   D. Absolute phrase (present): "The train leaving ahead of schedule, Vito missed his ride."

   E. Absolute phrase (past): "Their foundations weakened, buildings collapsed in the earthquake."

   F. Infinitive phrase: "To run a marathon, Keith had to train for a year."

   G. Appositive phrase: "Beautiful but aggressive birds, blue jays swarmed my feeders last winter."

10. Inverting sentences can create variety and help to emphasize the subject: "In the deep, cold water of Monterey Bay often lurk great white sharks."

ACTIVITY 18.15 Revising for Sentence Variety

Teaching Idea
If you don't have time to complete the whole paragraph, you might have students revise half of it.

Review the chapter summary, and skim back through the methods for creating sentence variety. Now revise the following student narrative paper. Think in particular about restructuring the paragraph to vary sentence lengths, types, and beginnings. You will need to add or drop a few words, but keep the organization and content largely intact.
Answers will vary.

The Clown Princess

My daughter Monique is four. She is the most comical child I know. Sometimes I have a bad day. She will find a way to make me laugh. I remember one day I was in the kitchen cooking. All of a sudden, I heard the television volume go up. The volume went up in the living room. Monique had put in her favorite noncartoon movie. The name of the movie is *Hope Floats*. My son was there. His name is Marquise. Baby Mariah was there too. They were also watching the movie. Next, I heard Monique run to her room. I wondered what on earth she was doing. A few minutes later she made her dramatic entrance. She was decked out in high-heels and a purple boa. She also had on a purple skirt. She held a fuzzy purple fan. On her head was a bright fuchsia hat with a purple feather. But the articles that got the most attention were her Marilyn Monroe elbow-length white gloves. She also had a strand of fake pearls.

Now was

Sandra Bu

You." Mor

a gray sky

sail on dr

the reaso

Monique f

She dippe

pinched h

sand. She

sang, "oh

politely s

kitchen. T

sister. She

too young

house. My

fun ways.

to smaller categories. We have already seen this concept illustrated as a "Language Line" like the one below:

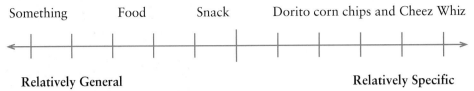

Something	Food	Snack	Dorito corn chips and Cheez Whiz

Relatively General   Relatively Specific

If a friend asks you to go to the store to pick up "something," what will you come back with? If your friend says "food," do you need to know more? If your friend really has a preference, maybe he should be specific: "a large bag of Dorito corn chips and a small can of Cheez Whiz." When writers want to create a clear image, they choose the most specific words possible, particularly concrete nouns and verbs. By narrowing the group to which the word belongs, you can more clearly communicate your meaning.

First drafts are often filled with general language. When revising for word choice, you should search your vocabulary, sometimes supplementing your search with a dictionary or thesaurus (a book containing synonyms of words), for the word that conveys the most precise meaning. Besides nouns like "food" from the example above, we often choose verbs that lack strength, as in the following sentences:

A. Jennifer made an attempt to say she was sorry.

B. Lilah is sleepy as she gets into the van.

C. Sam does hard work when he gets the products up on the shelves.

These sentences are clear enough, but they lack punch, largely because of bland verbs. Here is one way to revise them:

A. Jennifer stuttered, "I . . . I . . . I'm sorry."

B. Lilah's eyelids droop as she fumbles her way into the van.

C. Sam struggles with the 50-pound bags of dogfood as he hoists them onto the shelves.

As you revise, be especially alert to forms of the verbs *be, do, have, make,* and *get,* all of which can cause your sentences to lose energy.

Along with using general nouns and verbs, writers sometimes fall into the "very, really, extremely" habit. They say, "It's very hot out," "She's really smart," and "He is extremely mean." Typically, four out of five of these empty intensifiers in a draft should simply be eliminated, and often they can be replaced with more precise words. In the examples above, *scorching, brilliant,* and *brutal* would convey the meaning more effectively.

Other overly general words that add little to your writing are *thing, nice, pretty, handsome, good looking, good, bad, interesting, fun, great, young, old, happy,* and *sad.* This sentence contains nothing but vague words:

A very nice young man, who used to be happy but now is sad, no longer has much fun and has few interesting things to say.

Notice how much clearer and more effective this version is:

John Kelley, a sophomore in high school, used to be optimistic and happy but was devastated when his parents were divorced. He no longer talks to even his closest friends about his feelings and has become a virtual recluse.

(Most of the general terms have been replaced with more specific words.)

CAUTION! When using a thesaurus, choose words you know.

Teaching Idea
If you approach active verbs from the perspective of general versus specific, you can begin with an example like the verb *to move* and become increasingly specific with *to walk* and then *to saunter.*

HINT: *Be, do, have, make,* and *get* are often weak verbs.

Teaching Idea
Rather than banning adverbial intensifiers like *very,* you might challenge students to find alternate, more precise expressions for three out of four of them.

ACTIVITY 19.1 Revising for Specific Word Choice

Discuss the differences between relatively general and relatively specific words. Next, revise the following sentences to make them clearer and more interesting by substituting more specific words. Pay particular attention to the subjects and verbs, but also look for other vague words such as *very*, and either delete or replace them.

EXAMPLE

The person's child ~~very~~ often got into her lap.

Revised: Anita's three-year-old daughter often crawled up into her mother's lap.

Answers will vary.

1. Someone made contact with an object, and it went over some part of a fence somewhere out there.

   Jack smashed the ball over the left-field fence.

2. A person moved very quietly toward an animal standing near some vegetation.

   Ethan crept up on a deer grazing near a clump of birch trees.

3. A man was occupying himself in a boat on a really small body of water.

   An old man was bait fishing from a rowboat on a pond.

4. At the place where the big machines do jobs, one that pushes earth around had a problem with the gas flow and quit running.

   At a construction site a bulldozer stalled from a clogged fuel line.

5. In a building full of interesting books and other great things, some young people made conversation in extremely quiet voices.

   Three teenagers were whispering in the library.

6. Some time ago the structure was damaged in a natural disaster.

   Last year the Pacific Grove water tower sprang a leak in an earthquake.

7. Feeling the situation was hopeless, the nice person made an attempt to control himself but had to sit down and let his emotions get out.

   Feeling hopeless, Brian tried to control himself but collapsed in a chair and sobbed.

Teaching Idea
To give students additional practice with the concept of abstract versus concrete, see Chapter 5, Activity 5.2.

Choosing Concrete Words

Just as you can choose specific words to clarify ideas and images, you can favor concrete over abstract terms. **Abstractions** are ideas, qualities, emotions, and processes—expressed in terms like *equality, friendship, happiness,* and *evolution,* general terms that we understand through specific examples. When you think of *friendship,* for instance, you probably picture a group of people talking and laughing. Without specific examples, abstract terms can be hard to understand.

To help illustrate abstract terms, we rely not only on specific words but also on concrete ones. Concrete terms we know through our senses: sight, sound, touch, smell, and taste. You can hold a can of Sprite, for example, feeling its coolness and slick aluminum sides. You see that the can is green, feel that it weighs about 12 ounces, and taste the sweet soda in it. Popping the top, you hear it; splashing the liquid into a glass, you see and hear the bubbles rising. *Sprite* is clearly a concrete term. So is *handshake,* whereas *friendship* is not. *Tears* are concrete, but *sorrow* is not.

Teaching Idea
To help students understand how concrete words can often be used to develop abstractions, ask them to give some examples of a term like *democracy* in action (people voting, congressional debates, etc.). Ask what words in their example can be known through the senses (voting: punch cards and stylus, people standing in long lines, etc.).

Abstractions are needed for thinking and communicating because they establish large ideas quickly. You can then illustrate them with specific, concrete examples.

Your writing will be more compelling when you rely on concrete, specific words to develop more abstract terms. Compare the following paragraphs, the first with most of the abstract terms underlined. Which paragraph seems most vivid? Which one best communicates the concept of intense activity?

A. When the ocean recedes, leaving the tide pool behind, a beautiful and deadly world is revealed. Sea creatures struggle for life and often find death. They battle with one another, challenging each other's power in their quest for existence and continuity. This community is alive with marine animals moving about their world, chasing and escaping one another, searching for mates, trying to evade each other's snares. Large and small, brilliantly colored and drab, slow moving and graceful, frantic and powerful—the tide pool is a study in intense and frenzied life.

B. But when the tide goes out, the little water world becomes quiet and lovely. The sea is very clear and the bottom becomes fantastic with hurrying, fighting, feeding, breeding animals. . . . Starfish squat over mussels, and limpets attach their million little suckers and then slowly lift with incredible power until the prey is broken from the rock. And then the starfish stomach comes out and envelops its food. Orange and speckled and fluted nudibranchs slide gracefully over the rocks, their skirts waving like the dresses of Spanish dancers. And black eels poke their heads out of crevices and wait for prey. . . . Hermit crabs like frantic children scamper on the bottom sand. . . . Here a crab tears a leg from his brother. The anemones expand like soft and brilliant flowers. . . .

Teaching Idea
To see the rest of the Steinbeck tide pool excerpt, turn to Unit Six.

If you prefer paragraph B, then try the same strategy that John Steinbeck, the author of this passage, uses so well by illustrating abstract ideas in your own writing with concrete, specific examples.

ACTIVITY 19.2 Revising for Concrete Words

Working in a group, read through paragraph B above, discuss the differences between concrete and abstract terms, and then underline all the concrete terms.

Writing Concisely

Eliminating Redundancies

Another quality to strive for when revising for style is **concision**—saying what you mean with no wasted words. In the rush of getting ideas onto paper, writers often include everything that pops into their minds, so first drafts often resemble this:

> Let me tell you for a moment about what it means to communicate clearly to other people in words when you are going to a job interview where you hope to find work. Some kinds of advice are more worth listening to than others, and I have always thought the best sort of advice that one person can give to another is the kind of suggestions that get straight to the point.

To revise for concision, we need to eliminate unneeded repetition, imprecise words, and stalling phrases and get to the point:

> Communicating clearly will help you do well in a job interview.

Teaching Idea
Students struggling to reach a minimum word count sometimes try to "pad" their work. You might point out that the unneeded words will only bog their writing down and that you will simply cross out the excess.

By shrinking the wordy passage from 73 words to 11, we increase economy and clarity. The point in trimming deadwood from sentences is not to cut all repetition—writers often use repetition for emphasis—and not merely to write short sentences. You simply want to remove words that interfere with your meaning. In revising for economy and clarity, you need to reduce or eliminate the following:

- Redundant expressions
- Empty and padded phrases
- Excessive qualifiers and emphasizers
- Unnecessary examples, details, and explanations
- Inflated clauses and phrases

Revising to Eliminate Redundant Expressions

Some unnecessary words creep into sentences as **redundant expressions**—words that repeat an idea that has already been expressed, as in this example:

> <u>Currently</u> today, as we <u>gather</u> <u>and come together</u> as a <u>group</u> of unemployed <u>people</u> <u>who are out of work</u>, although our numbers are few <u>and there are not many of us</u>, we can still push for decent jobs.

Eliminating the redundant phrases gives us a clearer, more concise sentence:

> Today as we who are unemployed gather, although we are only a few people, we can still push for decent jobs.

Here are several pairs of words and phrases to watch for as you revise:

REDUNDANT PAIRS

adequate enough	gather together	proceeded to go
circle around	heavy in weight	red in color
climb up	hopes and wishes	return again
continue on	if and when	small in size
cooperate together	important essentials	square in shape
each and every one	intentionally try	sum total
few in number	link together	terrible tragedy
first and foremost	old antiques	true facts
free gift	past history	

ACTIVITY 19.3 Eliminating Redundant Expressions

Using the preceding chart, revise the following sentences to eliminate redundant
expressions. Be careful not to cut any important ideas.

EXAMPLE

~~In this day and age each and~~ every one ~~of us~~ today has the right to
affordable health care ~~that is inexpensive enough that no one is left
without it.~~

Revised: _Everyone today has the right to affordable health care._

Answers will vary.

1. If everyone in this country would cooperate together, we could
   overcome our past history of failure to meet the needs of our poor.
   If everyone in this country would cooperate, we could overcome our
   history of failure to meet the needs of our poor.

2. Although Horace is small in stature, he is aggressive, and he skates
   well enough and with sufficient skill to be on the team.
   Although Horace is small, he is aggressive, and he skates well
   enough to be on the team.

3. If we return again to the Lake of the Ozarks for the presentation on
   time-share condos, we are guaranteed to get a free gift this time.
   If we return to the Lake of the Ozarks for the presentation on time-
   share condos, we are guaranteed a gift.

4. Scaling back the space program would be a terrible tragedy for
   humanity and all the people living on earth because space research
   continues to make critically essential discoveries that affect everyone's
   life on the planet.
   Scaling back the space program would be a terrible tragedy for humanity because
   space research continues to make essential discoveries that affect everyone.

5. Heavy in weight but mostly full of liquid water, watermelons are best eaten when their pink color deepens to a red color.

   Heavy but mostly full of liquid, watermelons are best eaten when their pink deepens to red.

6. Everyone on the committee, meaning all the people who are discussing the issue, continues to circle around the first and foremost problem.

   Everyone on the committee continues to circle the foremost problem.

7. Missing her children terribly, Margaret had fond hopes and wishes to gather them together again once more on Christmas Eve to celebrate as they once had.

   Missing her children terribly, Margaret hoped to gather them to celebrate Christmas Eve.

Revising to Reduce Empty and Padded Phrases

Teaching Idea
You might want to reiterate that there are good reasons to use some of these terms on occasion.

In addition to repeating words and using redundant phrases, writers can bog readers down with empty and padded phrases. **Empty words** and **phrases** are best deleted. The following list gives a few common words and phrases that can be dropped from a sentence, usually without altering the meaning in any way:

EMPTY WORDS AND PHRASES

absolutely	certain	in kind	really
actually	character of	in terms of	situation of
area of	definitely	kind of	sort of
aspect of	element of	manner	thing
awfully	extremely	nature of	type of
basically	factor	quite	very

Padded phrases are stock expressions that use more words than needed to make the point—for example, *due to the fact that*, which simply means *because*:

A. <u>Due to the fact that</u> we are understaffed, no one goes home early.

B. <u>Because</u> we are understaffed, no one goes home early.

Because is a simple, concise replacement for the padded phrase. The following is a list of common padded phrases with more concise substitute words:

PADDED PHRASES	CONCISE SUBSTITUTES
at the present time, at this point in time, at the present moment, in this day and age	now, today
during that time, in the time when, in those days	then, when
at all times	always
despite (regardless of) the fact that	although

due to the fact that, the reason is because, for the reason that, considering the fact that	because
located close by	near
in the event that	if
by means of	by
form a consensus of opinion	agree
a large number of	many
few in number	few
aware of the fact that	know
refer back	refer
in the final analysis	finally
sufficient amount of	enough
make contact with	contact, meet
for the purpose of	for
in a situation in which, in the event that	when, if
is in a position to, has the opportunity to	can
it is important (crucial/critical) that	must
there is a chance that	may
during the time that	while
all of a sudden	suddenly

ACTIVITY 19.4 Reducing Empty and Padded Phrases

Revise the following sentences by crossing out the empty and wordy phrases and substituting more concise ones from the preceding list.

EXAMPLE

~~Considering the fact that~~ summer is almost over, we will ~~actually very~~ soon be back in school ~~again~~.

Revised: _Because summer is almost over, we will soon be back in school._

Answers will vary.

1. If the committee would form a consensus on this one issue, we could, in the final analysis, be out of this situation of constant debate and all go home.

   If the committee would agree on this issue, we could go home.

2. Some of the team members may not be aware of the fact that there is a chance the coach has an ulcer.

   Some of the team members may not know the coach may have an ulcer.

3. Located close by I-435 and Nall is a jogging trail that a large number of people run on daily considering the fact that they need exercise.

Near I-435 and Nall is a jogging trail that many people run on daily.

4. It is absolutely essential that Sheila and Maureen make contact with their supervisor despite the fact that it is after working hours.
Sheila and Maureen must contact their supervisor, although it is after working hours.

5. In a situation in which CO_2 and other greenhouse gases continue to rise, the earth will warm by several degrees, which is a sufficient enough increase in heat to cause catastrophic coastal flooding.
If CO_2 and other greenhouse gases continue to rise, the earth will warm by several degrees, causing catastrophic coastal flooding.

6. At this point in time, currently, it is the consensus of opinion among many political commentators that Maurice Jones, a kind of eloquent speaker, may become a candidate for senator.
Many political commentators agree that Maurice Jones, an eloquent speaker, may become a candidate for senator.

Removing Excessive Qualifiers and Emphasizers

Teaching Idea
You can save the material on qualifiers and emphasizers for your work in Chapter 16 on persuasive writing.

Even when you have thoughtfully trimmed redundant and empty expressions from your work, unnecessary qualifiers and emphasizers may remain. **Qualifiers** such as *often, usually,* and *frequently* are important in writing, especially in persuasion, because they can soften your tone and keep you from overstating your case. But qualifiers can be overused, cluttering a text and making writers seem unsure of themselves. Consider the following sentences:

A. In my opinion, we should probably lower the drinking age to maybe 18 or possibly 19 because, for the most part, young adults are responsible enough to choose when, where, and how much they drink, most of the time, except for when they are not being responsible, which they are not, admittedly, some of the time.

B. We should lower the drinking age to 18 because most young adults are responsible enough to choose when, where, and how much they drink.

Sentence A bogs the reader down with qualifiers such as "in my opinion" and "probably," whereas B is direct and concise yet still qualifies sufficiently by keeping the qualifier "most." Below is a list of common qualifiers (for more on qualifying, see pp. 395–397):

COMMON QUALIFIERS

almost	for the most part	maybe	often	seldom
apparently	frequently	might	perhaps	sometimes
can	in my opinion	more or less	possibly	try
could be	may	occasionally	seemingly	usually

Emphasizers such as *of course, clearly,* and *obviously* are also important in writing because they help you direct readers' attention to points you want to stress. However, as with too many qualifiers, you can unnecessarily clutter a text with too many emphasizers, making yourself sound arrogant. Consider the following sentences:

A. As everyone knows, 18-year-olds are obviously considered adults in the eyes of the law, and as anyone can plainly see, the simple fact that 18-year-olds have to assume adult responsibilities means that, of course, they should be, inevitably, allowed to legally drink.

B. Because 18-year-olds are considered legal adults and have to assume adult responsibilities, they should be allowed to drink.

Sentence A clearly overemphasizes, bogging readers down and possibly irritating them, whereas B is direct and concise yet still makes its point. Below is a list of common emphasizers:

COMMON EMPHASIZERS

all	crucial	invariably	undoubtedly
always	definitely	never	unequivocally
certainly	every time	obviously	unmistakably
clearly	everyone can see that	of course	unquestionably
critical	inevitably	plainly	vital

ACTIVITY 19.5 Removing Unneeded Qualifiers and Emphasizers

Discuss the following sentences, and then cut qualifiers and emphasizers wherever you feel there are too many of them. You may need to add words or restructure a sentence, but keep the main ideas intact.

EXAMPLE
When enough time has passed, most Americans ~~inevitably~~ forget the broken campaign promises of politicians and, ~~unquestionably, as anyone can see~~, will ~~certainly~~ reelect the greatest liars of the bunch.
Revised: <u>When enough time has passed, most Americans forget the broken campaign promises of politicians and reelect the greatest liars of the bunch.</u>

Answers will vary.

1. Although it seems to me that most people would like to feel safe in their homes, keeping loaded handguns at their bedside, for most people, might not be the very best possible solution to their safety concerns, in my opinion.
   <u>Although people want to feel safe in their homes, keeping loaded handguns at their bedside is not the best way to ensure their safety.</u>

2. Jailing people for smoking marijuana might just possibly waste taxpayers' money, may be an injustice to some of those imprisoned,

and could drain some of the resources for dealing with at least a few of the serious crimes.

Jailing people for smoking marijuana wastes taxpayers' money, is an injustice to those imprisoned, and drains resources for dealing with serious crimes.

3. Most people who love one another might find it helpful in their relationship to try to communicate as often as they can stand to about issues that they are not likely to agree on, unless they don't think they can talk about a really tough issue, in which case it might be all right for them to skip it occasionally.

People who love one another should communicate most clearly on the issues they are least likely to agree on.

4. It should be obvious to any clear thinker that state lotteries are legalized gambling and that supporting the system will inevitably lead to greater state involvement in gaming, with racetracks and, undoubtedly, riverboat gambling in the near future.

State lotteries are legalized gambling, and supporting the system often leads to greater state involvement in gaming, such as racetracks and riverboat gambling.

5. I think that everyone will agree that parents should definitely be held responsible for their children's education, and the way to deal with this critical issue, obviously, is to withhold tax credits from all parents who allow their children to fail subjects in school.

Parents should be held responsible for their children's education, and one way to do this is to withhold tax credits from all parents who allow their children to fail subjects in school.

Removing Unnecessary Examples, Details, and Explanations

Teaching Idea
If you teach the process-analysis chapter, this example will show overexplaining and detailing of steps.

Along with unneeded repetition, writers can be wordy by including more **examples, details,** and **explanations** than necessary. First drafts can be wordy because writers lose sight of their audience, forgetting what readers already know or want to know about a subject.

Consider the following paragraph response written to remind an *adult* of steps to take before mailing a letter:

Look closely at the front of the envelope, in the general area of the center, to see if you have remembered to write the proper and complete address where you want the letter to go. Remember to put the person's, company's, school's, or any other institution's name at the top of the outgoing address; and then on the very next line under the first line, put the street address with numbers first, that is, before the name of the street, road, boulevard, or drive. Then on the bottom line, under the middle line, write out the destination, beginning with the city and progressing through the state and possibly country if you are sending the letter out of the United States. Also be sure to write out all the numbers of the zip code (those numbers that help the post office route your mail properly). When you have accomplished this task, repeat it in more or less the same way as you check your return address, which should be in the upper left corner of the envelope you want to mail. Find a stamp that you have to lick or one that already has adhesive on the back, lick or in some other way, possibly using a sponge, dampen the stamp that needs to be wet in order for it to stick; and then affix it to the upper right corner of the envelope. The final step is to seal the envelope, which you can do again by licking or using the same sponge, or you might have envelopes that already have adhesive on them if you are lucky. Now seal it, and you are finished with the job.

If this process paragraph seems too long, it is because the writer has lost sight of what the audience needs and wants to know. Here is a concise revision:

> **Address the envelope properly, include your return address, stamp the envelope, and seal it.**

The longer version might be the rough draft of an explanation to children who have never before addressed an envelope. However, even for this audience, the writer should cut much of the unnecessary explanation and many of the examples. As you draft, you should be open to new ideas and include specific examples, but during revision, you should prune any that are not essential.

ACTIVITY 19.6 Removing Unneeded Examples, Details, and Explanations

Read through the following paragraph, and revise it to remove unneeded examples, details, and explanations. The purpose of the paragraph is to *briefly* explain to an adult how to light a charcoal fire. As you read, ask yourself, "How much of this information would I need to start a charcoal fire?"
Answers will vary.

To successfully light a charcoal fire for grilling, there are four basic steps, but there is a lot to know about each one. First off, what kind of grill do you have? If it is a gas or electric grill, you have an easy task. Just turn it on. If, on the other hand, you have a small Weber or other type of grill that has to use the kind of fuel you can buy in almost any supermarket, meaning charcoal, then the process becomes more complicated. Do you want to buy matchless charcoal or the kind of charcoal that requires charcoal starting fluid and a match or some other lighting device? Of course, there are several brands of charcoal, but if you choose the kind that requires fluid and a match, then pay for the bag, take it to your car, drive home, and take the charcoal out onto your deck or patio or driveway or wherever you plan to do your grilling. After you get there, open the bag with a knife or a pair of scissors or maybe you can just pull that little string that hangs down. Next, cover the bottom of the grill on the inside with some kind of fire-resistant material like aluminum foil and pour the briquettes (small pieces of charcoal that are sort of square and rough around the edges) out of the bag so that the charcoal covers the bottom of the grill. Now pour just enough fluid on the briquettes so that a film of the liquid covers most of the top at least. Now you are ready to work the charcoal into a pile that has roughly the shape of a pyramid, meaning a pile about 6 inches high at the pointed top tapering down to a kind of round-shaped bottom. The final step is to stand back at least at arm's length and, using a match, lighter, or a piece of paper that you have rolled up and lit with a match or lighter, carefully light the edge of the pile of charcoal. Be sure to stand back immediately so that you won't run the risk of having the flames leap up and possibly scorch your hand or arm or even your face.

Reducing Inflated Clauses and Phrases

The last important method for writing more concisely is to reduce clauses to phrases and phrases to single words where appropriate.

REDUCING PHRASES TO SINGLE-WORD MODIFIERS

A. Hannah ran to answer the phone ~~in an~~ eager ~~way~~.

Hannah <u>eagerly</u> ran to answer the phone.

B. The wolf could not blow down the house <u>built of bricks</u>.

The wolf could not blow down the <u>brick house</u>.

C. Most people appreciate the beauty ~~of~~ a sunset.

Most people appreciate a <u>sunset's beauty</u>.

REDUCING CLAUSES TO PHRASES OR SINGLE-WORD MODIFIERS

Teaching Idea
These clause/phrase reductions can also serve as a quick reminder about essential versus nonessential word groups.

A. Ernest Hemingway, ~~who is~~ <u>a well-known writer</u>, was a big-game hunter.

Ernest Hemingway, <u>a well-known writer</u>, was a big-game hunter.

B. The man ~~who is~~ <u>wearing a red vest</u> is my grandfather.

The man <u>wearing a red vest</u> is my grandfather.

C. Elephants, ~~which are~~ <u>the largest land animals</u>, may weigh 5 tons.

Elephants, <u>the largest land animals</u>, may weigh 5 tons.

D. The painting ~~that is~~ <u>hanging in the library</u> is from the nineteenth century.

The painting <u>hanging in the library</u> is from the nineteenth century.

Your response is probably "huh?" Stringing multisyllable words together generally produces writing that is hard to understand. The above sentence is an extreme form of "thesaurus" writing—exotic word hunting—and it obscures rather than clarifies meaning.

Here is a revised version:

A steady diet of television can make the brain flabby.

Your choice of words depends on your **writing context,** and sometimes you will have good reasons to use some "big" words. If you are writing for an audience knowledgeable in a certain field—say, doctors, mechanics, or restaurant managers—you will often use specialized terms that they understand, though the terms might be unfamiliar to others. People writing for a medical audience would not need to define terms like *otoscope* or *platelets,* for example. Sometimes you might choose a longer word for variety (*additionally* in place of *also* or *and*). However, in general, favoring more common—and often smaller—words will make your writing clearer.

In the following passage, how many words of more than one syllable did the writer, Joseph Ecclesine, need to express himself?

> Small words move with ease where big words stand still—or worse, bog down and get in the way of what you want to say. There is not much, in all truth, that small words will not say—and say quite well.

ACTIVITY 19.8 Revising Unneeded Big Words

Discuss the following sentences, and then revise them by "translating" the unneeded big words into more everyday language. Consult a dictionary if necessary, and keep the basic meaning of the sentence the same.

EXAMPLE

The Boy Scouts gathered their paraphernalia and prepared themselves for the coming arduous adventure into the wilderness.

Revised: *The Boy Scouts gathered their gear and prepared for their backpacking trip.*

Answers will vary.

1. Shannon attempted to purchase an automobile yesterday but did not succeed.

   Shannon tried to buy a car yesterday but failed.

2. Those who obtain a proficiency with computers can anticipate increased marketability.

   Learning computer skills will make a person more marketable.

3. The facade of the edifice is deteriorating with rapidity.

   The front of the building is rapidly crumbling.

4. Andrea received an equitable remuneration for her laborious toil.

   Andrea was paid fairly for her hard work.

   _____

5. Chen hypothesized that the communiqué in his mail receptacle

   contained abominable information.

   Chen guessed that the letter in his mailbox held bad news.

   _____

Avoiding Slang and Colloquial Expressions

Clichés

Just as using a lot of multisyllable words affects your tone, so does using slang and colloquial expressions. **Slang terms** are typically short-lived, invented words used by groups to express a meaning members understand but outsiders often do not. Slang can be colorful and often expresses strong emotions, as in the following expressions: *stressed out, freaked out, psyched out,* and *wired.*

Colloquial terms are similar to—sometimes indistinguishable from—slang but are typically understood by a wider audience—for example, words like *kid* for "child" or *hang out* for "spend time with."

Slang and colloquialisms are appropriate for informal gatherings but are usually avoided in more formal writing. Academic writers almost never use slang and use colloquial terms only on occasion, to vary their tone. If you want to achieve a relatively formal tone, replace all slang and most colloquialisms with more standard usage.

ACTIVITY 19.9 Translating Slang

Choose any five of the terms below and discuss their meaning. Next, write a sentence using the term as slang and then another sentence replacing the term with more formal language. You may need several words to convey your meaning, perhaps by describing a scene, and you may find that your interpretation of a slang word varies from that of others in your group.

Teaching Idea
You might remind students that there are often synonyms that can replace slang expressions, such as *overreacted* for *freaked out,* but that several words might be needed.

EXAMPLE

When I told my grandmother about the car wreck, she <u>freaked out.</u>

Revised: <u>When I told my grandmother about the car wreck, she hugged me</u>
<u>and began sobbing.</u>

EXAMPLE

Ethan was <u>busted</u> for stealing a car.

Revised: <u>Ethan was arrested for stealing a car.</u>

SLANG AND COLLOQUIAL EXPRESSIONS

airhead	busted	dude	hassle	paranoid	stressed out
awesome	chill	dumped on	hit on	pig	together
babe	chill out	freaked out	hot	psyched out	wasted
boost	cool	gig	laid back	psyched up	whacked out
bummed	diss	go postal	nerd	rip off	wired

Answers will vary.

1. Slang version: Jenny is whacked out if she thinks that I stole her purse.

   Revision: Jenny is insane if she thinks that I stole her purse.

2. Slang version: Allen ripped off a stereo last night.

   Revision: Allen stole a stereo last night.

3. Slang version: "Don't be so paranoid!"

   Revision: "Don't be so worried!"

4. Slang version: Isabella has a laid-back attitude.

   Revision: Isabella has a relaxed attitude.

5. Slang version: We were so wasted that we didn't even know the pigs had busted us.

   Revision: We were so drunk that we didn't even know the police had arrested us.

ACTIVITY 19.10 Revising Colloquial Expressions

Revise the following sentences by replacing the colloquial expressions with more formal language.

EXAMPLE

Tony was in a bind.

Revised: Tony had a problem.

Answers will vary.

1. Dale's boss keeps giving him the runaround.

   Dale's boss keeps misleading him.

2. "Did you catch the *Star Trek* rerun last night?"

   Did you watch the Star Trek rerun last night?

3. "I think that it's time to hit the road."

   "I think that it's time to leave."

4. "Sarah, you're driving me up a wall with that racket!"

   "Sarah, you're annoying me with that racket!"

5. "If you're not careful, Rachel will try to pull another fast one on you."

   "If you're not careful, Rachel will try to deceive you."

Controlling Denotation and Connotation

Links to Dictionary and Thesauri

Words have objective, literal meanings found in dictionaries, called **denotation,** but they also have more subjective, figurative meanings that people associate with them, called **connotation.**

Denotative meanings are usually easier for a writer to pin down than connotative meanings. When you look up the word *flag* in a dictionary, for example, you find this definition: "a piece of cloth, usually rectangular, of distinctive color and design, used as a symbol, a standard, a signal, or an emblem." Because a nation's flag is a symbol, however, it evokes different images and emotional responses from different people. For instance, the American flag arouses feelings of patriotism and a sense of national belonging in many Americans. It has positive associations—and connotations—for them. However, within the United States and abroad, there are those who see the flag as a symbol of oppression. To them, the flag has negative connotations.

To control your tone, you should be aware of the potential connotations words have for an audience. It is all too easy, especially in persuasive writing, to choose words that evoke a negative rather than a positive response. For example, how would you like to be characterized by a writer: as firm, assertive, insistent, aggressive, opinionated, or pushy? Most of us would prefer the more positive connotations of "firm" or "assertive" to the more negative associations of "aggressive, opinionated, and pushy."

ACTIVITY 19.11 Revising for Connotation

Review the following terms and discuss their connotations. Next, arrange each word group in a roughly ascending order from most negative to most positive.

Relatively Negative   Relatively Positive

EXAMPLE

restless, hyperactive, frantic, energetic, active

Reordered from most negative to positive: _frantic, hyperactive, restless,_
active, energetic

Answers will vary.

1. Quiet, reserved, shy, timid, withdrawn, reclusive
   reclusive, withdrawn, timid, shy, reserved, quiet

2. Frightened, apprehensive, hysterical, nervous, panicked
   hysterical, panicked, frightened, nervous, apprehensive

3. Odor, fragrance, stench, scent, smell
   stench, odor, smell, scent, fragrance

4. Thrifty, stingy, frugal, cheap, miserly
   miserly, stingy, cheap, frugal, thrifty

5. Slender, lean, thin, skinny, gaunt, emaciated
   emaciated, gaunt, skinny, thin, lean, slender

6. Innocent, childlike, unsophisticated, naïve, childish
   childish, naïve, unsophisticated, childlike, innocent

Eliminating Biased Language

Word Choice

Writers who are conscious of their readers usually try not to offend them. However, we sometimes unintentionally insult people because we don't realize the implications of our words. Without thinking, we convey negative impressions about race, religion, ethnicity, age, gender, social class, physical and mental abilities, body shape, and sexual orientation. When we do this, not only are we offending people, but also we are telling our reader that we are either insensitive or unaware, neither of which impression adds to a writer's credibility.

The largest group in this country that encounters discrimination in language is women. Writers who want to be sensitive to **gender bias** in language avoid using career and social stereotypes and pronouns that exclude women.

Career and social stereotypes take several forms, but in general they imply that men belong in one role or profession and that women belong in another (often lower-status) profession. Consider the following sentences:

SEXIST	A doctor must spend many years earning his credentials to practice medicine.
REVISED	Doctors must spend many years earning their credentials to practice medicine.
SEXIST	When the homeowner dusts, vacuums, and launders, she is doing required household maintenance.
REVISED	When homeowners dust, vacuum, and launder, they are doing required household maintenance.

Many doctors are women, and many men do household chores. These realities should be reflected in writing.

Another way to show that you are aware of women's presence in society is to avoid occupational titles and other group descriptions that include the word *man*. Here is a list of some common terms with alternatives that are not gender-biased:

anchorman = anchor	mankind = humanity, people
businessman = businessperson	manpower = personnel, workers
chairman = chair	newsman = reporter, journalist
congressman = representative	policeman = police officer
craftsman = artist	salesman = sales representative
fireman = fire fighter	stewardess/steward = flight attendant
foreman = supervisor	waitress/waiter = food server
freshman = first-year student	weatherman = weather reporter, forecaster
insurance man = insurance agent	
mailman = mail carrier	workman = worker

You can avoid using masculine pronouns to refer to groups that contain both genders by using a plural pronoun, dropping the pronoun, using a "his or her" combination, or alternating gender pronouns within a passage (as *A Writer's Workshop* often does).

OPTIONS TO PREVENT GENDER BIAS WITH PRONOUNS

GENDER BIAS	A student who studies his notes thoroughly should do well on his exam.
PLURAL PRONOUN	Students who study their notes thoroughly should do well on the exam. (*the* substituted for *his*)

CAUTION! The "he or she" method can easily be overworked and sound awkward.

CAUTION! When you alternate *he* and *she*, be sure the pronoun references are clear. (See Chapter 24 for help with pronoun reference.)

DELETED PRONOUN	A student studying notes thoroughly should do well on the exam.
HIS OR HER/SHE OR HE	A student who studies his or her notes thoroughly should do well on the exam.
ALTERNATED PRONOUNS	A student who studies his notes thoroughly should do well on the exam. The student will do particularly well if she focuses on the chapter summaries.

ACTIVITY 19.12 Revising Sexist Language

Revise the following sentences by replacing gender-biased language with appropriate alternatives.

EXAMPLE
"To boldly go where no man has gone before . . ."
Revised: "To boldly go where no one has gone before . . ."

_____

Answers will vary.

1. When a baby needs his diaper changed, find his mother in a hurry!
   a diaper, the parent

   _____

2. Dear Sir: I have heard a great deal about your company and the
   professionalism of your salesmen.
   Dear Mr. _____ /Ms. _____ , *sales force*

   _____

3. When the mailman dropped off my package, I thanked her.
   mail carrier

   _____

4. Jackie will be a freshman at JCCC this year.
   first-year student

   _____

5. If we had more manpower in this office, we could finish the job on time.
   personnel

   _____

6. Congressman Andrea Cambiano will now take questions from the
   newsmen.
   representative, press

   _____

Using Contractions Carefully

A **contraction**—two words joined with an apostrophe—is a small element that contributes to the tone of your writing. Contractions are common in everyday

Personification gives human qualities to animals and things, thereby creating a comparison and often establishing a mood. When we say that the sky looks angry or threatening, we are personifying, attributing emotions to the sky. Here are several other examples of personification:

PERSONIFICATION

A. Tired from the weight of years, the old barn leaned hard to one side.

B. The airbus, heavy with fuel and feeling its age, seemed reluctant to leave the runway.

C. The golden arches seemed to smile, saying, "Come on in. The fries are hot."

When you are using figures of speech like metaphors, similes, and personification, watch for clichés and worn expressions. **Clichés** are metaphors and similes that have had the life sucked out of them by overuse—for example, "He stood still as a statue" or "Her heart pounded like a drum."

Worn phrases are similar, but they are not always a comparison—for example, "live life to the fullest" or "a cut-and-dried solution." Because even old figures of speech have some power and are common in casual speech, they will occasionally sneak into your writing. However, since they are secondhand expressions, you should avoid them. Here is a brief list of some common clichés and worn expressions:

Teaching Idea
You might point out that spotting clichés in our own writing can be difficult because we have grown so used to them. Another pair of eyes is often required.

CLICHÉS AND WORN EXPRESSIONS

sent chills down my spine	hot as hell	cold as ice
seemed like an eternity	like two peas in a pod	butterflies in my stomach
couch potato	security blanket	
sparkle (gleam, spark, glint) in her (his) eye	iron out the wrinkles	a perfect little angel
	window of opportunity	glued to
thin as a rail (stick)	pushing the envelope	a step in the right direction
is a breeze	get a handle on	
velcroed to	live life to the fullest	see the light
make the project fly	take things one day (one step) at a time	a slap on the hand
no strings attached		few and far between
between a rock and a hard place	last but not least	life flash before her eyes
	seemed like only yesterday	
hated with a passion		winning isn't everything
break a sweat	go with the flow	
get the ball rolling	set in stone	up bright and early
moved like lightning	right on the money	brushed him (her) off
out in left field	bundle of energy	

ACTIVITY 19.14 Revising Clichés and Worn Expressions

Discuss the following sentences, and then revise them to eliminate clichés and worn expressions. You may "translate" the cliché into literal language or try for a fresh metaphor or simile.

EXAMPLE (CLICHÉ)

As I waited to take my algebra final, I felt butterflies in my stomach.

Revised (simile): *As I waited to take my algebra final, I felt like a beginning skier about to plunge down her first slope.*

Revised (literal language): *As I waited to take my algebra final, I was nervous*

Answers will vary.

1. They should act quickly, for their days are numbered.

   their time is limited

2. While driving on the highway, you can lose your life in the blink of an eye.

   instantly

3. Their relationship was doomed from the start.

   not likely to succeed

4. We need more jobs where money isn't everything.

   is less important

5. Everyone else was right on target, but Jason didn't have a clue.

   did not know

6. The last thing I want to do is to end up as another statistic.

   dead

ACTIVITY 19.15 Creating Metaphors and Similes

Teaching Idea
As in Activity 19.15, writers can discover similes by ending a thought with *like* or *as:* "Connor's depression left him feeling like _____."

Discuss with group members possible metaphors or similes for the following sentences. Imagining a scene as fully as possible can help. For instance, in the following example you might visualize a car with a wobbly wheel and then search for images that suggest a spinning object—pinwheel, Ferris wheel, carousel, Frisbee, or blender blades—or the drum of a washing machine. Try to avoid clichés. For number 6, create your own metaphor or simile, and explain its meaning.

EXAMPLE

The blown tire on Mayfield's car wobbled like *a washer with an uneven load.*

Meaning: *The wheels on a racing car move at high speeds, as does the drum inside a washing machine, and both are subject to stress. People can relate to a washer clonking around from an uneven load of clothes and see how the wheel might need the same immediate attention.*

ACTIVITY 19.17 Creating Overstatement, Understatement, and Irony

Discuss how you might revise the following sentences for overstatement, understatement, and irony. As you revise the sentences, expect that it will take some work to create interesting figures of speech. You may notice irony also working in understatement. Try to avoid worn phrases and clichés.

EXAMPLE

I don't feel appreciated at work.

Overstatement: _If I died tomorrow and fell on the floor, people would just step around me till they got tired of the nuisance, and then they would toss me in the dumpster out back._

Answers will vary.

1. Registering for classes can seem complicated.

    Overstatement: _Registering for classes can't be done by mere humans._

2. Freddy Krueger, from the *Nightmare on Elm Street* movies, is a spooky character.

    Overstatement: _Freddy Krueger makes me never want to walk into a dark house again._

3. Bill Gates is worth 65 billion dollars.

    Understatement: _Bill Gates has piled up a little spare change in his time._

4. Drunken driving kills thousands of people annually.

    Understatement: _Drunken driving has become something of a problem in this country._

5. A friend is doing poorly in college: He has not bothered to buy textbooks, seldom goes to class, and never studies for exams.

    Irony: _If you want to fail in school, you are going about it in the right way._

6. Elaine works hard, helps her friends, gives to charity, and is active in her community. She also is overly meticulous. Comment on this habit.

    Irony: _Now there is a serious character flaw for you._

Emphatic Repetition

Repetition can be a useful way to reinforce meaning and guide readers. Of course, repetition can also be useless, boring readers who wonder why the same word keeps repeating itself endlessly. Which of the following two paragraphs illustrates harmful repetition and which, helpful repetition?

A. <u>Television</u> is a mixed blessing. In small doses, <u>television</u> does not have to have the negative effects on our <u>kids'</u> health, behavior, and learning that <u>TV</u> often has in large amounts. In fact, most of us enjoy watching <u>TV</u> ourselves and with our <u>kids</u>; and, let's face it, we often need a break from the <u>kids</u> that the <u>TV</u> can provide. But, as tiring as it can be, we need to keep fighting the <u>TV</u> battle with our <u>kids</u>. We need to monitor what the <u>kids</u> watch on <u>TV</u> and how much. <u>Kids</u> cannot see very far down the road. <u>Kids</u> want what <u>kids</u> want when <u>kids</u> want it, regardless of the consequences. It is part of our job as parents to protect our <u>kids</u> from too much <u>TV</u>.

B. <u>Television</u> is a mixed blessing. In small doses, *it* does not have to have the negative effects on our *children's* health, behavior, and learning that *it* often has in large amounts. In fact, most of us enjoy watching TV ourselves and with our *family*; and, let's face it, we often need a break from the <u>kids</u> that the *box* can provide. But, as tiring as it can be, <u>we need to</u> keep fighting the TV battle with our <u>kids</u>. <u>We need to</u> monitor what *they* watch and how much. *Children* cannot see very far down the road. *They* <u>want</u> what they <u>want</u> when they <u>want</u> it, regardless of the consequences. It is part of our job as parents to protect *them* from themselves.

Paragraph A bogs the reader down and bores through unneeded repetition. On the other hand, paragraph B uses synonyms and pronouns to minimize unneeded repetition, keeping only what is useful for coherence. The author also creates special emphasis with the words "we need to" and "want."

In your own work, try occasionally repeating words that you want to especially emphasize, particularly in conclusions.

Copyright © 2006 The McGraw-Hill Companies, Inc. All rights reserved.

Teaching Idea
For more help with effective repetition, see the section "Connecting Sentences—Achieving Coherence" in Chapter 3.

Teaching Idea
For more practice to illustrate unnecessary repetition, have students compose a paragraph of four or five sentences and then deliberately revise it, overrepeating one or two words. Have them exchange versions and read each other's paragraphs aloud in pairs or groups.

ACTIVITY 19.18 Revising for Emphatic Repetition

Read through the following narrative paragraph and revise it for effective repetition. Replace any word you think is repeated unnecessarily, restructuring a sentence slightly if you think it is needed. Next, underline any *effectively* repeated phrase and explain how the repetition adds to the paragraph's meaning. Answers will vary. Effective repetition: "too tired."

Martin dragged into the house at the end of another exhausting workday. Martin had slept little the night before, and Martin had been kept on the job two hours past his regular quitting time. Martin collapsed on the sofa. Staring down at his work boots, Martin thought about unlacing his boots; his feet hurt. But he was too tired to manage it. Martin was too tired to unlace his boots, too tired to think about dinner, and far too tired to cope with the stack of unpaid bills on his dining room table.

CHAPTER 20

Working with Sentence Parts

What Are We Trying to Achieve and Why?

Teaching Idea
Because this is a foundational chapter, you might find it helpful to begin working students through it the first week of class and continue in small segments as the semester progresses until you finish it.

Most of *A Writer's Workshop* has focused on helping you discover, organize, develop, and revise ideas. However, once those ideas are in place, you must take the next step by expressing them in sentences that are clear to an audience. By learning the basic parts of a sentence, you will better manage them; and in seeing the relationship among the parts, you will punctuate more effectively as well.

Parts of Speech

Parts of Speech

All of the words in sentences fall into eight traditional categories, known as **parts of speech,** based on how they function.

THE EIGHT PARTS OF SPEECH

1. **Verbs** express an action or state of being: *run, is.*

2. **Nouns** name a person, place, thing, concept, or quality: *Tom, Idaho, rock, freedom, pleasure.*

3. **Pronouns** stand in place of a noun: *he, her, they, who, their, it.*

4. **Adjectives** describe nouns and pronouns: *hard* chair, someone *strong.*

5. **Adverbs** describe verbs, adjective, and adverbs: running *quickly, very* angry, *too* busily.

6. **Prepositions** shape nouns and pronouns into phrases: *on* the table, *near* her.

7. **Conjunctions** connect words, phrases, and clauses: cats *and* dogs, on my desk *or* in that drawer, they left *because* we left.

8. **Interjections** emphasize emotions: *Oh! Ouch!*

Teaching Idea
AWW treats articles as adjectives.

We seldom use all of the parts of speech in any one sentence, but we often use many in our most common expressions, as in the following sentence:

7 2 1 2 6 3 2 5 1 3 4
Because Timmy threw water on him, Tom immediately chased his younger
2 6 4 2 7 6 4 2
brother through the house and into the street.

Once we see examples from each category and how each works, we will learn where sentences begin and end and how to manage more complex sentences.

Verbs

Verbs, along with nouns, are the core of sentences. The verb expresses an action or state of being, and the nouns (or pronouns) perform or receive the action or experience the state of being. Verbs are of several types:

1. **Action verbs** show something happening—physically, mentally, or emotionally.

   A. Zeus *hurled* a lightning bolt across the sky.

   B. Aristotle *reflected* on the cause.

   C. Zeus's behavior often *angered* his wife, Hera.

2. **Being verbs** (or **linking verbs**) tell about a state of being. The verb *be* in its various forms (*am, are, is, was, were, been, being*) is the most common of these verbs. Others include *look, sound, taste, smell, appear, feel, seem, become, remain, get,* and *grow.*

   A. Sheryl *is* an intelligent woman.

   B. Max *seemed* very nervous.

   C. Hot chocolate with marshmallows *tastes* good in the winter.

3. **Helping verbs** help the main verb of a sentence express meaning. With the main verb, they create a unit called a **verb phrase.** Common

helping verbs include *be, have, do, may, might, must, can, could, should,* and *would.*

A. Martin *should be* making a decision.

B. Melanie *might have* finished the race.

C. Margaret *didn't say* anything to anyone.

Notice that the main verb is at the end of the verb phrase. When *be* is followed by another verb, *be* is a helping verb; when *be* is at the end, it is a being verb and the main verb.

In addition to a base form (*work*), verbs have an infinitive form (*to work*) and can occur in various tenses, which show action as present, past, or future: "John *works* today, *worked* yesterday, and *will work* again tomorrow." (For more on verbs, see Chapter 23.)

Nouns

As mentioned previously, nouns, along with verbs, form the core of our sentences, telling who or what is doing or receiving the action of the verb. Nouns can be relatively specific and concrete (*snow*) or relatively general and abstract (*cold*). (For more on this, see pp. 483–487.) Here are five categories:

1. **Proper nouns** name specific people (*Maria Gonzalez*), places (*Kansas City*), things (*Statue of Liberty*), and concepts (*Judaism*).

2. **Common nouns** name nonspecific people (*woman*), places (*city*), things (*statue*), concepts (*religion*), and qualities (*width*). Common nouns may be count or noncount nouns.

3. **Count nouns** name objects that can be quantified or enumerated: *rock, dress, car, trouble.* They generally form their plurals by adding an *-s* or *-es.*

4. **Noncount nouns** name objects that cannot be counted: *sunlight, music, air.* They have no plural form.

5. **Collective nouns** name a group that is considered a unit and so is grammatically singular: *team, family, gathering, band.* (For more on collective nouns and agreement, see Chapter 23.)

Nouns are often introduced by articles: *the, a,* and *an:*

- *The* introduces a noun that is referring to something specific or already known to the reader (*the* flock of sparrows that damaged my rice crop; *the* sun).

- *A* and *an* introduce a noun that is not referring to something specific or known to the reader (*a* flock of sparrows). Use *a* in front of words that begin with a consonant sound (*a* rock) and *an* in front of words that begin with a vowel sound (*an* egg). Keep in mind that it is the sound, not the letter, that matters: *an* F in chemistry, *an* hour, *a* used car.

Pronouns

HINT: Memorizing *who, which,* and *that* will help you identify relative (adjective) clauses. (See p. 543 for more on this.)

Pronouns are words that take the place of nouns. Like nouns, they can perform the action in a sentence ("*She* ran up a horrendous credit card debt") or receive the action ("Anna kicked *it* [the ball] downfield"). Because pronouns have no identity on their own, they must refer back to a noun. Readers can easily be confused if a writer does not *always* make the link between a pronoun and noun clear. Pronouns fall into the following categories (for more on pronouns, see pp. 576–586):

TYPES OF PRONOUNS

1. **Personal pronouns:** *I, you, he, she, it, we, they, me, her, him, us, them*
2. **Indefinite pronouns:** *all, any, anybody, anything, both, each, everybody, everyone, everything, few, many, more, most, much, nobody, none, no one, one, several, some, somebody, someone, something*
3. **Relative pronouns:** *who, which, that (whom, whose, what, whatever, whichever, whoever, whomever)*
4. **Interrogative pronouns:** *what, who, which, whom, whose*
5. **Demonstrative pronouns:** *this, that, these, those*
6. **Reflexive and intensive pronouns:** *myself, yourself, herself, himself, itself, oneself, ourselves, yourselves, themselves*
7. **Reciprocal pronouns:** *each other, one another*
8. **Possessive pronouns:** *my, mine, your, yours, her, hers, his, its, our, ours, their, theirs*

Adjectives

Adjectives are words that describe nouns or pronouns by answering questions like the following: *Which one? How many? What kind (shape, color, texture)?* Adjectives usually come directly before the word they modify. Many adjectives have three forms, indicating different degrees: *good, better, best; large, larger, largest; loud, louder, loudest.* (For more on adjectives, see Chapter 25.)

A. *The huge* Great Dane drooled on my arm.

B. Jonathan was *the best* child in the room.

Adverbs

Adverbs are words that describe verbs, adjectives, or other adverbs by answering the questions *when, where, why, how,* and *to what degree or extent.* An adverb is a flexible modifier, appearing before or after, and sometimes at a distance from, the word it describes. Consider the following sentences, in which *quickly* modifies the verb *scaled* and *too* modifies *quickly:*

A. Antonio *quickly* scaled the ladder.

B. *Too quickly* for safety, Antonio scaled the ladder.

Many adverbs are created by adding *-ly* to an adjective (*boldly* from *bold, happily* from *happy*), but many do not end in *-ly* (*then, sometimes, very, too*). (For more on adverbs, see Chapter 25.)

Prepositions

Prepositions come before nouns or pronouns, with which they combine in **prepositional phrases.** Many prepositions indicate location (*in, on, near*), but some do not (*during, except, despite*). Prepositional phrases function as adjectives (the skateboard *with* the broken wheel) and as adverbs (hiked *up* the mountain path).

PREPOSITIONS THAT SHOW LOCATION			OTHER PREPOSITIONS
above	beyond	onto	despite
against	by	opposite	during
ahead of	down	out of	except
along	from	outside	for
alongside	in	over	in addition to
among	in front of	past	instead of
around	inside	through	till
at	into	to	until
at the side (end)	near	toward	with
behind	next to	under	without
below	off	up	
beside	on	upon	
between			

HINT: Memorizing common prepositions will help you identify prepositional phrases.

Conjunctions

HINT: The acronym FANBOYS can help you remember the coordinating conjunctions.

Like prepositions, conjunctions connect sentence parts. The seven **coordinating conjunctions** are used to show an equal relationship between words, phrases, or clauses:

for	and	nor	but	or	yet	so

CONNECTS WORDS   Jesse *and* Frank James were outlaws.

CONNECTS PHRASES   On the playing field *or* in the classroom, we will do our best.

CONNECTS CLAUSES   Florence works at IHOP, *but* Greg works at Dillard's.

Correlative conjunctions also join words, phrases, and clauses but work in pairs. They include *both/and, either/or, neither/nor*, and *not only/but also*.

A. *Neither* eggs *nor* whole milk will clog arteries if consumed in moderation.

B. *Either* that dog goes *or* I go.

Conjunctive adverbs link only clauses, not words or phrases. Notice that they can express a relationship of ideas across sentences. Common conjunctive adverbs include *however, therefore, nevertheless, in fact*, and *consequently*.

A. I'm going to the symphony; *however*, Allen is going to the Pearl Jam concert.

B. I'm going to the symphony. Allen, *however*, is going to the Pearl Jam concert.

HINT: Memorizing a conjunction like *because* will help you remember the larger group of conjunctions.

The three types of conjunctions discussed so far link main clauses; **subordinating conjunctions,** in contrast, connect a subordinate clause to a main clause. (For more on main and subordinate clauses, see pp. 528–530.) A subordinating conjunction, then, signals an unequal relationship between the clauses: The subordinate clause, which it introduces, is less important in the sentence and cannot stand alone but needs the main clause to complete its meaning.

A. *Because* it is 95 degrees out, I am heading for the pool.

B. I am heading for the pool *because* it is 95 degrees out.

Here is a list of common subordinating conjunctions:

SUBORDINATING CONJUNCTIONS

after	as though	in order that	so that	whenever
although	because	now that	though	where
as	before	once	till	whereas
as if	even though	rather than	until	wherever
as long as	if	since	when	while

Interjections

Interjections are words used to express emotion. Mild interjections are set off with a comma ("*Well,* I won't be going to the movie"), and more emphatic ones are punctuated with an exclamation point ("*Oh, no!* Sophie forgot the tickets").

Identifying the Part of Speech a Word Belongs To

Teaching Idea
To help students identify parts of speech, try grouping them into these four categories: naming words (nouns/pronouns), action or being words (verbs), describing words (adjectives/ adverbs), and connecting words (conjunctions/ prepositions).

Identifying the part of speech a word belongs to is often fairly easy, and memorizing some of the "cue" words listed will help you. However, some words belong to more than one part of speech, and we therefore need to look carefully at their use in a particular sentence. For example, we can *light* a fire (verb), turn on a *light* (noun), or feel a *light* breeze (adjective). The best way to identify a word's part of speech is to think about how it *functions:* Does it name, describe, show action or being, connect, or express emotion?

ACTIVITY 20.1 Using Parts of Speech

Fill in the blanks with the type of word indicated in parentheses at the end of the sentence.

EXAMPLE
My whole family ___loves___ to go to the Renaissance Festival. (action verb)
Answers will vary.

1. Sharks ___swim___ in the deep, cold water of Monterey Bay. (action verb)

2. During the storm, a ___branch___ broke from the elm tree in our front yard. (noun)

3. The sound from the furnace would ___mysteriously___ disappear and then begin again. (adverb)

4. Hang gliding is a ___dangerous___ sport. (adjective)

5. Wild Bill Hickok was shot and killed ___in___ Deadwood ___at___ the age of 39. (prepositions)

6. Adolf Hitler was a dictator. ___He___ was responsible for the deaths of millions. (personal pronoun)

7. Honduras ___and___ Guatemala are both Central American countries. (coordinating conjunction)

8. Benjamin Franklin, ___who___ was one of the Founding Fathers, lived to be 84. (relative pronoun)

9. ___Although___ football is popular in America, soccer has more followers worldwide. (subordinating conjunction)

10. Just before the performance, Pavarotti ___seemed___ unwell. (being verb)

Recognizing the Verbs and Subjects of Simple Sentences

Teaching Idea
Being able to identify subjects and verbs is critical for students struggling to overcome sentence boundary and internal punctuation problems. Even after you leave this chapter behind, it helps to ask students periodically in class to identify the subjects and verbs in their sentences.

Knowing the parts of speech should make sentences seem less mysterious. To form sentences, of course, we don't need all the parts of speech. In fact, we can form a one-word sentence—"Stop!" As long as we have both a subject (in this case, *you* is understood as the subject) and a verb, and they represent a complete thought, we have a sentence. In this section, then, we focus on recognizing the basic parts of a **simple sentence** (sentence with one main clause): the subject—often a noun or pronoun—and verb. (For more on sentence types, see pp. 532–536.)

Simple sentences in English are usually ordered with the subject (S) coming before the verb (V), which is followed by the object (O), or word receiving the action, if there is one:

      S   V   O
      Eric cooked dinner.

Knowing this word order will help you find verbs and subjects and thus help you decide where a simple sentence begins and ends.

Recognizing Verbs

As we have seen, verbs include action words (*work*) and state-of-being words (*be, seem*). (They also include helping words such as *be, do,* and *have,* discussed further below.) One way to find verbs, then, is to ask which word shows action or state of being.

HINT: To recognize verbs, look for words that change their form to show tense.

Another is to ask which words change form to show tense: present, past, or future. You can test for tense by including the words *today, yesterday,* and *tomorrow.* Consider, for example, the sentence "Michael plays with his children":

A. Today, Michael *plays* with his children.

B. Yesterday, Michael *played* with his children.

C. Tomorrow, Michael *will play* with his children.

Because *play* changes form, it has tense and so is a verb.

Identifying verbs becomes more complicated when a simple sentence has several verbs. This can occur for two reasons.

First, we often use **compound verbs,** or two-part verbs, to create variety and concision (see Chapter 18). These two-part verbs can be hard to spot:

> Margaret skipped her lunch *but* later regretted it.

HINT: No comma is used with compound verbs.

CAUTION! Keep verb phrases together unless the sentence sounds most natural with the adverb after a helping verb. "Brian has quickly forgotten every answer on the exam" sounds less stilted than "Brian quickly has forgotten every answer on the exam."

Teaching Idea
You might want to mention the present progressive tense here to head off possible confusion with the participial phrase.

Simple sentences with compound verbs often use the coordinating conjunctions *and* and *but*, so be alert for these conjunctions.

Second, as we have seen, the main verb of a sentence often follows a helping verb like *be, do, have, may, might, must, can, could, should,* or *would.* Together they form verb phrases such as *"might have been singing"* or *"will be starting."* The verbs in these phrases sometimes become divided, often by an adverb, as in "Brian has quickly forgotten every answer on the exam."

Life gets even more complicated when we both split verb phrases and compound the verbs, as in the following sentence:

> I will soon be starting back to college and will probably enjoy all my classes.

Keeping these complications in mind will help you identify the subjects, verbs, and sentence boundaries of potentially tricky simple sentences like these.

One final factor can complicate the identification of verbs: Certain other word groups, called **verbals,** are easy to mistake for verbs because they look much like them. Notice that the italicized words in the following sentences are *not* verbs:

A. Jennifer has barely escaped *dieting* herself into a coma.

B. We are often told to *fend* for ourselves.

We will discuss verbals later in the chapter, but for now just remember that these kinds of words, which often have an *-ing* ending (diet*ing*) or a *to* beginning (*to* fend), are *never* the verbs in a sentence.

Recognizing Subjects

Subjects in sentences are usually nouns or pronouns located in front of a verb and answering the question of who or what is performing the action or experiencing the state.

<pre>
    S   V
</pre>
Glinda saved Dorothy from a sleeping spell.

Who saved Dorothy? Glinda. Glinda is the subject of the sentence.

As with verbs, there are various complications in identifying subjects. The subject of a simple sentence can be a compound subject, with two parts, as in sentence A, or even more, as in sentence B:

A. *Dorothy* and the *lion* became friends.

B. *Dorothy,* the *lion,* the *scarecrow,* and the *tin man* became friends.

Sometimes subjects have a describing phrase before, after, or within them:

C. *Dorothy*, a young girl from Kansas, and the *lion*, the *scarecrow*, and the

tin man became friends.

You might also write a sentence with one or more phrases as the subject (for more on phrases, see pp. 523–528):

INFINITIVE PHRASE   *To return* to Kansas was Dorothy's dream.

GERUND PHRASE   *Returning* to Kansas was Dorothy's dream.

There are several other situations that can make finding subjects more difficult. First, in command sentences, we often omit the subject:

Pass the salt, please.

In such sentences, the subject is understood to be *you*, the person who is expected to perform the command or request.

Second, in sentences that begin with the words *there* and *here*, the subject follows the verb, and in sentences that ask questions, the subject follows a helping verb:

A. There are four boys in the courtyard.

B. Here lies my best friend.

C. Will you come with me?

In this instance, simply rearrange the sentence mentally, putting the subject back into its usual slot.

A. Four boys are in the courtyard.

B. My best friend lies here.

C. You will come with me.

Finally, it is easy to mistake as subjects the nouns and pronouns within prepositional phrases attached to the subject:

A. The bitter taste [*of lemon peels*] makes him want to spit.

B. One [*of the girls*] wants anchovies on her pizza.

In these sentences, the nouns *peels* and *girls* cannot be subjects because they are within prepositional phrases. Since subjects *never* appear in prepositional phrases, one way of finding subjects is by mentally crossing out prepositional phrases in the subject part of the sentence.

It can also be hard to spot subjects and verbs in sentences with more than one clause, such as the following complex sentence:

subordinate clause   main clause (= simple sentence)
Although he did not run in it, Arthur watched the marathon on TV.

Each clause has a subject and a verb, and later in this chapter, we will look more closely at subjects and verbs in multiple clauses. (For more on verbs and subjects, see Chapter 23.)

Teaching Idea
Confusing subjects with nouns or pronouns in prepositional phrases is so common that you might want to write several more examples on the board. Students will find more help in the section "Subject/Verb Agreement" in Chapter 23.

ACTIVITY 20.2 Locating Verbs and Subjects

In the following sentences, underline the subject or subjects once and the verb or verbs twice. Look for the word(s) that expresses action or state of being, and then ask who or what is performing the action or experiencing the state of being.

EXAMPLE

Over the years, Clint Eastwood has become a fine director.

1. The United States still welcomes people from all over the world.
2. There are three good reasons not to take this trip.
3. Protecting the watershed of the river will help to protect the river itself.
4. One of the team's most outstanding players was awarded a scholarship to Michigan State.
5. To pilot commercial jets has always been Teresa's dream.
6. Montana and Wyoming are fighting more than the typical fires of a dry summer and are hoping for a quick end to their troubles.
7. Why has Hollywood seemingly lost interest in making classic westerns?
8. Warren might have quickly started the car but, in his nervousness, dropped the keys.
9. Please open the blinds and raise the window.
10. Residents of Central America and South America sometimes wonder about and resent the habit of many U.S. citizens of referring to themselves as Americans.

NOTE: In number 9, the subject *you* is understood.

Phrases

Teaching Idea
To reinforce comma usage—particularly for beginnings, middles, and ends of sentences—you can frequently point out how the rules apply to the phrases and clauses students are studying.

Knowing subjects and verbs will help you distinguish between clauses and phrases, the two word groups that make up sentences.

A **clause** includes a subject and a verb, whereas a **phrase** is missing a subject or a verb, or both. Because phrases can work as nouns, adjectives, or adverbs, knowing these parts of speech will help you manage phrases in sentences and will help you with their punctuation.

Here we will explore six kinds of phrases: prepositional, infinitive, participial, gerund, absolute, and appositive. (For more on phrases, see Chapter 18.)

Prepositional Phrases

Teaching Idea
Students often feel that sentence grammar is incomprehensible because sentence parts seem to have "no logic," that they can be moved here and there at random. It helps to stress that adverbial modifiers are the most maneuverable parts and that they can be identified by their function, answering the questions *when, where, why, how,* and *to what extent.*

A **prepositional phrase** begins with a preposition (*in, on, of, by*), ends with a noun or pronoun, and works as an adjective or adverb. Notice that prepositional phrases answer the same kinds of questions as do adjectives and adverbs.

ADJECTIVE

TELLS WHICH ONE   The pickup truck *with* the cracked windshield is mine.

TELLS WHO   The girl *in* the blue silk blouse is my date.

ADVERB

TELLS WHERE   Houdini escaped many times *from inside* a locked safe.

TELLS WHEN   Arthur talked *during* the whole movie.

TELLS HOW   I struggled out of bed this morning *with* great difficulty.

Prepositional phrases functioning as adverbs are often easy to move, for more sentence variety, clarity, and emphasis. Notice that we could reposition the prepositional phrase in any of the three sentences above. For example:

A. *With* great difficulty I struggled out of bed this morning.

B. I struggled out of bed *with* great difficulty this morning.

Sentences that begin with two or more prepositional phrases require a comma.

Infinitive Phrases

An infinitive can be formed by putting the word *to* in front of any base verb—for instance, *to run, to love,* or *to think.* Infinitives, along with gerunds and participles, are called **verbals** because they are verb forms that have a sense of action but do not function as verbs.

Infinitive phrases are formed by adding words, often nouns, after the infinitive: "*to run* a marathon," "*to love* one's country," "*to think* deep thoughts." Infinitives and infinitive phrases work as adjectives, adverbs, or nouns:

ADJECTIVE

DESCRIBES NOUN   Paula has a proposal *to present*.

ADVERB

DESCRIBES VERB   We practiced long hours *to win* the basketball game.

NOUN

IS SUBJECT   *To reach* the top was his driving ambition.

As with prepositional phrases, infinitive phrases that function as adverbs can often be moved within a sentence. For example, we could recast the adverb sentence like this: "*To win* the basketball game, we practiced long hours." Introductory adverbial infinitive phrases require a comma.

Participial Phrases

Participial phrases begin with either a present participle (base verb with *-ing*) or past participle (base verb with *-d/-ed/-n*). (For more on participles, see Chapter 23.) Participials can be single-word modifiers of nouns: *struggling* soldiers, *crashing* waves, *wrinkled* jacket, *forgotten* memory. As phrases, too, participials often work as adjectives. As in many of the following examples, they often include prepositional phrases:

PRESENT PARTICIPIAL PHRASE

A. *Skimming* close to the ground, the swallow caught a cricket in midhop.

B. Jamie bought 50 more lottery tickets, *praying* for a miracle.

C. The salesclerk *chewing* gum was the one who ignored me for 10 minutes.

PAST PARTICIPIAL PHRASE

A. *Exhausted* from three final exams in one day, Marilyn fell asleep in her seat.

B. Devin vowed to play his hardest, *thrilled* to finally be on the team.

HINT: Nonessential phrases, as in sentences A and B, require a comma.

HINT: Essential phrases, as in both C sentences, do not use a comma.

C. A bluegill *caught* on ultralight tackle can put up quite a battle.

Participial phrases can be *essential* to the meaning of the word they are describing, as they are in the two c sentences above, or *nonessential*, as they are in the two a and b sentences. (For more on punctuating essential and nonessential phrases, see Chapter 26.)

Nonessential phrases are set off with commas, and they can often be repositioned. For example, we might move the participial phrase in sentence B:

A. *Thrilled* to finally be on the team, Devin vowed to play his hardest.

B. Devin, *thrilled* to finally be on the team, vowed to play his hardest.

When shifting nonessential participial phrases, keep them close to the noun you want them to describe so as to prevent misreading. For example, the participial phrase in sentence A might seem to describe the cricket if recast this way:

The swallow caught a cricket in midhop, *skimming* close to the ground.

Also be wary of dangling and misplaced phrases that clearly modify the wrong word:

Skimming close to the ground, a cricket was caught by a swallow in midhop.

Gerund Phrases

The gerund, another kind of verbal, is formed by adding *-ing* to a base verb and is used as a noun—for example, *backpacking, swimming,* and *laughing*. **Gerund phrases** begin with a gerund and include other words. As shown in the following examples, gerunds and gerund phrases may appear in several places in a sentence:

A. *Backpacking* is a strenuous sport.

B. *Backpacking* in the Bob Marshall Wilderness is an unforgettable experience.

C. Ellen enjoys *laughing* at life's idiotic moments.

Although gerunds and many participials end in *-ing,* the gerund functions as a noun rather than as an adjective. Notice that the gerunds in sentences A and B are subjects and that the gerund in sentence c is an object. To see this difference between gerund and participial phrases, compare the following sentences:

PARTICIPIAL PHRASE *Backpacking* in the Bob Marshall Wilderness, Pauline learned the meaning of rugged.

GERUND PHRASE *Backpacking* in the Bob Marshall Wilderness is an unforgettable experience.

The first sentence uses *backpacking* as an adjective that tells about Pauline, the subject of the main part of the sentence; therefore, the phrase is a participial. The second sentence uses *backpacking* as the subject, so the phrase is a gerund. Whereas the participial phrase must be set off by a comma, the gerund phrase cannot be.

Absolute Phrases

The **absolute phrase** resembles a participial phrase in that it uses a present or past participle (*-ing* or *-d/-ed/-n*), but it differs in an important respect: A noun or pronoun always precedes the participle. Absolute phrases describe the rest of

HINT: No comma is used with gerunds or gerund phrases.

the sentence they are attached to, rather than a single word. For this reason, they can be in different places in a sentence, as shown by the following examples:

ABSOLUTE PHRASE—PRESENT

A. [The <u>wind</u> *blowing* steadily from the south,] we knew that the warm weather would last.

B. Coco said goodbye to her homeland forever, [her <u>eyes</u> *streaming* tears].

ABSOLUTE PHRASE—PAST

HINT: Absolute phrases require a comma.

C. Adam tried to appear at attention, [his <u>arm</u> *raised* in a stiff salute].

D. [The <u>thief</u> finally *locked* in a cell,] everyone felt more at ease.

You can create an absolute phrase by omitting a helping verb. For instance, without the *is*, the stand-alone sentence "The <u>wind is blowing</u> steadily from the south" becomes the absolute phrase in sentence A above.

Absolute phrases, like nonessential participial phrases, must be set off with a comma.

Appositive Phrases

An **appositive phrase** is a word group that renames a noun or pronoun. Appositives usually follow the word they are describing, but if describing the subject, they can be useful as sentence openers.

Most appositives are nonessential—giving useful but not vital information. Therefore, as with all nonessential material, we use commas. Here are several examples:

A. The <u>dolphin</u>, a *mammal*, lives in family units called pods.

B. A *mammal*, the <u>dolphin</u> lives in family units called pods.

C. The <u>dolphin</u>, a *mammal* known as a cetacean, lives in family units called pods.

HINT: Appositives usually require commas.

D. The <u>dolphin</u>, a *mammal* known as a cetacean that is still killed in large numbers by tuna fishers, lives in family units called pods.

In each case, the underlined appositive tells the reader a bit more about dolphins. These phrases are a handy way to add ideas or comments without distracting readers too much from the main flow of thought.

ACTIVITY 20.3 Identifying Phrases

Over each underlined phrase, write the type of phrase. Don't be confused when you find several phrases within a word group. Look at the overall structure, that is, at how the words work as a unit. For example, "Slipping on the ice, Ben fell" includes a prepositional phrase, "on the ice," within a participial phrase.

EXAMPLE

infinitive phrase

<u>To make it through her study session</u>, Jody drank two pots of coffee.

participial phrase
1. Perched on Jasmine's shoulder, the cockatiel always felt secure.

 gerund phrase   *prepositional phrase*
2. Jumping out of a plane is not Ethan's idea of a relaxing weekend.

 infinitive phrase
3. To find better jobs, many adults long out of school are returning.

 participial phrase   *prepositional phrase*
4. The new Corvette, redlining at 7,000 rpms, smoked down the interstate.

 participial phrases
5. Frantically chasing his tail, the puppy became so dizzy that he fell down.

 appositive phrase
6. Robert Downey, Jr., a man with questionable judgment and bad luck, is out of prison and looking for work.

 prepositional phrases
7. On a trip from Chicago to Denver, Joanne was stranded in airports for 36 hours.

 appositive phrase   *infinitive phrase*
8. Internet advertising, mostly obnoxious junk mail, continues to flood into our homes.

 gerund phrase
9. Having clear goals in life helps people succeed.

 participial phrase   *absolute phrase*
10. Stepping quietly into the room, his pipe glowing dimly, Holmes
 prepositional phrase
surveyed the scene of the murder.

ACTIVITY 20.4 Creating Phrases

Complete each sentence with the type of phrase(s) indicated in parentheses. Notice the use of commas with the phrases in these sentences.

EXAMPLE
Lilly sat (prepositional phrases) _at the end of the pier_ and waited.
Answers will vary.

1. In the morning Anna went (prepositional phrases) _out to the edge of the dock_.

2. _Dancing until 3:00 a.m._ (participial phrase), Lauren and Roy had the best evening of their lives.

3. _His stomach rumbling loudly_ (absolute phrase), Roger was so hungry that he nearly fainted.

4. _To reach their base camp_ (infinitive phrase), the climbers had to struggle up the cliff face till nearly dusk.

5. _Jogging for 30 minutes_ (gerund phrase) is good aerobic exercise.

ACTIVITY 20.7 Identifying Sentence Types

Underline each clause, and above it write its type (main clause or noun, adjective, or adverb clause). At the end of the sentence, write the sentence type (simple, compound, complex, or compound–complex). Remember that the type of sentence depends on the number and kind (main or subordinate) of clauses.

EXAMPLE

main clause   adverb clause
Children love to draw and paint from the earliest ages, and if adults

main clause
continue to encourage them, children will often carry their artistic

interests into adulthood. *Compound complex*

adverb clause   main clause
1. Although swimming is not the best sport for losing weight, it can be a

great aerobic workout. *Complex*

main clause   main clause
2. Carp are said by some to be delicious, but a person must know how

to prepare the fish properly. *Compound*

main clause
3. Many companies in the United States use underpaid foreign labor to

cut costs. *Simple*

main clause
4. Many trial lawyers are experts at bending the truth to help their

clients. *Simple*

adverb clause   main clause
5. Because scooters are becoming popular again, skateboarders and

roller bladers will have to make more room on the sidewalks and in

the streets for them. *Complex*

main clause   noun clause   adverb clause
6. I used to think that David was slow moving until I saw him jump up

from his chair to shake a centipede off his bare arm. *Complex*

main clause
7. Playing an instrument is a good way to learn music and bring joy

into a person's life. *Simple*

main clause   adjective clause   main clause continued
8. Fireflies, which are also called lightning bugs, produce their glow

through a process known as bioluminescence. *Complex*

adverb clause   main clause
9. When the weather permits, I love to grill just about anything out on

main clause
my deck, but my favorite food is hamburgers. *Compound-complex*

main clause   adverb clause   main clause
10. Jet planes cannot glide well, so if the engines malfunction, the plane

continued
is likely to crash. *Compound-complex*

ACTIVITY 20.8 Using Phrases and Clauses to Improve Readability

Review A Writer's Basic Sentence Grammar on pp. 536–537, and then discuss how to improve the clarity and flow of sentences in the following narrative. Keeping all the main ideas, revise the narrative by combining sentences and adding connecting words where needed (prepositions, such as *in, on,* and *near;* conjunctions, such as *because, when, and,* and *but;* and relative pronouns, such as *who, which,* and *that* will be particularly useful). Also try using -*ing* phrases ("closing the car door"). Leave the dialogue alone, and keep some short sentences for emphasis. Check your commas.

Teaching Idea

To expedite Activity 20.8, be sure that students review the sentence grammar chart. Then you can list several "cue" words on the board—prepositions, conjunctions, and relative pronouns. After students have written part or all of a paragraph, you might have them read their version aloud while you note similar sentence-combining strategies on the board.

To help with punctuation, you can give students the comma editing sheet included in the Instructor's Manual.

EXAMPLE

My older brother Jason should be on a special show called *America's Dumbest Criminals.* One night in May of 1998, Jason and his best friend, Ken, found a new white Nissan with the keys left in the door in the neighbor's driveway. This was temptation they could not resist. . . .

Answers will vary.

America's Dumbest Criminal?

My older brother Jason should be on a special show called *America's Dumbest Criminals.* One night in May of 1998, Jason found a new white Nissan. His best friend, Ken, was with him too. The car was in the neighbor's driveway. The car had the keys left in the door. This was temptation they could not resist.

"Hey, look at this," Jason said. "What an idiot to forget your keys."

"Yeah, it's their own fault if we borrow their car," replied Ken.

Both boys jumped in the car. Jason sat on the garage door opener. The door raised.

"Oh, crap!" Jason yelled. They leapt out of the car. Then they ran back home.

They watched the neighbors' house. They didn't see anyone reacting. Jason and Ken thought they were safe to try again. This time they figured they would be smart. They would bring along gloves to mask fingerprints. They climbed back into the car. Once again Jason sat on the garage door opener.

"Dammit, man!" Ken said. They were hiding in some nearby bushes. Still no one was stirring in the house. They tried for the Nissan again. This was the third time. This time they succeeded. So, off they went on their "well-planned" expedition.

They reached the major roads. Ken began to get paranoid. "Man, we just passed a cop. We're gonna get caught!"

"Shut up, dude," ordered Jason. "We're cool. How are they gonna know? The people are still asleep, remember?"

"Uhh . . ." said Ken, "because we're driving around with white gloves on, and it looks a little odd, don't you think?"

"Well then, we'll just take them off," Jason replied.

"Yeah, but when they get the car back, our fingerprints will be all over it."

Jason and Ken idled at a stoplight for a minute. My brother came up with his next brilliant suggestion. They would buy some Armor-All. Then they would wipe off all their fingerprints. Then they would park the car a few blocks from the owner's house. Well, they managed to clean the car half way up. They congratulated themselves on getting away with it. They taped the car key to the hood. Then they walked home.

But Jason had forgotten his gloves. Jason panicked. They went back to the car for them. But someone had called the police. The boys were arrested. Their situation got worse. They had parked across a city line. So they were prosecuted by two cities.

Older brothers and sisters are supposed to set an example. This is one older and "wiser" brother I learned never to follow.

A WRITER'S BASIC SENTENCE GRAMMAR

Having learned and practiced recognizing the basic sentence parts in this chapter, you now know more about how to control sentences. Words (parts of speech) build phrases; phrases grow into or are attached to clauses; clauses are sentences or are attached to them. Knowing how words work—to express action or state of being, name, describe, or link—you can now confidently revise your sentences to best express your meaning.

The following chart summarizes key sentence parts:

WORDS (8 KINDS)

verb, noun, pronoun, adjective, adverb, preposition, conjunction, interjection

PHRASES (6 KINDS)

prepositional, infinitive, participial, gerund, absolute, appositive

HINT: Words that begin prepositional phrases include *to, of, on, near, under, around, beside, against, at, by,* and *in.*

1. **Prepositional:** Phrase beginning with a preposition and ending with a noun or pronoun—used as adjective or adverb

   Example: "Erik ran *down* the hall and *through* the door."

2. **Infinitive:** Phrase beginning with *to* + base verb—used as a noun, adjective, or adverb

   Example: "*To arrive* at class on time, Erik finally set his alarm."

3. **Participial:** Phrase beginning with base verb + *-ing* or *-d/-ed/-n*—used as an adjective

   Example: "*Running* fast, Erik made it to class on time."

4. **Gerund:** Phrase beginning with an *-ing* word—used as a noun

   Example: "*Running* fast always wore Erik out."

5. **Absolute:** Phrase beginning with a noun followed by base verb + *-ing* or *-d/-ed/-n*—describes whole sentence

   Example: "Erik raced toward class, the door *closing* just in front of him."

6. **Appositive:** Phrase that renames a noun or pronoun—used as an adjective

   Example: "Erik, a chronic *oversleeper*, raced down the hall as the bell rang."

CLAUSES (2 KINDS)

main and subordinate (3 kinds): noun, adjective, adverb

1. **Main:** Clause with a complete thought—stands by itself

   Example: "Fran likes cheese pizza."

2. **Subordinate:** Clause without a complete thought—used with a main clause

   - **Noun:** Clause used as subject, object, or complement

     Example: "*That* Fran likes cheese pizza is obvious to everyone."

   - **Adjective:** Clause that follows and describes a noun or pronoun

     Example: "Fran, *who* is a close friend of mine, likes cheese pizza."

   - **Adverb:** Clause that describes a whole sentence

     Example: "*When* she goes to Italian Delight, Fran likes to eat cheese pizza."

HINT: Words that begin adjective clauses include *who, which,* and *that.*

HINT: Words that begin adverb clauses include *because, as, if, although, since, when, while, after, before,* and *until.*

SENTENCES (4 KINDS)

simple, compound, complex, compound–complex

1. **Simple:** "Aaron likes ice cream."

2. **Compound:** "Aaron likes ice cream, *so* he eats a lot of it."

3. **Complex:** "Aaron likes ice cream *because* it tastes sweet."

4. **Compound–complex:** "Aaron likes ice cream *because* it tastes sweet, *so* he eats a lot of it."

HINT: Words that join main clauses include *and, but, so, or, yet, nor,* and *for.*

HINT: The type and number of clauses determine the type of sentence.

CHAPTER 21

Coordination, Subordination, and Parallelism

What Are We Trying to Achieve and Why?

Chapter 20 helped us understand the parts of a sentence—what they are and how they work. This chapter takes us one step further, helping us understand the important role coordination, subordination, and parallelism play in ordering the ideas in a sentence.

Not everything in a sentence has equal weight, so writers need to signal when they expect the audience to pay special attention to some point.

- **Coordination** gives roughly *equal weight* to ideas.
- **Subordination** *stresses one idea* while deemphasizing another.
- **Parallelism** uses *similar structures* to achieve clarity and emphasis.

Chapter 21 will show you how to use each of these strategies in your writing.

Coordination

Using Coordination

When writers use **coordination,** they rely mainly on **coordinating conjunctions** (*and, but, or, so, yet, for, nor*) to link roughly equivalent sentence parts: words,

Coordination and Subordination

HINT: You should usually use a comma before the coordinating conjunction in a compound sentence.

Teaching Idea
You might discuss coordination and subordination in terms of general intellectual development. Children begin by speaking and then progress to writing, relying heavily on coordination. As they mature and their communication becomes more sophisticated, they begin to subordinate more. Of course, excessive coordination or subordination can make for difficult reading.

phrases, and clauses. When we say, "I'm going to the store to pick up some bread *and* milk," we are coordinating the two words *bread* and *milk* by using the word *and*. The two items are equally important. We might use the conjunction *or* to link two single words: "I'm going to the store to pick up Coke *or* Sprite." Again the linked words, *Coke* and *Sprite*, have the same value.

We regularly coordinate phrases as well as single words: "I'm in the mood *to crank* up the stereo *and to rock* till dawn." The infinitive phrases beginning with *to crank* and *to rock* are joined by the word *and*. Or we might say, "I am going to vote *in the morning or in the evening*." In this sentence, *or* links two prepositional phrases.

Few of us have problems in writing with linking words or phrases, but clauses can be more difficult. When we coordinate sentences with two or more main clauses—unless the clauses are very short—we should use a comma before the coordinating conjunction, as in the following examples:

A. Hitchhiking used to be looked on as an adventure, *but* it was always a risky way to travel.

B. Many of the Marlboro men have given up smoking, *or* they have died from it.

C. The Buffalo River, in Arkansas, has some of the most beautiful bluffs in the Ozarks, *so* be sure to bring your camera when you go.

It is important to choose the conjunction that expresses the relationship you want to show between main clauses. For example, sentence A would not communicate well if you tried to use *and, or, so, for,* or *nor* in place of *but.*

Sometimes, instead of using a coordinating conjunction, you can show coordination with a semicolon:

He quit his job; he was not fired.

You can also connect the two clauses with a semicolon and a **conjunctive adverb** such as *however, therefore, nevertheless, in fact,* or *consequently*. Conjunctive adverbs add emphasis or explain the connection, as in the following sentence:

He was not fired; *in fact,* he quit his job.

Note the semicolon before and the comma after *in fact.*

ACTIVITY 21.1 Coordinating Sentences

Choose the best coordinating conjunction for the following sentences, and write it in the space provided.

EXAMPLE
Maria adopted a Korean baby, ___*and*___ both have been happy ever since.

1. Life as a single person has many rewards, ___*but/yet*___ it can be terribly lonely.

2. Michael Johnson strained a hamstring, ___*so*___ he could not run the 200-meter in the Sydney Olympics.

3. Danny does not regret his decision to leave town, ___*nor*___ does Elaine regret her decision asking him to.

4. Skin cancer is frightening, ___*for*___ once the disease penetrates the lymph nodes, it is difficult to cure.

Below is a list of subordinating conjunctions that begin adverb clauses (for more on adverb clauses, see pp. 530–532):

SUBORDINATING CONJUNCTIONS

after	as though	in order that	so that	whenever
although	because	now that	though	where
as	before	once	till	whereas
as if	even though	rather than	until	wherever
as long as	if	since	when	while

ACTIVITY 21.2 Subordinating with Adverb Clauses

Fill in the blanks in the following sentences with clauses that work with the given subordinating conjunction. To be sure you have written a subordinate clause, underline the verb in each subordinate clause twice and the subject once.

EXAMPLE
When _____ I finish my homework _____, I will give you a call.
Answers will vary.

1. If _Donald survives the last mile of the marathon without collapsing from a heart attack_, he swears he will hang up his running shoes for good.

2. After _my friends arrive_, we will party till the refrigerator is empty.

3. Although _I have never thought of myself as much of a writer_, this composition class has given me new hope.

4. Once _Shawn's mom gets the sump pump working_, we can drain the basement.

5. I didn't realize that Gary Larson was truly demented until _I saw his cartoon of the chicken carrying a baby toward the chicken pen._

6. _Hugh is majoring in business,_ so that he will be marketable when he graduates.

7. _As Western medicine continues to advance_, some practitioners are looking to medicine of the East for solutions.

8. Write three sentences that contain an adverb clause. Remember to use a comma only to set off adverb clauses that *begin* sentences.
Answers will vary.

A. _____

B. _____

C. _____

Adjective Clauses

Almost as useful as adverb clauses for subordinating ideas within sentences are **adjective** (or **relative**) **clauses,** which generally begin with the relative pronouns *who, which,* or *that.* While adverb clauses work as adverbs (telling *when, why, where, how,* and *to what degree or extent*), adjective clauses work as adjectives, meaning that they describe nouns and pronouns, answering the questions *which one; how many;* and *what kind, shape, color, texture,* or *condition.*

Adjective clauses may be *essential* or *nonessential* to the meaning of a sentence. In both cases, though, they help condense information, making sentences more economical and fluid. Here are several examples. (for more on essential versus nonessential adjective clauses, see pp. 529–530):

HINT: Nonessential clauses require commas.

NONESSENTIAL ADJECTIVE CLAUSES

A. The mockingbird has an amazing range of musical voices.

The mockingbird is common to the Midwest.

The mockingbird, *which* is common to the Midwest, has an amazing range of musical voices.

B. Paul Bunyan is said to have created the Grand Canyon by dragging his ax along the ground one day.

Paul Bunyan is a giant out of folklore.

Paul Bunyan, *who* is a giant out of folklore, is said to have created the Grand Canyon by dragging his ax along the ground one day.

Neither of the underlined adjective clauses is essential to the meaning of the main part of the sentence, so they are enclosed with commas.

HINT: Essential clauses are not set off with commas.

ESSENTIAL ADJECTIVE CLAUSES

A. The woman is my sister.

The woman is wearing a bright red scarf.

The woman *who* is wearing a bright red scarf is my sister.

B. The Camaro ended up on its side in a ditch.

The Camaro almost got away from the highway patrol.

The Camaro *that* almost got away from the highway patrol ended up on its side in a ditch.

Both of the underlined adjective clauses are essential to the meaning of the main part of the sentence, so they are *not* enclosed with commas.

ACTIVITY 21.3 Subordinating with Adjective Clauses

Fill in the blanks in the following sentences with an appropriate clause. Note that commas are used to set off the nonessential clauses but not the essential clauses.

EXAMPLE

My best friend, <u>who has put himself and his children through school</u>, will graduate from college in the spring.

Answers will vary.

1. Paul Newman, who _____has given much money to charity_____, is still a fine actor.

2. Baseball is still the game that _____most defines the United States_____.

3. Babe Ruth is a baseball icon who _____hit 60 home runs in 1927_____.

4. SUVs that _____come equipped with four-wheel drive_____ are driven by many people who would never consider taking them off-road.

5. The Trojan Horse, which _____allowed the Greeks to enter Troy_____, was left outside the walls of Troy and presumed by the Trojans to be a gift from the gods.

6. Ireland is a country that _____has given birth to many fine poets, singers, and songwriters_____.

7. The Three Stooges were slapstick comedians who _____took hundreds of falls to entertain their public_____.

8. Write three sentences that contain adjective clauses. Remember to use commas only to set off nonessential adjective clauses.

Answers will vary.

A. _____

B. _____

C. _____

Avoiding Excessive Subordination

As with coordination, subordination can be too much of a good thing. When a writer puts more ideas into a sentence than readers can sort out, the writing becomes dense. The easy solution to the problem is simply to "unpack" a few of the sentences, splitting them into two or even three parts. Here is an example of overly subordinated writing:

People who are worried about the high risk of heart attack, which can strike both men and women even in their twenties, have several alternatives that can keep them healthy as long as they are willing to abide by some sensible rules for managing their lives in such a way as to bring their LDL cholesterol to within tolerable limits, which can be done through regular exercise and a low-fat diet, neither of which is beyond anyone's capabilities, although having to give up favorite foods can seem like a terrific sacrifice to many people who have made food a central part of their lives.

Now look at this revision:

People who are worried about heart attacks have several alternatives for remaining healthy. If they are willing to abide by some sensible rules (regular exercise and a low-fat diet), they can bring their LDL cholesterol to within tolerable limits. It is true, though, that giving up favorite foods can seem like a terrific sacrifice to many people who have made food a central part of their lives.

Notice that, aside from being clearer, the second version is shorter and more concise, without sacrificing any ideas.

Parallelism

Parallelism

When writers use **parallelism,** a form of coordination, they repeat similar grammatical structures for clarity and emphasis. The words may be in a series, list, or pair and are often connected by a coordinating conjunction like *and* or *but.*

Series

Items in a series should be the same grammatical type—nouns following nouns, verbs following verbs, and so forth—although slight variations are fine. In the third sentence, for instance, "watching television" is a phrase, not a single word.

NOUNS	Be sure to pick up <u>milk</u>, <u>eggs</u>, <u>bread</u>, *and* <u>coffee</u>.
VERBS	I will <u>swim</u>, <u>bike</u>, *and* <u>climb</u> my way through my vacation.
GERUNDS	Daryl plans to spend his vacation <u>reading</u>, <u>watching television</u>, *and* <u>sleeping</u>.
PREPOSITIONAL PHRASES	<u>On the playground</u>, <u>in the halls</u>, *and* <u>in the classroom</u>, the children played nonstop.

You should avoid this kind of nonparallel construction:

NONPARALLEL	Daryl plans to spend his vacation reading, watching television, and <u>he wants to sleep in</u> as much as possible.

There are two ways to make this construction parallel:

PARALLEL	Daryl plans to spend his vacation reading, watching television, and sleeping in as much as possible. (three parallel gerunds)
PARALLEL	Daryl plans to spend his vacation reading and watching television, and he wants to sleep in as much as possible. (parallel pair and separate main clause)

Lists and Outlines

Related to items in a series are lists, especially outlines. All outlines should be in parallel form. A sentence outline uses all sentences. A phrase outline uses the same kind of phrases (prepositional, participial, etc.):

FAULTY PARALLELISM	I. Hawaiian people 　A. The language they speak 　B. Worshipping gods 　C. Their culture

CORRECT
PARALLELISM

    I. Hawaiian people
       A. Language
       B. Religion
       C. Culture

Pairs

You can also use parallelism to balance pairs, usually with a coordinating conjunction, as in the following examples:

A. Bart loved to fish *and* to backpack.

B. As a child, Maryanne learned to whistle like a train *and* to hoot like an owl.

C. Ping-Pong requires fast reflexes *and* long arms.

D. I am going to Seattle by train, *but* Jenny is traveling to the city by boat.

Notice that sentence D is a compound sentence linking two main clauses that mirror one another in grammatical structure: subject, verb, and two prepositional phrases.

You can also use word groups called **correlative conjunctions** to pair ideas, as in the following sentence:

With my tax refund, I will have *either* the house painted *or* the driveway paved.

Here are several common correlative pairs:

either . . . or   neither . . . nor
both . . . and   not only . . . but also

When creating parallel phrases and clauses, you should be sure to include the words needed to balance both parts of the expression, without leaving any words out. In the following nonparallel examples, the first one has an unneeded infinitive, *to make,* and the second is missing the word *long.*

NONPARALLEL   Martin wanted recognition for his hard work rather than to make money.

PARALLEL   Martin wanted recognition for his hard work rather than money.

NONPARALLEL   Ping-Pong requires fast reflexes and arms.

PARALLEL   Ping-Pong requires fast reflexes and long arms.

When you use parallelism in a series, list, or pair, you can leave words out in front of phrases and clauses, as in the following examples:

A. The new beagle puppy chewed on magazines, (on) table legs, and (on) shoes.

B. Marlene ordered a chocolate shake, (a) hamburger, and (a) plate of fries.

C. I learned early to trust my parents, (my) close relatives, and (my) best friends.

D. I hope <u>that</u> my education encourages me to look inward, (that it)

guides me onward, and (that it) carries me upward.

Note that in sentence A, it would be incorrect to write "on magazines, on table legs, and shoes," dropping the final *on*. If you use the first two *on's*, you must finish the series using *on*.

Whether to include the words in parentheses above is an issue of style. Repetition often helps emphasize a point, and some people might find, for example, that sentence D above is more forceful with the *that's* left in.

ACTIVITY 21.4 Creating Parallelism

Complete the following sentences with parallel words, phrases, and clauses.

EXAMPLE
Margaret loves to dance, to ice skate, and _____to bowl_____.
Answers will vary.

1. Singing, writing, and ____painting____ are art forms.

2. Jerome will go either to the mall tonight or ____to the movies____.

3. We all feel unappreciated ____and lonely____ at times.

4. Brett wanted to spend his days surfing rather than to ____be chained to a desk____.

5. Grace is a woman who works hard and who ____is likely to succeed as a result____.

6. Neither the football team nor ____the basketball team____ made the play-off this year.

7. The horse bolted from the stable and then ____headed for the hills____.

8. Write three sentences containing parallel forms:
Answers will vary.

   A. _____

   B. _____

   C. _____

Run-Ons, Comma Splices, and Sentence Fragments

What Are We Trying to Achieve and Why?

Teaching Idea
Searching for a quick fix to their problems, many students rely entirely on periods or commas with coordinating conjunctions to correct comma splices and run-ons. Encourage students to experiment with several methods, including subordination, so they don't end up repairing one problem only to create another—lack of sentence variety.

Chapter 22 focuses on two common sentence problems that often occur in rough drafts: improperly divided and incomplete (fragmented) sentences. When the time comes to edit their work, writers sometimes find that ideas have lapped over onto one another and that it is difficult to determine where one main thought ends and another begins.

The key to determining sentence boundaries, and so to controlling **run-ons, comma splices,** and **fragments,** is locating *verbs* and *subjects,* as we practiced in Chapter 20. As you work through this chapter, make a habit of looking for the action (or state-of-being) word(s) in each sentence—the verb—and then asking yourself who or what is performing the action (or experiencing the state of being)—the subject.

Run-On Sentences and Comma Splices

Run-On Sentences Comma Splices

If two main clauses are run together as a single sentence, without any punctuation, the result is a **run-on** or **fused sentence.** If two sentences have been divided with a comma, the result is a **comma splice.**

Both kinds of errors can present problems for readers, as in the following examples:

RUN-ON   Greg says he will take all three of my shifts next week so I can go to the lake if my dad is in a good mood, he might give me the keys to the boat.

COMMA SPLICE   Greg says he will take all three of my shifts next week so I can go to the lake, if my dad is in a good mood, he might give me the keys to the boat.

When the first main thought ends with the word *lake*, we need to mark the spot with a strong break so readers know that a new main thought is beginning. A comma alone is not strong enough, but we can use one of the following methods:

- **End punctuation:** period, question mark, or exclamation point
- **Comma with coordinating conjunction** (*and, but, so, or, yet, for, nor*)
- **Semicolon**
- **Subordination:** words, phrases, clauses

Fixing Run-Ons and Comma Splices with End Punctuation

The easiest way to fix these two errors is by dividing the sentences with a period or other end punctuation (e.g., question mark or exclamation point).

FIXED   Greg says he will take all three of my shifts next week so I can go to the lake. If my dad is in a good mood, he might give me the keys to the boat.

However, a period is not always the best solution. If the sentences that are run together are short, using a period may create a "choppy" effect, as in the following example:

RUN-ON AND COMMA SPLICE   Paul Moller has been working on an air car for 37 years he is still not close to seeing it lift off the ground. He hopes to have it operational in his lifetime, most people do not think he will make it.

REVISED BUT CHOPPY   Paul Moller has been working on an air car for 37 years. He is still not close to seeing it lift off the ground. He hopes to have it operational in his lifetime. Most people do not think he will make it.

If correcting run-ons or comma splices with end punctuation creates a series of choppy sentences, you should try one of the other methods covered in this chapter. (For more on problems with sentence variety, see Chapter 18.)

Fixing Run-Ons and Comma Splices with Coordination

If a period is not the best choice, you might find that a comma and a **coordinating conjunction** like *and, but, or, so, yet, for,* or *nor* work better. These useful connecting words help readers understand the relationship between clauses.

For example, *and* lets readers know that the clauses are roughly equivalent and not dependent on each other. *But* and *yet* point out contrast, and *so* shows cause and effect. Revising our choppy example from above, we can eliminate the run-on and comma splice by using coordinating conjunctions:

FIXED   Paul Moller has been working on an air car for 37 years, and he is still not close to seeing it lift off the ground. He hopes to have it operational in his lifetime, but most people do not think he will make it.

(For more on coordinating sentences, see Chapter 21.)

Fixing Run-Ons and Comma Splices with Semicolons

A semicolon is an alternative to end punctuation or to a comma and a coordinating conjunction for fixing run-ons and comma splices. If the main ideas in the two clauses are closely related, then a semicolon might be a good choice.

RUN-ON	Knitting is not just for old folks many young people enjoy it too.
COMMA SPLICE	Knitting is not just for old folks, many young people enjoy it too.
FIXED	Knitting is not just for old folks; many young people enjoy it too.

A semicolon is probably the best choice for this sentence because the second main clause completes the statement made in the first clause. These two sentences work as a single unit of thought.

You can also separate the clauses with a semicolon and a **conjunctive adverb,** followed by a comma. Here is an example:

Western medicine has much to offer; *however,* Eastern medicine is also

a valuable resource.

Sometimes the conjunctive adverb can appear *within* a clause rather than between the two main clauses, in which case it is set off by commas:

Western medicine has much to offer; Eastern medicine, *however,* is

also a valuable resource.

Here is a brief list of common conjunctive adverbs: *however, therefore, nevertheless, in fact,* and *consequently.*

Fixing Run-Ons and Comma Splices with Subordination

A method for correcting run-ons and comma splices that also helps you eliminate unneeded words is **subordination.** When subordinating one main clause to another, you focus readers' attention on the idea contained within the main clause. You can change one of the clauses to a subordinate clause, a phrase, or even a single word. (For more on subordination, see Chapter 21.)

Notice the following examples:

RUN-ON	Jamie bought 50 more lottery tickets he was praying for a miracle.
COMMA SPLICE	Jamie bought 50 more lottery tickets, he was praying for a miracle.
FIXED: ADJECTIVE CLAUSE	Jamie, *who* was praying for a miracle, bought 50 more lottery tickets.
PARTICIPIAL PHRASE	Jamie, *praying* for a miracle, bought 50 more lottery tickets.
PARTICIPLE	Jamie, *praying,* bought 50 more lottery tickets.

Each of the revised sentences corrects the error—and eliminates unneeded words.

Here are several other examples that show how you can use subordination to fix problem sentences:

RUN-ON	Some Christmas carolers came to our house we served them hot chocolate.
COMMA SPLICE	Some Christmas carolers came to our house, we served them hot chocolate.
FIXED: ADVERB CLAUSE	*When* some Christmas carolers came to our house, we served them hot chocolate.
ABSOLUTE PHRASE	Some Christmas carolers *coming* to our house, we served them hot chocolate.
RUN-ON	We practiced long hours we wanted to win the basketball game.
COMMA SPLICE	We practiced long hours, we wanted to win the basketball game.
FIXED: ADVERB CLAUSE	*Because* we wanted to win the basketball game, we practiced long hours.
PARTICIPIAL PHASE	*Wanting* to win the basketball game, we practiced long hours.
INFINITIVE PHRASE	*To win* the basketball game, we practiced long hours.
INFINITIVE	*To win,* we practiced long hours.
RUN-ON	I had an unforgettable experience it was backpacking in the Bob Marshall Wilderness.
COMMA SPLICE	I had an unforgettable experience, it was backpacking in the Bob Marshall Wilderness.
FIXED: GERUND PHRASE	*Backpacking* in the Bob Marshall Wilderness was an unforgettable experience.
PREPOSITIONAL PHRASE	*On* my backpacking trip in the Bob Marshall Wilderness, I had an unforgettable experience.

(For help with changing independent clauses to subordinate clauses or phrases, review Chapters 18 and 20.)

ACTIVITY 22.1 Recognizing Run-Ons and Comma Splices

Decide which of the following sentences is correct, a run-on, or a comma splice. Underline each verb twice, ask yourself who or what is doing the action or experiencing the state of being, and then underline each subject once. You will find main clauses and a few subordinate clauses. Draw a line where the main clauses meet, and then at the front of each sentence, write "RO" for run-on, "CS" for comma splice, or "C" for correct.

EXAMPLE

   RO   I was having a great time | I didn't want to go home.

1.   *RO*   I think that I must have eaten too much | I'm feeling a little sick.

5. Although it is expensive, it is a special treat. To eat at the American Restaurant.

   <u>Although it is expensive, it is a special treat to eat at the American</u>
   <u>Restaurant.</u>

6. Two flight attendants were thrown onto the laps of passengers. The plane encountering heavy turbulence.

   <u>The plane encountering heavy turbulence, two flight attendants were</u>
   <u>thrown onto the laps of passengers.</u>

7. The funniest child in the family. Cicely seemed to have a joke for every occasion.

   <u>The funniest child in the family, Cicely seemed to have a joke for</u>
   <u>every occasion.</u>

8. Fishing in his pocket for a handkerchief. Martin finally found one. Buried underneath his car keys, wadded-up dollar bills, and rent statement. He handed the handkerchief to his fiancée, who was feeling depressed. Remembering how opposed her parents were to this marriage.

   <u>Fishing in his pocket for a handkerchief, Martin finally found one</u>
   <u>buried underneath his car keys, wadded-up dollar bills, and rent</u>
   <u>statement. He handed the handkerchief to his fiancée, who was</u>
   <u>feeling depressed, remembering how adamantly her parents were</u>
   <u>opposed to this marriage.</u>

Subordinate Clause Fragments

While sentence fragments are often phrases, they can also be subordinate clauses. As we discussed in Chapter 20, a **subordinate clause** contains a subject and a verb but not a complete thought. These clauses depend on main clauses to be complete.

Subordinate clauses come in three varieties—noun, adjective, and adverb— but adverb and adjective clauses are the ones that most commonly turn up as fragments. To identify adverb clause fragments, look for sentences that begin with one of these common subordinating conjunctions:

SUBORDINATING CONJUNCTIONS

after	as though	in order that	so that	whenever
although	because	now that	though	where
as	before	once	till	whereas
as if	even though	rather than	until	wherever
as long as	if	since	when	while

If a sentence begins with one of these conjunctions and is not attached to a main clause, it is a fragment. Adverb clause fragments can be fixed either by attaching them to the main clause or by dropping the subordinating conjunction to create another main clause, as in the following example:

ADVERB CLAUSE FRAGMENT	*Because* the Midwest drought and heat wave has lasted for a month. Much of what was once green is now withered.
FIXED: BY ATTACHING	*Because* the Midwest drought and heat wave has lasted for a month, much of what was once green is now withered.
BY DROPPING SUBORDINATOR	The Midwest drought and heat wave has lasted for a month. Much of what was once green is now withered.

Adjective clause fragments can usually be identified by one of these three common relative pronouns: *who, which,* or *that.*

These fragments can be fixed either by attaching them to the main clause or by dropping the relative pronoun and replacing it with a noun or pronoun as in the following example:

ADJECTIVE CLAUSE FRAGMENT	The first decent bicycle I bought was a Trek. *Which* has given me years of good service.
FIXED: BY ATTACHING	The first decent bicycle I bought was a Trek, *which* has given me years of good service.
BY DROPPING RELATIVE PRONOUN AND ADDING NOUN	The first decent bicycle I bought was a Trek. This bike has given me years of good service.

ACTIVITY 22.4 Recognizing and Fixing Subordinate Clause Fragments

Rewrite any of the following sentences that contain a fragment, or write "Correct." You may attach the fragment to a main clause or add a subject, whichever method seems best to you. When combining the subordinate clause with a main clause, be sure to punctuate correctly.

EXAMPLE
When the Renaissance Festival begins to advertise. I begin to think of all the food I will end up eating. While I am there.

Fixed: When the Renaissance Festival begins to advertise, I begin to think of all the food I will end up eating while I am there.

Answers will vary.

1. If Morgan joins the eco tour in Brazil. She will see some breathtaking rain forest canopy.

   If Morgan joins the eco tour in Brazil, she will see some breathtaking rain forest canopy.

2. We took the course in emergency CPR for children. Even though our daughter is grown. Because we hope to have grandchildren sometime soon.

Teaching Idea
You might also mention the
past participle -n/-en ending
of some irregular verbs.

The base form is the one you find listed in the dictionary: *walk, talk, eat.* The past tense of regular verbs is created by adding -*d* or -*ed* to the base form, whereas irregular verbs change their past tense in other ways, including vowel changes: *sing/sang, speak/spoke, drink/drank.* We usually form the past participle, like the past tense, by adding -*d* or -*ed* and the present participle by adding -*ing.* In the last form, an -*s* or -*es* is added to create almost all third-person singular present tenses: *he walks, she walks, it walks, somebody walks.*

We combine these five verb forms to create twelve tenses, which we can reduce to the three that we are all familiar with: present, past, and future.

Three Primary Verb Tenses

The **present tense** has several uses, in general showing action happening now: "The mockingbird *sings* in the tree." Here are four other uses:

- To show habitual action: "I *eat* breakfast every morning."
- To express general truths: "Spring *follows* winter."
- To discuss works of art: "*Romeo and Juliet* is not Shakespeare's best play."
- To refer to future events (sometimes): "Bruce Springsteen *begins* his concert soon."

Notice that only one form in the present tense differs from the others, the -*s* ending used with *he, she, it,* and many indefinite pronouns (*each, no one,* etc.):

I play	we play
you play	you (plural) play
he, she, it, everyone plays	they play

The simple **past tense** tells about actions occurring in the past that do not continue into the present. Regular verbs form the past tense by adding -*d* and -*ed* to the base: "Arnold *nailed* the horseshoe over his door." The action occurred one time and was not repeated.

I nailed	we nailed
you nailed	you (plural) nailed
he, she, it nailed	they nailed

Irregular verbs change their spellings in the past tense, sometimes radically: *fly/flew, creep/crept, eat/ate.*

Our final simple tense is the **future,** which is used to show anticipated action. We usually form this tense by adding the helping verb *will* to the base verb: "Claire *will dance* on Broadway this summer."

I will dance	we will dance
you will dance	you (plural) will dance
he, she, it will dance	they will dance

Helping Verbs

Teaching Idea
You might also want to
remind students of linking
verbs here (see the section
"Verbs" in Chapter 20).

To help verbs express tenses, English uses **auxiliary** or **helping verbs** with a main verb. The most common are forms of the word *be (am, are, is, was, were, been, being), do (does, did, done),* or *have (has, had).* Other typical helping verbs are *may, might, must, can, could, should,* and *would.* When combined with main verbs, helping verbs create phrases like the following:

A. We *were* running behind schedule.

B. Sabato *did* finish the contract yesterday.

C. The thief *had* stripped my Mustang before I got it back.

D. Mark *could have* gotten an internship last semester.

Perfect Tenses

While the simple present, past, and future tenses help express many essential time relationships, they do not cover them all. To discuss an action finished earlier in time than another, we use the **perfect tenses**—present, past, and future. To form a perfect tense, we put *has, have,* or *had* in front of a past participle (a base verb usually ending in *-d/-ed* for regular verbs).

The **present perfect** tells of actions begun in the past and finished at some unknown time or that continue into the present. If we mention a specific time, we use the **simple past** rather than the present perfect.

A. The spring rain *has* brought new life to the earth. (The rain happened at some point in the past.)

B. Alma and Mitch *have* both tried sleeping under a pyramid for their mental health. (They tried it at some past time, but the sentence does not indicate when or that they have stopped.)

C. Alma and Mitch both tried sleeping under a pyramid last night for their mental health. (They tried at a specific time: *last night.*)

The **past perfect** shows one action happening further back in time than another past action:

A. Emily *had* hoped to make the 1:00 flight, but her car stalled on the way to the airport. (Her hoping happened before the car stalled.)

B. As Martin walked into the crowd of friends, he suddenly realized that they *had* carefully planned this surprise party. (He realized after they planned.)

The **future perfect** shows an action that will be completed by or before some specific time in the future:

A. Isaac *will have* finished 200 lay-ups before the game next week. (Isaac will finish the drills in the future but before the more distant event of the game.)

B. Once dad searches the attic for the oven mitt, he *will have* looked everywhere. (The sentence specifies the time that the search for the mitt will be over.)

ACTIVITY 23.1 Distinguishing Simple Past from Present Perfect

Underline the correct verb form in the following sentences. Remember that the *simple past* is used for an action completed in the past, whereas the *present perfect*

1. "Hold down the racket! I (try/am trying) to concentrate."
2. I (go/am going) to school every morning at 8:00 A.M.
3. The wind (blows/is blowing) the chimes, and they are ringing softly.
4. Isabella (walks/is walking) across the stage to receive her associate's degree.
5. When a cold front (blows/is blowing) in, the fishing usually slows down.
6. As we speak, all the students (study/are studying) in the library.
7. Paul and Randy (install/are installing) the muffler right now.
8. Create three sentences of your own that use the present perfect tense:
   Answers will vary.
   A. _____

   B. _____

   C. _____

ACTIVITY 23.4 Distinguishing Simple Past from Past Progressive

Underline the correct verb form in the following sentences. Remember that the *simple past* tells that an action has been completed in the past, whereas the *past progressive* tells that the past action is ongoing.

EXAMPLE
I (worked/was working) in the back of the store when you called.

1. We (went/were going) to the store when mom was pulled over for speeding.
2. Jessica (typed/was typing) her composition when her computer crashed.
3. The men (smoothed/were smoothing) out the last section of sidewalk as the children (scratched/were scratching) their initials in the first section.
4. We (ate/were eating) at Rio Bravo when we heard the news about Paul's accident.
5. We (ate/were eating) at Rio Bravo last week, and this week we will try Margarita's.
6. Thinking about his plans for the evening, Allen said, "I (hoped/was hoping) that you would see *Casablanca* with me."
7. Virginia (spoke/was speaking) for two hours yesterday.
8. Create three sentences of your own that use the past perfect tense:
   Answers will vary.
   A. _____

   B. _____

   C. _____

Irregular Verbs

Regular verbs in English form their past tense by adding *-d* or *-ed* to the base or dictionary form (*walk/walked*), but **irregular verbs** are not so easy. The past tense and past participle of irregular verbs are usually spelled differently than the base form—sometimes just changing a vowel (*begin/began/begun*), but sometimes changing consonants (*prove/proved/proven*), and sometimes not changing at all (*cut/cut/cut*)! The only way to handle these forms is to memorize them and then refer to a dictionary when needed.

The most important irregular verb in English is *to be*. Because it is used so often both as a helper (*is* speaking) and on its own as a linking verb (John *is* a strong man), you should learn its seven forms (*am, are, is, was, were, been, being*):

Seven Forms of *To Be*

	SINGULAR	PLURAL
Present	I am	we are
	you are	you are
	he, she, it is	they are
Past	I was	we were
	you were	you were
	he, she, it was	they were
Past Participle	I had been	we had been
	you had been	you had been
	he, she, it had been	they had been

Here is a list of the principal parts of some common irregular verbs:

Common Irregular Verbs

PRESENT TENSE	PAST TENSE	PAST PARTICIPLE	PRESENT TENSE	PAST TENSE	PAST PARTICIPLE
awake	awoke	awoke/ awakened	draw	drew	drawn
			drink	drank	drunk
become	became	become	drive	drove	driven
begin	began	begun	eat	ate	eaten
bite	bit	bitten	fall	fell	fallen
blow	blew	blown	feel	felt	felt
break	broke	broken	fight	fought	fought
bring	brought	brought	find	found	found
build	built	built	fly	flew	flown
buy	bought	bought	forget	forgot	forgotten
catch	caught	caught	freeze	froze	frozen
choose	chose	chosen	get	got	got/gotten
come	came	come	give	gave	given
cost	cost	cost	grow	grew	grown
creep	crept	crept	go	went	gone
cut	cut	cut	hang	hung	hung
dig	dug	dug	hang	hanged	hanged
dive	dived/dove	dived	hear	heard	heard
do	did	done			

(Continued)

Subject/Verb Agreement

**Subject/Verb
Agreement**

In addition to understanding verb tenses, you need to understand how verbs agree with subjects. Singular verbs should be paired with singular subjects and plural verbs with plural subjects. Although it might seem confusing, the *-s* ending on a present-tense verb usually marks it as singular, whereas the same ending on a subject marks it as plural. We usually observe this distinction without thinking about it when we speak and write, as in the following two examples:

SINGULAR SUBJECT   My cat sleeps in bed with me.

PLURAL SUBJECT   My cats sleep in bed with me.

However, as we write more complicated sentences than these, we sometimes have trouble locating our subjects and verbs and then making them agree in number. The rest of this chapter will help you with subject/verb agreement problems.

Intervening Words

One of the most frequent trouble spots in our sentences occurs when a verb is separated from its subject by a number of words—as in this sentence. We often try to connect the verb (in this case, *occurs*) with the closest noun (*sentences*) instead of the actual subject (*one*). Here are several examples with the subjects underlined once and the verbs twice:

A. *The Matrix Reloaded,* one of the decade's many action-packed spectacles, stars Keanu Reeves.

B. The movie that we enjoyed more than all of the others is *Terminator II.*

C. Figures released today from the White House explain the president's proposal.

D. A box with 13 rolls or doughnuts is called a baker's dozen.

E. The defense attorney, along with union members, is protesting the ruling.

CAUTION! Subjects are never found within prepositional phrases.

Two steps can help you make subjects and verbs agree:

1. Locate the action or state of being word.
2. Ask, "Who or what is doing the action or experiencing the state of being?"

For example, in sentence C, what explains? *Figures* explain. Notice that sentence D has a prepositional phrase, "with 13 rolls or doughnuts," between the subject and verb. Subjects are never found within a prepositional phrase. (For more on subjects with prepositional phrases, see pp. 467–468.)

Also note that sentence e uses the phrase *along with,* one of a small group of phrases that do not affect the number of the subject: *in addition to, as well as, along with, plus, including,* and *together with.*

ACTIVITY 23.5 Agreement with Separated Subjects and Verbs

Underline the correct verb in parentheses twice and its subject once.

EXAMPLE
The <u>cars</u> on this lot (<u><u>cost</u></u>/costs) much more than I can afford.

1. The <u>undercover officer</u> standing among the teens at the concert (<u><u>blends</u></u>/blend) easily with the crowd.
2. <u>Some</u> of the most interesting sculptures in the museum, including one made entirely of soap, (<u><u>is</u></u>/are) on the third floor.
3. <u>Music therapy</u> along with other holistic healing methods (is/<u><u>are</u></u>) helping many people to overcome stress.
4. The <u>red-tailed hawk</u> in high winds (<u><u>needs</u></u>/need) to fly above them or land.
5. The <u>sound</u> of piston rods knocking (<u><u>makes</u></u>/make) most car owners a little sick.
6. A <u>stack</u> of red composite shingles (<u><u>sits</u></u>/sit) in Harold's pickup truck.
7. <u>One</u> of the cat's paws (<u><u>has</u></u>/have) a nasty infection.

Compound Subjects

In a **compound** or **two-part subject,** the verb usually becomes plural:

> <u>Firestone</u> and <u>Ford</u> <u><u>are accusing</u></u> each other in the latest round of blame fixing over blown tires.

However, some subjects may seem to be two-part but are actually singular:

> <u>My best friend and older brother,</u> Robert, <u><u>has helped</u></u> me through tight spots all my life.

Indefinite Pronouns

The singular **indefinite pronouns** in the following list require singular verbs when the pronouns are used as subjects:

SINGULAR INDEFINITE PRONOUNS

anybody	each	everyone	none	somebody
anyone	either	neither	no one	someone
anything	everybody	nobody	one	something

A. <u>Nobody</u> <u><u>wins</u></u> if <u>everyone</u> <u><u>is destroyed</u></u> in the battle.

B. <u>Anyone</u> who thinks she can do better <u><u>is</u></u> welcome to try.

C. <u>Everybody</u> <u><u>listens</u></u> closely to wolves howling in the distance.

When the doer of an action is relatively unimportant or unknown, the passive voice can be an effective choice. But active voice works best when—as in most cases—you want the real doer of the action to receive full attention. However, here are two examples of effective passive-voice sentences, both of which seek to emphasize the words in the subject position:

A. My friend's home was broken into last night. (A thief did it, but the focus is on the violation of the home.)

B. Six million Jews were exterminated during World War II. (The Nazis did it, but the focus is on the deaths rather than the perpetrators of the crime.)

ACTIVITY 23.7 Agreement with Reordered Sentences

Underline the verb in each sentence twice and the subject once.

EXAMPLE

In the middle of an angry crowd cowered two innocent bystanders.

1. From the back of the old Chevy station wagon clung three young boys, hitching a ride on their sleds.
2. This mess was made by someone.
3. When is Louis going to take the bar exam?
4. By the side of the road was a Ford Explorer with a flat tire.
5. Here are the best facilities for losing weight and toning up.
6. My flight was delayed by the ice storm.
7. There is a hole in the ozone over Antarctica that gets bigger each passing year.

Collective Nouns

In American English, words that stand for groups usually are treated as singular—for example, *army, committee, team, band, class, audience, crowd, gathering, group, herd, school,* and *flock:*

A. The group feels that its decision was just.

B. Our committee has beaten this issue to death.

However, if the members of the group are acting individually, it often sounds more natural to revise the sentence to reflect this—for example, "The members of our group are divided in their judgment."

Plural Nouns/Plural Verbs

While some nouns are collectively singular, others are always plural—for example, *scissors, pants, clothes,* and *fireworks:*

The scissors are in the drawer.

"False" Plural Nouns

Some nouns that end in -s are not plural—for example, *mathematics, physics, athletics, economics, statistics, measles, mumps, politics, ethics,* and *pediatrics.* Though titles may contain plural nouns—for example, *All Creatures Great and Small*—they take singular verbs. Sums of money, distances, measurements, and time units may also look plural, but when they are being used as a unit, they, too, are grammatically singular:

   A. Mathematics is my favorite subject.

   B. Thirty minutes is too long to spend listening to Dr. Parrish lecture.

   C. Twenty-five thousand dollars sounds like too much to spend on a car.

ACTIVITY 23.8 Agreement with Plural and Collective Nouns

Underline the verb in parentheses twice and the subject once.

EXAMPLE

Fireworks (is/are) a wonderful sight to many Americans on July Fourth.

1. *Jaws* (is/are) a movie that made many people reluctant to swim in the ocean.

2. The whole gathering (believes/believe) in the eminent destruction of earth.

3. The audience (applauds/applaud) enthusiastically, hoping for one more encore.

4. A whole flock of Canadian geese (is flying/are flying) through the airspace above La Guardia airport.

5. Five hundred dollars (is/are) too much for this guitar.

6. Athletics (brings/bring) many people together who otherwise might not meet.

7. The only pants I have (is/are) in the dryer.

8. Five hundred flat miles across Kansas (is/are) too far to drive to reach Denver.

CHAPTER 24

Pronouns

Reference, Agreement, and Form

What Are We Trying to Achieve and Why?

Teaching Idea
You might want to frame the discussion of pronouns in terms of writer- versus reader-based prose. The writer knows who or what he or she is referring back to, but the reader often does not.

Like verbs and nouns, **pronouns** are a common and important part of speech. Pronouns like *he, this, who, myself,* and *everyone* take the place of nouns and help create variety in your writing.

Without pronouns to replace nouns, we might be stuck with paragraphs like this one:

> The leopard crept stealthily through the dry grass, stalking the leopard's prey. As the leopard neared the antelope, the leopard's ears flattened, and the leopard's tail began to twitch in anticipation. Pausing for a moment, seeming to hold the leopard's breath, the leopard sprang from hiding to land on the antelope's back.

Clearly, the repetition of *leopard* becomes monotonous. To solve the problem, we can substitute pronouns, as in the following revision:

> The leopard crept stealthily through the dry grass, stalking her prey. As the leopard neared the antelope, the leopard's ears flattened, and her tail began to twitch in anticipation. Pausing for a moment, seeming to hold her breath, the leopard sprang from hiding to land on the antelope's back.

(For more on achieving variety and coherence through the use of pronouns, see p. 56.)

Teaching Idea
For a complete list of pronouns, see pages 516–517.

As useful as pronouns are, they present a built-in problem. Because they have no identity by themselves, they must refer to a noun to achieve meaning. If a friend were to say, "It was a horrible experience," you might respond, "What was horrible?" You cannot know until your friend says, "Root canal." Using a noun tells the reader exactly what the writer means.

Whenever you use pronouns, you must be sure that the reader knows what they are referring back to, and you must be careful to use the correct form of the pronoun. Chapter 24 will help us explore both of these areas.

Referring Clearly to a Specific Antecedent

Pronoun Reference

A pronoun refers to an **antecedent**—a word that the pronoun substitutes for, most often a noun but occasionally another pronoun or phrase. The antecedent is usually located before the pronoun, either within the same sentence or in a nearby sentence, as in the following: "Jim drinks hot chocolate. He likes it a lot." The words *he* and *it* take the place of *Jim* and *hot chocolate*.

Pronouns that are far removed from their antecedent can cause confusion. Consider the following sentences:

A. Eileen told Isabella that *she* would never be happy until *she* stopped

relying on men to define her existence.

B. After *she* made this statement, *she* apologized, not wanting to sound

like *she* was unkind.

In sentence A, readers cannot be sure who needs to stop relying on men. The confusion increases in sentence B. Who has said what? We can only guess. To clarify the meaning, we could recast the sentences this way:

A. Eileen told Isabella that Isabella would never be happy until she

stopped relying on men to define her existence.

B. After Eileen made this statement, she apologized, not wanting to

sound like she was unkind.

Now readers can understand the writer's meaning.

Pronouns that can be particularly confusing to readers are *it, they, them, this, that, these, those,* and *which*. These words should usually refer to a specific noun rather than a general idea, and they should be close to the noun they stand for to avoid unclear meanings, as in the following examples:

UNCLEAR   *They* rudely informed Jenna and Craig at the grocery store that *they* were out of mangoes.

Who informed Jenna and Craig—perhaps a store employee? The employee probably did not tell Jenna and Craig that the two of them were out of mangoes; the store was out.

REVISED   An employee at the grocery store rudely informed Jenna and Craig that the store was out of mangoes.

UNCLEAR   *It* made Jenna and Craig unhappy.

What made them unhappy: the lack of mangoes, the rudeness of the employee, or both?

REVISED The rudeness of the employee and the lack of mangoes made them unhappy.

UNCLEAR *This* taught them to prepare further in advance for parties, *which* will help *them* prevent *this* in the future.

What taught Jenna and Craig a lesson: the rude behavior, the lack of mangoes, or both? Is *which* referring to the parties—the closest noun—or the idea of preparing in advance? Is *them* referring to the parties—again, the closest noun— or to Craig and Jenna? What is the final *this* referring to?

REVISED This unhappy shopping experience taught Craig and Jenna to prepare further in advance for parties. The lesson will help the couple to avoid future unpleasant surprises when planning parties.

Pronouns are useful in writing, but they need to be clearly linked with their antecedents. Often the best fix for ambiguous pronoun reference is to replace the pronoun with a noun, as in the revised examples above.

ACTIVITY 24.1 Clarifying Pronoun Reference

Revise the following sentences for unclear pronoun reference by replacing the pronouns with nouns and writing the revised sentence in the space provided.

EXAMPLE

When I finally reached the admissions office, they told me my transcripts had been lost.

Revised: When I finally reached the admissions office, an employee told me my transcripts had been lost.

Answers will vary.

1. Nguyen and his wife planned a night walk over the Big Island's lava fields to see the hot lava oozing into the sea, which made them both a bit nervous.

Nguyen and his wife were nervous about their planned night walk over the Big Island's lava fields to see the hot lava oozing into the sea.

2. Many teachers are now aware that they have unconsciously discouraged girls from excelling in science and math. This is why they should now do better.

Because many teachers are now aware that they have unconsciously discouraged girls from excelling in science and math, these teachers will correct their former habits, and the girls should now do better.

3. Large asteroids seldom hit the earth, but when they do, they cause terrific destruction, which is a relief to me.

Though asteroids can cause terrific destruction, because they seldom hit the earth, I feel relieved.

4. Ann was talking to Eva when she saw the accident in the parking lot.

As she was talking to Eva, Ann saw the accident in the parking lot.

5. After the painters spoke with Jim and Kristi in their dining room, they moved the dining room table and then painted it.

After they spoke with Jim and Kristi in their dining room, the painters moved the dining room table and then painted the dining room.

6. Rainbow trout rest behind rocks in streams to conserve their energy and because they channel food toward them.

Rainbow trout rest behind rocks in streams to conserve their energy and because the rocks channel food toward them.

7. Sheila needed wire cutters or pliers to strip the insulation from the wire, so she asked her husband to hand it to her.

Sheila needed wire cutters or pliers to strip the insulation from the wire, so she asked her husband to hand the wire cutters to her.

8. Meat and dairy products are high in saturated fats and often have toxic chemicals in them. But they taste good and have many valuable nutrients. For these reasons, though, many people are trying to cut down on their consumption.

Meat and dairy products are high in saturated fats and often have toxic chemicals in them. But these foods taste good and also have many valuable nutrients. Because of the potential health hazards, though, many people are trying to cut down on their consumption of these products.

Agreeing in Number with the Antecedent

Pronoun-Antecedent Agreement

Not only must pronouns be clearly linked to their antecedents, but they also must agree in **number:** Singular nouns take singular pronouns; plural nouns take plural pronouns. Consider the following examples:

A. *The Night of the Living Dead* is a classic horror film, but there is much in *it* that is laughable.

B. Many *films* have tried to capture the essence of Mary Shelley's *Frankenstein,* but few of *them* have succeeded.

In sentence A, the singular pronoun *it* refers to the singular *film.* In sentence B, the plural pronoun *them* links with the plural noun *films.*

Difficulties with pronoun/antecedent agreement often occur when the antecedent falls into one of the following categories: **indefinite pronouns, collective nouns,** and **compound antecedents.**

Indefinite Pronouns

Indefinite pronouns as antecedents can be a problem because they do not refer to a specific person or thing. Although most are singular, a few are plural, and several (*all, any, enough, more, most, none, some*) can be either singular or plural, depending on what noun they connect with. Note the following list:

Indefinite Pronouns

SINGULAR			PLURAL
anybody	everybody	no one	both
anyone	everyone	one	few
anything	neither	somebody	many
each	nobody	someone	others
either	none	something	several

Singular indefinite pronouns take singular verbs even when the indefinite pronoun is connected to a plural noun. Note the following examples:

INCORRECT   *Each* of the *rock bands* play until midnight; then *they* move to the next gig.

Even though the noun *bands* is plural, the singular pronoun *it* refers back to the singular indefinite pronoun *each.*

CORRECT   *Each* of the *rock bands* plays until midnight; then *it* moves to the next gig.

INCORRECT   *Neither* of the *players* deserve to be benched for defending *themselves.*

Even though the noun *players* is plural, the singular pronoun *himself* refers back to *neither.*

CORRECT   *Neither* of the *players* deserves to be benched for defending *himself.*

Here are several more examples illustrating correct pronoun agreement:

A. *One* of the shoppers was trying to find *her* checkbook.

B. *Anyone* can learn to play a musical instrument if *he* or *she* practices enough.

C. *Most* of the athletes failed *their* drug tests. (The indefinite pronoun *most* is plural because the noun that is connected to it, *athletes,* is plural.)

D. *Most* of the coffee is in *its* container. (Here *most* is singular because the noun that is connected to it, *coffee,* is singular.)

HINT: Notice that sentence B uses "*he* or *she*" to overcome gender bias in pronoun usage. (For more on this strategy, turn to Chapter 19, pp. 502–503.)

Collective Nouns

In American English, most groups of things, animals, and people are treated as a single unit, that is, as individuals acting together as one—for example, *army, committee, team, band, class, audience, crowd, gathering, group, herd, school,* and *flock.* Pronouns referring to singular **collective nouns** are also singular:

A. The *group* feels that *its* decision was just.

B. Our *committee* has discussed the proposals, and *it* will accept the low bid.

However, if the members of the group are acting individually, the noun becomes plural, and so does the pronoun:

C. The *group* are divided in *their* judgment, *all* members arguing strenuously for *their* positions.

Compound Antecedents

We often use **two-part** or **compound nouns** connected with the conjunctions *and, or,* and *nor.* When the antecedent is linked by *and,* it is usually plural, requiring a plural pronoun:

A. *Wind and sun* suck moisture from the earth, and *they* can destroy a corn crop.

B. My *daughter and I* will be on *our* favorite float river by this time tomorrow.

When the antecedent is linked by *or* or *nor,* the pronoun should agree with the nearest part:

A. Either Mark *or* Luke will bring *his* Frisbee to the park.

B. Mark or his *brothers* will bring *their* Frisbees to the park.

C. Neither Mark nor his *friends* remembered to bring *their* Frisbees to the park.

When you are using a plural and singular compound antecedent, put the plural word second for smoother-sounding sentences:

AWKWARD   Neither the fans nor the *coach* could control *his* anger at the referee's decision.

REVISED   Neither the coach nor the *fans* could control *their* anger at the referee's decision.

ACTIVITY 24.2 Creating Pronoun Agreement

Underline the antecedent in each of the following sentences, and then write an appropriate pronoun in the blanks.

EXAMPLE
We are often told that anybody can be successful in this country if
he or she is willing to work hard.
Answers will vary.

1. Everyone would like a job that makes him or her happy.

2. A flock of Canadian geese was on its way south for the winter.

Teaching Idea
Refer students back to pages 502–503 for a discussion of gender bias in language and ways to prevent it.

3. Carl knew that the success of his latest CD depended on <u>many people</u> and that _____*they*_____ deserved recognition for _____*their*_____ help.

4. <u>Each</u> player, giving _____*his or her*_____ utmost, makes a team a winner or loser.

5. <u>Nobody</u> was able to move _____*his or her*_____ vehicle from the crowded stadium parking lot.

6. <u>Several</u> of the people at my party called the next day to say that _____*they*_____ had had a great time.

7. The <u>audience</u> broke into wild applause, and then _____*it*_____ pleaded for one more curtain call.

8. <u>Every</u> one of the girls should know that _____*she*_____ has an equal chance at the job.

9. <u>Either</u> of the boys will clean up the mess _____*he*_____ made if you bribe _____*him*_____ with candy.

10. Neither the director nor <u>any</u> of the actors thought that _____*they*_____ would complete the scene on schedule.

Choosing Proper Pronoun Case

Pronouns

Even after clarifying a pronoun's antecedent and checking for agreement in number, we can still have problems with **case**—the form a pronoun takes to show how it works in a sentence: as subject, object, or possessor.

Subjective Case

Pronouns used as subjects or subject complements are in the **subjective case:**

A. *She* <u>runs</u> 6-minute miles. (pronoun as subject)

B. The <u>person</u> to thank for breakfast <u>is</u> *she*. (pronoun as complement)

Objective Case

Pronouns used as objects (receiving the action of verbs), objects of prepositional phrases, and subjects of infinitives are in the **objective case:**

A. The whole <u>family</u> happily <u>greeted</u> *her.* (pronoun as direct object)

B. <u>Emily</u> <u>kicked</u> the ball to *him.* (pronoun as indirect object)

C. <u>Alex</u> <u>wanted</u> to share the secret with *you* and *me.* (pronouns as objects of preposition *with*)

D. <u>Patty</u> <u>asked</u> *him* to bring a green salad. (pronoun as subject of infinitive *to bring*)

CAUTION! *Its, whose,* and *your* are possessive pronouns; *it's, who's,* and *you're* are contractions.

Possessive Case

Pronouns used to show ownership are in the **possessive case:**

A. Is that *your* umbrella?

B. No, that one is not *mine.*

The following chart will help you choose the correct pronoun case:

Pronoun Case Chart

SINGULAR	SUBJECTIVE	OBJECTIVE	POSSESSIVE
First person	I	me	my, mine
Second person	you	you	your, yours
Third person	he, she, it, who, whoever	him, her, it, whom, whomever	his, her, hers, its, whose

PLURAL	SUBJECTIVE	OBJECTIVE	POSSESSIVE
First person	we	us	our, ours
Second person	you	you	your, yours
Third person	they, who	them, whom	their, theirs, whose

Solving Common Problems with Pronoun Case

Pronoun case often causes problems in three categories: compounds, comparisons, and *who/whom.*

Compounds

Difficulties with compounds occur when two pronouns, two nouns, or a noun and a pronoun are linked by *and* or *or,* as in the following examples:

SUBJECTS *Jerry* and *I/me* went to the Royals' game last night.

OBJECTS The game disappointed *him* and *I/me.*

OBJECTS OF PREPOSITION We left early, which was all right with *him* and *I/me.*

In each of these sentences, writers can be confused about which form of a pronoun to use. If we mentally cross out one of the pair, the remaining word will often guide us to the correct case:

A. ~~Jerry and~~ I went to the Royals' game last night. ("*Me* went to the Royals' game last night" does not sound right.)

Jerry and I went to the Royals' game last night.

B. The game disappointed ~~him and~~ me. ("The game disappointed *I*" does not sound right.)

The game disappointed *him* and *me.*

C. So we left early, which was all right with ~~him and~~ me. (You would not say "which was all right with *I.*")

So we left early, which was all right with *him* and *me.*

HINT: Being able to locate the verb and subject in your sentence will also help you determine case. If the pronoun is not a subject or a subject complement and does not show possession, it should be in the objective case.

Comparisons

We often make noun/pronoun and pronoun/pronoun comparisons using the words *than* and *as*. These comparisons can be confusing because they may leave words out of the sentence:

 A. Pauline sings more beautifully than *I/me*.

 B. Arthur is as competent as *he/him*.

If we add the missing verbs to sentences A and B, it becomes easier to determine the correct pronoun case. With the verbs in place, we can see that the pronouns are subjects and therefore must be in the subjective case.

 C. Pauline sings more beautifully than *I* (sing).

 D. Arthur is as competent as *he* (is).

By adding missing words to the following examples, we can see that the pronouns are direct objects and need to be in the objective case:

 A. This study guide will help you more than (it will help) *her/she*.

 B. Loud music distracts Jessica as much as (it distracts) *him/he*.

Sometimes choosing pronoun case will affect the meaning of your sentences:

 A. Ian cares for football more than me. (more than he cares for me)

 B. Ian cares for football more than I. (more than I care for football)

Who/Whom

The relative pronouns *who/whoever* and *whom/whomever* can also cause case problems. *Who/whoever* are used as subjects and *whom/whomever* have been traditionally used as objects, as in the following sentences:

| SUBJECT | *Who* will give Jenny a ride to the game? |
| OBJECT | I should give your house keys to *whom?* |

Although the distinction between *who* and *whom* has been fading—*who* often used in place of *whom*—most academic audiences expect the more formal usage of *whom*. However, if using *whom* seems awkward or overly formal, you can always recast the sentence so that the relative pronoun is unneeded or sometimes just drop it, as in the following example:

| FORMAL | The fastest swimmer *whom* Brandon had to face was his archrival from Shawnee Mission South. |
| LESS FORMAL | The fastest swimmer Brandon had to face was his archrival from Shawnee Mission South. |

ACTIVITY 24.3 Choosing Pronoun Case

For practice with two-part constructions, comparisons, and *who/whom*, underline the correct pronoun within parentheses in each sentence. Finding verbs and subjects will help you choose. Also, try crossing out one word of the pair and putting in the implied words.

EXAMPLE
We finally found a babysitter so that my wife and (me/I) could have a night out.

1. It made George furious to hear (she/<u>her</u>) and Jason laughing together.
2. Anna is the girl (who/<u>whom</u>) Tomas is taking to the prom.
3. The sergeant pointed at Carlos and (I/<u>me</u>) and said, "You are volunteering."
4. During the recital, Lewis could see that Amy was more bored than (him/<u>he</u>).
5. Few people have reacted as violently as (<u>they</u>/them).
6. The gold medal belongs as much to the rest of the team as (she/<u>her</u>).
7. My older brother and (me/<u>I</u>) started skateboarding before we began surfing.
8. My boss offered Richard and (she/<u>her</u>) a raise.
9. April is a girl (whom/<u>who</u>) never gives up.
10. (<u>She</u>/Her) and her friend will leave the party by midnight.

Avoiding Shifts in Person

As we saw in the Pronoun Case Chart on page 583, pronouns have number (singular or plural) and person (first, second, or third). **Person** is the perspective the author assumes when he or she writes: first person (*I, we*), second person (*you*), or third person (*he, she,* or *they*). Writers should be consistent in both number and person.

The most frequent shift error is from the first-person *I* or third-person *they* to the second-person *you*, as in the following examples:

Teaching Idea
To help students understand appropriate pronoun shifts, you might have them turn to the Unit Six essay "What Is Biodiversity and Why Should We Care about It?" Ask them why the author shifts to the second person in paragraphs 5 and 6.

| INCONSISTENT | *I* looked out the window as *I* sat in a huge jet cutting through the clouds. *You* could see tiny green irrigation rings on the ground 25,000 feet below, reminding *me* of the drought still in progress. |

| FIXED | *I* looked out the window as *I* sat in a huge jet cutting through the clouds. *I* could see tiny green irrigation rings on the ground 25,000 feet below, reminding *me* of the drought still in progress. |

| INCONSISTENT | To improve *their* lives, immigrants to America have often traveled westward. If *you* wanted to farm, ranch, or mine in the nineteenth century, the West was the place for *you.* |

| FIXED | To improve *their* lives, immigrants to America have often traveled westward. If *they* wanted to farm, ranch, or mine in the nineteenth century, the West was the place for *them.* |

CAUTION! Use *you* only when there is a good reason to directly address your readers.

Writers often mix persons in their work, but there should always be a good reason for doing so. The *I* of personal experience is sometimes used in introductions and conclusions but then avoided in the body paragraphs of an essay (except in a personal anecdote). You can use *you* occasionally in introductions and conclusions to address your readers directly, and you can use *you* often in process-analysis instructions (as in textbooks like this one). *We, us,* and *our* can help you connect with your audience, especially in persuasive writing. However, you should watch out for unnecessary shifts in person, such as the ones shown above.

When using the slightly more formal third person, you have several options to avoid an inappropriate second-person *you.* You can use third-person pronouns (*he, she, they*), or nouns that can take their place (*people, students, employees*), or you can leave the pronoun out altogether. Note the following examples:

INAPPROPRIATE PRONOUN SHIFT	Australia was first colonized by English convicts. You would have worked hard in those early settlements.
FIXED: THIRD-PERSON PRONOUN	Australia was first colonized by English convicts. *They* would have worked hard in those early settlements.
NOUN	Australia was first colonized by English convicts. The *colonists* would have worked hard in the early settlements.
PRONOUN DELETED	Working hard in the early settlements, English convicts first colonized Australia.

ACTIVITY 24.4 Avoiding Shifts in Person

In the following paragraphs, cross out the inappropriate pronouns, write in the appropriate word in the space above it, and change any verb affected by a pronoun substitution. You may need to make other revisions as well.

Answers will vary.

1. When I lived on the farm, I had to help with a lot of chores. I had to take care of my animals, and help my dad irrigate in the morning and evening, and I also had to help in the kitchen. ~~When you~~ [Now that I] live in a city, ~~you~~ [I] ~~end up with~~ [have] fewer responsibilities. All I have to do now is help my father with his lawn and landscaping business and help around the house. ~~You~~ [I] don't have all of the extra responsibilities in the city that ~~you have~~ [I had] on the farm.

2. People who downhill ski often love the sport and regularly risk terrible injury pursuing it. ~~You~~ [Some] might think that ~~you~~ [they] are too tough to get hurt, but skiers frequently break bones and, worse, rip their knee joints apart. Hurtling downhill at 40 to 50 miles an hour, ~~you~~ [a person] can easily run into a tree or another person, sending ~~you both~~ [both people] to the hospital. Skiers say that a fast run down the mountain is a lot like flying, but ~~you don't have~~ [there are not] all those trees, boulders, and people to dodge up in the sky.

CHAPTER 25

Adjectives and Adverbs

Words That Describe

What Are We Trying to Achieve and Why?

Teaching Idea
This chapter offers another opportunity to reinforce the value to students of knowing the function of phrases and clauses so that they can recognize and manipulate these structures. You might want to link the discussion here with the information on phrases and clauses in Chapter 20.

One of the ways that we add information to sentences is by using **adjectives** and **adverbs,** words that *describe* or *modify.* Phrases and clauses can also be **modifiers,** functioning as adjectives and adverbs.

Adjectives tell us about *nouns* and *pronouns:* "the *red* Mustang." **Adverbs** tell us about *verbs, adjectives,* and other *adverbs:* "She sings *melodiously.*" These modifiers are usually located close to the word they tell about, although adverbs in particular may be some distance from the word. The problems most likely to arise with adjectives and adverbs involve choosing the right forms, using them selectively, and attaching them clearly to the words they describe.

Adjectives and Related Word Groups

**Adjectives
and Adverbs**

Adjectives describe nouns and pronouns, telling of people and things—how many, what kind, color, shape, size, texture, or age, and so on. Here are two examples:

MODIFYING
A NOUN
A *tall* sycamore <u>tree</u> stands in my yard. (tells size)

MODIFYING
A PRONOUN
I'd like the *new* <u>one</u>. (tells which one)

Phrases and clauses also can function as adjectives, as in the following examples:

PHRASE
A sycamore <u>tree</u> *with an eagle's nest* stands in my yard. (gives further description)

CLAUSE
The sycamore <u>tree</u> *that fell on my house last night* was 110 years old. (tells which one)

Notice from the four sentences above that adjectives come before the noun they modify, whereas adjective phrases and adjective clauses follow the noun. In addition to coming before nouns, adjectives can follow linking verbs (*be, seem, feel,* and so on), as in these examples:

A. Louis <u>feels</u> *sick.*

B. He <u>is</u> *kind.*

Adverbs and Related Word Groups

Adjectives and Adverbs

Adverbs describe verbs, adjectives, and other adverbs, telling *when, where, why, how,* and *to what degree or extent* something was done. Here are some examples:

MODIFYING A VERB	Arthur *quietly* <u>entered</u> the room. (tells how)
MODIFYING AN ADJECTIVE	Arthur can be an *exceedingly* <u>quiet</u> man. (tells to what extent)
MODIFYING AN ADVERB	Arthur *very* <u>quietly</u> entered the room. (tells to what degree)

As with adjectives, phrases and clauses also can function as adverbs:

PHRASE	*On his tiptoes* Arthur <u>entered</u> the room. (tells how)
CLAUSE	*When everyone was sleeping,* Arthur <u>entered</u> the room. (tells when)

Adverbs that modify verbs and adverb phrases and clauses often allow us a great deal of freedom with placement. For example, we could recast the sentences above in several ways, including these:

A. Arthur <u>entered</u> the room *quietly.* (tells how)

B. Arthur <u>entered</u> the room *on his tiptoes.* (tells how)

C. Arthur <u>entered</u> the room *when everyone was sleeping.* (tells when)

HINT: Many adverbs are formed by adding *-ly* to the end of an adjective.

One way to identify adverbs is to look for the *-ly* ending often attached to adjectives to form adverbs (*bad/badly, happy/happily, sweet/sweetly,* and so on). However, this method is not foolproof because many adverbs do not have the *-ly* ending (*soon, too, very, already, often, quite, then, always, there,* and so on). Knowing how a word *functions* is the best way to determine what part of speech it is.

Comparative and Superlative Forms

Adjectives and adverbs often compare two or more things. Those that compare two things use an *-er* ending or the words *more* and *less,* forms known as **comparatives.** Those that compare three or more things use *-est* or *most* and *least,* forms known as **superlatives.** Here are some examples:

ADJECTIVE	COMPARATIVE	SUPERLATIVE
strong	stronger	strongest
beautiful	more beautiful	most beautiful
	less strong, beautiful	least strong, beautiful

ADVERB	COMPARATIVE	SUPERLATIVE
soon	sooner	soonest
easily	more easily	most easily
	less soon, easily	least soon, easily

A. Sam is *stronger* than Nick, but Ethan is the *strongest* of all.

B. Sam lifted the weights *more easily* than Nick did, but Ethan lifted them the *most easily* of all.

Often, as in these examples, one-syllable adjectives and adverbs take the *-er/-est* endings and those with two or more syllables appear with *more/most*.

Irregular adjectives and adverbs do not follow the pattern and so must be memorized. Here are the most common irregular forms:

IRREGULAR ADJECTIVES AND ADVERBS

good, well	better	best
bad, badly	worse	worst
far	farther, further	farthest, furthest

Even apart from their comparative and superlative forms, the words *good* and *well* can cause confusion. Keep in mind that *good* is an adjective, whereas *well* is often an adverb but sometimes an adjective, as in the following sentences:

A. Claire has a *good* dog.

B. Claire's dog performs *well*.

C. Claire's dog does not feel *well*.

In sentence A, *good* describes the noun *dog*; it is an adjective. In sentence B, *well* describes the verb *perform*, which makes an adverb. Sentence C has the linking verb *feel*, which connects *well* to *dog*, so *well* in this sentence is an adjective. As an adjective, *well* generally means "healthy, not sick."

The words *bad* and *badly* can also be confusing. Notice the following usages:

A. Puffy was a *bad* cat today.

B. Puffy behaved *badly* today.

C. Puffy felt *bad* today.

Bad is always an adjective, describing nouns (*cat*) and occurring before a noun, as in sentence A, or after a linking verb, as in sentence B. *Badly* is always an adverb, describing verbs—*behaved* in sentence C.

Avoiding Overuse of Modifiers

Teaching Idea
To connect this discussion of excessive modifiers with other strategies for making writing more concise, see the section "Using Specific and Concrete Language" in Chapter 19.

As helpful as adjectives and adverbs can be in building images and explaining things, we sometimes overuse them. Common culprits include adverbs like *very, really, extremely, awfully,* and *incredibly.* Occasionally these intensifiers are appropriate, but typically three out of four can be cut and the words they describe replaced with more specific words. For example, compare the following sentences:

A. The mercury was *very* high on that *extremely* hot, *awfully* uncomfortable day, making me feel *incredibly* bad.

B. The mercury topped 100 degrees on that blistering day, making me miserable.

If you think that sentence B has more force, then try to largely avoid the mushy intensifying adverbs of sentence A.

It is also not uncommon, especially in early drafts, to cram too many modifiers into one sentence, often simply stacking them in front of a word. Compare the following sentences:

A. A foul-tempered, cruel, 300-pound, gray-haired tyrant mother, whose breath constantly reeked of garlic and coffee, Carleta terrorized me as a child.

B. A foul-tempered, cruel, gray-haired tyrant, my mother terrorized me as a child. Carleta weighed 300 pounds, and her breath constantly reeked of garlic and coffee.

Sentence A stacks too many adjectives in front of the noun *mother*. Sentence B solves the problem by creating two sentences and redistributing the modifiers. Sometimes you will simply cut modifiers; other times you will weave them into your other sentences.

ACTIVITY 25.1 Correcting Problems with Adjectives and Adverbs

Correct the errors in the following sentences. If the wrong modifier is used, cross it out and write the correct one in the space provided. If too many modifiers are used, just cross out the ones you don't think are needed.

EXAMPLE
Though the room was noisy, he said ~~quiet~~, "My price is now 5,000 dollars."
quietly

1. When he saw his dad's truck in the driveway, Peter ran home ~~quick~~.
   quickly

2. We go to Sandstone ~~regular~~ to see outdoor concerts. *regularly*

3. With a 103-degree temperature and upset stomach, Aaron feels ~~badly~~ today. *bad*

4. Jennifer passed the soccer ball ~~direct~~ to her teammate who scored the winning goal. *directly*

5. This ~~really extremely very not~~ nice guy kept bothering me at a party that was already ~~awfully, really~~ incredibly boring. _____

6. Trisha Yearwood sang that last song ~~beautiful~~. *beautifully*

7. To make it to state competition, the team will have to play ~~good~~ all season. _____*well*_____

8. Six feet six, ~~broad-shouldered~~, potbellied, ~~gray-haired~~ and partly bald, my coach would glare at me with his cold ~~angry, squinting~~ blue eyes and say, "You're either lazy or stupid!" _____

9. Josh swore that if they came for him he would not go ~~quiet~~ to jail. _____*quietly*_____

10. Handle the crystal ~~careful~~ or you will break it. _____*carefully*_____

Avoiding Dangling and Misplaced Modifiers

Dangling Modifiers
Misplaced Modifiers

CAUTION! Participial phrases are especially prone to dangling.

Teaching Idea
You will find other references to misplaced modifiers in Chapter 18.

Another problem arises when modifiers are not clearly linked to the word they describe. When a modifier (single word or word group) occurs at the beginning of a sentence, it should describe the noun that follows. If it doesn't describe that noun, it is a **dangling modifier.** Here are several examples:

A. After finishing the meal, my eyelids grew heavy, and I dozed off.

B. Worn to a frazzle, the final exam had sucked out the last of Amy's energy.

C. To make it to the peak, the weather would need to favor the climbers.

D. As a civilian, his family had always come first.

As you can see, each sentence begins with a modifier that does not describe the noun that follows it. For example, in sentence A, *after finishing the meal* doesn't describe *eyelids;* it's obviously meant to describe *I*, later in the sentence. You can correct a dangling modifier by inserting a subject into the modifier or placing the noun it is intended to describe directly after it, as in the following examples:

A. After I finished the meal, my eyelids grew heavy, and I dozed off. OR

    After finishing the meal, I felt my eyelids grow heavy, and I dozed off.

B. Amy was worn to a frazzle, the final exam having sucked out the last of her energy. OR

    Worn to a frazzle, Amy felt that the final exam had sucked out the last of her energy.

Misplaced modifiers also appear to modify a word other than the one they are intended to modify, as in the following examples:

A. John called to the beagle in his slippers.

B. Paula put the calendar on her office wall covered with nature pictures.

C. The machinist drilled a hole in a piece of metal that was a half inch in diameter.

D. We saw a herd of cows from our car grazing in a harvested wheat field.

E. Billy only drank a glass of Pepsi. (meaning he did nothing but drink it)

Teaching Idea
If sentence E seems puzzling to students, you might mention that in this sentence Billy didn't *drop* or *spill*, but only *drank*, the Pepsi. In the clarified version E, Billy drank *only* a glass of Pepsi, *not* a Coke or chocolate milk.

To correct the misplaced modifier, you need to move it closer to the word it should describe, sometimes adding a word or two:

A. In his slippers *John* called to the beagle.

B. Paula put the *calendar* covered with nature pictures on her office wall.

C. The machinist drilled a *hole* that was a half inch in diameter in a piece of metal.

D. From our car we saw a *herd* of cows grazing in a harvested wheat field.

E. Billy drank only a *glass* of Pepsi. (meaning just one, and no more)

ACTIVITY 25.2 Correcting Dangling and Misplaced Modifiers

Rewrite the following sentences, adding whatever words might be needed to correct the dangling and misplaced modifiers.

EXAMPLE
Trying his best to make the team, Isaac's sweat-soaked shirt was proof of his effort.

Revised: Isaac was trying his best to make the team, and his sweat-soaked shirt was proof of his effort.

Answers will vary.

1. Rain soaked the highway that was pouring from the sky.
   Rain pouring from the sky soaked the highway.

2. Banging two pans together to wake him up, Tim groaned as his mother clanged them together once again.
   As Tim's mother banged two pans together to wake him up, Tim groaned, and his mother clanged them together once again.

3. To vote in national elections, polling booths should be open until midnight.
   So that all people can vote in national elections, polling booths should be open until midnight.

4. I felt sorry for the kitten at the pet store meowing in its cage.
   I felt sorry for the kitten meowing in its cage at the pet store.

5. At 73, Maria watched her grandfather run the Boston Marathon.
   Maria watched her 73-year-old grandfather run in the Boston Marathon.

6. Walking through the produce section, the peaches looked delicious.
   Walking through the produce section, I thought the peaches looked delicious.

7. I read about an insect in a magazine that is born, mates, and dies in one day.

   In a magazine, I read about an insect that is born, mates, and dies in one day.

8. Vito rode on the subway wearing only shorts and a T-shirt.

   Wearing only shorts and a T-shirt, Vito rode on the subway.

9. Elaine learned tae kwon do to defend herself at her community center.

   To defend herself, Elaine learned tae kwon do at her community center.

10. Emily went to the Halloween party at Lucy's house dressed like a witch.

    Dressed like a witch, Emily went to the Halloween party at Lucy's house.

CHAPTER 26

Commas, Other Punctuation Marks, and Mechanics

What Are We Trying to Achieve and Why?

Teaching Idea
Students often feel (sometimes rightly so) that punctuation is arbitrary and that marks need to go more or less wherever their current teacher says they are supposed to, even when this advice conflicts with what teachers in other courses have said. It can help to discuss punctuation as an imperfect but self-imposed system for achieving clarity.

After you have labored to gather, organize, and express your ideas, you have one final task as a writer: to make sure that your grammar, spelling, and punctuation are correct and support your hard work. This chapter focuses on punctuation—mainly commas but also other marks such as semicolons, colons, dashes, and parentheses.

Punctuation is essential for sorting our ideas into easily understood units of thought. To see this, notice how changes in punctuation from letter A to letter B are enough to dramatically change the meaning.

A. Dear John:

I want a man who knows what love is all about. You are generous, kind, and thoughtful. People who are not like you admit to being useless and inferior. You have ruined me for other men. I yearn for you. I have no feelings whatsoever when we're apart. I can be forever happy. Will you let me be yours?

Susan

B. Dear John:

I want a man who knows what love is. All about you are generous, kind, and thoughtful—people who are not like you. Admit to being useless and inferior. You have ruined me. For other men I yearn. For you I have no feelings whatsoever. When we're apart, I can be forever happy. Will you let me be?

Yours,
Susan

Your work is not likely to shift meaning this abruptly because you misuse a few commas, but you *are* likely to confuse or lose readers if you let punctuation and other mechanical problems pile up. Because commas typically cause the most concern, we will focus on them first.

Commas

Commas

Teaching Idea
Because most students rely heavily on the "pause and punctuate" method, it is worth acknowledging that it does work some of the time.

Because we use commas so often, writers have developed a system for placing this mark in an orderly way to help sort out ideas. This system of "rules" is not foolproof or even altogether logical, but it works reasonably well, and even professional writers adhere to it most of the time. Comma usage conventions are designed not to frustrate and confuse writers but to serve their needs. There *is* a controlling logic that works in punctuating by convention rather than by ear. Remember that writing is not simply transcribed speech: It is a more complex use of language that requires careful revision and editing. So the pause-and-punctuate method of placing commas will only help a writer about half the time. Fifty percent is not an average that most of us are happy with.

Learning to punctuate accurately depends on knowledge of sentence parts, knowledge you developed in working on Chapter 20. Once you can separate a main clause from a subordinate clause and are familiar with the different kinds of phrases, comma usage will make sense to you, at least most of the time. If you learn the three primary comma categories, in the next section, and the few secondary uses, in the section after that, you will greatly reduce any problems you have had with comma usage.

The Big Three Comma Categories

Teaching Idea
Because punctuating correctly so often depends on the ability to locate subjects and verbs, this is a good time to review the discussion of subjects and verbs in Chapter 20.

Commas are primarily used to separate and enclose. More specifically, they have three main uses:

THE BIG THREE COMMA CATEGORIES
1. To separate a main clause from introductory words or word groups
2. To enclose or separate nonessential words or word groups that come within or after a main clause
3. To separate two main clauses

To put commas in a sentence, first look for the main clause or main clauses in the sentence (see pp. 528–529). Once you locate a main clause, look for words or word groups that come *before, within,* or *after* it. Failure to use commas to

7. Nevertheless, RU 486, the abortion pill, has arrived in the United States.

8. Frightened by a legal system that has finally decided to care, deadbeat dads are beginning to pay their child support.

9. Climbing to the fifth floor of her apartment was a daily ordeal for Kendra. *C*

10. Write three sentences that use an introductory word group set off with a comma; underline the verb of the main clause twice and the subject once.

Answers will vary.

A. _____

_____

B. _____

_____

C. _____

_____

Commas That Set Off Nonessential Words and Word Groups

Teaching Idea
For more information on essential versus nonessential elements, you can direct students to Chapters 18, 20, and 21.

The second major reason for using commas is to set off **nonessential** words and word groups within or at the end of main clauses. *Nonessential* means that the words are not needed to complete the meaning of the sentence. If the words or word groups are cut, the main idea is still clear. Let's compare nonessential and essential word groups:

ESSENTIAL   The Dodge Caravan *that is leaking gasoline* is mine.

NONESSENTIAL   Dodge Caravans, *which are roomy family vehicles,* have hatchback doors.

In the first sentence, we need the *that* clause to identify which Dodge Caravan. In the second sentence, the *which* clause simply adds a comment, so the clause is set off with a comma.

Which clauses frequently signal nonessential material, and when they do, they must be set off with commas. *That* clauses signal essential material and so do not take commas. With *who,* both patterns are common:

ESSENTIAL   A bicyclist *who has survived cancer* might work even harder at his sport.

NONESSENTIAL   Lance Armstrong, *who has survived cancer,* may be the world's best bicyclist.

In the first sentence, the *who* clause identifies which bicyclist might work harder; not all cyclists, but perhaps those who have survived cancer. The second sentence uses a proper noun, *Lance Armstrong,* which identifies the athlete beyond question. Therefore, the *who* clause that follows is nonessential and so uses commas.

We often use nonessential word groups to enrich writing. However, when doing so, we need to signal with commas that the material is of secondary importance. Following, you will see examples of nonessential single words, phrases, and clauses. Notice that the introductory word groups from the previous comma category still require commas when shifted into the main clauses.

Words

CONJUNCTIVE ADVERB	I hope, *however,* to make it to the bank before it closes.
ADVERB	Gail, *unfortunately,* doesn't have enough money to buy that computer.
TRANSITIONAL WORD	The cat, *next,* decided to claw the new curtains.
PRESENT PARTICIPLE	Bobby, *smiling,* cradled his new catcher's mitt.
PAST PARTICIPLE	Susie, *excited,* ran to meet her mother.

Phrases

PRESENT PARTICIPIAL PHRASE	Wayne, *diving for the football,* snatched it from the air with one hand.
PAST PARTICIPIAL PHRASE	Susie, *excited by the sight of presents,* ran to meet her mother.
PRESENT ABSOLUTE PHRASE	Latashia coasted into her driveway, *the car running on fumes.*
PAST ABSOLUTE PHRASE	Terry, *his boat covered with a tarp,* felt it would survive the hailstorm.
INFINITIVE PHRASE	Tanya knew that, *to play lead guitar in the band,* she would need to practice hard.
APPOSITIVE PHRASE	Leslie, *an athlete with much experience,* could see that the game was headed for disaster.

We sometimes misuse commas because we confuse essential and nonessential participial phrases within or at the end of sentences. Compare the participial phrases that end the following two sentences:

A. We listened to the cottonwood leaves *rustling in the wind.*

B. We walked up the hill, *taking great pleasure in the sunny day.*

The present participial phrase in sentence A is essential, telling which cottonwood leaves the people listened to. We could rewrite it as an essential adjective clause, "*that were* rustling in the wind." The phrase in sentence B, in contrast, is nonessential, merely adding a comment about the people. Notice that, for this reason, we could easily shift the phrase in sentence B to the beginning of the sentence, whereas the phrase in sentence A must occur next to *leaves,* the word it describes. (If we tried to shift it to the beginning of the sentence, we would have a dangling modifier; see pp. 591–593.) Therefore, the phrase in sentence B is set off with a comma, but the phrase in sentence A is not.

Clauses

ADJECTIVE CLAUSE	Dmitri stayed at the Marriott Hotel, *which is one of the finest in the city.*
ADJECTIVE CLAUSE	Slobodan Milosevic, *who contributed to the deaths of thousands,* is no longer in power in the former Yugoslavia.

In both of these sentences, we know the adjective clauses are nonessential, because they follow proper nouns. Proper nouns themselves identify the person or thing, so what follows must be nonessential commentary.

The same logic applies to an adjective clause that begins with the word *where*. Note that it can be either essential or nonessential, as in the following examples:

A. Gary was not as popular in Topeka as he is in the city *where he now lives.*

B. Gary was not as popular in Topeka as he is in Dallas, *where he moved last fall.*

In sentence A, the *where* clause completes the meaning of the main clause, telling which city he is now popular in. Sentence B uses the proper noun *Dallas,* so the *where* clause becomes nonessential and is set off with a comma.
   (For more on nonessential versus essential word groups, see pp. 529–530.)

ACTIVITY 26.2 Commas with Nonessential Word Groups

In the following sentences, find the main clause and underline the verb twice and the subject once. Now use commas to set off nonessential word groups within and at the end of the main clauses. If a sentence is correct, do not insert a comma.

   EXAMPLE
   Kelsey chased after the soccer ball running at full speed.

   Corrected: Kelsey chased after the soccer ball, running at full speed.

   1. The motorcycle that is blowing oily smoke needs a ring job. C
   2. *Smithsonian* magazine which has Al Gore on its board of regents is filled with interesting articles.
   3. Dustin reacting quickly managed to save the child from falling overboard.
   4. Eboni exhausted dragged herself into the shower at 6:30 A.M.
   5. The wind which had blown continuously for three days whipped the edge of the flag to ragged tatters.
   6. The boxer hoping desperately for an opportunity to attack continued to backpedal around the ring.
   7. At midnight a time known as the "witching hour" Halloween parties reach their height.
   8. Gail's pediatrician who looked like she had bad news walked slowly toward us.
   9. I noticed the purple bruise developing under his left eye. C
   10. Write three of your own sentences that use nonessential word groups; underline the verb of the main clause twice and the subject once.
   Answers will vary.
      A. _____

         _____

      B. _____

         _____

      C. _____

         _____

HINT: Memorizing *and/but* will help you remember to edit for commas in two-part sentences.

Teaching Idea
It is worth stressing this misuse of a comma with a coordinating conjunction because it is so frequent in student writing, particularly when students are focusing on commas in compound sentences. You might direct students who are having trouble with this error to the discussion of coordination in Chapter 18 and unnecessary commas in this chapter.

Commas That Separate Main Clauses

The last major reason for using commas is to separate main clauses within compound and compound–complex sentences—sentences that use a coordinating conjunction (*and, but, or, so, yet, nor, for*) to join two main clauses. Here are some examples:

A. Five-year-old Addie wanted to climb the sweet gum tree in her backyard, *and* her mother wanted to stop her.

B. Jacob wanted to explain to his girlfriend what he was doing at the movies with another woman, *but* he couldn't think of a convincing excuse.

C. You can pay me now, *or* you can pay me later.

D. Michelle hoped to run in the Boston Marathon, *so* she trained all year.

E. Terrorists destroyed the World Trade Center on September 11, 2001, *yet* with this act they also began the destruction of their own organization.

Notice that, with two main clauses, a subject and verb appears on each side of the coordinating conjunction. Remember that coordinating conjunctions are used between words and phrases as well as clauses. If you tried to put a comma before every coordinating conjunction, you would have a mess. Consider the following sentence:

NO COMMA NEEDED   The willow trees were blowing in the wind *and* losing leaves and soon would be bare.

This sentence has only one main clause with a three-part verb, *were blowing, losing,* and *would be*. The words after *and* could not stand alone as a separate sentence. Use a comma before a coordinating conjunction only when the material before and after could be divided into two separate sentences, each ending with a period.

Another common error is using an unneeded comma before the subordinating conjunction *so that* when the *that* has been dropped, as in the following example:

NO COMMA NEEDED   Cinderella's cruel stepmother locked her in a room *so* [that] one of the stepmother's daughters might wed Prince Charming.

This *so* is not a coordinating conjunction; it is a subordinating conjunction that comes before an essential adverb clause.

When the main clauses are only a few words long, some writers omit the comma, as in the following example:

This deal stinks and you do too.

However, a comma between main clauses is never incorrect.

ACTIVITY 26.3 Commas to Divide Compound Sentences

In the following sentences, find the main clauses and in each underline the verb twice and the subject once. Now put commas before the coordinating conjunctions wherever needed. If a sentence is correct, do not insert a comma.

EXAMPLE

Nina asked her grandfather a question but he did not hear her.

Corrected: Nina asked her grandfather a question, but he did not hear her.

1. The California sea otter and the Chinese panda are endangered species. C

2. Sending large robots to distant planets is too expensive, but sending miniature ones is not.

3. Lois tried for years to play piano, yet she could not master the bass line.

4. Cell phones in college classrooms can be viewed as a blessing for those who need them or a curse for those who are startled by the beeping. C

5. The principal groaned in the midst of his nightmare and drifted back into dreams of being chased through the halls by students. C

6. Athletes should maintain at least a C average, or they should be benched until they raise their grades.

7. At first Cecelia favored the younger candidate for town council, but then she discovered his real priorities.

8. Russ was on his way to Madison Middle School, and he fervently hoped that Max, the class bully, would be absent again.

9. Tess wanted to win the lottery so she could quit work at the GM plant. C

10. Write three of your own compound sentences, underlining the verbs twice and the subjects once.

Answers will vary.

A. _____

_____

B. _____

_____

C. _____

_____

Secondary Comma Categories

While the Big Three comma categories account for most comma errors, several other structures that call for commas, discussed here as secondary comma categories, can also cause some confusion.

Items in a Series

When three or more words or word groups are listed in a row, a comma should follow each:

NOUNS	I'm going to Payless to buy some lumber, paving stones, and cement.
VERB PHRASES	We ran for the bus stop, missed the bus, and then chased it all the way to the next stop.
MAIN CLAUSES	Harry did the research, Albert organized all the sources, and Terry wrote most of the first draft.

Teaching Idea
Students will find more
information on ordering
adjectives in Chapter 28.

Coordinate Adjectives

When two or more **coordinate,** or equal, **adjectives** precede a noun (or pronoun), commas should be used between the adjectives:

It was a *long, hard* hike to get to the top of the mountain.

In this sentence, *long* and *hard* modify *hike* equally. We could also use the word *and* in place of the comma, and we could reverse the two adjectives, saying "a hard, long hike."

This sentence, in contrast, uses **cumulative adjectives:**

Two tired old men sat on a park bench.

The adjectives *two tired old* do not describe the noun *men* equally. Instead, each adjective adds meaning to the others: These are old men who are tired, and there are two of them. Notice that we could neither insert *and* between the words nor reverse them.

As discussed in Chapter 28, adjectives fall into various categories (adjectives of number, judgment, size, shape, age, color, location, and material). Adjectives from the same category occurring together are coordinate and use commas; adjectives from different categories are cumulative and do not use commas.

Another place *not* to use a comma is directly before or between two-word nouns, as in the following sentence:

Melanie changed the *filthy* furnace filter.

Because *furnace filter* is a single unit, no comma is needed.

Contrasting Expressions

We often contrast ideas using *not,* as in this sentence:

Frank, not Tony, deserves the promotion.

The phrase beginning with *not* is nonessential material and so is set off with commas.

Misleading Expressions

If a sentence might be misinterpreted without a comma, either insert a comma or restructure the sentence:

MISLEADING	He became angry when his opponent cheated and complained.
COMMA ADDED	He became angry when his opponent cheated, and complained.
RESTRUCTURED	When his opponent cheated, he became angry and complained.

Numbers, Addresses, Place Names, Dates, and Direct Address

When using numbers, addresses, place names, dates, and direct address, follow the conventions of standard comma placement:

- **Numbers:** 3,985,041
- **Addresses:** "Joanne lives at 4593 Connell Lane, Overland Park, Kansas."

Note: Adverb clauses that begin with *although, though,* and *even though* usually do use a comma even when they follow a main clause because these subordinating conjunctions announce strong contrast.

ACTIVITY 26.5 Removing Unnecessary Commas

In the following sentences, underline the verb of the *main* clause twice and the subject once. Next, cross out incorrect commas, leaving the correct ones.

EXAMPLE

While Roxanne tried on a new dress, her friend wandered around the department store, and finally decided to buy a new purse.

Corrected: While Roxanne tried on a new dress, her friend wandered around the department store and finally decided to buy a new purse.

1. Wandering listlessly, across the front yard, Helen felt that she had seen her better days pass her by, and wondered, if there was a chance that she still had a future.
2. Everyone, in the class thought, that singular pronouns like *everyone* should be plural.
3. The Saturn, missing its left rear taillight, was being followed closely by a highway patrol car. (Keep commas or delete both.)
4. The Suzuki Grand Vitara, costing less than several of its competitors, has a zippy, six-cylinder engine.
5. Arturo knew, that he was in trouble, when the conductor stopped practice the second time, and pointed at him.
6. Bruce Willis performed well in the movie, *Armageddon.*
7. The stillness in the air, and the sudden absence of animal activity made Gloria think that a big storm might be on the way. (Delete comma or add one after "activity.")
8. Dennis could see that quitting his job, and moving out of the city would not help him forget his first lost love.
9. The temperatures will remain in the hundreds, if the Jet Stream does not dip back down into the Midwest.
10. The insane engineer blew the whistle for five nonstop minutes as his train rumbled past the crossing at 3:00 A.M., waking residents, some of whom grumbled into their pillows and then dropped back into restless sleep. C

Teaching Idea
Sentences 3 and 7 can be used to illustrate the importance of the author's intent in determining essential versus nonessential ideas.

Other Punctuation Marks and Mechanics

In addition to commas, writers often use semicolons, colons, dashes, and parentheses to group and separate ideas. These are discussed here, along with some punctuation marks that serve other purposes and some other mechanics issues important to your writing.

Semicolons

Semicolons

If periods are full stops in sentences, bringing the reader to a temporary halt, and commas are half stops, mere split-second pauses, semicolons might be thought of as three-quarter stops, marks midway between the other two. We use semicolons in two ways: to separate main clauses without using a coordinating conjunction (such as *and* or *but*) and to separate word groups that are in a series and contain commas.

Separating Main Clauses

HINT: Semicolons are one method for correcting comma splices and run-on sentences.

Consider these two sentences:

A. Jakob Dylan is following in his father's footsteps; Bob Dylan is proud of his son.

B. Many books have been written about the Beatles; however, *The Beatles Anthology* has been written by the surviving Beatles themselves.

In both A and B, while a period could be used to separate the main clauses, the second main clause is so closely related to the first that the semicolon is a good choice. Notice that sentence B uses a conjunctive adverb, *however*, as well as a semicolon between the two main clauses. (Other common conjunctive adverbs include *therefore, nevertheless, then, in fact,* and *consequently.*) The semicolon dividing main clauses is one way to fix a comma splice or run-on sentence. (For more on comma splices and run-ons, see Chapter 22.)

Separating Word Groups in a Series

Look at this sentence:

When we go to the Renaissance Festival, we end up *devouring* turkey legs, sausages, and meat pies; *watching* the jousting, acting, and juggling; and *shopping* for clothing, art work, and musical instruments.

Each of the three main word groups in this sentence—the phrases beginning with *devouring, watching,* and *shopping*—has within it words that are separated by commas. To avoid confusion, we use semicolons, not commas, to separate the main word groups.

Colons

Colons

The colon has three primary uses: to introduce a list (as in this sentence), to separate closely related main clauses, and to introduce an appositive (nonessential describing word or phrase) at the end of a sentence. We also use the colon in the salutation of a business letter (Dear Professor Hastings:) and, sometimes, to introduce quotations (John Smith claimed: "There is no gold in the New World.").

When a colon introduces a list, the material before it must be a grammatically complete sentence. Do not use a colon to introduce a list that is needed to make the sentence grammatically complete, as in this example:

INAPPROPRIATE COLON INTRODUCING A LIST   Maria will bring: potato chips, soda, and pasta salad.

CORRECTED   Maria will bring the following items: potato chips, soda, and pasta salad.

Like a semicolon, a colon can be used to separate closely related main clauses:

SEPARATING MAIN CLAUSES   Lowell finally understood why his girlfriend would not return his calls: She had decided that they were through.

However, a colon should be used only if the second clause restates or completes the meaning of the first. In the example, it completes the meaning, by telling why.

Note: For grammatically complete sentences following a colon, the first letter may be either capitalized or lowercase.

Colons also introduce appositives:

INTRODUCING APPOSITIVE	Make your purchases on the basis of two criteria: cost and usefulness.

The sentence ends with an appositive, which describes the noun it follows, *criteria.*

Dashes

The dash is a versatile punctuation mark that can help writers in several ways: to set off a series that begins a sentence, to indicate an abrupt break in thought within a sentence, to enclose items in a series, and to emphasize a word or word group at the end of a sentence. (**Note:** A dash [—] is longer than a hyphen [-]. If your word processing program does not have a dash, use two hyphens to create it.)

BEGINNING SERIES	Three novels, one anthology of short stories, and two how-to books—my summer reading list is complete.
BREAK IN THOUGHT	I will arrive at the party—if Tony shows up to drive me—around midnight.
ITEMS IN SERIES	Last night Carrie packed all her necessities—clothes, shoes, and toiletries—but forgot to include her hair dryer.
FINAL WORD GROUP EMPHASIZED	Javier had worked hard at Sprint and deserved some recognition—and a salary increase.

Parentheses

Writers use parentheses primarily to enclose nonessential material. Since commas can often serve this function, writers usually reserve parentheses for more loosely related material:

> There were too many players on the team (and coaches, for that matter).

Quotation Marks

Quotation marks are used primarily to enclose the spoken and written words of others—that is, dialogue and quotations from texts. We also use quotation marks to enclose the titles of short creative works (stories, essays, poems, newspaper and magazine articles, songs, and episodes of television shows) and, occasionally, when referring to a word used as a word (*the word "dinosaur"*).

DIALOGUE	"I'll get Jamie out of the bath," said Albert.
QUOTATION FROM TEXT	In *The Voyage of the Beagle,* Charles Darwin writes, "In five little packets which I sent him, he has ascertained no less than sixty-seven different organic forms!"

Notice that the comma after *bath* and the exclamation point after *forms* are both placed inside the quotation marks.

Teaching Idea
You might suggest the dash to students who want to use a comma to separate compound elements at the ends of sentences. Of course, you'll want to stress that they should reserve the dash for special emphasis.

Teaching Idea
End dashes can also help students with some fragment problems.

CAUTION! Avoid overusing dashes; try to keep to one or two per page.

CAUTION! Note the possible confusion without the dashes: "Last night Carrie packed all her necessities, clothes, shoes, and toiletries . . ."

CAUTION! Avoid overusing parentheses; usually once or twice a page is enough.

Apostrophes

Apostrophes

CAUTION! *It's, you're, and who's are different from the possessive pronouns its, your, and whose.*

Apostrophes have two main functions: to indicate the omission of letters in contractions and to show ownership.

Contractions

Here are some common contractions: *wouldn't (would not), won't (will not), let's (let us), it's (it is), you're (you are), who's (who is/has)*. Be careful not to confuse *it's, you're,* and *who's* with the soundalike words *its, your,* and *whose,* which are possessive pronouns.

Possession

To show ownership for singular nouns and some plural nouns, we use the apostrophe and *-s* (*John's book, Stefanie's car keys, the cloud's shadow, the children's pet*). With most plural nouns, the apostrophe follows the *-s:*

> Adam and Darin owned the lemonade stand. It was the boys' stand.

The need for an apostrophe may not seem obvious in, for example, *an hour's wait, a dollar's worth of chocolate raisins,* or *a whole season's rain in one week.* To check whether an apostrophe is needed, you can restate the possessive word as an "of" phrase: *the car keys of Stefanie, the wait of an hour,* or *the rain of a whole season.*

Hyphens

Hyphens

Hyphens join word parts or words to make new words:

- **Prefixes:** ex-athlete, anti-Communist, self-respect, pro-democracy
- **Compound words:** son-in-law, go-between, look-alike, twenty-seven
- **Compound adjectives:** well-respected machinist, good-looking quarter horse, hard-fought contest, problem-solving attitude, hard-to-catch outlaw

Note: When the compound adjective follows the noun, no hyphen is used: "The machinist is well respected."

Hyphens can also be used at the end of a line of text to divide a word between syllables.

Capitalization

Capitalization

We capitalize proper nouns—the names of specific, unique individuals or things—and words derived from them. Here are some categories:

- **People, things, trademarks:** Mark, Camry, Coca-Cola
- **Professional titles:** Professor Oden, Doctor Franklin, Senator Edwards
- **Organizations, institutions, sports teams, companies:** the United Way, Centerville High School, Kansas City Chiefs, Sears
- **Nationalities, ethnicities, and races:** German, Russian, French, Korean, Syrian, African American, Hispanic, Asian
- **Languages:** Spanish, Mandarin, Swahili, Portuguese, English
- **Religions, followers of religions, deities, holy books:** Catholicism, Buddhism; Protestant, Hindu; Lord, Allah, Yahweh; Bible, Koran, Talmud
- **Historical documents, periods, events:** the Constitution, the Renaissance, the Vietnam War

- **Geographic names:** the Ozark Mountains, St. Louis, Pacific Northwest, Middle East
- **Days, months, holidays:** Saturday, April, Christmas
- **First word in a direct quote:** Margaret said, "No one agrees with you."
- **Titles:** books, stories, films, magazines, newspapers, poems, songs, and works of art: *The Catcher in the Rye,* "Down at the Dinghy," *Newsweek*

Note: Capitalize all words in titles except prepositions (*on, in, at*), coordinating conjunctions (*and, but, or, so, yet, nor, for*), and articles (*a, an, the*)—unless any of these words begin or end the title or follow a colon in the title (*Sleep-walking: A Comedy*).

Note: Do not capitalize the following: seasons (*spring*), plants (*rose, oak*), animals (*robin, ant*), school subjects (*biology, economics*).

Note that the categories above are proper nouns; do not capitalize words that are part of a name when they are used as common nouns. For example, capitalize *doctor* in *Doctor Johnson* but not in *Abby Johnson, who is a doctor;* capitalize *high school* in *Southwest High School* but not in *Tom's high school.*

Numbers

Numbers

Some writers prefer in most cases to indicate numbers with numerals instead of words. However, a more traditional treatment calls for spelling out numbers of one or two words (*three, fourteen, fifty-six*) and then using numerals for numbers of three words or more (101; 2,098; 5,980,746). Here are several other conventions for number use:

- **Numbers in dates:** January 3, 2001 (The endings *-st, -d,* and *-th* are not needed after dates.)
- **Numbers in series:** "The driveway was 140 feet long, 12 feet wide, and 6 inches deep." (Be consistent in using numerals or letters.)
- **Numbers that begin sentences:** "One hundred and thirty passengers died in the crash." (Spell out a number or recast the sentence.)
- **Percentages/decimals:** "The solution was 95 percent water." (Use numerals.)
- **Pages numbers:** "The authors state on page 34 . . ." (Use numerals.)
- **Identification numbers:** room 14, Interstate 35, channel 41 (Use numerals.)
- **Physical measures:** 6 miles, 12 feet (Use numerals.)
- **Times/ages:** 3 hours, 7 years old (Use numerals.)

Underlining and Italicizing

Italics

Most underlining or, with a word processor, *italicizing* is for the purpose of representing titles. The following list shows the categories of works whose titles should be underlined or italicized (shorter works are enclosed in quotation marks):

TITLES THAT SHOULD BE IN ITALICS (OR UNDERLINED)

Books: *The Ox-Bow Incident*	Long poems: *Beowulf*
Plays: *Hamlet*	Periodicals: *Newsweek*

Pamphlets: *Treating Lower Back Pain*

Long musical works: *Tapestry*

Television and radio programs: *Friends*

Published speeches: *Gettysburg Address*

Movies: *Spiderman II*

Works of art: Michelangelo's *David*

CAUTION! Don't be afraid to try italicizing for emphasis, but do it sparingly.

Other common uses include the following:

- **Emphasis:** "Luann said that she would *never* marry a man for money."
- **Names of specific airplanes, trains, ships, and satellites:** the space shuttle *Challenger*
- **Words and letters referred to as such:** "The word *very* is usually expendable."

ACTIVITY 26.6 Practicing Mechanics

In the following sentences in the *main* clauses, underline the verb twice and the subject once. Then correct the errors in the sentences. Check for semicolons, colons, dashes, quotation marks, apostrophes, capitalization, hyphens, numbers, and underlining/italicizing.

EXAMPLE

The essay Tony wrote called Diminished Capacity was praised by his teacher, who said, This essay should win the schools literary competition.

Corrected: the essay Tony wrote called "Diminished Capacity" was praised by his teacher, who said, "This essay should win the school's literary competition."

1. Harvey said, "there are many well-intentioned people maybe the majority who vote for a president based on a single issue." *(or —)* *^) or —*

2. Here are just a few of the car Manufacturers who have gotten into the mini-SUV line: toyota, subaru, suzuki, and nissan.

3. The recent arrival of the hybrid gasoline/electric cars is a hopeful sign for the environment; these cars might significantly reduce air pollution.

4. Some forget that it's the peoples will that is supposed to govern a democracy.

5. Juliet loves cool-Spring days (though she dislikes the rain) and says, *(or could be — or ,)* "after the earth has slept all winter, I can't wait for the first of Spring's Daffodil's."

6. *Forty-three* 43 sailboats set out for key west, Florida, but only *thirty-nine* 39 made it through the Hurricane. *no italics*

7. Thirty year old Alex Carroll has written a best selling book called
(italic or underline)
Beat the Cops: The guide To Fighting Your Traffic Ticket And Winning.

8. No till farming is an established method for conserving the soil.

9. The AARP organization begins sending out it's membership
applications to people when they turn 50. fifty
(italic or underline)

10. Madonnas CD Ray of Light was overseen by French Producer
Mirwais Ahmadzai.

CHAPTER 27

Spelling and Sound-alike Words

What Are We Trying to Achieve and Why?

Teaching Idea
Students who have special problems with spelling (such as those who are dyslexic) often have all but given up hope of dealing with the situation and also may have labeled themselves as unintelligent. To encourage these students in particular, you might stress spelling as only one skill among many, and one that they can improve.

An explanation or argument that in conversation impresses your listeners with its clarity and logic can, when you write it, be discredited altogether based on nothing more than misspelled words. Although spelling should be a low priority in drafting, when editing you should try to catch every misspelling because errors in spelling affect readers' perception of you. For example, even the brightest, most qualified job applicant who submits a résumé with miscellaneous misspellings and wrong choices of soundalike words, such as *there* instead of *their*, will have a hard time getting an interview.

English spelling is quirky at best, and everyone misspells words occasionally. Sounding words out often helps, but not always. A language that produces words like *knight, sign, sugar,* and *ocean* is bound to frustrate its writers. But there are patterns we can depend on to answer many spelling questions. This chapter will help you improve your spelling with some suggestions, some basic rules, lists of commonly misspelled words, and lists of soundalike words.

Some Suggestions for Help with Spelling

Spelling

The following list contains specific suggestions on how you can improve your spelling.

SUGGESTIONS TO HELP IMPROVE YOUR SPELLING

1. **Make a decision to work on your spelling.** If you want to improve, you can.

2. **Develop the dictionary habit.** Write with a dictionary close at hand. As you draft, put a question mark by words you are unsure of, and then

Teaching Idea
After students have turned in their first evaluated assignment, you might encourage them to track their errors, including errors in spelling and homonyms, and list them in the Improvement Chart in Appendix 2.

use your dictionary to find the correct spelling. If you try several letter combinations and still cannot find the correct spelling, mark the word and ask someone for help, perhaps a person in your editing group.

3. **Buy an electronic dictionary** programmed to search using approximate spellings.

4. **Take advantage of the spell-check feature** of your word processing software. Remember, though, that spell check is only a simple-minded device; it can't, for example, catch that you've used one word instead of another.

5. **Begin a personal spelling list** of words that you are unsure of or have misspelled in compositions. Pay particular attention to the ordinary words you use regularly and to sound-alike words. Because words like *photovoltaic* and *conundrum* are uncommon, you will probably be alerted to the need to check their spelling. It is the common—and commonly misspelled—words that are more likely to plague you.

6. **In editing, look closely at every word in every sentence.** Sound words out syllable by syllable, keeping in mind that sounding out doesn't always work.

7. **Try to remember pattern words** that are similar to and can help you with other words. If, for example, you are unsure of whether to double the *p* in the word *hopped* but are sure about the double *p* in *stopped*, *stopped* can help you with *hopped*.

8. **Test yourself on the lists of commonly misspelled words and soundalike words in this chapter.** Include in your spelling list any word that you misspell along with the correct spelling. It often helps to pronounce the word aloud several times, exaggerating the stresses on the syllables, such as *soph-O-more* or *math-E-mat-ics*.

9. **When you discover you have misspelled a word, make sure of the correct spelling** and then write the word several times, preferably within a sentence.

10. **Study the spelling patterns listed in this chapter.**

Some Useful Spelling Patterns

Much of spelling hinges on being able to break words into syllables and to recognize vowels and consonants. **Syllables** are simply units of sound—the way a word is divided in the dictionary—for example, *syl-la-ble* or *base-ball*. The vowels and consonants of English are as follows:

- **Vowels:** *a, e, i, o, u*
- **Consonants:** *b, c, d, f, g, h, j, k, l, m, n, p, q, r, s, t, v, w, x, y, z*

The letter *y* can function as either a consonant, as in *yes*, or a vowel, as in *pretty* (where it sounds like *ee*) and *fly* (where it sounds like *i*).

Doubling the Final Consonant

To determine whether to double the final consonant of a word when adding a suffix (an ending like *-ed*, *-ing*, *-er*, or *-est*), check to see if three conditions are met:

1. Is the word a single-syllable word (*pot*) or accented on the final syllable (*oc-CUR*)?
2. Are the last three letters of the word consonant–vowel–consonant (*p-o-t, occ-u-r*)?
3. Does the suffix begin with a vowel (*-ed, -ing*)?

If all three of these conditions are met, double the final consonant, as in the following lists:

Double Final Consonant

Single-Syllable Words	Words Accented on the Final Syllable
stun + ing = stunning	oc-CUR + ing = occurring
stop + ed = stopped	sub-MIT + ing = submitting
plan + er = planner	com-MIT + ed = committed
hot + est = hottest	pre-FER + ed = preferred

If any of the three conditions are lacking, do *not* double the final consonant:

en-ter + ing = entering (*enter* is not accented on final syllable)

ask + ed = asked (*ask* does not end in consonant–vowel–consonant).

slow + ly = slowly (*-ly* does not begin with a vowel)

Notice that the following words, while fulfilling conditions 1 and 3, do not fulfill condition 2, as none end in consonant–vowel–consonant:

Do Not Double Final Consonant

Single-Syllable Words	Words Accented on the Final Syllable
crawl + ing = crawling	despair + ing = despairing
stoop + ed = stooped	pretend + ing = pretending
plain + er = plainer	attend + ed = attended
slight + est = slightest	appear + ed = appeared

Dropping or Keeping the Final e

As a general rule, when adding a suffix to a word ending in *e*, you should do the following:

1. **Drop the *e* if the suffix begins with a vowel.** Common suffixes include *-ing, -al, -able, -ence, -ance, -ion, -ous, -ure, -ive*, and *-age*.

come + ing = coming	congregate + ion = congregation
survive + al = survival	fame + ous = famous
excite + able = excitable	seize + ure = seizure
precede + ence = precedence	create + ive = creative
guide + ance = guidance	plume + age = plumage

   Exceptions include *noticeable, courageous, manageable, dyeing*, and *mileage*.

2. **Keep the *e* if the suffix begins with a consonant.** Common suffixes include *-ly, -ment, -ness, -less, -ty*, and *-ful*.

definite + ly = definitely	taste + less = tasteless
advertise + ment = advertisement	entire + ty = entirety
like + ness = likeness	waste + ful = wasteful

   Exceptions include *acknowledgment, ninth, truly, wholly*, and *argument*.

Changing or Not Changing the Final *y* to *i*

When adding a suffix to a word ending in a *y:*

1. **Change the *y* to *i* if it is preceded by a consonant:**

   sky + es = skies   happy + ness = happiness

   rely + ance = reliance   healthy + est = healthiest

   marry + ed = married   merry + ment = merriment

   pity + less = pitiless   mercy + ful = merciful

2. **Do not change the *y* if it is preceded by a vowel:**

   enjoy + able = enjoyable   play + ful = playful

   deploy + ed = deployed   employ + ment = employment

   joy + ous = joyous   coy + est = coyest

   essay + ist = essayist

   Exceptions include *paid, said, laid, daily,* and *gaily.*

Note: When you are adding the suffix *-ing* to a word ending in *y*, always keep the *y: crying, studying, enjoying, saying.*

Forming Plurals: -s or -es

Most nouns form their plurals by adding *-s* or *-es* (*birds, batches*):

1. **If the word ends in *ch, sh, ss, x,* or *z,* add *-es:***

   snitch + es = snitches

   brush + es = brushes

   miss + es = misses

   box + es = boxes

   waltz + es = waltzes

2. **If the word ends in *y* preceded by a vowel, add *-s:***

   holiday + s = holidays

   Friday + s = Fridays

   monkey + s = monkeys

3. **If the word ends in *y* preceded by a consonant, change the *y* to *i* and add *-es:***

   theory + es = theories

   sky + es = skies

   fly + es = flies

4. **Some words ending in *o* add an *-s,* while others add an *-es.*** Here are a few common examples, which you might want to memorize:

o + *-s*	*o* + *-es*
pianos	tomatoes
memos	potatoes
solos	heroes
radios	mosquitoes

Using *ie* or *ei*

In most instances, use *i* before *e*, except after *c*, unless the *ei* sounds like *ay* as in *neighbor* and *weigh*.

ie

believe	piece
niece	yield

ei after c

conceive	receive
deceive	ceiling

ei That Sounds like ay

eighth	reign
weight	vein

Exceptions, which use *ei* where we would expect *ie*, include *caffeine, seize, height, leisure, neither, either, weird,* and *foreign*.

LIST OF FREQUENTLY MISSPELLED WORDS

a lot	completely	exaggerate	jewelry
accept	conceive	except	judgment
accommodate	conscience	experience	knowledge
acquaint	conscientious	fantasies	led
acquire	conscious	fascinate	leisure
adolescence	controlled	fictitious	length
advice	controlling	field	license
advise	convenience	foreign	likelihood
affect	council	forty	liveliest
all right	counsel	fourth	loneliness
already	counselor	friendliness	lonely
argument	criticism	fulfill	lose
beginning	criticize	government	maintenance
believe	curiosity	governor	marriage
beside	curious	grammar	mathematics
break	definitely	guarantee	mischief
breathe	dependent	height	moral
business	desirability	heroes	morale
calendar	despair	hypocrite	necessary
cannot	disappoint	immediately	ninety
capital	disastrous	independent	noticeable
career	discipline	interest	obstacle
character	effect	interfere	occasion
choice	eighth	interrupt	occurred
choose	environment	it's	occurrence
chose	equipped	its	occurring

opportunity	professor	success	unfortunately
parallel	quiet	suppose	until
particular	receive	surprise	usually
passed	referring	temperature	vacuum
past	relieve	than	vegetable
perform	reminisce	their	weight
personnel	rhythm	then	weird
piece	roommate	there	where
possess	sense	therefore	whether
practical	separate	they're	whole
precede	sergeant	threw	whose
preferred	shining	through	without
prejudice	similar	to	woman
principal	since	too	written
principle	sophomore	transferred	yield
privilege	strength	truly	you're
proceed	subtle	unconscious	your

Sound-alike Words

Word Choice

HINT: *A* and *an* are the indefinite articles; for more on their use, see pages 625–626.

A/An/And

A is an article used before nouns beginning with a consonant sound:

> *A* rose is a beautiful flower.

An is an article used before nouns beginning with a vowel sound:

> *An* iris is also a beautiful flower.

And links words:

> A rose *and* an iris are both beautiful flowers.

Accept/Except

Accept means "to receive":

> Olga *accepted* the silver medal.

Except means "excluding, other than, or but":

> Olga *accepted* the silver medal, *except* she still longed for the gold.

> Every member of the gymnastics team *except* Marina received a medal.

Advice/Advise

Advice means "an opinion or suggestion":

> Brent had some good *advice* to give to his younger brother.

Advise means "to counsel or give a suggestion":

> Brent *advised* his younger brother not to take their dad's car again.

Affect/Effect

Affect means "to influence or change":

Graduating from high school *affected* Matthew's career plans.

Effect usually means "the result":

The *effect* of Matthew's graduation was to change his career plans.

All Ready/Already

All ready means "prepared":

Are you *all ready* to go to the beach?

Already means "before or by this time":

Everyone was *already* prepared to go to the beach.

Are/Our

Are is a present tense form of *be:*

Wallace and Lupe *are* working on the proposal.

Our means "belonging to us":

Wallace and Lupe *are* working on *our* proposal.

Beside/Besides

Beside means "next to":

Brent sleeps with his cell phone *beside* him.

Besides means "in addition to or except for":

Besides his cell phone Brent also sleeps with his pager.

Brake/Break

Brake means "to stop or a device for stopping":

Most people *brake* when they approach a red light.

Break means "to separate something into pieces or destroy it":

Please don't *break* the vase.

Breath/Breathe

Breath means "the air we inhale":

Having climbed five flights of stairs, Austin was out of *breath.*

Breathe means "the act of filling our lungs with air":

Having climbed five flights of stairs, Austin needed to *breathe* deeply.

Choose/Chose

Choose means "to select":

"Sylvia, which mutual fund will you *choose?*"

Chose is the past tense of *choose:*

Sylvia *chose* the environmentally friendly fund.

Clothes/Cloths

Clothes means "something to wear":

Allyson is wearing business *clothes* this morning.

Cloths means "pieces of fabric":

> We will need several damp *cloths* to get the baby's face clean.

Conscience/Conscious

Conscience means "an inner sense of ethical behavior":

> Natasha's *conscience* troubled her when she took the promotion.

Conscious means "awake or aware":

> Natasha was *conscious* of her *conscience* troubling her.

Do/Due

Do means "to perform":

> When she discovered her error, Gabrielle had to *do* the budget again.

Due means "something owing or expected to arrive":

> Javier was *due* at 3:00 P.M.

Farther/Further

Farther refers to distance:

> It's *farther* to your house than it is to mine.

Further means "additional":

> I would like *further* practice before I embarrass myself onstage.

Hear/Here

Hear means "sensing a sound":

> At the Eagles' concert you are sure to *hear* "Hotel California."

Here refers to a place:

> Next month the Eagles will play *here* in this city.

Its/It's

Its means "ownership by a thing or animal":

> The horse hurt *its* hoof.

It's is the contraction of *it is*:

> The horse hurt *its* hoof, but *it's* going to recover soon.

Lead/Led

Lead is a metal and also means "to guide or be in front of":

> *Lead* is heavier than iron.

> Marco has been here before, so he will *lead* the way.

Led is the past tense of *lead*:

> Marco had been here before, so he *led* the way.

Loose/Lose

Loose means "unrestrained":

> I had a pocketful of *loose* change.

Lose means "to misplace":

> If you are not careful with all that *loose* change, you are likely to *lose* it.

Past/Passed

Past means "time before now":

> Michael spends too much time thinking about the *past.*

Passed is the past tense of the verb to *pass,* meaning "to go by":

> Haven't we *passed* this Dillard's sometime in the *past?*

Quiet/Quite

Quiet means "silent":

> At the end of the dock, all was *quiet.*

Quite means "very":

> At the end of the dock, all was *quiet* and *quite* still.

Sit/Set

Sit means "to be seated":

> If you don't mind, I will *sit* on the counter.

Set means "to place something":

> Please don't *sit* on the counter where we are going to *set* the plates.

Suppose/Supposed (to)

Suppose means "to assume or guess":

> I *suppose* Carmaletta will skate today.

Supposed can be the past tense of *suppose* but, combined with *to,* usually means "ought to":

> Carmaletta is *supposed* to skate today.

Their/There/They're

Their means "ownership by more than one":

> Cofia and Travis own that house. It is *their* house.

There refers to a place:

> Cofia and Travis live in that house over *there.*

They're is the contraction of *they are:*

> Cofia and Travis own that house. *They're* living in it.

Then/Than

Then means "afterward or at that time":

> Jocelyn went to the art exhibit and *then* went home.

Than means a comparison is being made:

> Jocelyn likes impressionist paintings better *than* pop art.

Through/Thru/Threw

Through means "moving from one side to another" or "finished":

> When he was *through* with his errands, Harvey drove *through* the parking lot at McDonald's.

Thru is a commercial shortening of *through,* used in naming places where you do business as you briefly pass by. *Thru* should not be used as a synonym for *through:*

> Harvey drove *through* the drive-*thru* at McDonald's.

Threw is the past tense of *throw:*

> When Harvey drove *through* the drive-*thru,* he *threw* five dollars to the cashier.

To/Too/Two

To means "toward" or marks an infinitive (*to talk*):

> Ashley went *to* the bank *to* get some money.

Too means "also, very, or excessively":

> Ashley arrived at her bank *too* late, and the other banks were closed, *too.*

Two is a number:

> Ashley was *too* late *to* get the *two* hundred dollars she needed.

Use/Used

Use means "to operate or work with something":

> I will *use* the lawnmower.

Used can be the past tense of *use,* but followed by *to, used* means "to be accustomed to":

> I am not *used* to the loud noise the lawn mower makes.

Whose/Who's

Whose shows ownership:

> Maxine found fifty dollars in the street but did not wonder long *whose* it was.

Who's is the contraction of *who has* or of *who is:*

> *Who's* got money for lunch?

> Maxine found fifty dollars, so she is the one *who's* buying lunch.

Were/Where

Were is the past tense of *are:*

> The clowns *were* squirting water all over the ring.

Where refers to a place:

> The clowns *were* squirting water only *where* they *were* supposed to.

Your/You're

Your shows ownership:

> Is that *your* Jeep?

You're is the contraction of *you are:*

> Oh, *you're* driving a rental.

ACTIVITY 27.1 Editing for Spelling and Sound-alike Errors

The following essay excerpt has many spelling and sound-alike errors. Applying the rules from this chapter—and using a dictionary—find each error, cross it out, and write the correct spelling above it.

Huddled
Hudled together in tiny dark windowless shacks, the first English

settlers in the New World struggled to survive the winter. Having little
experience   *planning*
expereince at rough living conditions, planing poorly, and often being

led by those unqualified for the job, the colonists in most of the early
dying their
settlements suffered terribly, many dieing there first year from
Beginning
starvation, illness, injury, and conflicts with Native Americans. Begining
progressing through
with the "lost colony" of Gilbert and Raleigh and progresing thru the
colonizing
Massachusetts Bay Company, early English attempts at colonizeing the

New World met with disaster.

Sir Humphrey Gilbert and his half-brother, Sir Walter Raleigh,
were   adventurers   colonizing
where the first adventures to try colonizeing America. Obtaining
possess
permission from Queen Elizabeth in 1578 to "inhabit and posses" any
by
land in the New World not claimed buy a "Christian ruler," they both

tried and failed several times. Gilbert, after two attempts, was drowned
colonies
in passage, and Raleigh had to abandon two more colonys in 1585.

Raleigh's final attempt was in 1587 with the infamous "lost colony,"

settled by more than a hundred people on Roanoke Island, near the

coast of North Carolina. It vanished without a trace within three years.
stopped until
After Gilbert and Raleigh, colonization efforts stoped untill 1607
companies
when James I allowed two companys, the London and Plymouth, to
neither   success
try again, but niether, at first, met with succes. The London Company

financed the first attempt (to be called Jamestown), which from the start
into
ran in to problems. On the four-month voyage across the Atlantic, thirty-

nine Englishmen died. Not knowing any better, the survivors located
mosquitoes
Jamestown near swampy ground that bred mosquitos and malaria.
preparing   storing
Instead of prepareing for winter by planting and storeing enough food,

the mainly gentlemen settlers searched for gold. As a result many
to
starved too death during the winter, and others died from disease. By

1608 only thirty-eight colonists were alive. Although Jamestown began to

prosper after 1630, between 1607 and 1624 80 percent of the colonists—
thousands
thousand of men, women, and children—died.

Often a noun is introduced in writing or speaking using *a* and then, after being identified for the reader or listener, is referred to with *the:*

FIRST USE	We watched *a* good ball game last night.
LATER USE	*The* game went into two extra innings before the Royals finally won.

If a plural count or noncount noun is general, do not use any article:

GENERAL PLURAL COUNT NOUN	Baseball *games* are an American pastime.
GENERAL NONCOUNT NOUN	Cold *air* blew through Carmen's apartment.

The articles *a* and *an* are used only before singular count nouns (*a train*, not *a trains*); *a* is used before words beginning with a consonant (*a car*, *a leaf*), and *an* is used before words beginning with a vowel (*an apple*, *an olive*).

Note: Some nouns begin with a silent consonant followed by a vowel and so require the article *an* (*an hour*, *an honest opinion*). Other nouns begin with vowels that are pronounced like consonants and so require the article *a* (*a useful tool*, *a utility knife*).

Note: Noncount nouns never use *a* or *an:* "We left water [not *a* water] running in the sink."

The following chart summarizes article usage:

Teaching Idea
While noncount nouns do not use *a* or *an,* you might point out that they can use *the.*

COUNT/NONCOUNT NOUN	GENERAL	SPECIFIC
Singular count noun: *car, bird, apple*	Use *a* or *an*	Use *the*
Plural count noun: *cars, birds, apples*	Use no article	Use *the*
Noncount noun: *weather, advice, flour*	Use no article	Use *the*

ACTIVITY 28.2 Using Articles

Find the article errors in the following paragraph. Cross out any incorrect articles, and add those that are missing by writing them above the line.

This was my first trip aboard *a* jet and my first trip to another country. I was excited to be up in *the* air with only 5 more hours till we would be landing in *A* Munich, Germany. Flight attendant walked by and offered me *a* Coke. "Yes, please," I said, trying not to look too excited, but the truth was that I could hardly wait to touch down. My parents had promised me this trip as *a* reward for finishing in *the* top third of my graduating class, and now we were finally here together at 30,000 feet, a few hours away from *a* week-long adventure.

Verbs

As we discussed in Chapter 23, **verbs** are the heart of writing, combining with subjects (nouns or pronouns) to create grammatical sentences. All sentences in English require a verb and subject (though the subject may only be implied in a command, as in "Leave the room!"). Verbs have three simple tenses—past, present, and future—and must agree in person and number with their subject: "Ronnell leaves tonight. Her friends leave tomorrow." Chapters 20 and 23 will help you to identify and use verbs correctly, but this section will give you other suggestions for handling questions common to non-native speakers of English.

Word Order

With regard to word order, remember the following:

- Verbs generally come after subjects in sentences: "Sasha dances well."
- Helping verbs precede action verbs in a verb phrase: "Sasha *will* dance tonight."
- A verb phrase may be separated by another word: "Sasha will *not* dance tonight."

Three Irregular Verbs—*to Do, to Have,* and *to Be*

As we saw in Chapter 23, **helping verbs** are used in verb phrases to form tenses and to add emphasis. Two irregular verbs that can work as either helping verbs or action verbs are *to do* (forms: *do, does, did, done*) and *to have* (forms: *have, has, had*).

ACTION VERB	I *did* the dishes right after dinner. (meaning "*completed* the job")
HELPING VERB	Olya *did* pay her credit card bill this month. (emphasizes *pay*)
ACTION VERB	Ramon *had* only 500 dollars to spend on the guitar. (meaning "*possessed*")
HELPING VERB	At one time he *had* hoped to have 1,000 dollars. (past perfect tense)

When used as a helping verb, *to do,* in all its forms, can help form questions, express negatives, and emphasize action verbs:

QUESTION	When *do* you plan on arriving?
NEGATIVE	I *do* not intend to answer the question.
EMPHASIZER	Leona *does* want to come to the party.

The irregular verb *to be* (forms: *am, are, is, was, were, been, being*) can either express a state of being (linking verb) or function as a helping verb:

STATE OF BEING	Em *is* in a good mood today. (links the subject, *Em,* to the feeling)
HELPING VERB	She *is* planning a party for fifteen friends. (present progressive tense)

ACTIVITY 28.3 Choosing Forms of *to Be, to Do,* and *to Have*

In the spaces below, write the correct form of the verbs *to be, to do,* and *to have.*

EXAMPLE
Sam ___*did*___ (to do) his homework last night before he went to bed.

1. Enrique ___*did*___ (to do) the laundry this morning.

2. Chen ___*did*___ (to do) send me a check last week.

3. Francesca __was__ (to be) feeling wonderful yesterday.

4. Ms. Pollard __was__ (to be) the best algebra teacher I ever had.

5. Coco __has__ (to have) the letter of recommendation from her history professor.

6. We all __have__ (to have) worked hard to make the performance succeed.

Modals

Other verbs that function as helpers are often called **modals**: *may/might, can/could, will/would, shall/should, must*. These helping verbs express requests, doubt, capability, necessity, and advisability:

REQUEST	*Would* (*will, could, can*) you pass the salt?
DOUBT	I *might* (*may*) go to the concert this weekend.
CAPABILITY	I *could* (*can*) ask Mae to come with me.
NECESSITY	Jade *must* meet her deadline or lose the contract.
ADVISABILITY	You *should* arrive at the airport at least one hour before your flight.

Teaching Idea
You might point out how important modals are in English for addressing one another courteously.

Modals help refine the meaning of main verbs and are especially useful in softening requests. For example, while eating dinner, you might say, "Pass the salt," as a command. Or you could reduce the command to a request, using one of the modals: "Would you pass the salt?"

Note: The base form of a verb always follows the modal, so be careful not to use the past tense or an infinitive:

NOT THIS	Francesca *should called* her mother this weekend.
BUT THIS	Francesca *should call* her mother this weekend.

ACTIVITY 28.4 Practicing Modals

In the following sentences, write the correct modal.

1. The sun is in my eyes. Please, __will__ you close the blinds? (request)

2. Ashwinder __might__ be able to visit her parents in New Delhi over Christmas. (doubt)

3. Crystal __can__ pick you up by 6:00 if you are ready to go. (capability)

4. If you want to do well on the exam, you __should__ study the whole unit. (advisability)

5. I __must__ make it to the bank by 5:00 if I want to get the loan. (necessity)

Stative Verbs

Stative verbs indicate that a subject will remain constant and unchanging for a certain time. *Understand*, for example, is a stative verb:

Ashwani *understands* calculus better than I ever will.

This sentence tells us that Ashwani knows calculus, and we assume that he is not likely to forget it in the near future. Be careful, however, not to use the present progressive tense with this kind of verb. It would be incorrect to write, "Ashwani *is understanding* calculus better than I ever will."

Here is a list of some common stative verbs:

COMMON STATIVE VERBS

be	hate	love	resemble
believe	have	mean	think
belong	know	need	understand
cost	like	own	weigh

Several verbs can be either stative or active, depending on their meaning, such as *weigh* and *look.* When they are active verbs, they can use the present progressive tense:

ACTIVE USE Tony *is weighing* himself to see how many pounds he must lose.

STATIVE USE Tony *weighs* so much that he knows he must lose some pounds.

ACTIVITY 28.5 Recognizing Stative Verbs

In the spaces provided in the following sentences, write "C" if the verb is correct and "I" if it is incorrect.

1. __C__ I believe that everything will turn out fine in the end.

2. __I__ Felipe is liking Maria and plans to tell her so.

3. __I__ I am hating the idea of taking another exam today.

4. __C__ Canadian geese are flying north as the weather begins to warm.

5. __I__ Rita has told us several times that she is needing more tuition money.

6. __C__ Neeva understands how to balance her checkbook.

Two-Word (Phrasal) Verbs

Another kind of verb that can be confusing is the **two-part** or **phrasal verb,** which consists of a verb followed by a preposition or adverb. For example, when you say, "Leon will *look over* the report," you do not mean that he will try to see across the report to something on the other side; you mean that he will read and think about the report. Phrasal verbs usually express a different meaning than the verb would have without the attached preposition or adverb. Dictionaries list phrasal verbs, and native speakers of English can help clarify their meaning.

Most phrasal verbs consisting of a main verb and an adverb can be split or remain together:

SPLIT   Travis will *drop* his sister *off* at school.

NOT SPLIT Travis will *drop off* his sister at school.

However, when a pronoun is used as the object, it must be placed *between* the two verb parts:

INCORRECT Travis will *drop off* <u>her</u> at school.

CORRECT   Travis will *drop* <u>her</u> *off* at school.

Teaching Idea
Learning phrasal verbs can
help non-native speakers
understand and use informal
language, but students should
be warned that informal and
idiomatic expressions are
usually not appropriate to
academic discourse.

Some phrasal verbs consisting of a main verb and a preposition are not separable:

NOT SEPARABLE   After that, Travis will *drop in* on his best friend.

We use many phrasal verbs in informal conversation that we would avoid in more formal writing, often finding a more concise substitute:

PHRASAL VERB   Professor Allen *drags out* class sessions with pointless anecdotes.

SUBSTITUTE   Professor Allen *prolongs* class sessions with pointless anecdotes.

(For more on idiomatic and overworked expressions, see Chapter 19.) Here is a list of common two-part verbs:

Common Separable Two-Part Verbs

VERB	MEANING	EXAMPLE
ask out	invite on a date	Gabrielle *asked* Sergei *out* to a movie.
ask over	invite to a place	Javier *asked* Marta *over* to his home.
back up	support	I hope my friends will *back* me *up*.
blow up	destroy	The construction crew had to *blow* the bridge *up*.
break down	disassemble	Sveta *broke* her tent *down* in the morning.
bring back	return	Frederick had to *bring* the videos *back*.
call off	cancel	The promoters had to *call* the concert *off*.
call up	telephone	Hector was too nervous to *call* Elena *up*.
carry out	do	The Marines *carried* their mission *out*.
cover up	hide	Politicians are always trying to *cover* something *up*.
drag out	prolong	Dad *dragged* the lecture *out* for an hour.
figure out	solve	Let's *figure* these bills *out*.
fix up	repair	We can *fix* this house *up* if we work hard.
get across	explain	Mom tried to *get* the message *across* to me.
give up	quit	Gebdao would like to *give* smoking *up*.
hand in	submit	The students all *handed* their homework *in*.
help out	assist	Friends *help* each other *out* in times of need.
lead on	entice, deceive	The salesperson *led* his customer *on*.
look up	search for	*Look* the number *up* in the phone book.

Common Nonseparable Two-Part Verbs

VERB	MEANING	EXAMPLE
call on	visit, ask someone	Professor Sung *called on* Amy to answer.
catch up (with)	reach	I *caught up* with the bus at the corner.
come across	discover	Jesus *came across* a great CD sale.
drop by	visit	My cousin *dropped by* unexpectedly.

(Continued)

Common Nonseparable Two-Part Verbs (*Continued*)

VERB	MEANING	EXAMPLE
drop out	leave	Too many teenagers are *dropping out* of school.
get along (with)	coexist	Everyone *gets along* with Alex.
get in	enter	Tomas *got in* the car.
get off	leave	The passengers *got off* the plane.
get on	enter	The passengers *got on* the plane.
get out of	leave, avoid	Ho Chul *got out of* the final exam.
get over	recover from	Marco *got over* the reprimand from his boss.
get through	complete	She finally *got through* the test questions.
get up	arise	I *got up* late for class this morning.
go over	review	*Go over* your packing list before the bus arrives.
look after	take care of	Tasha said that she would *look after* the baby.
look into	investigate	Principal Alvarez said he would *look into* it.
look out (for)	care for, be alert to	Rabbits must *look out for* foxes.
run into	meet accidentally	Kristin *ran into* Jamie at the hardware store.
run out (of)	finish a supply	We *ran out of* bread this morning.

ACTIVITY 28.6 Recognizing Phrasal Verbs

In the following sentences, underline the phrasal verb(s). Remember that sometimes the verb parts will be separated.

1. While driving my truck yesterday, I ran into a shopping cart.
2. Ping worked hard to fix his motorcycle up for the Saturday race.
3. I promised my father that I would look after my younger brother.
4. Sasha has decided to give fried foods up till he loses 10 pounds.
5. Maria's boss got over his anger by the time the crew got through with the job.
6. Professor Capelli told his students that they could not cover their lack of knowledge up by "padding" their essay exam responses.

Prepositions

Prepositions are words that link nouns and pronouns to sentences. As in the phrasal verbs in the preceding section, prepositions are often part of **idiomatic expressions**—phrases that may ignore grammar rules and that have a meaning beyond the literal definition of the words used. Many prepositions help show location (*near, around, against, beside*), some indicate time (*until, during, for, since*), and some can mean either time or location (*on, in, by, at*).

Multiple adjectives have a preferred order to follow, according to the category the word fits into:

THE PREFERRED ORDER FOR ADJECTIVES

1. **Determiners:** *this, these, that, the, a, an, some, many, my, our, your, all, both, each, several, one, two*
2. **Judgment:** *unusual, interesting, impressive, ugly, beautiful, inspiring, hopeful, smart, funny*
3. **Size:** *large, massive, small, tiny, heavy, light, tall, short*
4. **Shape:** *round, square, rectangular, wide, deep, thin, slim, fat*
5. **Age:** *young, adolescent, teenage, middle-aged, old, ancient*
6. **Color:** *white, black, blue, red, yellow, green*
7. **Adjectives derived from proper nouns:** *American, German, Kansan, Parisian, Gothic*
8. **Material:** *wood, plastic, cloth, paper, cardboard, metal, stone, clay, glass, ceramic*

Here are several combinations of adjectives:

A. *The beautiful tall ancient* redwoods should stand forever.

B. *Our brilliant young* daughter amazes people wherever we travel.

C. *Five amusing fat brown* squirrels chased each other through the trees.

In each of these sentences, the adjectives add meaning to the ones that precede them, so their effect is cumulative, and no comma is needed to separate them. Adjectives that modify or describe equally are said to be **coordinate** and *do* require a comma between them (*happy, hard-working* firefighter). In general, avoid "stacking" adjectives in front of nouns and pronouns. Try spreading the modifiers around within several sentences for better effect.

(For more on single-word adjectives, adjective phrases, and adjective clauses, see Chapter 25.)

CAUTION! If you use more than two or three modifiers at one time, the word they are describing becomes overloaded.

ACTIVITY 28.8 Ordering Adjectives

In each of the following sentences, either mark "C" for correct in the space provided or rearrange the adjectives so their order is appropriate.

1. _____ This green large cardboard box   This large green cardboard box

2. _____ My Asian young friend   My young Asian friend

3. _____ Each ceramic beautiful tiny bird   Each beautiful tiny ceramic bird

4. _____ Four old shrunken men   Four shrunken old men

5. _____ A Parisian wide boulevard   A wide Parisian boulevard

6. ___C___ A well-written big paperback book _____

Additional Readings

octopus add interest to the paragraph and help reinforce the dominant impression? (For more on personification, see pp. 505–509.)

Using the term murderer arouses our curiosity, as does the description

of stalking and killing prey.

6. Whether or not you are familiar with some of the creatures Steinbeck names, how do the metaphors and similes help you visualize them? What can you conclude about the value of comparisons in building description? (For more on metaphor/similes, see pp. 505–509.)

Answers will vary. One possibility: Nudibranchs, or sea slugs, is a term that few in the

class will know, but with the Spanish dancer and skirt image, most would now be able

to pick out the animal in an aquarium. Comparisons add color and clarity to images.

Narration

This personal narrative, by freelance writer Roger Hoffman, tells how the author as a 12-year-old took a dangerous dare. Though the event occurred many years in the author's past, he is able to recall a number of specific details of the setting, particularly the train, and some significant dialogue. As you read the story, ask yourself how Hoffman holds readers' attention, maintaining suspense until the end.

To review the elements of narrative writing, turn back to Chapter 6.

The Dare

ROGER HOFFMANN

1   The secret to diving under a moving freight train and rolling out the other side with all your parts attached lies in picking the right spot between the tracks to hit with your back. Ideally, you want soft dirt or pea gravel, clear of glass shards and railroad spikes that could cause you instinctively, and fatally, to sit up. Today, at thirty-eight, I couldn't be threatened or baited enough to attempt that dive. But as a seventh grader struggling to make the cut in a tough Atlanta grammar school, all it took was a dare.

2   I coasted through my first years of school as a fussed-over smart kid, the teacher's pet who finished his work first and then strutted around the room tutoring other students. By the seventh grade, I had more A's than friends. Even my old cronies, Dwayne and O. T., made it clear I'd never be one of the guys in junior high if I didn't dirty up my act. They challenged me to break the rules and I did. The I-dare-you's escalated: shoplifting, sugaring teachers' gas tanks, dropping lighted matches into public mailboxes. Each guerrilla act won me the approval I never got for just being smart.

Walking home by the railroad tracks after school, we started playing 3 chicken with oncoming trains. O. T., who was failing that year, always won. One afternoon he charged a boxcar from the side, stopping just short of throwing himself between the wheels. I was stunned. After the train disappeared, we debated whether someone could dive under a moving car, stay put for a 10-count, then scramble out the other side. I thought it could be done and said so. O. T. immediately stepped in front of me and smiled. Not by me, I added quickly, I certainly didn't mean that I could do it. "A smart guy like you," he said, his smile evaporating, "you could figure it out easy." And then, squeezing each word for effect, "I . . . DARE . . . you." I'd just turned twelve. The monkey clawing my back was Teacher's Pet. And I'd been dared.

As an adult, I've been on both ends of life's implicit business and 4 social I-dare-you's, although adults don't use those words. We provoke with body language, tone of voice, ambiguous phrases. I dare you to: argue with the boss, tell Fred what you think of him, send the wine back. Only rarely are the risks physical. How we respond to dares when we are young may have something to do with which of the truly hazardous male inner dares—attacking mountains, tempting bulls at Pamplona—we embrace or ignore as men.

For two weeks, I scouted trains and tracks. I studied moving boxcars 5 close up, memorizing how they squatted on their axles, never getting used to the squeal or the way the air fell hot from the sides. I created an imaginary, friendly train and ran next to it. I mastered a shallow, head-first dive with a simple half-twist. I'd land on my back, count to ten, imagine wheels and, locking both hands on the rail to my left, heave myself over and out. Even under pure sky, though, I had to fight to keep my eyes open and my shoulders between the rails.

The next Saturday, O. T., Dwayne and three eighth graders met me 6 below the hill that backed up to the lumberyard. The track followed a slow bend there and opened to a straight, slightly uphill climb for a solid third of a mile. My run started two hundred yards after the bend. The train would have its tongue hanging out.

The other boys huddled off to one side, a circle on another planet, and 7 watched quietly as I double-knotted my shoelaces. My hands trembled. O. T. broke the circle and came over to me. He kept his hands hidden in the pockets of his jacket. We looked at each other. BB's of sweat appeared beneath his nose. I stuffed my wallet in one of his pockets, rubbing it against his knuckles on the way in, and slid my house key, wired to a red-and-white fishing bobber, into the other. We backed away from each other, and he turned and ran to join the four already climbing up the hill.

I watched them all the way to the top. They clustered together as if 8 I were taking their picture. Their silhouette resembled a round-shouldered tombstone. They waved down to me, and I dropped them from my mind and sat down on the rail. Immediately, I jumped back. The steel was vibrating.

The train sounded like a cow going short of breath. I pulled my shirt- 9 tail out and looked down at my spot, then up the incline of track ahead of me. Suddenly the air went hot, and the engine was by me. I hadn't pictured it moving that fast. A man's bare head leaned out and stared at me. I waved to him with my left hand and turned into the train, burying my face in the incredible noise. When I looked up, the head was gone.

10   I started running alongside the boxcars. Quickly, I found their pace, held it, and then eased off, concentrating on each thick wheel that cut past me. I slowed another notch. Over my shoulder, I picked my car as it came off the bend, locking in the image of the white mountain goat painted on its side. I waited, leaning forward like the anchor in a 440-relay, wishing the baton up the track behind me. Then the big goat fired by me, and I was flying and then tucking my shoulder as I dipped under the train.

      A heavy blanket of red dust settled over me. I felt bolted to the earth.

11 Sheet-metal bellies thundered and shook above my face. Count to ten, a voice said, watch the axles and look to your left for daylight. But I couldn't count, and I couldn't find left if my life depended on it, which it did. The colors overhead went from brown to red to black to red again. Finally, I ripped my hands free, forced them to the rail, and, in one convulsive jerk, threw myself into the blue light.

      I lay there face down until there was no more noise, and I could feel

12 the sun against the back of my neck. I sat up. The last ribbon of train was slipping away in the distance. Across the tracks, O. T. was leading a cavalry charge down the hill, five very small, galloping boys, their fists whirling above them. I pulled my knees to my chest. My corduroy pants puckered wet across my thighs. I didn't care.

Questions for Analysis

1. Summarize the story's primary action in several sentences, and identify the climax. Name several word groups the author uses to keep the action connected from one paragraph to the next. (For more on time transitions, see p. 53.)

    - *Group of boys walking by a train track*

    - *O. T. daring the author to dive between the moving wheels*

    - *The author watching the trains and learning how to make his move*

    - *The author preparing to make the dive, making the dive, and surviving the dare*

    Climax: Hoffman rolling out from under the train

    Time transitions: after school, for two weeks, next Saturday, etc.

2. Showing and telling are crucial to effective storytelling. (For more on showing versus telling, see pp. 114–116.) What does Hoffman show us in paragraph 7, and how does this affect the suspense in the story?
    Hoffman shows how frightened he and O. T. are and heightens suspense
    by transferring Hoffman's property to O. T. The dangerous dive will be
    easier without the wallet and keys, and if the author does not make it,
    his best friend has the property—an impromptu will, perhaps.

3. What do you think the meaning of this story is for Hoffman, and where in the story does he make this clear?

The author marvels at what people will do for approval, though he does not moralize or shake a finger at those who take dares. Paragraphs 1, 2, and 4 discuss this.

4. If you think the introductory paragraph is effective, what makes it work? Look especially at the first sentence. Write out the thesis sentence.

The hook is well chosen to telegraph that a story involving danger will follow. Students will identify the thesis as the first or last sentence of this paragraph, but the last is a better choice.

5. If you think the concluding paragraph is effective, what makes it work? How does the last sentence reflect on the author and the need for approval that drove him to accept the dare?

The concluding paragraph creates several strong images that pull the story together.

Although the twelve-year-old Hoffman might have been highly embarrassed any other time at wetting his pants, coming after this close brush with death, he "didn't care" what the boys thought of his accident—at least temporarily above the need for peer approval.

6. Hoffman uses metaphors and similes in several places. Choose any two and explain how they add to the story. Does he also include any overly used metaphors (clichés) that he might have avoided? (For more on figures of speech, see pp. 505–512.)

Answers will vary. Two possibilities: silhouette = round-shouldered tombstone: association with death; cavalry charge = the group of boys: triumphing over the enemy train, completing the dare. Clichés: teacher's pet, monkey on back.

7. Specific words, sensory details, and active verbs are critical to effective storytelling. List several of each in paragraph 11 and tell how they add to the story.

Specific words (blanket of red dust, sheet-metal bellies), sensory details (thundered, settling dust, bolted to the earth), and active verbs (settled, thundered, shook, count, watched, ripped, forced, threw) help to put readers under the train with Hoffman here at the climax of the story.

Narration

Gary Soto—poet, essayist, and novelist—often writes about his childhood in California and the difficulties he and other Mexican Americans have faced as migrant workers in the San Joaquin Valley. The essay that follows is taken from a collection of his shorter works titled *The Effects of Knut Hamsun on a Fresno Boy.* As you read, notice how Soto enriches his narrative with metaphors and similes and how important the jacket is to the story.

The Jacket

GARY SOTO

1   My clothes have failed me. I remember the green coat that I wore in fifth and sixth grades when you either danced like a champ or pressed yourself against a greasy wall, bitter as a penny toward the happy couples.

2   When I needed a new jacket and my mother asked what kind I wanted, I described something like bikers wear: black leather and silver studs with enough belts to hold down a small town. We were in the kitchen, steam on the windows from her cooking. She listened so long while stirring dinner that I thought she understood for sure the kind I wanted. The next day when I got home from school, I discovered draped on my bedpost a jacket the color of day-old guacamole. I threw my books on the bed and approached the jacket slowly, as if it were a stranger whose hand I had to shake. I touched the vinyl sleeve, the collar, and peeked at the mustard-colored lining.

3   From the kitchen mother yelled that my jacket was in the closet. I closed the door to her voice and pulled at the rack of clothes in the closet, hoping the jacket on the bedpost wasn't for me but my mean brother. No luck. I gave up. From my bed, I stared at the jacket. I wanted to cry because it was so ugly and so big that I knew I'd have to wear it a long time. I was a small kid, thin as a young tree, and it would be years before I'd have a new one. I stared at the jacket, like an enemy, thinking bad things before I took off my old jacket whose sleeves climbed halfway to my elbow.

4   I put the big jacket on. I zipped it up and down several times, and rolled the cuffs up so they didn't cover my hands. I put my hands in the pockets and flapped the jacket like a bird's wings. I stood in front of the mirror, full face, then profile, and then looked over my shoulder as if someone had called me. I sat on the bed, stood against the bed, and combed my hair to see what I would look like doing something natural. I looked ugly. I threw it on my brother's bed and looked at it for a long time before I slipped it on and went out to the backyard, smiling a "thank you" to my mom as I passed her in the kitchen. With my hands in my pockets I kicked a ball against the fence, and then climbed it to sit looking into the alley. I hurled orange peels at the mouth of an open garbage can and when the peels were gone I watched the white puffs of my breath thin to nothing.

5   I jumped down, hands in my pockets, and in the backyard on my knees I teased my dog, Brownie, by swooping my arms while making bird calls. He jumped at me and missed. He jumped again and again, until a tooth sunk deep, ripping an L-shaped tear on my left sleeve. I pushed Brownie away to study the tear as I would a cut on my arm. There was no blood, only a few loose pieces of fuzz. Damn dog, I thought, and pushed him away hard when he tried to bite again. I got up from my knees and went to my bedroom to sit with my jacket on my lap, with the lights out.

6   That was the first afternoon with my new jacket. The next day I wore it to sixth grade and got a D on a math quiz. During the morning recess

Frankie T., the playground terrorist, pushed me to the ground and told me to stay there until recess was over. My best friend, Steve Negrete, ate an apple while looking at me, and the girls turned away to whisper on the monkey bars. The teachers were no help: they looked my way and talked about how foolish I looked in my new jacket. I saw their heads bob with laughter, their hands half-covering their mouths.

Even though it was cold, I took off the jacket during lunch and played 7 kickball in a thin shirt, my arm feeling like braille from the goose bumps. But when I returned to class I slipped the jacket on and shivered until I was warm. I sat on my hands, heating them up, while my teeth chattered like a cup of crooked dice. Finally warm, I slid out of the jacket but a few minutes later put it back on when the fire bell rang. We paraded out into the yard where we, the sixth graders, walked past all the other grades to stand against the back fence. Everybody saw me. Although they didn't say out loud, "Man, that's ugly," I heard the buzz-buzz of gossip and even laughter that I knew was meant for me.

And so I went, in my guacamole-colored jacket. So embarrassed, so 8 hurt, I couldn't even do my homework. I received Cs on quizzes, and forgot the state capitals and rivers of South America, our friendly neighbor. Even the girls who had been friendly blew away like loose flowers to follow the boys in neat jackets.

I wore that thing for three years until the sleeves grew short and my 9 forearms stuck out like the necks of turtles. All during that time no love came to me—no little dark girl in a Sunday dress she wore on Monday. At lunchtime I stayed with the ugly boys who leaned against the chain-link fence and looked around with propellers of grass spinning in our mouths. We saw girls walk by alone, saw couples, hand in hand, their heads like bookends pressing air together. We saw them and spun our propellers so fast our faces were blurs.

I blame that jacket for those bad years. I blame my mother for her 10 bad taste and her cheap ways. It was a sad time for the heart. With a friend I spent my sixth-grade year in a tree in the alley, waiting for something good to happen to me in that jacket, which had become the ugly brother who tagged along wherever I went. And it was about that time that I began to grow. My chest puffed up with muscle and, strangely, a few more ribs. Even my hands, those fleshy hammers, showed bravely through the cuffs, the fingers already hardening for the coming fights. But that L-shaped rip on the left sleeve got bigger, bits of stuffing coughed out from its wound after a hard day of play. I finally Scotch-taped it closed, but in rain or cold weather the tape peeled off like a scab and more stuffing fell out until that sleeve shriveled into a palsied arm. That winter the elbows began to crack and whole chunks of green began to fall off. I showed the cracks to my mother, who always seemed to be at the stove with steamed-up glasses, and she said that there were children in Mexico who would love that jacket. I told her that this was America and yelled that Debbie, my sister, didn't have a jacket like mine. I ran outside, ready to cry, and climbed the tree by the alley to think bad thoughts and watch my breath puff white and disappear.

11   But whole pieces still casually flew off my jacket when I played hard, read quietly, or took vicious spelling tests at school. When it became so spotted that my brother began to call me "camouflage," I flung it over the fence into the alley. Later, however, I swiped the jacket off the ground and went inside to drape it across my lap and mope.

12   I was called to dinner: steam silvered my mother's glasses as she said grace; my brother and sister with their heads bowed made ugly faces at their glasses of powdered milk. I gagged too, but eagerly ate big rips of buttered tortilla that held scooped-up beans. Finished, I went outside with my jacket across my arm. It was a cold sky. The faces of clouds were piled up, hurting. I climbed the fence, jumping down with a grunt. I started up the alley and soon slipped into my jacket, that green ugly brother who breathed over my shoulder that day and ever since.

Questions for Analysis

1. Summarize the main action in this story and identify the main conflict. What does most of the tension/conflict stem from, and what is the resolution of that conflict?

   Soto finding his new jacket, trying it on and quickly rejecting it, feeling like he is suffering at school because of the jacket, blaming the jacket for his shortcomings over the next few years, and sitting down to dinner with his family. Tension/conflict: Soto with his mother, but more importantly, with the jacket, Soto "loses" the battle.

2. Why does Soto tell us this story? What is his point? How does the jacket relate to the conflict in the story, and what does it show about the author's life?

   The ugly jacket mirrors the unpleasantness of Soto's young life: his poverty, awkwardness around girls, problems with school bullies, and troubles in school.

3. Personal narrative often reveals much about a person's life circumstances and character. What do readers learn about Soto's life and character from this story?

   Answers will vary. Students should include some of the following: Life circumstances: Soto is poor; he has a dog, a sister, a "mean" older brother, a best friend, and a mother who provides for him. Soto also has academic trouble and he fights. Soto's character: sensitive, self-conscious, awkward around girls, obedient to his mother, active, rationalizing, impulsive.

4. Soto uses many metaphors and similes and several instances of personification. Locate one of each of these figures of speech, and tell how they enrich the story.

   Answers will vary. Metaphors: The jacket is "the ugly brother," hands are "fleshy hammers," grass stalks are "propellers." Similes: "arms feeling like Braille," "forearms . . . like the necks of turtles," girls like "loose flowers." Personification: The jacket is a "stranger," "an enemy," and an

"ugly brother," and the "faces of the clouds were piled up, hurting."

5. Although most personal narrative includes direct dialogue, this essay does not. Locate two instances of indirect dialogue, and tell what readers learn about Soto from it. Could direct dialogue have also been used effectively in these places? Why or why not?

Answers will vary. In paragraph 2 Soto describes the jacket he wants. Indirect dialogue

is probably better here since direct dialogue would slow the story unnecessarily.

However, paragraph 10 might benefit from direct dialogue to characterize both Soto and

his mother during their argument. (Of course, it can also be argued that indirect

dialogue throughout heightens Soto's sense of alienation.)

6. Writers sometimes achieve emphasis by using sentence fragments and short sentences. In paragraph 3, locate a sentence fragment and a short sentence, and comment on how they add to the meaning of the scene.

"No luck. I gave up." These two statements characterize much of Soto's

condition throughout the three years he lived with the jacket.

7. Comment on the introduction. How does it arouse readers' curiosity and focus the story?

The introduction begins with an interesting hook, hinting at conflict,

and focuses readers on the essay's main image, the jacket.

8. Comment on the conclusion. Does it satisfactorily wrap up the story? How does Soto's final comment about the jacket relate to the significance of the story?

Some students will think the conclusion is too ambiguous. Some discussion points: Soto

reinforces his poverty (the children gag over the powdered milk), he reiterates the image of his

mother's fogged-over glasses (she doesn't see the world clearly—or at least the way the young

Soto sees it), the clouds are hurting, and the jacket is still there—"that green ugly brother." There

is a bleakness to the conclusion that complements much of the mood of the essay.

Illustration

"Rambos of the Road," an essay written by Martin Gottfried for *Newsweek* magazine, illustrates with two extended examples and many shorter ones an assertion about people's driving habits. As you read through this essay, imagine that Gottfried has just said to you, "I think drivers in America are getting crazier and more violent by the minute," and you have responded, "Show me what you mean." Does the author provide enough detailed examples and explanations to help you understand his position?

To review the elements of illustrating through examples, turn back to Chapter 7.

Rambos of the Road

MARTIN GOTTFRIED

1   The car pulled up and its driver glared at us with such sullen intensity, such hatred, that I was truly afraid for our lives. Except for the Mohawk haircut he didn't have, he looked like Robert DeNiro in *Taxi Driver*, the sort of young man who, delirious for notoriety, might kill a president.

2   He was glaring because we had passed him and for that affront he pursued us to the next stoplight so as to express his indignation and affirm his masculinity. I was with two women and, believe it, was afraid for all three of us. It was nearly midnight and we were in a small, sleeping town with no other cars on the road.

3   When the light turned green, I raced ahead, knowing it was foolish and that I was not in a movie. He didn't merely follow, he chased, and with his headlights turned off. No matter what sudden turn I took, he followed. My passengers were silent. I knew they were alarmed, and I prayed that I wouldn't be called upon to protect them. In that cheerful frame of mind, I turned off my own lights so I couldn't be followed. It was lunacy. I was responding to a crazy as a crazy.

4   "I'll just drive to the police station," I finally said, and as if those were the magic words, he disappeared.

5   **Elbowing fenders:** It seems to me that there has recently been an epidemic of auto macho—a competition perceived and expressed in driving. People fight it out over parking spaces. They bully into line at the gas pump. A toll booth becomes a signal for elbowing fenders. And beetle-eyed drivers hunch over their steering wheels, squeezing the rims, glowering, preparing the excuse of not having seen you as they muscle you off the road. Approaching a highway on an entrance ramp recently, I was strong-armed by a trailer truck so immense that its driver all but blew me away by blasting his horn. The behemoth was just inches from my hopelessly mismatched coupe when I fled for the safety of the shoulder.

6   And this is happening on city streets, too. A New York taxi driver told me that "intimidation is the name of the game. Drive as if you're deaf and blind. You don't hear the other guy's horn and you sure as hell don't see him."

7   The odd thing is that long before I was even able to drive, it seemed to me that people were at their finest and most civilized when in their cars. They seemed so orderly and considerate, so reasonable, staying in the right-hand lane unless passing, signaling all intentions. In those days you really eased into highway traffic, and the long, neat rows of cars seemed mobile testimony to the sanity of most people. Perhaps memory fails, perhaps there were always testy drivers, perhaps—but everyone didn't give you the finger.

A most amazing example of driver rage occurred recently at the 8 Manhattan end of the Lincoln Tunnel. We were four cars abreast, stopped at a traffic light. And there was no moving even when the light had changed. A bus had stopped in the cross traffic, blocking our paths: it was normal-for-New-York-City gridlock. Perhaps impatient, perhaps late for important appointments, three of us nonetheless accepted what, after all, we could not alter. One, however, would not. He would not be help-less. He would go where he was going even if he couldn't get there. A Wall Street type in suit and tie, he got out of his car and strode toward the bus, rapping smartly on its doors. When they opened, he exchanged words with the driver. The doors folded shut. He then stepped in front of the bus, took hold of one of its large windshield wipers, and broke it.

The bus doors reopened and the driver appeared, apparently giving 9 the fellow a good piece of his mind. If so, the lecture was wasted, for the man started his car and proceeded to drive directly *into the bus*. He rammed it. Even though the point at which he struck the bus, the folding doors, was its most vulnerable point, ramming the side of a bus with your car has to rank very high on a futility index. My first thought was that it had to be a rented car.

Lane merger: To tell the truth, I could not believe my eyes. The bus driver 10 opened his doors as much as they could be opened and he stepped directly onto the hood of the attacking car, jumping up and down with both his feet. He then retreated into the bus, closing the doors behind him. Obviously a man of action, the car driver backed up and rammed the bus again. How this exercise in absurdity would have been resolved none of us will ever know for at that point the traffic unclogged and the bus moved on. And the rest of us, we passives of the world, proceeded, our cars crossing a field of battle as if nothing untoward had happened.

It is tempting to blame such belligerent, uncivil and even neurotic 11 behavior on the nuts of the world, but in our cars we all become a little crazy. How many of us speed up when a driver signals his intention of pulling in front of us? Are we resentful and anxious to pass him? How many of us try to squeeze in, or race along the shoulder at a lane merger? We may not jump on hoods, but driving the gauntlet, we seethe, cursing not so silently in the safety of our steel bodies on wheels—fortresses for cowards.

What is it within us that gives birth to such antisocial behavior and why, 12 all of a sudden, have so many drivers gone around the bend? My friend Joel Katz, a Manhattan psychiatrist, calls it, "a Rambo pattern. People are running around thinking the American way is to take the law into your own hands when anyone does anything wrong. And what constitutes 'wrong'? Anything that cramps your style."

It seems to me that it is a new America we see on the road now. It has 13 the mentality of a hoodlum and the backbone of a coward. The car is its weapon and hiding place, and it is still a symbol even in this. Road Rambos no longer bespeak a self-reliant, civil people tooling around in family cruis-ers. In fact, there aren't families in these machines that charge headlong with their brights on in broad daylight, demanding we get out of their way. Bullies are loners, and they have perverted our liberty of the open road into drivers' license. They represent an America that derides the values of decency and good manners, then roam the highways riding shotgun and shrieking freedom. By allowing this to happen, the rest of us approve.

Questions for Analysis

1. How many paragraphs are devoted to the introduction, and which of the introductory methods that we practiced in Chapter 12 is being used? Is the introduction effective? Why or why not?
   Paragraphs 1–4 use a narrative method. Effective: arouses the reader's curiosity and gives her a sense of the essay's direction.

2. The introduction contains one extended example to illustrate the author's thesis; which paragraphs contain the second extended example? Write out the topic sentence that begins this example. How does the example develop the author's thesis?
   Paragraphs 8–10. "A most amazing example of driver rage . . ." The idiocy and frustration that Gottfried wants us to see is quite clear in this futile and pointless face-off.

3. In which paragraphs does the author reiterate his thesis? Is this pointless repetition, or does it strengthen the essay? If so, how?
   Paragraphs 6, 7, 8, 11, 12, 13. Strengthens: Reminding readers of an essay's main point increases clarity and should be done periodically.

4. Which of the patterns of development is used to expand paragraph 7, and how does this paragraph strengthen the essay? (For more on PODs, see pp. 8–9.)
   Comparison/contrast. The contrast of the way it was (or should be) and the way it is now makes the current antisocial driving habits seem all the more extreme.

5. List several specific words and action verbs in the narrative description of paragraphs 8–10. How do they strengthen these paragraphs?
   Specific words: Manhattan, Lincoln Tunnel, New York City, Wall Street, etc. Active verbs: strode, folded, stepped, broke, wasted, started, rammed, etc. Both sharpen the picture so we can see the anger and senselessness of the confrontation, thus supporting the author's thesis.

6. What effect do the questions and the pronouns we, our, and us in paragraph 11 have on readers? (For more on questions, see p. 463. For more on personal pronouns and audience, see Chapter 24.)
   Questions are a good strategy for connecting with an audience and creating sentence variety. These pronouns are especially useful when a writer needs to even mildly criticize his audience.

7. How does the reference to Rambos in the title and paragraphs 12 and 13 reinforce the thesis?
   Most students will recognize the reference to the movie First Blood and Sylvester Stallone as the unstable Vietnam special forces' veteran.

8. Why does the author use a dash in paragraphs 7 and 11 to set off the last few words in each sentence? (For more on the dash, see Chapter 26.)

For emphasis.

_____

_____

_____

Classification

In the essay "The Ways of Meeting Oppression," Martin Luther King, Jr., classifies the ways people react to oppression and argues that one method is superior. As you read, notice how clearly the author states the methods and develops them through specific examples, several of which are biblical references. Are you convinced after reading this essay that King's method of choice is the best one?

To review the elements of classification, turn back to Chapter 8.

The Ways of Meeting Oppression

MARTIN LUTHER KING, JR.

Oppressed people deal with their oppression in three characteristic 1 ways. One way is acquiescence: the oppressed resign themselves to their doom. They tacitly adjust themselves to oppression, and thereby become conditioned to it. In every movement toward freedom some of the oppressed prefer to remain oppressed. Almost 2800 years ago Moses set out to lead the children of Israel from the slavery of Egypt to the freedom of the promised land. He soon discovered that slaves do not always welcome their deliverers. They become accustomed to being slaves. They would rather bear those ills they have, as Shakespeare pointed out, than flee to others that they know not of. They prefer the "fleshpots of Egypt" to the ordeals of emancipation.

There is such a thing as the freedom of exhaustion. Some people are 2 so worn down by the yoke of oppression that they give up. A few years ago in the slum areas of Atlanta, a Negro guitarist used to sing almost daily: "Been down so long that down don't bother me." This is the type of negative freedom and resignation that often engulfs the life of the oppressed.

But this is not the way out. To accept passively an unjust system is to 3 cooperate with that system; thereby the oppressed become as evil as the oppressor. Noncooperation with evil is as much a moral obligation as is cooperation with good. The oppressed must never allow the conscience of the oppressor to slumber. Religion reminds every man that he is his brother's keeper. To accept injustice or segregation passively is to say to the oppressor that his actions are morally right. It is a way of allowing his conscience to fall asleep. At this moment the oppressed fails to be his brother's keeper. So acquiescence—while often the easier way—is not the moral way. It is the way of the coward. The Negro cannot win the respect of his oppressor by acquiescing; he merely increases the oppressor's arrogance and contempt. Acquiescence is interpreted as proof of the Negro's inferiority. The Negro cannot win the respect of the white people of the South or the peoples of the world if he is willing to sell the future of his children for his personal and immediate comfort and safety.

4   A second way that oppressed people sometimes deal with oppression is to resort to physical violence and corroding hatred. Violence often brings about momentary results. Nations have frequently won their independence in battle. But in spite of temporary victories, violence never brings permanent peace. It solves no social problem; it merely creates new and more complicated ones.

5   Violence as a way of achieving racial justice is both impractical and immoral. It is impractical because it is a descending spiral ending in destruction for all. The old law of an eye for an eye leaves everybody blind. It is immoral because it seeks to humiliate the opponent rather than win his understanding; it seeks to annihilate rather than to convert. Violence is immoral because it thrives on hatred rather than love. It destroys community and makes brotherhood impossible. It leaves society in monologue rather than dialogue. Violence ends by defeating itself. It creates bitterness in the survivors and brutality in the destroyers. A voice echoes through time saying to every potential Peter, "Put up your sword."* History is cluttered with the wreckage of nations that failed to follow this command.

6   If the American Negro and other victims of oppression succumb to the temptation of using violence in the struggle for freedom, future generations will be the recipients of a desolate night of bitterness, and our chief legacy to them will be an endless reign of meaningless chaos. Violence is not the way.

7   The third way open to oppressed people in their quest for freedom is the way of nonviolent resistance. Like the synthesis in Hegelian philosophy, the principle of nonviolent resistance seeks to reconcile the truths of two opposites—the acquiescence and violence—while avoiding the extremes and immoralities of both. The nonviolent resister agrees with the person who acquiesces that one should not be physically aggressive toward his opponent; but he balances the equation by agreeing with the person of violence that evil must be resisted. He avoids the nonresistance of the former and the violent resistance of the latter. With nonviolent resistance, no individual or group need submit to any wrong.

8   It seems to me that this is the method that must guide the actions of the Negro in the present crisis in race relations. Through nonviolent resistance the Negro will be able to rise to the noble height of opposing the unjust system while loving the perpetrators of the system. The Negro must work passionately and unrelentingly for full stature as a citizen, but he must not use inferior methods to gain it. He must never come to terms with falsehood, malice, hate, or destruction.

9   Nonviolent resistance makes it possible for the Negro to remain in the South and struggle for his rights. The Negro's problem will not be solved

*The apostle Peter had drawn his sword to defend Christ from arrest. The voice was Christ's, who surrendered himself for trial and crucifixion (John 18:11).

by running away. He cannot listen to the glib suggestion of those who would urge him to migrate en masse to other sections of the country. By grasping his great opportunity in the South he can make a lasting contribution to the moral strength of the nation and set a sublime example of courage for generations yet unborn.

By nonviolent resistance, the Negro can also enlist all men of good 10 will in his struggle for equality. The problem is not a purely racial one, with Negroes set against whites. In the end, it is not a struggle between people at all, but a tension between justice and injustice. Nonviolent resistance is not aimed against oppressors but against oppression. Under its banner consciences, not racial groups, are enlisted.

Questions for Analysis

1. Classification requires a single organizing principle for focus. What is the SOP (single organizing principle) in this essay? Name two other possible ways to classify oppression.

   How people react to oppression. Other possible SOPs: levels of brutality, levels of freedom, length of bondage, that which is oppressed (physical, mental, emotional, spiritual).

2. Having a reason for a classification is important. What is King's purpose in writing this essay? What sentence is this most clearly stated in?

   King is strongly advocating nonviolent resistance as the best hope of achieving civil rights. First sentence of paragraph 8.

3. Classification essays can be organized by space, time, or importance. Name the major categories in this essay and method of arrangement, and then explain why you think King chose this organization.

   Arrangement: order of importance. King discusses nonviolence last to emphasize it most.

4. Is the introductory paragraph effective? Why or why not? Where is the thesis located?

   Effective: The introduction begins with the thesis, which works as a solid hook, and then offers background information that would interest King's audience.

5. Essays are usually developed through several patterns, such as cause/effect, comparison/contrast, and definition. Tell which of the patterns of development is used in paragraph 5 and how effectively.

   Cause and effect. Effectively: The effects mentioned help make King's case that violence is a bad choice, in turn leading to his proposal of nonviolence.

6. Paragraphs 4–6 deal with the issue of violence in responding to oppression. Why does King discuss violence at this length? What groups in his audience might be especially interested in King's message?

Violence is a natural response to oppression, and King constantly had to defend his position against the objections

of more radical leaders like Malcolm X. His nonviolent message is directed to African Americans but also to the

white community, reassuring them of King's nonviolent intent and perhaps thereby diminishing some opposition.

7. Is the concluding paragraph effective? Why or why not? What is King's expanded thought?
Effective: King repeats "nonviolent" as a connector, touches on his strongest point, and adds the thought of the struggle being between "justice and injustice."

Classification

Judith Viorst wrote this essay for *Redbook,* a magazine with an audience primarily of women. As you read, ask yourself how well targeted the author's examples and explanations are. Does she choose situations that many women could identify with, perhaps more so than men? Does she choose quotations from people who would be interesting to her readership? Notice the eight categories she groups friendships into. Do you think she misses any important types of friends?

Friends, Good Friends—and Such Good Friends

JUDITH VIORST

1   Women are friends, I once would have said, when they totally love and support and trust each other, and bare to each other the secrets of their souls, and run—no questions asked—to help each other, and tell harsh truths to each other (no, you can't wear that dress unless you lose ten pounds first) when harsh truths must be told.

2   Women are friends, I once would have said, when they share the same affection for Ingmar Bergman,* plus train rides, cats, warm rain, charades, Camus,† and hate with equal ardor Newark and Brussels sprouts and Lawrence Welk‡ and camping.

3   In other words, I once would have said that a friend is a friend all the way, but now I believe that's a narrow point of view. For the friendships I have and the friendships I see are conducted at many levels of intensity, serve many different functions, meet different needs and range from those as all-the-way as the friendship of the soul sisters mentioned above to that of the most nonchalant and casual playmates.

4   Consider these varieties of friendship:

5   1. Convenience friends. These are women with whom, if our paths weren't crossing all the time, we'd have no particular reason to be friends:

*Ingmar Bergman (1918–) is a highly praised Swedish film director.
†Albert Camus (1913–1960) was a French novelist.
‡Lawrence Welk (1903–1992) was an American band leader whose television show ran from 1951 to 1978 on ABC and was then syndicated until 1982.

a next-door neighbor, a woman in our car pool, the mother of one of our children's closest friends or maybe some mommy with whom we serve juice and cookies each week at the Glenwood Co-op Nursery.

Convenience friends are convenient indeed. They'll lend us their cups and silverware for a party. They'll drive our kids to soccer when we're sick. They'll take us to pick up our car when we need a lift to the garage. They'll even take our cats when we go on vacation. As we will for them. 6

But we don't, with convenience friends, ever come too close or tell too much; we maintain our public face and emotional distance. "Which means," says Elaine, "that I'll talk about being overweight but not about being depressed. Which means I'll admit being mad but not blind with rage. Which means that I might say that we're pinched this month but never that I'm worried sick over money." 7

But which doesn't mean that there isn't sufficient value to be found in these friendships of mutual aid, in convenience friends. 8

2. Special-interest friends. These friendships aren't intimate, and they needn't involve kids or silverware or cats. Their value lies in some interest jointly shared. And so we may have an office friend or a yoga friend or a tennis friend or a friend from the Women's Democratic Club. 9

"I've got one woman friend," says Joyce, "who likes, as I do, to take psychology courses. Which makes it nice for me—and nice for her. It's fun to go with someone you know and it's fun to discuss what you've learned, driving back from the classes." And for the most part, she says, that's all they discuss. 10

"I'd say that what we're doing is *doing* together, not being together," Suzanne says of her Tuesday-doubles friends. "It's mainly a tennis relationship, but we play together well. And I guess we all need to have a couple of playmates." 11

I agree. 12

My playmate is a shopping friend, a woman of marvelous taste, a woman who knows exactly *where* to buy *what,* and furthermore is a woman who always knows beyond a doubt what one ought to be buying. I don't have the time to keep up with what's new in eyeshadow, hemlines, and shoes and whether the smock look is in or finished already. But since (oh, shame!) I care a lot about eyeshadow, hemlines, and shoes, and since I don't *want* to wear smocks if the smock look is finished, I'm very glad to have a shopping friend. 13

3. Historical friends. We all have a friend who knew us when . . . maybe way back in Miss Meltzer's second grade, when our family lived in that three-room flat in Brooklyn, when our dad was out of work for seven months, when our brother Allie got in that fight where they had to call the police, when our sister married the endodontist from Yonkers and when, the morning after we lost our virginity, she was the first, the only, friend we told. 14

The years have gone by and we've gone separate ways and we've little in common now, but we're still an intimate part of each other's past. And so whenever we go to Detroit we always go to visit this friend of our girlhood. Who knows how we looked before our teeth were straightened. 15

Who knows how we talked before our voice got un-Brooklyned. Who knows what we ate before we learned about artichokes. And who, by her presence, puts us in touch with an earlier part of ourself, a part of ourself it's important never to lose.

16   "What this friend means to me and what I mean to her," says Grace, "is having a sister without sibling rivalry. We know the texture of each other's lives. She remembers my grandmother's cabbage soup. I remember the way her uncle played the piano. There's simply no other friend who remembers those things."

17   4. Crossroads friends. Like historical friends, our crossroads friends are important for *what was*—for the friendship we shared at a crucial, now past, time of life. A time, perhaps, when we roomed in college together; or worked as eager young singles in the Big City together; or went together, as my friend Elizabeth and I did, through pregnancy, birth, and that scary first year of new motherhood.

18   Crossroads friends forge powerful links, links strong enough to endure with not much more contact than once-a-year letters at Christmas. And out of respect for those crossroad years, for those dramas and dreams we once shared, we will always be friends.

19   5. Cross-generational friends. Historical friends and crossroads friends seem to maintain a special kind of intimacy—dormant but always ready to be revived—and though we may rarely meet, whenever we do connect, it's personal and intense. Another kind of intimacy exists in the friendships that form across generations in what one woman calls her daughter–mother and her mother–daughter relationships.

20   Evelyn's friend is her mother's age—"but I share so much more than I ever could with my mother"—a woman she talks to of music, of books and of life. "What I get from her is the benefit of her experience. What she gets—and enjoys—from me is a youthful perspective. It's a pleasure for both of us."

21   I have in my own life a precious friend, a woman of 65 who has lived very hard, who is wise, who listens well; who has been where I am and can help me understand it; and who represents not only an ultimate ideal mother to me but also the person I'd like to be when I grow up.

22   In our daughter role we tend to do more than our share of self-revelation; in our mother role we tend to receive what's revealed. It's another kind of pleasure—playing wise mother to a questing younger person. It's another very lovely kind of friendship.

23   6. Part-of-a-couple friends. Some of the women we call our friends we never see alone—we see them as part of a couple at couples' parties. And though we share interests in many things and respect each other's views, we aren't moved to deepen the relationship. Whatever the reason, a lack of time or—and this is more likely—a lack of chemistry, our friendship remains in the context of a group. But the fact that our feeling on seeing each other is always, "I'm so glad she's here" and the fact that we spend half the evening talking together says that this too, in its own way, counts as a friendship.

(Other part-of-a-couple friends are the friends that came with the marriage, and some of these are friends we could live without. But sometimes, alas, she married our husband's best friend; and sometimes, alas, she *is* our husband's best friend. And so we find ourself dealing with her, somewhat against our will, in a spirit of what I'll call *reluctant* friendship.) 24

7. Men who are friends. I wanted to write just of women friends, but the women I've talked to won't let me—they say I must mention man–woman friendships too. For these friendships can be just as close and as dear as those that we form with women. Listen to Lucy's description of one such friendship: 25

"We've found we have things to talk about that are different from what he talks about with my husband and different from what I talk about with his wife. So sometimes we call on the phone or meet for lunch. There are similar intellectual interests—we always pass on to each other the books that we love—but there's also something tender and caring too." 26

In a couple of crises, Lucy says, "he offered himself for talking and for helping. And when someone died in his family he wanted me there. The sexual, flirty part of our friendship is very small, but *some*—just enough to make it fun and different." She thinks—and I agree—that the sexual part, though small, is always *some*, is always there when a man and a woman are friends. 27

It's only in the past few years that I've made friends with men, in the sense of a friendship that's *mine*, not just part of two couples. And achieving with them the ease and the trust I've found with women friends has value indeed. Under the dryer at home last week, putting on mascara and rouge, I comfortably sat and talked with a fellow named Peter. Peter, I finally decided, could handle the shock of me minus mascara under the dryer. Because we care for each other. Because we're friends. 28

8. There are medium friends, and pretty good friends, and very good friends indeed, and these friendships are defined by their level of intimacy. And what we'll reveal at each of these levels of intimacy is calibrated with care. We might tell a medium friend, for example, that yesterday we had a fight with our husband. And we might tell a pretty good friend that this fight with our husband made us so mad that we slept on the couch. And we might tell a very good friend that the reason we got so mad in that fight that we slept on the couch had something to do with that girl that works in his office. But it's only to our very best friends that we're willing to tell all, to tell what's going on with that girl in his office. 29

The best of friends, I still believe, totally love and support and trust each other, and bare to each other the secrets of their souls, and run—no questions asked—to help each other, and tell harsh truths to each other when they must be told. 30

But we needn't agree about everything (only 12-year-old girl friends agree about *everything*) to tolerate each other's point of view. To accept without judgment. To give and to take without ever keeping score. And to *be* there, as I am for them and as they are for me, to comfort our sorrows, to celebrate our joys. 31

up every hour of every day. And we have trouble launching a few shuttles per year safely.

6   The issue is not whether an economy that is stimulated by population growth is good, bad, or indifferent. The above calculations show that growth is impossible except in the very short run. The real issue is what kind of world will the people of the present and next few generations leave for the people and other creatures of the next few millennia.

7   According to UCLA professor and biologist Jared Diamond, the coming century will witness one of the worst extinctions in the history of life on Earth. Roughly one-half of the 30 million species that are estimated to end will become extinct, courtesy entirely of human beings. If yet additional population and economic growth of the sort that some people espouse actually occurs, then the extinction rate will be even worse. A combination of far too many people, greed, and unbridled technological power is destroying the natural world.

8   Each person plays a role in the population equation. If you and your spouse have two children and four grandchildren, then you are reproducing at replacement levels (zero population growth). But if you have four children and they, in turn, each have four children so that you have 16 grandchildren, then that is roughly equivalent to the 2% per year growth rate that characterizes the world as a whole.

9   Each of us has his or her own system of values. For me, a planet with relatively few people, each of whom can live with dignity and a high quality of life, is far superior to a world where too many people, awash in pollution, stretch resources to the breaking point, and where billions struggle to survive at mere subsistence levels.

Questions for Analysis

1. If you think the introductory paragraph is effective, what makes it work? Look especially at the hook (first sentence) and the thesis sentence. Write out the thesis sentence.

   Effective. The question as a hook draws readers in and begins to introduce the issue of religion, one source of conflict with the author's position. The thesis is another question that delays the persuasive intent of the essay: Couples should limit themselves to two children.

2. What is the author's purpose, is it stated or implied, and what paragraph reveals it most clearly?

   Implied. Zuckerman's essay is persuasive, largely relying on logical appeals to move people to limit the number of children they have. The clearest statement of the thesis is in the conclusion.

3. Writers sometimes use a transitional paragraph to summarize part of their essay and then move readers into the next discussion point. Which paragraph in Zuckerman's essay functions this way, what is it transitioning from, and what point is it moving the reader to? What effect does any statement in this paragraph have on the thesis?

   Paragraph 6: moves from the population statistics to the effect of animal extinction. The last sentence ("The real issue is what kind of world . . .") clarifies the issue and the author's position.

4. If you think the concluding paragraph is effective, what makes it work? How does the author try to connect with the reader?

    Effective: The author shows conviction for his position without becoming

    strident or confrontational. His use of "for me" is effective qualifying, and the

    ethical appeal of what is best for all people is another strong concluding appeal.

5. Is this primarily an essay dealing with causes, effects, or both? What effects are discussed in paragraphs 3 and 4 and in paragraph 7?

    Effects. Paragraphs 3 and 4: explosive population growth measured in

    statistics; paragraph 7: the accelerated rate of species extinction.

6. Cause-and-effect essays often explore problems and solutions. What paragraph is developed this way, and what is the author's point in this paragraph?

    Paragraph 5: Zuckerman anticipates objections to his argument,

    suggests potential solutions, and shows that they will not work.

7. The author addresses his audience in the third person ("people") and first person ("we") but also speaks to them in the second person ("you"). In what paragraph does Zuckerman speak to his readers as "you," and what effect is he trying to achieve? Is this use of second person effective or might it alienate his audience? Why or why not?

    Paragraph 8: The author is trying to emphasize that his audience is part of the problem—but also

    part of the solution. He is careful not to accuse his readers but to include them. This use of "you"

    is effective, and you might contrast it to the pronoun shift problems illustrated in Chapter 24.

Cause and Effect

Brent Staples is a journalist who writes about the negative effects—as an African-American male—he has on the people around him. Staples uses a number of well-illustrated examples to show these effects and points out that men of his race are themselves often endangered simply by being black. As you read this essay, try to put yourself in the author's shoes. Have you ever been frightened by someone who appears menacing? Have you ever perceived yourself to be frightening to others? How have these experiences altered your behavior?

Black Men and Public Space

BRENT STAPLES

My first victim was a woman—white, well dressed, probably in her early twenties. I came upon her late one evening on a deserted street in Hyde Park, a relatively affluent neighborhood in an otherwise mean, impoverished section of Chicago. As I swung onto the avenue behind her, there seemed to be a discreet, uninflammatory distance between us. Not so.

Yorkers hunching toward nighttime destinations seem to relax, and occasionally they even join in the tune. Virtually everybody seems to sense that a mugger wouldn't be warbling bright, sunny selections from Vivaldi's *Four Seasons*. It is my equivalent of the cowbell that hikers wear when they know they are in bear country.

Questions for Analysis

1. Does this essay deal primarily with causes or effects? Give several examples to support your response.

   Answers will vary. Primary effects: The introduction illustrates the effect that

   Staples has on a young white woman. Paragraph 3 explains the effects that

   Staples has on drivers. Paragraph 7 tells of the effects on Staples's behavior of

   his seeing people imprisoned and murdered in his childhood.

2. Where in the essay does Staples also discuss causes?

   The introduction explains what causes the woman to run from Staples:

   his appearance and race. Paragraph 7 tells what caused Staples to

   avoid confrontational behavior: seeing people imprisoned and murdered

   during his childhood.

3. Where is the thesis located?

   Paragraph 2: "the ability to alter public space in ugly ways."

4. If you think the introductory paragraph is effective, what makes it work? What effect does the hook have on the introduction? Is the introduction effective? Why or why not? Comment on the hook and the sentences that follow. What effect might they have on readers?

   The introduction is effective: The hook arouses readers' curiosity with

   the words "my first victim" and continues to build suspense as the

   introduction progresses.

5. Is the conclusion effective? Why or why not? How does it connect with paragraph 11? What is the expanded thought? What statement is Staples making with the cowbell simile?

   Answers will vary. The conclusion is effective. It continues the discussion from paragraph 11 of the

   measures (effects) the author has taken to reduce his menacing appearance (expanded thought).

   With the cowbell simile, Staples reinforces the danger he is regularly exposed to and also, like the

   hiker, is able to warn the "bears" to get out of the way before there is a confrontation.

6. What is the author's purpose in adding the information in the second half of paragraph 5, beginning with "I understand"?

Staples anticipates a likely reader question or objection. He clarifies his

position, making himself appear more reasonable and thus more

appealing to the audience.

7. In what paragraphs does Staples characterize himself in a way that makes it seem ironic that people would mistake him to be a violent person? *Answers will vary. Paragraph 2: "scarcely able to take a knife to a raw chicken." Paragraphs 6 and 7: He talks about his childhood and consciously avoiding trouble.*

Process Analysis

Caroline Rego, a longtime consumer advocate, wrote this article to show readers how to protest when they receive poor service or shoddy merchandise. The author gives practical suggestions for dealing with personal confrontations and writing effective letters of complaint. Notice as you read that Rego lays out her suggestions in several paragraphs, illustrating them with specific examples and explaining her points carefully. Paragraphs 5 and 6, in particular, benefit from positive and negative examples: "Do this, not that."

The Fine Art of Complaining

CAROLINE REGO

You waited forty-five minutes for your dinner, and when it came it was 1 *cold—and not what you ordered in the first place. You washed your supposedly machine-washable, preshrunk T-shirt (the one the catalogue claimed was "indestructible"), and now it's the size of a napkin. Your new car broke down a month after you bought it, and the dealer says the warranty doesn't apply.*

Life's annoyances descend on all of us—some pattering down like 2 gentle raindrops, others striking with the bruising force of hailstones. We dodge the ones we can, but inevitably, plenty of them make contact. And when they do, we react fairly predictably. Many of us—most of us, probably—grumble to ourselves and take it. We scowl at our unappetizing food but choke it down. We stash the shrunken T-shirt in a drawer, vowing never again to order from a catalogue. We glare fiercely at our checkbooks as we pay for repairs that should have been free.

A few of us go to the other extreme. Taking our cue from the crazed 3 newscaster in the 1976 movie *Network*, we go through life mad as hell and unwilling to take it anymore. In offices, we shout at hapless receptionists when we're kept waiting for appointments. In restaurants, we make scenes that have fellow patrons craning their necks to get a look

21 Notice that the P.S. says what you'll do if your problem isn't solved. In other words, you make a threat—a polite threat. Your threat must be reasonable and believable. A threat to burn down the store if your purchase price isn't refunded is neither reasonable nor believable—or if it *were* believed, you could end up in jail. A threat to report the store to a consumer-protection agency, such as the Better Business Bureau, however, is credible.

22 Don't be too quick to make one of the most common—and commonly empty—threats: "I'll sue!" A full-blown lawsuit is more trouble, and more expensive, than most problems are worth. On the other hand, most areas have a small-claims court where suits involving modest amounts of money are heard. These courts don't use complex legal language or procedures, and you don't need a lawyer to use them. A store or company will often settle with you—if your claim is fair—rather than go to small-claims court.

23 Whether you complain over the phone, in person, or by letter, be persistent. One complaint may not get results. In that case, keep on complaining, and make sure you keep complaining to the same person. Chances are he or she will get worn out and take care of the situation, if only to be rid of you.

24 Someday, perhaps, the world will be free of the petty annoyances that plague us all from time to time. Until then, however, toasters will break down, stores will refuse to honor rainchecks, and bills will include items that were never purchased. You can depend upon it—there will be grounds for complaint. You might as well learn to be good at it.

Questions for Analysis

1. List the steps Rego lays out for dealing with people in person. Then list the steps (sections) in the letter of complaint.
    Personal confrontations: Act businesslike and important, complain in person if possible, and complain to the right person. Answer letter: Explain the problem, soften up the reader, explain what you want, and use a PS.

2. Readers often want to know the why behind a suggestion and need to be warned if something may go wrong. How does the author explain (including defining words) and warn in paragraph 6?
    Rego defines what she means by "businesslike and important." If the complainer acts "puffed up," shouts, or threatens, though, the effort may backfire.

3. What is the author's most important suggestion for successful complaining? Do you agree with the author? Why or why not?
    Paragraph 8: Complain to the right person.

4. How many paragraphs does the author use to introduce her process, and where is the thesis located? How effective is this introduction, and why do you think so?

Paragraphs 1–5 introduce the process. The thesis is the last sentence in paragraph 4. The intro-

duction is effective, beginning with a series of common consumer problems, developing with other

specific examples, using figures of speech and active verbs, and then clearly stating the essay's focus.

5. Process-analysis essays can be dry, even boring, reading, so writers often try to enliven their style by creating a friendly tone and varying sentence patterns. List instances in paragraphs 1–9 where you think the author's style is especially engaging. Consider these elements: metaphor and simile; understatement; short sentences; dashes; pronouns like *you, us,* and *we;* active verbs; dialogue; and ellipsis points.

    Answers will vary. Paragraph 1: you scenarios; paragraph 2: dashes, active verbs

    (dodge, grumble, scowl, etc.); paragraph 3: us/we; paragraph 4: understatement

    ("don't win any prizes"), metaphor; paragraph 5: dialogue, and more.

6. What suggestions does Rego give in paragraph 23?

    Be persistent and complain to the same person.

Comparison and Contrast

In the essay "Grant and Lee: A Study in Contrasts," Bruce Catton compares and contrasts the two leading generals of the North and South during the Civil War. The author's purpose is not to argue for the superiority of one general over the other but rather to give readers some insight into the two men. As you read, think about which of the two you most identify with. Do you think the differences between the two men are still represented as divisions between the North and South in our country?

To review the elements of comparison and contrast, turn back to Chapter 11.

Grant and Lee: A Study in Contrasts

BRUCE CATTON

When Ulysses S. Grant and Robert E. Lee met in the parlor of a modest house at Appomattox Court House, Virginia, on April 9, 1865, to work out the terms for the surrender of Lee's Army of Northern Virginia, a great chapter in American life came to a close, and a great new chapter began.

These men were bringing the Civil War to its virtual finish. To be sure, other armies had yet to surrender, and for a few days the fugitive Confederate government would struggle desperately and vainly, trying to find some way to go on living now that its chief support was gone. But in effect it was all over when Grant and Lee signed the papers. And the little room where they wrote out the terms was the scene of one of the poignant, dramatic contrasts in American history.

Lee the dazzling campaigns of Second Manassas and Chancellorsville and won Vicksburg for Grant.

16   Lastly, and perhaps greatest of all, there was the ability, at the end, to turn quickly from war to peace once the fighting was over. Out of the way these two men behaved at Appomattox came the possibility of a peace of reconciliation. It was a possibility not wholly realized, in the years to come, but which did, in the end, help the two sections to become one nation again . . . after a war whose bitterness might have seemed to make such a reunion wholly impossible. No part of either man's life became him more than the part he played in their brief meeting in the McLean house at Appomattox. Their behavior there put all succeeding generations of Americans in their debt. Two great Americans, Grant and Lee—very different, yet under everything very much alike. Their encounter at Appomattox was one of the great moments of American history.

Questions for Analysis

1. Essays that compare and contrast organize material by the block or point-by-point method and sometimes both. In this essay, which paragraphs are devoted exclusively to Lee and which to Grant? Are these paragraphs comparing or contrasting?

    Lee: 5, 6, 10; Grant: 7–9, 11. Contrasting.

2. Which paragraphs discuss the similarities of the two generals? Has the method of organizing shifted? Are the comparison paragraphs arranged by the block method or point-by-point?

    12–16. Yes. Point-by-point.

3. Transitional words are particularly important when moving from one paragraph to another in comparison/contrast essays. Identify the transitional words in the first sentences of paragraphs 9–13.

    Yet, and that, on the other hand, so, yet.

4. Identify the topic sentence in paragraph 5, and explain if it is effective or not. Which example uses cause and effect for development?

    First sentence. Effective: The examples and explanations in the paragraph clearly support the topic sentence. The leisure class will bring about several effects. . . .

5. Contrast the views of Lee and Grant toward their communities as discussed in paragraphs 5 and 9. What is the fundamental difference between the two men?

    Lee's community is rural, agricultural, and local; Grant's community is the nation.

6. If you think the concluding paragraph is effective, what makes it work? What final thought does Catton leave us with?

    Effective: connector, brief summary, and expanded thought. Grant's and Lee's behavior set the tone for reconciliation.

Comparison and Contrast

Russell Baker is a well-known columnist and essayist noted for his humor and insight into human behavior. In "A Nice Place to Visit" Baker contrasts Toronto to New York City, using irony and overstatement extensively to make his point. (For more on these figures of speech, see Chapter 19.) You might notice that many of the author's paragraphs are brief, a convention of newspaper articles. As you read the article, how do you respond to Baker's humor? How do you think a resident of New York City would respond?

A Nice Place to Visit

RUSSELL BAKER

1   Having heard that Toronto was becoming one of the continent's noblest cities, we flew from New York to investigate. New Yorkers jealous of their city's reputation and concerned about challenges to its stature have little to worry about.

2   After three days in residence, our delegation noted an absence of hysteria that was almost intolerable and took to consuming large portions of black coffee to maintain our normal state of irritability. The local people to whom we complained in hopes of provoking comfortably nasty confrontations declined to become bellicose. They would like to enjoy a gratifying big-city hysteria, they said, but believed it would seem ill-mannered in front of strangers.

3   Extensive field studies—our stay lasted four weeks—persuaded us that this failure reflects the survival in Toronto of an ancient pattern of social conduct called "courtesy."

4   "Courtesy" manifests itself in many quaint forms appalling to the New Yorker. Thus, for example, Yankee fans may be astonished to learn that at the Toronto baseball park it is considered bad form to heave rolls of toilet paper and beer cans at players on the field.

5   Official literature inside Toronto taxicabs includes a notification of the proper address to which riders may mail the authorities not only complaints but also compliments about the cabbie's behavior.

6   For a city that aspires to urban greatness, Toronto's entire taxi system has far to go. At present, it seems hopelessly bogged down in civilization. One day a member of our delegation listening to a radio conversation between a short-tempered cabbie and the dispatcher distinctly heard the dispatcher say, "As Shakespeare said, if music be the food of love, play on, give me excess of it."

7   This delegate became so unnerved by hearing Shakespeare quoted by a cab dispatcher that he fled immediately back to New York to have his nerves abraded and his spine rearranged in a real big-city taxi.

8   What was particularly distressing as the stay continued was the absence of shrieking police and fire sirens at 3 A.M.—or any other hour, for that matter. We spoke to the city authorities about this. What kind of city was it, we asked, that expected its citizens to sleep all night and rise

refreshed in the morning? Where was the incentive to awaken gummy-eyed and exhausted, ready to scream at the first person one saw in the morning? How could Toronto possibly hope to maintain a robust urban divorce rate?

9   Our criticism went unheeded, such is the torpor with which Toronto pursues true urbanity. The fact appears to be that Toronto has very little grasp of what is required of a great city.

10   Consider the garbage picture. It seems never to have occurred to anybody in Toronto that garbage exists to be heaved into the streets. One can drive for miles without seeing so much as a banana peel in the gutter or a discarded newspaper whirling in the wind.

11   Nor has Toronto learned about dogs. A check with the authorities confirmed that, yes, there are indeed dogs resident in Toronto, but one would never realize it by walking the sidewalks. Our delegation was shocked by the presumption of a town's calling itself a city, much less a great city, when it obviously knows nothing of either garbage or dogs.

12   The subway, on which Toronto prides itself, was a laughable imitation of the real thing. The subway cars were not only spotlessly clean, but also fully illuminated. So were the stations. To New Yorkers, it was embarrassing, and we hadn't the heart to tell the subway authorities that they were light-years away from greatness.

13   We did, however, tell them about spray paints and how effectively a few hundred children equipped with spray-paint cans could at least give their subway the big-city look.

14   It seems doubtful they are ready to take such hints. There is a disturbing distaste for vandalism in Toronto which will make it hard for the city to enter wholeheartedly into the vigor of the late twentieth century.

15   A board fence surrounding a huge excavation for a new high-rise building in the downtown district offers depressing evidence of Toronto's lack of big-city impulse. Embedded in the fence at intervals of about fifty feet are loudspeakers that play recorded music for passing pedestrians.

16   Not a single one of these loudspeakers has been mutilated. What's worse, not a single one has been stolen.

17   It was good to get back to the Big Apple. My coat pocket was bulging with candy wrappers from Toronto and—such is the lingering power of Toronto—it took me two or three hours back in New York before it seemed natural again to toss them into the street.

Questions for Analysis

1.   What is the author's thesis, and where do you find it? Name several places where Baker reiterates it.

Paragraph 1: Toronto is a more civilized, relaxed, cleaner city than New

York City. Baker reiterates his thesis with each point he raises—for

example, courtesy, cab drivers, baseball park behavior, noise, and

garbage.

2. How is this article arranged—by the block or point-by-point method? If the author had chosen the other method, would the presentation be as effective? Why or why not?

    Point-by-point. Because Baker wants to discuss a number of points primarily by developing the Toronto side of the comparison, point-by-point is probably a better choice. The block method would be more likely to produce a well-developed paragraph or two on Toronto but underdeveloped paragraphs on New York City, unless Baker added more material.

3. List the points that the author compares between the two cities. Explain how any one of these points is developed, including the use of specific details.

    Main points: level of hysteria, courtesy, baseball park behavior, sirens, garbage, dogs, subway, vandalism, consideration of pedestrians. Answers will vary. Baker supports his point about the limited vandalism in Toronto by citing the undamaged subway and speakers attached to the board fence.

4. Baker presents an ironic, humorous persona in this article. (For more on persona, see pp. 393–395.) Choose one instance of irony—saying one thing but meaning the opposite—and explain how it adds to your appreciation (or dislike) of the article.

    Answers will vary. Baker discusses the "failure" of Toronto residents to be ill-tempered and confrontational due to an "ancient pattern of social conduct called 'courtesy.'" Baker uses irony to gently jab the New Yorker who might be rude, approving of behavior like throwing beer bottles and toilet paper rolls at baseball games.

5. Overstatement—exaggerating for effect—is used in many places in this article. Choose one instance of it, and explain how it adds to your appreciation for (or dislike of) the article.

    Answers will vary. Paragraph 4: "Yankee fans may be astonished to learn . . ." Paragraph 7: "This delegate . . . fled immediately back to New York." Paragraph 8: "the absence . . . of sirens" at any hour. The overstatement that favors Toronto diminishes the implied criticism of New Yorkers' behavior because the criticism is viewed in part as a joke, although Baker wants his essential points to be taken seriously.

6. Comment on the author's use of the dash and the rhetorical questions in paragraph 8. What does Baker accomplish with each?

    The dash adds emphasis and heightens the overstatement. In answering the rhetorical questions, readers respond as Baker wants them to. "What kind of city was it . . . ?" A wonderful city. "Where was the incentive" to behave badly? Not in Toronto.

7. What do you think of the conclusion? Of course it is brief (a journalistic convention), but is it effective? Is irony still operating in this paragraph? What is the expanded thought?

    We might believe that after the positive experiences Baker has had in Toronto he is less than happy to be back in New York. The final sentence can be interpreted in several ways: it is difficult to change a person's behavior; people need positive reinforcement from those around them to behave well; at heart Baker is a New Yorker, and he is affirming this in the end.

Definition

Lynda W. Warren, a psychologist and psychology professor, and Jonnae C. Ostrom, a clinical social worker, discuss a group of people known as "pack rats," or excessive savers, in this article published in *Psychology Today.* The authors are surprised to learn that compulsive savers are not only older people reacting to the deprivation they felt during the Great Depression; rather, pack rats are often young and can be found in every economic bracket. As is common in definition essays, you will find the term explored through the brief definition strategies listed in Chapter 15—synonyms, negation, comparisons, formal definition—and several of the patterns of development, especially cause and effect.

They've Gotta Keep It: People Who Save Everything

LYNDA W. WARREN AND JONNAE C. OSTROM

1   Most of us have more things than we need and use. At times they pile up in corners and closets or accumulate in the recesses of attics, basements or garages. But we sort through our clutter periodically and clean it up, saving only what we really need and giving away or throwing out the excess. This isn't the case, unfortunately, with people we call "pack rats"—those who collect, save or hoard insatiably, often with only the vague rationale that the items may someday be useful. And because they rarely winnow what they save, it grows and grows.

2   While some pack rats specialize in what they collect, others seem to save indiscriminately. And what they keep, such as junk mail, supermarket receipts, newspapers, business memos, empty cans, clothes or old Christmas and birthday cards, often seem to be worthless. Even when items have some value, such as lumber scraps, fabric remnants, auto parts, shoes and plastic meat trays, they tend to be kept in huge quantities that no one could use in a lifetime.

3   Although pack rats collect, they are different from collectors, who save in a systematic way. Collectors usually specialize in one or a few classes of objects, which they organize, display and even catalogue. But pack rats tend to stockpile their possessions haphazardly and seldom use them.

4   Our interest in pack rats was sparked by a combination of personal experience with some older relatives and recognition of similar saving patterns in some younger clients one of us saw in therapy sessions. Until then, we, like most people, assumed that pack rats were all older people who had lived through the Great Depression of the 1930s—eccentrics who were stockpiling stuff just in case another Depression came along. We were surprised to discover a younger generation of pack rats, born long after the 1930s.

5   None of these clients identified themselves during therapy as pack rats or indicated that their hoarding tendencies were causing problems in any way. Only after their partners told us how annoyed and angry they were

about the pack rats' unwillingness to clean up the growing mess at home did they acknowledge their behavior. Even then, they defended it and had little interest in changing. The real problem, they implied, was their partner's intolerance rather than their own hoarding.

Like most people, we had viewed excessive saving as a rare and 6 harmless eccentricity. But when we discussed our initial observations with others, we gradually came to realize that almost everyone we met either admitted to some strong pack-rat tendencies or seemed to know someone who had them. Perhaps the greatest surprise, however, was how eager people were to discuss their own pack-rat experiences. Although our observations are admittedly based on a small sample, we now believe that such behavior is common and that, particularly when it is extreme, it may create problems for the pack rats or those close to them.

When we turned to the psychological literature, we found surprisingly 7 little about human collecting or hoarding in general and almost nothing about pack-rat behavior. Psychoanalysts view hoarding as one characteristic of the "anal" character type, first described by Freud. Erich Fromm later identified the "hoarding orientation" as one of the four basic ways in which people may adjust unproductively to life.

While some pack rats do have typically anal-retentive characteristics 8 such as miserliness, orderliness and stubbornness, we suspect that they vary as much in personality characteristics as they do in education, socioeconomic status and occupation. But they do share certain ways of thinking and feeling about their possessions that shed some light on the possible causes and consequences of their behavior.

Why do some people continue to save when there is no more space 9 for what they have and they own more of something than could ever be used? We have now asked that question of numerous students, friends and colleagues who have admitted their pack-rat inclinations. They readily answer the question with seemingly good reasons, such as possible future need ("I might need this sometime"), sentimental attachment ("Aunt Edith gave this to me"), potential value ("This might be worth something someday") and lack of wear or damage ("This is too good to throw away"). Such reasons are difficult to challenge; they are grounded in some truth and logic and suggest that pack-rat saving reflects good sense, thrift and even foresight. Indeed, many pack rats proudly announce, "I've never thrown anything away!" or "You would not believe what I keep!"

But on further questioning, other, less logical reasons become apparent. Trying to get rid of things may upset pack rats emotionally and may 10 even bring on physical distress. As one woman said, "I get a headache or sick to my stomach if I have to throw something away."

They find it hard to decide what to keep and what to throw away. 11 Sometimes they fear they will get rid of something that they or someone else might value, now or later. Having made such a "mistake" in the past seems to increase such distress. "I've always regretted throwing away the letters Mother sent me in college. I will never make that mistake again,"

Questions for Analysis

1. In which sentence do you first learn the authors' focus for this essay? How do they define the term "pack rat"?
    Paragraph 1: "This isn't the case, unfortunately, with people we call 'pack rats' . . ." Defined: "those who collect, save or hoard insatiably . . ."

2. Write out the synonym the authors give in paragraph 25 for the term "pack rat."
    "Excessive savers."

3. The authors define through negation in paragraph 3. What do they tell us that pack rats are not?
    Collectors.

4. Which of the patterns of development (for more on this, see pp. 8–9) do the authors mainly use in paragraphs 9–23?
    Cause and effect.

5. Which one of the paragraphs in this essay begins with a question, and what is the authors' purpose in using it?
    Paragraph 9: This is a developmental question, a topic sentence that unifies the rest of the paragraph.

6. Drawing from traits and behaviors the authors describe in the article, write out a 10-point profile of a pack rat. What is the essential, defining trait of a pack rat?
    Answers will vary. Obsessive/compulsive, hoarders, miserly, orderly, stubborn, anxious, depressed, insecure, indecisive, controlled by their possessions, reclusive. Compulsive saving.

7. Are paragraphs 25 and 26 an effective conclusion? Why or why not?
    Answers will vary. Effective: The questions in paragraph 25 cause readers to reflect, to realize that there is still more to find out about pack rats. Paragraph 26 injects a note of humor into an otherwise fairly serious essay. Some will find it appropriate, and others not.

Definition

In the essay "What Is a Dad?" Bob Brannan offers several defining elements of fatherhood. Because this is an extended definition, you will find many of the patterns of development represented, as well as points common to brief definitions: synonyms, negation, comparisons, and formal defining. As you read, ask yourself if the designated audience—young married men who have just learned they are about to become fathers—would be interested in the examples and explanations provided.

What Is a Dad?

BOB BRANNAN

"Honey, it's going to be a girl!" my wife of ten years said to me as I paused near the top of the living room steps. I looked at the half a dozen pink balloons bouncing on the ceiling and at Beth smiling from above me at the head of the stairs. "Wonderful," I thought, and then immediately, "Oh, no!" Fatherhood was rushing at me like a space shuttle coming in with its payload from outer space, and I wasn't prepared. I dropped my briefcase on the landing, gave her a hug, and lied convincingly: "That's the best news I've heard this year." As we talked over the details of the sonogram, I thought hard about what lay ahead for us and about what I was going to become—a dad. I didn't know then much of what a dad was supposed to be, but I was sure it involved a lot more than just providing food, clothing, and shelter. And that's exactly what the past three years of raising a little girl has taught me: Being a dad is one of the hardest yet most rewarding jobs there is.

I had thought that being a father meant being a child again, just a quick time travel back to the days of bare feet and endless summers, becoming a friend and playmate. Well, I was wrong . . . and right. Fathers can and should play with their children, the more the better. But that's not how I spent the first year with my daughter. No one had prepared me for the seemingly endless routine of feeding, burping, cleaning, rocking, and diaper changing that came with the territory. It wasn't until Lauren was fairly secure on her feet that we were able to play the way I had anticipated. But for the past two years we have been inseparable companions, creating fantasy games, role playing every Disney character that Walt ever helped bring into the world, and both learning to sing lots of drippy songs—God help whoever has to listen.

But becoming a good father requires more than just a willingness and ability to become young again; a man must become fiercely, wholeheartedly protective. Of course we should be alert to the more predictable dangers for our children (put the gate across the stairs, pad all the sharp corners, put the locks on the cabinets, cover all the electrical outlets), but there is another world of potential hurt out there that most of us know next to nothing about. What if your son wakes up at three in the morning coughing uncontrollably? How about the ear infection and runny nose that never seem to go away? What do you do about those angry red welts that appear on, migrate across, disappear from, and then reappear on your little girl's skin? You might think that modern medicine and an enlightened, caring pediatrician could solve the problems. But often this is not so. Fathers and mothers are frequently on their own in this. If we care deeply for our children, we spend a lot of time finding out for ourselves how to help them.

4   However, the parent's life isn't all *that* dismal. Many fathers have supremely healthy children, which leaves the dads with more time for one of the most important roles he will play in his child's life, teacher. Yes, fathers-to-be, whatever you have done for a living up till this point, now you are a teacher. While some might view themselves more as a boss, benevolent monarch, or dictator, the truth is that we will be spending a large part of the next eighteen years (at least) trying to teach our children how to become happy, healthy, complete human beings. All the areas we work with from the initial ABCs and counting to restraining our anger—often at them!—to appreciating a spring daffodil or majestic sunset, all of these lessons, well taught, mark us as the most crucial teachers there can be. If we do our small jobs well, we slowly remake the world.

5   So what is a dad, really? As far as I can tell, he is a man who bravely and foolishly, with only limited vision, steps into a difficult lifelong role that he begins with almost no experience and ends, if he is lucky, having learned a little. Along the way he has profited immeasurably: he has had an attentive, enthusiastic playmate who laughs at his stupidest jokes and thinks his voice impressions are incredibly brilliant; he has become less selfish, if not selfless, learning to put the needs of another ahead of his own; and he has grown by giving daily without counting of his knowledge and wisdom, whatever they may be, as he teaches his son or daughter to the best of his ability. I suppose, in the end, the true measure of a good father is one who loves his children beyond himself—perhaps all others—and who can hope that the adult he has helped shape will for all her life be able to look back at the man and, at least on occasion, say, "I love you, dad."

Questions for Analysis

1. Extended definitions often grow from several patterns of development. Name two from paragraph 2, and explain how they add to the paragraph.
   Patterns: comparison/contrast and process analysis. The contrast between baby chores and toddler playtime helps readers see what fathers face. The process description of the baby chores works the same way—specific examples.

2. If you think the introductory paragraph is effective, what makes it work? Look especially at the hook (first sentence), the author's use of "I," the brief dialogue, revealing thoughts, and the thesis sentence. Write out the thesis sentence.
   Effective: The hook draws readers in, the "I" of personal experience adds credibility, the dialogue adds interest, and the thesis clearly predicts the direction of the essay.

3. If you think the concluding paragraph is effective, what makes it work? Why does the author use a question as the first sentence? What are the effects of being a father that the author lists?

   Effective: The conclusion uses a connector, summarizes, and adds an

   expanded thought: Fatherhood helps a person to grow. The question

   serves as transition. Effects: all of sentence 3.

4. Brief definitions often include negation, comparisons (often as metaphor/ simile), and synonyms. List each paragraph in which these occur, and explain how they add to your understanding of "fatherhood."

   Introduction: Negation shows the author's lack of knowledge about parenting.

   Introduction: The space shuttle simile develops the idea of how new and alien the

   experience felt. The synonyms parent and dad are used for father in several paragraphs.

5. What words in the topic sentence of paragraph 3 relate back to paragraph 2, and are they an effective connector?

   "More than just a willingness and ability to become young again." Yes.

6. Choose any paragraph and explain how the examples help develop the author's points.

   Answers will vary. One possibility, dangers, in paragraph 3: Predictable dangers

   can be controlled; other dangers require a skeptical attitude toward facile

   answers, a willingness to question and seek out the best solutions.

Persuasion

In the essay "Abortion, Right and Wrong," Rachel Richardson Smith argues for a broader perspective on the issue of abortion. As you read, think about the author's persona—how she presents herself to the audience—and her position on abortion. For an argument to be successful, does it need to convert a listener, or can it merely ask for greater tolerance and respect?

To review the elements of persuasion, turn back to Chapter 16.

Abortion, Right and Wrong

RACHEL RICHARDSON SMITH

I cannot bring myself to say I am in favor of abortion. I don't want anyone to have one. I want people to use contraceptives and for those contraceptives to be foolproof. I want people to be responsible for their actions; mature in their decisions. I want children to be loved, wanted, well cared for.

I cannot bring myself to say I am against choice. I want women who are young, poor, single or all three to be able to direct the course of their lives. I want women who have had all the children they want or can afford or their bodies can withstand to be able to decide their future. I want women who are in bad marriages or destructive relationships to avoid being trapped by pregnancy.

3   So in these days when thousands rally in opposition to legalized abortion, when facilities providing abortions are bombed, when the president speaks glowingly of the growing momentum behind the anti-abortion movement, I find myself increasingly alienated from the pro-life groups.

4   At the same time, I am overwhelmed with mail from pro-choice groups. They, too, are mobilizing their forces, growing articulate in support of their cause, and they want my support. I am not sure I can give it.

5   I find myself in the awkward position of being both anti-abortion and pro-choice. Neither group seems to be completely right—or wrong. It is not that I think abortion is wrong for me but acceptable for someone else. The question is far more complex than that.

6   Part of my problem is that what I think and how I feel about this issue are two entirely different matters. I know that unwanted children are often neglected, even abandoned. I know that many of those seeking abortions are children themselves. I know that making abortion illegal will not stop all women from having them.

Absolutes

7   I also know from experience the crisis an unplanned pregnancy can cause. Yet I have felt the joy of giving birth, the delight that comes from feeling a baby's skin against my own. I know how hard it is to parent a child and how deeply satisfying it can be. My children sometimes provoke me and cause me endless frustration, but I can still look at them with tenderness and wonder at the miracle of it all. The lessons of my own experience produce conflicting emotions. Theory collides with reality.

8   It concerns me that both groups present themselves in absolutes. They are committed and they want me to commit. They do not recognize the gray area where I seem to be languishing. Each group has the right answer—the only answer.

9   Yet I am uncomfortable in either camp. I have nothing in common with the pro-lifers. I am horrified by their scare tactics, their pictures of well-formed fetuses tossed in a metal pan, their cruel slogans. I cannot condone their flagrant misuse of Scripture and unforgiving spirit. There is a meanness about their position that causes them to pass judgment on the lives of women in a way I could never do.

10   The pro-life groups, with their fundamentalist religious attitudes, have a fear and an abhorrence of sex, especially premarital sex. In their view abortion only compounds the sexual sin. What I find incomprehensible is that even as they are opposed to abortion they are also opposed to alternative solutions. They are squeamish about sex education in the schools. They don't want teens to have contraceptives without parental consent. They offer little aid or sympathy to unwed mothers. They are the vigilant guardians of a narrow morality.

11   I wonder how abortion got to be the greatest of all sins? What about poverty, ignorance, hunger, weaponry?

The only thing the anti-abortion groups seem to have right is that abortion is indeed the taking of a human life. I simply cannot escape this one glaring fact. Call it what you will—fertilized egg, embryo, fetus. What we have here is human life. If it were just a mass of tissue there would be no debate. So I agree that abortion ends a life. But the anti-abortionists are wrong to call it murder. 12

The sad truth is that homicide is not always against the law. Our society does not categorically recognize the sanctity of human life. There are a number of legal and apparently socially acceptable ways to take human life. "Justifiable" homicide includes the death penalty, war, killing in self-defense. It seems to me that as a society we need to come to grips with our own ambiguity concerning the value of human life. If we are to value and protect unborn life so stringently, why do we not also value and protect life already born? 13

Mistakes

Why can't we see abortion for the human tragedy it is? No woman plans for her life to turn out that way. Even the most effective contraceptives are no guarantee against pregnancy. Loneliness, ignorance, immaturity, can lead to decisions (or lack of decisions) that may result in untimely pregnancy. People make mistakes. 14

What many people seem to misunderstand is that no woman wants to have an abortion. Circumstances demand it; women do it. No woman reacts to abortion with joy. Relief, yes. But also ambivalence, grief, despair, guilt. 15

The pro-choice groups do not seem to acknowledge that abortion is not a perfect answer. What goes unsaid is that when a woman has an abortion she loses more than an unwanted pregnancy. Often she loses her self-respect. No woman can forget a pregnancy no matter how it ends. 16

Why can we not view abortion as one of those anguished decisions in which human beings struggle to do the best they can in trying circumstances? Why is abortion viewed so coldly and factually on the one hand and so judgmentally on the other? Why is it not akin to the same painful experience families must sometimes make to allow a loved one to die? 17

I wonder how we can begin to change the context in which we think about abortion. How can we begin to think about it redemptively? What is it in the trauma of loss of life—be it loved or unloved, born or unborn—from which we can learn? There is much I have yet to resolve. Even as I refuse to pass judgment on other women's lives, I weep for the children who might have been. I suspect I am not alone. 18

Questions for Analysis

1. A good argument defines its issue early. Where in the first few paragraphs do we learn what the issue is in this essay?
   Paragraphs 1 and 2.

2. What is the author's position on the issue, and in which paragraph is it most clearly stated?

    People should recognize the complexity of the abortion issue and

    become more tolerant of each side—paragraph 8.

3. How would you characterize the author's persona? (For more on persona, see pp. 393–395.) What points in the essay make you feel this way?

    A person who is concerned, sincere, troubled, reasonable, and fair. Her position, her self-

    presentation as a mother (one who has experienced unplanned pregnancy, childbirth, and

    child rearing), her insight into the feelings of women who decide to have an abortion, etc.

4. Strong arguments require clear terminology and refutation of opposing reasons. In which paragraph does the author define a key term? How does the definition help refute a pro-life reason?

    Paragraph 13: Richardson Smith refutes the charge that abortion is

    "murder" by naming three examples of justifiable homicide.

5. In which paragraph does the author deal with the issue of the fetus as human? Does her position support pro-life or pro-choice?

    Paragraph 12. Pro-life.

6. All arguments grow from assertions supported by detailed examples and explanations. Identify the topic sentence in paragraph 9, and then list the examples the author offers to support her assertion.

    The second sentence. Pictures of fetuses in metal pans, cruel slogans,

    and misuse of Scripture.

7. What three reasons does the author list in paragraph 6 that support the pro-choice position?

    Unwanted children, children having children, and abortion continuing

    whether illegal or not.

8. To preserve their credibility by limiting overstatement, writers qualify frequently in argument (using words like *seems, might, often,* and *frequently*). Name three instances of qualifying in paragraphs 5–7. (For more on qualifying in argument, see pp. 397–398.)

    Paragraph 5, seems; paragraph 6, part of, often, all women; paragraph 7,

    can, sometimes.

Persuasion

"What Is Biodiversity and Why Should We Care About It?" comes from the book *The Global Citizen*, written by Donella Meadows in 1991. The author argues that people do not care enough for their planet, that if we continue to destroy plant and animal habitats we will ultimately destroy ourselves. As you read this article, imagine yourself as part of Meadows's target audience—people who are interested in the environment but not well informed on matters like "biodiversity." Does the author hold your interest and speak persuasively to you, or do you feel alienated at any point, as if the author is reprimanding you?

What Is Biodiversity and Why Should We Care About It?

DONELLA MEADOWS

1 Most of us have grasped the idea that there's a hole in the sky over the South Pole that could give us skin cancer. We are beginning to understand that a global warming could inundate Miami Beach and make New York even more unbearable in the summer. There is another environmental problem, however, that doesn't have a catchy name like "ozone hole" or "greenhouse effect," and that hasn't yet entered the public consciousness. It's the loss of biodiversity.

2 Bio-*what*?

3 Biodiversity sounds like it has to do with pandas and tigers and tropical rain forests. It does, but it's bigger than those, bigger than a single species or even a single ecosystem. It's the whole, all of life, the microscopic creepy-crawlies as well as the elephants and condors. It's all the habitats, beautiful or not, that support life—the tundra, prairie, and swamp as well as the tropical forest.

4 Why care about tundras and swamps? There's one good reason—self-interest. Preserving biodiversity is not something to do out of kindness of our hearts, to express our fondness for fuzzy creatures on Sunday mornings when we happen to feel virtuous. It's something to do to maintain the many forms of life we eat and use, and to maintain ourselves.

5 How would you like the job of pollinating all trillion or so apple blossoms in the state of New York some sunny afternoon in May? It's conceivable, maybe, that you could invent a machine to do it, but inconceivable that the machine could work as efficiently, elegantly, and cheaply as honeybees, much less make honey.

6 Suppose you were assigned to turn every bit of dead organic matter—from fallen leaves to urban garbage to road kills—into nutrients that feed new life. Even if you knew how, what would it cost? Uncountable numbers of bacteria, molds, mites, and worms do it for free. If they ever stopped, all life would stop. We would not last long if green plants stopped turning our exhaled carbon dioxide back into oxygen. The plants would

not last long if a few beneficent kinds of soil bacteria stopped turning nitrogen from the air into fertilizer.

7   Human reckoning cannot put a value on the services performed for us by the millions of species of life on earth. In addition to pollination and recycling, these services include flood control, drought prevention, pest control, temperature regulation, and maintenance of the world's most valuable library, the genes of all living organisms, a library we are just learning to read.

8   Another thing we are just learning is that both the genetic library and the ecosystem's services depend on the integrity of the entire biological world. All species fit together in an intricate, interdependent, self-sustaining whole. Rips in the biological fabric tend to run. Gaps cause things to fall in unexpected ways.

9   For example, attempts to replant acacia trees in the Sahel at the edge of the Sahara desert have failed because the degraded soil has lost a bacterium called rhizobium, without which acacia trees can't grow. Songbirds that eat summer insects in North America are declining because of deforestation in their Central American wintering grounds. European forests are more vulnerable to acid rain than American forests because they are human-managed, single-species plantations rather than natural mixtures of many species forming an interknit, resilient system.

10   Biodiversity cannot be maintained by protecting a few charismatic megafauna in a zoo, not by preserving a few greenbelts of even large national parks. Biodiversity can maintain itself, however, without human attention or expense, without zookeepers, park rangers, foresters, or refrigerated gene banks. All it needs is to be left alone.

11   It is not being left alone, of course, which is why biological impoverishment has become a problem of global dimensions. There is hardly a place left on earth, where people do not log, pave, spray, drain, flood, graze, fish, plow, burn, drill, spill, or dump.

12   Ecologists estimate that human beings usurp, directly or indirectly, about 40 percent of each year's total biological production (and our population is on its way to another doubling in forty years). There is no biome, with the possible exception of the deep ocean, that we are not degrading. In poor countries biodiversity is being nickeled and dimed to death; in rich countries it is being billion-dollared to death.

13   To provide their priceless service to us, the honeybees ask only that we stop saturating the landscape with poisons, stop paving the meadows and verges where bee food grows, and leave them enough honey to get through the winter.

14   To maintain our planet and our lives, the other species have similar requests, all of which, summed up, are: Control yourselves. Control your numbers. Control your greed. See yourselves as what you are, part of an interdependent biological community, the most intelligent part, though you don't often act that way. Act that way. Do so either out of a moral respect for something wonderful that you did not create and do not understand or out of a practical interest in your own survival.

Questions for Analysis

1. Evaluate the introduction. Does the first sentence arouse readers' curiosity? Do the middle sentences speak to the audience's interests and knowledge? Does the paragraph indicate what the article will be about? What pronouns help connect the writer to the audience?

   The hook works well as does the other information, establishing a connection with the audience of shared knowledge, and Meadows clearly states the topic of the article. Pronouns of accommodation are us and we.

2. Effective arguments quickly clarify their issue. One way to do this is by defining terms. In which paragraph does Meadows begin to define her key term, and what specific examples does she use to illustrate her definition? Has the author made a mistake by not also defining the term *ecosystem*? Why or why not?

   Paragraph 3. Meadows cites specific animals and habitats. Students should be able to determine from the introductory audience definition that most of the author's readers would be familiar with the term ecosystem.

3. Persuasive writing gives people reasons to accept a writer's position. What is the author's primary reason to support her position, where does she first state it, and how clearly does she explain it? What objection or misconception in this paragraph does she anticipate and counter?

   Primary reason: self-interest, stated in paragraph 4. Meadows begins to clarify her point by anticipating the potential objection of some who might feel that preserving biodiversity is primarily an act of kindness rather than self-interest.

4. Without support, reasons are unconvincing. What paragraphs does Meadows devote to supporting her primary reason? What main examples does she offer for support in paragraphs 5 and 6? Does the author's use of *you* in these paragraphs seem appropriate? Why would she combine *you* with a question as the first sentence in paragraph 5?

   Support for paragraph 4: paragraphs 5–9; paragraph 5: bees and pollination, paragraph 6: recycling organic matter. The pronoun you is appropriate because Meadows wants to directly address her audience; neither we nor people would work as well in this instance. Questions are useful for engaging an audience.

5. Because writers regularly combine the patterns of development in supporting their ideas, you will find several in this article, including cause and effect. Locate two instances of cause and effect, and explain how effectively they are used to help make the author's point.

   Cause and effect in paragraphs 6 and 9. Paragraph 6 effectively establishes a causal chain, and paragraph 9 uses three specific examples to illustrate negative effects.

6. All arguments deal with counterreasons and objections to the author's position. What is the counterreason offered in paragraph 10, and how well does Meadows refute it?

Counterreason: Biodiversity can be maintained with wildlife preserves.

Meadows has established in paragraphs 5–9 that diversity is essential

and that it must be planetwide to avoid chain-reaction extinctions of

beneficial species.

7. Connecting paragraphs in essays is important to ease readers from one idea into the next. What connecting methods does Meadows use to link paragraphs 1–4?

Paragraph 2 repeats a word and uses a question: "Bio-what?" Para-

graph 3 repeats biodiversity. Paragraph 4 repeats tundras and

swamps, using a question.

8. How effective is the concluding paragraph? What points does the author remind us of; what is the expanded thought? What device does Meadows use to keep from having to criticize her audience, even though she does use the pronoun *you*?

The conclusion is effective. Meadows links the lead sentence to her final body

paragraph, connects with her thesis, touches on two strong reasons for

supporting her position, and reminds readers that they, too, are part of the

biological community. She uses the animal voices to ask for change.

9. The author uses a number of stylistic devices to create clarity and interest, including the dash, italics, questions, metaphor, and personification. Locate an instance of each one of these, and explain how it strengthens the writing. (For more on figures of speech, see pp. 505–512.)

Answers will vary. Paragraph 4, dash for emphasis; paragraph 2, italics for

emphasis; paragraph 4, question used to develop a point; paragraphs 7 and 8,

metaphors of "gene library" and "biological fabric" for emphasis and clarity;

paragraph 13, personification of honeybees to promote emotional appeal.

Writing a Research Essay

What Are We Trying to Achieve and Why?

Setting the Stage

Writing research essays is a common academic task, one with which most of us already have some experience. In fact, the research paper is simply an extension of what you have been doing as you worked through the assignments in *A Writer's Workshop:* developing a focused idea with detailed examples and clear explanations. However, research requires you to go one step farther. Instead of relying entirely on your own personal experience and general knowledge, now you will find out what other people have to say, and you will use their ideas to help explain your own. In this appendix, you will learn how to find, select, use, and document information as you craft a well-developed, source-supported essay.

Linking to Previous Experience

Most of us have written essays that relied on sources outside our personal experience. For example, many high school students are assigned to write research essays, and most take short-answer or full essay exams that require them to present information—facts, statistics, names, dates, and so forth. In this text, you may already have worked with Chapter 17, which discusses how to include textbook sources in an answer to an essay-exam question. Also, throughout the text, you have worked on focusing and developing ideas, the basis of all writing. Finally, you have had to bring together ideas—a task that research requires—as you combined the patterns of development (illustration, cause/effect, process analysis, and so on) in essays for different purposes.

Determining the Value

Analysis (breaking something into its parts) and **synthesis** (combining ideas) are basic to the way we think. Without being able to *analyze*, say, a recipe for German chocolate cake to determine its ingredients, you wouldn't be able to *synthesize* the ingredients—put them together—to make that tasty treat. When you analyze and synthesize the ideas you discover through research, you improve your critical thinking skills, which will help you succeed in and out of college. Research has the added benefit of increasing your knowledge as you read and analyze the articles you use in your essays. Lastly, being able to cite respected authorities increases your credibility with readers and listeners.

Developing Skills and Exploring Ideas in Writing Research Essays

The following skills will help you write effective research essays:

- Quoting sources selectively and accurately.
- Integrating quotations from sources smoothly.
- Paraphrasing and summarizing ideas from sources.
- Avoiding plagiarism.
- Using in-text citations for all sources that you quote, summarize, or paraphrase.
- Preparing a Works Cited page.

Quoting Sources Selectively and Accurately

Incorporating Source Information

One useful method for bringing ideas from sources into your essay is quotation. **Quoting** a source means placing the author's words within quotation marks and then acknowledging the author by name, either within the sentence or within parentheses, usually at the end of the quotation. You should not use quotations merely to fill up space. Rather, you should include quotations when you have good reasons for doing so, as in the following:

- The author's wording is particularly memorable. A well-turned phrase often includes metaphors, similes, and other figures of speech (see Chapter 19).
- The material is loaded with statistics, names, dates, and percentages and so would be difficult to reword.
- The author of the quotation would be recognized by and be significant to the audience.

One other point to remember as you quote a source is to do so accurately. You are bound by convention to reproduce each word, punctuation mark, and even error as it appears in your source. If you want to economize by cutting part of a quotation, indicate the missing words with **ellipsis points**—three spaced periods—as in the following example:

"Like much of Mars, the butterscotch plain is . . . pretty dull."

When you need to add a word or two to clarify a point within a quotation or make it fit grammatically within your sentence, use **brackets** [ ], as in the following example:

"Like much of Mars, the butterscotch [meaning yellow] plain is . . . pretty dull."

If you notice an error within a quotation, you can show readers that it is not your mistake by writing the word *sic* within brackets after the error, as in this example:

"Like much of Mars, the butterscotch plane [sic] is . . . pretty dull."

Integrating Quotations from Sources Smoothly

When you quote a source, be sure to include information in your lead-in so that readers are not left to guess at the significance of the quotation. The following examples show how you might leave readers confused by a quotation or help them understand your meaning by introducing and explaining the idea:

Quotation Not Introduced

Oliver Norton says, "It's dustier than the road to death, drier than Dorothy Parker's martinis, colder than the devil's kiss."

Quotation Explained

The author, Oliver Norton, explains how hostile the environment is on Mars with these images: "It's dustier than the road to death, drier than Dorothy Parker's martinis, colder than the devil's kiss."

In addition to clearly introducing and explaining the significance of a quote, writers can vary the verbs they use to introduce quotations by using words in the following list:

says	offers	continues	remarks	argues	claims
explains	gives	adds	tells	maintains	challenges
states	mentions	expands on	reveals	asserts	admits
comments	discusses	points out	presents	denies	acknowledges

If you want to use a quotation that would be longer than *four* lines when reproduced in your essay, you should put it in **block quotation** form by indenting it 10 spaces from the left margin, double-spacing between lines, and omitting quotation marks around the information:

The surface of this part of Mars is barren and arid:

> It's dustier than the road to death, drier than Dorothy Parker's martinis, colder than the devil's kiss. Like much of Mars, the butterscotch plain is inhospitable, empty, ancient, and, when it comes down to it, pretty dull. But a few hundred meters to the south, over a shoal of low, uneven hummocks, the landscape changes. (Norton 8)

Note the author's last name and the page number in parentheses following the quotation. Full publication information would be provided in a "Works Cited" list at the end of the essay.

Paraphrasing and Summarizing Ideas Carefully

Two more methods for bringing ideas from sources into an essay are paraphrasing and summarizing. When you **paraphrase,** you put a passage into your own words, changing *both* the source's words and the arrangement of those words. Because you keep most of the main ideas from your source, a paraphrase is about the same length as the original. When you **summarize,** you reword the original text but keep only main points, leaving out supporting points, casual commentary, and most examples. Summaries are generally much *shorter* than the original. When you paraphrase or summarize, you must read a text closely and understand it well enough to report it accurately.

Read the following paragraph, written by Oliver Norton for *National Geographic,* and the paraphrase and summary that follow.

Original Text

Landscapes like this are changing the way geologists look at Mars. They've long been fascinated by the planet's distant past. Now they're getting ever more excited by the mysterious processes shaping its present—thanks in large part to the planet's apparent iciness. Martian ice is not a novelty in itself; for years geologists have expected to find it frozen into the soil at mid and high latitudes. The excitement comes from a growing suspicion that the ice doesn't just sit there but has a dynamic role to play. That it moves from place to place around the globe. That it reshapes the texture of the surface. And that it may sometimes produce fleeting traces of liquid water. (Norton 8)

Paraphrase

Oliver Norton states that geologists are becoming more interested in recent forces shaping the planet Mars because the scientists are beginning to suspect that ice in the soil helps change the landscape. Norton says that geologists, who have studied Mars for many years, have known about ice there for a long time and supposed that it might be found in the planet's soil in middle and upper latitudes. However, the scientists didn't realize that the ice might alter the surface of Mars. Now they theorize that the ice might liquefy in small amounts and that as it travels it erodes surfaces. (8)

Summary

Scientists have recently begun to suspect that ice on Mars may liquefy in small amounts and that as the ice moves it changes the face of the planet (Norton 8).

Three problems commonly occur when writers use paraphrase and summary: misinterpreting the source's ideas, omitting an idea or adding one that should not be there, and using too many of the author's words and a word arrangement that is too similar to the original.

Original Text

Martian ice is not a novelty in itself; for years geologists have expected to find it frozen into the soil at mid and high latitudes. The excitement comes from a growing suspicion that the ice doesn't just sit there but has a dynamic role to play. (Norton 8)

Misinterpreting and Leaving Ideas Out

> The author says that finding ice on Mars was not a surprise to geologists, who thought it would be all over the place. But now they are interested because they are sure the ice affects the planet's surface (Norton 8).

Notice that the original text says geologists thought the ice would be in a specific location, in the soil and at "mid and high latitudes." Also, the scientists are *guessing* at the dynamic function of ice; they are not "sure," as the distorted paraphrase claims. It is often difficult to report accurately what one of your sources intends, so it is important to read your material several times until you are sure you understand it.

ACTIVITY A.1 Paraphrasing and Summarizing Effectively

Read the original text below, taken from the article on Mars by Oliver Norton, and read the paraphrase. Then tell how, specifically, the paraphrase has been distorted.

Original Text

> Water will stay liquid only if it's warm enough and at high enough pressure. Drop the temperature, and it will freeze; drop the pressure, and it will vaporize. Physics seems to say that Martian midlatitudes are far too cold for liquid water to persist for any length of time at the surface. (Norton 15)

Distorted Paraphrase

> Oliver Norton discusses the physical properties of liquid when he notes that it will flow when it's warm and disappear when there is too little air pressure on it. Physicists are sure that Mars is too cold for water to be there.

Answers will vary.
Norton does not say that water will flow when it's warm; he says that it will be liquid. He says that it will "vaporize," not disappear, when pressure drops. Also, the source does not say that physicists are "sure," he says that "physics seems to say."

Avoiding Plagiarism

Avoiding Plagiarism

Another common problem in research writing is **plagiarism**—the theft of someone else's words or ideas. Sometimes people consciously represent another person's work as their own, deliberately plagiarizing. This is a serious academic offense that can result in a failing grade for an essay or for the entire course. But more often inexperienced writers either fail to document words or ideas from their sources or reword carelessly. Consider the following example of accidental plagiarism:

Original Text

> Then in the 1970s this Mars too was killed. Orbiting spacecraft—first Mariner 9 and then the two Viking missions—showed there was much more to the Martian surface than craters. Mariner 9 saw volcanoes twice as tall as any on Earth. There were canyons as deep as the Earth's deepest ocean trenches. (Norton 14)

Accidental Plagiarism

> In the 1970s this Mars too was destroyed. Orbiting spaceships, the first being Mariner 9 and then two Viking ships, were able to show there was a lot more to the surface of Mars than craters. Mariner 9 showed volcanoes two times as tall as any on Earth. Also there were canyons as deep as the Earth's trenches (Norton 14).

Even though the author of the plagiarized paragraph cited Norton, because the author included too many of the source's words in the same order and with the same sentence structures, this paragraph is unacceptable. To avoid accidentally plagiarizing, keep these two suggestions in mind:

1. If you use more than two or three of the source's words in a row, use quotation marks (remember, however, that quotations must be justified).
2. Carefully read the passage you will cite, and then *look away from it* as you "translate" the information into your own words. It is difficult to avoid plagiarizing if you shift your eyes back and forth between your source's words and your own.

Here is one way to eliminate plagiarism by paraphrasing and selective quoting:

Plagiarism Eliminated

> The author tells of the changing views scientists have had of Mars, including the shift "in the 1970s when this [image of] Mars too was killed." Whereas scientists had thought that the surface of Mars was largely riddled with craters and little more, they learned otherwise. Several space ventures, Mariner 9 and Viking, discovered volcanoes higher than any of Earth's and canyons to match those of our deepest ocean trenches (Norton 14).

Although it is critical to acknowledge your sources—their *ideas* as well as their exact words—some ideas and information are so widely known that they are considered to be everyone's property, or **common knowledge.** You do not need to cite the source of common knowledge. For example, most educated people know that the Holocaust took place in World War II, that there are seven continents, and that the United States was attacked by terrorists on September 11, 2001.

ACTIVITY A.2 Avoiding Plagiarism

Read the following original text, taken from the article on Mars by Oliver Norton, and compare it with the plagiarized paraphrase. Then rewrite the paragraph, "translating" Norton's words, quoting selectively, and changing the word arrangement.

Original Text

> Today Mars looks a lot more like a globe of ice than it ever has before. But it also looks like something shucking that ice away, something moving on, something undergoing change. Whatever else Mars turns out to be, it won't be a useless, changeless lump in the universe. (Norton 30)

Plagiarized Version

> Nowadays the planet Mars looks much more like a globe of ice than ever. Yet it also seems like something that is shucking that ice away, something moving along, a thing that is changing. The author says that Mars won't turn out to be a useless, unchanging lump in the universe (Norton 30).

Plagiarism Eliminated
Answers will vary.

_____

_____

_____

_____

Citing Sources within Your Essay

After choosing information to quote, summarize, or paraphrase, you must credit the author of the information within your essay. You do this to direct readers to a **Works Cited** page, on which you list all sources used in the essay. If the author of the information you are citing is well known to your audience or has impressive credentials, you should state his or her name in the sentence that introduces the information, as in "Mark Twain once said, . . ." You may also place the author's last name in parentheses near the source material in your paragraph, most often at the end of a sentence. Remember that you must cite summaries and paraphrases as well as direct quotations.

The following examples follow the MLA (Modern Language Association) format for citing sources within text:

Author Mentioned in Your Text
When the author's name is mentioned within your sentence, leave the name out of the parenthetical citation:

Professor Davis explains that vampires have left a profound mark on

literature (125).

Author Not Named in Your Text
Include the name of the author within the parenthetical citation at the end of the sentence if you have not used the name in your own text:

Some literary experts maintain that vampires have left a profound mark on

literature (Davis 125).

Two- or Three-Author Source
Include the names of all the authors:

The Lord of the Rings trilogy is the cornerstone of current fantasy fiction

(Senter, Harris, and Hogan 66).

More Than Three Authors
Include the first author's last name and then use the Latin abbreviation *et al.*, meaning "and others":

As we become familiar with the literature of vampires, we will see the

relationship many politicians have with society (Davis et al. 5).

Corporate Author
A work may be attributed to an institution rather than a person:

The best way to protect the land is to involve the people who live there

(Nature Conservancy 32).

Unknown Author

When the author is unknown, use the whole title of the work, if it is short, or the first significant words in the title, within quotation marks:

> The best way to protect the land is to involve the people who live there
>
> ("Saving the Land" 32).

Author of Several Works

If you use more than one work by the same author, include the first significant words from the title of each source within quotation marks, and include the author's last name:

> The Japanese Samurai was akin to the medieval European knight
>
> ("History," Halligan 77).

Several Sources Giving the Same Information

Include both sources, separated by a semicolon:

> Celtic music has undergone a rebirth in recent years (Broomfield 21;
>
> Russell 9).

Indirect Source

When using a quotation that your source has taken from someone else, use the words *qtd. in*, short for "quoted in." In this example, Williams has quoted Antle:

> As Jay Antle has remarked, "Storm chasing is not for the faint hearted"
>
> (qtd. in Williams 321).

Preparing a Works Cited Page

Bibliomaker

To help readers locate sources used in an essay, writers following the MLA format create a Works Cited page, which lists in alphabetical order all of the sources quoted, summarized, or paraphrased in the essay. Note that you do not include all sources you have looked at, just the ones you have used. The Works Cited page comes on a separate page after the conclusion of your essay. Follow these guidelines when creating your Works Cited page:

> **GUIDELINES FOR CREATING A WORKS CITED PAGE**
> 1. Center the words "Works Cited." However, do not underline them or use quotation marks around them.
> 2. Alphabetize the authors by last name.
> 3. Begin each name at the left margin.
> 4. Indent each line beneath the name within an entry by five spaces.
> 5. Double-space all lines in and between the author entries.

(To see a model Works Cited page, turn to p. A-21.)

The following examples will help you build your Works Cited page. (For more information on citing sources, visit the MLA website at http://www.mla.org.

Books

BOOK BY ONE AUTHOR

| Author's last name first | Title | City of publication | Publisher | Date |

Jackson, Stanley. Melancholia and Depression. New Haven: Yale UP, 1986.

The second line of each entry is indented
five spaces. All lines are double-spaced.

Book by Two or Three Authors

Hershman, Jablow, and Julian Lieb. Manic Depression and Creativity.
Amherst: Prometheus, 1998.

Chappelle, Sean, Maria Cox, and Steven Fenton. As the Last Rain Forest
Falls. New York: McGraw-Hill, 2003.

Book by More Than Three Authors

Rose, Michelle, Margo Schnipper, Russel Binelli, and Michael Cohen. The
Myth of the Bermuda Triangle. New York: Harper, 1999.

Note: The abbreviation *et al.,* meaning "and others," may be used after the first author's name, replacing the other author names.

More Than One Book by the Same Author

Martin, Melanie. Raising Children the Easy Way. Fort Worth:
Harcourt, 2001.

———. When Time-Out Is No Longer Enough. Fort Worth: Harcourt, 2002.

Note: Three hyphens substitute for the author's name.

Book with an Editor

Bellenir, Karen, ed. Mental Health Disorders Sourcebook. Detroit:
Omnigraphics, 1996.

Work in an Anthology

Dinesen, Isak. "Sorrow-Acre." The Norton Anthology of Short Fiction. Ed.
R.V. Cassill. 4th ed. New York: Norton, 1990.

Encyclopedia Article

Turk, Alexander. "Paleontology in the Twentieth Century." The New
Encyclopaedia Britannica: Micropaedia. 15th ed. 2002.

Periodicals

MAGAZINE ARTICLE: WEEKLY

| Author's last name first | Title | Name of publication | Date | Page numbers |

Caruthers, Faith L. "Where Is Osama Now?" Newsweek 7 Feb. 2003: 44–48.

Magazine Article: Monthly

Lamb, Bertrand. "Learning to Talk to Your Teen." Parenting May 2004:
120–23.

Journal Article with Consecutive Paging over Several Issues

Sturbenz, Michael. "Alzheimer's: The Earliest Onset." Journal of Applied
Psychology 64 (1999): 840–47.

Note: 64 = volume; 840–47 = page numbers.

Journal Article with New Paging in Each Issue

Walsh, Catherine. "Perspectives: Suicide of Author Michael Dorris."
America. 176.16 (1997): 7.

Note: 176.16 = volume 176; issue 16, 7 = page number.

Newspaper Article

Cowley, Frank. "Kudzu: Meet Your New Neighbor." New York Times 14 Jan.
2001, late ed.: C2+.

Note: ed. = edition, if known; C2+ = pages continue.

Editorial or Unsigned Letter to the Editor

"No Child Left Behind, and No School District Left Funded." Editorial. Free
Press News 4 Sept. 2003: A12.

Note: A = section.

Electronic Sources

Website

"Depression." 4 Jan. 1999. Mayo Clinic Health Information. 24 Mar. 2000.
<http://pr.quick.SDV2001/02DWK/mayo/depression~risk>.

Note: 4 Jan. 1999 = date website was created; 24 March 2000 = date the site was
accessed.

Article in Online Newspaper

Nagourney, Adam, and Jodi Wilgoren. "Dean's Campaign Alters Approach
after Iowa Loss." New York Times on the Web 22 Jan. 2004.
12 June 2004. <http://www.nytimes.com/2004/01/22/politics/22
CAMP.html?th>.

Note: 22 Jan. 2004 = date the article appeared; 12 June 2004 = date the article
was accessed.

E-mail

Bronson, Carter. "Getting Out the Vote." E-mail to Danny Alexander.
22 Jan. 2004.

Other Sources

Interview

Williams, Carmaletta. Personal interview. 4 Dec. 2004.

Film or Video

The Lord of the Rings: The Two Towers. Dir. Peter Jackson. Perf. Elijah
Wood, Ian McKellen, and Viggo Mortensen. Wingnut Films, 2003.

Television Program

"Living Dinosaurs." Narr. Lance Gunderson. Dir. Maureen Fitzpatrick. The
Learning Channel. 7 Nov. 2004.

Music Recording

Dayne, Taylor. Soul Dancing. Arista, 1993.

WRITING A RESEARCH PAPER
Summarizing the Assignment

This assignment asks you to choose a topic and develop an essay of about three
pages that uses information you find in books, magazines, and newspapers and
on the Internet to support your thesis. You will rely on outside sources for most
of the information in the essay, but you may also include personal experience if
it helps to develop your ideas. Your instruction will tell you how many sources
he or she wants you to use, but three to five can be adequate for a short research
essay. This assignment, more than any other this semester, requires careful planning and efficient use of your time.

Establishing Audience and Purpose

Limiting your audience will help you to focus your research. If your readers are
knowledgeable, you do not need to explain terms and ideas that are basic to
your topic, and you can focus on a more specific aspect of your topic. In other
words, you can discuss more about less. For example, in researching the making of *The Lord of the Rings* movies for a group of J. R. R. Tolkien fans, you could
assume they know the story well, so you would not need to provide a plot
overview and an in-depth explanation of the main characters. You might focus
your essay on the director's most notable departures from the book, discussing
why he did so and what the films may have gained or lost in the process. A less
knowledgeable audience might not be able to follow or even be interested in a
topic focused on the differences between the books and films. These readers
might enjoy a broader discussion of the location, sets, and acting challenges.

Your purpose may be to entertain, persuade, or inform, but supporting your
ideas with sources—introducing, rewording, and explaining them correctly and
effectively—should be your top priority.

Working through the Writing Assignment

Discovering Ideas

Look to your own life for topics. What activities do you enjoy? What do you do well? What do you want to know more about? You might connect your research with a college subject (perhaps in another course you are taking this semester), choosing a topic that lets you learn more about your major or furthers your knowledge in a certificate program. You could pick a job-related topic. Maybe you have read an article in the paper recently or heard a talk show discussion that makes you want to know more about a subject. There are many possibilities. Whatever your topic, remembers that it must be researchable and well focused. The topics list below may help with ideas:

Topics List

- **People:** musician, athlete, politician, artist, writer, religious leader, criminal
- **Political processes:** primaries, presidential campaigning, voting, federal court appointments, presidential vetos, passage of legislation in Congress, filibusters
- **Political issues:** Patriot Act, Americans with Disabilities Act, No Child Left Behind Act, term limits, campaign finance reform, farm subsidies, age discrimination, NASA funding, missile defense shield, North American Free Trade Agreement (NAFTA), affirmative action, school vouchers, North Korean nuclear program, gun control, campaign finance reform
- **Mysterious places, things, or events:** Bermuda Triangle, UFOs, Stonehenge, Easter Island figures, paranormal abilities (clairvoyance, telekinesis, etc.), supernatural creatures (ghosts, vampires, etc.), alien abductions
- **Cultural traditions:** Japanese tea ceremony, American Fourth of July, Chinese New Year, African-American Kwanza, Passover, Mexican Cinco de Mayo, Mardi Gras, Native American Green Corn Festival, Kashmiri Shivratri Festival
- **Vacation spots:** Cancún, Mexico; Vail, Colorado; Orlando, Florida; New Orleans; New York City; San Francisco; Seattle; Cape Cod, Massachusetts; Padre Island, Texas; Montreal, Quebec
- **Sports:** baseball, football, basketball, soccer, lacrosse, golf, skateboarding, figure skating, NASCAR racing
- **Family issues:** disciplining children, divorce, "deadbeat" dads, single parenting, home schooling, teaching a child to read, childhood immunizations, rethinking Ritalin use with attention deficit hyperactivity disorder (ADHD)
- **Films:** *The Last Samurai, The Lord of the Rings: The Return of the King, House of Sand and Fog, Elf, Finding Nemo, Pirates of the Caribbean: The Curse of the Black Pearl, Friday Night Lights*
- **TV issues:** violence, sex, advertising targeted to children, TV program ratings, high-definition TV broadcasting, watching too much TV
- **Health issues:** cigarettes; alcoholism; eating disorders such as obesity, anorexia, and bulimia; organic foods; irradiated foods; genetically altered foods; meat processing; vegetarianism; food additives; recombinant bovine growth hormone (rBGH) in milk; Atkins diet; labeling foods to show country of origin; sleep deprivation; Mad Cow disease; severe acute respiratory syndrome (SARS); medical marijuana; Alzheimer's disease

- **Environment:** Clean Water Act, Clean Air Act, Endangered Species Act, Kyoto Protocols, preserving wetlands, saving the Everglades, drilling in the Arctic National Wildlife Reserve (ANWR), cutting old-growth forests, snowmobiling in Yellowstone National Park, global warming, oil spills, alternate energy sources

- **Career programs:** nursing, welding, paralegal, fire science, medical technician, dental hygienist, emergency medical technician

- **National security:** 9/11, airport security, reform of the CIA, missile defense shield, Patriot Act, energy independence, renovating the energy grid, biological warfare, cyber security, disaster response

- **Crime:** serial killers, guns in school, gang violence, cyber theft, juvenile justice, white-collar crime, prison overcrowding, minimum sentencing

Prewriting

**Using the Library
Using the Internet**

After choosing a topic, you need to find your slant on it (narrow it) and then gather sources. It is helpful to prewrite even before heading to the library or logging onto the Internet, perhaps using clustering or listing, to discover what you already know about the topic and to begin to find a direction for your research. Olivia Lutz, the author of the student model in this chapter, picked clinical depression to explore and began with this list:

Depression

- Mental illness: What is it exactly? Who can have it?
- Does it run in families?
- Who does have it: any well-known people?
- Other mental illnesses: schizophrenia, dementia, Alzheimer's?
- What kinds of depression are there?
- What causes it?
- Affects many people
- Affects all kinds of people
- Affects teenagers
- Makes people miserable: affects family relationships and friendships, keeps people at home, makes them do poorly at work, causes people to hurt themselves
- Can be hidden.
- How can it be treated?
- What do people feel like who are clinically depressed? Why don't they get treatment?

As Olivia reviewed her notes, she began to focus on these exploratory research questions: "What are the causes, effects, and kinds of depression; how is it treated; and how do people feel who suffer from this illness?" She knew that as she researched she might change her focus, adding or cutting ideas, depending on the information she found, her changing interests, and the length requirements of the assignment.

The next step in the process is gathering sources. Your college or local community library offers books, periodicals (magazines, newspapers, journals), and Internet access. A good way to begin collecting information is by looking up your topic in a general reference encyclopedia such as *Encyclopedia Britannica* or

Encyclopedia Americana, which may help you narrow your topic and direct you to other sources. You will find these sources listed in the library's online catalog, which usually contains books and periodicals, as well as in other online databases the library subscribes to. If your instructor takes your class to the library for a tour and practice run with the online catalog and databases, take advantage of this help. Additionally, remember that the reference librarians are experts at retrieving information and are usually happy to explain how the catalog and databases work and to help you track down material.

The Internet, and in particular the World Wide Web, is a vast network of computers. It is also a valuable resource, but it can bog you down with information overload. A search for a broad topic using a search engine—a computer program that helps you locate sites on the World Wide Web that contain words you enter—is likely to produce hundreds of thousands of references, only a few of which will be useful in your essay. For example, a search using the term *depression* on the popular search engine Google will yield over 26 million hits, few of them useful. Narrowing the search by using the search engine's advanced search screen produces a list, with the most relevant pages appearing first. For example, the accompanying screen shows the results of an advanced search for all pages that contain the word *depression* and the phrase *family relationships* on Google. Note that phrases should be enclosed in quotation marks. Another problem with Internet research is that many of the websites are trying to sell something and/or are written by people with questionable credentials. Databases that many college libraries subscribe to, such as EBSCOhost and InfoTrac, on the other hand, contain information that has been critically reviewed by at least one editor and that has appeared in magazines, newspapers, and journals throughout

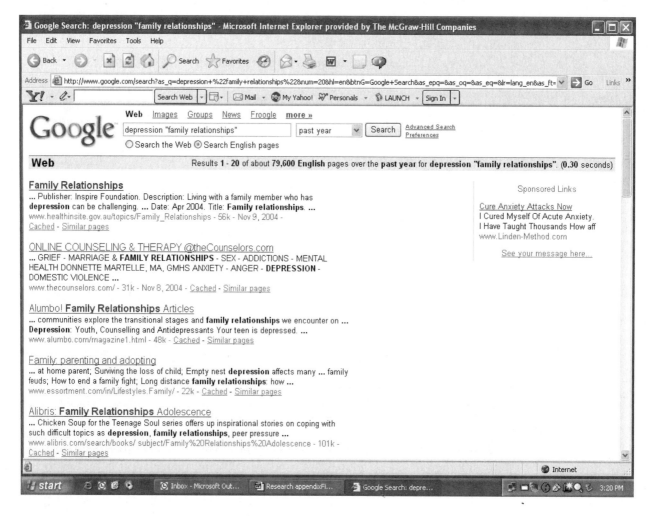

the country. You can be more certain of finding quality sources when you rely on these "refereed" databases.

However, information from any source should be carefully examined before using it in a research essay. When you evaluate your sources, consider these points:

Source Evaluation Tutor

CAUTION! Abstracts of articles—brief summaries—often do not provide enough information for useful citation. It is best to locate—and use—the complete article.

QUESTIONS TO ASK WHEN EVALUATING SOURCES

1. **Is the source current enough to be useful?** For example, if you are reporting on computer processing speeds, an article from 2000 would not have current information, although it might still give useful background.

2. **Is the source clearly presented?** Do you understand the material well enough to use it in your paper?

3. **Is the source accurate?** Are any claims being made or facts/statistics presented that seem wrong? If, for instance, you have found a web page that claims astronauts have never landed on the moon, you should suspect the author's credibility—and sanity.

4. **Is the source complete?** Is enough information given to answer questions you and your audience might have about the topic?

5. **Does the source have a particular point of view, or bias?** Especially if your purpose is persuasive, the opinions and attitudes of your sources will influence how your readers view your work. For instance, if you are arguing to snowmobilers that snowmobiles should be banned from national parks, how likely are they to be convinced by information from a group on either side of the issue? Statistics from a more neutral organization or a government agency, however, might be more convincing.

6. **Is the author well respected and qualified to write the article?** The author's qualifications can be difficult to determine, but here are some ways to check them out: Look for credentials such as an M.D. or a Ph.D., check any bibliographic information about the author at the beginning of the article, and look for references to the author in other sources.

You can record paraphrases, summaries, and quotations from sources you decide to use in a notebook, on note cards, or in a computer file—whatever works best for you. However, be sure to indicate your source on each note, and keep a separate list of all the publication information for the Works Cited page. For books, include the author, title, publishing company, city of publication, and year of publication. For periodicals, include the author; title; periodical name; volume number, issue number, and date; and page numbers of the article.

PREWRITING—SUMMING UP

1. **Prewrite to find a topic.**
2. **Limit your topic with a research question or rough thesis.**
3. **Begin gathering sources, preferably from library catalogs or databases.**
4. **Evaluate and select your sources.**
5. **Record your paraphrases, summaries, and quotations, and choose a method for organizing your sources: notebook, note cards, or computer file.**
6. **Write out the publication information for each source you will need to list on the Works Cited page.**

Organizing Ideas

With your sources collected, you can select and organize the information that answers your research question. If you listed points in your prewriting, you can now arrange them into a **working outline,** based on the sources you found and the points you are still interested in. You may well have changed your focus from the research question you started with, adding or deleting points. For example, Olivia Lutz refocused her essay, cutting the idea of treatment for depression and coming up with this thesis and forecasting statement: "What causes this illness, what are its effects, what forms does it take, and what does it feel like to be in the grips of depression?"

It is less time consuming and frustrating to plan your paper in advance than to cut major sections after you have written them. Here is a rough outline for Olivia's essay:

1. Begin with statistics to show how serious depression is.
2. Work in the idea of what it feels like to be depressed.
3. Give some history on the causes of depression.
4. Tell about current thinking on the causes of depression.
5. Tell about the effects of the illness.
6. Describe the types of depression.
7. End with more on how it feels to be depressed.

The benefit of a rough outline is that it helps you separate the information you have gathered from your sources into the major blocks of information that will support the ideas in your essay.

You may organize your essay in several ways, depending on your purpose and patterns of development. If your goal is persuasion, you may find order of importance the best choice, arranging reasons and refutations from least to most powerful. If you are primarily giving information, you may arrange paragraphs by space, time, or importance. The annotated model, for example, arranges body paragraph 1 chronologically and body paragraph 4 by order of importance.

Remember to begin each body paragraph with a topic sentence and a connector like the transitions below (for more on connectors and transitions, see pp. 53–58):

- **Locating or moving in space:** above, against, around, behind, below, on, in
- **Moving in time:** after, at last, awhile, first, immediately, next, now, often, then
- **Adding material:** again, also, and, in addition, furthermore, as well as
- **Giving examples:** for example, for instance, another, one reason, in fact
- **Comparing:** alike, also, both, in the same way, similarly
- **Contrasting:** in contrast, although, but, differs from, even though, however
- **Cause/effect:** and so, as a result, because, consequently, since, so, then
- **Summarizing/concluding:** finally, in brief, in other words, in short, to summarize

> **ORGANIZING—SUMMING UP**
> 1. **Use a rough thesis sentence to focus your essay.**
> 2. **Create a working outline.**
> 3. **Plan on beginning each body paragraph with a topic sentence.**
> 4. **Use transitions to connect your body paragraphs.**

Drafting

With the preliminary work out of the way, you are almost ready to write a first draft. But before moving ahead, review the drafting suggestions in Chapter 1, page 12. As you draft, be sure to do the following:

1. **Weave information from your sources into each paragraph.** This is a synthesis paper, one that develops your ideas by combining quotations, summaries, and paraphrases.
2. **Interpret each source:** Introduce it, lead away from it, and explain its significance.
3. **Avoid plagiarizing.** Use your own words and sentence structures.
4. **Include parenthetical citations,** even in your rough draft. This will keep you from having to scour your sources for hours trying to find which author belongs to which bit of information in your final draft. It will also help reduce accidental plagiarism.
5. **When in doubt, document.** If you are not sure whether some information or idea is common knowledge, it is best to cite it. You can always delete the citation if it is unneeded.

Revising Drafts

To review the lists for revising first, second, and final drafts, see Chapter 13.

ANNOTATED STUDENT MODEL:
"Why Do I Feel This Way?"

Olivia's purpose is to communicate information about clinical depression for an audience that needs the knowledge—people who suspect that someone in their life may be afflicted with the illness. Notice that she develops her ideas largely through causes and effects, carefully introducing and then explaining her sources.

Olivia Lutz

Professor Brannan

English 106

April 7, 2000

Why Do I Feel This Way?

Depression is the most common of all psychological disorders, affecting nearly everyone occasionally. However, when a person is unable to conduct his or her life normally, depression becomes a problem requiring treatment. Over 17 million Americans have this terrible medical condition, which costs the country a shocking amount, totaling $43 billion in 1992 from decreased work productivity (Nemeroff 44). Not only does depression hurt the economy; clinical depression kills. Each year 15 percent of those who are severely depressed may commit suicide (Nemeroff 44). Regardless of its severity, about a third of the people with depression don't know they have it, and two-thirds don't seek treatment ("Depression" 1). After studying the suicide of successful author Michael Dorris, Catherine Walsh believes that "human beings—no matter what their accomplishments or level of self-awareness—are vulnerable" and can slide into depression (7). What causes this illness, what are its effects, what forms does it take, and what does it feel like to be in the grips of depression?

People have studied the causes of mental disorders for centuries and are still finding new information about depression almost daily. In the earliest Greek medical texts, depression or "melancholia" was associated with the "four-element theory," which maintained that physical and mental health corresponded with the four basic elements of fire, air, earth, and water, seen in people as the four "humors" of blood, phlegm, yellow bile, and black bile (Alexander 30). Melancholia was thought to result from excessive black bile (Alexander 32). During medieval times scholars made further progress in the study of depression. A sixth-century

Last name and page number in upper-right corner

Your name, professor's name, course name, and date double-spaced at left margin

Title centered

Introduction begins weaving sources into text.

Using author's name to introduce quotation

Combining quotation with summary

Thesis with forecasting statement

Topic sentence

Paragraph arranged by time

Lutz 2

Byzantine physician, Alexander of Tralles, went beyond the four-element theory of causes for medical conditions, realizing that depression is centered in the brain (Alexander and Selesnick 60). Researchers have made many advances in the study of depression since these early observations. Today we understand that this illness may have many causes—biological, psychological, and genetic—and that high stress and traumatic events can trigger it (Bellenir 161).

Science has also learned that biochemical changes in the brain can cause psychological diseases, such as depression. This illness is generally linked with the depletion of serotonin, a molecule that certain brain cells use to communicate with each other. Having too little serotonin negatively affects the hypothalamus, which controls our appetite, libido, and sleep, and the amygdala, which affects our emotions. Depressed patients with low serotonin levels have the greatest risk for suicide (Nemeroff 46).

The effects of depression can be hard to detect since everyone experiences them occasionally. Symptoms can be slow thinking, somberness, apathy, loneliness, insecurity, and low interest in normal daily activities. People suffering from depression will often become indecisive, slow their speech, abandon interests, cry frequently, neglect themselves, become inhibited, and, in severe cases, attempt suicide. Appearance, also, usually reflects a person's descent into depression. People with this disorder can look unattractive, aged, expressionless, and sloppy in their grooming and dress (Hershman and Lieb 35-36). In order for a doctor to diagnose a person with depression, the patient must show some of these symptoms nearly every day for at least two weeks.

If a person is diagnosed as clinically depressed, the next step is to find out how severe the condition is. The mildest form is called seasonal affective disorder or SAD. Short spurts of depression related to changes in a person's life are common traits of SAD, and these cases are usually not treated. Bipolar disorder, also called manic-depressive disorder, is a more

Topic sentence

Defining terms, summarizing source, and explaining effects

Topic sentence

Source with two authors

Topic sentence

Lutz 3

severe form and is characterized by recurrent cycles of depression and mania, extremely low and high periods that seriously affect judgment. Another type of depression, dysthymia, can last two years or longer but is not usually disabling, and some sufferers can have short periods of feeling normal. However, dysthymia can make people feel like their lives are hardly worth living, as one person suffering from the illness wrote: "Lately I've felt like a shell of a person, just barely getting through the day. I just barely get out of bed, then I just sit by the TV and watch my day go by" (qtd. in Jackson 3). This person had a normal life only while around people, but days without company were spent entirely in bed. The worst form of depression is major depression. The symptoms are severe, such as overwhelming grief and mood disturbance, and can last for more than two weeks at a time ("Depression" 1).

Symptoms of depression can be mild or severe; however, even if symptoms are not obvious to others, a person with depression may be struggling on the inside. The French composer Hector Berlioz once wrote:

> It is difficult to put into words what I suffered—the longing that seemed to be tearing my heart out by the roots, the dreadful sense of being alone in an empty universe, the agonies that thrilled through me as if the blood were running ice-cold in my veins, the disgust with the living, the impossibility of dying. . . . (qtd. in Jamison 19)

Even with all the advances we have made in the study of depression, the number of people suffering from this illness is rising. If we want to help ourselves and our loved ones to remain mentally healthy, we should know the signs of depression, even though sometimes we may have to look closely to see them. The silent sufferers who mask their symptoms and deny even to themselves that they have an illness may be the ones who need our help the most.

Marginal annotations:

Paragraph arranged by importance—"the worst"

Useful block quotation to emphasize author's final point

Block quote indented ten spaces and double-spaced

Quoting source within source

Lutz 4

Works Cited

Alexander, Franz G., M.D., and Sheldon T. Selesnick, M.D. History of
    Psychiatry: An Evaluation of Psychiatric Thought and Practice
    from Prehistoric Times to the Present. New York: Harper, 1966.

Bellenir, Karen, ed. Mental Health Disorders Sourcebook. Detroit:
    Omnigraphics, 1996.

"Depression." 4 Jan. 1999. Mayo Clinic Health Information. 24 Mar.
    2000. <http://pr.quick.SDV2001/02DWK/mayo/depression~risk>.

Hershman, Jablow, and Julian Lieb. Manic Depression and Creativity.
    Amherst: Prometheus, 1998.

Howells, John G., ed. World History of Psychiatry. New York: Brunner/
    Mazel, 1975.

Jackson, Stanley. Melancholia and Depression. New Haven: Yale UP,
    1986.

Jamison, Kay. Touched with Fire. New York: Free Press, 1993.

Nemeroff, Charles B. "The Neurobiology of Depression." Scientific
    American. 278.6 (1998): 42–49.

Walsh, Catherine. "Perspectives: Suicide of Author Michael Dorris."
    America. 176.16 (1997): 7.

Do not underline
or put quotation
marks around
words "Works
Cited."

Double-space all
lines within and
between author
entries.

Indent each line
beneath name
within entry by
five spaces.

Finish each entry
with period.

Appendix Summary

1. Research essays use print and other sources to develop a topic.

2. Sources must be analyzed (taken apart) and synthesized (put together).

3. Evaluate sources for currency, accuracy, completeness, objectivity, and credibility.

4. Weave sources into your paper using *selected* quotations, summaries, and paraphrases.

5. Introduce and explain all sources—especially quotations.

6. Use block quotations when the text would appear in your paper as five or more lines.

7. To avoid accidental plagiarizing, when you use more than two or three words in a row from a source, put them in quotation marks. Also, look away from your source when summarizing or paraphrasing.

8. Information that is common knowledge does not need to be cited.

9. When you cite authors within your essay using MLA format, either include the author's name in the introduction to the quotation, paraphrase, or summary, or place the author's last name along with a page number from the work within parentheses at the end of your sentences.

10. All sources used in a paper must be identified on a Works Cited page.

11. Focus your research efforts with a research question or rough thesis sentence.

12. Write a rough outline to help you manage your sources.

13. Include parenthetical citations even in your rough drafts.

14. Edit your final draft carefully, several times.

CREDITS

Text Acknowledgments

Baker, Russell, "A Nice Place to Visit." Copyright © 1979 by The New York Times Co. Reprinted with permission.

Catton, Bruce, "Grant and Lee: A Study in Contrasts." Copyright © 1958 by U.S. Capitol Historical Society. All rights reserved. Reprinted with permission.

Gottfried, Martin, "Rambos of the Road." Copyright © 1986 by Martin Gottfried, author of twelve books, including *Balancing Act—The Authorized Biography of Angela Lansbury,* and a biography of Arthur Miller. Reprinted with permission.

Hoffmann, Roger, "The Dare." First published in The New York Times. Copyright © 1986 by Roger Hoffman.

King, Jr., Martin Luther, "The Ways of Meeting Oppression." Reprinted by arrangement with the Estate of Martin Luther King Jr., c/o Writers House as agent for the proprietor New York, NY. Copyright © 1958 by Martin Luther King Jr, copyright renewed 1991 Coretta Scott King.

Meadows, Donella, "What Is Biodiversity, and Why Should We Care about It?" From *The Global Citizen* by Donella H. Meadows. Copyright © 1991 by the author. Reproduced by permission of Island Press.

Morton, Oliver, "Mars Revisited," *National Geographic* January 2004. Used by permission of the National Geographic Society.

Rego, Caroline, "The Fine Art of Complaining." Reprinted by permission of Townsend Press.

Smith, Rachel Richardson, "Abortion, Right and Wrong." Copyright © 1985 by Rachel R. Smith. Reprinted with permission.

Soto, Gary, "The Jacket" from *The Effects of Knut Hamsun on a Fresno Boy: Recollections and Short Essays* by Gary Soto. Copyright © 1983, 1988, 2000 by Gary Soto. Reprinted by permission of Persea Books, Inc. (New York).

Staples, Brent, "Black Men and Public Space." Copyright © 1986 by Brent Staples, who writes editorials on politics and culture for The New York Times and is author of the memoir, *Parallel Time: Growing Up in Black and White.* Reprinted with permission.

Steinbeck, John, "The Great Tide Pool," from *Cannery Row* by John Steinbeck. Copyright © 1945 by John Steinbeck. Renewed © 1973 by Elaine Steinbeck, John Steinbeck IV and Thom Steinbeck. Used by permission of Viking Penguin, a division of Penguin Group (USA) Inc.

Viorst, Judith, "Friends, Good Friends—and Such Good Friends." Copyright © 1977 by Judith Viorst. Originally appeared in *Redbook.* Reprinted by permssion of Lescher & Lescher, Ltd. All rights reserved.

Warren, Lynda W. and Jonnae C. Ostrom, "They Gotta Keep It: People Who Save Everything." Originally titled "Pack Rats: World-Class Savers." Copyright © 1988 by Sussex Publishers. With permission from *Psychology Today magazine.*

Zuckerman, Benjamin, "Two by Two, We'll Fill the Planet." Copyright © 1991 by Benjamin Zuckerman, Professor of Physics and Astronomy, UCLA. Reprinted with permission.

Photo Credits

INDEX